AFRICA'S WORLD WAR

To the memory of
Seth Sendashonga

GÉRARD PRUNIER

Africa's World War

Congo, the Rwandan Genocide,
and the Making of a Continental Catastrophe

OXFORD
UNIVERSITY PRESS

2009

OXFORD
UNIVERSITY PRESS

Oxford University Press, Inc., publishes works that further
Oxford University's objective of excellence
in research, scholarship, and education.

Oxford   New York

Auckland   Cape Town   Dar es Salaam   Hong Kong   Karachi
Kuala Lumpur   Madrid   Melbourne   Mexico City   Nairobi
New Delhi   Shanghai   Taipei   Toronto

With offices in

Argentina   Austria   Brazil   Chile   Czech Republic   France   Greece
Guatemala   Hungary   Italy   Japan   Poland   Portugal   Singapore
South Korea   Switzerland   Thailand   Turkey   Ukraine   Vietnam

Published in North America
by Oxford University Press
198 Madison Avenue
New York, 10016

Published in the United Kingdom in 2009
by C. Hurst & Co. (Publishers) Ltd.

www.oup.com

Oxford is a registered trademark of Oxford University Press

Library of Congress Cataloging-in-Publication Data
Prunier, Gérard.
Africa's world war : Congo, the Rwandan genocide, and the making
of a continental catastrophe / Gérard Prunier.
p.   cm.
Includes bibliographical references and index.
ISBN 978-0-19-537420-9
1. Congo (Democratic Republic)—History—1997–
2. Rwanda—History—Civil War, 1994—Refugees.
3. Genocide—Rwanda.
4. Political violence—Great Lakes Region (Africa).
5. Africa, Central—Ethnic relations—Political aspects—20th century.
6. Geopolitics—Africa, Central.
I. Title.
DT658.26.P78   2009
967.03'2—dc22   2008020806

1 3 5 7 9 8 6 4 2

Printed in the United States of America
on acid-free paper

CONTENTS

ABBREVIATIONS

AAC: Anglo-American Corporation.

ABAKO: Alliance des Bakongo. Led by Joseph Kasa Vubu, it was the political expression of the Bakongo tribe at the time of the independence of the Congo in 1960.

ACRI: African Crisis Response Initiative. The U.S.-sponsored structure that had been developed in the late 1990s in the hope of creating a kind of "peacemaking" African multinational force.

ADF: Allied Democratic Forces. A multiethnic Ugandan guerrilla group created in 1996 in Zaire by fusing elements of the ADM, NALU, and UMLA to fight the Museveni regime.

ADM: Allied Democratic Movement. A Baganda anti-Museveni guerrilla movement created in 1996. See *ADF*.

AEF: French Equatorial Africa.

AFDL: Alliance des Forces Démocratiques pour la Libération. The umbrella rebel organization created in October 1996 in eastern Zaire under Rwandese tutelage to spearhead the fight against Mobutu's regime. See *CNRD*; *MRLZ*.

ALIR: Armée de Libération du Rwanda. Anti-RPF movement based in the Congo, led by former FAR officers. At times referred to by its more political name PALIR, or Peuple Armé pour la Libération du Rwanda.

AMFI: American Mineral Fields International.

AMP: Alliance pour la Majorité Présidentielle.

ANACOZA: Alliance of North American Congo-Zaire Associations. Congolese association in the United States from which AFDL recruited quite a number of cadres.

ANC: African National Congress. The main South African nationalist organization that fought against apartheid and swept into power in the 1990s.

ANC: Armée Nationale Congolaise. (1) Name of the Congolese Armed Forces after independence before the country changed its name to Zaire, whereby ANC was renamed FAZ. (2) Under the same appellation, name given by the RCD (Goma faction) to its armed forces in 1998.

AND: Agence Nationale de Documentation. One of Mobutu's most feared secret services, headed for a long time by his close adviser Honoré N'Gbanda.

ANR: Agence Nationale de Renseignements. Kabila's new secret police after taking power.

ASD: Alliance pour la Sauvegarde du Dialogue Inter-Congolais.

AZADHO: Association Zairoise des Droits de l'Homme. The largest human rights association in Zaire, which became ASADHO (Association Africaine des Droits de l'Homme) after the overthrow of Mobutu.

BCMP: Bourse Congolaise des Matières Précieuses.

BDK: Bundu dia Kongo. A political/religious Congolese sect.

BOSS: Bureau of State Security. Apartheid South Africa's secret service.

CCM: Chama cha Mapinduzi (Party of the Revolution). The Tanzanian party born from the fusion between the continental TANU (Tanganyika African National Union) and Zanzibar's Afro-Shirazi Party (ASP) after the 1964 island revolution. CCM remained a single party for over twenty-five years when the country opened to multiparty politics.

CEEAC: Communauté Economique des Etats de l'Afrique Centrale.

CFA franc: Communauté Financière Africaine. The common currency of former French African colonies

CIAT: Comité International d'Accompagnement de la Transition.

CND: Centre National de Documentation. One of Mobutu's internal spying organizations.

CNDD: Conseil National de Défense de la Démocratie. The mostly Hutu organization created in exile in Zaire by former Burundi interior minister Léonard Nyangoma in February 1994. See *FDD*.

CNDP:	Congrès National pour la Défense du Peuple.
CNL:	Conseil National de Libération. The ephemeral left-wing Congolese "government" of 1963–1965.
CNRD:	Conseil National de Résistance pour la Démocratie. New name of the PLC in the mid-1990s, one of the four anti-Mobutu organizations that joined to create the AFDL.
CNS:	Conférence Nationale Souveraine. The national Zaire reform conference that convened between August 1991 and December 1992. It then turned into the HCR and HCR/PT.
CONAKAT:	Confédération des Associations Tribales du Katanga. Created in November 1958, it was at first the political expression of Katangese regionalism. It developed later into an instrument of the "genuine Katangese" (i.e., opposed to the Baluba immigrants from Kasaï) and led the secession of the province against the Leopoldville government.
CZSC:	Contingent Zairois de la Sécurité des Camps. The armed unit raised by UNHCR to ensure the security of the Rwandese refugee camps in Zaire.
DDRRR:	Disarmament, Demobilization, Rehabilitation, Reintegration, and Resettlement.
DEMIAP:	Direction Militaire des Activités Anti-Patrie. President Laurent-Désiré Kabila's military secret service created in November 1997.
DGSE:	Directorate-General for External Security. (French Secret Service).
DISA:	Direciao de Informaciao de Segurança de Angola. The MPLA secret police.
DMI:	Directorate of Military Intelligence. The Rwandese military secret service.
DRC:	Democratic Republic of Congo.
DSP:	Division Spéciale Présidentielle. President Mobutu's elite force recruited among his Ngbandi tribe and other related ethnic groups from the northern Equateur Province.
ESAF:	Enhanced Structural Adjustment Facility.
ESO:	External Service Organization. The Ugandan external secret service.
FAA:	Forças Armadas Angolanas. The name taken by the supposedly unified MPLA-UNITA Angolan army after the Bicesse

Agreement of 1991. After the 1992 breakup it remained the name of the MPLA forces.

FAB: Forces Armées Burundaises. The Burundese regular army.

FAC: Forces Armées Congolaises. The new national army created by President Laurent-Désiré Kabila after he took power in 1997.

FALA: Forças Armadas de Libertação de Angola. The UNITA army.

FAPLA: Forças Armadas Populares de Libertação de Angola. The name of the MPLA forces until the Bicesse Agreement of 1991.

FAR: Forces Armées Rwandaises. The army of the former Rwandese regime overthrown in July 1994. It reorganized in Zaire and kept fighting, at first independently and then either as part the FAC or with ALIR.

FARDC: Forces Armées de la République Démocratique du Congo.

FAZ: Forces Armées Zairoises. The national army of Zaire, it collapsed under the impact of the 1996 rebellion and invasion.

FDD: Forces de Défense de la Démocratie. At first the military arm of the Burundese CNDD, which later split from its mother organization under the leadership of Jean-Bosco Ndayikengurukiye.

FDLR: Forces Démocratiques de Libération du Rwanda. Anti-RPF Hutu guerrilla group based in the eastern DRC.

FLC: Front de Libération du Congo. Supposedly unified Congolese rebel movement regrouping MLC and the various RCD factions. Largely a paper organization.

FLEC: Frente de Libertação do Enclave de Cabinda. The Cabinda Enclave rebel movement. Closely linked to UNITA, it later split into two fractions. The largest one was FLEC/FAC (Forças Armadas de Cabinda), led by Henriques Nzita Tiago, followed by FLEC-Renovada, led by Jose Tiburço Luemba.

FLN: Forces de Libération Nationales. A military fraction of the old PALIPEHUTU Burundi opposition group which split in 1993 under the leadership of Kabora Kossan.

FNL: Forces Nationales de Libération.

FNLA: Frente Nacional de Libertação de Angola. First Angolan anti-Portuguese rebel movement, created in 1961 by Holden Roberto.

FNLC: Front National de Libération du Congo. The organization created by the former Katangese Gendarmes from their Angolan exile after the collapse of Tshombe's regime. They carried out the two unsuccessful Shaba invasions of 1977 and 1978 and later joined the victorious AFDL.

FRD: Forces de Résistance de la Démocratie. Rwandese democratic opposition party created in exile by Seth Sendashonga and Faustin Twagiramungu in 1996. It went into eclipse after the assassination of its first founder in May 1998.

FRODEBU: Front pour la Démocratie au Burundi. Hutu opposition party created in exile by Melchior Ndadaye in 1986 and legalized in May 1990.

FROLINA: Front de Libération Nationale. A Burundi Hutu guerrilla group led by Joseph Karumba.

FUNA: Former Uganda National Army. Former soldiers of Idi Amin's Uganda National Army who, after being defeated by the Tanzanians in 1979, regrouped in southern Sudan. Inactive throughout the 1980s, they were recycled by the Sudanese Military Intelligence in the late 1990s to fight the Museveni regime.

GSSP: Groupe Spécial de la Sécurité Présidentielle.

HCR: Haut Conseil de la République (High Council of the Republic). The embryo democratic national assembly of Zaire born out of the CNS. Convened between January 1993 and January 1994 before turning into the HCR/PT.

HCR/PT: Haut Conseil de la République/Parlement Transitoire (High Council of the Republic/Transition Parliament). A product of the fusion between the HCR and the old Mobutist pseudo-parliament. HCR/PT theoretically lasted until the end of the Mobutu regime but lost most of its actual relevance with the resignation of its president, Monsignor Monsengwo, in January 1996. (See *CNS*.)

HIPC: Heavily Indebted Poor Countries.

ICG: International Crisis Group.

ICRC: International Committee of the Red Cross.

ICTR: International Criminal Tribunal for Rwanda.

IDP: Internally displaced persons. Refugees who have not crossed an international border.

IMF: International Monetary Fund.

IOC: Integrated Operations Centre. A UNREO spin off, it was in charge of coordinating the evacuation of the IDP camps in southern Rwanda.

IRIN: Integrated Regional Information Network.

ISO: Internal Service Organization. The Ugandan internal secret service.

JMC: Joint Military Command.

LDF: Local Defense Force. The Rwandese government local militia.

LRA: Lord's Resistance Army. Millenarian guerrilla movement active in northern Uganda since 1987.

LSA: Lord's Salvation Army. Original name of the LRA between 1987 and 1992.

MAGRIVI: Mutuelle des Agriculteurs des Virunga.

MDC: Movement for Democratic Change. Zimbabwean opposition party.

MDR: Mouvement Démocratique Républicain. Largest of the prewar Rwandese opposition parties, it was heir to the old PARME-HUTU ethnic movement of pre-independence days. There was an ambiguity between the "old" party, identified with ethnic ideology and anti-Tutsi persecutions, and the "new" party, supposedly more democratic.

MESAN: Mouvement d'Evolution Sociale de l'Afrique Noire.

MIB: Mission d'Immigration des Banyarwanda.

MIBA: Société Minière de Bakwanga.

MLC: Mouvement de Libération du Congo. Congolese rebel group created in 1998 by Jean-Pierre Bemba to fight the regime of Laurent-Désiré Kabila. Turned into a political party during the Congolese transition.

MMD: Movement for Multiparty Democracy. Zambian opposition party launched in the 1980s to challenge the single-party UNIP. It won the October 1991 elections.

MNC: Mouvement National Congolais. Created in October 1958 by Patrice Emery Lumumba, it was the main nationalist party at the time of independence.

MNF: Multinational intervention force.

MONUA: Mission des Observateurs des Nations Unies en Angola. The UN peacekeeping mission (1994–1999) that followed the failure of UNAVEM.

MONUC: Mission des Nations Unies au Congo.

MPLA: Movimento Popular de Libertaçao de Angola. The ruling party in Angola since independence in 1975.

MPR: Mouvement Populaire de la Révolution. President Mobutu's single party, created in 1967.

MRC: Mouvement Révolutionnaire Congolais.

MRLZ: Mouvement Révolutionnaire pour la Libération du Zaïre. The small South Kivu anti-Mobutu movement created by Anselme Masasu Nindaga. (See *AFDL*.)

MRND: Mouvement Révolutionnaire National pour le Développement. In Rwanda, the late President Habyarimana's single party whose cadres played a key role in the genocide.

NALU: National Army for the Liberation of Uganda. A guerrilla movement formed by the Bakonjo tribe of western Uganda in 1988 to fight the Museveni regime. Into eclipse after 1992, many of its fighters later went into the ADF.

NDF: Namibian Defense Force. The Namibian regular army.

NGO: Nongovernmental organization.

NIF: National Islamic Front.

NRA/NRM: National Resistance Army/Movement. The guerrilla movement organized by Yoweri Museveni and his friends in Uganda. It has been in power since January 1986.

OAU: Organization of African Unity.

OECD: Organization for Economic Cooperation and Development.

PALIPEHUTU: Parti pour la Libération du Peuple Hutu. Clandestine Burundi Hutu opposition party created in exile by Remy Gahutu in 1980.

PALU: Parti Lumumbiste d'Action Unifié. Left-wing political party in Zaire created by former Lumumba associate Antoine Gizenga. Has links with the old PSA.

PARENA: Parti du Renouveau National. Burundi Tutsi opposition party created in August 1994 by former president Jean-Baptiste Bagaza.

PARMEHUTU: See *MDR*.

PCT: Parti Congolais du Travail. Congo-Brazzaville's single party created in 1968.

PDC: Parti Démocrate Chrétien. A small Rwandese prewar opposition party which became a special target for the RPF when it started its confrontation with the Catholic Church. In April 1999 PDC President Jean-Népomucène Nayinzira changed its name to Parti Démocrate Centriste (Democratic Party of the Center) in the hope of severing the implied Catholic connection.

PDSC: Parti Démocrate Social Chrétien. Anti-Mobutu opposition party led by André Bo-Boliko, a member of USORA.

PL: Parti Libéral. A minor Rwandese opposition party.

PLC: Parti de la Libération Congolais. Small guerrilla group created in 1986 around Beni which later contributed to the bigger Zairian rebellion of 1996 under the label of CRND.

PPRD: Parti Pour la Reconstruction et le Développement.

PRI: Parti Républicain Indépendant. Anti-Mobutu opposition party led by Jean Nguza Karl-I-Bond, a member of USORA. Nguza's break with USORA led to the creation of UFERI.

PRP: Parti pour la Réconciliation du Peuple. Burundi royalist party created in 1993 by Tutsi politician Mathias Hitimana.

PRP: Parti de la Révolution Populaire. Anti-Mobutu guerrilla movement created in 1967 by Laurent-Désiré Kabila.

PSA: Parti Solidaire Africain. A left-wing nationalist party in the Congo at the time of independence. It became the nucleus of the radical Kwilu rebellion led by Pierre Mulele in 1963–1968 and constituted one of the political tendencies later reincarnated in PALU.

PSD: Parti Social Démocrate. A prewar Rwandese opposition party that slowly died out after the RPF monopolized power.

RCD: Rassemblement Congolais pour la Démocratie. Congolese rebel group created in 1998 to fight the regime of Laurent-Désiré Kabila. It later split into several factions, which were supposed to be reunified by merging into the FLC. Became a political party during the Congolese transition.

RDR: Rassemblement Démocratique pour le Retour. The "new" political movement created in the Rwandese refugee camp by

	the former génocidaire leadership to try to regain international credibility.
RPA:	Rwandese Patriotic Army. The new army created in Rwanda in 1994 after the RPF took power.
RPF:	Rwandese Patriotic Front. A political movement created in 1987 by Rwandese exiles living in Uganda. From October 1990 on it carried out a guerrilla insurgency against the Habyarimana dictatorship, finally winning the war in July 1994 and taking power in the wake of the genocide.
RTNC:	Radio Television Nationale Congolaise.
SADC:	Southern African Development Community. Regroups all the southern African states plus Rwanda, Uganda, and the DRC.
SADF:	South African Defense Force. The South African army.
SARM:	Service d'Action et de Renseignement Militaire. Zairian military intelligence service often used for internal repression against civilians. It had a commando unit entirely made up of Ngbandi soldiers commanded by Mobutu's brother-in-law.
SASMIP:	Service d'Achat des Substances Minérales Précieuses.
SNIP:	Service National d'Intelligence et de Protection. The "new" Zairian Special Service created in 1990 to "humanize" the former FIS and FAS previously led by "Terminator" Honoré N'Gbanda. SNIP was under the command of Gen. Likulia Bolongo.
SOMINKI:	Société Minière du Kivu.
SPLA:	Sudanese Peoples Liberation Army.
SSR:	Security Sector Reform.
SWAPO:	South West African Peoples Organization. Namibian nationalist movement created in 1960 with South African Communist Party help; it achieved power in 1990.
TNA:	Transitional National Assembly.
TPDF:	Tanzanian People's Defense Force. The Tanzanian army.
UDEMO:	Union des Démocrates Mobutistes.
UDI:	Unilateral Declaration of Independence. The November 1965 proclamation of Rhodesian independence by the white minority-led government of Ian Smith. It resulted in fourteen years of conflict until the 1979 Lancaster House Conference on Zimbabwean independence.

UDPS: Union pour la Démocratie et le Progrès Social. Zairian opposition party led by long-time Mobutu opponent Etienne Tshisekedi. A USORA member organization.

UFERI: Union des Fédéralistes et des Républicains Indépendants. A pro-Mobutu political party born of the fusion of Nguza Karl-I-Bond's PRI (after it broke with USORA) with Gabriel Kyungu wa Kumwanza's Parti Fédéraliste Démocrate Chrétien. Reincarnated as UNAFEC after the fall of Mobutu.

UMHK: Union Minière du Haut Katanga. The Belgian mining concern that dominated the economy of Congo's Katanga province and played a key role in its secession from the Léopoldville government in 1960. It was nationalized in 1966 and renamed Générale des Carrières et Mines du Zaïre (GECAMINES) in 1971.

UMLA: Uganda Muslim Liberation Army. An anti-Museveni Muslim guerrilla group created in 1996. (See *ADF*.)

UNAFEC: Union Nationale des Fédéralistes Congolais. The new name of UFERI after the fall of Mobutu.

UNAMIR: United Nations Assistance Mission to Rwanda. The military body supposed to help Rwanda and which, after evacuating the country during the genocide, came back and stayed on until 1996, but without much effect.

UNAR: Union Nationale Rwandaise. Rwandese royalist party that fought against the Kasa Vubu regime alongside the left-wing Congolese rebels of 1964–1965.

UNAVEM: United Nations Angola Verification Mission. The failed UN mission to supervise the voting in Angola (1991–1994).

UNHCR: United Nations High Commission for Refugees. Among the various specialized UN agencies, it was the most important player in the Great Lakes crisis.

UNHRFOR: United Nations Human Rights Field Operation for Rwanda.

UNIP: United National Independence Party. Led by Kenneth Kaunda, it was the main nationalist party in Zambia before becoming the country's single party for twenty years.

UNITA: União Nacional para a Independência Total de Angola. Anti-Portuguese rebel movement created in 1966 by Jonas Savimbi. It fought the MPLA until Savimbi's death in 2002. Later turned into a legal political party.

UNREO: United Nations Rwanda Emergency Office. The UN body supervising all emergency operations after the genocide. It was supposed to act in coordination with UNAMIR but was largely autonomous.

UNRF: Uganda National Rescue Front. This was initially a West Nile–based guerrilla organization created by former Idi Amin minister Moses Ali to fight the second Obote regime (1980–1985). When Moses Ali became a minister in Museveni's government, disaffected Aringa tribesmen launched UNRF II with Khartoum's support.

UPA: Uniao de Populaçiao de Angola.

UPC: Uganda Peoples Congress. Created in 1961 by Milton Obote, it dominated Ugandan politics until 1985.

UPDF: Uganda People's Defense Force. The name taken by the Ugandan NRA when it became the regular Ugandan army.

UPRONA: Union pour le Progrès National. Burundese nationalist party founded in 1957 by Chief Léopold Bihumugani and later led by independence hero Prince Louis Rwagasore.

USORA: Union Sacrée de l'Opposition Radicale et Alliés. An anti-Mobutu political cartel which regrouped the UDPS, the PRI. and the PDSC after the collapse of the Conférence Nationale Souveraine.

WNBLF: West Nile Bank Liberation Front. An anti-Museveni guerrilla group created in Zaire by former Idi Amin commander Juma Oris in 1994.

ZANU: Zimbabwe African National Union. Initially based on some Mashona sections, it was the main nationalist party in the anti-Rhodesian struggle, later becoming a single party after independence under the name of ZANU/PF (Patriotic Front).

ZAPU: Zimbabwe African Peoples Union. ZANU Matabele-based rival nationalist party.

ZCSC: Zairian Camp Security Contingent. FAZ elements paid by UNHCR to ensure refugee camps security in eastern Zaire during 1995–1996.

ZDI: Zimbabwe Defence Industries.

ZNA: Zimbabwean National Army.

GLOSSARY

The language from which the term originates is marked thus: Fr. for French, Kin. for Kinyarwanda, Lin. for Lingala, Port. for Portuguese, Sw. for Swahili, Lug. for Luganda.

abacengezi (Kin.):
"Infiltrators." Name given by the RPF to the ex-FAR, former Interhamwe, and later ALIR combatants who infiltrated back into Rwanda after 1997 to try to overthrow the new regime.

abacunguzi (Kin.):
"Liberators." Play on the word *abacengezi* by the local Hutu population in northwest Rwanda.

abakada (Kin/Fr.):
A Kinyarwanda corruption of the French word *cadre* combined with the Kinyarwanda prefix *aba* meaning "people." These are the young men recruited by the RPF to extend its control over the rural areas. They are largely a law unto themselves.

abanyanduga (Kin.):
People from the *nduga* (i.e., south-central) area of Rwanda. The *abanyanduga* did not particularly like the Habyarimana regime and were often not supportive of the genocide. This gave them a reputation as "friends of the Tutsi," which neither endeared them to their fellow northern Hutu nor really protected them from the heavy hand of the RPF.

abazungu (Kin.):
Derived from the Swahili word *Wazungu,* meaning white people.

afande (Sw.):
From the Turkish *efendi,* meaning "sir." Roughly equivalent to *lieutenant,* it was brought to east Africa by the British army usage of Egyptian army ranks in the late nine-

	teenth century. A respectful term used by the RPA for officers whose ranks it did not want to make public.
assimilados (Port.):	Name given in Angola to those natives who had learned Portuguese and were deemed more civilized than the rest. (See *évolués.*)
autochtones (Fr.):	The word, meaning "natives," in French is used in the two Kivu provinces to designate non-Kinyarwanda speakers as opposed to the Kinyarwanda-speaking population, who are thus implicitly assigned the position of "foreigner" or "immigrant."
Banyaviura (Sw.):	Name given to the mostly Tutsi Rwandese migrants to Katanga who formed a small community of office workers for the mining companies during the Belgian era.
bapfuye buhagazi (Kin.):	"The walking dead." Name given to the genocide survivors, whether Tutsi or Hutu, who had usually lost most of their relatives.
candonga (Port.):	Name given in Angola to the parallel economy.
contratados (Port.):	"Those under contract." A form of indentured labor akin to temporary slavery, practiced in the Portuguese colonies.
creuseurs (Fr.):	"Diggers." The illegal gold or diamond miners in Zaire. (See *garimpeiros.*)
dawa (Sw.):	Literally "medicine." Although the word still retains its ordinary sense it is also the term used for the "magic medicine" that a number of millenarian-oriented fighting groups (Simba rebels in the Congo in 1964–1965, Alice Lakwena's rebels in Uganda in 1986, Mayi Mayi guerrillas in the DRC since 1996) use in the hope of gaining protection from enemy fire.
evolué (Fr.):	"Evolved." Name given by the Belgians to the Congolese natives who had reached an "appropriate level of civilization." (See *assimilados.*)
gacaca (Kin.):	A form of conflict resolution in traditional Rwandese culture which the government

tried to adapt to the postgenocide legal process. This adaptation was difficult because traditional *gacaca* was supposed to deal with misdemeanors rather than with blood crimes.

garimpeiros (Port.): Illegal miners in Angola. (See *creuseurs.*)

gendarmerie (Fr.): A corps of rural military police similar to the French *Gendarmerie,* the Italian *Carabinieri,* or the Mexican *Rurales.* It is a major component of military forces in Rwanda.

génocidaires (Fr.): "Those who committed the genocide." The term was at first purely descriptive. It later acquired a political meaning when it was applied to people who had not taken part in the genocide but who were considered hostile to the new regime.

gutunga agatoki (Kin.): "Pointing the finger." A process by which real or supposed génocidaires are denounced. *Gutunga agatoki* became a national sport in postgenocide Rwanda, with people often denouncing each other for political or economic advantage.

ibipinga (Kin.): "Destroyers." A term used by the RPF regime to stigmatize their enemies, whether Tutsi or Hutu. The term implies a nasty underhanded way of being an opponent.

icyihuture (Kin.): "De-Hutuized," that is, turned into a Tutsi. A form of social promotion within the Banyarwanda.

imitima yarakomeretse (Kin.): "The disease of the wounded hearts." The state of mind in which the genocide survivors live.

indigenas (Port.): "Natives." All those in the Portuguese colonies who were not assimilados.

Interahamwe (Kin.): "Those who fight together." The name of the former MRND politicomilitary militia. The *Interahamwe* were at the forefront of the genocide and did most of the killing. After the genocide, while the real *Interahamwe* kept operating in Zaire, noncompliant Hutu within Rwanda were called *Interahamwe* as a term of political opprobrium.

Ingo (Kin.):	See *Rugo*.
Inyangamugayo (Kin.):	"Those who hate dishonor." People recruited to be a moral reference in litigation following the genocide. They often ended up in practice being part of the problems they were supposed to solve, even turning into a government militia in some communes.
Kabaka (Lug):	Traditional title of the king of Buganda.
Kinyarwanda (Kin.):	The Rwandese language. There are many Kinyarwanda speakers in the Congolese Kivus.
kubohoza (Kin.):	"To liberate." The word was at first used by militias of the opposition parties during 1990–1994, when they often violently "liberated" (i.e., brutalized) their pro-government opponents. After the genocide the word was transformed ironically to mean "liberate for one's benefit" (i.e., confiscate Hutu properties).
kwitaba inama (Kin.):	To answer the call to a meeting, an expression transformed by a grim pun into *kwitaba imana* ("answer the call of God"), that is, to die, because of the RPF killings during "peace meetings."
matumbo (Port.):	From the Portuguese word *mato* meaning "the bush." Used as a derogatory term in Angola to talk about the black African peasants of the interior. (See *preto*.)
mestiços (Port.):	Half-caste or mixed-blood person in the former Portuguese colonies.
mugaragu (Kin.):	"Client" in traditional Rwandese quasi-feudalism.
mundele (Lin., pl. Mindele):	A white person in western, northern, or central Congo, equivalent to *Muzungu* in Swahili-speaking Katanga or Kivu.
musseques (Port.):	Angolan shanty towns whose population has played a key political role in the civil war.
Mwalimu (Sw.):	"The schoolteacher." Nickname of Tanzania's former president Julius Nyerere.
Mwami (plural "Abami"; Kin.):	"King" in Kinyarwanda and in several of the Kivu languages. There were many *abami* in

the small kingdoms that preexisted "Ankole" and the Kivus.

nokos (Lin.): Literally "uncles." Name given to politically influential Belgians during the colonization of the Congo. Later used for the "big men" of Laurent-Désiré Kabila's regime.

preto (Port.): Black (derogatory); see *matumbo*.

retornados (Port.): "Those who have returned." Bakongo from Angola who had lived in exile in Zaire and returned home after independence in November 1974. (See *zairenses*.)

rugo (ingo in the plural; Kin.): The basic Rwandese peasant compound.

shebuja (Kin.): "Patron" in traditional Rwandese quasi-feudalism.

soba (Port.): Angolan colonial chiefs; the title is still used today.

songamana (Sw.): From the verb *kusonga*, "to press together." A form of crowd control using humiliation practiced by the RPA where many people are made to squat tightly together on the ground while being hectored by an officer.

umugaragu (Kin. Pl. Abagaragu): Client.

`wakombozi (Sw.): "The liberators." The name was first used by the pro-Obote Ugandans who had come back to Uganda in the wake of the Tanzanian army overthrow of Gen. Idi Amin's dictatorship in 1979. Their excesses soon made them thoroughly unpopular. The term was applied to the NRA in 1986 and later taken to Rwanda by the RPF in 1994. (See *Kubohoza* for a word of related etymology in Kinyarwanda.)

wazungu (Sw.): White people. Used in Uganda and the Congo, same as *abazungu* in Rwanda.

Zairenses (Port.): Literally, "Zairians." Name given to the Angolan Bakongo retornados after their return to Luanda.

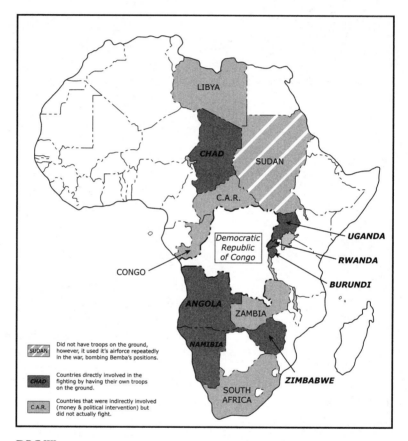

DRC War

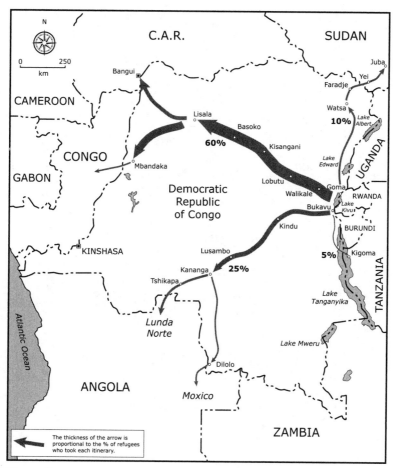

Hutu refugees

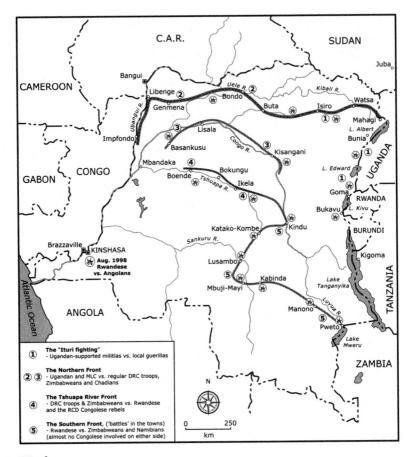

The "Ituri fighting"
① - Ugandan-supported militias vs. local guerillas

The Northern Front
② ③ - Ugandan and MLC vs. regular DRC troops, Zimbabweans and Chadians

The Tshuapa River Front
④ - DRC troops & Zimbabweans vs. Rwandese and the RCD Congolese rebels

The Southern Front, ('battles' in the towns)
⑤ - Rwandese vs. Zimbabweans and Namibians (almost no Congolese involved on either side)

War fronts

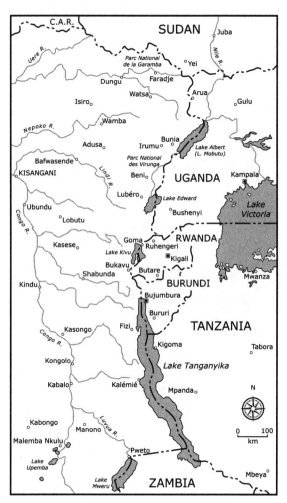

Great Lakes Region

INTRODUCTION

In 1885, at the heyday of European imperialism, Africa was a continent apart. It had no nation-states, no caliphate, and no empire. It did not even have the crude military dictatorships that at the time passed for states in Latin America. It was a continent of clans, of segmentary tribes and of a few sacred monarchies. Societies were what mattered, and the state was a construct many could live without. Boundaries did exist, but not in the European sense. They were linguistic, cultural, military, or commercial, and they tended to crisscross and overlap, without the neat delineations so much beloved by Western statesmen since the treaties of Westphalia. Colonial European logic played havoc with that delicate cobweb of relationships. New borders were drawn not so much in violation of preexisting ones but according to a different logic. African borders had been porous membranes through which proto-nations were breathing, and the colonial borders that superseded them were of the pre-1914 cast-iron variety. Then, within those borders, vast enterprises of social and economic rationalization were undertaken, all for the good of the natives, of course, and for the greater prosperity of the empire. African social and cultural ways of doing things were neither taken into account nor questioned; they were simply *made obsolete*. Karl Marx and Rudyard Kipling agreed: empire was *progressive*. The Europeans rationalized African cultures to death. And it is that contrived rationality that they bequeathed to Africa when they walked away from the continent in the 1960s.

The problem was that this rationality had not had time to filter down from the exalted spheres of government and philosophy to the real lives of ordinary people. Marxists would have said that, after seventy-five years of colonization, the administrative superstructure bore little relationship to the productive infrastructure. The Europeans had destroyed a traditional culture, planning to rebuild it along wonderfully rational lines at a later date. But history forced them to walk away before they could complete their supposedly benevolent alternative system, thus giving renewed tragic relevance to Antonio Gramsci's famous remark that the moment when the Old is dead and the New is not yet born is a very dangerous moment indeed.

Because independence occurred right in the middle of the cold war, political evolution was frozen until further notice. France took as its special responsibility the supervision of the cold storage equipment and turned it into a dearly beloved consolation prize for its waning role as a superpower. As a result Paris was loath to acknowledge the geopolitical earthquake that took place in 1989, and the notion that this primarily European event could have African consequences was not accepted. President Mitterrand's extremely traditional political worldview did not help.

The Rwandese genocide acted in this fragile African and international environment like the bull in the proverbial china shop because it was at the same time both typically "African" and typically un-African. Its deep-seated causes reached far back into the precolonial culture of Rwanda. But it could never have occurred without the manic cultural reengineering of the Belgian colonial authorities. It was both a traditional logic gone mad and a totally modern artifact. In other words, it was a contemporary African social phenomenon.

To think that an event of such magnitude, of such concentrated evil and of such political inventiveness could be kept bottled up in the 26,000 square kilometers of the official Rwanda state was naïve. But many people, including this author, hoped against hope that it could be. As for the self-styled "international community," its standardized worldview could not hide the fact that as far as Africa was concerned it had willy-nilly inherited the mantel of the former colonial empires. Reluctantly trying to face a catastrophe of unheard-of magnitude, the international community attempted to deal with it in the stilted humanitarian style usually dispensed by the United Nations. And although the UN Assistance Mission for Rwanda had been the ultimate experience in toothlessness, further bureaucratic remedies were nevertheless proffered after the genocide to a world spinning out of control, as if they would suffice to steer it back on course. Refugee camps were mushrooming, with armed murderers and hapless peasants living side by side, sharing the unreal bounty dumped on them by distant authorities who were choosing not to choose. Victorious victims were cradling their weapons in anticipation of a looming military solution. The diplomatic rout was almost absolute. The French, stunned by defeat and the torrents of blood they had unwittingly helped to shed, were incapable of coherent reaction. Shamed by their post-Somalia passive acquiescence to the genocide, the Americans were trying their hand at steering a situation they did not even begin to understand. And Marshal Mobutu, the longest-serving friend of the former free world, was clumsily trying to reformat the whole thing according to the obsolete parameters he was familiar with. Through a mixture of diplomatic routine and woolly good intentions, more septic material kept being injected into the already festering sores. By mid-1996 the infection was totally out of control.

Let me be clear: the Rwandese genocide and its consequences did not *cause* the implosion of the Congo basin and its periphery. It acted as a *catalyst*, precipitating a crisis that had been latent for a good many years and that later reached far beyond its original Great Lakes locus. This is why the situation became so serious. The Rwandese genocide has been both a product and a further cause of an enormous African crisis: its very occurrence was a symptom, its nontreatment spread the disease.

In Zaire itself what passed for a government structure was so rotten that the brush of a hand could cause it to collapse. A few mortar shells dislocated it beyond recognition. Paris was stunned for the second time, while Washington gleefully boasted about "New African Leaders." And all the peripheral conflicts started to roll down into the Congo basin like so many overripe toxic fruits. In Burundi the civil war that started in 1993 had never stopped. Sudan and Uganda were still at each other's throats and ready to jump, flailing, into the Congolese ring. The so-called Angola Peace Agreement was but a breathing spell between two periods of military campaigns. In Zimbabwe an ethnopolitical elite that had lost any sense of moderation or financial decency was keen to jump in with bright visions of political investments designed to counter South African economic expansion northward. Even in distant Namibia a weak government afraid of the new South African imperialism was ready to follow its supposedly strong protector in Luanda into the general melee.

Then there were the nervous onlookers, with no immediate connections to the coming maelstrom but with many invisible links reaching into it: Brazzaville and Bangui, where separate conflicts were forever on the edge of blending with those across the great rivers; Tripoli, where Colonel Gaddafi's perennial grand diplomatic design was back on the drawing board after years of Lockerbie freezing; Lusaka, where President Chiluba was trying to make up for a disintegrating economy by a flurry of diplomatic activism; and Pretoria, where the accession of the African National Congress to quasi-absolute power had created a situation of absolute economic need to empower the blacks without disenfranchising the whites.

All this is what we could call "the modern state logic of the confrontation," and it provides a first layer of explanation. Africa was teeming with geopolitical problems that suddenly all found a common locus. But something else is needed to explain the lightning spread and later the sluggish intractability of the conflict. Behind the competing egos of the politicians and the trendy appetites of the new African imperialisms lay some things that are deeper and thicker and that the politicians themselves were quite unable to fully understand and, even less, control.

First is the uncertainty of Africa's multiple identities. Governments can manipulate what exists; they cannot create what does not. The violence of the so-called Congolese conflict, which for a while became a continentwide war, was the product of unsettled questions that the Rwandese genocide had brushed raw. What is a country in Africa? What is a legitimate government? Who is a citizen? Why do we live together? Whom should we obey? Who are we? Who are the "others," and how should we deal with them? None of these questions had been answered, except by the dry legalistic proviso of the Organization of African Unity charter guaranteeing the intangibility of the former colonial borders. Pretending to answer so many vital questions with one paragraph in a forty-year-old treaty designed for a now obsolete context was unrealistic.

Then comes the problem of legitimacy. At independence, being black was legitimate enough to qualify as president of a newly decolonized state. Later, U.S. cold war interests and French neocolonialism helped buttress existing governments. The collapse of the communist empire shook up these arrangements, which had never taken the ordinary African into account. Ordinary people on the continent began to insist on being treated like citizens and not like subjects. *Democracy* became a new byword. But the problem was that democracy as a form of government presupposes a certain degree of social integration, the existence of a political class with some concept of the national interest, and a minimum of economic development. None of these existed. The African political class was largely made up of "tropical gangsters,"[1] and the continent's economy was a stagnating swamp. Attempts at democracy, although inherently hopeful, tended to end badly either through violence or, more often, through the deliberate perversion of the new institutions, which were promptly emptied of any democratic content. Nevertheless these failures did not help the now beleaguered dictatorships that remained under pressure from their rapidly organizing civil societies and from a newly politically correct international community. Dictators such as Mobutu had not been asked too many questions as long as they helped the West fight international communism. To their great surprise they were now held accountable for previously irrelevant items such as human rights and good governance. Only in Paris were these uncomfortable innovations largely spurned as "Anglo-Saxon hypocrisy." As a result, caught between impotently fermenting democratic ideals and the realities of persistent institutional authoritarianism, Africa started to drift into a de facto legitimacy vacuum.

To this second layer of explanation economists, cynics, and anthropologists will add a third one, equally deep, equally thick, and equally beyond the control of the politicians: the social impact of the contemporary African economic rout, with its corollaries of extreme poverty and corruption.

Precolonial African economies were essentially subsistence economies, usually producing a small surplus that was used to trade in luxury goods for purposes of social prestige. Empire attempted to change all that. The natives were now supposed to work for two purposes: producing raw materials for the benefit of the centers and making money so that they could buy in their distant peripheries the manufactured goods produced by those same centers. As they were only moderately interested in fulfilling these foreign-imposed goals, the natives were deemed lazy and were brutally coerced into working. The end of empire did not basically change these "progressive" orientations, and the pattern imposed by today's World Bank and the International Monetary Fund is not essentially different from the old colonial system except for two things: mass media cultural seductions have replaced the whip as an inducement to perform, and trade has been multilateralized away from the old empire monopolies. Apart from that, the old evils of deteriorating terms of trade, agricultural monoproduction, the lack of industrialization, and an abysmally low level of manpower qualification are still there. Infrastructures left by colonization have seldom been improved and in most places have greatly deteriorated. The elegant solution to all that used to be the revolutionary struggle of the oppressed masses; today it is called poverty alleviation through globalized free trade. In both cases the result is the same: very little.

But Africa has had to go on living anyway. And year after year there are more and more young Africans trying to make a living out of a stagnant traditional agriculture and in a very slowly expanding urban job market. Abstract economic terms are translated every day into social and cultural hunger and frustration. Unemployment, underemployment, and make-believe jobs are politely subsumed under the heading "informal economy." In such a context, the violent tearing of an already threadbare social fabric is bound to have enormous and unforeseen consequences. The Rwandese genocide provided just such a violent rending.

Since 1960 France had played a disproportionate role in propping up the African theater of the cold war conflict. With or without U.S. help, France had been playing policeman at the four corners of the continent, taking the protection of its economic interests as a reward for its violent involvement. The Rwanda debacle took Paris by surprise. France had started in the good old spirit of propping up a friendly neighborhood dictatorship and it had wound up with 800,000 unexpected dead bodies. The shock felt by Paris was primarily cultural: How could France, the birthplace of Voltaire, Victor Hugo, and Victor Schoelcher,[2] the self-appointed best friend of Africa, be responsible for such a mess? The French power structure could understand neither its own errors nor the tremendous impact they were going to have in the post–cold war context.

The catastrophe then reverberated clear across the continent under the eyes of a stunned and unbelieving audience, knocking down all the worn-out props in the process, including the central one, Mobutu himself. But given the state of Africa in the late twentieth century, such a radical change was bound to have effects not only at the visible state level but also at the deeper levels of identity perception and economic survival. The quasi-continentwide conflict was the logical consequence of that triple conundrum.

It was thus impossible to analyze the conflict strictly in state-versus-state terms (or state-versus–nonstate villains), as the international community has tried to do. States of sorts do exist in Africa, and they are indeed part of that tragic game. But they are far from representing the whole story. It is within that gap in perception that the heart of the problem lies. Diplomats are by nature conservative, and they tend to strive for the fantasyland of a balanced status quo, all the while fearing the possible hell of a Kaplan-like "coming anarchy." And although reality mostly tends to hover somewhere in between, they cannot resign themselves to the probability of a protracted crisis. International diplomacy is at present desperately trying to patch up a worn-out and contradictory social order in Africa, first by convincing itself that African states are "normal," in the etymological sense, and then by convincing these states to make peace with each other while at the same time trying to format the nonstate elements into entities acceptable to the UN and the World Bank. The complicated patchwork of local contradictions blending into the general mess is either not perceived or is ritually dismissed as "African complexities."

This is probably due not to incapacity but to two other elements. First, there is a massive lack of genuine interest. Africa is too peripheral to the contemporary interests of the so-called world community to actually be part of it. The September 11 crisis and its vast consequences only accelerated the process of Africa's international marginalization. As Senegalese president Abdou Diouf presciently said to a high-ranking French civil servant back in 1985, "Our last trump card is our capacity for nuisance." African heads of state now periodically issue dark warnings about HIV-AIDS, illegal immigrants, and the terrorist-breeding potentialities of the continent. But even this feeble attempt at blackmail is seldom taken seriously. Compared to the Middle East, Africa carries only a limited fear factor.

Second, there is the very low pain threshold of the economically developed Western world. This threshold is so low that we cannot even tolerate watching the pain of others on television. So one of the diplomats' jobs—a rather thankless task, I should say—is to remove the visible signs of pain from the CNN broadcasts before they can prevent Western spectators from going about their familiar domestic pleasures. Humanitarian action is then resorted to as an adequate substitute for political decisions. High-protein supplementary feeding is brought in, a vaccination campaign is undertaken, reassuring shots of black babies with white nurses are displayed, and then the cameras roll off. Mission accomplished.

These combined factors—a fatal attraction for what U.S. National Security Adviser Anthony Lake once called "a quick fix solution," the lack of a genuine interest at the government level, and the short attention span of the general public—have given us the "Great Lakes crisis" storyboard of the past thirteen years:

1994: Genocide in Rwanda. Horror.

1995: Festering camps. Keep feeding them and it will eventually work out.

1996: Refugees have gone home. It is now all over except in Zaire.

1997: Mobutu has fallen. Democracy has won.

1998: Another war. These people are crazy.

1999: Diplomats are negotiating. It will eventually work out.

2000: Blank

2001: President Kabila is shot. But his son seems like a good sort, doesn't he?

2002: Pretoria Peace Agreement. We are now back to normal.

2003: These fellows still insist on money. What is the minimum price?

2004: Do you think Osama bin Laden is still alive?

2005: Three million Africans have died. This is unfortunate.

2006: Actually, it might be four million. But since the real problem is Al Qaeda, this remains peripheral.

2007: They have had their election, haven't they? Then everything should be all right.

The result is rather strange. A situation of major conflict is reduced to a comic book atmosphere in which absolute horror alternates with periods of almost complete disinterest from the nonspecialists. Massive levels of physical violence and cultural upheavals are looked upon from a great distance by theoretically powerful international institutions who only dimly understand what is actually happening. There is a great use of stereotyped categories ("advance warning," "failed state," "humanitarian emergency," "confidence-building process," "national reconciliation," "negative forces," "national dialogue," "African ownership of the peace process") which are more relevant to the Western way of thinking than to the realities they are supposed to address. The desperate African struggle for survival is bowdlerized beyond recognition, and at times the participant-observer has the feeling of being caught between a Shakespearian tragedy and a hiccuping computer.

Which does not mean that African leaders are at all put off by this cognitive dissonance. Many have learned the new ropes. They know that if talked to with the proper, politically correct vocabulary the international community can be immensely useful. Never mind the fact that the international community hardly understands what is going on. This very ignorance is part of the African players' basic tactical kit. Since 1994 gaining the moral high ground from where you can shell your enemies with UN supplies has been a routine part of every battle. Humanitarianism is seen as the mainstay of international diplomacy, and diplomacy becomes the pursuit of war by other means.

At this point the situation begs an obvious question: What is going to come out of all this? Is Africa falling apart, or is it going through the pangs of some kind of rebirth? The answer is, probably both. The Rwandese genocide is an example of an atrociously violent leap into some form of modernity. The lack of previous economic and social modernization was not its *cause,* but it created the conditions of its feasibility. And the "Congolese" conflict that it spawned belonged to the same domain. In a totally different context, differential modernity is at work. The warlords, the peasants, the dashing instant neocapitalists, the refugees, the *kadogos,* the traders, the NGO employees, the satellite phone providers are all part of an enormous transformation whose historical consequences are still unknown. Diplomats, international bankers, humanitarians, and businesspeople are all by nature impatient with the erratic events strewing that dark and meandering path. Their impatience is understandable, but it is not realistic. History cannot be hurried along, and Africa is at present going through a major historical transformation. The present calls for an "African government" are unrealistic and premature. But they reflect a desire to jump-start an approved form of modernity. Change does not automatically mean either progress or decay because history is not teleological. But change is irreversible, and Africa is morphing: out of the old clichés and into an unknown future shape.

This book is a modest effort at stating the problem correctly and more or less trying to understand it. Rarely have ground reality and diplomatic discourse been more at variance than in the case of today's African crises. To cite a famous title, *Africa works*[3]—but only in a queer sort of a way—and *toward what* is still unknown. The "Congolese" conflict, with its accompaniment of horrendous suffering, was part and parcel of that vast transformation. For the time being its most violent aspects have subsided, although many of the basic questions that had gone into its making have stubbornly refused to give way to the diplomatic blandishments: Will Joseph Kabila manage to keep his contradictory regime working? And if so, toward what end? Will Rwanda obligingly withdraw to its overcrowded rural slum, or will it manage its transformation into the African Singapore Paul Kagame is dreaming of? Will all the peripheral conflicts that for over four years globalized themselves into the Congolese cockpit accept deconstruction into separate cases amenable to a light diplomatic treatment?

Whatever happens, one thing is certain: the relatively tame post- or neocolonial Africa of the cold war years is now definitely dead and something else is on the way to being born. This difficult birth will occur mostly outside the presence of an otherwise engaged international community. This leaves unresolved the enigmatic case of the "new" South Africa, winner by default of a conflict it did not fight. In a now largely indifferent world, almost nobody but South Africa has the combination of international weight, economic wherewithal, and emotional engagement with the continent. The two other imperialisms still playing themselves out in today's Africa are much narrower. China's is a blunter, cruder version of Leninist nineteenth-century imperialism, entirely designed around global resource exploitation. As for U.S. imperialism, it is selectively focused on siphoning off Gulf of Guinea oil, with a more recently added "war on terror" security sideshow in the Horn. Both China and the United States can live without Africa. South Africa cannot.

Apartheid crumbled and the Rwandese genocide took place within the same time frame. Both events shook the world; neither was really understood; and both were later semi-forgotten in the wake of September 11. But African history stubbornly went on, and it is in that now disconnected history that the "Congolese" conflict marked a watershed. To what end is not yet clear, even if South Africa's increasingly unavoidable presence is bound to be a part of whatever develops. The New Partnership for Africa's Development, "African Union," *Can Africa Claim the 21st Century?*[4]—the world is now faced with the equally believable possibilities of an African Renaissance or an African Anarchy, neither of which will really engage its attention. An enormous and inchoate process is now at work, and may God help the men and women who are both its actors and its often powerless raw material.

AFRICA'S WORLD WAR

1

RWANDA'S MIXED SEASON OF HOPE
(JULY 1994–APRIL 1995)

The immediate aftermath

To live in Rwanda after July 1994 meant living with the consequences of the genocide. And the genocide in Rwanda could not be compared to other, similar crimes committed elsewhere because its massive horror had been carried out within the confines of a small, tightly knit community.[1]

Other genocides have been committed by strangers killing other strangers, and their violence was often engulfed in the wider violence of large international wars or revolutions. Here, attempts by revisionist historians notwithstanding, reducing the phenomenon to a simple consequence of the war is impossible. It was a hill-by-hill and a home-by-home thing. And it is this neighborly quality, this grisly homespun flavor, that contaminated the world of the survivors after the killing had stopped. Western readers should beware of too close a parallel with the Jewish Shoah during World War II. To understand the complexity of the postgenocide situation in Rwanda, one should imagine a world in which many of the German SS would have had Jewish relatives and in which the postwar State of Israel would have been created in Bavaria instead of the Middle East. The following might help us feel how the complexity of the genocide in Rwanda created an almost insane world:

- A Hutu couple, professors at the University of Rwanda, take into their home the sixteen-year-old son of a mixed Hutu-Tutsi family, hoping to protect him. The boy's father, a Tutsi, is killed in the genocide. The couple run to Cyangugu with the boy, seeking the protection of the French army then involved in Operation Turquoise.[2] After the war, the boy's Hutu mother gets her son back and has his saviors arrested for "complicity in the genocide."[3]

- A Hutu trader hides his mixed-parentage relatives. To protect them, he gets a gun but never uses it. The Rwandan Patriotic Front (RPF) comes to power. He flees to Zaire, as do the local *Interahamwe* militiamen.[4] They get back to Rwanda before him and occupy his land. Then they use his possession of an unauthorized gun to denounce him as a *génocidaire,* get him arrested, and keep his farm.[5]

- A Tutsi man escapes being killed by the *Interahamwe* because he is a very popular fellow on his hill. He pleads with the killers for the lives of his wife and son. The militiamen grant him the life of his wife but murder his son "because he is an arrogant Tutsi." Hearing of his miraculous escape, the man's niece (also a Tutsi), whose whole immediate family has been wiped out, runs to him and begs him to save her. The *Interahamwe* return and, refusing to listen to the uncle's pleading, kill the eighteen-year-old girl. After the RPF victory the man becomes the local *bourgmestre* (mayor). A few weeks later he goes to Kigali on administrative business. He gets arrested for "not having protected his niece," in reality because some local people want his job. Five years later he was still in jail.[6]

- A Tutsi RPF soldier falls in love with a Hutu girl. Relatives try to stop the marriage by saying she was involved in the genocide and get her arrested. The young soldier frantically begs anybody who can help him save his beloved. Through the agency of one of his officers he gets the girl freed. He then gets arrested for "interfering with justice" and spends eighteen months in jail.[7]

- Célestin Sebulikoko, a Tutsi businessman who used to finance the RPF during the war, runs to the RPF-held area of Byumba in May 1994 to flee the killers. He then gets killed by the RPF in obscure circumstances, probably over a business rivalry. The "official" excuse is that he was a member of the Mouvement Révolutionnaire National pour le Développement (MRND).[8]

- A young Tutsi from inside Rwanda joins the RPF during the war. His whole family is destroyed during the genocide. He comes back home and finds Tutsi émigrés from the diaspora in Burundi who have returned to Rwanda and occupied his farm. They get him thrown in jail as a *génocidaire* and he manages to get out only with the help of his commanding officer.[9]

- Antoine Sibomana, bourgmestre of Mbazi commune, has protected many Tutsi during the genocide and saved the children of the Hutu Human Rights activist Monique Mujawamaliya. When the fighting gets close to his hill he shepherds his whole flock to Burundi. Contacted there by agents of the new government who tell him they know of his honorable behavior, he comes back with his people. He is arrested three days later with no reason given.[10]

2

- A Hutu peasant and his Tutsi wife have both managed to survive the genocide. After the RPF victory Tutsi extremists come to their hill and threaten him. He and his wife run for safety to an internally displaced persons (IDP) camp near Kibungo. There she is killed by Hutu extremists who accuse her of being "a government spy."[11]

The list could be almost endless. Genocide was so intertwined with everyday life that it could be used at every turn to secure an economic advantage, to settle an old grudge or to cover one's tracks.[12] Many people were killed by former *Interahamwe* simply because they might give evidence against them.[13] Other people quickly found out that having survived the genocide could be a profitable business. They created "accusation cooperatives," which would sell their denunciations of real or supposed *Interahamwe* activities to those who could use such testimonies for economic or political benefit. In January 1995 two hapless Angolan businessmen who were so denounced ended up in jail under the accusation of being "mercenary militiamen" because somebody wanted their dollars.[14] There were many young women and girls pregnant from rape by Hutu killers trying to arrange for abortions, which the collapsed medical system was unable to provide. Tutsi survivors, called *bapfuye buhagazi* ("walking dead") by the diaspora Tutsi who had come back, were often looked on with suspicion. They were caught in a nightmarish world between their Hutu neighbors, some of whom had been their saviors and some who had tried to murder them, and strange returnees from abroad who often accused them of compromising with the killers in order to save their lives. As for Hutu survivors, they were looked on as *génocidaires* by the returnee Tutsi and as traitors by the sympathizers of the old regime.[15] Nobody was automatically innocent, and suspicion was everywhere. Worse, there was very little solidarity between Hutu and Tutsi survivors. Widows' associations, mainly Tutsi, at times refused to let Hutu widows join, especially if the dead husband had been a Hutu. The first anniversary of the genocide in April 1995 clearly showed that some in the new regime were intent upon getting as much political capital as they could out of the occasion, and Hutu survivors were marginalized. The "Tutsification" of the genocide thus subtly started to turn it exactly into what its perpetrators had intended it to be: an ethnic rather than a political massacre.[16]

The civilian returnees themselves, although in a better spiritual position, soon found out that life in postgenocide Rwanda was anything but normal. While in exile they had maintained a sense of unity that was fostered by their common situation. RPF consciousness raising and the hopes and fears

3

linked with the war had reinforced this impression. Now, having "returned" to a country many of them did not know, they were confronted with the triple conundrum of dead relatives, limited economic opportunities, and cultural strangeness. They were discovering that, paradoxically, Tutsi survivors often had more in common with their Hutu neighbors than with themselves. They started to divide and quarrel according to their synthetic "tribes of exile," that is, the countries where they had spent their years away from Rwanda. There were "Zairians," "Burundians," "Tanzanians," and "Ugandans," as well as those from more exotic places not ranking high enough in terms of returnee numbers to constitute a serious network of solidarity. If these distinctions did not matter too much in daily life, they mattered a lot as soon as politics, business, or the military was involved. Networks and mafias emerged, struggling for political control and economic advantage in the midst of the ruins. The biggest fish in that dangerous pond was of course the Rwandese Patriotic Army (RPA) itself, the armed branch of the RPF. The RPA leadership was mostly "Ugandan," a fact that was to acquire growing importance as the political and military situation in the region progressively slipped into further disintegration.

Most of the Hutu who had stayed in the country were there because they had not managed to run away in time.[17] Because many sympathizers of the opposition parties had been killed and many of the *Interahamwe* followers were in exile, the remaining Hutu population belonged to that vast middle ground that is the mainstay of any civil society. But in Rwanda "middle ground" did not mean moderates. Years of relentless political propaganda had taken their toll and most people displayed an attitude of sullen resentment toward the new government. It was perceived as a conquerors' regime, not as a legitimate one. Many Hutu showed little or no sensitivity toward what had just happened and equated their own real but limited plight with the massive horrors suffered by the Tutsi. Some even denied that any genocide had taken place at all and attributed the many deaths to "the war." Incredibly gross remarks could be heard, such as that of a Hutu woman walking by a heap of decomposing corpses and snarling, "Why don't they clean up this mess? It stinks." Because this was at a time when "Tutsi fundamentalists" were organizing solemn reburial ceremonies of abandoned corpses, it did not augur well for any policy of national reconciliation.

This poisoned spiritual climate was made even worse by the state of material chaos in which the country was plunged. The former government had fled to Zaire, taking all the money from the Central Bank and herding into exile approximately 2.1 million people (out of a postgenocide population of about 6.9 million) as an immediate human buffer and a future political pawn in case of negotiations. In the south of the country there were over 500,000 people living in IDP camps left over from the so-called Safe Humanitarian Zone created by the French during Operation Turquoise and perhaps another 500,000 living wherever the war had pushed them. This left about 3.6 million people living in roughly "normal" conditions, that is, only 45 percent of the prewar population. Given the extremely fertile nature of the Rwandese soil, food was not too much of a problem. But transport was, as most vehicles had been either destroyed or taken to Zaire by retreating government forces. In the midst of the general confusion, over 700,000 Tutsi from the diaspora were in the process of coming back from their countries of exile, those from Uganda bringing with them vast quantities of cattle (probably about one million head), which started to invade the Mutara area and even the Akagera National Park, competing for grazing space with the wildlife. Empty houses and even unoccupied farms were taken over by the newcomers, who assumed that all those who had gone into exile were *génocidaires*. One of the reasons for the fierce competition for urban properties was that the "old caseload refugees"—the Tutsi returnees coming from abroad—were sociologically quite different from the victims of the genocide. Roughly the same numbers came back (around 700,000) as had been killed (800,000). But the victims had been ordinary Rwandese, with a majority of rural dwellers. The newcomers were not peasants; they had lived in exile in situations where access to land was restricted, and many of them had no experience in agriculture. Furthermore, the notion of being isolated in the hills surrounded by a majority of Hutu, right after the genocide, was not very appealing. So they tended to congregate in the towns and to look for and monopolize the moneyed jobs. These were not high-paying jobs since there were not enough of those to go around anyway. Returnees would take *any* salaried job, and this meant pushing the Hutu out of the towns—and out of the jobs. This contributed to further social tensions in the country. To make things worse, over 150,000 houses had been destroyed, and even without any illegal occupations there would not have been enough houses to go around. There were also nearly 300,000 children without parents, both "unaccompanied minors" floating around and survivors in "minor-headed households" on the farms, living lives of incredible fear and loneliness, at times miles away from the nearest adult. Most of the police were dead or had fled abroad with the former government. So had most of the judges, school-teachers, doctors, and nurses. The various ministries had only a skeleton staff left, and even the churches, which were full of dead bodies, were closed. The majority Catholic Church, which should have provided some form of moral guidance in the midst of the disaster, was in fact deeply tainted by the geno-cide. The Church hierarchy had been very close to the former regime and it remained unrepentant after the genocide, in spite of its sullied record.[18] Many Hutu priests had refused to help not only lay Tutsi but even their fellow Tutsi clergy members. Nuns running orphanages and schools had delivered their Tutsi charges to the killers and pushed Tutsi sisters out of the community and to their deaths. Church buildings that had been considered places of refuge had become tombs, one priest going even as far as organ-izing the destruction of his own church with a bulldozer, burying under its ruins a packed group of Tutsi refugees whom the killers had not managed to extricate from the building. Some priests who had fled to Goma were bold enough to write to Pope John Paul II,

The population fears to fall back into the pre-1959 slavery.... This is a vast plot prepared a long time ago.... It is an anti-Catholic movement supported by some priests who work with the RPF. Some have become Muslims and others dug mass graves financed by the RPF.... This explains the anger of the people.... Let us forget about this International Tribunal where the criminals will be both prosecu-tors and judges.[19]

The accusation that the Hutu were in fact the victims and not the perpe-trators of the genocide was common in Church circles, which helped sup-port some of the early revisionist propaganda churned out by friends of the former government. The Catholic Church was using the fact that about half of its clergy had been killed to wrap itself in martyrs' shrouds, omit-ting to say that most of the victims were Tutsi and that the Hutu priests who were killed trying to protect their flocks were often considered traitors by their fellow Hutu clerics. The Anglican Church, although much smaller than its Catholic counterpart, was just as compromised in the genocide. But perhaps due to the more critical tradition of Protestantism it was the only Church to do an honest bit of soul-searching and try to understand what had happened, questioning its type of evangelization, its relationship with the regime, and its weaknesses on the ethnic question.[20]

In such a landscape of almost total misery and destruction the attitude of the new government was critical, in moral as well as practical terms. And that too was soon going to add another disquieting dimension to the knot of problems Rwanda had become.

The politics of national unity

The government that was inaugurated on July 19, 1994, was a genuine government of national unity. It was fully in the spirit of the Arusha Peace Agreements of August 1993 which the *génocidaire* regime had sought to destroy. The new president, Pasteur Bizimungu, was an RPF Hutu who had been a government civil servant in the 1980s. Of the twenty-one ministries, the lion's share (eight) had gone to the RPF; the rest were evenly distributed, with four ministries going to the Mouvement Démocratique Républicain (MDR; the main opposition party under the former government), three to the Parti Social Démocrate (PSD), three to the Liberals, two to independent personalities, and one to the small Christian Democratic Party. In ethnic terms fifteen of the new ministers were Hutu and only six were Tutsi. After such a catastrophe the new cabinet looked like a small miracle of reason in a sea of madness.

But the international community was not entirely happy with the new cabinet and there was pressure for a "broadening of the political base" before any form of economic aid could be resumed. Of course this pressure came mostly from Belgium and from the Social Christian Party, which had been very close to the Habyarimana regime. But the U.S. government, various international bodies, and even the UN kept harping on the same theme. It was obvious that "broadening" meant "get more former government Hutu onboard." The advice was ambiguous, a bit like asking Bundeskanzler Konrad Adenauer in 1949 to include former Nazis in his government for the sake of national reconciliation. But Seth Sendashonga, an RPF Hutu and the minister of the interior, got a green light from Gen. Paul Kagame, the vice president, minister of defense, and regime strongman, for cautious "broadening." Since it was out of the question to negotiate with the *génocidaires*, Sendashonga tried dealing with former prime minister Sylvestre Nsanzimana and former minister of agriculture James Gasana. Neither of them had had anything to do with the genocide, but both refused cabinet positions out of political caution. Insisting on the "political broadening" of the national unity government as a precondition for resumption of economic aid was a narrow obsession, given the global nature of the catastrophe.[21] Financial help was absurdly stuck on technicalities, and although $1 billion in humanitarian aid had been pledged, it was impossible to find

7

$4.5 million to pay Rwanda's arrears to the World Bank in order to release $250 million in available loans.[22] It was the European Union that unilaterally broke the deadlock in November 1994 by giving $88 million without preconditions.[23]

Indeed, the question of economic aid could not be separated from political considerations. But the problem was not the "broadening" that the international community blindly kept insisting on during those early days. Having "moderate criminals" in government would not have helped very much. But there were other, very serious concerns that had started to develop almost from day one *within* the government of national unity itself, and those were definitely not addressed by the international community.

In November 1994 the MDR, the main RPF coalition partner in the cabinet, published a radically critical report on the general situation.[24] It made eight fundamental points of varying importance: (1) the fundamental law had been violated because the transitional government period of existence had been set at five years instead of a maximum of two; (2) the "new army," which was supposed to be born out of a fusion of mostly Tutsi RPA elements and new recruits, was very slow in coming together; (3) there was no separation of powers, and the executive acted independently from Parliament; (4) the RPF should clarify its juridical status, whether as a party or as something else; (5) tribunals should quickly be set up to try those responsible for the genocide; (6) a stop must be put to illegal property seizures; (7) a stop must be put to arbitrary detentions and murders, especially in military camps; and (8) there should be a commission of inquiry to check the growing talk about a double genocide.

The first point was clearly self-serving: as a mainstream party the MDR could count on a good share of the Hutu vote, and it was trying its luck at pushing an obviously premature electoral agenda. Points 2, 3, and 4 were more serious since they dealt with the way the new Rwanda was supposed to work: an ethnic army, a towering executive, and an overwhelming RPF were not recipes for even embryonic forms of democracy. Of course, *democracy* was itself a loaded word in the Tutsi-Hutu context,[25] and the MDR's "innocent" appeal to the ballot box was far from free of ethnic calculations. So was the RPF's refusal to address the problem. Points 5 and 6 were even more serious because arrests, which had started in a haphazard way in July, kept happening but without getting more organized. *Gutunga agatoki*, "pointing the finger," was still the dominant mode of bringing about charges. Detainees were shoved into the jails, and when those were full they were pushed into any available closed space, including metallic containers for cargo, with tiny air vents and no toilets, where many died of suffocation and diseases. From 1,000 prisoners in August 1994 the numbers had risen to 6,000 at the end of the year and kept growing exponentially to reach 23,000 by March 1995.[26]

The judicial system was in ruins. Justice Minister Alphonse-Marie Nkubito had only one telephone line and two typewriters in his office. But a strange feeling was beginning to develop among the Hutu ministers in the cabinet: that the RPF was in no hurry to push for quick justice and that it wished to maintain full political control over justice proceedings. On October 28, 1994, the Rwandese delegation in New York presented a memo to the UN Security Council in which it tried to stop the creation of an international tribunal of justice for the genocide and asked instead for the creation of a national one. It also asked that war crimes be excluded from its mandate to avoid too close scrutiny of its own postgenocide behavior.[27] As for illegal property occupations, they were a major source of strife, and more and more people kept getting arrested as *génocidaires* over what were in fact real estate disputes.

But it was of course points 7 and 8 that were the gravest. About those the MDR document did not mince words: "In order for agricultural work to start again we must control insecurity which prevents the peasants from working in their fields since they are not even sure of being alive the next day." Point 8 about a "double genocide" was beginning to be bandied around as Hutu extremists in exile eagerly seized on rumors of RPF killings to confuse issues and develop a revisionist argument.[28] Nevertheless, the RPF did not seem very eager to have a thorough inquiry throw a clarifying light on the situation. Prime Minister Faustin Twagiramungu was extremely worried and soon returned to the subject in a public broadcast wherein he both accepted blame and begged his fellow countrymen to calm down: "We cannot deny that we have not provided security.... People are still being killed like by the earlier ones [i.e., the MRND].... We are all angry. But we cannot take spears and machetes and keep killing one another."[29]

Soon the subject had become so controversial that the prime minister and General Kagame agreed to a public debate to clarify the situation. It did not help much, since neither wavered on his position, Twagiramungu denouncing the insecurity and Kagame "defending the honour of the Army."[30] There was a slight drop in the arrest rate following the debate, but then it picked up again. And although the government of national unity managed to stay together, the tension kept growing, unabated. It was around that time that

9

General Kagame gave a long interview to the Belgian newspaper *Le Soir* which is worth quoting at length because all the main themes of the period are present:

There is no reason for people to be afraid.... There are more than a million victims, so there must be culprits: where are they? International opinion should be understanding of us. It is hard for justice to get started again.... Trials have to be well-prepared.... It is also certain that the arrest of high-ranking genocide suspects who live abroad, especially in Europe, would help appease tensions here.... How can we forget and forgive? If we did, everything would blow up sooner or later. You don't bury the feelings of people whose relatives lie in mass graves.... There are many criminals in those camps and our patience is nearing its end. We have waited a long time but there is no end in sight. Innocents must go home and the guilty be arrested. Nobody seems to want to put all that in order and so we are going to have to do it on our own.[31]

Everything is here. First, the denial of the problem ("There is no reason ... to be afraid"), coupled with an explanation of why survivors are furious. Then, a plea for the understanding of the West about the lack of justice ("Trials have to be well-prepared"); anger at the sloth and indifference of the West about *génocidaires* who are still free and about the Western-supported open sores of the refugee camps; pressure; tensions. And finally, the grim resolve that, once again, as in 1990 and 1994, "We are going to have to do it on our own."

Justice and the killings

Many foreigners have tended to see the need for justice in the Rwandese genocide as mostly the problem of an international tribunal dealing with high-powered criminals. This is partly true; an international tribunal was indeed created in November 1994, the small town of Arusha in Tanzania being chosen as its seat in February 1995.[32] But because this tribunal belongs more to the domain of the international community's paradoxical policies toward postgenocide Rwanda than to the domain of justice, I will deal with it in its proper place.

The true problem of justice, once the international community had flunked the test of speed and efficiency that could have put it on the reality track, had to do with what went on *inside* Rwanda.[33] And that was more than what the international community cared to know. From the beginning it was obvious that the situation was going to be hard to control. Prime Minister Twagiramungu had created an initial stir by saying that there should be at least thirty thousand people put on trial.[34] A few months later the figure, which initially had looked enormous, sounded understated. Through the *gutunga agatoki* system thousands were arrested: a mixture of genuine killers, hapless hangers-on, victims of property quarrels, cuckolded husbands, and common criminals. The RPF *abakada* had the run of the hills and they did as they pleased.[35] By early 1995, when the momentum really got going, 100 to 150 people were arrested every day, and the numbers kept growing: 44,000 in June 1995, 55,000 in November, 70,000 in February 1996, 80,000 in August, without any due process and without any prospect of achieving it. The conditions of detention became insane, with densities reaching 5.7 prisoners per square meter in the jail at Gitarama. In March 1995 twenty-two prisoners choked to death in an overcrowded room of the Muhima *gendarmerie* brigade,[36] and the same number were later beaten to death by their drunken jailers in a makeshift prison near Kibuye.[37] In Gitarama, where 6,750 prisoners crowded a jail with a capacity for 600, Médecins Sans Frontières witnessed a thousand deaths between October 1994 and June 1995.[38] It was common for prisoners to develop ulcers or even gangrene of the feet from days of not finding enough room to sit down.[39] Of 183 places of detention listed by the Red Cross,[40] only sixteen were actual jails. The rest could be anything, including holes dug into the ground, covered with corrugated iron sheets weighted down by cement blocks. There were only thirty-six judges left, together with fourteen prosecutors, of whom only three had had any sort of legal training.[41] In February 1995 in the central jail of Kigali, only 1,498 out of 6,795 detainees had had a chance of seeing a magistrate at any point since their arrest.[42] Most prisoners' files were empty or nonexistent. But trying to free even innocent detainees was a perilous exercise. In October 1994, when Judge Gratien Ruhorahoza attempted to free forty people who had no files, he was kidnapped by the military and later murdered. Twenty-six of the 270 magistrates left after the genocide (out of about 800) were arrested as *génocidaires* when they tried freeing detainees they considered innocent. The Liberation Commission created by the Justice Ministry in October 1994 reviewed about one hundred cases between its creation and April 1995, freeing only fifty-eight prisoners. In any case, former prisoners were in danger because in the popular mind arrest was often equated with guilt; several prisoners were murdered after their liberation.

When considering this justice disaster, the most ironic aspect of the situation was that the main perpetrators of the genocide remained free.[43] Most of them were just over the border in Zaire and in lesser numbers in Tanzania.

11

Many of the key political actors of the former government were living in Nairobi, where President Daniel arap Moi had given them tacit protection because of his strong dislike for Ugandan President Yoweri Museveni, a close ally of the new regime in Kigali.[44] The International Criminal Tribunal for Rwanda (ICTR) had drawn up a list of about four hundred genocide suspects in April 1995 but had not managed to enforce its search warrants. This apparent toleration of the intolerable acted as a permanent irritant both on ethnic relations inside Rwanda and on the relations of the new regime with the international community. It also helped reinforce two different feelings the RPF had about the outside world: "We are alone and we have to rely purely on ourselves," and "These foreigners are so weak and incoherent that they are unlikely to react no matter what we do." It is unfortunate that both feelings were not far from the truth.

But it did not seem that the regime was really willing to improve the justice situation. Given the incredible pileup of untried cases and the pitiful state of the Rwandese justice system, the obvious answer would have been to bring in outside legal resources, a suggestion that was made by several human rights organizations and by the ICTR.[45] But in July 1995 the Rwandese government adamantly refused even a temporary loan of foreign judges, deeming it to be "unconstitutional and a breach of the sovereignty of the Rwandese people."[46] The government never changed its position, even when the number of detainees passed the 100,000 mark in 1997. The feeling of many Hutu collaborators of the new regime was that the RPF did not want the situation to be resolved. As long as *gutunga agatoki* remained the rule, as long as jail was an ever present threat hanging over the whole Hutu community, guilt and fear combined to keep everybody in line, and the growing RPF monopoly on power was unlikely to be challenged by people who could at any time be accused of being *génocidaires*. Moreover, any serious attempt at a global settlement of the justice situation would have had to examine more closely the growing body of allegations made against the RPF itself. And this was something that was definitely not wanted by the new regime.

The problem of the RPF killings is probably one of the most controversial in the vastly conflicting body of writing and studies on the Rwandese genocide. Among the supporters of the RPF regime it is an infamous accusation spread by former *génocidaires* intent on sullying the good name of an otherwise respectable government. Indeed, one cannot but wince when one hears some of the most outrageous statements made by members of the former regime.[47] But although the notorious theory of a "double genocide" does not stand up to serious inquiry, a simple display of moral indignation is not quite sufficient to dismiss the notion of the RPF committing horrendous crimes since it started moving toward absolute power with the onset of the genocide.[48]

To understand the violence of the RPF, it is necessary to go back a bit to its Ugandan origins. The hard core of the RPF was made up of men who were young boys in Uganda in the early 1980s. They grew up as refugees in the violence of the Ugandan civil wars.[49] Their first experience of blood came with the Idi Amin massacres of the 1978–1979 war with Tanzania, then with the 1979–1980 countermassacres committed by the so-called *wakombozi*. Later they suffered from the anti-Rwandese pogroms of 1982 and joined Museveni's guerrilla forces.[50] There they not only fought, but they also witnessed the government army massacring civilians in the Luweero region. Once they won the war they were quickly pressed again into combat, this time in the north, against the troops of the "prophetess" Alice Lakwena. Now the tables were turned; this time *they* were the "forces of law and order" and it was the local population who were the insurgents. They in turn committed massacres, to such an extent that President Museveni had to send special military judges to the north to curb his own army. One of these judges was Paul Kagame, and some of the men he had to judge were later his subordinates in the RPF. The whole life history of these men even before they set foot on Rwandese soil had been full of the sound and the fury of civil war, with its attendant atrocities and civilian massacres, committed against them, around them, or by them. For them violence was not exceptional; it was a normal state of affairs.

And the violence did not let up once they started fighting in Rwanda, as their beloved charismatic leader, Fred Rwigyema, was murdered by his own comrades within days of the attack.[51] Since I got this crucial event wrong in 1995, some elaboration is called for.[52] The RPF had attacked Rwanda from Ugandan territory on October 1, 1990, under the leadership of Fred Rwigyema, the Rwandese Tutsi former chief of staff of the Ugandan army and long-time personal friend of Yoweri Museveni. Rwigyema had known Museveni since their student days together and their involvement in the revolutionary movement in Mozambique in the 1970s. On the third day of the offensive, Rwigyema held a staff conference with three of his close associates, Commanders Peter Banyingana, Chris Bunyenyezi, and Stephen Nduguta. A strong argument soon developed between Rwigyema and two of his aides,

Nduguta remaining a silent bystander. The reasons for the argument were multiple. Rwigyema was a highly politicized and competent guerrilla strategist. He was keenly aware of the deadly potential of the Hutu-Tutsi identity split and wanted to proceed slowly, politicize the Hutu peasantry, wait for the government to make mistakes, and gradually get the rural masses on his side. Not so for Banyingana and Bunyenyezi, who wanted power and wanted it quickly, without giving much thought to the problems they would encounter later. The argument became heated, and Banyingana drew out his pistol and shot Rwigyema in the head. In the resulting confusion Nduguta slipped away, went back to Uganda, and told President Museveni what had happened. Museveni was shocked and sent his trusted brother Salim Saleh to Rwanda, where he found Rwigyema's body in a swamp, buried it properly, arrested the two culprits, and brought them back to Uganda for interrogation and eventual execution.

But there is more to that story. Paul Kagame had had a close relationship with both Peter Banyingana and Chris Bunyenyezi since he had spared their lives in 1988 when he was a roving army judge in northern Uganda and they had been detained for committing atrocities against the civilian population. Besides, he was a cool and collected type of person, in direct contrast to the more volatile personalities of the other two. Kagame belongs to the Bega clan, which is famous in Rwanda for having usurped power through the Rucunshu coup d'état; his own great-grandfather, Kabare, killed young King Rutarindwa in December 1896.[53] Fred Rwigyema, on the contrary, was a Muhindiro, a member of the purest royal lineage of the Nyiginya dynasty. Although remote in time, these events are still vividly present in the minds of most Rwandese today, and many friends of Rwigyema now living in exile believe that the hapless Banyingana and Bunyenyezi were manipulated in order to murder their leader. There is of course no concrete proof for this Shakespearean betrayal of a much-loved man by his comrades-in-arms, only some circumstantial evidence that would not stand up in a court of law. Yet many are the former members of the RPF who remain persuaded that Rwigyema's murder was a carefully contrived plot to eliminate a brilliant man whose combination of royal legitimacy and revolutionary charisma made him a probable future national leader.[54]

So violence dogged the steps of the former National Resistance Army guerrillas as they moved into Rwanda. Of course, during the four years of the war the movement recruited large numbers of young fighters who came from different backgrounds. But the top level of the officer corps remained

"Ugandan." And there is quite strong evidence that the "Ugandan" officers did not hesitate to kill a number of young francophone Tutsi recruits, especially those coming from the refugee community in Burundi, because they felt that, as the recruits were better educated, they could threaten the officers' future control of the movement.[55] Moving from that background into the genocide was a quantum leap into witnessing even more massive horrors and hardening the RPF's culture into the use of casual instrumental violence. Direct population control by such a force after July 1994 was unlikely to resemble anything like the workings of a civilian administration.

The first rumors of RPF violence started during the genocide itself, when NGO and UN High Commission for Refugees (UNHCR) workers in Tanzania were told by fleeing refugees about massacres committed by advancing RPF forces.[56] These and other cases were later corroborated by research for the massive report on the genocide written by Human Rights Watch Africa.[57] Shocking as these stories may have been, they had to be seen in the context of the war and of the genocide. But what is in a way more interesting was the apparent global disdain of the RPF for the safety of the Tutsi victims. RPF soldiers of course helped Tutsi civilians threatened by *Interahamwe* when they would chance upon them, but they never planned their military operations so as to try saving as many as possible. And when there was talk of a foreign intervention force to stop the genocide, although it was a very dim possibility, the RPF unambiguously opposed it, to the dismay of some longtime human rights activists who had fought for the lives of the Tutsi civilians since 1990.[58] I will return to this point at the end of this section, where I discuss the patterns and meaning of the RPF killings.

What finally brought these massacres to light was the Gersony Report episode. Robert Gersony, an experienced American freelance consultant who had done extensive work in combat zones in Africa, particularly in Mozambique and Somalia, was hired by UNHCR to do a refugee survey in the hope of facilitating refugee return.[59] He and his assistants started their work with broad sympathy for the RPF, as was common among those who had been confronted by the horror of the genocide.[60] Between early August and late September 1994 Gersony conducted about two hundred interviews inside Rwanda at ninety-one different sites located in 41 of the country's 145 communes, mostly in the Kibungo, Gisenyi, and Butare areas. He also did interviews in nine refugee camps. He ended up having to face a terrible reality: the RPF was carrying out a massive campaign of killings, which could not be considered simply as uncontrolled revenge killings even if some of the murders belonged to that category.[61] His informants all told the same story: the first RPF soldiers they saw were nice and cheerful and there was no problem with them. But a day or two later other soldiers came. These, obviously selected killer teams, assembled the people for a "peace and reconciliation meeting," which they attended without fear and during which they were indiscriminately slaughtered. Gersony's conclusion was that between early April and mid-September 1994 the RPF had killed between 25,000 and 45,000 people, *including Tutsi*.[62] The UNHCR, which had commissioned the study for quite a different purpose, was appalled. The news went all the way up to UN Secretary-General Boutros Boutros Ghali, who ordered Kofi Annan, then assistant secretary-general, and Kamel Morjane, UNHCR director for Africa, to rush to Kigali. Annan briefed President Bizimungu, Vice President Kagame, Prime Minister Twagiramungu, and Interior Minister Sendashonga and gave each of them a copy of the report. He told them that he personally believed in its general validity but hoped that the killings were not deliberate. He also promised that the UN would embargo the document to give the new government a chance to stabilize.[63] The report was indeed embargoed: its very existence was denied and Gersony was instructed never to talk about it publicly. Although he was called to Kigali and asked to personally brief the Rwandese cabinet, he has kept his word to this day, giving his suppressed report an almost mythical dimension. The United Nations Assistance Mission to Rwanda (UNAMIR) tried some desultory investigations but was either prevented from going when mass graves were revealed (September 1994 in Butare) or operated in such a clumsy way that it did not manage to "discover" what everybody else knew about. My own uneasiness about the Gersony Report spurred me into some direct research when I went back to Rwanda for the first time after the genocide in January 1995. It was unfortunately not very difficult to meet massacre witnesses, even if one had to go through a wall of lies. Apart from the understandable RPF denials, there were also quite a few hopeful lies by Hutu who desperately wanted the government of national unity to work in spite of everything.[64] But testimonies were plenty, both in Rwanda and abroad, and many were heart-rending because they involved getting hit by both sides. For example, a mixed-parentage doctor who had lost nine Tutsi members of his family to the machetes of the *Interahamwe* then lost eighteen members of his Hutu family when they were killed by the RPF on April 15, 1994, in the Kanazi sector of Sake commune (Kibungo prefecture).[65] Then there were the frequent stories of people who had been called to a meeting by the RPF and who, when they expected in typically Rwandese fashion to be told what the new power wanted them to do, would be slaughtered indiscriminately. The practice had started very early, with the Kigina massacre (Rusumo commune, Kibungo prefecture) on May 15, 1994, and its pattern was followed quite regularly, including probably the biggest massacre of the early period at the Arboretum in Butare.[66] This led the population to joke with typical gallows humor that *kwitaba inama* ("answer the call to a meeting") was in fact *kwitaba imana* ("answer the call of God"). Liberal Hutu who had fought the dictatorship and seen their families engulfed in the genocide were not spared. Many who managed to go to Byumba in the hope of getting protection from the RPF were killed within days of their arrival.[67] But not all were killed, and the reasons for surviving could be puzzling. I met a former PSD militant from Cyangugu who had lost her family in the genocide, who then managed to cross the border into Zaire, went up to Goma, and from there reentered Rwanda to join the RPF forces in Byumba. She started to work with the new authorities and discounted as slander the rumors of killings she had heard. But one day she had a puncture late at night while driving an RPF military vehicle and she asked an old Hutu peasant to help her change the tire. Taking her for an RPF fighter (she was dressed in a uniform), he asked her why they killed people. She asked him what he meant, so he took her to a banana plantation and showed her many dead bodies roughly covered with banana leaves, saying that this was the work of her friends. Shaken by the experience, she started to investigate the rumors she had heard and discovered many burial sites around Byumba. After the fall of Kigali she was transferred to the capital and from there went abroad to a Rwandese diplomatic mission and eventually into political exile. Asked why she thought she had been spared in Byumba, she said that it was because she knew Prime Minister Twagiramungu well (he hails from Cyangugu, like her) and that the RPF did not want to create a scandal by killing somebody close to a man it still needed at the time.[68]

Because there were many dead bodies and because the RPF did not wish to attract attention,[69] disposal areas were set up in a variety of places to incinerate the corpses. Several of the men who worked in two of these centers in Masaka and Gabiro have testified to several people, giving precise and believable details about the corpse disposal process.[70]

All this begs several questions. First, what about the reactions of the Hutu cabinet ministers while all this was going on? I have discussed the massacres at length with Faustin Twagiramungu and Seth Sendashonga, probably the two main Hutu political actors of the period, and the answers are complex. They believe there was a certain amount of necessary toleration of the massacres, the feeling that they were caught in a horrible but unavoidable logic: the Tutsi had lost three-quarters of a million of their people and the situation could not be settled without some blood on the other side. They were resigned to *some* blood but started getting worried when there seemed to be no end in sight. Then there was also a feeling of powerlessness: to stop the killing they had to set a new political agenda and it might take some time; in the meantime they had to be realistic. Since they were kept well informed by their own parallel intelligence network this did not prevent them from protesting to Kagame. Sendashonga wrote him over four hundred memos on the killings and insecurity during his thirteen months in the cabinet, but Kagame was careful never to answer in writing.[71] At first he kept wavering between partial admission, feigned surprise, and blunt denial, and then later he simply stopped answering. The Hutu ministers were so conscious of the potential catastrophe their eventual resignations could cause that they swallowed it all in the name of national unity. Until the Kibeho slaughter pushed them over the brink.[72]

Then there is the vexing question of the foreigners: Were they all blind, deluded, or accomplices? This is a complex issue that I discuss in more detail in the section on the international community's attitudes. But suffice it to say here that it was a bit of all three plus a lot of material problems. There were 154 NGOs in Rwanda in 1995, and the least one can say is that their display of foolishness was amazing. Of course some of them, such as Médecins Sans Frontières and Oxfam, gave quite a good account of themselves. But on the international NGO scene Rwanda was the place to be if you wanted to get funding, just like Ethiopia in 1985 or Somalia in 1992. So everybody rushed to Rwanda, whether or not they had something to contribute. The NGOs were there "for purely humanitarian purposes" and carefully kept away from the local politics, which they did not understand anyway.

As for the UN human rights operation, it was a sad joke.[73] Underfunded and staffed with largely incompetent young people, most of whom spoke no Kinyarwanda or Swahili or even French, it did practically nothing. I met in Kibuye a group of "human rights monitors" who seemed to spend most of their time swimming in Lake Kivu and sunbathing, their only French-speaking member being then on leave. The monitors who spoke French and were eager to work were usually prevented from doing so by their director, who seemed to mostly fear rocking the boat in any way. He was not the only one. In January 1995, when trying to visit a dubious mass grave site near Kibungo while on an unofficial UNHCR visit, I was prevented from doing so by the UNHCR country director, who accused me of "wanting to create problems with the government."[74] With such attitudes the RPF did not have to worry too much about being found out.

There was also a major problem of logistics and administration, which partly explains why foreign workers could not at times see what was going on literally under their noses. To quote from a contemporary report about Byumba prefecture,

Apart from the main paved road leading to Kigali, secondary roads are generally in poor condition, thus hampering easy access to the communes situated furthest from the Field Office. Modern communication means are virtually nonexistent. As is the case in most of the country local authorities are mostly "old caseload returnees"[75] who have spent the last thirty years outside the country.[76]

Finally, there was the problem of the RPF itself. Were these killings attempts at a "second genocide," as the former *génocidaires* and their friends were trying to say? Or were they only the unavoidable revenge killings that one could expect after such a horror? Or was it something else altogether? I personally tend to think that it was something else for a number of reasons. First, there was the callous indifference to the fate of the Tutsi civilians "from inside," which did not fit well with a simple ethnic reading of the situation. The RPF had known since 1992 that the resolve of Hutu Power ideological extremism was such that maybe not a full-scale genocide but at least numerous massacres were a distinct possibility. Yet, as we have already seen, when the genocide did start, saving Tutsi civilians was not a priority. Worse, one of the most questionable of the RPF ideologues coolly declared in September 1994 that the "interior" Tutsi deserved what happened to them "because they did not want to flee as they were getting rich doing business with the MRND."[77] During the very early days of the massacres, RPF soldiers often did not distinguish Tutsi from Hutu when they killed people, seeming to assume that the remaining Tutsi were "collaborators" of the *Interahamwe*. Which brings us back to the brutal military culture of the RPF. The mainly Tutsi RPF had decided to "liberate" Rwanda and to create a "new democratic Rwanda" free from ethnic domination. Around 1992–1993 this goal seemed genuine enough to bring a limited number of liberal Hutu to its side. But what actually happened later bore no resemblance to these theories. The theories were thrown to the winds and what

19

remained was used only for window dressing, barely hiding brute force and cold-blooded political calculations.

Then there is the style of the killings. Unlike the killings carried out during the genocide, these new massacres were decentralized, secret, limited, and fluctuating. If we bring these characteristics together with the callousness displayed toward the internal Tutsi population we have something that resembles neither the genocide nor uncontrolled revenge killings, but rather a policy of political control through terror. The RPF seemed to trust nobody in Rwanda, not even the Tutsi survivors who were felt to be "contaminated." Thus the killings do not appear to be separate from other aspects of RPF policies, such as building a national unity front (later discarded), keeping the judicial process as a Damocles' sword above all Hutu heads, or carefully designing a propaganda line to exploit the outside world's guilt. These policies are coherent, and their focal point is undivided political control.

During the first period of violence (April to September 1994), the killings were rather indiscriminate; some genuine revenge killings took place together with the programmed terror killings. After that there was a period of relative calm which seemed a response to fears of negative Western reactions.[78] When those were dispelled and the killings resumed in January 1995,[79] there were fewer and they were more focused. The victims mostly belonged to four categories: (1) friends and family of the *génocidaires*, (2) educated people, (3) old PARMEHUTU[80] members, and (4) *ibipinga,* that is, opponents, people who did not think and behave "right." What these people had in common was their constituting an actual or potential elite, capable of giving shape to a politically amorphous peasant mass. Whether the victims had actually intended to act in a political way was completely beside the point. The point was that they had some capacity to do so. The RPF vision of the Hutu masses seems to have been that of a permanent danger to be kept at bay by random mass killings to instill fear and to be defanged by neutralizing real or potential leaders. Death was the preferred method during the first period, but later marginalization became sufficient once the emergency period was over. Terrorizing a group into submission does not require annihilating it. Therefore there was not even an *attempt* at a second genocide. The point was simply to get a compliant Hutu mass that would do agricultural work and keep minding its simple business without any ideologues, *génocidaires* or not, putting ideas into their heads. Some members of the Hutu elite came to realize the situation, which was clearly articulated by Gen. Léonidas Rusatira, a democratic former Forces Armées Rwandaises

(FAR) officer who had opposed the genocide and later joined the RPA. After his flight into exile in November 1995 he wrote in an open letter:

I joined the RPA on 29 July 1994 in the hope of enabling all my fellow country-men to live together . . . but instead I went on a deadly obstacle course for the next sixteen months[81] and this finally convinced me that the present regime in Kigali deserves no confidence and does not want a genuine reconciliation between Tutsi and Hutu.... . It only wants to consolidate its power without any form of sharing and hopes to keep it forever. The plan of the elite in Kigali is to decapitate through any available means the Hutu elite, *and to let live a voiceless mass of peasants only good enough to toil the earth for their masters.*[82]

Then there is another key question: Were these killings systematically or-ganized? Given the size of Rwanda, the discipline of the RPA, and the RPF's tight political control, it is almost impossible that they were not. Work par-ties to bury bodies and the use of crematoria in several areas hardly suggest improvisation. The evidence points to an original tactical pattern. Apart from the early *kwitaba inama* killings, which were large and systematic, the later killings were small and decentralized. A "bad" family would be blown up with grenades or burned alive in their house, a civil servant would be ambushed on the highway and shot, a man would be kidnapped and his body would later be found in a banana grove. The killings were routinely attributed to *Interahamwe* cross-border raids, and there were indeed a lot of such attacks. It was often quite difficult to tell if people had been killed by *Interahamwe* or by the RPA, and popular wisdom would usually look at the personality of the victims to try to decide from which side the blow came. Contrary to the former regime, the RPF never boasted about its violence, even indirectly, and it denied any responsibility unless caught red-handed. And then excuses were made, often quite convincingly.[83] After the initial period of *kwitaba inama* the further killings felt more tolerated than insti-gated, although they were not random. It was almost like an adaptation of free market economics to political assassination. The top RPF leadership only had to tacitly condone a variety of killings ("dangerous people," profes-sionals, independent-minded civil servants, Hutu businessmen) for those to happen automatically in the tight economic situation, with the returnees' need for jobs in the monetarized sector. With their culture of conflict the RPF officers were men for whom violence was a profession and who took it to be an integral part of their daily lives, a "solution" to many problems.

The key question was whether there was any resolve to punish their crimes. Obviously there was none. Or rather, there was the usual window dressing;

some RPA privates and NCOs were arrested, tried, and even condemned but *exclusively* for what could be proved beyond any doubt to be common crimes: murdering a man to steal his motorbike, shooting people in a bar while drunk, and so on. The visible perpetrators were always at the bottom of the social or military scale, and so were their victims. When important people such as the prefect Pierre-Claver Rwangabo,[84] the businessman Gervais Birekeraho,[85] or the banker Aloys Karasankwavu[86] died, nobody was ever arrested. Similarly, no important perpetrators were ever brought to justice, or when they were, only symbolic sentences were passed.

The final question concerning the killings is speculative: Were they useful, even from the point of view of cold-blooded realpolitik and Tutsi security? In other words, was the choice of control through calculated violence the only workable option for the political arm of the Tutsi minority after the genocide? It is very doubtful. Because even if the vast majority of the Hutu were not supportive of the new regime they were not automatically opposed to it. There was a sullen semi-acceptance of change depending on a variety of factors: real justice, the economic situation, the refugee problem, army behavior, national reconciliation, and the fate of the government of national unity. If those elements had progressively evolved in the right direction, the former *génocidaire* regime would slowly but surely have lost its appeal, even if fantasies about Hutu Power were probably bound to linger in the collective mind for some years.

Then why kill? The answer seems once more to come from the peculiar culture developed by the RPF since its Ugandan days. The RPF Tutsi were soldiers, good soldiers but only soldiers. And General Kagame was probably the epitome of the RPF soldier.[87] As soldiers they knew only the gun, and the gun had worked well for them in the past. Whatever they had set out to do by force of arms—fighting Idi Amin, overthrowing Obote, overthrowing the Hutu Republic in Rwanda—they had eventually achieved. Their self-confidence was strong, their political vision embryonic, and they had a limited but efficient bag of tricks to deal with the international community. As General Kagame boasted to a British journalist, "We used communication and information warfare better than anyone. We have found a new way of doing things."[88] This might have been slightly exaggerated, but it was not altogether wrong. The UN had not been able to stop a genocide; how would it dare interfere with "the victims" who were now "restoring order"? From that point of view the difference of tone between speeches given in Kinyarwanda in the hills and speeches made in English within earshot of foreigners in Kigali is revealing. The RPF calculated that guilt, ineptitude, and the hope that things would work out would cause the West to literally let them get away with murder. The calculation was correct. Thus "national reconciliation" came to take on a very peculiar coded meaning. It meant in fact the passive acceptance of undivided Tutsi power over an obedient Hutu mass. Above that mass the Tutsi were in theory supposed to all be equal, but, to borrow from Orwell's formula in *Animal Farm,* the RPF Tutsi were more equal than the others. A number of compliant but hopeful Hutu kept acting as intermediaries, greasing the wheels of the system and providing the foreigners with the edifying picture of national reconciliation in progress. But all those who believed that their collaboration with the regime had provided them with sufficient credentials to act in a politically autonomous way eventually fell foul of the RPF power structure, which could not tolerate any independent political activity.[89]

Belonging to a culture in which obedience to authority is a long national tradition, the Hutu peasant masses complied.[90] But their compliance was superficial: minds and souls were not won and the future remained fraught with dangers.

And of course, there was no way for the moderate Tutsi to dissociate themselves from this strategy. With the smell of death still in the air, the decomposed bodies carefully husbanded by the new regime in nerve-straining ceremonies,[91] the pain of having lost whole families, the fear that it could happen again, the knowledge that among the Hutu many were totally unrepentant and hoped for a new occasion to kill again, how could even the most liberal-minded Tutsi criticize "his" regime?

Here we may pause and generalize a bit because understanding this process brings us to the very center of the whirlpool that was later to suck in a massive chunk of the African continent and to set in motion a radical new questioning of the whole postcolonial order. If we stand back, we see a group of victorious military men who forcibly brought an apparent "solution" to a monstrous crisis (the genocide) in the face of Western incompetence and vacillation. Subsequent Western guilt turned their might into right regardless of what they were actually doing. So when another massive problem followed (the refugee camps in Zaire), for them the "obvious" way to solve it was once more through the resolute use of force. Again the Western world reacted with stunned incompetence. And it "worked." By then the conclusion for those who were later nicknamed "Soldiers without Borders" was unavoidable: they could "solve" more and more of their problems in the same manner and the international community would only stand by. So they removed President Mobutu, whose absolute decay only required a slight push; tried to gain control of Zaire/Congo; then tried to overthrow their own Mobutu replacement when he did not prove pliable enough, all the while hoping to solve their own overpopulation and poverty by further conquests. But what the rough Rwandese men of war did not realize was that Zaire/Congo was at the heart of a soft continent. It was the epitome of a world rendered fragile by thirty years of postcolonial neglect and exploitation. And the West, which was the implicit guarantor of that postcolonial order, rotten as it may have been, was caught napping at every turn. From Burundi to Sudan and from Angola to Brazzaville, many different forms of conflict pathologies had developed around the rim of the Congo basin, ready to blend in. It would not have mattered if Rwanda had been isolated in a neutral corner of Africa. But the space into which these increasingly brutal military "solutions" were playing themselves out was (and remains) so vitally connected to the rest of the continent that, as in Berlin in 1885, the whole of Africa's future was now at stake. But by then, contrary to nineteenth-century imperialist Europe, the post–cold war Western world was only marginally interested. In spite of the usual diplomatic platitudes, Africa was now increasingly on its own, whether moving toward further decay or toward yet unforeseen recomposition and reorganization.

Rwanda outside Rwanda: the world of the refugee camps

The end of the war and the end of the genocide were accompanied by a massive wave of Rwandese refugees fleeing their country toward Zaire, Tanzania, and even conflict-torn Burundi.[92] They did not run far, settling with UN and NGO assistance in enormous refugee camps located almost directly on the border with Rwanda. Contrary to other refugee exoduses from countries at war, this was not the flight of individuals wishing to escape danger; rather, just as the genocide had been, it was an organized system of mass mobilization for a political purpose. The refugees settled in their camps in perfect order, under the authority of their former leaders, ready to be used for further aims. As Joël Boutroue wrote from his experience as senior UNHCR staff member in the camps, "Discussions with refugee leaders . . . showed that exile was the continuation of war by other means."

With about thirty-five camps of various sizes, Zaire was at the core of the problem. The most formidable locations were the five enormous camps of Katale, Kahindo, Mugunga, Lac Vert, and Sake around Goma, the administrative capital of North Kivu province. Together they held no fewer than 850,000 people, including the 30,000 to 40,000 men of the ex-FAR, the army of the genocide, complete with its heavy and light weapons, its officer corps, and its transport echelon. To the south of Lake Kivu, around Bukavu and Uvira, thirty smaller camps held about 650,000 refugees. There were also 270,000 people in nine camps in Burundi, and another 570,000 in eight camps in Tanzania.[93] But apart from the large Benaco camp in Tanzania, practically all the politicians and military men had gone to Zaire, where President Mobutu's sympathy for their fallen regime afforded them greater freedom of movement.

From the beginning these camps were an uneasy compromise between genuine refugee settlements and war machines built for the reconquest of power in Rwanda. The majority of the people were in a state of shock and, as good Rwandese, were waiting for orders. As one refugee told a French journalist,

Very clever people have pushed us into fleeing two months ago. FAR troops were opening the way with a lorry and we had to follow them, forced from behind by other soldiers with guns. They pushed us like cows.... . Anyway, we do not know what to think because our leaders are not around just now. We are waiting for a new burgomaster to give us our orders.[94]

They did not have to wait long. As soon as UNHCR tried to organize the first repatriations it had to stop because both the refugees and the aid workers came under threat from these "leaders" through their *Interahamwe* henchmen. About 140,000 people managed to return, mostly on their own, during the first two months. But by September 1994 rumors of the violence inside Rwanda had combined with political intimidation inside the camps to turn the limited returnee flow to a trickle. By early 1995 it had stopped altogether.

The first aim of the political leadership was to gain control of the food supply, knowing it to be the key to their constituency's fidelity. Through a system of "electing popular leaders" who could front for the real, hidden political leadership, the former administrators gained control of humanitarian aid without exposing themselves.[95] Thus they could punish their enemies, reward their supporters, and make money through ration overcounting and taxation. Even a writer politically sympathetic to the refugees could not but remark, "There is a form of dictatorship in the camps."[96] First pick for food and health treatment was given to the former elite and to the ex-FAR soldiers.[97] The political order was ironclad, and those who disagreed or wanted

25

to return to Rwanda or were too frank with the humanitarian aid workers were subject to intimidation, even murdered.[98] This led at first to strong reactions from the humanitarian establishment, which found it extremely difficult to work under such conditions. In November 1994 fifteen NGOs, including CARE, Oxfam, and Médecins Sans Frontières, published a joint communiqué denouncing the situation. But the funding was good and it was always possible to rationalize one's presence with the idea that this was where the emergency was and that the people who would really suffer in case of agency withdrawal would be the ordinary peasants and not their criminal leaders. In the end, only Médecins Sans Frontières withdrew, first from the Zaire camps (November) and finally even from those in Tanzania (December).

Within their long orderly rows of *blindés*,[99] the refugees tried to rebuild some semblance of a normal life. Too normal perhaps. In the five camps around Goma there were 2,324 bars, 450 restaurants, 589 shops of various kinds, 62 hairdressers, 51 pharmacies, 30 tailors, 25 butchers, five iron-smiths and mechanics, four photographic studios, three cinemas, two hotels (including one two stories high, built entirely from scrap material), and one slaughterhouse, which was regularly supplied with locally purchased or sto-len cattle.[100] There were camp information bulletins and even newspapers. And, of course, there were the soldiers.

The first armed infiltrations back into Rwanda had started almost from the beginning.[101] The former leaders were quite open about their intentions. Former MRND secretary-general Mathieu Ngirumpatse declared that the army was at present being trained and redeployed and was just waiting a while before launching a full-scale invasion. This was empty boasting at the time since the defeat had been severe. But training was indeed taking place,[102] and military operations had resumed at a low level. On October 31, 1994, ex-FAR soldiers infiltrated from Zaire had killed thirty-six people near Gisenyi, starting a cycle that would not stop. In a blind continuation of the genocide, the infiltrators would target any Tutsi civilian they could find, but they would also kill Hutu civilians, almost at random, including in an area (the northwest) where they were popular, just to make sure the population was terrorized into helping them. Caught between RPF violence and ex-FAR terror, the northwest was going to be a small hell on earth for the next four years.

Did this militarization of the camps put the former regime in a position to seriously threaten the RPF in Kigali? Yes and no. In the short run, the ex-

FAR did not have the military capacity to seriously challenge the recent victors. But the future was much more uncertain, as the ex-FAR had started a process of rearming, practically in full view of the international community. The *génocidaires* had taken with them all of the Rwandese government's official financial resources, and they kept making money out of the camps themselves.[103] In addition they could call on the private resources of corruption money stashed away by their leadership in better times. They also went to their former arms suppliers, particularly in South Africa, and asked for completion of the partially fulfilled contracts they had signed while in power.[104] New suppliers were also found, such as when President Mobutu kindly took along Mrs. Habyarimana and her brother Séraphin Rwabukumba on a state visit to China in October 1994. They visited Chinese arms factories during their trip and were able to acquire five million dollars' worth of equipment at extremely competitive prices.[105] Off the record, a Chinese official later told a British journalist, "China practices a policy of allowing people to solve their own problems."[106]

The simplest way was still to buy from private arms merchants who were able to supply a whole array of cheap weapons from former Soviet bloc countries, no questions asked. The main suppliers seem to have been Bulgaria and Albania, through a variety of dealers[107] using Nigerian-, Ghanaian-, Russian-, and Ukrainian-registered planes.[108] Contrary to many rumors, France does not seem to have belonged to the dubious Rwanda *génocidaires* military suppliers club. The accusation was reasonable, however, since the French government had staunchly supported the former Rwandese regime and had even very likely violated the UN embargo during the last months of the war.[109] But it seems that by the time Operation Turquoise was over, authorities in Paris had decided that all was lost and that the *génocidaires* were both too compromising and too inefficient to be supported anymore.[110]

In spite of the danger the refugees represented for its eastern provinces, Zairian complicity in continued politicization and militarization was obvious. I will come back to the question of the refugee impact on the Kivus proper,[111] but the Zairian decisions concerning the refugees came from Kinshasa, from President Mobutu himself. He did not care much for the Kivus, an area that had been generally politically hostile to him since the civil war of the 1960s, and he saw in the refugees' arrival a multilayered political opportunity. It enabled him to blackmail the international community into reaccepting him into the mainstream diplomacy from which he had been excluded during the past few years;[112] it also allowed him to put proxy military pressure on his enemies in Kigali and Kampala; and finally he might use the refugees in local Kivu politics by distributing voter cards to them if he was forced to live up to his promise of a national ballot in 1997.[113] To achieve these diverse and complex objectives, Mobutu played one of the cat-and-mouse games he was notorious for: he announced repatriation deadlines and then dropped them; he promised to disarm the ex-FAR and helped them rearm on the sly;[114] he offered to help police the camps and did not do it; he promised to move the camps away from the border and forgot his word the next week. The former Rwandese leadership had free run of the country, and Gen. Augustin Bizimungu, former commander in chief of the FAR, often met with President Mobutu in Kinshasa or Gbadolite to coordinate strategies with him. He was actually in the company of the Zairian president when Mobutu went through the motions of a *refoulement* (forced repatriation) in August 1995. Far from being a threat to the refugees, even if fifteen thousand were actually pushed over the border and a few killed, the whole exercise was designed purely to panic the international community by showing how messy things would be if Zaire actually decided to kick the refugees out. The blackmail was quite successful, and Mobutu became again a major player in the eyes of the UN and the Europeans, and to a lesser degree of the Americans.

For the *génocidaire* leadership, Mobutu was an essential factor. Zairian protection enabled them not only to rearm and to keep harassing Rwanda militarily from their safe havens in the camps, but it also helped them pretend they were still a major actor to be reckoned with, a not so obvious proposition once the iron discipline of the camps was discounted. The ex-FAR were largely a spent force, still capable of murdering civilians (they did it on a regular basis during their cross-border operations) but not really capable of fighting a well-organized army. Their poor military performance when the moment of truth came in October and November 1996 is proof of that. Among the refugee rank and file there were widely diverging attitudes. Some intellectuals, mostly southern *abanyanduga*, were conscious of being caught in a dead-end situation with no choice but a potentially ineffective military option and were desperately trying to find help in creating a political alternative.[115] They were bitterly disappointed when former commerce minister François Nzabahimana created the Rassemblement Démocratique pour le Retour (RDR) at Mugunga camp in early April 1995. Although Nzabahimana himself had not been directly involved in the genocide, he was fully in sympathy with the former leadership's ideology, and the RDR was just an attempt at regaining a modicum of international respectability by pretending to be "new."[116] It did not work too well, especially because General Bizimungu immediately declared his support for the "new" organization. But UNHCR was so desperate for decent refugee leadership it could talk to that for a while everybody went through the motions of pretending it was in fact new. The new-old leadership knew that the political initiative had slipped out of its hands and desperately wanted the support of the international community to achieve some kind of negotiation. But the positions of the two sides were light years apart. On the same day Joseph Kalinganire, the information minister of the Rwandese Government in Exile, declared, "If the international community is not willing to put pressure on the RPF to negotiate with us we will have to come back by force,"[117] while General Kagame was saying, "One cannot say that the one million or so Rwandese outside the country were all killers."[118] His army had recently attacked Birava camp on April 11 and Mugunga on April 26, killing thirty-three, just to show that cross-border raids could work both ways. Both sides were angling for the support of the international community in their contradictory endeavors. But the difference was that although this support was vital for the former regime, which did not have it, the new government, which did, could actually do without, thus retaining a much wider margin of decision.

The international community's attitudes

The international community considered the Rwandese genocide with a complex mixture of shock and indifference. On the one hand, intellectuals, the humanitarian community, journalists, and politically aware sections of the general public were shocked that the solemn promise made after World War II and embedded in the 1948 Convention on the Prevention of Genocide could be violated in full view of the United Nations and the world's TV cameras. But on the other hand, Rwanda was a small and strategically unimportant country, the cold war was over, there were no economic interests involved, and for many of the ordinary men in the street Africans were savages from whom one could expect nothing better anyway.

But this was also the time when the rich post–cold war world was trying to convince itself that it was building a "new world order." The Gulf War of 1991 had not been too convincing, since the protective concern displayed for a small invaded country might not have been so vigorous if that country had not been rich in oil. The Somalia experiment had definitely been more altruistic. It had also been much less successful,[119] and its failure was a major cause of the weak international response to the Rwandese genocide, wrongly perceived as "another case of a failed state in Africa."[120]

So when the genocide was actually over and when the immensity of the horror became visible, the international community rushed into humanitarian aid with guilty relief, never-too-late-to-do-good, thus greatly helping the perpetrators of the very crimes it had done nothing to stop. The whole thing would have been funny if it had not been tragic. The only mitigating circumstance was that there was nobody else around who could be helped so quickly and effectively and there was a desperate feeling that *something needed to be done*. The financial cost of maintaining nearly two million refugees in camps was staggering; it was much higher than the cost of helping Rwanda itself, in which there were two and a half times as many people as there were refugees.

Cost of Humanitarian Refugee Aid		Cost of Humanitarian Aid to Rwanda
1994	$705m	$386m
1995	$592m	$362m
1996	$739m	$149m
TOTAL	$2.036b	$897m

Source: UNHCR. The refugee aid figures are multidonors and multiagencies. They should be considered approximate because of the problem of geographical breakdown. Total cost is calculated by computing Great Lakes humanitarian disbursements (on some items given as aggregates) + Zaire disbursements + Tanzania disbursements + one-third of Burundi figures to allow for the separate emergency in Burundi itself. Rwanda figures reflect *humanitarian* aid, not economic aid, which was much higher ($598.8 million in bilateral aid and $773.2 million in multilateral aid pledged in Geneva in January 1995).

When looking at the data in the table, we must keep in mind that there were around two million refugees, as opposed to over five million people in Rwanda proper. Thus these figures represent about $1.40 per capita per day in the camps against only $0.49 per capita per day in Rwanda itself, typical of the quantitative meltdown and the political vacuum that kept dogging the whole period. The joke in Kigali was that HCR stood for Hauts Criminels Rassasiés ("well-fed high criminals"). This massive financial effort did not even earn the international community any sympathy from the refugees, who felt that UNHCR was on the side of Kigali. A moderate refugee leader interviewed by Johan Pottier said, "Repatriation is not just a question of logistics, of trucks and leaflets. No, it is deeper than that. But HCR does not seem to understand."[121] How could it? The game was always seen, at least from the side of the heavy battalions of donors, as a number of *quantitative* and *technical* problems. Some NGOs of course tried to remind the international community that there were many *qualitative* and *political* problems as well, and that they were probably at least as important as, if not more important than the ones that were considered worthy of attention by the donors and the UN bureaucracy. Their efforts proved largely useless.

In many ways, the pattern of approaching the problem was similar to the one used before the genocide, when the international community was pushing for peace during the Arusha negotiations. The international community had been so obsessed with its preferred goal that it totally neglected the various factors that could run counter to it, including the preparation of the genocide. Now repatriation had to be achieved at all cost, the first casualty of that policy being truth, when Robert Gersony was effectively silenced for having uncovered the "wrong" facts.

Then the magic word had been *peace*; now it was *repatriation*. Every technical effort was made to achieve this predefined goal without pausing to think about what the various actors actually *meant* when they apparently agreed to it. But just as in the peace negotiations, it was the context that finally prevailed and completely submerged the technicalities, rendering them irrelevant.[122] The attitude toward the 1994 Gersony Report is an edifying case in point.[123] The U.S. government got wind of it and decided that showing the RPF as probably guilty of crimes against humanity would be bad for the United States, since it had done nothing about the genocide and would then be seen as partial to the side of the *génocidaires*. Under-Secretary of State for Global Affairs Tim Wirth was asked to rubbish the report as much as he could. Wirth went to Kigali and New York, reassured the RPF, attacked Gersony's methodology, hinted at a Hutu conspiracy, and leaked carefully chosen tidbits of information to the press. It worked. And an embarrassed UN press conference did not help.[124] Secretary-General Boutros Ghali decided to put the report into the hands of the UN Commission of Experts on Human Rights, which was then directly briefed by Gersony in Geneva in October 1994. To no avail. The commission went to Rwanda, stayed for a few days in quasi-tourist conditions, and gave its expert advice: although there was some evidence of "killings by Tutsi elements of Hutu individuals . . . they were not committed to destroy the Hutu ethnic group as such within the meaning of the 1948 Genocide Convention."[125] This was both substantially true and incredibly cynical: what it basically said was that, short of an attempted second genocide, limited killings were all right. The key elements the international community wanted to skirt were organization and intent because organized RPF killings at the time would have embarrassed everybody and threatened "quick repatriation." Therefore these elements did not exist, even if a duly commissioned independent expert had found out about them.

Concerning the refugees, there were three major parameters that were repeatedly neglected. The first and most obvious one was the militarization of the camps. The ex-FAR were there, in full view of everybody, doing their jogging and their calisthenics every morning, organizing, training, and marching. Their close association with the *génocidaire* leadership, whether original or slightly facelifted as the RDR, was public knowledge. Reports kept coming in about their efforts at rearmament. And practically nothing was done. In February 1995, after the camps had existed for six months, the UN finally succeeded in putting together an armed force to ensure a minimum of security. This force, called the Zaire Camp Security Contingent, was made up of soldiers from the Division Spéciale Présidentielle (DSP), the elite corps of the Zairian army. But in financially collapsed Zaire even the DSP was not paid regularly. The UN took fifteen hundred men, gave them new uniforms, and paid them. Nicknamed "Mrs. Ogata's troops"[126] (which they were not, unfortunately), after UN High Commissioner for Refugees Sadako Ogata, they behaved surprisingly well and brought back a measure of law and order to the camps. But their mandate did not include restraining ex-FAR activities. The ex-FAR general command was located on the Kivu lakeshore, in the *bananeraie* (banana grove) mini camp near Mugunga, and it would have been easy to surround it and to arrest the key military actors; without their officers, the men would have been easier to control. The idea was contemplated several times but never actually tried.[127] Nothing serious was done to stop ex-FAR arms purchases either. In view of this, it was hard to disagree with General Kagame when he accused the UN and the NGOs of "help[ing] an army in exile."[128] Ironically this help to an army in exile was carried out alongside a deliberate refusal to see what the new army in power was doing.

The second parameter was security in Rwanda itself, to quell the rumors and foster a feeling of security among the refugees.[129] The now thoroughly discredited UNAMIR II force was still inside the country, in the vague hope that it would help achieve the peace it had so tragically failed to keep a few months before. Great importance was put on the level of the UNAMIR II military presence: 5,500 troops, 320 military observers, and 120 civilian police had been authorized by the Security Council, but in June 1995 the Rwandese government tried to get these reduced to 1,800 men and to have their presence shortened. The secretary-general counterattacked and decided that 1,800 men "were not enough to carry out the mandate outlined by the Special Representative." After some haggling the UNAMIR II mandate was extended to December 8, 1995, and troop numbers were brought up to 2,330. This was felt to be an important diplomatic victory. The only problem was that UNAMIR II troops were, for all practical purposes, deaf, blind, and lame. Whether there were 1,800 or 2,330 of them was irrelevant. They were despised by everybody in Rwanda as the embodiment of arrogant powerlessness. Children laughed at the soldiers going into shops in full battle gear to obey UN regulations though they had not fired a single shot during the genocide. Interior Minister Sendashonga once remarked to me as a light UNAMIR tank was clanking by, "That is the only trace they will leave behind, their caterpillar tracks on the tarmac of our streets." In theory UNAMIR II could have stopped or at least detected some of the worst human rights abuses then being committed by the RPF-led government. But just as had been the case for UNAMIR I before the genocide, it was not supposed to engage in intelligence gathering. It clumsily tried once or twice to find out about some of the most obvious massacres, but because it was always giving advance notice of its movements and "cooperated" with the RPA, it never found anything. When it finally left ingloriously in March 1996, Special Envoy Shaharyar Khan, who had had time to ponder the riddle of the UN presence, could only conclude, "What Rwanda needs is a mini Marshall Plan and the UN is in no position to provide one."[130]

The third parameter was diplomatic resolve in dealing with the governments of Zaire and Rwanda.[131] Instead of appearing as a locus of international leadership, the UN looked like a cork bobbing up and down in a furious sea, barely able to react and totally unable to take the initiative. To be fair, one should keep in mind that the UN is weak when its strong members either do not support it or, worse, are in conflict over a given issue. This was the case over Rwanda: "Whenever France was ready to apply pressure on Rwanda . . . this was blocked by the U.S. Similarly whenever the U.S. wished to put pressure on Zaire this was blocked by France. Hence one could not expect much of the Security Council."[132] Why so? France's position was relatively understandable. It had been defeated, and since it could not openly support its horrible former friends it vented its frustrations through obstructionist tactics, all the while hoping to "put Mobutu back in the saddle," as a high-ranking French civil servant told me in early 1996. The U.S. position was more complicated. Although nobody in the international community had done anything to stop the genocide, the United States was probably the only country seriously embarrassed about that. This resulted from a variety of complex factors peculiar to U.S. politics, to the American psyche, and to America's view of its place in the world. First there was the presence of a large and vocal Jewish lobby that felt terrible about the genocide and had an instinctive sympathy for the new Rwandese government; then there was a feeling of cultural shame that had to do with being "the land of the free, the home of the brave," a role that did not stand out prominently during the terrible spring of 1994; and finally there was a notion that as *the* major world power the United States could not but have a great responsibility in such a momentous event. All this blended with the "good guys versus bad guys" preferred mode of American thinking; Department of Defense fascination for the RPA, which it was just then beginning to discover;[133] and simplified geopolitical "game plans" for the future of eastern and central Africa. The end result was growing and almost uncritical support for the RPF regime. With the United States pulling on one side and France pulling on the other, the UN was rudderless. In addition, it was divided according to "UNHCR geopolitics": the Goma UNHCR office pushed for early return because it was afraid of the destructive local impact of the camps and feared the highly politicized leadership; the Kigali office wanted staggered gradual returns because it was influenced by the security views of the Rwandese government; the Bukavu office wanted an early return but was less anxious than Goma because it was not in close contact with the noxious *génocidaire* circles; and the Special Unit for Rwanda and Burundi in Geneva preached caution because it had limited trust in the RPF promises. The result was inaction.

Apart from the refugee situation, the second major area of concern where the international community's attitude mattered was the question of justice. The ICTR had been created in November 1994 and installed in Arusha in February the following year. In April it had produced its own list of four hundred genocide suspects, supposed to be more neutral than the various lists produced in Rwanda itself. A year later it was still floundering about, complaining about "lack of means,"[134] not having even produced any indictment, much less judgments.

As I have argued elsewhere,[135] the magnitude of the crime required radical measures if justice had to have a *symbolic impact*. The problem was one of urgency. Hundreds of thousands had died, the culprits were known, and a fast-track process had to be used if we wanted to defeat the notorious "culture of impunity" so much talked about in international circles and about which so little had been done. If the whole exercise was to make sense for the ordinary Rwandese population, some people had to hang, and quickly. This was the only way to convince the Tutsi that the world cared about them in spite of its passivity during the genocide. It was also the only way to show the Hutu population that for once it was not the ordinary fellows who were going to pay the price, but the "big men." Perhaps more important even for the chance of a better future it was the only way to stop the RPF from using the excuse of "uncontrolled revenge" to push forward its agenda of organization and ethnic dictatorship.

Of course, if we keep in mind the utter spinelessness of the international community before, during, and after the genocide, the ICTR was probably all that it could come up with; expecting an African Nuremberg was probably too much to ask. But even when the ICTR got on the road, the punishments it meted out to the *génocidaires* failed to impress the Rwandese population. For them letting killers live on, and live in much better physical comfort than anything the ordinary person in Rwanda had, was a form, if not of pardon, at least of toleration. And they knew that pardoning obviously guilty "high criminals" could only perpetuate the impunity–revenge–counterrevenge cycle so that hundreds of thousands more would die from the unchecked direct and indirect consequences of their actions. We chose to go by the book of our laws because we wanted to please ourselves more than we wanted to heal the wounds of Rwanda. Two years after the genocide, when talking to a young Tutsi student in Europe, I could not but remonstrate angrily (and stupidly) with him for the RPF crimes in Rwanda. "Sir, we have had no justice. So now we kill. What can we do?" was his almost desperate answer. Just as the Hutu had used the blunders of Belgian colonial policies to legitimize ethnic dictatorship, so now the Tutsi were free to use the cowardice of the international community to legitimize their violence. In a way the *génocidaires* had won their political argument, and we had helped them win through our nice legalistic view of the situation. Prim and proper international law had left unattended a gaping moral loophole, and the ethnic ideology of the *génocidaires* had slipped through. Because the real Hutu killers had not been sacrificially executed, all Hutu were now regarded as potential killers. And all Tutsi had become licensed avengers. Many Tutsi and many Hutu did not want to be either. But we had provided them with procedural squabbles instead of the biblical justice that would have been commensurate with the magnitude of the crime. And they were now, almost all of them, inmates or wardens, living in the stifling prison built by the defeated but triumphant racist ideology.

FROM KIBEHO TO THE ATTACK ON ZAIRE
(APRIL 1995–OCTOBER 1996)

The Kibeho crisis

Somehow life went on in Rwanda at the beginning of 1995. Amid the ruins. With the killings and the "disappearances." With the government of national unity staggering on, hoping to provide a modicum of leadership in this broken society. The Rwandese had coined an expression for what so many people felt: *imitima yarakomeretse,* "the disease of the wounded hearts." The economy was in shambles; of the $598 million in bilateral aid pledged in January at the Rwanda Roundtable Conference in Geneva, only $94.5 million had been disbursed by June.[1] Of that money, $26 million had to be used to pay arrears on the former government's debt.[2] The perception gap between the international community and what was happening in Rwanda was enormous. The international community talked about national reconciliation and refugee repatriation, but suspicion was pervasive. *Gutunga agatoki* (showing with the finger) denunciations were commonplace: survivors denouncing killers, actual killers denouncing others to escape punishment, bystanders denouncing innocents to get their land or their house. Women survivors tried to band together to help each other, but even then, some Hutu widows might be refused access to the support groups because of ethnic guilt by association, and Hutu orphans in orphanages would be roughed up by Tutsi kids as "children of *interahamwe.*"[3] Some transport had restarted and the electricity supply was slowly becoming less erratic. Very few schools had reopened. The January 1995 public debate between Prime Minister Faustin Twagiramungu and Vice President Paul Kagame had not settled the matter of the violence, which everybody knew about but which the UN remained blind to.

This violence eventually led to the Kibeho massacre of April 1995 and to the unraveling of the national unity government. The process leading to the massacre is worth describing in detail because it offers on a small scale all the characteristics of what was eventually to take place in Zaire eighteen months later: nontreatment of the consequences of the genocide, well-meaning but politically blind humanitarianism, RPF resolve to "solve the problem" by force, stunned impotence of the international community in the face of violence, and, finally, a hypocritical denial that anything much had happened.

The problem initially stemmed from the existence of very large camps of internally displaced persons in the former so-called Safe Humanitarian Zone created by the French during Operation Turquoise in southwestern Rwanda. In late 1994 these camps had sheltered a population of about 350,000 persons,[4] and the United Nations had created a special Integrated Operations Centre (IOC) to handle the situation. The IOC started rather well, managing to repatriate about eighty thousand IDPs between its creation in October 1994 and January 1995. But this had been during a window of opportunity, coinciding almost exactly with the period of caution on the part of the RPF after it was given a warning through the Gersony Report. In January, when the "fateful conference" syndrome had dispelled RPF fears of Western sanctions and the killings had resumed, the IDPs refused to go back to the insecurity of the hills. "By the third week of February, Operation Retour [Return] had come to a virtual standstill."[5] But the government still insisted on closing the camps. As the former director of the United Nations Rwanda Emergency Office (UNREO) wrote,

The government's hostility to the camps was profound, visceral. It stemmed from their link to the genocide. The camps were regarded as a product of Operation Turquoise... . A large portion of those who had taken shelter within Zone Turquoise were seen by the government as perpetrators of the genocide.[6]

This was of course a biased view on the government's part since the camps sheltered thousands of women and children as well as the men who might or might not have been *génocidaires*. But pressure was building rapidly on the government side to close down the camps, by force if necessary. The IOC, faced with the unwillingness of the IDPs to go back to what they knew to be a dangerous environment, kept wavering between appeals for more time, pleas to the IDPs to go back, and rather pointless bureaucratic "programs." While the RPF "day after day accused, criticised and demanded more cars. . . making many NGOs feel unwelcome and even threatened,"[7] the UNREO insisted on creating an expensive and cumbersome "integrated humanitarian computer database." The sophisticated database kept breaking down and ended up "costing much and contributing little."[8] But it enabled the IOC to issue "nice high quality maps and graphs . . . making operational reporting clearer, swifter and more impressive."[9] Meanwhile the RPA threatened the use of direct military force against the camps. As an anonymous UN field worker wrote at the time, "We are only actors insofar as the military co-operate with us.... . We will only be blamed when things will go wrong."[10] The field workers were caught in a terrible situation. On the one hand, the RPF establishment felt only contempt for them, tried to squeeze them to the utmost, and had no intention of going along with the politically correct schemes concocted in New York. On the other hand, their superiors insisted on computerized offices, proper procedures, and close cooperation with the government. But, as the former UNREO director was to write after the explosion, "The government was on board but never fully committed, allowing the humanitarian community to assume responsibility for an 'integrated' approach that in reality never existed."[11]

In fact, far from emptying, the camps were filling up with new arrivals fleeing from the terror in the hills. The IOC, caught between its desire for cooperation and the bloody reality, wavered between conflicting explanations, writing in the same report, "A deliberate campaign of disinformation continues to spread stories of harassment, arbitrary arrests and murder in the home communes," and a few lines further on, "Unfortunately people return to the camps, fearing for their personal safety. There have even been reports that some people are fleeing the communes and entering the camps for the first time."[12] On April 6 1995, the ceremonies commemorating the first anniversary of the genocide were the occasion for the spectacular proper reburial of six thousand victims. Feelings were running high and the resolve to do something drastic was building up. On April 17 the *préfet* of Butare announced that all the IDP camps in his prefecture were to be closed forthwith, and the next day the operation started. What happened then is best described in the clear cold language of the military:

On Tuesday 18 April at 0300 hrs two battalions of RPA soldiers surrounded Kibeho camp. The RPA used the expedient measure of firing shots in the air to move the IDPs along. One woman was shot in the hip and ten people, mostly children, were trampled to death... . [The soldiers] torched many of the huts so that the IDPs would not return. At 1630 hrs the RPA fired warning shots and nine more IDPs were killed in the resulting stampede.[13]

The same evening Jacques Bihozagara, the Tutsi RPF minister of reha-bilitation, gave a press conference, where he declared, "Today's operation is an integrated operation based on the strategy elaborated by the Integrated Task Force," adding in a dismissive way, "There are rumours that if the IDPs return home they will be killed... . If that were the government's intention then it would have gone ahead and killed the people within the camps. After all, the camps are still within Rwandan territory." The last part was very revealing of the RPF's train of thought: national sovereignty had to be reestablished over this former Turquoise nest of *génocidaires*, and since this was their territory they could kill whomever they wanted to. Eighteen months later, the question of the borders was not to stand in the way of repeating the operation on a much wider scale in Zaire.

In striking contrast, Minister of the Interior Seth Sendashonga, another RPF member but a Hutu, rushed to Kibeho the next day to try to stop the catastrophe from getting worse. Upon his return to Kigali, he called an emer-gency meeting of the UN and NGOs to get means of transportation quickly because he knew that the RPA could not be restrained much longer. He also briefed Prime Minister Twagiramungu, President Bizimungu, and Vice President Kagame on what had happened. Kagame told him with a straight face that in his capacity as defense minister he would make sure that things remained under control.[14] The next day the soldiers opened fire again, kill-ing twenty and wounding sixty. Then they surrounded Kibeho camp. What happened next has been graphically described by an eyewitness:

[There were] about 150,000 refugees[15] standing shoulder to shoulder on a moun-tain plateau the size of three football fields... . For the last sixty hours the refugees have been forced to relieve themselves where they stand or where they have fallen. The stench takes my breath away... . The refugees do nothing, say nothing, just stare at the Zambians.[16] . . . The two roads winding through the mountains to Kibeho have been closed. Food and water convoys from aid organisations are be-ing stopped and sent back. The government has forbidden all refugee aid... . The first time I witness the consequences of the UN non-intervention policy I fly into a rage... . A group of refugees, about six of them, break away from the crowd and start running into the valley. Rwandan troops start firing immediately. We see the refugee fall dead. I scream at Capt. Francis [Zambian officer] "Stop them! Do something!" . . . He answers: "We have been ordered to co-operate with the Rwan-dan authorities, not to shoot at them." "Even if they kill innocent people before your eyes?" "Yes," he answers.[17]

In fact, this was only the beginning. At noon on Saturday, April 22, the soldiers opened fire on the massed crowd, first with their rifles and later with

60mm mortars as well. They slowed down for a while after lunch, then resumed firing until about 6 p.m. In the words of Linda Polman, a journalist who was still with the Zambian Blue Helmets, "All we could do was to drag away the corpses." But they were beaten to it by the RPA, which started burying the corpses during the night of April 22–23. At daybreak the Australian Medical Corps, which had thirty-two men on the spot, started counting the bodies. They were up to forty-two hundred before being stopped by the RPA. In their estimate, there were still about four hundred to five hundred uncounted. Adding to that figure what the RPA had buried during the night, a not unreasonable estimate would stand at over five thousand casualties. There were many wounded, but not as many as in a combat situation because the RPA troops had bayoneted or shot many at close range.[18]

Seth Sendashonga rushed back to Kibeho on the morning of the April 23. Although he was a minister, albeit a Hutu one, he was turned back by the army; more corpse removal work had to be done before the civilians were allowed in. President Bizimungu arrived in the afternoon and was told that there had been about three hundred casualties, something he accepted without discussion, even showing displeasure when a Zambian officer tried to give him the figure computed by the Australian medical team.

Back in Kigali some of the NGOs, such as Médecins Sans Frontières and Oxfam UK, complained to the UN. To no avail. The Ministry of Rehabilitation issued a short report saying that "casualty estimates which were confirmed by some UNAMIR commanders stand at about 300... . The cause of the incident which resulted in the deaths of so many was traced to the criminal gangs in the camps who were determined to make the [repatriation] process fail."[19] This line of argumentation was to be strictly adhered to by the RPF. The "three hundred" deaths were "unfortunate," but they had been caused by a génocidaire hard core who had used the "ordinary" IDPs as a human shield. The proof was that this armed hard core was still holed up in Kibeho, refusing to move. The army would have to clear out the sixteen hundred people still in the camp.

But what had happened to the others? They were being "repatriated" rather forcefully, mostly on foot, beaten and attacked on the way by angry civilian crowds, falling dead by the roadside due to dehydration and exhaustion.[20] How many survived this grueling ordeal? It is hard to say since the IOC figures on this point are totally out of kilter. On April 24 the IOC announced that there were 145,228 IDPs who had returned to the Butare prefecture. But on April 26 the figure had fallen to 60,177. Even if we take the lowest estimate of the precrisis Kibeho population, that is, around 80,000, this means that at least 20,000 people "vanished" *after* the massacre. Some journalists picked up on the discrepancy in figures, which became even bigger as time went on and as all the other camps were closed by force in the wake of the Kibeho slaughter.[21]

What followed was even more shameful. Interior Minister Sendashonga had asked for an international commission of inquiry, only to be severely rebuffed by Kagame. General Kagame wanted a tame commission, and he got it. After Bizimungu went with the press to Kibeho and publicly dug up 338 bodies, that figure became "official." The "independent" commission of inquiry was made up of nine handpicked lawyers and diplomats from France, Canada, Belgium, Pakistan, the United States, and Holland under the sharp leadership of Christine Omutonyi. They met and talked in Kigali between May 3 and 8, never doing any field inquiry. Their conclusions followed the government line absolutely. There had been "a fear of rearming" and "military training had been observed to take place. ... There [was] evidence that firearms were captured."[22] The loss of control had come when "there had been firing from the IDPs and the RPA suffered casualties... . The RPA responded by firing into the crowd." And finally, as a conclusion: "Due to logistic and time constraints, it was not possible to determine the exact number of fatalities." Yet a year later, the Independent International Commission of Inquiry Report could be quoted with approval in a Swiss academic study on the international protection of displaced persons,[23] and to this day the figure of 338 fatalities has never been officially questioned, although everybody knows it to be false. In fact, the Kibeho tragedy stood as a kind of dress rehearsal for much bigger things. As usual, the lack of response to one crisis was bound to lead to a bigger crisis further down the road.

The collapse of the national unity government

Kibeho was the beginning of the end for the government of national unity created in July 1994. Its guiding principle, born out of the war, the Arusha Agreement, and the genocide, was that power should be shared among the various components of the Rwandese society, Tutsi and Hutu, francophones and anglophones, survivors from the interior and returnees from abroad. The social and political makeup of the cabinet, which had been picked on July 19, 1994, was a fair approximation of that ideal. But there was a steady struggle to maintain the high hopes of the beginning in the face of the growing bad faith of the RPF, which formally pretended to respect the letter of the Arusha Agreement while repeatedly violating its spirit. Whether it was on justice,[24] on dealing with the problem of illegally occupied properties, on physical security, or on the reorganization of the economy, the RPF did not even act as the biggest fish in the pond: it acted as a shark, imposing its solutions, furthering the material interests of its members, and chewing up whoever swam in the way. The Kibeho crisis, and especially its aftermath, was to prove too much of a strain for the fragile remnants of "national unity."

Seth Sendashonga, the pugnacious RPF interior minister, had bombarded Kagame with memos about killings and "disappearances" for the previous nine months, always hoping against hope that somehow things would be brought under control. In a few days Kibeho shattered any remaining hope that Kagame himself and the military nucleus surrounding him were perhaps rough but ultimately had good intentions. During the Kibeho crisis no effort was made to sort out the guilty from the innocent, the Hutu being collectively treated as murderers deserving to be shot without trial. When Sendashonga tried to obtain some redress, not only for the sake of justice but also to preserve the very notion of a government of national unity, he was dryly told to mind his own business. Contrary to President Bizimungu, who clung to his seat for the next five years in the elusive hope of giving weight and content to his paper-thin presidency, Sendashonga realized after Kibeho that the constitutional avenues for a progressive democratization of the regime existed in theory but were closed in practice.[25] The RPF "Ugandan" Tutsi hard core wanted full power, would tolerate only patsies, and was ready to use any tactics, including mass killings, to achieve this purpose. For a liberal Hutu who had staked everything on the reforming and democratic views proffered by the RPF in its guerrilla days, the blow was hard. Still, both Sendashonga and Twagiramungu tried to salvage what they could from the ruins of their democratic efforts. There was still a faint glimmer of hope in the fact that the political divide did not follow purely ethnic lines. Some Tutsi, especially among the francophone Tutsi who found themselves systematically marginalized by the "Ugandans," were beginning to have second thoughts about the new regime. Thus the journalist Jean-Pierre Mugabe, himself an RPF veteran, could write in his newspaper almost exactly at the time of Kibeho,

There are many Tutsi extremists. They are everywhere in the civil service and we have decided to denounce them. They have arbitrarily arrested many Hutu, as if all Hutu were *Interahamwe*. For these extremists even the Tutsi survivors of the

43

genocide are *Interahamwe*. Today many of the Tutsi are just as vulnerable as the Hutu.[26]

Those were brave words indeed, and the future was to show how true they were. But in April 1995 this was definitely a minority opinion within the Tutsi community. The genocide was still fresh in everybody's minds, there were still hollow-eyed children in the hills playing with skulls and bones, *imitima yarokomeretse* was the common ocean of suffering in which everybody was trying to swim, and the Tutsi community still mostly trusted the RPF.

In the short run, Sendashonga decided to stop the arrests. Fifteen prisoners had suffocated to death in the days following Kibeho after being brutally shoved inside the tiny cells of the Rusatira detention center.[27] He went public about his decision, declaring on the radio, "Of late many criminals have been arrested following the closure of the Kibeho camp, thus making the prisons full beyond their capacity.[28] . . . Due to prison overcrowding many inmates are now dying of suffocation."[29] Even if Sendashonga had prudently used the word "criminals" to talk about the new detainees, his declaration was in direct contradiction to a speech made by General Kagame a few days earlier, when he said, "Over 95% of the former Kibeho people have returned to their homes and are in good shape.... . The few who were arrested were arrested because of their crimes."[30] Kagame was furious, and the tensions within the cabinet rose one notch further. They soon got even worse when Maj. Rose Kabuye, the RPF mayor of Kigali, decided to create residency permits for all city dwellers.[31] Not only was it announced that the permits would be delivered "only to blameless persons," but it was also decided that the permits would be green for the old residents and blue for the returnees from Zaire. This set off a panic in the Hutu population and crowds stampeded the offices to try to get the precious document. Sendashonga canceled the whole exercise, thereby provoking Kagame even further.[32] A few days later, Jean-Damascène Ntakirutimana, Twagiramungu's chief of staff, resigned and fled the country, declaring,

The RPF bases its policies on the domination of one ethnic group by the other, as if the painful experience of the fallen regime had served for nothing.... . The situation is getting worse: arbitrary killings, arrests, tortures, a stalled justice, double talk on the refugee question, repression of the press.... . Pressures should be applied on the regime by those countries that support it to bring it to its senses.[33]

By then, the Directorate of Military Intelligence (DMI), which took it upon itself to monitor all aspects of Rwandese society, looked on every

Hutu member of government as a potential traitor and defector. In a memo leaked to the press, the DMI wrote that it was "keeping under scrutiny opposition politicians, especially those of MDR and other extremist forces,"[34] a rather paradoxical statement since the MDR was Faustin Twagiramungu's party and a leading signatory of the Arusha Agreement. The memo explicitly wrote that Sendashonga, Minister of Finance Marc Ruganera, and Vice Prime Minister and Minister for the Civil Service Col. Alexis Kanyarengwe were all being watched constantly. All three were Hutu.

Since "disappearances" and assassinations went on unabated, Sendashonga took the drastic decision to disband the so-called Local Defense Forces (LDFs). Set up after the genocide in theory to replace the almost nonexistent police, the LDFs had soon turned into groups of thugs controlled by the local RPF *abakada*. Many of the arbitrary arrests, disappearances, and murders could be traced to them, something even Radio Rwanda admitted.[35] But they were the RPF's eyes and arms in the hills and Kagame was incensed. A campaign of calumnies developed against Sendashonga, who was seen by the RPF hard core as the soul of resistance to their undivided control. Because nothing could be said against him directly, the calumnies concentrated on his brother.[36] It was in that poisoned atmosphere that Prime Minister Twagiramungu decided to call for an extraordinary council of ministers on security matters. The council met on August 23 and went on for three days, soon turning into a stark confrontation between Kagame and Sendashonga. The minister of the interior received the backing of Twagiramungu and Ruganera, which was to be expected, and more surprisingly of the Tutsi minister of women's affairs, Aloysia Inyumba. This had to do with Inyumba's old idealism and also with the fact that she was keenly aware, as a minister, of the deep concern of women, Tutsi women included, about the mounting violence. Sensing that he had nothing more to lose, Prime Minister Twagiramungu reproached Kagame for choosing 117 Tutsi out of the 145 newly appointed *bourgmestres*. This was clearly overstepping the unspoken agreement never to mention ethnicity in the cabinet in an aggressive way. But it was too late. Sendashonga stood his ground on the disbanding of the LDF, saying that it would not lessen but would, on the contrary, improve security. This was on the third day of the cabinet meeting and everybody knew that the showdown had come. Kagame said ironically to Sendashonga that since he seemed to know more than he about security, perhaps he could take over the Ministry of Defense, or even the whole government. He then got up and left the room, bringing the meeting to an end.[37]

After mulling over the events for two days, Prime Minister Twagira-mungu announced his resignation. President Bizimungu, furious and not wanting to allow him the moral advantage of resignation, came to Parliament on August 28 and asked for a public vote to fire Twagiramungu. Fifty-five raised their hand in support, six abstained, and none voted against.[38] The next day Sendashonga, Minister of Transport and Communications Immaculée Kayumba, Minister of Justice Alphonse-Marie Nkubito, and Minister of Information Jean-Baptiste Nkuriyingoma were all fired.[39] Sen-dashonga's and Nkubito's firings were politically crucial, but the firing of Nkuriyingoma, a relatively junior figure, was simply due to his being candid about the crisis when speaking to the media. As for Immaculée Kayumba, the only Tutsi of the lot, she was fired for three reasons: she personally got on Kagame's nerves; as minister for communications she had not managed to cut off the telephones of the sacked ministers quickly enough, allowing them to speak freely to the international press; and it seemed like a good idea to fire a Tutsi minister, to avoid making the global sacking look ethnically motivated. Sendashonga and Twagiramungu were placed under house arrest and their personal papers ransacked. Nevertheless they were able to get out of it alive, finally managing to leave the country toward the end of the year. The government of national unity was dead, even if its pretended existence was going to be carried over with diminishing credibility for another five years, until the April 2000 presidential crisis.

The refugees and the Kivu cockpit

As the government of national unity collapsed in Rwanda, the problem of masses of refugees sitting practically on its borders and controlled by the forces of the former government went on without any hope for a solution. Although there were over 470,000 Rwandese refugees in Tanzania, for a number of reasons the main problem centered around those in Zaire.[40] One reason was the position of Marshal Mobutu, who, although largely reduced to practical impotence in the Kivus, still tried to manipulate the situation, both for purposes of local and national politics and for reinstating himself to his former international position through blackmail.[41] Another reason had to do with the terrain itself, in the geographical, demographic, and political senses. The Kivus, North and South, were not simply two provinces of Zaire. They had been an essential factor in the 1960s revolt against the Leopoldville government;[42] they were an extension of the ethnic and political problems of Rwanda itself; they were a zone of high-density population with demographic and tribal contradictions of their own; they were connected with the Rwenzururu conflict in Uganda;[43] and they were the backyard of the civil war then going on in Burundi. It was easy to predict the impact of one and a half million refugees with an extremist political leadership, plenty of weapons, and a history of recent genocide when they suddenly burst upon this fragile human environment.

It is crucial to keep in mind both the fragility and the interconnectedness of the Kivus if we want to understand the process that turned a genocide in the tiny country of Rwanda into what eventually became a continentwide war. The Kivus were (and have remained) a high-danger zone on the continent. Conflicts had started there before the global war of 1996, and they have proven extremely difficult to control even after the generalized conflict receded. They would remain so even after the successful Congolese elections of 2006.

The slide from what had been a nationally focused genocide into a global war had one basic cause: there was no political treatment of the genocide in Rwanda by the international community. No efforts were made to prevent it, no efforts were made to stop it, and no efforts were made to remonstrate with those who spoke in the name of the victims when they started to abuse their role.[44] Mature political treatment was replaced by humanitarian condescension and diplomatic bickering. As a result over two million refugees poured over the borders of Rwanda, complete with all the trappings of quasi-sovereignty, including an army, a treasury, and a complete set of criminal politicians. Because the treatment of the crisis, or should I say the nontreatment, was purely humanitarian, the situation was allowed to fester. In Tanzania, where the political and social makeup of the refugee asylum areas was basically sane in spite of extreme poverty, this did not create too grave a problem. But the Kivus were a highly complex and volatile environment in a country that, due to the corrupt leadership of his lifetime president, had sunk below the level of even the most deficient African polities. And the international community did not react to that any differently than it had reacted to the Rwandese genocide: it sent in the humanitarian battalions, ready with plastic tents, emergency food from our groaning farm surplus stocks, and devoted health care workers out to relieve human pain and suffering. The political side of the equation remained solidly blocked at zero. The following section examines how the results, which could be expected, eventually came to materialize.

The area of Zaire known as the Kivus (North and South) is about four times the size of Rwanda. But even though these provinces are bigger and less densely populated than Rwanda, they are far from empty. The population patterns are closely linked to the ethnic and political situation. To understand the situation better, consider North and South not separately, but in sequence.

North Kivu: ethnicity and the land conflict. The two dimensions of ethnicity and land are intimately linked. For example, the table specifies the densities in North Kivu as humans per square kilometer.

Zone	1957	1984
Goma	59	286
Rutshuru	26.4	91
Masisi	38.9	101
Walikale	2.1	6

Source: J. C. Willame, *Banyarwanda et Banyamulenge* (Brussels: CEDAF, 1997), 39.

These figures show that the rate of growth is very high, whereas the densities are very unevenly distributed, depending on the various areas of the province. Densities are one dimension; the nature of the population is another. In North Kivu the local population is made up of the so-called *autochtones*[45] and of Kinyarwanda speakers. There have been Kinyarwanda speakers in North Kivu since time immemorial and they were divided into many small communities (Banyabwisha, Bafumbira migrants from Uganda) that did not have any special relationship problems with their autochthon neighbors. Then came the Mission d'Immigration des Banyarwanda (MIB), created by the Belgians in 1937 to bring agricultural workers from an already over-populated Rwanda into what was seen as an underpopulated Kivu. During its eighteen years of existence the MIB imported about eighty-five thousand Banyarwanda from Rwanda, mostly into North Kivu, although some were sent down to Katanga to work in the mines.[46] They settled in various areas, but with a preference for the Masisi and Walikale zones, then thinly populated. The newcomers, both Tutsi and Hutu, tended to reinforce the community feelings of those Kinyarwanda speakers who were already present. Given their growing numbers (today they represent about 40 percent of the population province-wide, with peaks of over 70 percent in Masisi) this tended to create resentment among the autochthons, especially among the smaller tribes, such as the Bahunde and Banyanga, who already tended to be marginalized by the majority Banande.[47] This was due to the fact that the Banyarwanda presence seemed at least partly sponsored by the Belgians and to the fact that their concepts of landholding did not mesh easily with those of the locals. With the support of the colonial administration they received "customary rights" to local tribal lands, which did not imply possession in the Western sense. But the social transformations brought about by colonization tended to weaken the powers of the local lineage chiefs over land attribution, replacing those by more individual and monetarized transactions.[48] The Banyarwanda were seen as taking advantage of this new order of things to turn their "acquired customary land rights" into permanent ownership, and a very tense situation developed during 1960–1965, when the first civil war totally upset the forms of government inherited from the colonial administration. Contrary to the South, North Kivu was not directly touched by the war. But the war was often a pretext for local administrators to persecute the Banyarwanda and to illegally seize their land. This finally led to a limited outburst of violence in 1965, *after* the war had stopped in the rest of the country.[49]

President Mobutu did not mind. For him the North Kivu Banyarwanda, especially the Tutsi, were an interesting political investment. The region was potentially rebellious and the Banyarwanda were in a difficult position, especially since many new arrivals had come after the massacres of Tutsi in Rwanda between December 1963 and January 1964. Therefore, using the Banyarwanda was good politics since they could not get a local power base independent from the central government. This led to the promotion of the Banyarwanda in the postwar years, especially during 1967–1977, when Barthélémy Bisengimana, a Tutsi refugee from Rwanda, was Mobutu's righthand man as the chief of the presidential office. With the support of Bisengimana many Kivu Tutsi went into lucrative businesses and "acquired" land, especially land that had been abandoned by Belgian farmers in 1960 or confiscated from them during the 1973 exercise in "Zairianization." The land grabbing reached such incredible proportions that in 1980 the Land Ministry in Kinshasa had to cancel the "attribution" of 230,000 hectares (575,000 acres) to the notorious Munyarwanda businessman Cyprien Rwakabuba. At a time when the average amount of land per person in Kivu was 0.81 hectare (2 acres),[50] such insolent agrarian "success" won the Banyarwanda very few friends. Even if many of them did not partake of the riches corruptly acquired by their elite, the whole community became stigmatized.

Parallel to the land struggle, there was another battle about citizenship. In January 1972, at the height of his power, Bisengimana had managed to get the Political Bureau of the Mouvement Populaire de la Révolution (MPR) to pass a citizenship decree[51] whereby all persons originating from "Ruanda-Urundi" and residing on then Belgian Congolese territory in or before January 1950 were automatically Zairian citizens (Article 15).

When Bisengimana fell from power in 1977 there was intense pressure to change the law, and a new one was passed on June 29, 1981 (Law 81-002), abrogating the famous Article 15. Although the new law had vague provisions for the eventual "acquisition" of Zairian nationality, it left this important point to political arbitrariness.[52] The results were immediate. In 1987 elections could not be organized in North Kivu because nobody was capable of saying exactly who was or was not Zairian in order to draw polling lists. Then, using the 1981 law, local Banande worthies counterattacked and tried to cut down Banyarwanda landholdings and businesses.[53] They managed to get the support of the Bahunde and Banyanga minority tribes (each one representing 5 percent of the North Kivu population), who had always been at the wrong end of the deals, whether it was the Banyarwanda or the majority Banande who had been on top. To further their aims they used the democratization movement then taking place in Zaire. The autochthons sent delegates to the Conférence Nationale Souveraine (CNS) in Kinshasa and managed to bar Banyarwanda from taking their seats at the Assembly under the pretext that they were not Zairians. Then they used the CNS decisions to completely overhaul the local administration in North Kivu, putting new judges and police in place who were Banande, Bahunde, or Banyanga. The whole justice and repressive apparatus then became slanted against the Banyarwanda.

In the meantime, war had broken out in neighboring Rwanda and the Tutsi-Hutu conflict there was carried over to Kivu. President Habyarimana and his clan had organized a pro-Kigali network under the guise of a peasant association, the Mutuelle des Agriculteurs des Virunga (MAGRIVI). While the RPF recruited young Zairian Tutsi into its ranks, the MAGRIVI did the same thing with Hutu, thus deeply dividing the Banyarwanda community at the very moment when it was under assault from the autochthon tribes. Tensions rose and finally broke into open violence in February 1992. To paraphrase the title of a contemporary report by Médecins Sans Frontières, the French medical NGO, the struggle for land had burst into interethnic conflict.[54] After a period of low-intensity skirmishes during 1992, violence escalated when a "large number" of Hutu Banyarwanda were killed by armed Bahunde militiamen at the Ntoto market near Walikale on March 20, 1993. Within ten days, after about a thousand Banyarwanda had been slaughtered, they counterattacked, doing some killing of their own. By August the casualties numbered around 20,000 and there were about 250,000 IDPs of all tribal origins.[55] President Mobutu himself came to North Kivu, set up residence in Goma, and deployed several thousand elite troops from the famed Division Spéciale Présidentielle (DSP). Violence abated by late 1993 and negotiations were undertaken by local leaders in November. By February 1994 an uneasy peace had been reestablished. It was to be shattered five months later by the arrival of 850,000 Hutu refugees from Rwanda.

South Kivu: the Banyamulenge and the memories of 1965. Although similar to North Kivu in climate and vegetation, South Kivu is different because it is less populated, which results in less pressure on land problems. While there are 102 humans per square kilometer in Uvira Province, the southern Fizi-Baraka area has only 13.[56] The question of ethnicity and nationality is also posed in different terms. Here, the main "nonnatives" are the Barundi, who probably represent up to 15 percent of the population. Curiously, they have had only limited problems with their autochthon neighbors (mostly Bavira and Bafulero), unlike the much smaller Banyamulenge group.

The Banyamulenge are a group of Banyarwanda migrants who have come from Rwanda at various points in history.[57] The first arrivals might go back as early as the seventeenth century.[58] But they seemed to have especially come at the close of the eighteenth century from the southern Kinyaga region, to escape the growing power of Mwami Rwabugiri in Rwanda.[59] Some came to escape the repression unleashed after the Rucunshu coup d'état of 1896. But in any case they were few in number and they were mostly Tutsi. Their Hutu *abagaragu* (clients) had been *icyihuture*, turned into Tutsi, thus dissipating any intragroup social tension. They settled on the Itombwe plateau above the Ruzizi plain, where the altitude (up to 3,000 meters) prevented normal agriculture but where they could pasture their cows. They received further influxes of migrants in 1959, 1964, and 1973, as anti-Tutsi persecutions took place in Rwanda. Poor and somewhat aloof from their Bafulero and Babembe neighbors, they played an almost involuntary political role during the civil war, when the Simba rebels,[60] on the run from Jean Schramm's mercenaries and government soldiers, came up the plateau and started killing their cows to feed themselves. The Banyamulenge, who up to that point had had no group involvement in the rebellion,[61] then turned

solidly against it, later accepting weapons from the Mobutu forces and joining in the slaughter of the remaining rebels. Because many of those in the
area were drawn from the neighboring Babembe tribe, this created a durable
resentment between the two groups.[62]

After the war, in a political context that was favorable to them, the Banyamulenge expanded, some moving southward to Moba and Kalemie in
northern Katanga, others going down into the Ruzizi plain, where a few
became chiefs among the local Barundi through gifts of cattle, and still others going to work in the provincial capital, Bukavu, or in the mushrooming
gold boomtown of Uvira.[63] They supplied meat and milk to the *creuseurs*,
the illegal but not clandestine gold diggers, and made a fair living. Unlike
the North Kivu Banyarwanda, they had only a very small educated elite and
no political connections in Kinshasa.

But the bloody memories of 1965 remained between them and the autochthon tribes, feeding an ever present low-key tension. Even their name,
Banyamulenge, meaning "those from Mulenge" (a village on the Itombwe),
was chosen in the early 1970s to avoid being called Banyarwanda and being seen as "foreigners."[64] Thus when the war broke out in Rwanda, the
RPF recruited widely among the Banyamulenge, who went to fight there
not so much for the liberation of a country that was not theirs but to gain
military experience and to acquire weapons for a possible future showdown
with their neighbors. But going to fight in another country's civil war was
an ambiguous course of action for people who wanted to be accepted as
Zairians. One of them, Monsignor Gapangwa, bishop of Uvira, was not
able to decide clearly which were the various motivations of the young RPF
volunteers, mentioning "a search for security, opportunism, joining as mercenaries or perhaps finding a solution to their questions about nationality."[65] Like the Banyarwanda in North Kivu, they followed the ebb and
flow of the legal status of Kinyarwanda speakers in Zaire. But their position was different. In North Kivu the Banyarwanda were 40 percent of a
population of about 2.8 million, and getting rid of them belonged to the
domain of wishful thinking. But in South Kivu the Banyamulenge were a
much smaller proportion of the population and understandably felt more
threatened. Their enemies tried to belittle them by saying that there were
no more than 35,000 of them,[66] while they themselves tried through dubious computation to push their numbers up to 400,000.[67] The reality stands
probably at around 60,000 to 80,000, a very small fraction (3 to 4 percent)
of the approximately 2.4 million people who live in South Kivu. Thus, here

as in North Kivu, the question of the relationship between Kinyarwanda speakers and their autochthon neighbors remained a barely healed sore that the arrival of the refugees was going to reopen.

The impact of the Rwandese refugees on the Kivus. To understand exactly what happened, we must steer clear of two diverging ideological interpretations.[68] The first, which we could call pro-RPF, sees the Kivus as an extension of Rwanda, where "extremists" and "negative forces," inspired by Rwandese Hutu *génocidaires* (almost a pleonasm, in this view) are systematically pursuing the annihilation of the Banyamulenge and the North Kivu Tutsi.[69] This interpretation, which was supported internationally by pro-Tutsi NGOs and the U.S. government,[70] tends to overlook RPA human rights abuses in the Congo, or at least excuse them as simply unfortunate collateral damage in a war of self-defense. The second interpretation, which we could call anti-RPF,[71] sees the autochthon tribes as innocent lambs savagely attacked by evil Banyarwanda predators. This view, which is mostly supported by the Kivu civil society and its European NGO allies, used to dwell on the evil of the Hutu in 1994–1996 but has since shifted its ideological aim to the evil of the Tutsi while trying to hide or minimize violent racist outbursts on the part of the Kivu tribes as "legitimate anger." The reality is of course much more complex, as I have tried to show. The struggle for land in North Kivu, the memories of the civil war in the South, the problems of citizenship and of dual loyalty on the part of the Kinyarwanda speakers, general poverty, overpopulation, the collapse of the Zairian state, the ambitions of politicians who kept manipulating local feelings and contradictions for their own benefit—everything converged into making the Kivus a dangerous and volatile environment, with many links to the radical evil of the genocide that had just happened in Rwanda. It was obvious that the irruption of masses of desperate and belligerent refugees in that environment would create a major problem, fraught with potentially devastating consequences for the future. Beyond simplified ideological explanations, we can now look at the situation created by this refugee exodus.

The first point to remember is that the numbers involved were huge: during July and August 1994 a total of 850,000 refugees arrived in the Goma area of North Kivu, another 332,000 moved to Bukavu in South Kivu, and another 62,000 came to the Uvira zone, where 255,000 Burundese had also been settled since the 1993 explosion in Burundi. The second point to keep in mind is the peculiar nature of their "refugee" character. Although the great mass of the people were indeed genuine refugees, they were manipulated by a highly ideological political and military leadership that had no intention of sitting idle in Zaire while waiting for the "humanitarian emergency" to resolve itself. The refugees were seen by their leaders as a political trump card that could be used to manipulate the international community, seduce President Mobutu, and threaten the new government in Kigali. The third point is that the whole thing was extremely expensive. Figures are hard to compute given the intricacy of bilateral, multilateral, and NGO financing, but the figures in the table give an idea of the order of magnitude.

	1993	1994	1995	1996	1997
Great Lakes Region	8.29	446.74	317.14	613.68	307.99
Zaire	18.11	154.47	166.20	104.40	56.57
Tanzania	11.27	61.23	79.51	11.88	19.57
Burundi	18.76	133.24	72.44	37.69	28.67

Source: UN/OCHA. Figures are in U.S. $ millions. The Great Lakes global figures are not a sum of the various geographical figures but a separate line for multinational attributions disbursed together.

With these figures, we can compute a ratio of about 60 percent of Zaire-directed disbursements against 40 percent of disbursements for Tanzania and Burundi. Thus, if we add 60 percent of the global Great Lakes figures to the specific Zaire disbursements, we arrive at the total expenditure for refugees in Zaire, still in millions of U.S. dollars.

1993	1994	1995	1996	1997
23.08	422.51	356.48	472.61	241.36

The pattern is clear. Figures leap upward with the 1994 emergency, settle a bit during 1995, jump again with the 1996 "war of the camps," and settle down again, albeit at a rather high level, after the mass of refugees go home, flee westward, or die. But the financial impact was devastating, especially at the local level. It contributed to disorganizing the local economies, whetting dangerous appetites, and, through aid theft and resale, to financing the "Hutuland" war.

In addition, there is a fourth and major point to remember: the refugees had a heavily disruptive impact on the environment, whether we take the word in its social, political, economic, or ecological sense. This had been obvious from the very beginning, even as soon as the August 1994 cholera epidemic was over.[72] The refugees behaved as if in a conquered country, cutting firewood without authorization, stealing cattle, plundering crops, setting up illegal roadblocks, and, this not in an anarchic, disorganized way, but, on the contrary, clearly responding to the directives of a sinister and powerful political leadership. In a letter addressed to Kamel Morjane at UNHCR Headquarters in Geneva, the local envoy, Joël Boutroue, wrote worriedly, "Neither our mandate nor the means at our disposal match the requirements needed to address the regional crisis."[73] There were two documents appended to Boutroue's letter. One was a collectively signed memo from the Goma branches of all the Zairian opposition parties (Union pour la Démocratie et le Progrès Social [UDPS], Parti Démocrate Social Chrétien, and others), written on October 28 and complaining about the refugees:

[They have] destroyed our food reserves, destroyed our fields, our cattle, our natural parks, caused famine and spread epidemics, who benefit from food aid while we get nothing. They sell or give weapons to their fellow countrymen,[74] commit murders both of Tutsi and of local Zairians.... They must be disarmed, counted, subjected to Zairian laws and finally repatriated.

The second memo was written by members of the civil society on November 18 and was even graver. It recommended a December 31, 1994, repatriation deadline and focused expressly on the security aspect of the situation. It gave the precise locations of nine ex-FAR training centers and an arms depot and denounced the local assistant director of the Service National d'Intelligence et de Protection (SNIP), a certain Muhuta, as a paid accomplice of the ex-FAR who trafficked in weapons with them. As early as August 1994 the UNHCR had written to New York to ask for a number of emergency measures:

1. Totally disarm the ex-FAR troops, collect all arms and military equipment and gather them in a secure place far from the border.

2. Isolate and neutralise the civilian leaders.

3. Set up a mechanism to deal with the perpetrators of crimes.

4. Ensure maintenance of law and order in the camps through the deployment of police.[75]

The creation of the Zaire Camp Security Contingent[76] was a partial fulfillment of recommended measure 4, but none of the other measures were ever even attempted. Repatriation started well, as long as the refugees did not fully realize what was going on inside Rwanda. A total of 215,312 refugees returned between July 1994 and January 1995. But then, according to a UNHCR report, "the repatriation movement grounded to a halt."[77] There were only 3,770 repatriations in May, none in June, and 1,900 in July. At the same time, 11,248 new refugees flowed out of Rwanda. The killings that had resumed inside Rwanda were having their effect on refugee choices.

This was the time President Mobutu chose to implement his Operation Rehabilitation. It had been carefully planned with the French from way back. Jacques Foccart[78] had discussed it with the Zairian president when he went to Kinshasa during the genocide, in April 1994.[79] They met again when the veteran of the French geopolitical games in Africa invited Mobutu in private to his Cavalaire country home on August 17, 1995. They went together to Mobutu's neighboring residence at Cap Martin, where they received a phone call from President Jacques Chirac. The French president persuaded Mobutu to accept all the points former president Jimmy Carter was then mediating between him and Secretary-General Boutros Ghali: stop the "hate" radio broadcasts, stop the weapons deliveries to the ex-FAR, move the camps away from the border area, and accept more UN observers. In exchange Mobutu would be reinstated in his old role of central African kingpin with French backing. Mobutu agreed to everything, then went on to brutally push fifteen thousand refugees over the border on August 19, just to give proof of his nuisance capacity. After five days of panic he drew back his claws and proclaimed his desire to cooperate.[80] The French were somewhat taken aback by his methods but said nothing.

Meanwhile the security situation had gotten totally out of control. The ex-FAR had tried to needle the new regime, but the RPA retaliated and then went on the offensive. The Kigali UNHCR office counted fifty-two armed incidents in August 1995, forty in September, thirty-one in October, and only eighteen in November, showing a progressive decrease in the combat capacity of the former regime's troops.[81] They tried to make up inside Zaire for the war they were losing on the Rwanda border. Given the extremely tense situation, as sketched in the preceding section, they did not find it difficult to again set fire to the Masisi and Walikale areas. The idea was simple: they might be in this for longer than they would wish and should therefore develop a secure territorial base. They could use the local Hutu population both against the Tutsi and against the autochthon tribes to carve out a territory for themselves. The military operations were under the command of the former FAR chief of staff Gen. Augustin Bizimungu and they had the blessing of President Mobutu, who, in spite of his promises to the French government, had no intention of relinquishing his one trump card in the Kivus.[82] The result of these manipulations was a renewed explosion of violence in North Kivu.

The war restarted in October 1995 and immediately produced new refugees, this time Zairian Tutsi fleeing the *Interahamwe* and ex-FAR into Rwanda. By February 1996, according to UNHCR, there were thirty-seven thousand Tutsi refugees in Rwanda, half of them native Zairians and the other half refugees of the 1959 massacres who had once sought asylum in the Belgian Congo. The situation was paradoxical because many of the expulsees had been thrown out of their own country, while many other "refugees" were citizens of their country of asylum. But the RPF government had no intention of letting these potentially useful refugees simply melt into Rwandese society, and it forced UNHCR to accept, albeit with some reluctance, opening camps almost directly on the border, practically within shooting distance of the Hutu camps on the other side. Sadako Ogata complained to the UN secretary-general that the situation was slowly becoming intolerable:

The recent influx from Masisi to Rwanda now stands at 9,000 persons. The Government of Rwanda insists that these persons are Zairians and is determined to keep them at the Petite Barrière camp site, 800m from the border.... . The repatriation program remains at an impasse. As you know, 25% of the refugee camps in Zaire are within five kilometres while the rest are less than 30 kilometres away from the Rwandan border. Confronted with these worrying developments the international community should consider urgent measures to prevent a further deterioration in the security situation.[83]

Of course, the international community remained totally passive. Secretary-General Boutros Ghali knew that the Americans were not happy with him and that he needed French and francophone African support if he wanted to get reelected. Getting in the way of Jacques Foccart and President Chirac's plans was not the best way to achieve that, and he remained prudently silent. Which does not mean that he was not aware of the situation; as early as May 1995 he had confided in a meeting with Emma Bonino, European commissioner for humanitarian affairs:

I have no confidence in the Rwanda government.... . They want revenge.... . As for the Hutu they are preparing their military return to Rwanda from the refugee camps.... . We would need to intervene militarily but nobody is ready to do it.... . It would be cheaper than to feed them for the next ten years. Aid helps women and children but also those who are rearming and preparing to go to war.... . I can't say it publicly but we should impose a political conditionality on aid, it is the only language they will all understand.[84]

In the meantime the *Hauts Criminels Rassasie's* kept getting their rations, their fuel, their health care, and the benign neglect they needed to keep operating. In the words of a later commentator, "The West treated what was essentially a political problem as a humanitarian crisis."[85] Some of the NGOs did not mind because, as Samantha Bolton from Doctors without Borders USA was to admit after the catastrophe, "Everybody made a lot of money in Goma. We were on TV all the time. It was a good fund-raiser to say you were working in Goma."[86]

By early May the fighting in Masisi had spread to the adjoining Rutshuru territory and there were now nearly 220,000 IDPs.[87] In early April a contingent of the Forces Armées Zairoises (FAZ) had carried out Operation Kiama, fighting the Bahunde and Banyanga side by side with the ex-FAR and the local Hutu militiamen. There were rumors that President Mobutu wanted to install the Rwandese Hutu durably in North Kivu, give them bogus papers, and get them to vote in the planned May 1997 elections.[88] In the meantime he was bringing in more guns.[89] On May 14, 1996, a group of Tutsi IDPs was caught in a fight between local Hutu and Bahunde militiamen at the Mokoto Trappist monastery: 110 of them were slaughtered in full view of the Belgian monks, which caused a bit of a stir internationally.[90] Kinshasa was beginning to worry, not about the Kivu war, which it tolerated, but about its possible resulting backlash. The UNHCR was "irresponsible" and the camps it had opened in Rwanda were "sheltering bogus Zairian refugees; they are in fact teeming with RPA elements," complained Gen. Eluki Monga Aundu, the FAZ chief of staff.[91] This was not altogether wrong because if the refugees were not RPA, their young men were in fact being quickly militarized by the RPA through a crash training course. There were now 18,000 Tutsi refugees who had come from North Kivu into Rwanda in addition to the 37,000 who had already fled during 1995.[92] There was some concern in New York about the situation, and on May 29 a mission of information was dispatched to Goma. It produced no tangible results. There were some isolated independent warnings from NGOs,[93] but nobody seemed to realize the extent of the impending catastrophe.

At that point two elements were still missing for a general conflagration to take place: a cause that would push one of the main actors over the brink and a mediatized event that could be used as an acceptable casus belli to neutralize the international community. Burundi was to provide the first element and the Banyamulenge crisis of mid-1996 the second one.

The Burundi factor

Burundi had been in a state of upheaval since the murder of President Melchior Ndadaye on October 22, 1993. The failed putsch that led to his death had started a general crisis of *all* the institutions. The army, of course, because it was half within the putsch and half outside it. and the civil service as well since many civil servants were appointees of the Front pour la Démocratie au Burundi (FRODEBU) who were accused of having organized the massacres of Tutsi that followed the assassination.[94] This resulted in a triple political struggle in the months following the failed coup: the Tutsi-dominated army kept undermining the still FRODEBU-dominated civilian government; Tutsi civil society extremists who were bent on bringing down what they saw as a *génocidaire* government kept organizing strikes and demonstrations; and Hutu extremists who considered Hutu moderates still in the government as "stooges" took up arms against it.

There were four different Hutu guerrilla groups. The oldest one was Parti pour la Libération du Peuple Hutu (PALIPEHUTU), created in 1980 by Rémy Gahutu and led after his death in 1990 by Etienne Karatasi, who lived in exile in Denmark. In 1993 PALIPEHUTU split on the support of President Ndadaye. The "historical" nucleus wanted to collaborate with the Hutu president, but some radical members with racist agendas disapproved of Ndadaye's ethnic collaboration policies. PALIPEHUTU's military chief, Kabora Kossan, split from the organization to create his own Forces Nationales de Libération (FNL). In the south of the country a former schoolteacher, Joseph Karumba, created a locally based guerrilla group in Nyanza-Lac called the Front de Libération Nationale. And finally, when the government collapsed after the failed October 1993 putsch and the murder of President Ndadaye, former interior minister Léonard Nyangoma fled to Zaire and created a political movement in exile, the Conseil National de Défense de la Démocratie (CNDD), which had a military arm, the Forces de Défense de la Démocratie (FDD), led by a young intellectual, Jean-Bosco Ndayikengurukiye.[95] Although all these groups were out to overthrow the formerly Tutsi-dominated Burundi government, they diverged widely on a number of points. Some, like CNDD and even PALIPEHUTU, accepted the principle of negotiation. Not so with Kabora Kossan's men, who chose a totally military option. The split was different on the question of ethnic tolerance: apart from CNDD, which had a relatively mature political view of ethnicity,[96] the other groups were militantly racist and dreamed of treating the Tutsi the way the Rwandese *Interahamwe* had done during the genocide.

But as the level of guerrilla actions slowly increased during 1994, new armed groups sprang up within the towns as well, including in the capital, Bujumbura. The Tutsi militias were at times linked to political parties, like the *Imbogaraburundi* ("those who will bring Burundi back") who worked for the Parti du Renouveau National (PARENA) of former President Jean-Baptiste Bagaza, or the *Sans Echec* ("those who never fail"), who were close to Mathias Hitimana's Parti pour la Réconciliation du Peuple. Others, like the *Sans Défaite* ("the undefeated"), the *Sans Pitié* ("the pitiless ones"), and even the *Sans Capote* ("those who never wear condoms") were loose cannon, ready to hire themselves to the highest bidder among the small Tutsi extremist parties. On the Hutu side FRODEBU had its *Inziraguhemuka* ("those who did not betray"), while the FDD had infiltrated militants called *Intagoheka* ("those who never sleep"). In the poor and mostly Hutu Kamenge section of Bujumbura, Pascal Gashirabake, a roughneck former mechanic nicknamed Savimbi for his resemblance to the Angolan leader, raised a small army out of the former youth street gang called the Chicago Bulls. Actually, street gangs were often the raw material from which the politicians carved out their militias. Many youth gangs were biethnic before the violence started, but after October 1993 they found it profitable to split along ethnic lines and to start working for "the big men." They got guns from the politicians and demonstrated or killed for them.[97] On the Tutsi side the militias were at times reinforced by young men (and even young women) from good families, especially when the university became a battlefield for the factions.[98]

The violent death of President Cyprien Ntaryamira on April 6 1994,[99] did not result in a general explosion for a number of reasons, which also explain why there was not a genocide in Burundi. First of all, there were still a lot of moderates left on both sides, even if at times they looked like an endangered species. These moderates often worked discreetly at defusing crises while their more extremist colleagues vociferated. Also, contrary to the fears of both ethnic groups, there was no systematic genocidal planning on either side, and no prepared means of carrying it out. And finally, daily violence has a way of undercutting itself. In a country that had been provocatively termed by two British journalists "the land that lost its head,"[100] there simply were not the means, the organization, nor the resolve to carry out a genocide. Instead there were "small massacres which kept bubbling on,"[101] a kind of settling down to a life of daily fear, of occasional violence, of perpetual tension. Delivery trucks were ambushed, peasants bringing their produce to the market were shot at, grenades were tossed, often at random, in places of worship, in bus parks or in bars, and guerrillas, as well as killing Tutsi, mercilessly killed those Hutu who did not want to cooperate with them. Then, more often than not, the army came right after them, accused the peasants of helping the guerrillas, and killed some more. Ahmedou Ould Abdallah, the former UN special representative in Burundi between September 1993 and October 1995, declared tiredly at the time:

The extremist elements do not want any solution. They play for time, one does not know what for.... I did not see any good will in June when the government [FRODEBU] was dragging its feet and I did not see it either in July when it was the turn of certain fractions of the opposition [Union pour le Progrès National (UPRONA) hard-liners and small Tutsi parties] to drag their feet. Currently [late July 1994] there is a deadlock.... This is childish behaviour when the population is in such a desperate situation. The security forces are tired. Since October 1993 they have been trying to hold the floodgates; they have to provide security in the country and ensure security at the border. And in the meantime all the politicians are just sitting at the Hotel Novotel, talking.[102]

It was becoming obvious that some modicum of coexistence had to be found, and the man who managed its precarious negotiation was Prime Minister Anatole Kanyenkiko, a liberal UPRONA Tutsi. Kanyenkiko's idea was not revolutionary or even very innovative; it was simply an effort at common sense. Because the struggle for power between the groups had everything to do with money, positions, and patronage, he would try to share those according to the rough proportionality of each group's political weight (which of course did not mean demographic importance), taking into account as best he could the various private interests and nuisance capacities of the various "political parties" (i.e., coalitions of appetites). Haggling went on for about six weeks, and on September 12, 1994, a power-sharing agreement was signed.

The problem was that most of the signatories acted in absolute bad faith. As soon as the agreement was signed the Tutsi extremists started what Professor Filip Reyntjens has called a "creeping coup":[103] strikes, forced business closings, procedural guerrilla tactics to challenge the nomination of Hutu appointees, use of the still Tutsi-dominated justice system to obstruct what could be obstructed, and an effort at de-legitimizing the FRODEBU government in the press. On the other side, the "moderate" Hutu politicians did very little to discourage the extremist guerrillas, which kept operating even after the power-sharing agreement had been signed.

Under increasing pressure from extremists in his own camp, UPRONA Prime Minister Kanyenkiko was forced to resign in early 1995, declaring in his resignation speech, "Today, a handful of politicians from all sides are refusing to draw lessons from the Rwandese tragedy which happened at our doorstep. They want to lead the country towards a similar tragedy."[104] Although understandable, this moralistic interpretation was wrong. The Burundian politicians were not mad fanatics. They were simply cunning and greedy, cold-blooded poker players. Most of them (and not "a handful") were engaged in a short-sighted game of brinkmanship in which they expected to come out ahead *without* a genocide. They thought they could *control* the situation, kill their enemies, and get away with it. The prize was undiluted power, or at least majority power. The power-sharing agreement could not work durably because there was always a group somewhere that felt somehow slighted, that thought its rightful demands had not been met. The Tutsi had formally lost power through an election in 1993, but they had retained enough of it through their control of the army, parts of the civil service, and the judiciary to effectively sabotage any power-sharing agreement.[105] The result was ceaseless confrontation at all levels, with a rough balance of terror preventing genocide by either side.

This begs a question: Why did the general population accept its role in this ghastly scenario? The answer is tragically simple: because of poverty and the absence of an economy independent from state patronage. The articulation between an economic dead end and violence has been extremely well explained by a (Tutsi) Burundian university professor who is worth quoting here at some length:

A growing part of the peasantry gradually realized [during the 1970s and 1980s] that, through the system of export cash crops, it was caught in a situation that completely blocked the way of any social and economic promotion for its children. In turn these children realized that they could not escape from an agricultural economy whose remuneration steadily decreased... . The state remained the only hope.... For these poor educated youths, these low-ranking civil servants and their peasant families, Ndadaye was more than a president, he was a king, a god, the only hope.[106]

But after July 1993 the shoe was on the other foot. Even if President Ndadaye was the "only hope" for the Hutu, he was not God and the economy remained as structurally limited under his leadership as it had been before. It was now the Tutsi's turn to be afraid, and the fight for patronage was on:

The nominations of Hutu in the administration after July 1993, followed by the replacement of both Tutsi and Hutu UPRONA civil servants, down to such level as communal secretaries and marketplace watchmen . . . frightened a lot of people into thinking that they were going to lose not only the symbols of their hegemony but their permanent sources of monetary income and familial patronage. The press magnified the feeling and the UPRONA party played on it.... . Demonstrations organized by UPRONA to protest against losses of employment can be seen in the perspective of this organized panic This led some of the members of the armed forces to think that the whole of Burundi society was in a state of upheaval.[107]

This was a self-fulfilling evaluation. By killing Ndadaye these same members of the armed forces actually drove the whole of Burundi society into a state of upheaval. Regarding patronage, the fear of loss (Tutsi) or hope of gain (Hutu) became sharper than before because the economic situation went from bad to worse as the insecurity spread. Thus the downward spiral became extremely hard to escape: Tutsi and Hutu fought each other to retain access to patronage in a state-dominated economy that their very conflict made poorer by the day, and growing poverty in turn kept ensuring a steady supply of resolute and desperate supporters for the political class. The press played a dreadful role in this process. Most newspapers were without a shred of professional ethics, mixing facts with commentaries or even outright fabrications. Violent, vulgar, and outrageously partisan, they ceaselessly contributed to destabilization in the name of press freedom.[108] The prize probably could go to the Tutsi extremist paper *Le Carrefour des Idées*, which did not flinch from asking in one of its headlines: "Do the Hutu have a soul?"[109] or from offering a front-page bounty of one million Burundian francs for the head of Léonard Nyangoma.[110] The worst is that no legal action was ever taken against these publications, which usually sold better than the serious papers.[111]

This created a climate of slow-motion civil war. But there were no compactly held territory and no battle lines in this war. The two sides were hopelessly intertwined because they had lived side by side before the conflict and because the insurgents never had the military means to cut off certain areas. During the October 1993 massacres, the Tutsi had run to the little towns and villages, even to schools, factories, and hospitals that were isolated in the rural areas but that had an enclosure and could be turned into a strong point for defense. They had remained there, under thin army protection, at times forming their own armed militias. Going back to farming was hazardous, and they often saw their Hutu neighbors pick their crops. Hutu guerrillas and Tutsi militias raided and counterraided. The army tried to control the situation, at times neutrally, at times siding openly with the Tutsi militias. Whatever the fight pattern, the combatants usually suffered fewer losses than the civilians.

In such a climate the power-sharing agreement of 1994 never had much of a chance. Bujumbura itself became a battlefield, with such areas as Kamenge, Cibitoke, Kinama, and Gasenyi turning into Hutu bastions while the Tutsi entrenched themselves in Musaga, Buyenzi, and Ngarara. The showdown ended when the army ethnically cleansed the whole city between March and June 1995, pushing thousands of Hutu into the surrounding hills or all the way to Zaire. Then the army went after the IDPs, whom it accused of supporting the guerrillas. By early 1996 the situation appeared totally out of control. The "small massacres" had finally bubbled over,[112] and there was a growing fear of genocide among the international community, even if, as I showed earlier, the prerequisites of a genocide did not really exist.[113] Former president Nyerere tried to organize negotiations between UPRONA and FRODEBU in Tanzania in the hope that they could talk more securely outside the country than in Burundi itself, but the conversations failed. By then more of a hostage than a real head of state, President Sylvestre Ntibantunganya went to the Arusha regional summit of June 25–26, 1996, with a radical request: the international community should intervene militarily to reestablish a minimum of law and order. This was a radical turnaround; when the idea had been first mooted by UN Secretary-General Boutros Ghali in January, it had been rejected out of hand by UPRONA. President Ntibantunganya had gone along with the UPRONA rejection at the Tunis mini-summit[114] because he knew that the Burundian army and the Tutsi extremists would not accept it. And as soon as UPRONA Prime Minister Antoine Nduwayo, who had backed the president's position in Arusha, came back to Burundi he was denounced by his own party as "guilty of high treason." Paradoxically, the radical PALIPEHUTU guerrillas agreed with UPRONA in their rejection of foreign intervention.[115]

It was in that extremely tense climate that two successive massacres came to push the situation over the brink. First, on July 3, Hutu guerrillas hit the Teza tea factory, killing between sixty and eighty people. Then, on July 20, three hundred displaced Tutsi were killed at the Bugendana camp. Rumors were rife of an imminent intervention by the regional powers or by the UN, although plans were extremely confused. When President Ntibantunganya went to the Bugendana funeral, the crowd pelted him with stones. He fled directly from the funeral site to the U.S. Embassy in Bujumbura, expecting a coup at any time. In fact, the coup took four days in coming because the Bururi Tutsi community was divided about who should carry it out, former President Pierre Buyoya or his radical predecessor, Jean-Baptiste Bagaza. The army NCOs and the Tutsi extremist militiamen preferred Bagaza; the officers and the Bururi elders were for Buyoya, with the argument that "Bagaza is too radical for the Abazungu [Europeans]." Buyoya got the support and took power in a bloodless coup on July 26.

Buyoya, the army, and the semi-moderate elements of UPRONA had carried out the coup both to finish off the FRODEBU-led regime that had come out of the June 1993 election and to stop the threatening slide into anarchy. But the coup could not achieve any sudden turnaround of the situation. There were still rumors of a possible UN intervention, even if nobody in New York seemed too enthusiastic about it.[116] But the regional summit that met in Arusha on July 31 was very hostile and clamped radical economic sanctions on Burundi. The prime movers of the hostility toward Buyoya were the Ugandan and Tanzanian governments, for two different reasons. Tanzania had long been semi-supportive of the Hutu guerrillas because former President Nyerere, who remained the real master of Tanzanian diplomacy despite his retirement, had never believed in the good sense of having an independent Rwanda and Burundi. He could be quite frank about it, such as when he declared at a private meeting in Washington, DC in September 1996:

We might succeed to bring a political solution to Burundi. But we must not leave Rwanda and Burundi hanging there, they are too small and unviable. The real problem is the pushing of space. Rwanda and Burundi were part of Tanganyika before World War I. If Tanganyika, Rwanda, and Burundi hadn't been broken up after the Versailles Treaty, you wouldn't be hearing about Tutsis and Hutus today. Even now . . . if we can give them space, if we can find a solution for five or six years, then we can make them part of East Africa which is growing up again.[117]

Unknown to most of his American hosts, "Mwalimu" had of course a rather radical solution in mind "for the next five or six years," since he was at the time putting the finishing touches to his general plan for the attack on Zaire. The Buyoya coup had made his long-term strategic planning harder because it would tend to reinforce the Tutsi regime, which he wanted to crack open. If Nyerere's position had nothing to do with Buyoya as an individual, this was not the case with Uganda's Museveni. Shortly after Mwalimu's visit Amama Mbabazi, Museveni's roving diplomatic troubleshooter, also went to Washington and declared in defense of the Arusha Summit sanctions, "The Tutsi dominate the Army and the civil service in Burundi. We must open them to the Hutu, there is no other way. We must find an adequate system of power-sharing, as we have in Uganda."[118] If this was apparently more politically correct than Mwalimu's reasoning it is probably because it was said in public. But the reality was that Museveni could not stand Buyoya, whom he reproached for two reasons: overthrowing his friend Bagaza in 1987 and organizing elections in 1993. The first reason was very affective: Museveni was grateful to Bagaza for his help during his own bush war[119] and generally agreed with his authoritarian style. He thought that Bagaza was the right man to negotiate with Nyangoma and that peace could come from this rapprochement of opposite extremisms.[120] For the same reason he disliked Buyoya, whom he saw as a wet and a fool for having organized the June 1993 elections. Museveni thought that Africa was not ripe for multiparty politics[121] and that Burundi, of all African countries, was probably one of the least ripe. But Museveni's and Nyerere's views, although diversely motivated, converged on one key point: Buyoya was not the man they wanted in power in Burundi. Mwalimu would not have minded a continuation of Ntibantunganya's weak presidency, and Museveni would have liked a Bagaza coup. But both were unhappy and Buyoya could expect hostility from them.

This was not the case with Rwanda, which was very concerned about the situation in Burundi. Rwanda knew that if the Burundi regime imploded, it would have to deal with at least half a million Tutsi refugees.[122] In addition, it could expect a radical Hutu regime to provide the ex-FAR and *Interahamwe* with military bases. Rwandese troops had started to operate alongside the Forces Armées Burundaises (FAB) as early as 1995, collaborating with the Tutsi militias to attack the Rwandese Hutu refugee camps in Burundi.[123] In early August 1996 RPA contingents crossed the border to support the FAB in large-scale antiguerrilla operations.[124] The situation had grown worse on the ground as the rebel Hutu forces were now trying to cut off Bujumbura's food supply and had managed to knock down electric power lines, plunging the capital in darkness. There was a sense of urgency in Kigali. In a tense and hurried effort, the two governments managed to deport the last 85,000 Rwandese Hutu refugees left in Burundi back to Rwanda.[125] On August 17 the Rwandese delegation at the Kampala regional meeting could not disagree with Uganda and Tanzania and had to half-heartedly approve the confirmation of sanctions against Burundi, but it then immediately set about undermining them. On August 30 the United Nations gave the new president of Burundi a two-month ultimatum to negotiate with the rebels. Buyoya answered, "Peace will not be made at the Security Council,"[126] a statement certainly not politically correct but definitely prophetic. Rwanda could not afford to let Burundi boil over. For Kigali the last element of the situation had now fallen into place and the time had come for action.

General Kagame goes to war

If it was the situation in Burundi that gave the final call for action in General Kagame's judgment, it was far from being his only reason to move. The basic cause that led the Rwandese leadership to attack Zaire in September 1996 was the presence of the large, partially militarized refugee camps on its borders. But there was also a broader view, which was a systematic trans-African plan to overthrow the Mobutu regime in Zaire. Already in November 1994, in the wake of the Rwandese genocide, Museveni had called a meeting in Kampala of all the "serious" enemies of Mobutu to discuss the idea of overthrowing him.[127] The conclusion had been that the time was not yet ripe. In early 1995 former president Nyerere had relaunched the idea, developing contacts with a number of African heads of state with the purpose of cleaning up what they looked upon as the shame of Africa. The heads of state involved were the presidents of Eritrea, Ethiopia, Rwanda, Uganda, Zimbabwe, and Angola. Mwalimu himself occupied the place of President Mkapa because the really important issues of Tanzanian diplomacy had always remained his prerogative.[128] His basic reasons for launching this unconventional effort were coherent with his lifelong choices: socialism and pan-Africanism. Nyerere felt that a new generation of African leaders had recently come to the fore who were committed to the basic ideals of something that might not be called "socialism" but that was a basic and radical concern for the social and economic welfare of their populations. At the top of the list were Presidents Issayas Afeworki of Eritrea and Meles Zenawi of Ethiopia, whom he admired for having put an end to the thirty-year-long Eritrean conflict.[129] President Museveni and his protégé, General Kagame, were next. To these young men Mwalimu was ready to add the older leftists whom he had supported during the years of the anti-apartheid struggle, Robert Mugabe of Zimbabwe and Agostinho Neto's heir, José Eduardo dos Santos, of Angola. As an enormous and unmentioned counterpoint to the project, there was the victory of the anti-apartheid forces in South Africa and the ascension to power of President Nelson Mandela. But Mwalimu had no intention of asking the new South African leadership to get into the act of overthrowing Mobutu, even if he knew that he could count on its sympathy. There were too many reasons against it. South Africa needed time. South Africa should use the moral authority of Nelson Mandela to act as a referee rather than get into the fight itself. And, last but not least, Mwalimu knew that all was not for the best between the African National Congress and its friends in Luanda and Harare and that getting them to collaborate on the ground might be difficult. Rwanda, because of the refugee question, was of course to be the entry point and the spearhead of the operation. Never mind that General Kagame probably had scant regard for the inclusion of Rwanda into either a resurrected version of Deutsche Ostafrika or a modernized version of the East African Community. In the short run he was satisfied to be able to count on a regional alliance to back him. A Rwandese journalist summed up the situation quite publicly when he wrote,

The present situation in Burundi is largely a result of Zairian support for PALI-PEHUTU and CNDD. The final attack on Burundi would be a catastrophe for Rwanda because the plan is to allow Nyangoma to take power in Bujumbura and to bring the *Interahamwe* back in Rwanda. But Zaire should be careful. The RPA can fight back. In which case the Great Lakes Region might witness the end of the Mobutu dictatorship.[130]

Hard to put it more clearly. But by August 1996, as Burundi was heating up and Kagame's resolve to deal with the camps had reached the decision point, this grand anti-Mobutu design was still somewhat hazy. On July 7, when Issayas Afeworki and Meles Zenawi stopped in Entebbe to have pre-OAU talks with Museveni, the connection between the Burundi situation that was to be discussed in Yaounde and the grand plan for Zaire was discussed, but only in a most general way.[131] General Kagame could not afford to wait for these plans to coalesce, especially since he was soon going to be handed a perfect *casus belli*, courtesy of a totally blind Zairian political class. His decision to act alone had been made, and he practically said so to his U.S. hosts during a late August trip to Washington, DC: "I delivered a veiled warning: the failure of the international community to take action would mean Rwanda would take action.... . But their response was really no response at all."[132] Meanwhile the conflict in Masisi that I described in the section on North Kivu had rekindled the latent tensions around the citizenship question of the South Kivu Banyamulenge, especially at a time when President Mobutu was planning his 1997 election strategy to satisfy the donors and still maintain power. In North Kivu he was in the process of creating a Hutuland in collaboration with Gen. Augustin Bizimungu and the Rwandese refugees. Their gratitude would be translated into votes. But in the South he knew that the main tribes, Babembe, Barega, Bashi, Bafulero, strongly disliked him and had supported the Simba rebellion in the 1960s. But these same tribes were also hostile to the Banyamulenge, both as "foreigners" and as former supporters of Mobutu himself during the 1960s civil war. Mobutu's tactics then were to try to use one of these hatreds against the other and to reap the benefit. In other words, the Banyamulenge had to be used as a sacrificial goat for his electoral plans. He had several good local tools. First, there was Anzuluni Bembe, a Mubembe delegate to the Conférence Nationale Souveraine and later president of the Haut Conseil de la République/Parlement Transitoire, who had betrayed his constituency by siding with the government when in Kinshasa and who got stoned by villagers when he went back home in 1991. He learned his lesson and was now ready to turn against the Banyamulenge so as to satisfy both his tribesmen and the government. Anzuluni had teamed up with Mobutu's young vice prime minister in charge of foreign affairs, Jean-Marie Kititwa Tumansi,[133] a Murega, who knew that his fellow tribesmen would appreciate getting their hands on the cattle of the Banyamulenge. Everybody in South Kivu knew that it was only a question of time before the Banyamulenge would be hit. The Banyamulenge themselves were aware of it, and they had started acquiring weapons. They got weapons from Kigali of course, but they also got them from a rather unexpected source: the Zairian "government" itself. The FAZ and Gen. Eluki Monga Aundu started to sell to the Banyamulenge the weapons President Mobutu had just acquired to reinforce the FAZ garrisons in the east. In July 1996 Kongolo Mobutu, one of the president's sons, had gone to Bukavu and up to the Itombwe to sell the Banyamulenge the arms then stored at Panzi Military Camp. When asked if he did not think that this was a dangerous thing to do in the present context, he shrugged his shoulders and said that for years he had sold FAZ weapons to the União Nacional para a Independência Total de Angola (UNITA), so why should there be a problem?[134]

As part of his contingency planning, General Kagame had started to infiltrate Banyamulenge RPA veterans in civilian clothes into South Kivu in early July,[135] and they picked up the weapons hidden for them on the plateau. The first RPA commando sent to support them was infiltrated during the night of August 31 to September 1 from Cibitoke in Burundi and clashed with the FAZ at Businga, losing three men.[136] The timing was perfect because the other side seemed totally blind to reality and the governor of

South Kivu, Lwasi Ngabo Lwabanji, and his *commissaire* in Uvira, Shweba Mutabazi, had just decided to make their move. On September 14 a group of 286 Banyamulenge civilians showed up at the Rwandese border in Cyangugu, telling tales of terror and massacre. For the past two weeks groups of armed Babembe and Barega thugs sponsored by the local Zairian authorities had been killing and looting the Banyamulenge at random. More refugees soon showed up, telling the same grim stories.[137] Symmetrically, the Banyamulenge militia, largely made up of RPA veterans, moved in to surround Bukavu. On September 9 the city closed down with a general strike and the population marched "against the Rwandese invaders" while the FAZ clashed around Lemera with unidentified armed elements;[138] 117 Banyamulenge took refuge inside the UNHCR office in Uvira. On September 12 a strong motorized RPA contingent from Ndenzi camp near Cyangugu crossed at night into Burundi and then into Zaire through the Gatumba border post.

In a note typical of the total confusion then prevailing in the area Zairian Foreign Minister Kamanda wa Kamanda complained that the UNHCR was "collaborating with a plan of invasion of South Kivu by Banyamulenge elements infiltrated from Rwanda."[139] There was in fact a real basis for what sounded like a paranoid delusion. When the UNAMIR forces departed from Rwanda in September 1995 they had left behind over two hundred vehicles in running order as a "gift to the people of Rwanda." These included sixty-four troop carriers, which had of course been snapped up by the RPA and which were used in the Gatumba invasion. Because they had been poorly repainted, the large UN markings on their sides were still showing through, leading eyewitnesses to think that the UN was ferrying the invading troops into Zaire.[140]

Meanwhile more Banyamulenge refugees were fleeing to the Rwandese borders while their armed brothers skirmished with the FAZ. General Kagame, quite unperturbed, coolly flew down to South Africa for four days (September 18–22), where he met Thabo Mbeki, Foreign Minister Alfred Nzo, and Vice Minister for Defense Ronnie Kasrils. One of his main concerns was to make sure that the large arms contracts he had signed with Armscor on his previous visit would be honored, and it seems he got reassurance on that point.[141] As soon as he returned, heavy artillery fire was directed at Bukavu from Cyangugu,[142] the purpose being to keep FAZ forces pinned down in their positions while more RPA troops crossed the border.

The Kigali government kept saying that it had nothing to do with what was going on in South Kivu. But the Rwandese press was not so coy. In its September 23 issue, the magazine *Imvaho Nshya* editorialized, "Zaire is only reaping the harvest of what it sowed yesterday when it gave asylum to the Rwandese and Burundese refugees." Some local geopoliticians were even giving a clear idea of what the government had in mind: "As a new fact, it would now be more interesting for Rwanda to cooperate with a Kivu Republic than with big Zaire."[143] The refugees were certainly the cause of the attack, but General Kagame was already considering the next steps.

The pace soon quickened. While the FAZ and the Banyamulenge militia were skirmishing around Fizi and Mwenga between September 30 and October 5, President Bizimungu invited all the press and diplomatic community in Kigali to an extraordinary briefing at the former Méridien Hotel, renamed Umbano, on October 3. He pulled out a map of Rwanda that purported to show that large areas of North Kivu and smaller parts of South Kivu had been tributaries of the former Rwandese monarchy.[144] He then said, "If Zaire gives back its Rwandese population, then it should also give back the land on which it lives." Probably fearing that he had gone too far, he quickly added, "Rwanda has no territorial claims and respects the intangibility of national borders."[145] Part of the irony is that on the map he showed, the Banyamulenge area does not appear and is definitely not drawn as a former tributary area of the kingdom of Rwanda, something that is clear from all historical accounts.

But history was being made and, as is often true, it had rather rough edges. On October 6 the Banyamulenge militia attacked the Lemera hospital, killing thirty-four patients and three nurses, which caused Sadako Ogata to declare the next day that there was now "a very dangerous security situation." By then this was already an understatement. South Kivu Governor Lwabanji ordered all the Banyamulenge to leave the country, passing through a "corridor," or else "be treated as rebels." Gen. Monga Aundu arrived in Kivu on October 10, and the next day Firmin Ndimira, Burundi's prime minister, said that his country was not involved. General Aundu declared a state of war in South Kivu, identifying the RPA as the enemy. Ideological fantasies were running wild; the South Kivu Parliamentary Group denounced "a plot by the international community, hatched by foreign powers and the United Nations against Zaire in order to fulfil the expansionist ambitions of Rwanda and Burundi," adding that the aggression was carried out by "Rwandans, Burundians, Ugandans Somalians and other Ethiopians,"[146] a strange mixture of political fact and racial fiction. The broadcast ended with a call to "support the self-defence actions undertaken by the local people," which in clear language meant "Kill the Banyamulenge."

But it was already too late for that because the Banyamulenge themselves were now on the offensive. On October 13 they had attacked the Runingo Burundian refugee camp near Uvira, killing four, injuring nine, and causing nineteen thousand to flee headlong into the hills.[147] The South Kivu clashes had changed dimension and turned into a major conflict. Rwanda had crossed that magical imaginary line the colonialists had called a *border*. A taboo had been broken and nothing would be the same any more. But if the international community had been caught floundering about helplessly, the Rwandese themselves had made a move into the unknown whose importance they did not realize at the time. They had moved into that immense soft underbelly of the African continent called Zaire, and they did not even begin to realize the twin fragilities of that world and of the continental environment in which it was enmeshed. This double ignorance was to have enormous consequences. What many Africans were later to dub "Africa's First World War" was about to begin.

3

THE CONGO BASIN, ITS
INTERLOPERS, AND ITS ONLOOKERS

When General Kagame sent his army across the Zairian border in September 1996 he had a clear main purpose: countering the military threat posed to the new Rwandese regime by the remnants of the former regime who were rearming under the cover of the refugee camps. Conceivably this could have been a limited operation in the manner of the Israeli army hitting Hezbollah across the border into Lebanon. But the regional environment into which this move was going to take place was radically different from that of the Middle East. Borders were porous, populations were highly heterogeneous, and their distribution did not correspond to the border limits; conflicts overlapped and intermingled in ways that made them influence each other even when they were of a completely different nature. Central to the whole gathering storm was the huge sick blob of Zaire. Zaire was so "soft" in the 1980s and early 1990s that practically anybody could walk in and do whatever he liked in its territory; it took only bribes paid to the border guards. Any amount of military equipment could travel anywhere over Zairian territory with a minimum of problems. In the past Mobutu had had "policies" that he was relatively able to promote, such as supporting the Frente Nacional de Libertação de Angola (FNLA) in the Angolan civil war. But after the democratization process began in 1990 his capacity to control territory shrank radically and his capacity to project his influence beyond Zaire's borders disappeared. He was able only to act passively, for example, by giving the Sudanese government a right of passage through Zairian territory to bypass Sudanese Peoples Liberation Army (SPLA) positions in western Equatoria and attack Ugandan territory. This created two categories of proto-actors in the future "Congolese wars," categories that I have called here "interlopers" and "onlookers": those who stepped inside Zaire in order to act and those who stood outside looking in, trifling with the margins, permanently on the verge of falling in.

The interlopers were of two types: the "official" interlopers, those who had been invited in by President Mobutu, and the "unofficial," those whom Mobutu did not like but about whom he could do little given the sorry state of the FAZ.

Throughout the 1980s and early 1990s the official interlopers had been represented mainly by the Angolan guerrilla movement União Nacional para a Independência Total de Angola (UNITA), which had been supplied, courtesy of the CIA, from the Kamina base in Katanga.[1] UNITA could freely use Zaire as a rear base in its conflict with the ruling Movimento Popular de Libertação de Angola (MPLA). Later also welcome was the much smaller National Army for the Liberation of Uganda (NALU), started by Obote's secretary of state, Amon Bazira, in the foothills of the Ruwenzori Mountains to fight Yoweri Museveni's new regime installed in Kampala since January 1986. The West Nile Bank Liberation Front (WNBLF), another anti-Museveni movement, created in the 1990s, later also carried out hit-and-run attacks on Uganda's northwestern province of West Nile. Then, after the 1993 murder of Burundian president Melchior Ndadaye in Bujumbura, Léonard Nyangoma found ready asylum for his CNDD (Conseil National de Défense de la Démocratie) rebel movement in the Uvira-Bukavu area, from where he could attack Burundi. The latest addition to this collection was the Rwandese refugees, who, after August 1994 and with the implicit toleration of UNHCR and the quasi-official blessing of Mobutu, could re-arm and plan to attack Rwanda.

In the "invited guests" category one should also add the Sudanese army. The reason for tolerating Sudanese troops operating against the SPLA on Zairian territory was that Ugandan President Museveni sympathized with the SPLA, that Mobutu disliked and feared Museveni, and that the enemy of my enemy's friend was regarded as my friend, making Khartoum's forces welcome on the Zairian side of the border.

But this toleration of armed groups fighting various enemies of Mobutu automatically brought about a reaction, with all the adversaries of these armed guests also entering Zairian territory to battle it out with their foes. For Angola this meant that MPLA troops were periodically crossing the border in hot pursuit of UNITA guerrillas. It also meant that in 1977 and

74

1978 the Angolan government attempted to overthrow Mobutu by providing logistical support to the former Gendarmes Katangais,[2] who set out to invade Shaba.

In the Sudan the SPLA considered that, since the Sudanese army was free to operate through Zaire, it had no reason to refrain from doing likewise. And because after 1993 Uganda started to give the SPLA support, as a service to Museveni SPLA combatants would chase the Zaire-based antigovernment Ugandan guerrillas into their own rear bases, something the Ugandan army was loath to do for fear of the international consequences.

The only regional fighting groups that had never invited themselves into Zaire were the Burundian and Rwandese armies. But when they decided to cross into Zaire in September 1996, their much broader political agenda turned the former hide-and-seek operations of the 1980s and early 1990s into a thing of the past. The sudden Rwandese assault on the refugee camps was frontal and it was total. But it soon became apparent that it would not be limited to its initial target. The Rwandese invasion was taking place in a regional environment already undermined by years of complex and largely unnoticed conflicts. Force of habit caused the Western powers to consider the Mobutu regime as perhaps unpleasant but something that could stagger on for a while yet. There was still, lingering from the 1960s, the specter of an enormous zone of chaos at the heart of Africa.[3] The Rwandese assault had thus a dual effect: on the one hand, it exploded the myth of Mobutu as the only possible ruler of Zaire; on the other hand, it brought tumbling down into the vast Congolese basin a multiplicity of particular conflicts, each with its own logic, its own history, and its own independent actors. Once they had all rolled in and meshed with local Congolese problems, disentangling them from their involvement in order to return home became a daunting task. The RPF military elite, with its view of the continent mostly limited to the Great Lakes region and a highly militarized conception of politics, completely failed to realize the size of the Pandora's box it was cracking open.

Into the Zairian vortex

The huge land mass successively called the Congo Free State (1885–1908), the Belgian Congo (1908–1960), the Congo Republic (1960–1971), and now Zaire was not a nation-state but an arbitrarily cut chunk of the African continent. Almost 60 percent of its 2.3 million square kilometers (905,000 square miles) is covered with thick tropical forest; the rest is savannah, with the exception of the mountainous Kivus in the east, whose physical and human geography is part of the Great Lakes highlands. Bordering on seven different countries, the Zaire-Congo is the heart of the continent, but a weak heart, that was faintly pumping its life fluids into an oversize and flabby body. There was a simple reason for this: both the climate and the human-to-land occupancy ratio were and always had been unfavorable. In addition, the ruthless private economic exploitation of this huge space by King Leopold II of Belgium in the late nineteenth century had resulted in a quasi-genocide that had durably traumatized the population.[4]

Later Belgian colonization was a strange affair. A mixture of state capitalism, colonial anthropology run amuck, Church-sponsored paternalism, and forced labor, it was a unique blend that both protected the natives and brutalized them, made enormous amounts of money and ran progressive social protection programs, did everything and its opposite, but that always followed the beacon of a single idea: Africans were children whom you could spank or reward, depending on the circumstances, but whom you should never trust or treat seriously.

Apart from South Africa, the Belgian Congo was the most industrialized and "developed" territory on the continent. By 1958, on the eve of independence, 35 percent of all adults were in salaried employment, a proportion unknown elsewhere in Africa.[5] But this "development" was deceptive: out of the whole salaried workforce, barely fifteen hundred could be termed "professionals," while the others were unqualified workers, farm laborers, petty clerks, and assorted *fundi* (artisans and repairmen). By the time of independence in 1960 there were only *seventeen* university graduates out of a population of over twenty million. The Belgian paternalistic system needed disciplined, semiqualified drones; it did not need people who could take responsibility: the whites were there for that. The problem came when Brussels, suddenly shoved forward by the strong winds of British and French decolonization, shifted from total denial of any "native problem" to a hurried flight from both colonization and any form of responsibility.[6] Improvised elections in May 1960, the only real elections to be held in the Congo before those in 2006, produced a fractured Assembly wherein twenty-six "political parties," which were in fact tribal coalitions, tried to negotiate a democratic regime. The almost immediate secession of the mineral-rich province of Katanga followed by four years of civil war led to a CIA-sponsored coup in 1965 which brought to power a former colonial army sergeant, Joseph-Désiré Mobutu.

Mobutu is a fundamental political phenomenon of contemporary Africa, and the subsequent thirty-two years of his unbridled power constitute one of the most catastrophic examples of dictatorship in a continent that has displayed an impressive array of those during the past half-century.[7] Protected by the Americans, who saw him as their most reliable cold war ally on the African continent, Mobutu ran the Congo, which he renamed Zaire, as a poorly managed private estate. At once greedy and munificent, violent and funny, clever and ignorant, he was a tyrant out of Suetonius whose limited horizon stopped at the preservation of his undivided power. He never seems to have given a thought to the fact that he destroyed his country in order to keep ruling it. His undoing was to come with the end of the cold war, which had been the great justification for his regime.

The turning point was the year 1990, when the whole system started to go awry. Mobutu had had opponents before but never any structural threat to his regime. The remnants of the 1960s radical guerrillas had either been crushed militarily, like Pierre Mulele's *maquis* in Kwilu, or pushed into irrelevancy, like Laurent-Désiré Kabila's PRP in South Kivu.[8] Etienne Tshisekedi's Union pour la Démocratie et le Progrès Social (UDPS) had been more of a problem because of its Kasai Baluba constituency, but it could be accommodated. And the violent challenge of the Angolan communist-backed Gendarmes Katangais invasion in 1977 had been contained through classical cold war tactics of foreign military intervention. But 1990 was something else; the world was changing and the aging dictator did not know what to make of it.

In January and February 1990 President Mobutu decided to tour the whole country. He had been shaken by the violent death of the Romanian dictator Nicolae Ceaucescu, who had been a personal friend, and his political acumen told him that something new was happening. Mobutu was surrounded by sycophants and largely cut off from the people,[9] which made this trip a rude awakening for him in spite of all the *animation* and popular dancing usually organized for such circumstances. He came back with an impression of dangerous discontent at every level. His answer was to make a historic speech on April 24, 1990, proclaiming a "Third Republic" in which the press was to be free, Christian names and Western business suits were to be allowed again,[10] and the MPR would lose its monopoly on political representation. Of course, he intended to maintain control over the whole process. But the pressure had been building for too long and the political agitation that developed as a result scared him, causing an overreaction: on the night of May 11–12, 1990, DSP commandos were unleashed on the campus of the University of Lubumbashi, killing dozens of students.[11]

This was the mistake he could not afford to make in the international context of the time. All the financial abuses that he had committed and had been allowed to get away with in the past were suddenly brought to the fore. In rapid succession Belgium, the United States, and the World Bank cut Zaire off. All had previously had excellent reasons to do so, but they had to wait until the cold war was over and the old dinosaur[12] was made redundant before they decided to act. Now Mobutu had to bite the bullet, and on August 7, 1991, the Conférence Nationale Souveraine (CNS) was solemnly inaugurated.[13] But the wily old man had not lost his talent for manipulation: if there were to be several political parties, there could also be *too many* parties, so as to make the whole thing unmanageable. The unmanageability worked beyond his wildest dreams: when the CNS started to disintegrate Kinshasa blew up as the unpaid FAZ started to loot the city.[14] Large segments of the population soon joined the soldiers in an orgy of pillaging and often of sheer gratuitous destruction of anything that was a symbol of Mobutism. The CNS was suspended on January 19, 1991. Pressure mounted. On February 16 the one-million-strong Church-led *Marche de l'espoir* (March of Hope) ended in tragedy when police and the army opened fire on the unarmed marchers, killing seventeen, according to the authorities, or forty-nine, according to Médecins Sans Frontières. The CNS reopened on April 6 in an atmosphere of extreme urgency. The delegates by then knew that whatever their petty quarrels and divisions, they were in a historic position, with the eyes of the whole country trained on them. But the old dinosaur could still bite, and he showed it by increasingly ethnicizing the political situation in order to make it unmanageable.

In 1990 Mobutu had appointed Kyungu wa Kyumwanza as governor of Shaba Province. Kyungu was a Muluba from Katanga who was a co-founder of UDPS together with Tshisekedi. But after he was jailed he made a deal with Mobutu: to get his release he defected from the party. In Shaba he soon became a vocal proponent of a return to "Katangese autonomy." The former prime minister Nguza had created his own political party, the Union des Fédéralistes et des Républicains Indépendants, and collaborated with Kyungu in Shaba. In September 1992 the governor ordered a massive roundup of Kasaian Luba.[15] Tens of thousands were arrested, their properties confiscated or looted, they were regrouped in concentration camps and deported "back to Kasaï" (where many of the youngest ones had never

78

been). There were an untold number of victims, probably several hundred at least. This agitation and confusion contributed to undermine the CNS, especially because there were sporadic outbursts of looting in the interior (Mbandaka in October, Kisangani and Goma in December). On August 15 the CNS elected Tshisekedi prime minister against Mobutu's wishes, and on December 6 Mobutu closed down the Assembly.

With aid cut off after years of economic decay most sources of financing for the government had dried up. Mobutu then cold-bloodedly resorted to printing huge quantities of increasingly worthless currency. The inflation rate became insane: 4,130 percent in 1991, 2,990 percent in 1992, 4,650 percent in 1993, and 9,800 percent in 1994. The new five million Zaire note which was introduced in late 1992 was the straw that finally broke the shopkeepers' patience: they refused it as legal tender. Because the army had been paid with these new worthless notes it exploded into another looting spree, from January 28 to February 2, 1993, and completely ransacked the capital, killing French Ambassador Philippe Bernard in the process. The country was tottering on the brink of anarchy. The CNS had been reopened under the name Haut Conseil de la République (HCR) under Monsignor Monsengwo's presidency and was trying to back Tshisekedi as prime minister, though Mobutu had named Faustin Birindwa for the position. The whole of 1993 was spent in deadlock, with two prime ministers, two Assemblies (the HCR and the old Mobutist Parliament), and increasingly chaotic provinces.[16]

Mobutu could still rely on a measure of French support, and in September he was invited to the Franco-African Summit in Mauritius, where he talked with President François Mitterrand. Mitterrand asked him to support the democratization of the country and Mobutu promised he would. He knew that he had very little support left from Brussels or Washington; Paris appeared to be his last hope. He managed to eventually wear down Monsignor Monsengwo's resistance and get the prelate to embrace a mythical "third way" between the executive and Tshisekedi's opposition. On January 14, 1994, the HCR was dissolved, and nine days later Laurent Monsengwo agreed to fuse it with the old Mobutist Parliament, creating the Haut Conseil de la République/Parlement Transitoire (HCR/PT).

To buy time Mobutu kept promising the West anything it wanted. The diplomatic skies seemed to be clearing since the 1994 Rwandese genocide and its subsequent refugee exodus had put Zaire back on the international community's map. "Free and fair elections" for 1997 had even been promised, and the old dinosaur looked as if he had won yet another battle. In fact, he and his regime were dying, both physically and metaphorically. He was soon to be diagnosed with advanced cancer of the prostate, and the country had decayed into uncontrolled pseudo-feudal ethnic units. As for the Rwandese refugee question, far from providing the useful blackmailing card he had hoped for, it was rapidly turning into an uncontrollable disaster. Which is why, when the RPA finally crossed the border in September 1996 and found nothing standing in its way, the ease with which its military campaign succeeded against the refugee camps eventually tempted the attackers into dealing the regime its deathblow and write the last chapter of a thirty-two-year rule.

The interlopers

Sudanese and Ugandans. Sudan's independence process had mainly been an Arab affair,[17] but until the 1980s, in spite of the long drawn-out conflict between northern and southern Sudan and in spite of the Ugandan civil violence of the Idi Amin and Obote II regimes, there had been little cross-border interference.[18] Things changed with the advent of Yoweri Museveni's rise to power in Kampala on January 25, 1986,[19] and even more when the radical National Islamic Front (NIF) took over in a bloodless military coup in Khartoum during the night of June 30 to July 1, 1989. One of the main problems came from a (wrong) personal inference. In the 1960s both Yoweri Museveni and Col. John Garang, the SPLA leader, had briefly been students at the University of Dar-es-Salaam, then the Mecca of young African left-wingers. When Museveni came to power the Sudanese regime was immediately persuaded that Uganda would become a rear base for the Sudanese rebel movement, although there were no signs that such a plan existed.[20] The whole "radical student theory" was based on a mistake in the first place, for Museveni and Garang had attended Dar-es-Salaam University at different times, and they had hardly known each other during the two or three months when both had been there. Fantasies notwithstanding, there was no "Dar-es-Salaam left-wing old boys' network."[21] As for Ugandan support for the SPLA, it was nonexistent until 1993, and there were times when a simple appointment with the Kampala SPLA representative (who did not even have an office) could cause the poor man to be questioned and briefly detained by the Ugandan police for "unauthorised political activities."[22] Museveni was extremely careful not to antagonize Khartoum, and if he finally resorted to helping the SPLA it was only because his policy of noninterference failed in the end to produce any results.[23]

The NIF 1989 putsch brought to power a government even more hostile to Kampala than Sadiq al-Mahdi's had been.[24] The cause was ideological rather than factual because, contrary to the former democratic regime's pro-Western orientation, the NIF had a strong anti-U.S. position.[25] The Muslim Brothers stood for militant Islam; they were looking forward to a medium-term future when Islamization would reach the Great Lakes, and even to a long-term future when it would sweep the whole continent.[26] In that long-range strategic view, Uganda stood in the way.

Up to 1989 there had been sporadic efforts by Khartoum at helping anti-Museveni forces in Uganda. The first attempt was very early on, in 1986, when the new Ugandan regime had to face resistance from the defeated Acholi in the north.[27] The former chief of the Ugandan Military Council Army, Acholi Brig. Basilio Okello, had crossed into Sudan after being defeated by Museveni's NRA and been given help by the Sudanese army. This first attempt at interfering with the new Ugandan regime did not work out very well because the political guerrilla movement Brigadier Okello and his friends launched was soon bled of its men and equipment by a strange millenarian cult led by a young prophetess, Alice Auma, nicknamed Lakwena, "the messenger." Alice's mystic leadership was more attractive for the bitter and disoriented young Acholi soldiers who had just lost power than the conventional political manifestos of Brigadier Okello and his former government associates.[28] She and her band of combatants smeared with *dawa* (magic medicine) pushed back the NRA in the north, fought their way down to the south, and were stopped only by superior firepower as they were nearing Jinja in October 1987. Alice, who was wounded, took refuge in Kenya and the movement almost collapsed. But Joseph Kony, her nephew or cousin, declared that he had also had visions and laid claim to the rebellious prophet's mantle, creating the Lord's Salvation Army (LSA). Between 1988 and 1993 he kept a small guerrilla war going in north Acholi, in almost impenetrable terrain close to the Sudanese border. Up to late 1991 his position remained extremely difficult because the SPLA was on the other side of the border and was very hostile to the LSA. Although the Sudanese rebels were not getting any help from Museveni at the time, they were careful to stay on good terms with him because Uganda was a major conduit for humanitarian aid channeled by trucks from Kenya to SPLA-occupied Equatoria. The 1991 fall of Colonel Menguistu's regime was to prove a boon for Joseph Kony and his men as the SPLA, which had been close to the former communist regime, suddenly lost its main source of support. Soon after, in August 1991, the Sudanese rebel movement split into two mutually hostile wings when its Nuer and Dinka units started fighting each other. The Sudanese government, which had already taken an interest in the Kony rebellion but had not been able to access it geographically, started to make contact with it after its two successful offensives of early 1992 and late 1993. The Sudanese government had acquired control of several stretches of the Sudan-Uganda border and Kony was invited to Juba by the Sudanese Military Security; there, in exchange for a symbolic smattering of Islam (some of the fighters took Muslim names and pretended to convert), he got serious military aid. The Lord's Resistance Army (LRA),[29] which had been down to about three hundred fighters in mid-1993, was suddenly up to over two thousand well-equipped troops by March 1994 and was in a position to raid the whole of northern Uganda.

It was then that the situation began to get seriously internationalized. The Khartoum government approached President Mobutu sometime during mid-1994 and got his approval to run supply convoys from Wau in Bahr-el-Ghazal down to northern Uganda through the Central African Republic and the Uele Province of Zaire. Not only did the LRA now get some of its supplies through Zaire, but Sudanese Army Security contacted Kakwa and Aringa former Idi Amin soldiers who had been living in the area since 1979 and reorganized them into a fighting front.[30] The WNBLF was born in November 1994 in Faradje and, with Sudanese help, immediately started harassing Ugandan forces in West Nile from the Zairian side of the border.

This was bound to attract some kind of Ugandan reaction, but not right away, in the "triple border" zone. There was another region further to the south, around the Ruwenzori and Virunga volcanic chain, where trouble between Uganda and Zaire had long been endemic. On the Ugandan side this was an area of long-running conflict between the central government and the Bakonjo and Baamba tribes, who live astride the Uganda-Congo border. In the early 1900s the Bakonjo had been arbitrarily made subjects of the Tooro kingdom because the Tooro monarchy had allied itself to the colonial occupation and the British wished to reinforce it vis-à-vis its anti-British neighbor, Bunyoro. The Bakonjo and their Baamba neighbors took their subject position with patience but ended up asking the colonial authorities for their own district in the 1950s. Their request was denied, and they launched a low-intensity guerrilla struggle against the British, which they kept going through all the independent governments following decolonization. This movement was called Rwenzururu and became famous in a kind of local folk epic.[31] After years of struggle the Rwenzururu leadership finally signed an armistice with the Obote II government in August 1982. The man who had been instrumental in this reconciliation was himself a Mukonjo, Amon Bazira, who understood that the movement was by then largely middle class and that it was possible to co-opt it with some commercial advantages. But Bazira, who was a staunch supporter of the Uganda Peoples Congress (UPC), left Uganda in 1985. He later approached President Mobutu and President Daniel arap Moi of Kenya, who each had their own reasons for disliking the new Ugandan regime. They both supported a revival of the Bakonjo rebellion under the new label of the National Army for the Liberation of Uganda, a much grander sounding name than Rwenzururu. In fact NALU was just a cut-rate version of Rwenzururu without the popular appeal. But money could do wonders in an impoverished peasant milieu in a marginal region of Uganda. NALU soon grew enough to become an irritant, and in 1992 Bazira was shot dead in a Nairobi street, most likely by Ugandan agents.

Museveni, who had always seen Mobutu as the African stooge of imperialism incarnate, was even further angered by the NALU episode and started looking for ways of getting back at the Zairian dictator. He found them on the other side of the Virunga Mountains, across from the Ugandan town of Kasese, where the waning of the Congolese rebellion in 1965 had left lingering guerrilla remnants around Beni. Later, in 1986, groups of young Batembo, Bahunde, and Banande who resented Mobutu's protection of local Banyarwanda land grabbing, started a new low-intensity antigovernment operation under the leadership of Joseph Marandura's son on the other side of the Virunga Mountains, across from the Ugandan town of Kasese.[32] They called their movement the Parti de Libération Congolais (PLC), but their activity was mostly limited to raiding Ugandan border villages to steal goats and chickens. In 1988–1989 they were severely mauled by the FAZ and had to withdraw either north, all the way into Garamba National Park, or deeper into the Beni Forest.

As we have already seen,[33] in November 1994 President Museveni discussed the possibility of overthrowing Mobutu with a number of Congolese opponents. Although they decided not to act at the time, this had not prevented the Ugandan External Service Organization (ESO) from helping the PLC. Col. Kahinda Otafiire, one of the key Ugandan Secret Service operatives and a friend of President Museveni, had recruited into the PLC a young, idealistic, and dynamic young Mutetela named André Kisase Ngandu. Over the next two years Kisase was going to become "Uganda's man" in eastern Zaire, looking for ways of eventually turning the PLC from a micro-guerrilla band into a more serious military force. In the meantime, in spite of its limited size, the PLC could be used to retaliate in case of Zairian incursions.

On June 17, 1994, a group of undisciplined Zairian soldiers crossed the Ugandan border near Arua in West Nile and looted everything they could get, taking back with them two Ugandans as prisoners.[34] As this came in the wake of some WNBLF cross-border actions, the ESO sent the PLC boys across from Bundibugyo to attack the FAZ in reprisal. They were allowed to retreat back into Uganda after their hit-and-run raid, and Uganda's Ministry of Foreign Affairs denied the whole thing on September 2.[35] At the same time Kampala was pressuring UNHCR to repatriate the so-called Amin's refugees from Province Orientale since they provided the ready pond where Sudanese agents were fishing for WNBLF recruits.[36] Meanwhile, arms trafficking kept growing between Zaire, Sudan, and northern Uganda, with disastrous consequences for the civilians.[37] But soon a new dimension was going to be added to this already strained situation.

In January 1995 a Muslim group calling itself the Uganda Muslim Liberation Army (UMLA) formally declared war on the National Resistance Movement (NRM) government. The reasons given for this in its communiqué were rather hazy: the UMLA accused Museveni of having killed Muslims in 1979 at Nyamitaga, near Mbarara,[38] and later in 1983 at Butambala, near Mpigi.[39] But there were two interesting points in the document: first, there was an obvious effort at presenting Museveni as an enemy of the whole Ugandan Muslim community by using somewhat contorted "historical" arguments;[40] second, most of the document's signatories were Muslim Baganda, a completely new development: in the past, and notably during the 1981–1986 bush war against Obote, the Baganda Muslim community had given the NRA discreet but significant support. Historically it is not exaggerated to say that in early 1981 it was the timely financial and political support of Prince Badru Kakungulu that enabled Museveni to turn his small band of outlaws (he had twenty-six men) into a more efficient armed organization.[41] It was soon apparent that the puzzle of this role switch had more to do with Baganda factional politics than with Islam. During the bush war of 1981–1986 and its immediate aftermath the Baganda, who had been the main target of Obote's repression, supported the NRA. But soon after the end of the war the old and well-known ultramonarchist tendencies that had triggered the whole Ugandan catastrophe back in the 1960s began to resurface. The monarchists, in an effort at resuscitating their movement, targeted Museveni for a number of imagined ills designed to mobilize Baganda opinion against the central government. It was partly to appease these neomonarchists that Museveni restored the kingdom of Buganda in 1993, albeit in a diminished and nonpolitical form.[42] But this "clipped restoration" was exactly what the neomonarchists could not accept. A number of them secretly created the Allied Democratic Movement (ADM) in London in January 1995. Later ADM documents are politically very crude,[43] but they belie the tradition of the men who had pushed Kabaka Mutesa II into his ill-conceived confrontational politics of the 1960s. In the 1990s, even though the new Ugandan regime enjoyed the full support of the United States and even though the Soviet Union had disappeared, these same people still called Museveni a communist. Talking with them made one feel like a time traveler, for their argumentation in the late 1990s was still pure 1965 Kabaka Yekka vintage, complete with its right-wing cold war rhetoric.[44] These were upper-class Protestant Baganda, but political opportunism was soon going to bring them into a most unnatural alliance with the radical Muslim UMLA Lumpenproletariat.

In fact, the ADM and the UMLA were born at the same time and both were led by Baganda. But there was a clear sharing of responsibilities: the ADM recruited among ordinary Baganda (who are mostly Christians), while the UMLA recruited beyond the very small Baganda Muslim community and also got non-Baganda Muslims, who tend to be at the bottom of Ugandan society.[45] The two rebel movements complemented each other and cleverly exploited the complex interweaving of ethnic and class politics typical of most of today's Africa: the core leadership of the two organizations was the same (radical Baganda neomonarchists in search of troops to fight Museveni), but the rank and file was anything they could pick up, mostly very poor people from a variety of tribes. The movement soon grew impressively. Later it was interesting to talk with Uganda People's Defense Force (UPDF) officers, who seemed puzzled as to what the guerrilla force was all about. There were two things that seemed to deeply disturb them: one, that the guerrillas were not an ethnic group; two, that the prisoners they captured in Bundibugyo told them they had been promised money to fight. The going rate was about 500,000 shillings for an ordinary fighter (enough to buy a kiosk from which to sell cigarettes and sodas at the bus stop) and 5 million shillings for an officer (enough to buy a taxi). The UPDF officers were NRA veterans who said, "We fought for an ideal. How can these people fight for money, especially so little money?" It was hard for them to accept that, though their "ideal" had brought them a certain bit of prosperity, they were now facing the very people whom the "Ugandan economic miracle" had passed by. The notion that this social marginalization was not attached to any given tribe, as had been the case in the past, seemed even stranger.[46]

Since the 1987 monetary reform Uganda has averaged a 5 percent yearly rate of economic growth, which puts it in the very limited group of IMF African success stories of the past fifteen years.[47] But the product of that growth has been extremely unevenly distributed. NRM cadres and their political cronies skimmed the cream off the top and very little was left for ordinary Ugandans. The Baganda conservatives who hated Museveni knew they could play on that growth-induced social marginality. They were bourgeois, but they knew that there was a Lumpenproletariat they could use, either among the young rural unemployed or among the city street kids. And because the Muslim community represented a very large proportion of that Lumpenproletariat, for historical reasons going back to the place of Muslims in Uganda's colonial society, a satellite Muslim organization was an essential tool both in recruiting and in getting outside support from the Sudan. This was a strange alliance, and the good Protestant Anglo-Baganda bourgeois leadership that prided itself on its monarchic extremism felt somewhat ill at ease about this tactical alliance with Khartoum's radical Islam.[48]

The first UMLA military efforts proved abortive. Its forces were defeated in a series of encounters at Buseruka, near Lake Albert in Bunyoro, on February 20–28, 1995. The survivors fled to Zaire, where they settled near Bunia. The reasons for their defeat were simple: they were city boys (and girls: approximately 20 percent of the guerrillas were female) without much knowledge of the terrain; they were a multiethnic group with almost no local sympathies;[49] and their armament was limited. But in Bunia they soon made interesting new contacts. The Sudanese Army Security Services were at the time using the Bunia airfield to bring supplies both to the Rwandese *Interahamwe* and to the WBNLF. Both groups were hostile to the NRM regime and therefore worth supporting, from Khartoum's point of view. Although based in Zaire, this was a Sudan-driven operation because Mobutu was far too weak to provide anything except the physical ground from which to operate. But in Bunia the Sudanese found the vanquished UMLA fighters licking their wounds and took them in hand. Although Khartoum already knew about the UMLA, it had so far worked more closely with the radical Ugandan Muslim movement known as Tabliq. The Tablighi Jama'at, born in India in the 1920s, had initially been a pietist and revivalist Muslim sect that started to spread worldwide in the 1950s and eventually reached Uganda.[50] Tabliq "missionaries" had penetrated the Uganda Muslim Youth Association in the early 1980s, at a time when the Uganda Muslim community was still trying to recover from its embarrassing association with the Idi Amin dictatorship. By the 1990s the result of this initially rather mild faith renewal movement was the birth of a native Ugandan militant fundamentalism with strong connections to the Sudan.[51] In 1991 the Tabliq occupied by force the Kampala Central Mosque; four people were killed, many were wounded, and hundreds were jailed and later tried in huge public trials. Whatever help Khartoum had channeled to the nascent UMLA before 1995 had gone through the Tabliq movement of Sheikh Jamir Mukulu, which had strong connections with the international fundamentalist networks and with Sudan.[52] It was from the Khartoum-sponsored fusion between ADM and UMLA in Zaire that the present Allied Democratic Forces (ADF) was born.[53] But the key element in that union was that the Sudanese operators soon realized that without a good peasant grounding in local realities, the guerrillas would be defeated again. This is why they worked at incorporating the guerrilla force into the remnants of NALU, the old Bakonjo Rwenzururu movement of the Ruwenzori Mountains.[54]

In August 1995 the Sudanese army operating inside Zaire with WNBLF support took the small strategic towns of Kaya and Oraba from the SPLA in order to secure their supply lines and disrupt those of the SPLA. They celebrated their victory by shelling the Sudanese refugee camp at Koboko on Ugandan territory from the Zairian side of the border. The Sudanese government was then at its most militant, having tried to assassinate Egyptian President Hosni Mubarak in June in Addis-Ababa during an OAU meeting, and President Museveni felt there was enough international leeway to allow him to retaliate strongly. So the UPDF attacked the LRA *inside* Sudan in September and October 1995, pushing all the way to Owinyi-Kibul in a common operation with the SPLA.

On the Zaire front Crispus Kiyonga, who was President Museveni's Bakonjo representative, felt obliged to deny Ugandan support for the PLC,[55] but the relationship had become common knowledge in Bundibugyo since PLC fighters were taking part in the local coffee-smuggling operations from Zaire that partially financed their movement. Through the early months of 1996 both the old NALU and the Tabliq networks kept recruiting young men in their different social environments. But the Sudanese had not yet managed to bring them together and an early UMLA-Tabliq attack on Kisoro ended in failure.[56] The Muslim community was split between its pro-Museveni and pro-Khartoum choices, and in June 1996 the Tabliq tried to murder Suleiman Kakeeto, a moderate Uganda Supreme Muslim Council leader who had publicly disavowed the guerrillas; as for Sheikh Jamir Mukulu, he fled to Khartoum just before the Internal Service Organization (ISO) could arrest him.[57]

Meanwhile, fighting was spreading in the north and in West Nile. The result of this increase in military operations was that Uganda was forced to go back on the demobilization program it had started with World Bank support in 1994, with a target of cutting down the UPDF from 90,000 to 40,000 men.[58] In June 1996 the Ministry of Defense had to review its budget and reinvest the $29 million it had so far saved through the demobilization exercise, after letting go about 12,000 men.

As the Rwandese army began to launch its operation against the refugee camps in South Kivu in September, it was immediately obvious that given the degree of Sudanese support for the Zaire-based Ugandan guerrillas, Kampala was going to take advantage of the general conflagration to do its own bit of cross-border cleanup.[59] The question was: Up to where and with what political agenda? The answers would become clearer only gradually, in the following months, after the refugee problem was taken care of in the most brutal and radical fashion.

Far from the Great Lakes: the Angolan conflict. Although the Angolan conflict was also to play a fundamental role in the later Zairian conflagration, its nature was fundamentally different from the Sudanese-Ugandan transborder skirmishes just described. First, Angola is a very large country (1,246,000 square kilometers, or almost half a million square miles), and the fighting was spread out over its territory rather than limited to the relatively small areas where Zaire, the Sudan, and Uganda meet; second, Portuguese colonialism was in a category of its own and so was its legacy; third, Angola was a key theater of cold war struggles, which had left an enormous backlog of conveniently forgotten unpaid political bills; and fourth, Angola is a much richer country than either the Sudan or Uganda, which allowed its process of national destruction to be carried out with an impressive array of military means quite unknown in other parts of the continent, except for Ethiopia.

The Portuguese colonization of Angola theoretically dated to the sixteenth century, but in practice less than 15 percent of the territory was under actual government control at the time of the 1885 Berlin Conference, and it was between that date and the fall of the Portuguese monarchy in 1926 that the takeover of the hinterland was carried out in a very painful manner.[60] Portuguese colonialism had been archaic in several ways. Its economic policies harked back to a kind of outmoded physiocratic model that, if it had been a permanent temptation for the French or the British, had never been applied elsewhere in Africa with such a relentless absolutism. This trait was to leave an enormous legacy to the postcolonial state in terms of its love for totalitarian state control. Another unusual feature of Portuguese colonization was the large white presence throughout the colonial period, a white presence that not only kept growing but even greatly increased just as the colony exploded into revolt.

Number of Whites in Angola

1869	1902	1931	1940	1950	1960	1970
3,000	13,000	60,000	44,000	79,000	172,000	335,000

Sources: Gervase Clarence-Smith, "Capital Accumulation and Class Formation in Angola," in David Birmingham and Phyllis Martin, eds., *History of Central Africa* (London: Longman, 1983), 2: 191; G. Clarence-Smith, *The Third Portuguese Empire (1825–1975): A Study in Economic Imperialism* (Manchester, UK: Manchester University Press, 1985). Figures have been rounded off to the nearest thousand; the huge 1970 figure includes over 50,000 soldiers.

Many of the whites were uneducated, and in 1960 an estimated twenty thousand were jobless, living by selling lottery tickets, begging, shining shoes, or pimping for their African wives and concubines.[61] Sexual promiscuity had resulted over the years in a large number of *mestiços*,[62] whose social and class interests were distinct from those of the whites and from those of the native Africans, but were often quite close to those of the *assimilados*, the educated blacks the Portuguese were co-opting into their culture on the basis of language.[63] The general impression given by the Portuguese system is of a Creole time warp somehow keeping an increasingly precarious foothold in the contemporary world.

The cost of living was high and salaries were modest.... Bachelors lived in small hostels where alcoholism and prostitution were rife.... The effects of this persistent poverty were a mixture of radicalism and racism.... Some Whites, like the radicals in Algeria, went as far as joining the clandestine Communist Party. But radicalism generally went together with a virulent racism. Newly arrived immigrants were provided with a shelter and some form of income, often at the expense of the Africans. Skin colour was used as much as possible to gain advantage and the discourse of the Whites was as racist as that prevalent in South Africa and Rhodesia.... This mixture of poverty, radicalism, solidarity and racism accounted for the hysterical determination of the white community not to give in to African nationalist demands in 1961, in strong contrast with the Belgian Congo.[64]

Luanda's first nationalist organization was the MPLA, founded in 1956; it was practically an overseas offshoot of the then clandestine Portuguese Communist Party. The movement was the political expression of the semi-Portuguese proletarian petty bourgeoisie that both hated Salazarist oppression and feared the rural African masses.[65] Both traits were going to last. In that same year another movement was created in Leopoldville, the União das Populações de Angola (UPA). Its leader, Holden Roberto, was a Mukongo assimilado. But he was also a Baptist, and the religious difference was to prove a key factor in the contribution to the nationalist movement. The UPA was "black African" with a nativist ideology and a Protestant support network. The war of independence started in early 1961.

The UPA, which was soon renamed Frente Nacional de Libertação de Angola (FNLA), was essentially a Bakongo movement. Most of its adherents were Bakongo, and they came from all the Bakongo territories, including the Cabinda Enclave, the French Congo, and the Belgian Congo. But other black Angolans also tended to gravitate toward the FNLA, as the MPLA was perceived as the party of radical whites, assimilados, and mestiços.[66] The FNLA was at ease in Leopoldville,[67] which was not the case with the Marxist MPLA. The movement's leadership left for Brazzaville as soon as Massemba-Debat's radical coup provided them with a more congenial environment (in November 1963), and it began training a small armed militia with the help of the Cubans, who had just arrived in Brazzaville to support the new regime. In 1964 Jonas Savimbi, an Ovimbundu assimilado and FNLA militant, decided to break away from the Front, which he found "too ethnically oriented," meaning controlled by Bakongo elements. By 1966 he had created his own organization, UNITA, which recruited mostly among the Ovimbundu and which began to fight the Portuguese from the east.[68] Savimbi based himself in Zambia, where he made contacts that were to stand him in good stead later. His small movement was seen by the Portuguese as an ideal spoiler for the much more dangerous FNLA and MPLA, and the colonial army concluded a nonaggression pact with him, the better to fight the other two movements.[69] In this cutthroat climate outside support for one or the other movements immediately took on an added internal dimension. By November 1974 the MPLA and the FNLA were fighting each other in an effort to control the Zairian border and the capital. On

January 15, 1975, the Portuguese Movimento de Forças Armadas, which had overthrown the fascist regime in Portugal, got the three movements to sign the Alvor Agreement, which provided for a tripartite government at independence. But the MPLA, which had been gaining increasing control of the capital, decided to dispense completely with the Alvor Agreement and to kick out all UNITA and especially FNLA militants from Luanda. On November 11, 1975, it proclaimed unilaterally the Popular Republic of Angola, which was soon recognized by the Eastern Bloc, by the European powers, and by most Third World countries, but not by the United States. A new civil war had taken the place of the independence struggle.

The civil war was immediately internationalized when the South Africans decided to intervene and were progressively deployed between November 1975 and January 1976. Encouraged by the U.S. nonrecognition of the new Angolan state and by the South African intervention, the FNLA thought that the time was ripe to take Luanda by storm. But it had overestimated its military strength and underestimated the amount of support brought in by Cuba[70] and the USSR. In January 1976 the FNLA was smashed by Russian heavy artillery fire and withdrew in disarray to the Zaire border. Mobutu then sent his troops into the war, but they were also promptly and decisively defeated. For all practical purposes the FNLA then disappeared from the Angolan political equation, leaving no other option for the anti-MPLA actors, the United States and South Africa, but to support Savimbi and his fledgling UNITA.[71]

The stance the United States took against the MPLA was straight cold war strategy, but for Pretoria the situation was more complicated. The main motivating factor, apart from opposing the rise of a communist-backed regime in Angola, was to protect South African control over South West Africa. This former German colony had been given to Great Britain as a Mandate Territory after World War I and retroceded by London to its South African colony. But when the 1948 election brought the South African National Party to power, leading to the proclamation of apartheid and the subsequent break between Pretoria and the Commonwealth, it left South West Africa in the hands of a regime that was isolated by international reprobation. Given the mineral riches of South West Africa and its strategic importance as a buffer state against subversion by the African National Congress (ANC), Pretoria was strongly committed to its security. During the 1960s the South West Africa People's Organization (SWAPO) had worked in close collaboration with the Angolan FNLA and, when he broke with Holden Roberto, with Savimbi's UNITA.[72] But in 1976, given the rise to power of the MPLA, SWAPO had to make a sudden about-face and fight its former UNITA allies in order to be able to stay in Angola at all. The break was particularly cruel because, since it knew UNITA's internal organization very well, SWAPO could betray it effectively to the MPLA, and many UNITA militants were killed. Savimbi then became a resolute enemy of his former friends and betrayed all the information he had on SWAPO bases to the notorious South African Secret Service, which made good use of it.[73] But by 1976 the situation did not look very promising for the South Africans: the FNLA had collapsed, there were now thirty-six thousand Cuban troops in Luanda, and the ill-prepared 1975–1976 campaign into Angola by the South African Defense Force (SADF) had been less than conclusive from a military point of view. The poor SADF showing in Angola brought about active support for SWAPO, under the condition that the Namibian movement would actively fight its erstwhile ally UNITA in the south. The UN then voted a new resolution asking for "the withdrawal of South Africa's illegal administration of Namibia and the transfer of power to the people of Namibia with the assistance of the United Nations."[74] In Pretoria's eyes the UN had just become an objective ally of Moscow and Havana and military means were the only answer. At a secret conference in December 1977 the SADF top brass persuaded the South African prime minister John Vorster to move across the border. Vorster's unenthusiastic endorsement was taken as an absolute green light by the military, who in May 1978 attacked the Kassinga SWAPO refugee camp inside Angola, killing over six hundred civilians. Pretoria's so-called Total National Strategy policies, outlined in a key 1977 Defense White Paper, recommended nothing less than "coherent military, diplomatic and economic actions aiming at the creation of a South African–dominated cluster of interdependent states in Southern Africa."[75] UNITA had become a part of that grand strategy.

In the United States the 1980 election of President Ronald Reagan radically modified the rules of the international game when Assistant Secretary of State for Africa Chester Crocker pronounced his famous "linkage" speech,[76] making the application of UN Resolution 435 dependant on the withdrawal of Cuban troops. This was an unacceptable approach for Luanda; determining to win militarily at all cost, the MPLA purchased over a billion dollars' worth of weapons from the Eastern Bloc during 1986–1987. But there were key political changes under way in the Soviet Union and Fidel Castro knew that he might not have too much time left to win some kind of decisive victory before he would be forced to the negotiating table. But if

Soviet Perestroika was putting indirect pressure on Havana's commitment to the MPLA,[77] Pretoria was feeling another kind of constraint: the degradation of its economic and financial situation. In 1988 South Africa's external debt had reached $24 billion, $12 billion of which was due for repayment in 1990–1991.[78] In the words of a South African analyst, "Foreign debt repayment may have been one of the single biggest factors putting pressure on South Africa to end its occupation of Namibia."[79] On December 22, 1988, a tripartite UN-guaranteed agreement was signed in New York between Angola, Cuba, and South Africa. SWAPO, whose fate was being decided, was not invited to attend. The Cubans had until July 1, 1991, to go home; during the same period the South African government would comply with UN Resolution 435 and organize free and fair elections in Namibia, with SWAPO participation.[80] SWAPO had been handed a victory by the MPLA as a ready-made package, and this after years of being used by Luanda as an auxiliary military force in the war with UNITA. This godfather role toward Namibia was decisive, and it was going to remain a permanent feature of the relationship between the two countries.

The New York Agreement was a fine piece of diplomatic work. The only problem was that it had nothing to say about the situation in Angola itself, where the war went on as before. After years of harping on Savimbi-the-puppet-of-the-South-African-racist-regime the MPLA had begun to believe its own propaganda. The propaganda was partly true; Savimbi had indeed played South Africa's game. The man had an absolute single-mindedness which enabled him to adapt to any circumstances or to any ally as long as this served his long-term strategy. But he was nobody's puppet, and the problem of having a Lusophone Creole elite numbering 500,000 at best ruling a country of over 12 million Africans remained. Worse, the war had now turned the MPLA into a subculture of its own, with its own rules, tricks, and arrangements.

Oil was a big part of the problem. From its humble beginnings in the Cabinda Enclave during the Salazar years, oil had grown to represent Angola's major economic resource, and it was going to grow even more in future years until its value peaked at 89 percent of government revenue in 1997.

Angola's Oil Production (in barrels per day)

1973	1988	1994	1995	1999
172,000	470,000	580,000	680,000	770,000

Source: Sonangol, Angola's national oil corporation.

The oil economy had grown out of Cabinda and then pervaded the whole Angolan economic landscape. But it employed only ten thousand people and tended to concentrate rather than distribute wealth.[81] Between the war and the neglect of productive investments, traditional and even plantation agriculture had fallen by the wayside. A whole *candonga* (black market) economy had grown around the empty bunkers of "socialist production," social and health facilities had collapsed, and it was only the Cuban doctors who managed to keep minimum service going; prostitution and delinquency were rife, and the whole public sector ran almost exclusively on kickbacks and payoffs. This did not prevent the favored members of the *nomenklatura* from living well and from practicing in their private lives the capitalist opposite of the socialist asceticism they were preaching every day in public. The old left-wing ideals of the past had been buried, together with the pretence of nonracialism. The MPLA had become a single party in the best communist tradition: intellectual and press freedoms were unknown, the radio was controlled, there was a single (compliant) trade union, and the Direcião de Informacião de Segurança de Angola (the MPLA's secret police) was a looming threat in people's daily life.

As for Jonas Savimbi, he had been a tough fighter and an astute politician from his early days with the FNLA, but he had also been a systematic tyrant, a megalomaniac, and a killer. If the MPLA had developed an oil-based *nomenklatura*, UNITA had built its own *candonga* economy, in which its *garimpeiros* (illegal miners) exploited secret diamond mines, mostly in Lunda Norte Province, making up to $600 million or $700 million per year on the world market.[82] Often the two *candonga* families would blend, as when officers of the Forças Armadas Populares de Libertação de Angola (FAPLA) either organized their own *garimpeiros* networks to sell the diamonds on the black market[83] or even dealt directly with UNITA to commercialize the enemies' gems. Savimbi ruled his outfit with an iron hand, and diamond thieves and dissenters were regularly shot. Violence was not reserved for high-ranking movement members: soldiers were regularly shot for misdemeanors, ordinary peasants were mercilessly taxed and their children press-ganged into the Forças Armadas de Libertação de Angola (FALA). Nevertheless, UNITA not only survived but even thrived. Why? First and foremost there was a basic unspoken reality nobody wanted to acknowledge publicly: the MPLA was not the legitimate representative government of Angola, and this for three reasons: it had refused to abide by the 1975 Alvor Agreement, which provided for a realistic tripartite government, and it was and had remained the political expression of a Creole class of *mestiços* and *assimilado* blacks. These were unified by their use of the Portuguese language, their transnational Lusophone culture, and their fear and disgust of the *pretos* ("blacks"), of the *matumbos* (boorish bush dwellers), and of the deeply African peasant masses.[84] There were plenty of reasons for the international community to remain silent about these facts. It was not politically correct to say that the "progressive" MPLA was a cultural holdover of Portuguese colonization, and moreover there was a form of unconscious racism: the MPLA Creole elite was "more like us," the whites, the civilized people. They spoke a European language and they talked in intellectual terms. As for Savimbi, he had concentrated in his persona a near-perfect cornucopia of all the contradictory evils of postmodern demonology: Maoism, Salazar's fascism, South Africa's apartheid, Ronald Reagan, the CIA, and antiwhite racism, and, last but not least, he had dared to threaten U.S. oil companies in 1992. Short of being a Nazi child molester, it is hard to do worse in terms of political image. But this international image was in complete contradiction to the internal perception of many of the despised *matumbos*. For them Savimbi was a hero. Never mind that Savimbi himself was a pure product of the *assimilado* group. He stood for the *matumbos*, and many *matumbos* stood for him.

The December 1988 New York Agreement had taken care of the Namibian problem,[85] but not the Angolan one. President Mobutu had organized a major meeting among African heads of state in Gbadolite in June 1989, where Savimbi and José Eduardo dos Santos[86] had been able to meet, but the results had been inconclusive. It was only on May 31, 1991, that the two mortal enemies signed a peace agreement at Bicesse in Portugal. The main features of the agreement were the decision to hold free and fair elections within a year and a process of fusion between FAPLA and FALA, setting an unreasonable target of fifty thousand men for the unified Forças Armadas Angolanas.[87]

The country lay in ruins. There were almost one million IDPs and another 760,000 refugees in Zaire and Zambia. The 1990 per capita income was 45 percent of its 1974 level, and agricultural production had practically caved in. The financial situation was critical, with the service of the national debt representing roughly 30 percent of the value of exports.[88] Military expenditures stood at around 60 percent of the total budget, and the signing of the Bicesse Agreement did not prevent the government from immediately spending another $25 million for military hardware from Spain.[89]

After many delays and much mutual bickering elections were set for September 29 and 30, 1992. The UN created a special mission to "verify" them: UNAVEM, the United Nations Angola Verification Mission.[90]

The opening up of the Angolan political landscape to multipartism had some interesting consequences. Nobody could be sure of a monopoly any more: two UNITA generals, N'Zau Puna and Tony Da Costa Fernandes, had defected to start their own party, and several other small parties had appeared, with limited constituencies and a hope of making their voices heard. Savimbi, who was not used to democratic politics, was conducting an unnecessarily aggressive campaign in which he managed in a record few weeks to threaten the foreign oil companies ("We will re-negotiate your contracts"), to scare not only the *mestiços* but practically all the city dwellers by sounding more *matumbo* than it seemed possible, and to antagonize UN-AVEM members through clumsy militaristic and propagandistic displays. All the nice people wanted him to lose but were scared of what the monster would do if he did. The elections carried out on schedule were of the tropical variety: phantom polling stations, unreliable voters' lists, lost ballot boxes, and variable geometry results. UNAVEM claimed to have verified that 53.7 percent voted for the MPLA and 34.1 percent for UNITA, with the balance going to the small parties.[91] As for the presidential election, it was even more fantastic, with first results giving 51.54 percent to dos Santos and 38.83 percent to Savimbi. This meant that dos Santos was elected president on the first round. On second thought, the results were changed to 49.57 percent against 40.09 percent, and it was decided to organize a second round. Savimbi called the whole process "a masquerade"[92] and called for verification. Within days the atmosphere in Luanda became particularly electric. Fearing for his life Savimbi fled the capital on October 8, and everything finally exploded on October 31. The bloody events of that day and night were called by the MPLA "the battle for the cities" and by UNITA "the All Saints Day massacre." Fifty percent of UNITA's three hundred soldiers and two thousand cadres in Luanda were killed.[93] Symbolically Jeremias Chitunda and Salupeto Pena were among the dead; they were respectively Number 2 and Number 3 of the rebel movement and had negotiated the Bicesse Agreement, which was now coming apart. Within days the war had started again.

It restarted badly for the MPLA, which immediately began losing ground and responded by panicky massacres of civilians accused of being UNITA supporters.[94] The hysteria reached its peak after UNITA took the strategic oil town of Soyo on the coast. Because Soyo is close to the Zaire border, the fall of the city was blamed on the Bakongo, and during Luanda's infamous "bloody Friday" (January 22–23, 1993) over one thousand were slaughtered in the streets of the capital.[95]

In April talks restarted between the two warring factions in Abidjan. The tone of the international community was distinctly anti-UNITA: President Clinton threatened to recognize the MPLA government as legal,[96] and in June the UN voted Resolution 843. Savimbi had become a kind of tragic Falstaff, the former boon companion of the West during the period of its worst anticommunist excesses whom everybody now wanted to get rid of in order to forget those shameful years. But the brute refused to die and even claimed he had a cause. The country was now cut in two, with one administration (MPLA) in Luanda and another (UNITA) in Bailundo. Deprived of any foreign support and making less money from its diamonds than the MPLA was making from its oil, UNITA started to lose ground. In September 1993 the UN voted a global embargo on UNITA, which drove it to finally sign the Lusaka Peace Protocol on November 20, 1994. But both sides were acting in bad faith, waiting for the other one to make a mistake.

With over half a million barrels per day the Angolan oil economy had entered the big league, and foreign oil companies were now careful to harmonize their political positioning with their exploration interests. As for American oil companies, they never had any problem dealing with the Angolan Marxist state their government was actively fighting. In Cabinda Cuban troops even stood guard, protecting the Chevron oil wells against possible attacks by U.S.-supported rebels of the Frente de Libertação do Enclave de Cabinda (FLEC). But now Luanda wanted to diversify its weapons supply channels and so started to get closer to the French oil company Elf Aquitaine.[97] The balance of trade showed a $3.1 billion surplus for 1995, but debt service was $1.6 billion annually and there was $5.66 billion in arrears. So every penny had to be squeezed out of the oil companies, especially since the MPLA was secretly rearming. UNITA was doing the same thing, using its diamond money.

Estimated UNITA Diamonds Revenue (in U.S. $ millions)

1992	1993	1994	1995	1996
600	600	600	320	700

Source: Global Witness, *A Rough Trade: The Role of Companies and Governments in the Angolan Conflict,* London, 1999, 4, quoting various years of the Economist Intelligence Unit's *Quarterly Reports on Angola.* The French diamond expert Olivier Vallée consid-

97

ers these figures to be much too high and puts UNITA's net yearly diamond income at around $200 million. Professional sources in Antwerp lean toward a $450 million to $500 million yearly figure for 1992–1997.

UNITA had occupied most of the Kwango Valley alluvial diamond sources since 1992, and many of the problems encountered in carrying out the fusion of territorial administrations between the two rival movements had to do with the control of the diamond-producing areas. Savimbi was quite blunt about it, saying, "UNITA has controlled two thirds of the diamonds production since 1993. We are not going to give it up."[98] Both sides were rearming, but UNITA, which was under embargo, had to do it secretly. According to the findings of the Fowler Report, the best source on the diamonds-for-guns UNITA circuit, the main sources of supply were Bulgaria and very likely Belarus and Russia, who "did not provide substantive replies" to the panel's questions.[99] The countries providing fake end-user certificates were Zaire, Burkina Faso, Congo-Brazzaville, and Togo. Given the extremely close relationship of French-speaking African countries with Paris, it is not hard to see why France had a bit of a problem with President dos Santos. But the situation was ambiguous because during the 1992–1995 period of cohabitation in Paris, before Jacques Chirac was elected president, Interior Minister Charles Pasqua had become closely associated with Pierre Falcone and Arkadi Gaydamak, who had just concluded a large financial deal between Russia and Angola.[100] The contracts were initially for $300 million but soon mushroomed to $450 million and later reached $642 million. The deal involved a discounted repurchase of Angola's public debt toward the former Soviet Union (which stood at $8 billion in 1993) and payment of the debt in exchange for the supply of military hardware.[101]

We can now see the whole ambiguity of the French position: on the one hand, as the Fowler Report shows, Paris was, if not an accomplice, at least a godfather of UNITA's sanction-busting operations through its African protégés; on the other hand, through the whole SOFREMI-Brenco-Paribas-Simportex[102] affair, France was also, if not the supplier, at least a facilitator of the MPLA's rearmament campaign. UNAVEM had fallen by the wayside after the October 1992 explosion, and a small structure had been set up after the signing of the Lusaka Peace Protocol to monitor its application. It was known under its French acronym MONUA (Mission des Observateurs des Nations Unies en Angola) and was desperately trying to collect weapons, monitor encampments, support moves toward a government of national unity, and ensure respect for the Peace Protocol. It was a hard job. Out of a population of 12,486,000 there were 1,345,300 IDPs and an additional 2,161,000 persons considered by the UN as "affected by the conflict."[103] Skirmishing was happening off and on, with UNITA complaining that the MPLA was slowly encroaching on its diamond territory. But open war was more or less kept at bay for the time being. The Great Lakes explosion was going to upset that extremely precarious balance.

Standing by, trying to keep out: three uneasy onlookers. Northern Rhodesia was administered from 1899 to 1924 by the British South African Company and then retroceded in that year to the Colonial Office because the company did not know what to do with the territory. Four years later copper was discovered in the north, close to the border with Katanga, and the colony started on a unique course of mining and industrial development. Unlike in Southern Rhodesia, there were few settlers, and most of the whites were employed by the administration or by the mining companies.[104] The economy was "developed," but it was also lopsided and totally dependent on the decisions of foreign companies, which were not even registered in the territory.[105] With such an economic kitty as a prize the whites tried to keep the territory to themselves, first against London and then against the rising tide of black nationalism when Macmillan's famous "winds of change" started blowing. Because there were not enough of them they pooled their efforts with those of the much larger and politically active white settler population of Southern Rhodesia. The result was the creation of the ill-fated Federation of the Rhodesias and Nyasaland[106] in 1953. The attempt at settler control lasted ten years and was defeated by the steady rise of African political parties. The United National Independence Party (UNIP), created in 1959, was finally led to electoral victory by Kenneth Kaunda, and Zambia became independent in October 1964.

The whole process had been extremely civilized and Zambia had become free without as much as a single shot being fired. President Kaunda believed in a form of Gandhi-like civil disobedience, with which the British authorities were very familiar by the 1950s. The problem was that his exotic version of Britain's welfare state rested on the extremely fragile base of a single-product economy: in 1964 the 632,000 tons of copper produced in Zambia represented 47 percent of GNP, 53 percent of tax revenues, and 92 percent of export revenues.[107] Things were fine as long as copper prices remained high. Kaunda supported all the guerrilla movements in southern Africa: the Zimbabwe African Peoples Union and the Zimbabwe African National Union, the Angolan UNITA, the Namibian SWAPO, and South

Africa's ANC. Zambia was then the epitome of the front-line state, battling at the same time apartheid, Portugal's late fascism, and Ian Smith's Unilateral Declaration of Independence regime in Salisbury; Kaunda's "humanism" refused superbly to condescend to miserable problems of financial plumbing and much preferred to seek prestigious compensation in a worldwide diplomatic merry-go-round.[108] But by the 1980s, with falling copper prices, inefficient management, and padded payrolls, Zambia's nationalized mining economy was obviously sinking and "privatization" became the battle cry of the new Movement for Multiparty Democracy (MMD) launched by Frederick Chiluba in the late 1980s. In October 1991 Chiluba swept into power with 75.8 percent of the vote, since most Zambians seemed to think that all their problems came from Kaunda as a person and from the UNIP barons as a group. But within months the system had reproduced itself and turned Chiluba into a free-enterprise version of Kaunda (who took kickbacks from private contractors instead of directly dipping into the public treasury) and MMD into a mirror image of UNIP. What remained, in spite of the appalling drop in living standards, was the basic mildness and decency of Zambian society.[109]

As for the gathering storm clouds, they mostly came from UNITA's long familiarity with the Zambian political landscape, dating back to 1964, when Savimbi moved to Lusaka after his break with Holden Roberto's FNLA. The Angolan war had dragged on and Savimbi had been jailed and then deported for having attacked the Benguela railway, Zambia's vital rail link to the Atlantic Coast. But he retained many friends in Lusaka. By the late 1980s, as the nationalized copper economy and the UNIP state were sinking together, Savimbi's diamonds began to come in very handy for members of the elite who had to face hard times. More military equipment started to fly in, to supplement the large arsenal that UNITA kept in Zaire. There were air connections with Mozambique, Zaire, Togo, and Burkina Fasso. The end of Kaunda's presidency did not mark an end to the system. On the contrary. As the economy kept shrinking, the lure of UNITA's diamonds grew. Discreet airstrips were built in various parts of the country,[110] and the names of some of the new MMD elite (Vice President Christian Tembo, Minister of Commerce Enoch Kavindele, Minister of Defense Ben Mwila) appeared in the now semi-free press as "good friends of Jonas Savimbi." Contrary to what had happened in many other African countries, the help given to UNITA came only from powerful men, not from the government as a body, and it was given mostly for financial reasons.

But with this money and these weapons also came a new and most un-Zambian surge of violence in which the government could not but get embroiled: former finance minister Ronald Penza was shot at home in 1998 in what was described by Africa News Service as "a clumsy attempt at simulating armed robbery in which the police then shot all the suspects," and FAPLA started to chase FALA fighters across a Zambian border whose neutrality looked more and more dubious. The local population suffered from the firefights, especially when FAPLA attacked the Angolan refugee camps. By late 1996, as the "peace process" dragged on in Angola and the Rwandese army was about to attack Zaire, Zambia was still a "neutral" country. But its neutrality depended on what would happen around it, particularly in Zaire, Angola, and Zimbabwe. Within months all of them would be part of the global conflict.

Extending from Zaire's northern border, the Central African Republic is perhaps the most marginal and forlorn state on the whole continent. Called everything from "Upper Ubangi" to "Ubangi-Chari," it was indeed, as Pierre Kalck aptly wrote, "the most neglected of France's colonies" after having been "the last blank space on the map of Africa."[111] Ubangi-Chari was a meeting point of tribes: the Sara from the north, the Azande from Zaire, the Gbaya from the west, all nesting, not always peacefully, around the central mass of the Banda. It was also a meeting point between the savannah lands of Sahelian Africa to the north and east and the great forest of central Africa in the south and west. The opposition between the "river people" of the south and the "people of the savannah" of the north remains a fundamental contradiction of the territory to this day. But basically Ubangi-Chari was a point of passage, densely crisscrossed by navigable rivers. The nineteenth-century ravages of the slave raids from the Sudan had left it broken, despondent, and largely shapeless.

The French treated it particularly shabbily because they did not see any use for it except to block expansion from the Congo Free State toward the Nile (Leopold tried hard in the 1880s and 1890s) or any southwesterly British move toward the Congo. For Paris Ubangi was just a plug used to stand in other white men's way. Because it was a financial burden the Ministry of Colonies tried to make it self-supporting by selling it conditionally to what were known as "the big concessionaire companies."[112] As Pierre Kalck wrote,

In order to save money the management of the big companies contracted with perfect social misfits[113] who were ready to accept poor salaries and very hard working conditions.... . These agents soon became little local tyrants who enjoyed "hitting the niggers" to satisfy their neuroses.[114]

In the 1920s the system was given a facelift by renaming the hated "concessions" and calling them "commercial monopolies." They were strictly the same thing. At the behest of some friends the famous writer André Gide went to the Congo, as it was still called, and came back horrified by what he discovered. He wrote upon his return, "I am now inhabited by an immense wailing, I now know things I cannot tolerate. What demon drove me to Africa? I was in peace. But now I know and I must speak." The travel memoir in which he described the companies' abuses created a scandal;[115] there were discussions in Parliament, and then, as usual, the companies got the whole thing quashed. There was even worse by then: the construction of the (in)famous 600-kilometer-long Congo-Océan railway between the Pointe Noire harbor and Brazzaville. Thousands of laborers were recruited by force in the "useless" Ubangi-Chari and shipped downriver to Brazzaville to work on the "useful" railway. The construction lasted from 1921 to 1934 with an incredibly high mortality rate, "one dead man for each railroad tie laid," in the words of the investigative journalist Albert Londres.[116]

Strangely enough, immediately after World War II this tragic colonial backwater produced a man who was probably the most gifted and the most inventive of French Africa's decolonization generation of politicians: Barthélémy Boganda. Boganda was a Catholic priest who got elected to the Paris Parliament on a "colonial" seat in November 1946.[117] Coming from the small Ngbaka tribe he soon proved able to reach an audience far beyond the limits of his ethnic group, even including a number of progressive-minded white *colons* in his political party, the Mouvement d'Evolution Sociale de l'Afrique Noire (MESAN). It was typical of Boganda that the movement he created did not make any reference to Ubangi-Chari as such but instead tried to deal with the much bigger problem of understanding what were going to be the boundaries of the new independent states soon to be born. Coming from such a hopeless colony as Ubangi-Chari and possessing a sharp and imaginative mind, he saw that "countries" such as the one he might soon be saddled with had no economic viability. In May 1957, when he inaugurated a form of limited self-government for the colony, he boldly called for the building of "the Latin United States of Africa," which in his view should have regrouped French Equatorial Africa as a whole, the Belgian Congo, Ruanda-Urundi, and the Portuguese territories to the south. He clearly envisioned France as a the patron needed for this federation, which he saw as a counterweight to the powerful British-influenced bloc of southern African states (South Africa, the Rhodesias, Bechuanaland, and Nyasaland). But on November 29, 1959, as he was flying from Berberati back to Bangui, his plane blew up in midair. Although the probability of foul play was very high, there was no commission of inquiry,[118] and Ubangi-Chari became independent on August 13, 1960, under the name Central African Republic and under the lackluster leadership of a *de facto* one-party state dominated by MESAN luminaries Abel Goumba and David Dacko. Within six months Dacko had manipulated Parliament in order to marginalize Goumba and grab all the power.[119] Within another five years the country was in such difficult economic straits that Army Chief of Staff Jean-Bedel Bokassa was able to easily organize a bloodless coup, seizing power on December 31, 1965.

Although General Bokassa was a relative of Barthélémy Boganda, he was a very different kind of man. Both were born in the small village of Bobangi in the Lobaye region, Boganda in 1910 and Bokassa in 1921. Both shared the same terrible early trauma of having their fathers beaten to death by French concessionaire company agents. Bokassa was six when his father was killed "for being insubordinate," and his mother died of despair within a few weeks. The boy was raised by his grandfather and went on to join the army in 1939. He did not fight during World War II, but he fought for three years in French Indochina (1950–1953), where he was much decorated and acquired French citizenship.

The regime he was to create in the Central African Republic after grabbing power in 1965 was one of the strangest on the continent and can only be compared with Idi Amin Dada's in Uganda. Bokassa's charismatic leadership style corresponded perfectly to that described by Max Weber: "The term 'charisma' will be applied to a certain quality of individual personality by virtue of which he is considered extraordinary and treated as endowed with supernatural or at least specifically exceptional powers or qualities…. How these qualities would be ultimately judged from any ethical, aesthetic or other such point of view is naturally indifferent for purposes of definition."[120] Bokassa's leadership was not ethically or aesthetically very pleasing, but it worked for nearly fourteen years. The main traits of his power were magic, theatrical violence, and larger-than-life grotesque displays of showmanship. His anger was used as a means of terrorizing the population: he kicked to death his driver because he suspected him (wrongly) of having driven his wife to an amorous appointment; he publicly smeared strong pepper on the genital organs and in the eyes of people he accused of a variety of misdeeds, including one of his sons; he emasculated and gouged out the eyes of Dacko's last security chief and then cut off his head and ordered it to be displayed in schools throughout the country for educational purposes;[121] he permanently carried a stick with a big *J* for *Justice* carved at the top and would beat people with it if he felt they deserved it. His decisions were sudden and without appeal: several times he sent judges to jail when he thought they had passed an unsatisfactory judgment and in some cases specified a new sentence that would be immediately applicable, up to and including the death penalty. His violence was often linked to magic, as when he killed his wife's seamstress because his witch doctor asked him for the fresh liver of a young woman.[122] And it seemed to work, since all plots against him failed, at times spectacularly so, as in February 1976, when one of his officers tossed a grenade at him and it did not explode. He turned any situation to his advantage: when he was poisoned during a trip to neighboring Chad he came back on a stretcher and gave an impromptu speech at the airport, declaring to a fascinated crowd, "Those colonialist bastards tried to kill me but they cannot.... . I am Jesus Christ, I am the reincarnation of Barthélémy Boganda."[123] Although the violence was constant and very public, it was also limited. Bokassa killed individually, he never destroyed whole categories of enemies, and although he systematically favored his Ngbaka tribe, he never persecuted the others.[124] He delighted in being totally unpredictable, shouting in public at Kurt Waldheim that he was "an imperialist pimp," insisting on calling General de Gaulle "Daddy"[125] and offering to attack Paris with a paratroopers' regiment and shoot up the French rebel students during the 1968 riots. He converted to Islam in October 1976, received money for his conversion, and then abjured it in January 1977. By then he had decided to crown himself emperor and felt it would be nice if the pope could come for the occasion, as he had attended the coronation of Napoleon I in 1804. The pope refused, but the coronation on December 4, 1977, was right out of a novel by Evelyn Waugh, with an enormous fake two-ton throne, a tiara studded with six thousand small but real diamonds, thousands of guests, fifty thousand dollars' worth of champagne, and a gilded carriage pulled by eight white horses.

Bokassa's personal assets were vast, eclectic, and growing all the time.[126] He owned restaurants, garages, pharmacies, hardware stores, a brick factory, farms, diamond mines, office buildings, a sawmill, a food canning plant; he monopolized cement imports and palm oil production; he had thirty thousand elephants killed by the army and sold the ivory; he manufactured clothes, recorded music, raised pigs and oxen, built his own slaughterhouse and coffee-processing plant, and owned a cinema, where he would sit and watch the movie of his own coronation. Nothing was too small for his profit: he advertised the flights of his presidential plane to Paris when it flew there on diamond-selling trips and sold tickets to the public. He made a great show of drinking and eating to excess; he had thirty-five legitimate children from many women as well as many other unacknowledged ones; and when his Romanian mistress was foolish enough to sleep with an officer of his guard, he had the man publicly cut up into little pieces. The image is of an ogre of legend, of a larger-than-life creature who wants to physically own his territory, manipulate it like an object, possibly even eat it.[127] It was only in former Ubangi that such a regime could exist, where the dictator incarnated the country rather than ruled it, faced no organized political opposition, had no civil society to contend with, could walk all over the prostrate body of an amorphous land.

The French tolerated his eccentricities because of the strategic role played by the Bouar military base in the Chadian conflict. Throughout the 1970s Gaddafi's pressure was growing on Chad and France had decided to resist it, with discreet U.S. approval. The Bouar base was vital. As for Bokassa, he was not anti-French but rather possessed by what one could call "aggressive Francophilia" on the model of the expression used by Ali Mazrui about Idi Amin.[128] France could live with that. But when he quelled school riots in April 1979 by packing dozens of school kids in airless cells where nineteen eventually suffocated to death, there was an international scandal and the OAU imposed a commission of inquiry. Emperor Bokassa I got nervous and flew to Tripoli, promising Gaddafi he would reconvert to Islam and give him the Bouar base to attack the French from the south. This was too much for Paris, and on September 20, 1979, French Air Force transport planes flew into Bangui from Ndjamena and simply removed the problem.[129]

But removing Bokassa and bringing back Dacko[130] was not enough to make the Central African Republic viable. In spite of a bevy of French advisers at every government level, in spite of the presence of a large French army contingent, in spite of French economic aid Dacko lasted only two years. He was overthrown in September 1981 by Gen. André Kolingba, a quiet and professional army man whose eventless twelve-year rule gave the impression that he had finally "normalized" the Central African Republic and brought it up to the ordinary standards of the French neocolonial system[131] to the point of accepting democratic elections and losing them in October 1993. The elections were won by Ange Félix Patassé, a northern Gbaya-Sara who finally put an end to rule by the "river people."[132] Jean-Paul Ngoupande, who became his prime minister, described him as "intellectually, an eclectic mixture of Third World radicalism tinged with Marxism and populist nationalism . . . but laced with cynicism and a crude perception of the country as divided between two blocks, the 'nice savannah people' who have suffered and the 'evil river people' who made them suffer. . . . And more than everything his everyday political style is marked by the influence of Jean-Bedel Bokassa."[133] Which of course does not make for a very coherent or orthodox way of dealing with public affairs. He was arrested at the Paris airport in September 1979 with a gun in his pocket, as he was trying to get on a Tripoli-bound plane.[134] During his eleven years of exile in Togo during the Kolingba presidency he seems to have been involved in highly dubious business dealings which he never denied when they were made public.[135] His lackluster performance after 1993, the corruption of a new "get-rich-quick" group of businessmen around him, and his erratic administrative style made his hold on power in what former prime minister Ngoupande calls "a non-existent state" tenuous at best. His army mutinied in April 1996 because it was not paid, and it was only the intervention of French troops that managed to restore order. In a sort of nihilistic challenge to their desperate condition the soldiers not only looted but destroyed everything that symbolized wealth or prestige, including a cigarette factory that was razed to the ground, most Bangui downtown stores, and the MOCAF brewery, which was thoroughly trashed.[136] In November 1996 the Central African army mutinied again. Part of the problem, apart from the nonpayment of salaries, was that the army had retained a Yakoma and "river" majority since the Kolingba presidency, whereas the Presidential Guard was solidly Sara and "savannah." Both were at each other's throats, while the civilian population, which was neither, was caught in the middle.[137]

By late 1996 the Central African Republic was a rudderless ship, with a discouraged civil service, a divided and rebellious army, and a mostly "informal" economy, its porous borders crisscrossed by *zaraguinas*,[138] the Sudanese army, SPLA guerrillas, Chadian poachers, and even Ugandan rebels in the extreme southeast. Tottering on the brink of nothingness, it was going to be suddenly affected by the distant Rwandese genocide when fleeing former *génocidaires* chased by the RPA ended up crossing the Ubangi into its territory.

In medium-size Congo-Brazzaville the population of 2.7 million is extremely unevenly distributed, with over 60 percent living in the towns, mostly in Pointe Noire and Brazzaville, which are both in the south. The neglected, sparsely populated, and rural north contains only 20 percent of the people. This lopsided distribution has had major effects in heightening tribal tensions and exacerbating the impact of urban problems on politics.[139] Brazzaville-Congo's ethnic distribution is relatively simple if compared with huge countries like Zaire or Angola: a cluster of Kikongo-speaking tribes in the south, the Teke group in the center, and a variety of small related northern tribes collectively known as Mbochi. But the problem is that, unlike in Zaire, the tendency of the various ethnic groups has not been toward regional regroupings but, on the contrary, toward militant fragmentation. Thus the coastal Vili around Pointe Noire have developed a political identity separate from their other Bakongo brethren, and so have the Lari around Brazzaville. The various Teke groups have both mixed with and fought against their Bakongo neighbors. The northerners have obstinately clung to a variety of subidentities (Bangala, Koyo, Mboko, Kabonga), even though they are in fact very closely related; in the north some of those identities (Ngbaka, Banza) overlap with those in the Central African Republic.

The "middle Congo," as the country was called during colonial times, was placed at the center of what became French Equatorial Africa (AEF). The other AEF territories (Chad, Ubangi-Chari, and Gabon) were poorer and/or landlocked, which gave the Congo the role of a regional capital at the heart of a small empire. This explains the oversized development of Pointe Noire and Brazzaville, which were harbor and administrative capital, respectively, for a much larger territory than the Congo itself. It also explains the higher degree of education found at an early stage among the native population, a tradition that has survived right down to our time.[140] Congo's first president at independence was a Mukongo priest, Father Fulbert Youlou, who ordered his cassocks from Christian Dior, was waited on by a special body of nuns, and spent money wildly. He was overthrown in August 1963 by an exasperated populace.[141] In "intellectual" Brazzaville Alphonse Massemba-Debat started the left-wing drift that was going to be so typical of Congolese politics over the next twenty-eight years. He called himself a "Bantu social-ist," which caused a disagreement with his prime minister, Pascal Lissouba, who saw himself more classically as a "scientific socialist." Both were southerners like Youlou,[142] but the majority of the army came from the northern tribes and they soon decided to turn that asset into political power. On July

31, 1968, Capt. Marien Ngouabi, a Kouyou officer, overthrew Massemba-Debat, a year later creating the Parti Congolais du Travail (PCT), a sort of elitist communist party that was to culminate at 1,475 members in 1974. Zigzagging between right-wing coup attempts and left-wing guerrilla insurrections by way of purges and selective political murders, the PCT-led Congo started on a long career of tropical Marxism that has been aptly described as "an ideological swindle."[143] It is not impossible that some of the younger officers took their Marxism seriously and saw themselves as defenders of an oppressed peasantry, but for the majority of the army the PCT was just an instrument of privilege and of northern political domination over the more populated south, which would have had its way in any kind of election. The dictatorship of the proletariat was in fact the dictatorship of Mbochi officers,[144] and the oil boom, which started in 1973, soon fueled corruption and heightened the competition for power. But given the PCT's hegemonic position the competition came from *inside* the party rather than from outside, causing frequent upheavals and purges.[145]

This did not prevent Brazzaville from turning into one of the most vibrant African capitals, partly due to its own tradition of intellectual life and partly due to the influence of the robust Zairian popular culture just across the river in Kinshasa.[146] In March 1977 President Marien Ngouabi was murdered in obscure circumstances,[147] and his successor, Gen. Joachim Yhombi-Opango, never quite managed to get things under control. His power was soon threatened by Gen. Denis Sassou-Nguesso, another PCT northern officer, with a slightly different ethnic inscription (Mbochi instead of Makwa). In February 1979 Sassou-Nguesso took power and threw his predecessor in jail, where he left him to languish for the next thirteen years. Sassou soon enacted another constitution[148] and brought the PCT brand of tropical Marxism to a point of near perfection. In May 1981 the Treaty of Mutual Help and Friendship with the Soviet Union gave the regime a solid political and military backing, while the growth of economic and oil cooperation with France ensured the possibility of vast overspending, particularly through bloating the civil service:

The number of civil servants doubled between 1970 and 1979 although their salaries did not increase in keeping with inflation... . Even poorly paid the civil servants were slightly better off than many other people... . But even more than the expenses in salaries what grew completely out of control were the expenses in equipment for the ministries. They were multiplied by three between 1980 and 1982. Nevertheless it was hard to find a single photocopy machine in working order in most ministries and there was a constant dearth of chairs and tables in the schools. But it is true that it is easier to steal money on the funds earmarked for equipment than on the salaries themselves.[149]

This padding of payroll to prevent social unrest was possible only because of the "understanding" attitude of the French oil company Elf, which controlled most of the oil production. By international standards Sassou accepted a very low return on oil exploitation, on the condition that Elf be prepared to pay oil dividends ahead of schedule. So by the time the PCT regime collapsed in 1991 under the weight of its own incompetence, coupled with the fall of its Soviet protector, Brazzaville's oil revenues were mortgaged ten years in advance, until 2002.

Unsurprisingly, the final blow that brought the system down came from France. At the momentous Franco-African Conference at La Baule in June 1990, President François Mitterrand announced that French economic aid would in the future be linked to increased democratization.[150] Obediently, most of the francophone African dictatorships started to display at least some signs of political transformation. Benin, nicknamed "the Latin quarter of Africa," showed the way, and the Congo-Brazzaville was next in line. On February 25, 1991, it opened a national conference that was to last three and a half months and dismantle the "workers state" of the prior twenty-two years. But now the main problem was that the command economy it had created was also in many ways a "command society," which encouraged educational development but did not provide it with any outlet apart from a bloated civil service, which the IMF now wanted deflated. In a massively urbanized society where over 60 percent of the citizens were younger than eighteen this was an explosive mix. And the mix did explode.

The apparent catalyst was once more tribal politics. After a short transition period the August 1992 elections brought to power Pascal Lissouba, Massemba-Debat's former prime minister of the mid-1960s. Lissouba was a southerner from a very minor tribe. He was thus faced with two difficulties in ethnopolitical terms: an obvious one, keeping the now frustrated northerners in line, and a more delicate one, building an alliance of minor tribes that would give him a power base in the south. Faced with a crisis in Parliament and believing that the electorate would support him, Lissouba chose to dissolve the Assembly and call for another election in October 1992. This is when the situation started to get out of hand.

The army was still mostly northern and therefore pro-PCT. The new president made a deal with the Israeli private security firm Levdan, which started to train a special militia for him, the "Aubevillois," from the name of the Aubeville Social Centre for Youth, which they used as a meeting place.[151] This was not seen with pleasure in France, whose army had always considered that security in former French colonies was its special preserve. But this was just the beginning of the process: Lissouba found that he did not have enough money to pay for the hefty Levdan contract (around $50 million), so he offered in exchange a cut in the Marine III offshore oil permit to Naphta Inc., an Israeli petroleum company with close ties to Levdan.[152] With an empty treasury, pressing needs opened by the hopes following democratic change,[153] and a national oil production already mortgaged for the next ten years, President Lissouba had only two solutions: either get new and better terms from Elf[154] or else introduce new players in the oil game. He chose to try Elf first, asking for $200 million on good collateral, the new N'Kossa oil field then getting under production. Elf refused. But in a way the small Naphta contract had opened a psychological breach in the Elf monopoly and Lissouba did the unthinkable: he contacted the U.S. company Occidental Petroleum (Oxy) and asked for money up front. He was offered a facility costing $150 million secured by the same Congolese government's share of the N'Kossa permits that Elf had refused as collateral for the loan. This sent alarm bells ringing both in Paris (at Elf and in government circles, which at the time were almost one and the same thing) and in Brazzaville itself, where the PCT reacted as if it were still in power, sending one of its top members, Rodolphe Adada, to the United States to get Oxy to cancel the deal. The tension rose by several degrees when the PCT-MCDDI[155] opposition refused to recognize the results of the June 1993 legislative elections, which seemed to show a reinforcement of the presidential camp. By July 1993 Brazzaville exploded into wild urban riots which, with periods of lull between bouts of fighting, were going to last until February 1994. These eight months of violence caused only a limited number of casualties,[156] but they led to a massive and artificial reethnicization of society that severely dented the country's self-confidence.[157]

Why "artificial" reethnicization? Because the "new tribes" that appeared during this conflict, and that were later to take part in the even more violent battles of 1997–1998, were very far indeed from being the primeval ethnic entities ethnologists might have studied some years before in the same area. First, there was the phenomenon of urbanization: all the southerners lived in the same parts of town and had intermarried; therefore, since it was southerners who were fighting each other,[158] they had to create new artificial distinctions among themselves, using the "real" ethnic markers as a base but turning them into new synthetic "tribes." The militias were the tools of this transformation.[159] Second, there was the question of the ethnicization of the regions when their ethnic makeup did not allow them a large and coherent enough stake in the civil war; thus the so-called Niboleks were born, their name being an aggregate from the southern district names of *Ni*ari, *Bo*uenza, and *Lek*oumou. The "Niboleks" were "really" Bouissi, Nzabi, Voumbou, or Bembe; or, if one prefers, they were "really" Teke and Kongo, the global identities that regroup the smaller tribes along language lines.[160] But the "real reality" were the militias, the politically induced groupings of young urban unemployed and semi-educated youths who fought for lack of a future, to get some money right now, and to do as in the Kung Fu and U.S. action movies they had watched when idling away their unemployed lives.

By early 1994 the fighting had slowly died down without any clear settlement being reached. Even if Lissouba was still in power, the net victor was Sassou-Nguesso, who had sat it out while the southerners were destroying each other. Lissouba had had to backtrack on the Oxy oil deal and was back begging from Elf; everybody knew that Elf had discreetly supported the Cobra militias of Sassou-Nguesso during the war, all the more discreetly since the Cobra did not fight much themselves but instead passed on this support to Bernard Kolelas and his Ninja, who were the ones actively confronting the government. The militias had survived the war and shared the meager resources of the *quartiers* (neighborhoods) among themselves, setting up their own racketeering systems. But there were 10,000 men in the militias and the army was 20,000 strong, with 12,000 officers and NCOs (northerners in their majority) and only 8,000 privates of all tribes. The demilitarization agreement that had followed the end of the fighting provided for the militias' integration into the army. Because it would have radically altered that structure the northerners resisted it.

On the oil front President Lissouba compounded his mistake of 1993 by antagonizing Angola. Right from the beginning, when FLEC leader Da Costa became prominent among the cadres of the Aubeville Centre, it was obvious that Lissouba had overestimated the possibilities of change brought about by the collapse of the Soviet Union; he wanted, if not to annex the Cabinda Enclave, at least to bring it within his sphere of influence. But given the fact that over 50 percent of Angola's oil came from Cabinda alone, it was unlikely that Luanda would accept such a change without a fight. Sassou's Soviet alliance had brought him to the MPLA side of the Angolan conflict, and Lissouba seemed to think that the demise of the Soviet Union opened the possibility of an alliance reversal for the Congo. On August 15, 1995, Jonas Savimbi stood by his side on the Brazzaville podium, where the thirty-fifth anniversary of Congo-Brazzaville's independence was celebrated. This did not go unnoticed in Luanda, and at that moment Pascal Lissouba became a marked man in many eyes: Paris did not look with much sympathy upon a francophone African head of state who had broken the ranks;[161] Elf suspected him of favoring "foreign" (i.e., non-French) oil companies;[162] former President Sassou-Nguesso, who had gone to live in Paris, was planning his comeback; and the Angolan leadership considered him a dangerous UNITA ally. The situation was extremely fragile. Given Brazzaville's very close relations with Zaire, the destabilization of the Mobutu regime concurred in pushing the internal Congolese situation over the brink, especially when, as in the Central African Republic, a number of former *génocidaires* arrived in the country, with the Tutsi RPA in hot pursuit.

4

WINNING A VIRTUAL WAR
(SEPTEMBER 1996–MAY 1997)

Rwanda in Zaire: from refugee crisis to international war

Laurent-Désiré Kabila and the birth of the AFDL. Shortly after the start of the concerted Banyamulenge-RPA attack on South Kivu a new Zairian rebel political movement was announced, the Alliance des Forces Démocratiques pour la Libération du Congo-Zaire (AFDL). The agreement creating this new movement was supposed to have been signed in Lemera in South Kivu[1] on October 18, 1996. The signatories were the representatives of four hitherto little-known rebel groups: Deogratias Bugera (ADP),[2] Laurent-Désiré Kabila (Parti de la Révolution Populaire [PRP]), Anselme Masasu Nindaga (Mouvement Révolutionnaire pour la Libération du Zaïre), and André Kisase Ngandu (Conseil National de Résistance pour la Démocratie).[3] Bugera was a North Kivu Tutsi who worked as an architect in Goma. Masasu Nindaga was a little known half-Mushi, half-Tutsi political activist from Bukavu.[4] The first thing to notice about the makeup of this weak "alliance" is that the Banyamulenge who were to be the spearhead of the early military operations did not have any representative among the high command. This was later to cause serious problems when the Banyamulenge developed a sense of alienation from the rest of the AFDL, feeling that they were being used. Neither the ADP nor the Mouvement Révolutionnaire pour la Libération du Zaïre had any military forces, and both were largely paper organizations with very few militants. Kisase Ngandu was definitely more serious, both in military and in political terms. In fact he was the only one among the four who could boast a real fighting force (about four hundred men) and a network of sympathizers extending from Bunia to Goma.

The fourth signatory, Laurent-Désiré Kabila, must be examined in more detail because he had been a minor but nevertheless definite player in the troubled days that followed the independence of the Congo.[5]

Laurent-Désiré Kabila was born in November 1939 in the small regional center of Jadotville (Likasi) in northeastern Katanga. He was a Muluba,[6] and he soon became involved in intra-Baluba politics during the civil strife of the early 1960s. He followed the Baluba movement of Jason Sendwe in 1959 that battled the Confédération des Associations Tribales du Katanga (CO-NAKAT),[7] although his own father was a CONAKAT sympathizer who was executed by fellow Baluba in November 1960. This seems to have been one of the factors that pushed the young Kabila away from tribal politics and toward the more generous abstract generalizations of Marxism-Leninism.[8] Kabila joined the rebels of the Conseil National de Libération in Stanleyville in 1964 and was sent to the South Kivu–northeastern Katanga area.[9] He later came back to Stanleyville, then in full anarchy, but had to leave in a hurry just as the Belgian paratroopers were about to land. The white mercenary forces operating at the service of Mobutu's army soon joined them and unleashed a reign of terror. It was this rather inauspicious moment that the famous Latin American revolutionary Ernesto "Che" Guevara picked to come to the rescue of the "African Revolution."[10] Guevara had left Cuba in April 1965, traveling to the eastern Congo by way of Prague, Cairo, Dar-es-Salaam, and Kigoma. The small band of Cuban revolutionaries was supported by Tanzania because Julius Nyerere hated Moise Tshombe, whom he considered to be a neocolonialist stooge.[11] But Tanzanian logistics were amateurish at best and the military situation almost desperate. Kabila, who was supposed to be Guevara's link with the Conseil National de Libération remnants abroad,[12] hardly showed up at all. When he finally came to the combat zone he brought along crates of whisky and a retinue of sleazy mulatto women, eliciting icy comments from the rather puritanical Argentinean.[13] Guevara nevertheless tried to make a go of it but was extremely disappointed both by the military capacities and by the level of political consciousness of his comrades-in-arms. When Tshombe was dismissed by Kasa Vubu in October 1965, Nyerere let the Cubans know that their presence in the Congo was not welcome anymore and Che had to withdraw.[14]

After creating the PRP Kabila for a time thought of continuing a classical guerrilla struggle against the Mobutu regime. Most of his fighters were Babembe and he had a few weapons. But as was usual with him, he remained more the politician than the military man; the guerrillas' true field commander during the 1970s and 1980s was Calixte Mayawila. Nevertheless, in spite of spending more time in Dar-es-Salaam and in Europe than in *hewa bora*,[15] Kabila remained in full political control of his front, to the point of developing a Mao-like personality cult around his distant image.[16] In 1975 he kidnapped four zoologists working with the chimpanzee specialist Jane Goodall in Tanzania and only freed them against a $500,000 ransom. This was the start of a transformation in the guerrillas' operations which progressively turned more and more toward a business venture: "Gradually the Zairian Army set up a commercial alliance with the PRP. Calling the area a 'high security risk zone' justified the demand for a huge amount of aid from Kinshasa so as to be able to fight the 'outlaws.' This situation was skilfully exploited by Kabila as the trade in gold and ivory from the PRP-controlled areas was increasingly directed at the Zairian Army officers. In the end the situation became quite ludicrous: the Army officers declared the zone to be extremely risky but no one really wanted to leave when appointed elsewhere."[17]

Kabila even engaged in ordinary swindles, such as the time in 1978 when he sent his comrades crates of "weapons" from the coast with only two layers of Kalashnikovs on top and nails to fill the rest of the box.[18] The "weapons" had been paid for in gold. In November 1984 and in June 1985 the PRP tried twice to attack Moba but was beaten back both times. Calixte Mayawila then not only surrendered to the FAZ but even led them against his former friends. Kabila gave up and moved to Tanzania for good, setting up several businesses in Dar-es-Salaam.[19] Some of his commanders (Sylvestre Lwetsha, Willy Dunyia) stayed around the Fizi-Baraka area and kept a very low-intensity armed movement going. Kabila traveled around the region for his business. But he always laced his business with politics, just in case. He was right never to give up pretending because the pretence eventually paid off in real terms. In September 1996 he met the Ugandan journalist Adonya Ayebare in Kampala and told him that he was "drawing a new business plan."[20] This was quite true: he had just become the new local cover for the Rwandese attack on Zaire, in charge of making a foreign invasion look like a national rebellion.

Erik Kennes wrote, "It is still unclear how Kabila got 'recycled' into the 1996–1997 war" and suggested that it was Museveni who introduced him to Kagame as a once and future Congolese rebel. My own research shows a slightly different pattern. When Kagame made the decision to attack Zaire, probably sometime during the first half of 1996, both he and Museveni started to look for "suitable Congolese" to act as local cover and both started to push their choices. Bugera and Masasu Nindaga, being Tutsi, were Kagame's choices. Kisase Ngandu, who had worked with the Ugandan External Service Organization for several years, was Kampala's choice. Nyerere got worried about this division between the two allies, and because he very much wanted his long term anti-Mobutu plan to come to fruition he suggested Kabila as an added element to the future AFDL mix. This was both because Kabila was neutral between Museveni and Kagame and because he was under practically complete control of the Tanzanian secret services, which considered him harmless and easy to manipulate.[21] In any case, he soon became, if not the real leader of the AFDL (his position was simply that of spokesman), at least its most visible personality.

The bogey of the multinational intervention force. On October 11, 1996, Monsignor Munzihirwa publicly denounced "the repeated attacks of Rwanda on Eastern Zaire" and "Kigali's lying discourse about the refugees."[22] The same day the U.S. NGO Refugee International called on the international community to "immediately act in concert to stop Zaire from executing ethnic cleansing" and to "assist the Banyamulenge displaced, most of whom will seek refuge in Rwanda."[23] The battle lines were drawn.

Given the importance of steadying the threatening situation in Burundi, the first target of the RPA-Banyamulenge forces was the Burundian refugee camps. On October 17 they attacked several of those near Uvira, killing thirty-one and sending forty thousand into flight.[24] By Saturday, October 19, there were over 100,000 refugees fleeing in all directions, and by Monday their numbers had reached 250,000. There were only three thousand assailants, but the refugees knew that the FAZ did not have any desire to fight for "foreigners" and that their own CNDD-FDD had limited military means. In the midst of such mayhem the U.S. State Department declaration that it would "support UNHCR's efforts for a safe return of the refugees"[25] sounded either like a weak bleating (if taken at the security level) or a warning that Washington was in fact strategically aware of what was going on. Then suddenly, on October 22, mysterious "armed men" attacked the Kibumba and Katale camps in North Kivu.[26] By the 25th several of the camps had come under heavy artillery fire, both from mortars inside Zaire and from heavier guns firing from Rwandese territory. The United Nations began to worry, declaring in its regional bulletin, "The ultimate objective of the Banyamulenge is unclear as the conflict ostensibly began as an exercise in self-defence. The possibility of some kind of master plan linking attacks in North Kivu and the South Kivu conflict is hard to discount entirely."[27]

116

Kigali's foreign minister, Anastase Gasana, went on the air to declare, "The Zairian crisis is a purely internal affair and in no way involves Rwanda,"[28] while somewhat contradictorily President Pasteur Bizimungu was asking for "a second Berlin Conference."[29] On October 28 Kinshasa appointed two DSP generals as governors of Goma and Bukavu. But it was too late. Bukavu was taken by storm on the 29th and Munzihirwa was killed in cold blood by some of the Banyamulenge attackers.[30] On October 30 French President Chirac called for African leaders to meet and discuss the situation in Zaire.[31] General Kagame immediately pooh-poohed the idea, but that night his forces started shelling Goma with long-range artillery firing from Rwandese territory. In New York the UN General Assembly seemed paralyzed because, as the AFP representative remarked, "There are enormous inhibitions among Council members due to a feeling of guilt towards Rwanda. Very few delegates are ready to criticise Kigali, at least openly."[32] Kigali knew it and took full advantage of the situation. On November 1 the RPA attacked Goma, both on land and from the lake,[33] all the while denying that it was doing anything. Two days later Rwandese Radio declared, "The foreign media continue to implicate Rwanda in the eastern Zaire crisis.... But we must stress that the current conflict . . . involves Zairians fighting against Zairians."[34]

Meanwhile, more refugee camps had come under intense attack; in the south the panic was general and the refugees were fleeing where they could, either northward up the lake's western shore or westward toward Shabunda. The Banyamulenge had corralled thousands of Burundian refugees and were herding them toward the border, where the Burundian army was waiting for them. They were screened, and a number were shot immediately. The others were pushed farther east under army surveillance. At the same time some of the FDD guerrillas who had been cut off from their main body fought their way into Burundi, hoping to go clear across the country and come out on the other side, taking refuge in Tanzania. The sweep was fierce and little quarter was given. In the first three days of November the International Committee of the Red Cross buried more than four hundred dead in and around Goma, most of them women and children.[35] The victims were a mixture of local inhabitants who had been killed by the retreating FAZ during bouts of looting and refugees who had been killed by the attacking mob of Mayi Mayi warriors, RPA regulars, and former Masisi refugee Tutsi militia.[36] Two headlines from the French daily *Le Monde* sum up the political contradiction the French camp was in at the time: "France is ready to take part in a humanitarian intervention in Zaire" and "Kinshasa is in a near state of siege while politicians wait for President Mobutu as if for their savior."[37]

The 115,000 refugees from Kahindo camp, 195,000 from Kibumba, and an unspecified number from among the 210,000 in Katale had taken refuge in the giant Mugunga camp after coming under heavy attack. By November 8 Mugunga had reached a total population of over 800,000.[38] There was no certainty as to what the attackers, now in control of Goma, would do with Mugunga, where the last forces of the ex-FAR were swamped by civilian refugees. The U.S. government did not sound very keen to get involved, declaring, "We want to co-operate with our partners in solving the crisis in Eastern Zaire. But we must make sure that these plans are sound, logical and that they would work."[39] This was partly a result of the Somalia syndrome and also partly due to the fact that other segments of the U.S. government were physically supporting the operation without making that fact public. As the crisis unfolded it became obvious that decision making in Washington was taking place at several levels simultaneously and that they were not always in agreement with each other.[40] But the general tone of the U.S. approach to the crisis was of support for the Kigali regime and its actions; U.S. Gen. George Joulwan, head of NATO, even described General Kagame as "a visionary."[41]

After the taking of Bukavu, whose last defenders had been FDD Burundian guerrillas, the mixture of RPA and Congolese rebel troops pushed southward.[42] They were soon joined by a group of about sixty African American mercenaries. According to English-speaking Zairians who had occasion to talk with them, they had been privately recruited in the United States and flown to Uganda, from where they had been taken by road to Kigali and later to Bukavu. The way their passage from the United States had been facilitated by Customs and police suggested undeniably that they were on some kind of unofficial government mission.[43] They were soon battling the FDD at Mwenga and Kiliba.[44]

There was increasing international concern about the refugees because it was not clear whether they were caught in the middle of a battle or were themselves the target of that battle. There was ambiguity on both sides because, as Kisase Ngandu declared, "The Hutu are fighting for Mobutu. We cannot counter-attack because the refugees are in the way. Get them out of the way of our forces, that is all we want."[45] By "the Hutu" he obviously meant the ex-FAR, even if "the refugees" were of course also Hutu. And he added, "We will let the refugees return to Rwanda, what we want is to liberate Kinshasa." The expression "humanitarian corridors" began to appear. Mobutu had accepted a "neutral" force proposed by Canada, and on November 7 State Department spokesman Nicholas Burns declared that the United States would provide "logistical support." On the same day Amnesty International tried to bring a bit of clarity back into the debate by issuing a communiqué reminding everybody that people should not be moved against their will; "humanitarian corridors" should not become "one-way valves to funnel people back to the country they have fled"; and members of armed militias should not be considered refugees. It was increasingly obvious that the refugees had become political pawns. France and the pro-Mobutu West African francophone states pretended to back a multinational intervention force (MNF) to save the refugees; what they really wanted was to save Mobutu. On the opposite side the United States was dragging its feet on the MNF question (and Rwanda was openly opposing it) because it was increasingly collaborating in trying to bring Mobutu down, while not caring too much about what would happen to the refugees, or even, in the case of Rwanda, wanting them back under control, dead or alive.[46] Similarly among foreign NGOs and political parties, pro-Hutu groups saw the refugees as innocent lambs about to be slaughtered, while the pro-Tutsi groups saw them as largely killers who were getting their comeuppance.[47]

On November 8 fighting started around Mugunga, and UN Secretary-General Boutros Ghali called for the rapid creation of a multinational intervention force, fearing the possibility of "genocide by starvation."[48] In spite of frantic diplomatic activity from Paris, negotiations were still bogged down. The British press made "the West" in general responsible for the delay,[49] while the French press clearly accused the United States.[50] President Mobutu had moved from Switzerland to his villa of Roquebrune-Cap Martin on the Riviera on November 4, leaving the Kinshasa political class in a state of expectant confusion. Prime Minister Léon Kengo wa Dondo had agreed to the multinational force, Information Minister Boguo Makeli had rejected it, the opposition parties UDPS and PDSC had refused to take a position but said that humanitarian aid should be distributed in Rwanda and Burundi, *not* in Zaire.

Meanwhile, in Kivu the AFDL was systematically trying to adopt the posture of a new government authority, Kabila declaring, "Mr Chrétien [Canadian Prime Minister] ignores me and this is a grave mistake because we are now the real power."[51] Nevertheless lucid observers such as Colette Braeckman could reasonably ask,

The four parties which together have created the AFDL never took part in the CNS democratic transition process. Instead they look rather like "leftover 1960s" guerrillas . . . who had even in the past collaborated economically with the Zairian Army. Are they now supposed to represent the core democratic opposition to the Mobutu regime?[52]

On November 11 the AFDL expelled the entire international press corps from Goma; the final big push against Mugunga was being prepared and it did not want foreign journalists to witness what promised to be messy. In a perfect display of diplomatic hypocrisy White House Spokesman Michael McCurry declared on November 12, "There is a real reluctance here to go headfirst into a situation we do not fully understand." The next day President Clinton even said that yes, the United States would commit troops to a Zaire intervention force.[53] But this was just playing for time while the Rwandese army was preparing for the final assault.

Late on the afternoon of November 13 Rwandese mortars opened fire at close range on the Mugunga camp. They fired off and on all night, and the infantry attacked the next morning. The ex-FAR fought for a few hours and then withdrew westward in the early afternoon, leaving one million refugees in a state of confusion and panic. They then split up into three groups, the main one heading east toward Rwanda, and two smaller ones heading west toward Walikale. In west Africa this was seen as another defeat; Ivory Coast president Henri Konan Bédié declared, "We [francophone Africans] feel enraged because we are powerless to confront this situation."[54] By the morning of Friday, November 15, hundreds of thousands of refugees were crossing east into Rwanda, the same border they had crossed west into Zaire when fleeing the RPF twenty-six months before.

In the meantime, totally unnoticed in the general commotion caused by the explosion of the camps and the massive return of so many refugees, another event was taking place, which would eventually bring Uganda into the war: the ADF guerrillas, which the Sudanese Secret Service had been preparing for months, had been forced into emergency action on November 13 because, after the taking of Ishasha by the Congolese rebels, they had felt that their rear base at Kasindi in Zaire had now come under threat.[55] Museveni phoned Mobutu (who seemed genuinely surprised) and told him he would enter Zaire in hot pursuit in case of a renewed attack.[56] Trying to turn necessity into opportunity, ADF leader Ssentamu Kayiira issued a communiqué saying that his men were fighting "to reintroduce multi party politics in Uganda, stop Museveni's nepotism giving all the juicy jobs to

Westerners [meaning people from Ankole and Kigezi, not Europeans] and re-establish cordial relations with Uganda's neighbours."[57] There seemed to be a slight problem of political coherence among the rebels: while the Tabliq component of ADF was preaching through its mosque circuit that it was fighting for an Islamic state with Jamal Mukulu as its president, Bakonjo prisoners told UPDF interrogators that they were fighting because they had been promised that they would finally get their autonomous kingdom.[58] In any case, Museveni had made a decision: he would have to go into Zaire to get the ADF, and since the rebels were moving north it seemed to be a good time. The internationalization of the war was now an unavoidable fact.

The refugee exodus. After mid-November 1996 the Rwandese refugees were the object of a raging controversy centering on how many of them there were. How many were there in the camps at the time of the attack? Various head counts had been conducted by UNHCR during the prior few months, giving the following results:

Goma Area	Bukavu Area	Uvira Area
(counted Mar. 31, 1996)	(counted Aug. 30, 1996)	(counted Sept. 6, 1996)
Rwandese: 715,991	Rwandese: 305,499	Rwandese: 75,948
Burundians: 2,000	Burundians: 2,000	Burundians: 145,518

Source: UNHCR Regional Special Envoy's Office, Kigali, September 26, 1996.[59]

Now the question was, what happened to them once the shooting started? The Burundian refugees were the first ones to be hit and to flee. But over half of them were caught by the Rwandese-rebel forces and herded toward the Burundi border. These (numbering 77,000) were coyly put by UNHCR in the category of "spontaneous returns."[60] Another 23,000 slowly trickled back over a period of eight months, until June 1997, while an estimated 10,000 managed to make their way independently to Kigoma in Tanzania. Taking into account the very uncertain counting methods of returnees at the border, this leaves a gap of between 25,000 and 40,000 Burundian refugees disappeared, presumed dead.

The problem of the Rwandese is much more complicated. Just to give an idea of the order of magnitude of the uncertainty, in early 1997 the United Nations boasted about a precise 726,164 refugees having "self-repatriated" in mid-November 1996,[61] but by early 1997 it had revised that estimation to a prudent 600,000.[62] In fact, nobody really knew. The human torrent that had crossed the border away from the North Kivu camp disaster on Friday, November 15, was estimated at first in the evening at "around 100,000 persons."[63] The next day UNHCR admitted that "the registration system at the border [was] breaking down." Figures started to get extremely subjective, depending on the personal preferences of who was issuing them. Ray Wilkinson, the UNHCR spokesman, declared on November 15, "The 700,000 refugees of North Kivu are all heading home,"[64] but the next day he thought that only 350,000 had crossed the border; at the same time, Eric Mercier of Médecins Sans Frontières was putting the figure at 500,000.[65] On November 18 the UN offered further details about its statistical procedures: the flow, starting on the 14th, was evaluated at between 10,000 and 12,000 people per hour. It started in the afternoon and kept going evenly until the evening of the 18th. Counting on a ten-hour-a-day flow (the barrier was closed at night) the figures came to the following:

Friday, November 15:	60,000
Saturday, November 16:	120,000
Sunday, November 17:	120,000 (full day, but the flow is slowing down)
Monday, November 18:	40,000 (same as above)
Tuesday, November 19:	5,000 (the flow had become very thin)
Wednesday, November 20:	5,000
Thursday, November 21:	5,000
Friday, November 22:	5,000
Saturday, November 23:	5,000
Sunday, November 24:	5,000[66]
Monday, November 25:	1,016, the first precise head count. The rush was over.

So what do we have? A grand total of 371,000 returnees out of a base population of over 800,000 in North Kivu at the beginning of the exodus.[67] In South Kivu it was even worse: very few refugees had crossed the Cyangugu barrier in spite of Rehabilitation Minister Patrick Mazimpaka talking about "massive daily crossings."[68] In fact, numbers now became pawns in the diplomatic tug-of-war about whether or not there should still be a multinational intervention force and what its purpose should be. Michela Wrong summed it up perfectly:

Until recently many Zairian politicians believed they would be saved by the arrival of a multinational force with a humanitarian agenda of feeding one million Hutu refugees. By stopping the rebel operations such an intervention could allow the

Army to recapture lost ground and shore up the tottering regime. But yesterday's apparent return of hundreds of thousands of refugees to Rwanda has suddenly changed the picture.[69]

The Americans seized the moment. On November 18 a U.S. State Department spokesman declared, "The mass return of nearly half a million Rwandese refugees from Zaire obliges the U.S. to review its plans in the African Great Lakes crisis." In case the point was not clear enough, U.S. Defense Secretary William Perry added, "We might not go. We are not the Salvation Army."[70] The intervention momentum was lost. Canadian Gen. Maurice Barril, who was supposed to take command of the MNF, declared the situation to be "unclear, with remaining refugee estimates varying from 100,000 to 500,000.... It is necessary to be better informed about conditions on the ground to study the military choices which could be made."[71] The numbers game continued raging. "The RPF regime denies the existence of the 700,000 refugees left in Zaire," declared the Rwandese opposition group Forces de Résistance de la Démocratie,[72] while General Kagame said at a press conference, "The majority of the refugees have returned.... There are only a few scattered refugees remaining in Eastern Zaire.... International agencies are inflating the numbers of those left behind for their own purposes."[73] Sylvana Foa, the UN spokeswoman, declared that the United Nations believed there were still 746,000 refugees in Zaire and that the problem was not resolved. Boutros Ghali's preference for high figures was probably not entirely independent from his pro-French position. U.S. Ambassador Robert Gribben in Kigali did not agree with those numbers, writing, "Most of the refugees still in Zaire are either Zairian or Burundians and the number of Rwandese refugees are nothing like those put forward by aid agencies.... They are in the twenties of thousands rather than these vast numbers." This infuriated the NGO Refugees International, which asked for the recall of the ambassador. Overflights and satellite pictures gave a different, more sober, story.[74] There were very large numbers of Rwandese refugees left in eastern Zaire, although they were probably somewhat less than the 700,000 UN figure. There was one relatively small group west of Masisi, another larger group north of Sake, enormous numbers heading west of Bukavu toward Shabunda, and smaller numbers heading south around Fizi. All in all, the total number was probably between 600,000 and 650,000.

In all the hubbub about refugees, the Zairian rebels had been almost forgotten. But at a meeting held in Goma on November 20 André Kisase Ngandu declared, "Now we have to think for ourselves.... Our main problems are how to use taxes, a fair administration and freedom for all of Zaire." He was increasingly vocal and he recruited easily. To the young men who joined him he was clearly saying that the main problem they were going to have was how to deal with the very heavy "protection" they were getting from the Rwandese. Those who joined him were usually those who wanted to bring Mobutu down but who did not trust Kigali. As a result Kigali considered him with growing distrust.[75] This did not go unnoticed by Kabila, who took exactly the opposite tack, behaving in a very subservient way toward "the tall ones," as everybody called the Tutsi. Kabila even acquired at the time the ironic nickname Ndiyo Bwana ("yes sir" in Swahili) because it was his usual answer to whatever the Rwandese were telling him. But the time was not yet ripe for the Rwandese to activate him. First they had to finish dealing with the refugee question.

Rumors were now beginning to filter out indicating that the RPA and its local auxiliaries were killing the refugees left behind in Zaire. In mid-November, near the temporary camp at Chimanga, Zairian peasants found 310 bodies and buried them.[76] The Dutch paper *De Standaard* published interviews and excerpts from the diary kept by a refugee since October 20. He described how the Rwandese army was hunting down the refugees, systematically killing all the males between the ages of ten and fifty, and how he had personally seen heaps of bodies he estimated at 120 or 150 people. He added that the *Interahamwe* had also killed an estimated 500 people in Mugunga on the last day, after one of their numbers had been murdered and after they understood that most refugees were too tired and too dispirited to risk another dash in the jungle.[77]

But the full extent of the massacres was not to be understood until the publication several months later of a report compiled during those terrible days in Kivu.[78] This report was questioned at the time because it was anonymous. Its author was Father Laurent Balas, a French priest who had lived in Kivu for the past six years and who spoke Swahili. The reason he initially testified anonymously was that he was still living in Goma and so his life would have been in danger had his name been made public.[79] Contrary to some allegations made at the time, Father Balas did not harbor any anti-Tutsi feelings. In late October 1996 he had saved forty-two Tutsi who had taken refuge in his house when the Bukavu anti-Banyamulenge pogroms extended to the northern capital, and he had nearly been lynched while trying to take seven Tutsi women across the border to Gisenyi.[80] His testimony was simply a spontaneous reaction to the new horror he now had to witness and which the international media, to his pained surprise, did not report on at the time. He was keen to point out that the refugees were the victims of a deliberate murder campaign and not simply of the fighting:

If it was only for the fighting the Hutu refugees would have no more reason to flee than the local Zairian peasants. What they are fleeing are the massacres perpetrated by the Tutsi "rebels." . . . The "rebel" discourse is to say that all the refugees who have not gone back to Rwanda are *génocidaires*... . But UNHCR estimates that only about 7% of the refugees took part in the genocide which means that many innocents have not gone back... . Calling the refugees *génocidaires* . . . is similar to the *inyenzi* ("cockroach") name used by the *interahamwe* themselves during the 1994 genocide so that they could kill with a lighter heart... . There are mass graves everywhere; but they are carefully concealed and looking for them is extremely dangerous. [There follows a description of several mass burial sites and of random dumping grounds for corpses.] . . . On 24th December the "rebels" captured two young Congolese Hutu and used them as guides to take them to refugee locations. One of the guides commented: *Waliwauwa wote wakimbizi wale, wote kabisa, hata moja aliyepona* meaning: "They killed them all these refugees, everyone of them, not a single one survived." . . . Tens of thousands have been murdered and hundreds of thousands will be made to die of exhaustion, of sickness, of hunger ... . Will that be an end to the problem of the 1994 *génocidaires*? This is far from sure. The *interahamwe* and ex-FAR who committed most of the murders are young and strong. They run fast and they have weapons... . The refugees who are getting murdered are not the killers; they are families who cannot run faster than the children with them and who are fleeing and dying as a group.

Father Balas regretted that the media maintained an almost complete blackout on the massacres even after he contacted the Paris daily *Le Figaro* and Radio France Internationale. The international community's attitude toward the problem was cavalier at best. For example, when Maurice Barril declared that there were no refugees left in eastern Zaire, he based his declaration on having spent half a day around Sake in December 1996, driving on the open road in a Rwandese army jeep.

Many refugees had returned to Rwanda willy-nilly; many others were dead; but there were still several hundreds of thousands in Tingi-Tingi, near Lobutu, in Shabunda, or scattered here and there in the Virunga forests. They were to be part of the next episode, as the "rebels" were now regrouping and preparing for their next move.

The long walk into Kinshasa

War and diplomacy. Confused discussions about the relevance of the MNF sputtered on inconclusively at the Stuttgart meeting on November 25, 1996. Meanwhile the United States (or rather, some elements thereof) had swung into action. On that same day Peter Whaley, acting deputy chief of mission of the U.S. Embassy in Kigali, crossed the border to meet Kabila in Goma. Both men later refused to make any comment about their meeting.

The U.S. military involvement in the region had started right after the genocide, when a contingent of sixty American soldiers arrived in Kigali on July 31, 1994. U.S. officials were greatly impressed by Kagame's leadership and characterized him as "a brilliant commander, able to think outside the box."[81] In early 1995 the U.S. army started a training program for the RPA. It was a large program that brought RPA officers to the United States as well as U.S. army personnel to Rwanda. The fact that the Department of Defense Joint Combined Exchange Training Program did not require congressional approval did make matters simpler when the department wanted to help the Rwandese army.

When asked about the program during a December 1996 congressional hearing, Ambassador Richard Bogosian said that the training "dealt almost exclusively with the human rights end of the spectrum as distinct from purely military operations." Considering the massive human rights violations committed by the RPA that I described in the first two chapters of this book, that part of the training must not have been very successful. As for the military aspect, since the RPA was probably the African army with the best experience in unconventional warfare on the whole continent, it should have been able to train the Americans and not the other way around. In fact, under the respectable technical guise of "training," this was largely a psycho-political covert relationship in which the Rwandese RPF managed to hook the Americans. Half through guilt, half through admiration, some segments of the U.S. Department of Defense slowly slipped deeper and deeper into cooperation with the RPA, probably feeling that they were doing what some State Department diplomats really wanted them to do but did not have the guts to take responsibility for.[82]

The U.S. army and the CIA opened several communications monitoring stations in Uganda, first on Galangala Island in the Ssese archipelago on Lake Victoria, then at Nsamizi Hill near Entebbe, and finally in Fort Portal.[83] During 1995–1996 large U.S. Air Force transport planes (C-141s and C-5s) landed very frequently at the airport in Kigali, somewhat less often at Entebbe. When questions were asked, the answer was always the same: they were "carrying aid for the genocide victims."[84] That aid must have been very heavy. But it seems to have answered needs quite different from those of the genocide survivors, who never reported any particular largesse on the part of the Americans. At that time the RPA acquired a large quantity of excellent communication equipment and many nonlethal military supplies (vehicles, boots, medicines). Once the war started it seems that these supplies were supplemented by secondhand former Warsaw Pact weapons and ammunition which were either flown directly to Goma or air-dropped at convenient points along the advancing AFDL lines. The U.S. Air Force was by then using slower and more rugged C-130s for these operations.[85] Apart from this direct logistical support to the AFDL, Washington operated a multipurpose anti-Mobutu machine which ranged from the half-humanitarian, half-military support given by the International Rescue Committee, long rumored to have been an NGO close to sensitive segments of the U.S. administration, to the soothing testimony given on the question of the missing refugees by Assistant Secretary of State to the Bureau of Population, Refugees and Migration Phyllis Oakley in December 1996. After some American arm-twisting at the UN the U.S. Ronco Consulting Corporation got a large de-mining contract in Rwanda to remove more mines than had ever been laid during the war. This had the advantage of legitimizing the impressive U.S. military air traffic since "supplies" were needed. It was an impressive performance which was completely different in style from the heavy-handed U.S. interventions during the cold war. It was stealthy, light, and indirect, with the one remaining superpower on earth easily running circles around a frustrated French diplomacy still caught up in the inefficient old web of its questionable Franco-African friendships.[86]

Meanwhile things were getting more and more out of control on the Zairian side. Tshisekedi had come back from his meeting with Mobutu in Cap Martin saying that the ailing president had made him prime minister, and he was welcomed back in Kinshasa by huge crowds.[87] But Mobutu denied the appointment, and Tshisekedi had to be restrained by force from entering "his" office at the prime minister's official headquarters. On the ground the AFDL was cautiously moving ahead, taking Butembo (November 26) and Beni (November 30). In Beni the AFDL received support from the Ugandan army, which had crossed the border mostly to crush the ADF base at Kasindi. The Ugandans denied the crossing.[88] But the situation was uncertain. On paper at least the FAZ remained quite a large army and its reactions were still untested. But the Zairian armed forces were not united; they were a clientele-based series of independent bodies, all organized around the person of Mobutu, "radiating around him like the spokes of a wheel."[89] The most powerful body was the Division Spéciale Présidentielle (DSP), twelve thousand strong on paper,[90] under the command of General Nzimbi, Mobutu's nephew. Its soldiers were mostly Ngbaka and its officers were Ngbandi, from the president's tribe. It had its own artillery and armor and totally escaped control by the FAZ chief of staff.[91] Then there was the Garde Civile, a kind of military police entirely made up of Ngbandi under the command of General Kpana Baramoto. Its theoretical strength was ten thousand, but because Baramoto was the most powerful man in Zaire after the president, nobody would have dared to count the actual number of troops. Then there was the Service d'Action et de Renseignement Militaire, a special elite corps of three thousand men (mostly Ngbandi, of course) under the command of Mobutu's brother-in-law General Bolozi. There was also the Service National d'Intelligence et de Protection (SNIP) under General Likulia Bolongo.[92] And finally there were the regular FAZ, the ordinary foot soldiers, who were pretty much abandoned to their fate and seldom saw a payday.

In theory all this added up to around eighty thousand men;[93] in practice there were at the most around fifty thousand, with probably less than half at anything like fighting capacity.[94] The officer corps was not only ridiculously large (fifty generals and over six hundred colonels), but it was also split by rivalries between officers trained in Belgium, in the United States, or in France, who formed their own factions in addition to the tribal divisions.[95] Most of the top ranks were natives of Equateur Province; almost all the professionally inclined officers belonging to other areas had been purged or even killed over the years.[96] The winners of that negative selection process were absolute gangsters; their corruption was such that when the managing directors of a number of public companies were changed by decree in 1991, the top officers besieged the offices with armed men and tanks to try to impose their own candidates for the jobs. But by then Mobutu was so weakened that he threatened to resign instead of shooting them.[97] Such was the army that the AFDL was going to have to "fight." In fact, the AFDL mostly saw it running away; the only fighting during the campaign was done by foreigners. The FDD Burundians fought in South Kivu, and the Rwandese ex-FAR and *Interahamwe* fought at the Osso River and at Shabunda. Angolan UNITA regiments defended in Bunia and, during the only large-scale battle of the war, fought at Kenge before everything fell apart.

128

On December 17, 1996, Mobutu came back from his Cap Martin villa to a triumphant welcome by over a million people in Kinshasa. This spontaneous popular movement for such a discredited man was a sort of warning for the future: Mobutu was disliked, but he was the old devil everyone knew, while there was great fear and uncertainty concerning the foreign forces silhouetted behind Kabila.[98] FAZ Chief of Staff Eluki Monga Aundu had been fired in November[99] and briefly replaced by Baramoto. When he came back President Mobutu replaced him with the only general who still commanded a minimum of respect among military and civilians alike: Gen. Mahele Lieko Bokungu. Mahele, who was a graduate from the prestigious French Army Officer Academy of Saint-Cyr, had fought courageously in Shaba in 1977 and 1978 and had stood, pistol in hand, in the way of his pillaging troops in 1991. He was supposed to be the candidate Paris had groomed to replace Mobutu. But the type of support he then got from France to help him fight off the invasion was nothing short of catastrophic when he received a bunch of mercenaries who looked like a cross between Frederick Forsyth's "dogs of war" and the Keystone Kops. In many ways they were a typical product of the declining capacities of Françafrique.[100] When the ailing Mobutu asked Dominique de Villepin and Fernand Wibaux to help him recruit some mercenaries in October,[101] he had in mind the likes of "Mad Mike" Hoare, Jean Schramme, and Bob Denard. But they were all either dead or retired. All that the French could come up with were a bunch of Bosnian Serb veterans recruited through a shady telecommunications company.[102] The first mercenary contingent arrived in Kinshasa in December. By early January 1997, Col. Christian Tavernier had set up his command post in Kisangani, with a so-called White Legion of 276 men under his orders. Their only serious trump card was their small air wing, consisting of four Aermacchi MB-326 light fighter bombers and four powerful Mi-24 Russian combat helicopters.[103] They were so hopeless that they did not even manage to use them correctly.[104] They spent their days getting drunk and aimlessly harassing civilians.[105] They did not have proper maps, they spoke neither French nor Swahili, and soon most of them were sick with dysentery and malaria. General Mahele privately complained, "The French want me to regain control of the situation and they do not even manage to supply me with the simplest things."[106] Confused efforts were made: on January 12 two giant An-124 cargo planes chartered by a British company arrived from Belarus with 200 tons of weapons which they delivered to Kisangani;[107] several MiG fighters came from China, but there were no trained mechanics capable of taking them out of their crates and putting them back together. On January 24 the French Ministry of Foreign Affairs finally issued a denial about any recruitment of mercenaries; nobody believed it, and it did not matter anyway.

On December 25 the rebels took Bunia. For the first time there was a bit of serious fighting because UNITA sent some men to the eastern front. Many vanished in the jungle as they were trying to make their way on foot or with broken-down trucks all the way from Kamina to Upper Zaire.[108] But others were flown directly to Bunia and tried to stand their ground. UNITA Gen. Abilio Kamalata ("Nuna") was killed during the assault, along with several of his men. It was after the fall of Bunia that Kabila and his minders started to seriously take stock of the situation:[109] they now controlled a 600- to 700-kilometer strip stretching from Uvira to Bunia, with Walikale as its westernmost point, and they had to make a decision on their final strategic objectives. In the eyes of many observers they appeared to have achieved their final aims: smashing the refugee threat and getting control of a few little gold and diamond mines.[110]

So far the FAZ had proved to be no match for the combined AFDL, RPA, and UPDF forces, and AFDL was now recruiting easily, even if it was obvious that the new soldiers would not be operational for several months.[111] The first local problem started when a group of Mayi Mayi fighters attacked AFDL Banyamulenge near Butembo on January 3, killing eleven. The North Kivu Mayi Mayi had supported the invaders in October, when they attacked the Rwandese Hutu refugee camps, a logical move given the fact that the armed wing of the refugees had been steadily encroaching on their lands for the past two years in an effort at creating a "Hutuland" rear base for their war with Kigali. But now that the ex-FAR and *Interahamwe* were fleeing west, they feared, not Hutu, but Tutsi domination and they turned against the Tutsi-supported Alliance.

The strategic choice was made in late 1996, and it was made for all-out war. On January 4, 1997, the AFDL decided that its four components were now fused into one. Four days later the AFDL military leader Kisase was killed by the RPA.[112] He had always been a thorn in the side of the Rwandese because of his openly nationalistic attitude, which often brought him into conflict with his RPA minders. There was a famous occasion when he stopped the RPA from taking a large electric generator from Goma Airport to Rwanda, saying that it belonged to the Congolese state and that he was accountable to that state and not to Kigali. And there were numerous occurrences of public speeches when he had voiced his defiance of the overbearing Rwandese. The RPA had never managed to keep him under control, while Kabila accepted the nonstop day-and-night presence of six to ten Tutsi "guardian angels" around him. After the AFDL "consolidation" everything went very quickly: since he was "a nationalist" the Rwandese asked him with some irony to go and take care of this newly developing Mayi Mayi problem. At the last moment, as he was heading to Butembo, his bodyguards were removed and replaced by some of Kabila's.[113] Kisase was careless enough to go anyway, and they killed him. Kabila then lied about the murder on January 17, saying that Kisase "had been wounded by the Mayi Mayi, was hospitalised and would soon be back." This was a portent of things to come in terms of his future style of government.

On January 2 Zairian Prime Minister Léon Kengo wa Dondo announced "a total and crushing offensive [*offensive totale et foudroyante*], which will spare no enemy, Zairian or foreign."[114] Then he did nothing. In the meantime two key Luanda officials, National Security Adviser Gen. Helder Viera Dias ("Kopelipa") and MPLA Secretary-General Lopo do Nascimiento, arrived in Bukavu.[115] Their job was to assess the strengths and weaknesses of the Alliance and the degree of involvement of UNITA on the Zairian government's side. Since the 1994 Lusaka Peace Agreement UNITA and the MPLA were in a situation of "no peace, no war," which did not stop them from skirmishing on the fringes of their respective areas of control. The two MPLA envoys were a bit wary because they knew that the RPF had long-standing relations with UNITA.[116] But they realized that circumstances had changed, and they decided that Kagame now needed them and would collaborate in their strategy of strangling UNITA. Between February 12 and 25, 1997, two battalions of "Tigers" were flown to Kigali from Luanda on big Ilyushin Il-76 cargo jets.[117] They were later to play a decisive role in the war.

Meanwhile the AFDL-RPA forces had carefully started to move to cut off the various access points to Kisangani, their next target. Mahagi, just across the Uganda West Nile border, was taken on January 29 by thirty Ugandan soldiers. The move was denied two days later by President Museveni himself in a radio interview: "We are not in Zaire.... Dissident groups have been present there for thirty years, lumumbists, the Tshombe group, Mulele groups and others. They are the ones who have taken up arms."[118] On the day Museveni was making this disingenuous claim his troops reached Watsa in the north, forcing Tavernier's mercenaries to flee back to Kisangani. Watsa was taken to be the stepping stone for Uganda's coming attack on southern Sudan. By then Alliance forces were moving in three directions at once: southward, where they occupied Kalemie on February 3;[119] northward, where they occupied Aru on February 2; and westward, where they had been fighting for the Osso River crossing on the Walikale-Lobutu road since mid-January. This last front was the only one where some serious fighting took place. Beyond the river was the large Tingi-Tingi Rwandese refugee camp, and the ex-FAR were doing their best to stop the RPA advance.[120] But the Alliance forces had started moving southwest as well, taking Shabunda on February 6, a move that opened the road to mineral-rich Kasai and Katanga.

The Ugandans were fulfilling an agenda of their own, which had more to do with the Sudan than with Zaire. President Museveni had declared, "We have run out of solutions with the Sudan. We are now seeking a solution on the battlefield."[121] By then the war had generalized and the Ugandan army had taken prisoner some former FAZ soldiers among the ADF guerrillas operating in the Kasese area,[122] while the Sudanese were air-dropping supplies to the Lord's Resistance Army in northern Uganda in the hope that it could hit the UPDF hard enough to stop it from joining the battle in Zaire. But the LRA was more of a terrorist outfit than a regular guerrilla force: between January 7 and 9 it had killed 312 civilians in Lamvo County, near Kitgum,[123] a move that only strengthened Museveni's resolve to deal directly with the Sudanese. In early February the Uganda National Rescue Front II guerrilla group, led by Ali Bamuze, attacked the village of Midigo (Aringa County) in West Nile.[124] This move had been encouraged by the Sudanese Secret Service, which was anxious because the main body of West Nile guerrillas (the WNBLF) was crossing over from its bases in Zaire and surrendering in large numbers to the Ugandan army.[125] By then the Sudanese were desperately trying to coordinate with Colonel Tavernier and the FAZ remnants in Upper Zaire, but they were crumbling so fast that the Sudan border now lay open. On the other side Museveni was now working with the SPLA to try to squeeze the Ugandan rebels in northeastern Zaire in a three-pronged assault coordinated with the AFDL-RPA forces then moving northward. The next step would be to push them back into southern Sudan.

Faced with these dynamics, reactions both from Kinshasa and from the international community were extremely weak. On February 17 three Zairian Air Force Aermacchi MB-326 light strike aircraft dropped a few bombs on the Bukavu market, killing nineteen civilians and wounding thirty-seven.[126] This action was totally useless from a military point of view. The next day in New York the United Nations passed Resolution 1097 demanding an end to hostilities, the withdrawal of all external forces, including mercenaries, the protection and security of all refugees, and an international peace conference for the Great Lakes crisis. None of these demands had the slightest effect on the situation.

By early March Alliance forces and their foreign allies were moving at great speed in all directions: Kindu fell without fighting on March 3, followed the next day by Manono. The road to Katanga was now open. In the north the combined forces of Congolese rebels, the RPA, the Ugandan army, and SPLA Sudanese rebels had pushed the last FAZ remnants to the Sudanese border. Inside Sudan SPLA forces besieging Yei had captured the supplies air-dropped by the Sudanese Air Force for the beleaguered garrison, and on March 13 the town fell. But the Ugandan rebels then moving northward to escape the trap in Zaire did not know it; they were trekking up on foot from Morobo toward Yei, together with bedraggled remnants of the FAZ and some Sudanese regulars, a column of over four thousand men, women, and children. They fell into a major SPLA ambush halfway to Yei on March 12: two thousand people were killed, over one thousand captured,[127] and the rest, including wounded WNBLF Commander Juma Oris, fled in disarray toward the safety of the Sudanese army garrison in Juba.[128]

President Museveni briefly stopped in Paris on a return flight from the United States on March 11. His interview with President Chirac was icy because he denied the presence of UPDF troops in Zaire, something the French had fully documented through their Commandement des Opérations Spéciales commandos. But French efforts were increasingly irrelevant: on March 13 at a meeting in Brussels France was still trying to convince the European Union of the need for a military intervention;[129] two days later Kisangani fell into rebel hands. Tavernier's mercenaries did not even try to resist but instead fought the FAZ to get into the fleeing helicopters. It now looked increasingly likely that the Mobutu regime was on its last legs. On March 17 Kabila refused a cease-fire, saying, "Only direct talks with Mobutu might bring some kind of a pause."[130] Two days later Jacques Foccart, the Grand Old Wizard of French African policy, died at his home in Paris, a symbol that the end was near.[131]

On March 20 the French army pre-positioned one hundred troops in Brazzaville, with five Transall transport planes in case foreign civilians would need to be evacuated from Kinshasa.[132] Mobutu was back from the Riviera the next day, so sick he could hardly walk out of the plane.[133] Four days later there was an OAU general meeting in Lome which all the main play-ers felt it mandatory to attend: Honoré N'Gbanda, André Boboliko, and Gérard Kamanda wa Kamanda from Kinshasa; Bizima Karaha and Gaëtan Kakudji for the AFDL;[134] Howard Wolpe for President Clinton; African Affairs Adviser Michel Dupuch for President Chirac;[135] and, of course, UN Secretary-General Kofi Annan. All they had to go by was Resolution 1097, and it was not much: Kabila declared the next day, "We will never enter into any kind of power-sharing arrangement with the Kinshasa government."[136] Mbuji-Mayi, the diamond capital, fell without fighting on April 5. A week earlier Jonas Mukamba Nzemba, managing director of the Société Minière de Bakwanga (MIBA), had declared that he was ready to work with the AFDL.[137] This meant that the rebel movement was now out of the woods, both physically and figuratively: coming into Kasai meant that the rebels were out of the dense central forest and could look forward to easier opera-tions in the savannah area; the road to Kinshasa was now open. Also, getting the cooperation of the largest diamond company in Zaire meant that they were likely to begin accessing some kind of self-financing. As we will see in the next section, the signal was not lost on the international mining com-munity, which was soon beating a path to Kabila's door.

There was now panic in Kinshasa. President Mobutu fired Prime Minister Kengo wa Dondo, who had reached maximum unpopularity,[138] and tried to replace him with Etienne Tshisekedi. AFDL agents secretly came to see the old opposition leader and warned him that accepting would mean his political death.[139] He accepted nevertheless, generously offering the AFDL six portfolios in his future cabinet. Because all the remainder was going to his UDPS party, he managed to antagonize both sides at the same time, and the last Mobutists refused him. After some comical scuffling he was again prevented from taking his position, and Mobutu, who by then was nearly dying, named SNIP boss Gen. Likulia Bolongo as prime minister on April 11. Three days later Lubumbashi fell to the combined AFDL-RPA–Katangese Tiger forces.[140] There was not much fighting even if the local UFERI militia of Katanga's governor Kyungu wa Kumwanza theoretically sided with the last few DSP troops left. Their contribution was mostly to loot the city before it fell. The attackers surprised them by entering Zambia and then attacking from the southeast when everybody expected them to come from inside Zaire, through Kasanga or Likasi.[141] A few days later and without any form of consultation Kabila proclaimed himself president of the now renamed Democratic Republic of Congo.

The old Congo Free State blue flag with the yellow star was brought back and preparations were made for the march on Kinshasa. Troops started to move on the Kamina-Kananga axis to join up with columns coming down from Mbuji-Mayi and with new Angolan reinforcements coming up through Tshikapa.[142] By now even the "official" U.S. forces were a bit worried about what was happening. On February 13 a joint meeting of the U.S. State Department, the Defense Intelligence Agency, the CIA, the Deputy Joint Chiefs of Staff, and the National Security Council had taken place in Washington to decide on a more coherent strategy. There were more meetings on March 24 and 29 and April 2 with NSC African Affairs Director Charlie Snyder, National Intelligence Agency African Affairs Director William Foltz, Security Adviser Shawn MacCormack, DIA member William Thom, and Ambassador Simpson. There was a lurking fear that things had gotten out of hand and that the war could globalize from the Central African Republic to Zambia and from Angola to the Sudan.[143] The consensus was that somehow Kabila was getting out of control and that he should be brought back into line. His declaration that any foreign forces on Congolese soil would be considered "enemy" did not sound nice, with U.S. forces poised in Brazzaville for an eventual evacuation. Ambassador Simpson hurried back to Kinshasa to try to convince the Mobutist generals to avoid a disastrous last stand. The United States feared a bloodbath that would have been immediately used by the French as proof of Washington's evil intentions. In a secret memo to the French government retired general Jeannou Lacaze had darkly warned, "A great battle is about to happen [in Kinshasa] because as the FAZ are retreating they get more compact and able to resist.... . Contrary to what has happened in Kisangani or Lubumbashi they will not hesitate to oppose a strong resistance to the rebel forces."[144] This was a nightmare scenario for Washington, and President Clinton sent his UN ambassador, Bill Richardson, to Kinshasa, where he met President Mobutu on April 28. The game plan was to try to convince the old dictator to step down without too much of a fuss. Mobutu was sick and cranky and asked for guarantees for himself, his friends, his family, and his money. Richardson made all kinds of vague promises and then flew down to Lubumbashi to meet Kabila. He managed to get him to agree to a meeting with Mobutu. Nelson Mandela was also active behind the scenes, trying to find a neutral place for the fateful conference. After discarding Brazzaville (the Alliance refused because Lissouba was considered to be a UNITA crony and therefore distrusted by Luanda), Libreville (same refusal, because Bongo was seen as too pro-French), Lome (same thing), and Lusaka (this time it was Mobutu who felt he might not come out of it alive), the South African president found a creative solution: he would go himself to Pointe Noire and guarantee Mobutu's physical security for a conference aboard the South African navy ship *Outeniqua*. The conference finally took place on May 3–4, but without any result; during the conference the Alliance announced that its forces had taken Kikwit, practically without fighting. Mobutu, sicker than before, simply went back to Kinshasa.

But there was still one battle to be fought before everything would be over: Jonas Savimbi realized that Zaire was lost and that he had to intervene one last time. In an interview published in 1999 he said this:

In Zaire we had hospitals, equipment and personnel. We had to get everything out. So we fought Kabila at Kenge, 70 km from Kinshasa. We stopped his progress for about a week, enough to remove everything. Then we left. There was nothing else to do anyway. Mobutu was sick and tired and power was slipping out of his hands. His army had no more will to fight.... I picked up the phone and I called Madeleine Albright, who was so keen on us leaving the way open for Kabila so that he could overthrow Mobutu. I told her: "Mrs Secretary of State, we are just taking care of our business. We stopped Kabila at Kenge but we will not prevent him from taking power." She was quite happy.[145]

After the battle of Kenge it was just a matter of days before everything would be over. Mobutu went to Libreville on May 8 for one last nostalgic meeting with the Françafrique old guard: Bongo, Patassé, Lissouba, and Equatorial Guinea President Obiang Nguema. They had no miracle solution, but they advised on one last trick: a third man. According to this plan Mobutu could try to recall the old CNS hero Archbishop Laurent Monsengwo. On May 11 the HCR/PT offered him the position of prime minister. The poor man was in Brussels and had not even been consulted. He gave a dilatory answer, and that was the end of it. On May 16 Mobutu fled Kinshasa; his top officers did the same. Baramoto and his friend the "Grand Admiral" Mavua Mudima (who never had a fleet to command but was a keen businessman) flew to South Africa in Baramoto's private jet. General Nzimbi, who a few days earlier had vowed to die fighting, simply took a small canoe across the river to Brazzaville. Many others tossed away their uniforms and tried to melt into the civilian crowds. The next day the victorious Alliance troops entered the capital without a fight. The last victim of the war was General Mahele, who had conducted his own parallel negotiations with the rebels, thus earning himself the enmity of the last

Mobutists. He was shot at Camp Tshatshi by Mobutu's son Kongolo who then fled to Brazzaville.

The mining contracts: myths and realities. "With the full backing of the Clinton administration … AMF and its partners stood ready to expand their plans… . But something would first have to be done about Zaire's pro-French leader, Marshal Mobutu Sese Seko. Mobutu continued to favour French, Belgian and South African companies over those from the United States and Canada. A safe platform was needed from which an attack could be launched on Mobutu and his French and Belgian mining benefactors. That platform would be one of the poorest and most densely-populated tinderboxes in Africa: Rwanda."[146]

This extreme form of neo-Leninist conspiracy theory, although not shared by most analysts who wrote about the fall of the Mobutu regime, was nevertheless often used as a kind of prudent noncommittal background by journalists. But when American Mineral Fields International (AMFI) signed what was described as a "one billion dollar contract" with Laurent-Désiré Kabila on April 16, 1997, many were a bit shaken. Because all close observers who had been to the field during the war knew about the poorly hidden U.S. cloak-and-dagger involvement and because Washington kept obstinately denying it, that big contract suddenly started to look like the proverbial smoking gun.

And yet, in spite of the obvious U.S. interest in seeing Mobutu go, every single one of the premises on which this interpretation rested was false.

Let us first deal with some of the general assumptions underpinning this line of reasoning, Madsen's being only an explicit version of what others only hinted at. "Zaire's pro-French leader, Marshal Mobutu": here is a judgment with at least one fragment of truth in it. By 1991 or 1992 at the latest Mobutu knew that his time with Washington was up; because he was clever and well aware of the pathological anti-American feelings of a large majority of the French,[147] he played that card for all it was worth. I remember the head of the Africa Elysée cell at the time, Bruno Delaye, fuming (and this while the Rwandese genocide was not yet completely over), "It is out of the question to let the Anglophones decide the destiny of French-speaking countries in Africa." The same gentleman told me a bit later, "Mobutu has to be put back firmly in the saddle so that he will be part and parcel of any future solution." But did this mean that French mining interests in Zaire benefited as a result of that circumstantial diplomacy? Not so, simply because there were hardly any such interests.[148] Two years later, when the war started, the only French mining investment in Zaire was not even purely

French, it was a share of the Belgian Union Minière, which exploited copper and cobalt in Shaba-Katanga. The one other French investment in the country, the Société Minière du Kivu (SOMINKI), which had belonged to the Empain-Schneider group, had been sold in early 1996 to a Cluff Mining–Banro consortium.[149] So if it is correct to say that Mobutu, more by force than by choice, had to side with Paris against Washington, this did not at all mean that such an alliance brought economic benefits to the French.[150]

Second wrong assumption: Mobutu was anti-U.S. (and anti-Canadian). This does not make any sense either. Mobutu had been put in power and kept there with U.S. help. He was quite desperate at having lost that trump card with the collapse of the Soviet Union, and if Washington's support could have been bought back simply by dishing out a few mining contracts, he would have been only too glad to oblige. But contrary to many conspiracy theorists' allegations, the Americans were not very interested in Zairian mining riches. When Canadian companies came in, they were welcomed. And when one big U.S. company (Barrick Gold) finally showed up in mid-1996 it had no problem buying out the Kilomoto complex from Cluff-Banro.

There was no French dominance and no reluctance on Mobutu's part to see the Americans come in. In fact, neither the French nor the Americans had large mining interests in Zaire. Mining interests in Zaire were extremely diversified, and if any countries had more weight than others it was still the two old actors from the colonial days, South Africa and Belgium.[151]

Finally, a third bit of debunking: if Rwanda was indeed "poor, densely-populated and a tinderbox," it was in no shape or form a "platform" for the Americans. Regardless of the opinion one has of President Kagame's leadership it is absolutely necessary to recognize that he is nobody's puppet, that his decisions are not dictated by any foreign power. This is always the problem of conspiracy theories applied to Africa: they purport to denounce the evil visited upon Africans by ill-meaning foreigners and they end up with Africans looking like perfect dolts, manipulated here, pushed there, used for this, deceived into that. In thirty-seven years of studying Africa I have seen more whites manipulated by blacks than the other way around. But lingering postcolonial racism makes it hard for the victims to admit to themselves that they have been taken for a ride; the implicit notion that all things being equal the white fellow is smarter than the black one is still the unspoken assumption of a large number of white diplomats, international civil servants, and businesspeople. Conspiracy theorists do not represent an exception: their evil whites are more cleverly evil than their evil blacks, an assumption I seriously doubt. General Kagame was no more a puppet of the Americans than President Mobutu was a puppet of the French. As to his reasons for invading Zaire, we have already seen several that were quite local, and those others I discuss later on have had little to do with Washington's game plan, which in Kigali has always been considered more of a resource to be tapped than an obligation to be obeyed.

Zaire might have been a "geological scandal," but it was not the center of the mining world. Actually, as with most other things in the country, its share of the mining world market has kept going down, more sharply so since the beginning of the 1990s. By the late 1990s it represented only 0.7 percent of the value of minerals produced in the world.[152]

A brief synopsis of the Zairian mining world and of how it was affected by the 1996–1997 war would go roughly like this. The old mining dinosaurs (Union Minière, Gécamine) were still surviving in Shaba by digging up some copper and scrounging the cobalt left over in the old copper tailings. Between 1988 and 1996 copper production fell from 506,000 tons to 38,000 and cobalt from 10,140 tons to 5,300. The technical condition of the production apparatus was a disaster. In Mbuji-Mayi MIBA was the biggest diamond producer in the country, but not by much: it produced between six and nine million carats (valued at between $55 million and $90 million, depending on market price fluctuations) out of a total of fifteen to seventeen million carats. The various diamond purchasing *comptoirs,* some of them run by major companies like De Beers and others by individuals, were making an estimated $300 million to $400 million a year, and contraband diamonds directly sold by diggers on the black market represented approximately another $100 million. Which meant that MIBA, with all its paraphernalia of taxes, predation by the government, and theft by employees was simply the biggest comptoir but not the biggest commercial system on the market.[153] In addition, SOMINKI was surviving in Kivu with a much reduced production of gold (10 to 20 kilograms a month), Australia's Anvil Mining operated a small zinc mine near Lubumbashi, and China's State Mining Company had signed an agreement with Kinshasa to exploit two copper and cobalt mines at Ruashi and Etoile but had not yet put them into production. In that troubled and sick landscape there were very few new investment plans taking shape as the 1990s drew to a close.[154] Apart from the already mentioned purchase of the Kilomoto branch of SOMINKI by Barrick Gold in August 1996 there were only two significant investment projects in the mid-1990s. The first one was the Fungurume cobalt mining project in Shaba, which was developed as a joint venture (Tenke Mining) between Gécamines and a mining newcomer, the Swede Adolf Lundin. Over $1 billion in planned investments was announced but not actually disbursed. The other one was for two projected joint ventures between U.S.-based AMFI and South Africa's Anglo-American, one for a zinc mine-cum-smelter at Kipushi and the other for mining cobalt in Kolwezi. AMFI and Anglo-American quarreled, broke up their joint venture project, and dropped everything in October 1996.[155] But it was the same Kolwezi project that eventually resurfaced in April 1997 as the miracle "one billion dollar contract" with Kabila, this time as a purely AMFI deal. And it was on that old-new contract that the whole U.S. mining conspiracy theory was built, largely because AMFI's director, Jean-Raymond Boulle, based his company in Hope, Arkansas, Bill Clinton's hometown.

But who was Jean-Raymond Boulle, and what was his company? Boulle was born in 1950 in Mauritius. He is a French-speaking British citizen and a tax resident of Monaco. In the early 1970s he worked for De Beers as a diamond purchaser, first in Sierra Leone and then in Zaire. He did well, and by the late 1970s he was working directly for CSO in London, at the top of the organizational chart. But he did not like being a small man in a big pond and he resigned in 1981, preferring to work as a freelance diamond buyer in his familiar African hunting grounds. By 1989 he had enough confidence to launch his own company in partnership with Robert Friedland, a Chicago-born former hippy who had spent a good many years traveling between Indian ashrams and Oregon new-age farms. Together they created Diamond Field Resources, which set up shop in Hope, Arkansas, because the two business associates wanted to mine the Crater of Diamonds deposit in an Arkansas state park. It was in the process of setting up that operation (which met with fairly stiff opposition from conservationists) that Boulle first met Bill Clinton, governor of Arkansas. Crater of Diamonds proved to be a somewhat disappointing project, but in 1994 Boulle had an unexpected stroke of luck: while exploring for diamonds in Newfoundland he discovered what was then the world's largest deposit of zinc at Voisey's Bay. He drove a hard bargain and got Falconbridge and Inco, the two largest Canadian mining concerns, in a bidding battle for the deposit. It was sold for $4.3 billion, but then Boulle had to contest several lawsuits (with the Inuit natives, with some of his financial backers, with his partner Friedland) before managing to get his share. When he finally did, he had over $1 billion net cash in his pocket. With this money he created a new company, American Mineral Fields International, in partnership with his brothers Franco and Bertrand, whom he sent as agents to Russia and Guinea, respectively. As chief executive of his own company he could now go back to Africa. His May 1996 announcement of the Kipushi-Kolwezi joint ventures agreement with the giant Anglo-American must have felt like a triumph for the former AAC employee.[156] Breaking it must have felt even better, and signing the April 16 contract with Kabila was the crowning achievement of his career so far.

So adherents of the U.S.-mining-conspiracy-behind-the-fall-of-Mobutu theory would have us believe that a French-speaking Mauritian British passport holder, freelance diamond prospector, and chance billionaire who never operated in the United States before the mid-1980s was the man chosen by dark and powerful American interests to take over Zaire through a war of conquest sponsored by the president of the United States himself because he happened to be from Arkansas where Boulle had once had some (minor) mining projects. This does not make sense. It makes even less sense if one tots up a few additional facts: (a) Boulle eventually moved out of the Arkansas backwaters and set up shop in London; (b) his "miracle $1 billion contract" was attacked in an international court of law after the war by none other than his old employer Anglo-American, who argued, through Gécamines, that the contract was in breach of some of their own previous contracts signed with Mobutu for the same area; and (c) after almost two years of litigation Boulle resold his rights to AAC in an out-of-court settlement, making a very large amount of money and getting a 20 percent share of the future company, which will certainly one day mine the cobalt at Kolwezi. It was obvious from the start that Boulle was playing a well-known game for smaller independent mining companies: Go find a big deal (which you do not have enough money to bring into production), make a lot of publicity, hold on to it for a while, then sell to one of the majors, who will have either the money to exploit it or else enough financial strategic depth to be able to wait for ten or twenty years until the conditions are ripe. As for the U.S. "conspiracy," it was nowhere in sight during this game between an international independent and his former South African bosses.

Actually, the whole process was much more typical of the workings of modern transnational capitalism than of the old style imperialism proposed by conspiracy theorists. Yes, the Americans were involved in the fall of Mobutu; no, it was not to control mineral riches, which they could have acquired perfectly well in a simpler way—unless one wants to believe that

President Clinton started a war in order to enable former President Bush to steal something he already owned.[157]

This does not mean that there were no backdoor dealings with the AFDL during the war. But those started only after the rebels had taken the mining capital Lubumbashi and when it looked increasingly likely that the Mobutu regime would not last much longer.[158] The first to come was Nicholas Davenport, head of De Beers in Kinshasa, who flew to Lubumbashi together with some Union Minière officials and a World Bank representative on April 18, 1997. But Boulle, true to his freelance approach, had been in contact with the rebels for the previous three months. He even facilitated similar contacts between Tenke Mining and the AFDL when the rebel forces started marching south.[159] On April 16 Boulle signed the mythical contract, and, according to experts, the up-front cash he put up at the time was less than $40 million. But he also loaned his private Learjet to both Kabila and his "minister of mines," Mawampanga Mwana Nanga,[160] something that was of precious help during the war. The unconfirmed rumor is that he made $400 million two years later when he resold his rights to Anglo-American.

By early May a real charter flight of twenty-eight financiers (representatives of Morgan Grenfell, First Boston Bank, Goldman Sachs, and others) flew into Lubumbashi when it became obvious that Kabila was going to be the next president.[161] But it looked more like a case of bandwagon jumping than like a long-standing conspiracy.

By then the AFDL had acquired new confidence. No more ultimatums and empty declarations, but actions: in Mbuji-Mayi the Lebanese diamond traders were asked for $960,000 in back taxes,[162] and De Beers had a nasty shock when it tried to take "its" latest diamond consignment, worth about $3 million, out of town: Mawampanga told the South African team that they must tender for the lot. When De Beers protested that it would be a breach of their purchase agreement the "minister" replied that they themselves were in breach of contract since they had been buying diamonds from black market dealers who had mined them illegally on MIBA concessions. The De Beers men asked for orders from headquarters and were told to pay $5 million. They also did not contradict Mawampanga's subsequent public statement when he said that the South African company would break with the Mobutu regime and deal with the AFDL in the future.[163] A few weeks later Mobutu had become a memory. And, according to the mining expert Jean-Claude Sémama, who as a Frenchman should not be too soft on the "Anglo-Saxons," "The political change did not seem to have benefited U.S.

mining companies. There are two possibilities: either they tried to appropriate resources but did not manage to do it; or else the media image is simply false."[164] But once the mining myths were disposed of there remained another major problem concerning the war: What had happened to those refugees who did not return to Rwanda in mid-November 1996?

The fate of the refugees. As we have seen, refugees fleeing the RPA-AFDL attacks in the Kivus mainly took two directions: a very large group of perhaps 350,000 started to walk toward Lobutu, while a smaller group of around 150,000 went down toward Shabunda. A very small group of mainly former ex-FAR and *Interahamwe* walked up to the Sudan.[165] And, perhaps most neglected of all, many (perhaps nearly 100,000) remained in the Kivus, hiding in the forests on the foothills of the Virunga or trying to take refuge among native Congolese Hutu populations around Masisi and Walikale. In the words of Jean-Hervé Bradol, then a member of the Médecins Sans Frontières mission in Kigali, "They had entered the Bermuda Triangle of politics."[166] Those who suffered the most in the short run were the ones who remained in the east without being able to get to the refuge of the forests. The RPA-AFDL troops were hunting them down like rabbits and were helped in their task by Mayi Mayi guerrillas, especially in North Kivu, where they were simply carrying on with the pre–Rwandese genocide Masisi war that had restarted with the arrival of the Rwandese refugees in the summer of 1994.[167] This resulted in, among other acts of violence, the Nyamitaba massacre of November 21, 1996, when several thousand refugees were killed by the Mayi Mayi.[168]

The main group of refugees started to walk toward Walikale after the *Interahamwe* had killed several of their numbers to deter them from turning east.[169] They managed to reach the Lobutu area, where they settled in two huge camps, at Amisi and Tingi-Tingi, with a combined population of at least 170,000 people. Another 100,000 refugees were rolled in a southwesterly direction toward Shabunda. Both groups eventually settled, in very difficult circumstances. The frenzied refugees number game slowly died down after the MNF idea collapsed. The Americans had continued to underestimate the refugees left in Zaire,[170] while the French kept clamoring that "an international force . . . is more than ever necessary."[171] But everybody knew that the MNF issue was dead. The Rwandese government even gloated about it, Patrick Mazimpaka declaring, "Those refugees about whom the international community is so worried, we found them, we repatriated them. And the international community should reward us for all the savings we allowed it to make."[172] In typical U.S. newspaper clipped style, an American journalist gave a simplified summary of the situation: "In the last two months a rebel force few had ever heard of before solved a problem in Eastern Zaire that the United Nations and western democracies could not solve in two years. Using quick and decisive military strikes (and, some unconfirmed reports claim, leaving piles of massacred bodies) the rebels have separated hundreds of thousands of Rwandese refugees from the Hutu militants who have virtually held them hostage and have sent the refugees packing back to Rwanda."[173]

End of story. At least, that was the story sold in the media. But at about the same time things started to move for the refugees in Tanzania. After the mid-November exodus Tanzanian President Ben Mkapa had declared to the press, "Repatriation of refugees now seems more feasible,"[174] and the Tanzanian Permanent Secretary to the Ministry of Home Affairs Colonel Magere had told UNHCR, "Following the mass return of Rwandese refugees from Eastern Zaire and the developments which have taken place, the Rwandese refugees in Tanzania have no longer any legitimate reason to continue to refuse to return to Rwanda."[175] The refugees knew it and they immediately started to flee the camps, walking to Rusumo, hoping to get anywhere—Kenya, Malawi, Zambia—except to Rwanda.[176] But the pressure for repatriation was tremendous. UNHCR issued a joint communiqué with the Tanzanian authorities telling the refugees to return. The Tanzanian army was brought in; two Italian priests from Rulenge Parish who were telling the refugees that they had a right to decide whether to go or stay were arrested and deported to Italy, and UNHCR vehicles were used to truck the refugees back over the border. By the end of December practically all the Tanzanian refugees were home; there had been 3,200 arrests at the border and only two deaths.[177] The Tanzanian repatriation was considered again as "voluntary," which reinforced the notion that whoever was running away from the Rwandese army in Zaire must be a *génocidaire.*

The refugees who settled around Lobutu and Shabunda enjoyed a precarious respite of a few months while the Alliance was sorting itself out militarily and politically and consolidating its eastern base. But by early 1997 the AFDL and the Rwandese forces started to move west. The first attack occurred at Katshunga, forty-five kilometers northeast of Shabunda, on February 4 and sent 30,000 to 40,000 refugees fleeing toward Pangi.[178] Most of them were overtaken by the AFDL-RPA forces, which were moving faster than the refugees because they had vehicles and the road was passable.

The attackers immediately separated out the young males and "shots were heard." The survivors were then herded back toward Bukavu.[179] Those who managed to escape started on a long southwest trek that eventually took them all the way to the Angolan border by way of Kindu, Lusambo, Mbuji-Mayi, and Luiza.[180] But they were harassed all the way, at times by innovative tactics. Because the refugees were hungry and exhausted, the Alliance forces would let the humanitarians take the lead, and when the refugees heard that some help had arrived, they would come out of the forest. Then the military, who were not far behind, would pounce and kill them. An RPA commander told a worker with Médecins Sans Frontières, "All those who are in the forest have to be considered enemies." Some of the humanitarian NGOs chose to withdraw, fearing that their help was in fact lethal for the refugees.

Meanwhile the Alliance was also attacking around Lobutu; the sharp fighting on the Osso River had mostly been carried out by Rwandese on both sides. In Kigali U.S. Ambassador Gribben, as usual strongly in support of the attackers, made short shrift of the humanitarian quandary, writing in a cable to Washington, "We should pull out of Tingi-Tingi and stop feeding the killers who will run away to look for other sustenance, leaving their hostages behind…. If we do not we will be trading the children in Tingi-Tingi for the children who will be killed and orphaned in Rwanda."[181] Such a message implied that helping the refugee camps would somehow sustain some kind of war effort by the ex-FAR against Rwanda itself. In fact, the truth was almost completely the opposite. The fleeing ex-FAR had stuck with the refugees, partly out of simple solidarity, partly to use them as human shields and reservoirs of humanitarian aid, partly because they wanted to keep their constituency. But when it became obvious that the situation of the camps might end in absolute collapse they started to think about alternative strategies. Gen. Augustin Bizimungu then flew back to Kinshasa,[182] while Col. Gratien Kabirigi reorganized his best fighting troops (about five thousand men) and turned them around, going back eastward through the forest to avoid both the fleeing refugees and their pursuers.[183]

The humanitarian situation in Tingi-Tingi and Amisi was terrible, with thirty to thirty-five people dying every day, mostly small children. By early February a cholera epidemic had started and the humanitarian workers were short of just about everything.[184] On February 14 Sadako Ogata, the UN-HCR high commissioner, begged the Alliance forces not to attack Tingi-Tingi; when they finally did anyway most of the refugees fled toward Kisangani and others ran into the jungle. From that moment on what had been a very difficult humanitarian situation became a particularly atrocious one.[185] To make everything more confusing, this was the moment when Father Balas's testimony about the killings in Kivu was released. This testimony, which was vital, was ill timed in terms of helping the public understand the situation because it did not refer to what was then happening near Kisangani but to events that had happened four months earlier in Kivu. Public opinion was in upheaval, with pro-Hutu and pro-Tutsi hurtling accusations at each other in perfectly bad faith.[186]

By late February the former Tingi-Tingi refugees had resettled somehow in a string of camps stretching over a hundred kilometers south of Kisangani, from Ubundu to Lula by way of Kasese and Biaro. There were between 120,000 and 140,000 people, in a state of total dereliction. Some Médecins Sans Frontières doctors said of their charges that they were "not so much patients but rather pre-cadavers." In March a representative of the World Food Program who flew over the Kisangani–Tingi-Tingi road said it was "strewn with hundreds of bodies lying along the roadside, apparently dead or dying."[187] At the same time, at the other end of the trail, bedraggled survivors of the November camp fighting who had been hiding in Kivu since then finally emerged starving from the bush; on April 1 20,000 to 30,000 refugees appeared out of nowhere at a village called Karuba at the northern end of Lake Kivu. They were former residents of Katale and Kahindo who had fled to the bush when the artillery fire started coming down and who were finally surrendering.[188] They (and others later) were careful to wait until some UN-HCR personnel were around so as to avoid being killed upon emerging.

Around Kisangani the main humanitarian problem was the same that had already turned working in Tingi-Tingi into a nightmare, that is, constant and capricious restriction of access to the refugees. Expatriate staff were not permitted to stay overnight in the camps and were forced to commute every day over very bad roads, reducing their working time to absurdly short hours. Mortality kept rising; the health status of the refugees was described as "catastrophic" by Médecins Sans Frontières. Permission to airlift the worst cases was denied. Even airlifting unaccompanied sick children was refused by the Alliance[189] under the pretext that there were still ex-FAR in the area.[190] On April 17 about two hundred Rwandese soldiers were flown into Kisangani and immediately replaced the Katangese Tigers who had so far escorted the humanitarian workers. They were part of a killer team dispatched directly from Kigali. They were reputed to carry in their knapsacks small cobbler's hammers which they used to silently and efficiently smash skulls.[191] First they did a bit of psychological preparation, telling the local population that the six villagers who had been killed near the Kasese camp on April 20 had been killed by the refugees. This enabled them to recruit some of the villagers, whom they needed for the large burying job they were about to carry out. Then, on April 21, after the humanitarian workers were forbidden to come, they hit the camps. Humanitarian workers were not allowed back in until the 25th, and by that time the camps were totally empty. There had been about 85,000 people between Kasese 1, Kasese 2, and Biaro camps.[192]

Reports of these abominable events were filtering out, but only weakly.[193] Belgian Secretary of State for Cooperation Reginald Moreels gave an interview in which he talked about the massacres, but without giving sufficient detail.[194] There seemed to be a great reluctance (Bradol's "Bermuda Triangle of politics") at officially condemning what the RPA-Alliance forces were doing for a variety of reasons: first, as Patrick Mazimpaka had pointed out, the West was relieved that the blocked refugee situation was finally "taken care of," albeit in atrocious fashion; second, given the fact that the refugee problem was in itself a product of the 1994 horror, there seems to have been an unspoken compact among the various Western actors[195] not to prevent the Rwandese from carrying out their revenge since it was the West's lack of reaction during the genocide that had made it possible in the first place. But this compact was not universal, and some elements of the international community were trying to react, albeit in a state of complete and contradictory disarray.[196] The first so-called Garreton Report on the human rights situation in Zaire was a step in the right direction,[197] but it caused violent protests from the Alliance-Rwandese forces, which did not appreciate its severe judgment. The situation became even more conflictual when Garreton was sent back to Zaire in April as the situation was worsening. He flew to Kigali only to be refused entry by the AFDL for being "partial." He was not able to carry out his mission and had to fly back to New York after hearing what he could from those who dared to approach him. Still, some of his conclusions can stand for the whole horrible episode:

One cannot of course ignore the presence of persons guilty of genocide, soldiers and militia members, among the refugees… . It is nevertheless unacceptable to claim that more than one million people, including large numbers of children, should be collectively designated as persons guilty of genocide and liable to execution without trial… . The accounts heard or read by the mission show that most of the acts of violence attributed to AFDL were carried out against refugees inside the camps.... . Very often the targets were neither *Interahamwe* combatants nor soldiers of the former FAR. They were women, children, the wounded, the sick, the dying and the elderly, and the attacks seem to have had no precise military objective. Often the massacres were carried out after the militia members and former FAR soldiers had begun to retreat.[198]

This Rwandese tragedy played out in the Congo was going to have grave diplomatic consequences for Laurent-Désiré Kabila after he finally assumed power. But before closing off the topic, I have one last remark about the casualty figures, which have been such a bone of contention. In its final tally of the situation the UNHCR decided on the following figures:[199]

Number of Rwandese refugees in eastern Zaire (Sept. 1996):		1,100,000
Repatriations from eastern Zaire:	Spontaneous:	600,000
	By land:	180,000
	By air:	54,000
	Total:	834,000
Refugees located in Angola:		2,500
	In Congo-Brazzaville:	20,000
	In the Central African Republic:	3,800
	Total:	26,300
Refugees remaining in Zaire:		26,300
Total refugees location unknown:		213,400

Over 200,000 refugees had thus officially disappeared. But even this already large figure rests on the assumption that there were really 600,000 returnees in November 1996. And as we have seen, that is likely to have been an optimistic evaluation. So if we consider the fact that UNHCR admits to another 35,500 Burundian refugees with a "location unknown" status, which is a polite way of saying they are dead, and if we take into account the very probable exaggeration of returnee numbers, the total refugee death toll should be considered to be around 300,000, an estimate that UNHCR High Commissioner Ogata considered possible.[200]

5

LOSING THE REAL PEACE
(MAY 1997–AUGUST 1998)[1]

Kabila in power: a secretive and incoherent leadership

Laurent-Désiré Kabila arrived in Kinshasa almost stealthily on May 20, 1997, and he was not seen publicly till his swearing in ceremony nine days later. This bizarre behavior corresponded to something all parties involved in the problems of the new Congo were soon going to realize: the new president was a political Rip van Winkle whose conspiratorial political style had been frozen at some point back in the 1960s and who still lived in a world seen strategically as a deadly struggle against imperialism and tactically as a mixture of conspiracies and informal economics. This was going to be painfully obvious in the way he picked his cabinet, "bypassing both the country's impressive civil society and the squad of opposition politicians led by Etienne Tschisekedi."[2]

There were two main problems with the cabinet President Kabila announced on July 1, 1997: its heterogeneity and its diaspora origins. The minister of the interior, Mwenze Kongolo, was an "ANACOZA recruit" who had moved from a minor legal job in the United States;[3] Raphael Ghenda, now minister of information and cultural affairs, was an ultraleftist admirer of Kim Il Sung who had spent the past thirty years in exile in France and Belgium; Justine Kasa Vubu, daughter of Congo's first president and minister for the civil service, was a UDPS activist who had been living in exile in Algeria, Switzerland, and finally Belgium for the past thirteen years; Bizima Karaha, the minister of foreign affairs, had lived and worked as a medical doctor in South Africa; the chief of staff and future successor, Abdoulaye Yerodia Ndombasi, was said to be a "Lacanian psychoanalyst" who had been living in Paris;[4] Etienne Mbaya, minister of national reconstruction, had spent years living in precarious exile in Germany; Mawampanga Mwana Nanga, the new minister of finance, was another ANACOZA recruit from the United States, where he taught agricultural economics. Over half of the cabinet members came from the diaspora and represented a bewildering array of personal and professional experiences which precluded any possible idea of teamwork. And it was the same thing for the various advisers, who, without being officially in power, often had more power than the ministers themselves. These were Moïse Nyarugabo, Kabila's Munyamulenge personal secretary; Aubert Mukendi, a Muluba from Kasai who was his chief of staff and quasi–prime minister; the AFDL's official boss, Déogratias Bugera; and *primus inter pares* Paul Kabongo, head of the new Agence Nationale de Renseignements (ANR), a sort of reincarnation of the Mobutist SNIP. Kabongo, whose last known occupation was as a bar owner in a Madrid suburb, had no special qualifications apart from being a personal friend of the new president. But for a while he was the only one who had permanent access to Kabila, day or night, and he did not refrain from making everybody understand that he was on top of it all. Then, on August 21, without any warning, he was jailed and lost all his mysterious influence. There was going to be more and more of the same style of leadership, especially at the level of the military. For the first few months there was no minister of defense, no known chief of staff, and no ranks; all officers were Cuban-style "commanders" called "Ignace," "Bosco," "Jonathan," or "James," who occupied connecting suites at the Intercontinental Hotel and had presidential list cell-phone numbers. None spoke French or Lingala, but all spoke Kinyarwanda, Swahili, and, quite often, English. Twenty-seven-year-old Anselme Masasu Nindaga, who called himself a "general," told anybody who cared to listen that *he* was the army boss; nobody contradicted him until he also was jailed in November, after which President Kabila said that he had never been chief of anything and that he was "only a former Rwandese Army corporal" anyway. When the Belgian journalist Colette Braeckman asked Kabila what was the actual army command structure apart from himself he answered, "We are not going to expose ourselves and risk being destroyed by showing ourselves openly.... We are careful so that the true masters of the army are not known. It is strategic. Please, let us drop the matter."[5] This only contributed to further fueling the rumors of Rwandese control over the Congolese armed forces. Government business was transacted in an atmosphere of permanent improvisation "verging on anarchy,"[6] whether at home or abroad. On a state visit to Tanzania President Kabila simply decided in the midst of his trip that he had more important things to do in Kinshasa, picked up the phone, talked to President Mkapa, and drove to the airport, leaving his hosts in total confusion. Shortly after, he told former president Nyerere that he needed to see him and that he would come and visit him at his home village in Butiama. Then he called and said he had flown instead to Bujumbura, then under an embargo, and that he had just thought he could mediate between President Buyoya and the rest of the region. It was a comment that Nyerere, who had just initiated the Arusha peace process and had arranged for a special mediator, did not really appreciate. Kabila also stood up President Mubarak, who was waiting for him at Cairo Airport in late February 1998 with a red carpet and a guard of honor, simply phoning him two days later to say that "he had been feeling tired." Everything seemed arbitrary. A young French doctor who spent several weeks in detention[7] later said that anybody could be jailed under the most bizarre pretexts and be brutally treated, like the foreign minister's chief of staff, who was brought into detention during the doctor's stay and was severely whipped: "People were denouncing each other from Ministry to Ministry, between one service and another, from office to office. Anything could land you in jail, from an accusation of conspiracy to some bit of black marketing."[8]

Contrary to what often happens in Africa, the problem at first was not the new government's ethnopolitical balance, which was reasonable enough, even if the Equateur Province was understandably largely absent.[9] The problem was that Kabila kept promising the same thing to different people and giving contradictory answers to the same question asked at different times. He also had multiple "special advisers" who all thought they had direct access to the chief. He seemed to think that pitting these various men (and the groups they represented) against each other would enable him to remain in full control of what one hesitates to call "the state apparatus." But most of the time these convoluted ploys, which were a direct inheritance from his old conspiracy days,[10] only resulted in confusion, sterile infighting, and paralysis. As a result, "ethnic problems" soon developed because the Kasaians were played against the Katangese, the Balubakat against the Lunda, and the Tutsi against all the others.[11]

Thus in September 1997 Emile Ilunga, who with Deogratias Symba had been one of the key actors in swinging support from the Gendarmes Katangais behind the AFDL in late 1996, blasted the new regime:

151

Four hundred of our men have been arrested in Lubumbashi with General Delphin Muland, and detained upon orders of the Rwandese.... Confusion prevails.... Masasu says he is Commander-in-Chief: where is the decree? Mawampanga is arrested and then rehabilitated: where are the official documents?[12] Everything is done orally. What is Kakudji doing at Gécamines?[13] Kabila has no coherent political project and the recent fighting in Kivu is a result.[14] If we have to use revolutionary means to change that situation, we are ready for it.[15]

In fact, the Tigers swallowed their pride and did not do anything and General Muland was eventually freed from jail on November.[16] The key to that erratic situation was the almost complete lack of institutionalization, which turned every conflict of competence into a personality conflict and then into an ethnic one.

Apart from a blurry populist and "anti-imperialist" stance that never quite seemed to find ways of expressing itself beyond mere denunciations, Kabila seems to have had only the vaguest notions of what he actually intended to do after overthrowing Mobutu.

Interviewer: What model of democracy do you see as suitable?

Kabila: I cannot say now, you are asking too much. Being a head of state is not like being in a restaurant. I have to have time to think about it.[17]

One of the key struggles in the installation period of the new regime concerned the place of the AFDL as an organization. Deogratias Bugera and his Rwandese backers were pushing for a one-party state because they knew that in the Congo, unlike in Rwanda, they could never manage to contain the existing opposition parties. Aubert Mukendi and a number of other people around "Mzee"[18] were pushing for a fully multiparty system, albeit with some controlling devices to avoid the Mobutu-induced "party anarchy" of the CNS period. Kabila fluttered between the two, seeming at first to encourage the one-party approach,[19] but then slowly downgrading the importance of the AFDL, until he finally sacked Bugera in June 1998, replacing him with the much tamer Vincent Mutomb Tshibal.[20]

The single-party question was linked to the all-important point of deciding on how to deal with the long-standing nonviolent anti-Mobutu opposition. From that point of view the Ugandans had given Kabila totally different advice from that of the Rwandese. As early as May 1997 they had told the old conspirator that he would be well advised to follow the example they had set in January 1986, after they took power, and to create a "broad-based government" in which all moderate opponents would be invited to take part. Then he could always secure the system by keeping a politically and tribally safe hub at the center of that liberal wheel. "Unfortunately that fool did just about the opposite," complained one of his former interlocutors.[21] President Museveni was appalled at the crude way Kabila treated the old anti-Mobutu opposition, declaring publicly, "He should include opponents in his cabinet. Not doing it is a mistake. I don't know what he is afraid of."[22] The Ugandan leader knew from experience that political inclusion was the best way of sterilizing opponents and pleasing the Western donors at the same time. In comparison to Mobutu, Kabila was a soft dictator, but his clumsy defiance managed to both irk the donors and spur his opponents into more virulent action at a time when he could hardly afford to choose such a path of confrontation.

The first arrests in mid-June 1997 could pass as a post-Mobutu cleanup operation since they mostly concerned former ministers, bankers, and managing directors of state enterprises. But the old anti-Mobutu human rights organization AZADHO immediately understood and denounced a "downward drift into totalitarianism coupled with an indifference to the summary justice meted out by AFDL forces."[23] Foreigners were hoping things would turn out all right. Acting U.S. Assistant Secretary of State for African Affairs William Twaddell spoke about his country's "critical engagement," and European Union representative Jacques Poos put on a brave face, declaring, "Kabila has a firm will to base the future of the Congo on the same values as ours: democracy, respect for human rights and building a legal state."[24] The old rebel Antoine Gizenga and his Parti Lumumbiste d'Action Unifié were the first ones to test the political waters by organizing a small-scale demonstration on July 25; the police opened fire, three demonstrators were killed, and fifty-four were arrested.[25]

Security services were among the first institutions the new regime paid attention to, and it quickly became obvious that the ANR was the new SNIP and that Direction Militaire des Activités Anti-Patrie (DEMIAP) had replaced the old Service d'Action et de Renseignement Militaire.[26] The repressive spirit remained. Political arrests began to multiply for the most varied reasons, running from the ordinary (Arthur Z'Ahidi Ngoma and Joseph Olenghankoy simply for being politically active) to the conspiratorial ("Commander" Masasu Nindaga after a shootout we will come back to). The final test was Tshisekedi himself, who had declared that he would defy the ban on open political activity. He was arrested in January 1998, on the anniversary of Lumumba's death,[27] and later relegated to his village in Kasai. By early 1998 an Amnesty International report could already display an impressive roster of political prisoners and denial of basic liberties.[28] To look tough and impress a new respect for law and order on the population, the regime also organized batches of collective public executions by firing squad.[29]

All in all the results were mixed. Most people were still grateful for the overthrow of Mobutu, even if they would have liked a more democratic approach to the transition. Confusion was perhaps expected, but the brutal authoritarianism created fear. This ambivalence was obvious in a series of opinion polls that were taken in early 1998 in the major Congolese cities. They showed that in case of a presidential election Kabila would definitely win over Tshisekedi, even if by a limited margin (33 percent of the vote in a first round against 20 percent). But they also showed that at the legislative level the UDPS would beat the AFDL with about 35 percent of the vote to 14 percent for Kabila's party.[30] In July Kabila "unbanned" Tshisekedi and allowed him to come back to Kinshasa.[31] Two days later the old "Lion of Limete" agreed to collaborate with the new regime. But in typical Kabila fashion, several of his aides were immediately put under arrest when they became a bit too active.

As for the international community, it sort of grumbled at the internal civil liberties and human rights violations, but it might have tolerated a certain amount of them had it not been for a more burning issue.[32] What really set it in a face-to-face duel with the new regime was the unresolved question of the fate of the Rwandese refugees.

Diplomacy and the refugee issue

To understand the incredible year-long trial of strength between the United Nations and the Kabila government over the Rwandese refugee issue, one has first to keep in mind what the toppling of Mobutu meant for Africa and how it came about. The fall of Mobutu was the wiping out of a fundamental blot of shame on the whole continent, the revenge on a feeling of permanent humiliation that had lasted for over thirty years. The man once described by a French diplomat as "a walking bank account with a leopard cap" had long embodied all that Africa felt was wrong in its relationship with the rest of the world: humiliation, toadying to the "imperialists," corruption, vulgarity, and violence coupled with powerlessness. The Alliance had been the hollow point of an Africa-wide bullet rather than a purely Congolese phenomenon.

In late 1996 it was Kabila who had cold feet about venturing west and it was the Alliance's foreign backers who had nudged him on.[33] The impetus, as we have seen, came mostly from Rwanda, which wanted a "final solution" to the problem of the Rwandese refugees, and from Uganda, which had decided that its undeclared war with Sudan would be solved laterally by doing battle in Zaire. But it also came, in a less obvious fashion, from the states of Africa's southern cone—Zimbabwe, South Africa, Namibia, and Angola—who still smarted at the memory of Mobutu's alliance with the CIA to support the FNLA against the MPLA, SWAPO, and the ANC. The former "front-line states" (Zimbabwe, Zambia, Tanzania) still saw in Mobutu the man ushered into and kept in power by Washington, right-wing white mercenaries, France, Belgium, Saudi Arabia, and the king of Morocco in order to bolster the South African apartheid regime.[34] Even if they now had the blessing of America's New World Order, all the African heads of states supporting the Alliance were old leftist sympathizers. From Nelson Mandela to Yoweri Museveni and from Robert Mugabe to Issayas Afeworki, *all of them* had sympathized with Moscow, Havana, or Beijing at some point in their career. Overthrowing the imperialist puppet was their triumph. On May 18, 1997, Thabo Mbeki made sure that he was the first African leader to fly into Kinshasa to congratulate Kabila on the downfall of "that man who stank."[35] In distant Kampala an opposition paper quoted approvingly one government member, Amanya Mushega, when he said in a speech, "The Great Lakes have been chosen by God to launch the struggle against the modern oppressive regimes of Africa.... . The current liberation crusade started in the bushes and caves of Luwero in Uganda."[36] The government paper printed a cartoon showing one member of Parliament telling another, "Kabila is using our [presidential] jet? I am going to query this!" while the other answered, "You don't have to: this is *kulembeka* in progress."[37] *Kulembeka,* meaning "our task, our duty." Removing Mobutu was Africa's *kulembeka.*

Of course, all noble historical tasks have a less noble underside. In 1995 Uganda exported $23 million in gold, mostly from its small mine in Kaabong. But in 1996 the figure climbed to $60 million and then to $105 million in 1997, an increase directly related to gold from the Congo, some given by Kabila and some bought cheaply from the local diggers. Meanwhile, in early 1997 the Rwandese Embassy in Brussels was trying to sell thirty-two tons of papain, a chemical produced exclusively in the Congo.[38] Then there were those monies transferred by the MIBA to the treasuries of Rwanda, Uganda, and others after the war.[39]

These were secondary aspects, the economics of the dream, so to speak; they did not really matter. But the question of the refugees was something else: it involved ethics and politics, seen from diametrically opposing points of view. Once Mobutu was gone, why did the international community keep trying to find out what had actually happened to the Hutu refugees during their headlong flight from the camps? It was perceived as disingenuous imperialist political nit-picking. This position was perfectly summed up by General Kagame when he told a sympathetic American journalist:

These are politically-motivated allegations, even at the highest levels of the international community. They are terribly wrong . . . in fact I think we should start accusing those people who supported those camps, spent one million dollars per day, supporting these groups who rebuilt themselves into a force of militarised refugees... . This is the guilt they are trying to fight off [by accusing us], this is something they are trying to deflect. [The victory of the pan-African alliance in the Congo has constituted a defeat for the international community, writes the author.] "They have not determined the outcome so this is something they cannot stomach... . Kabila emerges, the Alliance emerges, something changes, Mobutu goes, things happen, the region is happy about what is happening . . . and everything takes them by surprise. They are extremely annoyed by that and they can't take it.[40]

From Kagame's point of view, the international community, which had let 800,000 Tutsi who were under its care get slaughtered without lifting a finger, did not have the moral right to ask too many questions. And if it insisted, then it was being "political."[41]

But insist it did, and with obstinacy. The ambiguity of the situation was well perceived by Julius Nyerere, who, as both the father of the whole crusade and the continent's elder statesman, could see both sides of the story.[42] While in New York shortly after the war he said that Kabila "should not be pushed too hard" and that the West should not "demonise him, making him responsible for the crimes of others."[43] Which was both a way to admit that crimes had indeed been committed and that Kabila was probably not the principal perpetrator. But the Congolese president was caught on the horns of a dilemma well summed up by Colette Braeckman:

His was an impossible position: either he had to admit that at the time of the events he had no control over his army and then look like an absolute puppet; or else he had to shoulder the responsibility and run the risk of being accused of crimes against humanity, even perhaps of genocide.[44]

This was the moment Kagame chose to candidly admit what he had been denying indignantly less than five months before: that it was the Rwandese army that led the war.[45] This was perfect timing. Now impaled on one horn of the dilemma, the most humiliating one, Kabila chose to shake himself free and immediately impaled himself on the other horn by hotly claiming to have been in full control during the war.[46] Now there was no way he could unload the responsibility on Rwanda. Some of the Americans, especially in the State Department, started to feel a bit queasy. After Kabila declared in Windhoek that the UN Commission of Inquiry was a "French-inspired smear campaign," Acting Assistant Secretary for African Affairs Twaddell retorted,

The United States has a clear stake in the policy decisions taken by the new leadership in the Congo.... U.S.-Congolese relations will depend on progress in creating a broad-based transitional government, respect for human rights and co-operation with the UN-led probe into the alleged massacres.[47]

In fact the massacres had not stopped with the end of the war. During May there were more killings, in Mbandaka and around Biaro.[48] Small groups of stragglers were by now trying to make it back to Rwanda, or at least to a place where the media and humanitarian workers would guarantee their safety. At times this was not enough; at Shabunda a group of five hundred refugees were wiped out on August 14, *after* they had made contact with UNHCR, which could not protect them.[49] By then the AFDL had discreetly changed tack and was trying to catch up with the refugees still floating around. The aim was to protect them from the Rwandese, but it soon turned into something more ambiguous because there were ex-FAR and *Interahamwe* among the civilian refugees, and they offered the only thing they had left in exchange for their life: their fighting capacity. Thus by late 1997, Kabila slowly started mixing the safety of civilians with the recruitment of soldiers.[50]

The first UN investigation mission, led by Roberto Garreton in January 1997, resulted in a searing report Kigali did not appreciate at all. When Garreton went back with another mission in May he was blocked in Kigali by the Rwandese government and, unable to get to the field, eventually flew back to New York. This was the beginning of an incredible saga, wherein a Rwanda-controlled Kinshasa government stubbornly tried by all means, fair or foul, to block any further investigation into the fate of the refugees.[51]

157

On July 8 the UN agreed to a new commission without Garreton, a condition that was denounced by several NGOs as unethical, especially since an independent observer, Dr. Guy Mérineau from Médecins du Monde, had published almost simultaneously a whole page of eyewitness accounts of the massacres in a Paris newspaper.[52] Reconstruction Minister Etienne Mbaya first denied that the Garreton Report contained any truth and then accused France of "trying to destabilise our government."[53] Then, in a move fully coherent with the "*kulembeka* African Crusade" spirit described above, a number of African heads of state met in Kinshasa and issued a communiqué in support of the new Congolese regime. They said, among other things:

That there was a "persistent misinformation campaign against the DRC" (point 2).

That a commission of inquiry was fine, but that its mandate should start in 1993 (point 6).

That they totally and unequivocally supported the DRC government (point 7).

That they commended Kabila's "tireless efforts to restore order in the region" (point 10).

Under the presidency of "Comrade" Robert Mugabe,[54] then OAU chairman, the meeting was attended by the presidents of Zimbabwe, Uganda, Zambia, the DRC, Mozambique, Namibia, Ethiopia, Eritrea, the Central African Republic, and Rwanda. This was to be the last concerted effort by the regional leaders to block the inquiry. It also fitted briefly into the framework of analysis that saw in this concerted effort a continuation of the anti-Mobutu crusade, marking the emergence of "New African Leaders" under U.S. supervision.[55]

Reality soon reasserted itself in the shape of a new massacre when 833 people were killed by AFDL forces in the small fishing villages of Wimbi, Alela, Abanga, and Talama on the shores of Lake Tanganyika.[56] The victims were a mix of refugees and the local people who had given them shelter. This occurred shortly after Gen. Ndenga wa Milumba, the new 4th Brigade commander in charge of the Kivus and Maniema, declared, "There should be no prison for bandits, only public firing squads." His men had perhaps taken his words a bit too literally. Then 105 "new refugees," mostly Congolese with some Rwandese, managed to cross the lake and arrive at Kigoma. On August 27 the Congolese human rights organization AZADHO denounced the arrest of Robert Lukando, an eyewitness to some of the massacres who had been detained in Kindu as he was trying to make contact with a humanitarian organization.

By then the situation had turned into a regular diplomatic war: Secretary-General Kofi Annan named Ambassador Mohamed Sahnoun special envoy and sent him to Kinshasa after the Congolese government recused the new head of the commission, Kofi Amega, because he was Togolese and Togo "had had close relations with Mobutu."[57] After Sahnoun's arrival the commission got the go-ahead from the government, but UNHCR High Commissioner Sadako Ogata decided to withdraw from the DRC "in view of the complete disregard of international humanitarian norms in the handling of the remaining Rwandese refugees."[58] The next day Kagame's personal secretary, Emmanuel Ndahiro, commented that Ogata had "imaginary notions about the whole thing."[59] Kofi Annan then denied that he was "soft on Kabila," acknowledged that the commission's work was "not smooth sailing," but asked for "patience for a regime that is trying to take over in a country that has more or less collapsed."[60] The commission then gave an ultimatum to the government about letting it do its work, which drove Kabila to lash out at "western plots in the guise of humanitarian action."[61] The journalist Scott Campbell, who had managed to get to some of the former refugee camps, wrote, "The bones are still visible on the massacre sites but they are now being burned to hide the evidence."[62]

There was a strange duality of purpose within the mythical "international community." At about this same time I attended a UN meeting in New York (September 26–27) where people were wondering how to get regular cooperation restarted in the DRC in spite of the refugee business. Sir Kieran Prendergast, the representative of the secretary-general, even said with a note of anguish in his voice, "We are in a box. I ask you as experts: How can we get out of the box?" We could not, but it was interesting to see that the fate of the refugees was of concern to *some members* of the international community, whereas for many others the main worry seemed to be about how business as usual could be reinstated. The whole background of the genocide and its impact on the Kivus, which was repeatedly brought back into the discussion by Jacques Depelchin, the future leader of the Rassemblement Congolais pour la Démocratie (RCD), did not seem to register on the UN personnel, who appeared embarrassed by such painful and complicated considerations.

But business as usual could not work anymore in this situation, which was perfectly summed up by a headline in the *Economist:* "Kabila Sends a

Message to the World: Buzz Off!"[63] The *Washington Post* was even more explicit, asking in an editorial, "Will Congo self-destruct?"[64] The question was pertinent because the issue of the refugees loomed more and more menacingly over the proposed "Friends of the Congo" meeting, which was scheduled for early December with a view to restarting some kind of sorely needed economic cooperation. Some of Kinshasa's friends had creative ideas about getting out of Sir Kieran's "box." When French Minister of Foreign Affairs Hubert Védrine went to South Africa, his counterpart there, Alfred Nzo, started their meeting by simply denying that there had been any massacres at all, but when Thabo Mbeki said that "it was not possible to simply reject the inquiry without alienating the donors," this led one of his aides to suggest that it would perhaps be possible "to dilute their massacres into all the other massacres which have taken place in the region."[65] This was easier said than done with Kabila, who kept vociferating that the massacre eyewitnesses had been "manipulated," that all opposition politicians (including Etienne Tshisekedi) were "agents of Mobutu," and that the NGOs were guilty of "politicisation and smuggling."[66] A new UN mission finally got going and arrived at Mbandaka, only to find that there was no food or lodging.[67] Soon large "spontaneous" demonstrations forced them to flee for their own safety.[68] The UN still did not give up and sent another mission, only to find freshly emptied mass graves and more demonstrations, in which the local people accused the UN staff of having "desecrated the graves of our ancestors." Some of the witnesses who came forward to talk to them were immediately arrested.[69]

By then everybody was tired of the game and serious trouble began to develop.[70] The Friends of the Congo meeting in December had of course ended in failure, and the Americans were getting impatient with their loose cannon, the "New Leader." When President Clinton went to Africa on his grand diplomatic tour of the continent in March 1998 he decided not to go to Kinshasa but instead called President Kabila to a meeting in Entebbe. There he officially told him, "You have to help us help you."[71] He actually took Kabila aside and said, "We are fed up. You have six months to free the opposition politicians, stop harassing the civil society, NGOs, and the press and curb your army. If you fail to do that, in six months we drop you flat."[72] He did not even mention the refugee inquiry, which by now everybody had given up for lost. Kabila verbally acquiesced, although he never acted on his promises. The UN made one last try and sent another mission to Goma. Congolese police immediately arrested a Canadian UN staff member, searched his luggage, and briefly detained him. In spite of New York's furor, the U.S. State Department still intervened on Kabila's behalf and asked the UN to please not drop the inquiry and the Congo with it.[73] But this was going to be the last time. The UN did withdraw, and on June 30 it released a very severe report which was described by Kigali as "emotive and lacking in credibility," while the DRC ambassador in New York called it "a collection of unfounded allegations" and Kabila more simply "a pure fabrication."[74] He had won the battle, but he had lost the peace. The economy was in shambles, and new storm clouds were rising in the east.

The economy: an ineffectual attempt at normalization

The economic situation the AFDL government inherited from the Mobutu regime was catastrophic. The real downward spiral had started around 1990, when a combination of low copper prices and growing political and administrative confusion pushed up costs and reduced revenue. From sickly, the Zairian economy turned terminal. In a fertile country like Zaire people could still eat, but even agricultural production was stagnant because of an almost complete lack of investment in transport, fertilizer, pesticides, or even simple tools. With a population growing at 3 percent per year, per capita food production entered into a slow decline in the mid-1980s: because the cropping area had remained stable at around 7.8 million hectares, as had the production technique, the output remained stagnant for a rapidly expanding population. In ten years (1985–1995) per capita food production diminished by over 10 percent. Agricultural exports had declined only moderately until around 1992, but a negative price evolution had drastically reduced their value. And then, after 1992, commercial agriculture moved the same way as the mining and manufacturing sectors: sharply downward. Coffee production went from 92,000 tons in 1988 to 56,000 in 1996, palm oil production declined from 95,000 tons to 18,000 during the same period, and rubber practically disappeared. The mining and manufacturing situation was even worse, given the dependency of these sectors on imported spare parts and equipment. Copper production went from 506,000 tons in 1988 to around 38,000 in 1996, MIBA industrial diamond production fell from about 10 million carats in 1986 to 6.5 million in 1996, and cobalt went from 10,000 tons in 1988 to less than 4,000 tons in 1996. The effects on the balance of trade were drastic, with revenues dropping from about $1.3 billion in 1990 to $176 million in 1994. Because imports remained at a fairly high level for some time while exports declined, the external debt had risen to $12.8 billion by 1996, representing 233 percent of GDP, or 924 percent of the export capacity. Debt service was not paid and arrears had risen to over $800 million. Zaire had been suspended from the IMF in 1992 and never reinstated. The result was an almost complete collapse of the state financial capacity, with public revenue falling from 17 percent of GDP in the 1960s to less than 5 percent in 1996. Not having any more money the state practically stopped spending, and public investment in infrastructure fell to about 1 percent of GDP.[75]

Perhaps the most preoccupying effect of this collapse was the quasi-disappearance of the monetary system. With an inflation rate that the IMF calculated at an average 2,000 percent during most of the 1990s, prices shot up in an insane way.

Evolution of the Consumer Price Index (1990 = 100)

1988	1989	1990	1991	1992	1993
27	55	100	2,154	4,130	1,989,738

Source: Economist Intelligence Unit, *Zaire Country Report 1994*, 17.

The government started to print money as fast as it could, simply to keep a certain amount of fiduciary current irrigating the economy. Bills were printed in ever higher denominations and put into circulation as fast as possible, and their rapidly shrinking real purchasing value would then wipe them off the market in a way that made even the German hyperinflation of the 1920s look mild.

Currency Life Cycle

Bill Denomination (Zaire)	U.S. Dollar Equivalent	Life Duration (months)[76]
10,000	22.00	30
50,000	12.10	19
100,000	1.00	15
200,000	1.30	17
500,000	3.18	17
1,000,000	1.12	13[1].

Source: Hughes Leclerq, "Commentaire sur la situation économique récente de la RDC et ses implications pour la politique d'aide internationale," paper prepared for the UN Congo Expert Group Meeting, New York, May 1–3, 1998.

In December 1992 the system finally imploded: the Z 5 million bill was refused by everybody and had a zero life span. The government then tried to force it through by paying soldiers' salaries with the new currency, but the army rioted when its money was refused in the shops. In 1993 the government demonetized the old Zaire bills and introduced the "New Zaire." The result split the monetary system in two because Kasai refused the new currency and kept using the old one, which regained a certain value simply by not being printed anymore. But by 1994 the modern sector was operating entirely with foreign currencies, mostly U.S. dollars, which were either used directly in bills or held in special accounts in Zairian banks. This created a third fiduciary zone linked with international money transfers. As a result the actual total value of the money in private circulation within the country kept shrinking because foreign currency circulation was negligible inside.

Total Amount of Fiduciary Circulation (in U.S. $ millions)

Year	Value of Circulating Cash	Value of Bank Deposits	Total
1974	365	521	886
1989	337	260	597
1990	310	200	510
1993	127	blocked	127
1996	93	12	105

Source: Hughes Leclerq, "Commentaire sur la situation économique récente de la RDC et ses implications pour la politique d'aide internationale," paper prepared for the UN Congo Expert Group Meeting, New York, May 1–3, 1998.

The result of this evolution was the slow destruction of the monetary sector of the economy, pushing the whole economic system back to self-subsistence supplemented by barter. Paid employment shrank.

Paid Employment Evolution (in millions of people)

	1974	1989	1995
Total population	21.20	36.10	43.80
Active population	10.30	18.40	22.40
Population in paid employment	1.45	1.12	1.00
Ratio (in %)	14.10	6.10	4.50

Source: Prof. Hughes Leclerq, "Commentaire sur la situation économique récente de la RDC et ses implications pour la politique d'aide internationale," paper prepared for the UN Congo Expert Group Meeting, New York, May 1–3, 1998.

In plain language, the Zairian economy reverted to its precolonial, premonetary existence, but with three major differences. First, the precolonial economy had been a complex affair in which purely economic matters were intimately mixed with ritual, religion, social prestige, and cultural exchanges.

These rich precolonial complexities were by now largely dead. Second, the precolonial economy had served a population of probably fewer than ten million, whereas by 2000 there would be over fifty million Congolese. Third, the precolonial economy had operated as a system of peasant autarky supplemented by limited regional trade mostly made up of nonessentials. By now the people had been taught to expect that they could purchase a number of products and services from a circuit of commercial exchanges; thus the shrinking of the money economy turned what had been dignified scarcity into humiliating grinding poverty. The social consequences were enormous. Growing numbers of young people expecting to take part in the worldwide revolution of rising expectations were in fact forced down into a return to an autarkic economy now devoid of any cultural justification or prestige. Many understandably refused to accept it and gladly turned to soldiering when that option was offered. In late 1996 in the Kivus Kabila had no problem recruiting his *kadogo*. The only limit to enrollment was the available number of AK-47s. Later warlords were to be in the same position.

Faced with that disastrous situation and with the necessity of restarting the foreign aid flow, what was the AFDL government going to do? The first economic initiative was the proposals made for the Friends of the Congo December 1997 meeting in Brussels, the so-called Economic Stabilization and Recovery Program. There were three major objectives:

1. Macroeconomic stabilization, meaning an end to inflation, renewed tax collection, control of public expenditure, and rebuilding the practically dead banking system.

2. Rehabilitation of the transport and energy infrastructures.

3. Reversing the trend in the destruction of human capital by rebuilding the health and education sectors, demobilizing part of the army, and retraining a slimmed-down civil service.[77]

It was supposed to be a twelve-month program amounting to $1.6 billion, with the foreign donors putting up $575 million.[78] But the Friends of the Congo meeting was torpedoed by the refugee issue, and Finance Minister Mawampanga Mwana Nanga, who had prepared the whole plan, was demoted to minister of agriculture in January 1998.

The second initiative was potentially much more ambitious and far-reaching. It was the preparation of a National Conference on Reconstruction, at the behest of Reconstruction Minister Etienne Mbaya. It was supposed to be a sort of national economic forum, with over six hundred delegates from throughout the country coming to debate their needs and priorities. But both Kabila and his Rwandese minders started to panic at the idea, realizing that this would probably turn into a form of national conference where all grievances would be aired, including many noneconomic ones such as the lack of freedom and the overbearing presence of the Rwandese ringmasters.[79] The exercise was canceled, and the Ministry of Reconstruction was suppressed during the January 1998 cabinet reshuffle. Etienne Mbaya became the minister of planning, but there was nothing left for him to plan.

He tried anyway and launched a third initiative, called the Three-Year Minimum Program for nine priority areas: transport, agriculture, energy, mining, industry, health, education, security, and justice. The Ministry of Planning was supposed to identify the needs in all those areas, define investment strategies, and then find ways of financing them. The whole exercise was estimated at around $4 billion over three years. It was mostly a wish list, and with the ongoing fight about the Refugee Commission of Inquiry, it did not even begin to get off the ground.

Then, with some World Bank prodding, the government started a fourth project: to identify areas of possible private investment in the DRC. This must have been some kind of joke. Given the general economic, diplomatic, and political situation, only the wildest or the most inexperienced private companies would dare to put any money into the Congo.

To say the least, investors received little encouragement. The first mistake of the AFDL was to nationalize the Sizarail company as soon as they took Lubumbashi in April 1997. Sizarail was a South African–Zairian joint venture created in 1995 to run the railways in the south and east of the country. In August Sizarail's Belgian managing director, Patrick Claes, was arrested; this absurd move poisoned the AFDL's relations with Pretoria for many months at a time when the new government needed all the goodwill it could get.[80] And there were other acts of arbitrariness: AFDL "commanders" had commandeered the best houses belonging to the Mobutu elite, grabbed the cars, and were camping at the Intercontinental Hotel, where their unpaid bills had reached $8 million within a month of their taking Kinshasa.[81] All operations were done in cash, which at times was disbursed (in large quantities) to very bizarre recipients. When Presidential Chief of Staff Aubert Mukendi asked the famous singer Tshala Mwana the reason for the payment he was supposed to make to her, she burst out laughing and answered, "I give very special night concerts for the Chief and that is a very expensive service." Mukendi grumbled, but the money was disbursed.[82]

165

Before the end of 1997 the general impression of the populace in Kinshasa was that the new regime was slowly slipping into the bad old habits of the former elite, but on a much reduced scale because there was much less that could be taken.[83]

In the absence of aid blocked by the conflict over the UN Commission of Inquiry the government's financial situation was desperate. The two successive finance ministers, Mawampanga Mwana Nanga and then Fernand Tala Ngai, tried to negotiate the foreign debt situation so that at least new arrears in reimbursement would not continue to accumulate. The new Central Bank director, Jean-Claude Masangu Mulongo, was a U.S.-trained financier of impeccable orthodoxy who quickly managed to arrest inflation.

The U.S. dollar had fallen from NZ 180,000 to NZ 115,000 between May and July, and it kept going lower.[84] The failed Friends of the Congo meeting had left the DRC with the consolation prize of a "trust fund," to which U.S. Secretary of State Madeleine Albright had pledged $40 million, with another $85 million promised by the European Union.[85] This was woefully inadequate for a state in which the administration's cash flow had been reduced to the monthly $10 million paid by the Zimbabwean government or to small irregular payments made by Namibia.[86] Between March and July 1998 Finance Minister Fernand Tala Ngai kept playing a kind of hide-and-seek game with IMF President Michel Camdessus to try to unlock Congo's drawing rights without actually repaying accumulated arrears, and he eventually lost. The first semester of 1998 had brought only $65 million in foreign exchange,[87] while incompressible expenses amounted to $88.4 million. The government was reduced to paying pressing expenses directly with cash and to fiddle with diamond counter regulations for hand-to-mouth survival.[88] The banking system was dying and bankruptcy was looming. Kabila, who simply kept asking for an outright cancellation of the Congolese foreign debt, did not seem to realize that his defiant attitude toward the international community had become increasingly suicidal.[89]

Curiously, given his "anti-imperialist" fixation, he progressively went back to the old mining industry patterns which he had seemingly wanted to break during his seven-month conquest. In early January 1998 Gécamines canceled AMFI's miracle "billion-dollar contract" for noncompliance,[90] and AMFI countered almost immediately by suing, not the DRC government, but the Anglo-American Corporation. AMFI accused it (probably rightly) of being behind the move and asked for $3 billion in compensation for breach of contract.[91] Meanwhile Barrick Gold was beating a prudent retreat by deciding to fuse all its African holdings, which consisted mostly of the 81,000 square-kilometer OKIMO concession, into a joint venture with Anglo-Gold, the gold-mining branch of Anglo-American.[92] And then, to cap it all, AMFI and Anglo-American finally reached an agreement on the Kolwezi project in July. Thus, barely more than a year after Kabila's victory, all the grand designs of shifting Congolese mining away from the traditional South African and Belgian predators by using new untried U.S. minors had finally come full circle and the old majors were again in complete control. Of course, their control was over a field of ruins, but for them it did not matter. They had the financial means and the technical wherewithal to sit on temporarily useless concessions and wait for a day when conditions would be ripe for exploitation, something the young mining companies could not afford. The "takeover of the Congolese mining riches" had boiled down to what it had probably been meant to be from the start: a daring speculation designed to squeeze the old majors into buying back their place in the new system. As for the Congolese population, it remained as before, a mute witness to the whole operation. The only result was that its tax burden increased out of all proportion, reaching the punishing rate of 7.5 percent of GNP outside the oil and mining levies.[93] But the whole regional political situation was so preoccupying that worries about the economy were soon going to be overshadowed by more pressing concerns.

Between Luanda and Brazzaville: the DRC's volatile West African environment

In 1996, when the anti-Mobutu crusade started, practically all the countries surrounding what was then Zaire were in a state either of extreme fragility or even of open conflict. The Mobutu war and the period of uncertainty that followed it, up to the explosion of the new conflict, had not changed things fundamentally. But two of Zaire's neighbors in the west had drifted further into conflicts that were to interlock with Kinshasa's situation, especially since east and west were now becoming enmeshed.

The relationship between Congo-Rwandese to Congo-Brazzaville antedated the Kabila war by several years. The first Tutsi refugees had arrived in Kinshasa in 1993, at the time of the Masisi war. Given the good relationship between Mobutu and President Juvénal Habyarimana, they were seen as "enemies" by the Mobutist establishment even though they were Zairian nationals. They quickly migrated across the river to Brazzaville, where they were welcomed by the recently elected president Pascal Lissouba.[94] The link remained, and when they arrived as victors in Kinshasa they tried to influence Kabila in his favor. This pushed the ex-FAR, who had managed to cross into the Congo-Brazzaville, to seek out an alliance with Sassou-Nguesso. About three hundred of them remained in the capital, while the majority (over five thousand) went north to Likolela, eighty kilometers from Oyo, Sassou's fief. They were later to play a key role in the Congolese war of June to October 1997. Curiously, this ethnopolitical automatic alliance system tolerated an exception for the ex-DSP troops who had fled to Brazzaville and who were quickly integrated by Lissouba into his militia. The RPF apparently did not feel threatened by that particular alignment.

But the Rwandese-AFDL-Lissouba alliance did not extend to the relationship with Angola. Lissouba had had a long-running relationship with both UNITA and the Cabindan FLEC (Frente de Libertação do Enclave de Cabinda, an anti-MPLA guerrilla group, closely allied to UNITA), several of whose members had been active in his entourage. For his part, Sassou had always been on good terms with the MPLA due to their common Soviet links.

Presidential elections were scheduled to take place on July 27, 1997. The political climate deteriorated very quickly as the election date approached because everybody talked about the democratic process but nobody seemed to trust it. The main political actors (President Pascal Lissouba; his uncertain allies Bernard Kolelas and Jean-Pierre Thystère-Tchikaya; his challenger, Sassou Nguesso) all started to buy weapons and to equip the militias they had discreetly kept since the end of the 1993–1994 war.[95] A series of armed incidents (in Owando on May 10, in Oyo on May 14) caused dozens of casualties. According to some sources Kabila indirectly played a role in the final move that triggered the explosion when he warned his "friend" Lissouba that Sassou was planning to overthrow him.[96] Lissouba reacted by sending troops and six armored cars to "arrest" his rival in the early hours of June 5. This started major fighting, which was to last until October 15, killing about 8,000 people, turning almost 700,000 into IDPs, destroying a good section of Brazzaville, and costing Lissouba the presidency.[97]

The conflict was being fought on two fronts: one was a savage house-to-house urban militia war, the other a cutthroat effort to control the oil revenues. Since the end of the 1993–1994 fighting the Lissouba regime had been plagued by recurrent corruption centering on the use of the oil money. A certain degree of corruption would have been unavoidable, as in any poor Third World country with politically controlled access to large centralized

168

amounts of money. But what made it worse in the Congo were three factors: (1) the persistence of a poorly paid but bloated bureaucracy inherited from the days of the PCT "workers' state"; (2) the highly corrupt practices of the French oil company Elf; and (3) the nature of Nibolek tribalism. Lissouba himself being a Nzabi was not part of it since the Nzabi are considered to be a "Gabonese" tribe and are very few in the Congo; still, he depended on the southerners for his political survival, and their fractious politics had been amply demonstrated by the 1993–1994 fighting between various southern tribes and subtribes. Lissouba was thus forced to grease the wheels of administration beyond what could have been reasonably expected because every nomination of a Teke or a Loumbou had to be balanced by extending the blessings to Bembe, Vili, or Yombe beneficiaries. In a dispatch sent to the Ministry of Foreign Affairs in Paris two years earlier, Ambassador Raymond Césaire had perfectly summed up the situation:

Lissouba is drifting with his country rather than governing... . Democracy remains a completely foreign concept... . The only administrative services of the government which are still working are those which can bring direct financial benefits to those who are in charge... . The incompetence of most politicians is only rivalled by their determination to keep their privileges.[98]

The IMF had gone into an Enhanced Structural Adjustment Facility (ESAF) agreement with Brazzaville, and it was furious to see (in early 1995) that even as the budget showed a 6 billion CFA franc credit, civil servants still would not get their salary arrears paid. Or that the 142 large companies concentrated in Pointe Noire would together pay 2.5 billion CFA francs in taxes for their 104 billion CFA franc turnover, that is, only about 2.4 percent, because they were "well connected." But it was of course difficult for the IMF to integrate ethnopolitical considerations into ESAF planning.

After the war both Sassou and Lissouba were to accuse Elf of having supported their rival. In fact they were both right. As one analyst wrote,

'Elf has always had two parallel lines of intervention in Africa with the networks headed by André Tarallo and Jean-Luc Vermeulen respectively... . Now Denis Sassou Nguesso feels "the other fellows" have gone too far in support of the former President. He reproaches Elf for having paid his enemy Lissouba $20m into a FIBA bank account[99] on 20th September while he considers that Lissouba stopped being president on 31st August.[100]

To make sure that it would be on the winning side, Elf had played both camps at the same time. This meant, for example, that at no time during the

169

war was the fighting allowed to disrupt the regular pumping of oil from the coastal and offshore installations.

The RPF Tutsi in Kinshasa tried to help their Brazzaville friends up to the end. When the Angolans decided to intervene it was because they did not want Savimbi to regain on the other side of the river what he had just lost in Kinshasa;[101] hence the Rwandese who had taken control of the Agence Nationale de Renseignements managed to block the transfer of military supplies across the river to Sassou's forces. For a few days it looked as if the war might globalize in a completely crazy cross-alliance way: the Angolan FAA had brought BM-21 multiple rocket launcher batteries which were firing at Lissouba's forces from the DRC side of the river while Angolan-supported President Kabila had sent over six hundred *kadogo* to help Lissouba. In a desperate move Lissouba even ordered his artillery to fire on Kinshasa, hoping to force Kabila into a direct intervention on his side. But the Angolans acted quickly behind the scenes to threaten Kabila, curtail the Rwandese influence, and limit the AFDL's support for the Congolese government's camp.[102] Sassou's aide Pierre Oba was then frantically lobbying Angola's chief of staff, Gen. João Batista de Matos, for a direct intervention, which finally took place on October 11, when over one thousand FAA troops with armored support crossed the border from Cabinda.[103] Within five days the Lissouba camp had collapsed and the open phase of the conflict was over.

This short war offered a concentrate of practically all the problems plaguing the contemporary African political scene. In order of decreasing importance these were, first, a completely corrupt and selfish political class: all the various leaders had only one thing in mind, power, so as to grab as much oil money as possible. The claim to defend any sort of national interest beyond that of their own faction was a pure rhetorical device constantly betrayed by hard facts. The second problem was international interference by Western countries: the most guilty party was of course France, which turned a blind eye to Elf's shenanigans. In a great display of neutrality the oil company dealt with Claudine Munari and Nguila Mougounga for the Lissouba camp and with Rodolphe Adada for the Sassou side. Lissouba still being the legitimate power holder got the government oil revenues, while Sassou received royalties from oil wells in Angola that he had obtained for Elf in the past. Both promptly turned these monies into guns, which could be considered looting of natural resources from the Congolese people's point of view. Instrumentalized tribalism was a third catastrophe. Of course, the tribal raw material existed independently from the politicians, but as a Congo political observer wrote, "In 1997, all ethnoregional identities were completely restructured"[104] through the manipulation of the political leaders. The tribal raw material was explosive, and some of the leaders saw their own houses looted by their own militiamen, many of whom would have agreed with a looter then declaring to a journalist, "Why call it theft? When they push us to kill each other they call it 'human stupidity'; then they go and they drink champagne together, calling it 'national reconciliation'; for us, nothing. Did you ever see the son of a leader getting killed in this fighting?"[105] Poverty and urban unemployment, more than "tribalism," made militia recruitment easy. The "tribal" groups that were fighting each other in the streets of Brazzaville had very little in common with their ethnic ancestors whom anthropologists had studied fifty years before. Fourth, mercenary recruitment and weapons trafficking played a major role in the violence. Weapons were bought from the former Warsaw Pact countries, from South Africa, and from Angola. Mercenaries of various nationalities, including U.S., French, Israeli, South African, and Serb, were hired.

But these four disasters, which so excite the attention of the international community when it tries to "help Africa," were in fact secondary; they were tools, they were consequences of a deeply rotten social, political, and economic landscape; they were not the causes of the war. I will return in the last chapter to this touching humanitarianism that thinks it can prevent forest fires by banning the sale of matches.

Fifth and finally, the regional involvement looked almost mild compared to the previous factors. Yes, ex-DSP troops fought for Lissouba while his Rwandese Tutsi friends in Kinshasa tried to help him; yes, Chadians and ex-FAR Rwandese Hutu fought for Sassou; yes, in the end it was the massive Angolan military intervention that brought the fighting to an end, and that intervention, in turn, was triggered, at least partly, by the steady worsening of the relationship between UNITA and the MPLA in Angola itself, where the pretence of peacemaking looked every day more flimsy.[106] But none of these interferences were in themselves sufficient to cause the conflict. The Brazzaville fighting left massive humanitarian scars in southern Congo[107] and a legacy of bitterness and tension that resulted in protracted guerrilla fighting over the next few years, causing even more suffering than the urban clashes of 1997. As for the October Angolan invasion, it inaugurated a new era of Angolan military projection beyond its borders in an elusive search for "national security." But security was a commodity in increasingly short supply in the region.

The unquiet East: the Kivus and their neighbors

As we saw in chapter 2 the Kivus, both North and South, were densely populated and ethnically fragmented provinces where access to the land had created major political problems in the past.[108] The evolution from traditional patterns of land control to modern systems of land ownership had been accompanied by swindling and manipulations on the part of some members of the Kinyarwanda-speaking populations, who took advantage of their close relationship with the Mobutu regime in its early and middle years, thus creating durable anti-Banyarwanda feelings. Later, the political wind changed with the 1981 citizenship law, which was slanted against the Banyarwanda. Things became worse when the so-called *géopolitique* of the Conférence Nationale Souveraine (CNS) nearly totally blocked the Kinyarwanda speakers of eastern Zaire from entering the political debate of the late Mobutu years.[109] Even worse, the "ethnic feudalization" of the late Mobutu years drove the autochthon tribes into mutually hostile camps, even going as far as splitting some of them into hostile intratribal subgroups.[110] The result of this political decomposition between the 1960s and the 1990s was the endless fragmentation of an already fragmented political landscape. Because the dangerous Kivu tinderbox lay next to the burning braziers of Rwanda and Burundi from which ethnic sparks constantly flew, it was only a question of time before the conflagration spread. We saw in chapter 2 that the arrival of over one million refugees in mid-1994 created an insufferable situation, which the Rwandese government proceeded to "solve" by invading the Kivus and, from there, pushing clear across the continent, toppling Mobutu and installing in his place what looked like the perfect puppet regime.

So if we take the 1994 Rwandese genocide to be the initial match tossed in the (relatively) quiet postcolonial landscape, the individual fires of the refugee exodus, the nonpolitical treatment of the crisis by the international community, the refugee camps war, and the fall of Mobutu all fit as a series of logical consequences. Because the key geographical link for this spreading fire was the Kivus, simply swearing in Kabila as president of a "new Congo" was not enough to magically solve the eastern problem.[111]

This became obvious even before the war was over. The Rwandese-AFDL westward push had been made possible by a relatively stable alliance with the eastern populations, providing the advancing forces with a quiet rear base. But keeping this "peace" in the Kivus for the new regime hinged on several delicate conditions:

1. Continued support of the new government by the Mayi Mayi militias after the collapse of the ex-FAR and Mobutu, who had been their main enemies.

2. Keeping a clear distinction between "foreign Tutsi forces" (the Kigali regime, the RPA) and Congolese Kinyarwanda speakers.

3. Steering clear of the ethnic and subethnic factions playing among autochthon tribes.

4. Keeping six or seven of the main eastern "big men"—first among them Anselme Masasu Nindaga—happy and busy in Kinshasa.

5. Staying on the good side of the highly sensitive "civil society" and the Catholic Church.

All these things were easier said than done, and achieving them would have required remarkable diplomacy indeed. But Kabila paid little attention to this problematic periphery, choosing instead to remain embroiled in the confused handling of power at the center, described earlier.

As early as June 1997 the Babembe in South Kivu had created "self-defense" militias under the leadership of a man calling himself "Charles Simba," in distant homage to the Lumumbist rebels of the 1960s. They attacked Fizi, with the support of Burundian FDD fighters, claiming that "Laurent-Désiré Kabila had been sent by the Tutsi to attack Zaire."[112] Within weeks armed "Mayi Mayi" groups had sprung up everywhere among various tribes, all the way from Masisi to the Fizi-Baraka area. In late August five thousand Masisi Tutsi who had come under attack from Nande Mayi Mayi sought refuge in Goma under the protection of the RPA and the Forces Armées Congolaises (FAC).[113] On September 5 the army commander of Bukavu Airport was shot dead by Mayi Mayi.[114] In North Kivu the fighting was particularly sharp because a number of Tutsi pastoralists had moved over from Rwanda and Uganda with their cows and tried to settle in the Masisi-Walikale area. Local Congolese chiefs were deposed and replaced with Tutsi, causing massive retaliation. The fighting led to more than one thousand civilian casualties during September alone.[115] By then the situation was completely enmeshed with what was happening in northwestern Rwanda: thousands of Tutsi refugees fleeing the violence in North Kivu had crossed into Gisenyi prefecture, where they were put in large refugee camps. The fact that these camps were themselves very vulnerable became evident when the largest one at Mudende was hit on August 21 by an *aba-cengezi* commando coming from Kivu that killed 148 refugees while losing seventeen of their own.[116] The whole late part of 1997 and the early months of 1998 were filled with a monotonous litany of attacks and counterattacks by shadowy armed forces with all too clear purposes. The men attacking Rwanda from the Congo had three clear aims: kill as many Tutsi as possible, push the local Hutu population into open insurrection, and disorganize the Kigali administration to the point of making at least part of the country ungovernable. On the other side the RPA tried to do two things: militarily to contain the insurgency and politically to terrorize the civilian population into submission. The result was perfectly summed up by a peasant woman from Gisenyi: "Those who are not killed by the soldiers of the former army are killed by those of the new army. It is always the innocent ones who are the victims."[117] The United Nations Human Rights Field Operation for Rwanda (UNHRFOR), which was created after the 1994 genocide, practically stopped operating in early 1997. Its presence would have been useless anyhow since the UN had accepted a Rwandese government overview of its reports which had been systematically bowdlerized since January 1997.[118] This wave of violence had a massive effect on Rwanda's internal politics, reinforcing the hard-liners, and on March 28, 1997, the Rwandese cabinet was reshuffled, eliminating the last vestiges of independent Hutu political presence in the government.[119] In addition, the controversial policy of compulsory villagization, which had been decided on at a December 1996 cabinet meeting, was pushed into implementation, although its effect on the security situation seems to have far from offset its rather catastrophic socioeconomic impact.[120]

In Kinshasa President Kabila was still largely under the control of his Rwandese minders and had to try to carry out their policies in the Kivus. He did so at times with blind violence, such as in late September 1997, when large numbers of Mayi Mayi fighters who had surrendered to the AFDL forces were killed in North Kivu,[121] or when his forces swept more than two thousand refugees back into Rwanda and Burundi in November.[122] The new chiefs appointed by the government tried to enforce the "antigénocidaires" policy inspired by Kigali, which resulted in increased violence, because when they tried to block the movements of armed ex-FAR units they ended up in clashes with the local populations, who had often agreed to help the former Rwandese army out of hostility toward the RPA presence. Clashes with the local populations then favored the further recruitment of Mayi Mayi militias.[123] The situation ended up being so tense between the Congolese and Rwandese elements of the AFDL that the Kivu problems were bound to reverberate all the way to the top and affect the balance of power in Kinshasa itself.

This is what finally happened in November 1997 with the violent arrest of Anselme Masasu Nindaga.[124] Masasu Nindaga was in many ways emblematic of the Kivu conundrum. Born from the union of a Mushi father and a refugee Rwandese Tutsi woman, half-educated, flamboyant and immature, he was positioned at the crossroads of revolutionary politics and the "civil society" organizations of South Kivu. His hopping on the AFDL bandwagon in October 1996 suddenly propelled him to national importance and added a touch of warlordism to his profile. But being more of a Kivu homeboy than anybody else in the AFDL, he was more keenly aware than the purely Tutsi members (Bugera, Bizima Karaha) of the unpopularity of the AFDL back home. He had gone back to Bukavu in November for an extended visit and concluded that he had to strike an independent course, both as a matter of local political necessity and to further what he believed to be his own personal destiny.[125] He was arrested soon after returning to Kinshasa and his support within the AFDL led to armed clashes directly inside the presidential palace.[126] In typical Kabila fashion his arrest was later justified by saying that he had "kept a private militia, planned a coup and smoked hemp." The first accusation was true, the second unproven, and the third irrelevant. What was certain was that his arrest triggered a whole chain of consequences. First, the Rwandese commander James Kabarebe was declared to be the "real" chief of staff of the newly born Forces Armées Congolaises, and Masasu, who had previously been described as chief of staff, was derided as "a mere Rwandese corporal."[127] In the Kivus this violent switch of the army command from the hands of a local boy to those of a foreigner did not go down very well. The governor of South Kivu had to warn the population not to go on strike in support of Masasu, and clandestine leaflets attacking the government were distributed.[128] This gave a tremendous boost to the Mayi Mayi militias, who gained enough strength to attack Bukavu itself on December 11. Committees sprang up everywhere, trying to think up ways of "bringing back peace"[129] while violence increased. The situation appeared to have slipped sufficiently out of hand for Kabila to undertake a special trip to the east and make a public speech to a large audience in Bukavu on January 25, 1998. Unfortunately the speech proved to be more incendiary than soothing:

There is the Mayi Mayi phenomenon. People say it is an expression of popular discontent. This is absolutely false. It is in fact an insurrectional movement against

175

the established power and not a way of signalling the popular desiderata to the government. Mayi Mayi works in cahoots with the outside, with foreign powers. You want proofs? There are plenty. Even the Vatican is involved in this through Caritas and other similar stuff.[130]

What I wanted to do yesterday and could still do is to proclaim a State of Emergency. 24-hours curfew. Every house searched to look for proofs of belonging to Mayi Mayi. Whoever is caught will be shot on the spot. You might be crying. But you know me. I am a tough guy.[131]

In the same speech Kabila tried to defend the Banyamulenge, who were experiencing greater and greater difficulties in their relationship with the other Kivu ethnic groups. Actually supporting them in that way did more harm than good because Kabila looked like a puppet for the Kigali ventriloquists and therefore tended to draw the embattled Banyamulenge even further into a symbolic association with the hated Rwandese Tutsi.

In several ways the Banyamulenge situation was a concentrate of all that was wrong in the Kivus: prejudice, bad faith on both sides, conflicting historical rights, ethnicization of local politics, struggle for economic survival, and innocent civilians caught between the devil and the deep blue lake. The contradictions manifested themselves more acutely at the level of the newly forming army. Since the AFDL victory in April, former FAZ soldiers had been regrouped in various camps, supposedly to be "reeducated." In fact, the conditions of detention were atrocious and many died.[132] But the new army being born (the FAC) was riddled with tensions and contradictions. There were three basic sociological recruitment pools that contributed troops to the AFDL: the Banyamulenge of South Kivu; the so-called *kadogo*, child soldiers originating from various eastern tribes; and the mostly Lunda Katangese Tigers of the former FNLC. To these were added dashes of former FAZ just coming out of the hell holes of Kitona or Kamina, eager to regain some of their lost advantage and quite hostile to their former enemies. The mix was explosive. On February 23, 1998, when the new officers wanted to break up a mostly Banyamulenge unit in Bukavu to disperse its men into various regiments at the four corners of the Congo, the soldiers mutinied.[133] Their feeling was that they were abandoned by Kabila to the attacks of local Mayi Mayi militias, the Burundian FDD, and Rwandese ex-FAR and *Interahamwe* and that now, on top of everything else, the former FAZ were coming up inside the new FAC units for what they sniggeringly called "a return match." To make matters still more intractable, local units of the Forces Armées Burundaises sided with the Banyamulenge mutineers.[134]

The situation was also deteriorating sharply in North Kivu. Between February 20 and March 1 Butembo was the scene of fierce and confused fighting between local Mayi Mayi and mostly Katangese FAC troops supported by Ugandan soldiers. The Kivu cauldron was threatening to explode, with far-reaching consequences.[135] The final death toll was anywhere between fifty and three hundred. A few weeks later the new FAC 10th Brigade, which had been sent especially to the Kivus to try to restore order, attacked Ugandan ADF rebels near Beni. Between April 14 and 18 a combined force of six thousand FAC, UPDF, and RPA soldiers operated between Beni and Butembo, but the ADF rebels managed to evade them and most of the victims were Nande civilians. This did not contribute to a cooling off of tempers, and North Kivu Governor Kanyamuhanga, a rather mild person, was made responsible for the whole mess because he was a Tutsi.

This growing risk of conflagration in the east, although expressing itself in myriad complex confrontations, could nevertheless be subsumed under a general heading: Did the local population agree to be ruled by a government in Kinshasa not really independent but largely in the hands of a foreign state, that is, Rwanda, which was highly suspected of harboring expansionist views? People like the Banyamulenge, who, by being both Tutsi and Congolese, fell in between the hard choices, tended to be squeezed by both sides. Congolese opposed to the new regime of Laurent-Désiré Kabila, mostly people from the northern tribes who had lost power with Mobutu's fall or non-Baluba Katangese who had missed the boat when the power shift took place, began to jockey for the next round of confrontation.[136] Enemies of the Kigali and Bujumbura regimes discreetly accelerated their courtship of Kinshasa. As we saw, the protection of former refugees slowly blended into recruiting former FAR and *Interahamwe* into the new FAC, as the type of troops who, given their past, were most likely to be loyal to whoever rescued them and steadfast in their opposition to whatever Kigali chose to sponsor. As the likelihood for confrontation drew closer those FAC officers who did not like President Kabila started to manipulate the troop mix of the famous 10th Brigade in the east: fewer *kadogo* (they had a reputation for being faithful to "Papa" Kabila[137]), more disgruntled Tigers, more North Kivu Banyarwanda Tutsi, more Banyamulenge, more ex-FAZ with a chip on their shoulder.[138] By early May there were sixteen thousand FAC soldiers between the two Kivus, all with uncertain loyalties. A local UN expert correctly summed up the government's conundrum: "The danger is that the government's attempt at proving its own independence from those who assisted it in taking power will, if successful, provoke unrest in the East and, if unsuccessful, lead to further fragmenting of the DRC as other ethnic groups turn against the central authority."[139] It was obvious by that time that an explosion was becoming unavoidable.[140] The only question was the location of its fault lines since the extremely fragmented nature of the ethnopolitical landscape made them uncertain. After taking part in the UN secretary-general's DRC Resource Group Meeting in New York (May 1–3, 1998), where all the region's specialists were able to share their views, I came back to Paris perfectly sure that war was imminent. I then proceeded to issue strong warnings whose absolute uselessness made me once more seriously question the oft-vaunted concept of "conflict prevention."[141] The actors themselves tried to deny until the last moment that anything was amiss, as shown in this amusing little excerpt from Congolese radio and television:

Interviewer: This morning on Radio France Internationale we heard Mr Prunier who pretends to be a specialist in African and Congolese questions. He said that the situation in Kivu is verging on an explosion and that the Head of State has no more control over the region. What do you say?

Didier Mumengi, minister of information: This is one more example of the villainy of those adventurers who want to deal with an Africa without Africans.... The situation in the East is getting more and more stable. The Mayi Mayi warriors are disarming.[142] . . . This Mr Prunier is only a specialist in lies.... Any danger of the country breaking up exists only in that man's head.... His Congo is a pure figment of his imagination.[143]

What finally triggered the explosion was the decision by President Kabila to bring things to a head and to get rid of his Rwandese minders. On July 23 he flew to Havana in the company of Godefroid Chamuleso.[144] Probably reinvigorated by his contact with the old Marxist certainties, he went on the air on the evening of his return (July 27) and read a bizarre midnight communiqué ordering all Rwandese troops to leave the Congo. He thanked the Rwandese for their "solidarity" and the Congolese people "for tolerating and sheltering the Rwandese troops," a curious double back-handed compliment.[145] The next day the Rwandese troops started to leave. In Kigali Emmanuel Ndahiro, Kagame's righthand all-purpose man, pretended to take it coolly, saying that the withdrawal "had been already planned" and that only about one hundred RPA troops were left in the DRC. Kabila said that the decision had been made "to satisfy those who found it uncomfortable to be in the presence of foreigners." For good measure he added that FAC strength was now up to 140,000, an obvious gross exaggeration.[146]

178

There was one last little incident with their former chief, as James Kabarebe came to bid good-bye to the president.[147] The bodyguard in Kabila's office, which until recently had been made up of Rwandese Tutsi, had been changed to Balubakat soldiers. The colonel who commanded them asked Kabarebe to leave his sidearm at the guard's desk before entering the president's office, which he did. But the colonel had a doubt at the last minute and asked Kabarebe to let himself be frisked. "Commander James" reluctantly agreed and was found to carry a small .32 caliber pistol in his boot. The colonel confiscated it, fuming. Kabarebe grinned and said he had to be careful about his security. As he was about to step into Kabila's office the colonel shouted at him to take off his beret, saying that out of respect he had to appear bare-headed in front of the president. Kabarebe refused and a scuffle ensued. In the scuffle the beret was torn off his head—and a very small .22 caliber automatic fell to the floor. Had "Commander James" intended to assassinate Kabila? It seemed likely, even though he denied it heatedly. "In fact it really scared us," my informant told me, "it showed how daring these fellows were. He did not have a chance of coming out of there alive after he would have shot the President. And yet he was willing to try it."[148] Four days later the war broke out and "Commander James" was leading the attack.

6

A CONTINENTAL WAR
(AUGUST 1998–AUGUST 1999)

Commander Kabarebe's failed Blitzkrieg

Once more, the Kivus had been, if not the cause, at least the catalyst for a major conflict in the Congo.[1] Nevertheless, from the start antigovernment forces presented the new war not as a local problem but as a national and patriotic military uprising against an unworthy regime.[2] And indeed, the mutiny was not limited to the Kivus: in addition to fighting in Bukavu, Goma, and Baraka, there were also clashes in Kindu and Kisangani and, clear across the country, at Camp Tsatshi and Camp Kokolo in Kinshasa itself. Shooting was also heard at the Kitona base in Bas Congo Province, where the ex-FAZ were being "reeducated." Even though there was no mention of Rwanda, the almost perfect synchronism of the mutiny with the expulsion of Rwandese Hutu forces from the Congo could not but lead to suspicions of collusion between the DRC rebels and the Kigali government. Both sides strenuously denied the obvious.[3] But by August 3 RPA troops were moving across the border in support of the "rebels," and the first of three airplanes highjacked by the Rwandese army landed at Kitona on August 4 with "Commander James" on board.[4] Rwando-rebel forces fared differently in their various zones of operation, the troubled east proving to be the easiest, with all the key points in the Kivus falling within the first forty-eight hours.

The behavior of the "liberators" differed widely according to the style of the commanders and the local conditions: violence was very limited in Goma and moderate at first in Bukavu. But when some troops from the Bukavu garrison, which had remained faithful to the central government, withdrew to Camp Kavumu, the RPA unit that surrounded them arrested all the officers and their bodyguards and shot them on the spot.[5] In Kisangani the rebels were defeated and loyal FAC forces retook control of the city. The same thing happened at Camps Tshatshi and Kokolo in Kinshasa itself, where the limited numbers of Rwandese troops who had not yet been evacuated tried to fight their way out but were all killed.[6] The whole thing gave an impression of confusion, of lack of preparation, and the RPA-Banyamulenge forces left behind in Kinshasa seem to have been caught completely unaware by the actions of their comrades in Goma and Kigali.[7] Which in turn begs a question: What was the amount of planning on Kigali's side?

The answers seem to point at a very limited and improvised decision-making sequence. Two of my informants who were eyewitnesses to the facts concur on that point: "James [Kabarebe] came back from Kinshasa quite flustered and eager to strike back. Paul [Kagame] asked him what was going on and James told him bluntly: 'You are our chief; if you want to go on being our chief just let me handle this.' Paul was worried because contingency plans had been made before for such a situation but now James seemed decided to improvise."[8] And from another source: "I had been out of town and then I met James [Kabarebe], whom I had not seen for a few days, in the street in Kigali. I asked him what was going on and he laughed and said: 'Do you want to witness the taking of Kinshasa?' I said yes and he told me to go to the airport in Goma; we were leaving right away. Soon we were on our way to Kitona in one of the highjacked planes."[9]

Could such a major political and military operation be that spontaneously organized? Well, yes and no. As we saw in chapter 4 Kabarebe had used his position as commander in chief of the FAC to modify the ethnic composition of some of the army units in the east, especially the 10th Battalion and the 222nd Brigade, so as to have a majority of favorable forces.[10] Where he failed to do this, such as in Kisangani, where the 25th Brigade retained a largely local ethnic composition, the uprising failed.[11] As for the Kitona operation, it had a recklessness that seemed right out of a Hollywood action movie: Commander James and his boys landed in the middle of the camp, on a runway surrounded by troops with mortars and machine guns. But Kabarebe knew very well that the gaggle of troops in Kitona were in bad shape and not ready to fight unless somebody gave them food and weapons, along with the promise of some money and looting opportunities.[12] The soldiers present contented themselves with shooting the aircraft nose-wheel tire to prevent it from taking off again, and then they started talking. Within half an hour James had won them over to his side. He then immediately started to move on to Kinshasa with his motley force of twelve hundred airlifted RPA troops, plus whoever among the Kitona dwellers was fit enough to follow him.[13]

The first signs of a political organization of the rebellion came on August 6, when Arthur Z'Ahidi Ngoma claimed leadership of the uprising, declaring, "This is not a struggle of the Banyamulenge or a struggle of the Rwandese, it is a struggle of the Congolese people."[14] The rebels took Uvira on the same day, prompting Burundi's minister of defense to deny that FAB troops had crossed the border to help them.[15] On the west coast Kabarebe and his men took Moanda and Banana and President Kabila told his fellow countrymen to "prepare for a long war." Panic hit the region. President Nujoma of Namibia announced a special Southern African Development Community (SADC) meeting on August 5, and Robert Mugabe, Laurent-Désiré Kabila, Pasteur Bizimungu, Yoweri Museveni, Frederick Chiluba, Sam Nujoma, and Benjamin Mkapa all met at Victoria Falls on the 8th. The atmosphere was tense, with Bizimungu and Museveni, the "aggressors," considered with suspicion by all the others. The absence of Angolan President José Eduardo dos Santos made everybody nervous because nobody was quite sure of which side he would be on. Zimbabwe Defense Minister Moven Mahachi officially promised military aid to the embattled Congolese president.[16] Anti-Tutsi pogroms had started in the streets of Kinshasa, during which hundreds were arrested and dozens killed.[17] Congolese authorities were panicking; knowing that anti-Tutsi feelings ran high they often resorted to a shrill rhetoric, evoking sinister memories of the Rwandese genocide.[18] Rebel forces occupied Beni on August 10; Uganda denied any involvement.[19] The giant hydroelectric Inga dam was captured on the 13th, enabling Kabarebe to cut off the power to Kinshasa. Fearing for his safety in the capital President Kabila flew out to Lubumbashi, from where he was hoping to organize a last stand if he lost Kinshasa.[20] Never given to understatement, Bizima Karaha went on the air to say, "Kabila has fled after looting the Central Bank."

On August 16 the rebels went public as the Rassemblement Congolais pour la Démocratie (RCD) and announced the names of their leaders. The politicians were a strange mixture of former Mobutists, such as Alexis Tambwe and Lunda Bululu,[21] together with radical left-wingers (Jacques Depelchin, Ernest Wamba dia Wamba), regional barons (Mbusa Nyamwisi), UN and NGO figures (Z'Ahidi Ngoma, Joseph Mudumbi), and well-known representatives of Rwandese interests (Bizima Karaha, Déogratias Bugera, Moïse Nyarugabo). As for the military leaders, they were mostly known for owing their careers to their good relations with the RPA: Il-unga Kabangi had been a secondary school student in 1997 when he joined the AFDL. He then became Kabarebe's personal bodyguard, which led to his being put in charge of RPA-FAC relations during Commander James's tenure as FAC chief of staff. As for the soon-to-be-declared RCD military commander Jean-Pierre Ondekane, he was a former DSP officer from Mbandaka and later an agent of the Service d'Action et de Renseignement Militaire in Kinshasa who had been arrested by the AFDL in 1997. During his time of "reeducation" he had struck up a friendship with some Tutsi officers in charge of the program who got him out of the Kitona hell hole and put him at the head of the 10th Brigade in Goma in June 1998. In the words of the Belgian Congo specialist Jean-Claude Willame, "It was a team of well-known people but with even less coherence than the group which had been present around Kabila at the time of his emergence less than two years before. Their only common denominator was the frustration of having been excluded from power."[22]

The emergence of this hodgepodge organization caused the region to fret because the "rebels" were so obviously incapable of military or even political autonomy that the whole thing looked more like an invasion than a genuine Congolese uprising, and the political agenda of its sponsors was questioned. The key undecided player was, of course, President dos Santos, whose choice could tip the situation either way. On August 16 Kabila rushed to Luanda for an emergency meeting with him and with Namibian President Sam Nu-joma. Etienne Tshisekedi immediately asked the Angolan president "not to rush to the rescue of Kabila," even as the OAU condemned what it termed "an external intervention in the Congo."[23]

Meanwhile the rebels kept progressing. They occupied Aru near the Su-danese border, Lobutu on the edge of Province Orientale, Fizi on the road to Katanga, and Mbanza-Ngungu, 130 kilometers from Kinshasa, all on August 16. Foreigners started to evacuate the capital. The next day SADC defense ministers met in Harare in the presence of Joseph Kabila, Laurent-Désiré's son,[24] and decided to help the beleaguered regime. But South Africa was less than happy with this decision; South African Deputy Minister for Foreign Affairs Aziz Pahad declared on the 18th, "A military solution is not possible.... We don't want a whole new surge of ethnic violence erupt-ing. This is not an ethnic problem." Several of the SADC members close to South Africa (Lesotho, Swaziland, Mauritius, Botswana, the Seychelles) began to dissociate themselves from what looked more and more like a Zimbabwean-driven initiative. On August 19 a first contingent of four hundred Zimbabwean troops disembarked at Kinshasa's Ndjili Airport, and the next day two Congolese cargo planes flew to Grootfontein in northern Namibia and brought back twenty-one tons of weapons.[25] Rwandese Ambassador in Pretoria Benjamin Karenzi declared that his country was ready for full-scale war if Zimbabwe and Namibia did not withdraw their forces from the DRC, which prompted French Foreign Minister Hubert Védrine to say, "This is not just a DRC crisis anymore, it is a regional crisis and therefore one should take into account the strategies of Uganda, Rwanda, Burundi, Angola and others." This was the first official acknowledgment that the war had indeed gone continental.

Then, on August 21, President dos Santos finally decided to make his move: Angolan cargo planes flew large numbers of troops to Cabinda, from where they immediately attacked Moanda across the border. President Museveni threatened intervention, and Republic of Congo President Sassou-Nguesso, who had been hesitating, gave reassurance to Kabila's envoy Didier Mumengi that he was indeed on Kinshasa's side.[26] Mandela called a SADC summit in Pretoria, which neither Kabila nor his new allies attended. Congolese justice minister Mwenze Kongolo commented, "Young African fighters once relied enormously on President Nelson Mandela but now it seems that age has taken its toll," to which Mandela's aide Parks Mankhlana replied, "Comments like those are not worth responding to." Even Mandela's iconic status was no longer enough to prevent SADC from splitting right down the middle on the Congo issue, between a pro-Kinshasa camp (Angola, Namibia, Zimbabwe) and all the others lined up behind South Africa on a line of "understanding" for the Rwando-Ugandan-rebel side. As we will see later, the split went even further and deeper than within the confines of the SADC and was in fact threatening to engulf at least one-third of the African continent.

But in the meantime guns mattered more than words and the big ones were on the Angolan side. The Angolan expeditionary force in the Cabinda Enclave was supported by tanks, MiG 23 fighter bombers, and Mi-17 combat helicopters flown by South African mercenaries. Those proved to be particularly deadly: the Rwandese expeditionary force lost 50 percent of its men in the first two days. The Forças Armadas Angolanas (FAA) soon smashed their way into the western front: Banana, Boma, and Kitona all fell within forty-eight hours. Commander James was now largely cut off from any possibility of resupply from Rwanda,[27] and he lost no time in withdrawing his mauled battle corps to Matadi, where, during the next three days, several cargo flights landed to pick up the wounded and the survivors.[28] Some of these flights landed for refueling on UNITA-controlled airfields inside Angola.[29]

By now reassured, President Kabila flew back to Kinshasa on August 25. FAA helicopters kept attacking rebel columns that, strangely enough, kept rushing toward Kinshasa in a mad, headlong flight forward. These armed elements entered the capital on August 26, desperately trying to get to Ndjili Airport.[30] The lucky ones were killed on the outskirts of the city; the others fell into the hands of the Kinshasa populace, driven frantic by fear and hatred. The hapless soldiers plus a number of arbitrarily tagged civilian "rebels" were grabbed and beaten to death or burned alive with old tires.[31] Presidential Adviser Yerodia Ndombasi did not help quiet things down when he declared on the radio, "The rebels are scum, microbes which must be methodically eradicated. We are decided to use the most effective medicine."[32] These words, with their Rwandese genocide echoes, were immediately picked up by Rwandese propaganda and, perhaps more important, by the international media.[33] The Zimbabwean troops, which by now numbered twenty-eight hundred men, retook control of the Ndjili area in three days of fierce fighting (August 26–28) but did not venture outside Kinshasa to fully clear the Lower Congo province.[34] Elsewhere in the country the rebels were still progressing. They had taken Kisangani on the 23rd, Kalemie on the 26th, and Moba on the 30th. An RCD spokesman declared, "When we have taken Lubumbashi, we will be at ease."[35]

These were brave words indeed, but it was now obvious that Kabarebe's Blitzkrieg had failed.[36] Everybody began to realize that this was probably going to be a long drawn-out conflict, involving many different protagonists. All of Congo's neighbors were by now nervously eyeing the situation because they all realized that the tangle of alliances and interests was reaching from the Mediterranean to the Cape of Good Hope and that nobody could predict exactly how and where the chips were going to fall. And, with the cold war over, there was no clear "tactical map" of the situation. The French were vaguely supposed to be favorable to the rebellion,[37] but so were the Americans, a convergence of purpose that was rather unlikely. Africa's radar screen was blurred and the foreigners had turned theirs off. The continent was now largely on its own.

Heading for an African war

The regime of Laurent-Désiré Kabila had survived only because of the military intervention of foreigners. Without the Angolan combat helicopters and without the Zimbabwean troops, Commander James would have succeeded in taking Kinshasa before the end of August. Although given the open hatred of the Rwandese that had developed over the past fifteen months and the fact that his attack had exasperated these sentiments even further, what Kabila could have done with it would have been quite another matter. The whole adventure was fearfully improvised, like a second-rate remake of the events of late 1996, when the enemy was Mobutu and a large chunk of Africa stood united behind those who wanted to remove him. This time around the situation was much more complex because there was no single purpose behind either the attempt at overthrowing Kabila or the decision of some of his peers to help him stagger on. The continent was fractured, not only for or against Kabila, but *within* each of the two camps.

Kinshasa's friends: godfathers and discreet supporters. The main player in Kabila's survival scenario was President dos Santos, and his overriding motivation was the increasingly tense domestic situation in Angola itself, where the Mission des Observateurs des Nations Unies en Angola (MONUA) had been incapable of bridging the gap of distrust and hatred between the government and UNITA. But although the distrust was mutual, the attitude of the international community toward "these two appalling adversaries [was] far from even-handed."[38] The international community did not really seem to want to acknowledge that the November 1994 Lusaka Peace Protocol had been the result of military exhaustion and diplomatic arm-twisting rather than any genuine desire for reconciliation. New York and the three members of the Lusaka Troika[39] acted as if everything was normal, as if the MPLA was a democratically elected government and UNITA an unreasonable spoiler. MPLA violations were simply "not seen," while UNITA reactions to them were immediately pointed out as a sign of ill will.

The first and probably most important violation concerned the security of Jonas Savimbi and his close associates. After the 1992 massacre of UNITA forces in Luanda it was difficult for the rebel movement to trust the MPLA, especially since, although it learned new "politically correct" tricks, it seemed to have lost nothing of its old thuggish ways. There were many examples, such as the time three top UNITA men who had just given a press conference at the Méridien Hotel in Luanda were trapped in their elevator, which shot up to the twenty-third floor and then crashed to the ground.[40] Then there was the suspicious death of the famous UNITA general Arlindo Pena ("Ben Ben"), who passed away in a Johannesburg hospital on October 19, 1998, two days *after* the MPLA media had announced his death. Immediately after his demise the FAA General Staff sent a special delegation to South Africa to fetch the corpse and prevent the autopsy the family was demanding from being carried out.[41] These were the famous cases, but there were many other "ordinary" ones: "In the provinces of Huila, Kwanza Norte and Kwanza Sul, where UNITA has handed over the administration to the MPLA, hundreds of its supporters were arrested in February 1998. This followed a more general 'destruction programme' in which [were] . . . assassinated hundreds of UNITA militants and arrested another 400 since May 1997."[42]

Given such a track record it is hardly surprising that Savimbi was extremely reluctant to come to Luanda in person, especially since his personal status, which was eventually voted by Parliament after lengthy delays, was in total contradiction with the sanctions voted against UNITA at the international level and did not give him any security.[43] Demobilization was another one-sided charade. Over 50,000 of UNITA's 75,000 combatants had been demobilized by March 1998, but the MPLA had demobilized none of its soldiers. In addition, there were over 4,000 highly trained mercenaries classified as "security guards" who protected the diamond mining sites whom the government refused to include as combatants to be demobilized, although they, and the Rapid Intervention Police, were probably the best troops Luanda had. The same double standard applied in the case of diamond production; UNITA had surrendered all its diamond sites to the government by January 1998, expecting to get in exchange bundles of shares from the foreign companies that were buying the permits.[44] But the shares never materialized. The attitude of the international community remained completely biased against UNITA, no matter what actually happened on the ground. In June 1998 MONUA mediator Alioune Blondin Beye said, "It is abnormal that Savimbi's party remains armed" without any mention of the MPLA non-demobilization or of any possible UNITA security concern,[45] while U.S. Assistant Secretary of State for African Affairs Susan Rice declared in a speech symbolically given at the Agostinho Neto University in Luanda, "UNITA and Mr. Savimbi are undoubtedly the main causes of the derailing of the peace process and of the movement back towards war."[46] As Savimbi was later to remark, this was an attitude of "winner takes all, loser loses all."[47] So Savimbi "did not comply" with the terms of Lusaka by not putting his head on the block, and security started to slip. After June 1998 UNITA obviously decided that a renegotiation of Lusaka was not possible without war, and sporadic fighting erupted in Lunda Norte, Malanje, and Cuanza Sul provinces. Over twenty thousand refugees crossed the border into Katanga.[48]

It is in that context that Kabarebe's lightning attack on Kinshasa has to be seen. For dos Santos, having a loose cannon regime in the DRC brought back the ghost of Mobutu's pro-UNITA policies, at least potentially. And that was too much of a risk to run. But then, why did it take him so long (nineteen days) to make up his mind? Both the Rwandese and the Ugandans later claimed that they had had ironclad guarantees from Luanda that it would let them overthrow Kabila without interference.[49] It seems that these claims were largely due to wishful thinking. President dos Santos later complained to a visiting diplomat,

I just received a letter from President Museveni three or four days after they had launched their offensive. He was telling me not to worry, that everything would be all right. Now what is this? How would he have taken it if I had sent a large military force right up to his border and just notified him by letter two or three days later?[50]

Such neglect of accepted protocol had a far more serious underside. There were strong rumors that both Museveni and Kagame had been in contact with UNITA prior to August 2, 1998. Because these contacts did materialize later it is tempting to project them back in time, although I have not been able to substantiate the matter. But what is beyond any doubt is that there were close contacts between Arthur Z'Ahidi Ngoma and FLEC, UNITA's ally in the Cabinda Enclave. And since 58 percent of Angola's oil was coming out of the diminutive territory, Luanda was particularly nervous about anything having to do with Cabinda. Z'Ahidi Ngoma had met the FLEC-FAC leader Enriques Nzita Tiago in Paris in July through the agency of the notorious French influence peddler Michel Pacary.[51] Z'Ahidi Ngoma had promised FLEC that he would support their cause politically and perhaps even militarily in case of victory. By early August FLEC troops were poised to cross the DRC border and to help Kabarebe, but the FAA moved faster. The FLEC–Z'Ahidi Ngoma connection was already cause enough to worry Luanda. But in addition there was also the behavior of Commander James when he occupied Kitona. There were UNITA troops in the camp and also former "Zulu" Lissouba militiamen. James did not hesitate to take them on board, a move certainly due more to short-term opportunism than to any kind of long-term views. But was this not the main reason for Luanda's concern? Since the "rebels" and their backers seemed to have no other guiding principle than short-term lunges for the jugular, what could stop them from allying themselves with UNITA later on? Dos Santos had no security guarantee worth the name, and he had the practical proof of reckless behavior on the part of the invaders. What finally tipped the balance in favor of intervention was the resolute attitude of FAA Commander in Chief João de Matos. As dos Santos later told a CIA visitor, "He [de Matos] told me: 'Mr President, if you do not give me the order to intervene in the DRC I will do it anyway, with or without your approval.' "[52] Dos Santos added jokingly for the benefit of his American guest, "You know, in Africa, when your Army Chief talks to you like that, you listen!"[53]

To sum up Angola's position, one could say that the uncertainty surrounding the aims and alliances of the Rwando-rebels was not acceptable for the MPLA, who knew that its confrontational policy toward UNITA was bound to restart the war and who could not run the risk of seeing the rebel movement reacquire its old rear bases in the Congo. And then there were two other overriding considerations pleading for an anti-Rwandese choice. First, if Luanda had let Kabarebe and his friends take power in Kinshasa it would have had no control over them.[54] On the contrary, a militarily impotent and diplomatically ostracized Kabila was an ideal tool as Congolese head of state since his weakness would keep him pliable. Second, taking an even longer view of things, the MPLA was weighing the closeness between Museveni and Kagame on the one side and the South African leadership on the other. Of course the ANC was in power now, but South Africa remained South Africa, apartheid or no apartheid. Luanda knew that the ANC was in touch with UNITA[55] and that, just as the old white leadership had dreamed, the new black leadership saw Katanga and even the whole southern African cone as a natural sphere for South Africa's economic expansion. In a way, now that the psychopolitical block of apartheid had been removed, this made South Africa even more dangerous because it enjoyed universal recognition and support. Angola, which in spite of its large and well-equipped army and its growing oil-based economic clout remained a war-devastated country, preferred to move in close alliance with Zimbabwe, which shared its fear and resentment of the South African giant.

The case for Zimbabwe's intervention was less obvious, for two reasons: it had no security stake in the DRC and it had, on the contrary, many domestic problems that seemed to preclude the idea of foreign adventures. With rich mineral and agricultural resources, a small but coherent industrial base, and a sophisticated service sector, Zimbabwe at the beginning of the 1990s had the potential of being a small regional economic wonder. Of course, there were certain structural problems: an overweight public sector (37 percent of GDP), a very unequal land and wealth repartition wherein the white minority retained a socially dangerous predominance, and a tendency to overspend, which had led to dangerous rates of inflation (26 percent during 1990–1995). But the country retained many comparative advantages, not least its highly skilled workforce (by African standards), a dynamic civil society, an active stock exchange, and a solid infrastructure in terms of roads, banks, and telecommunications. But two things triggered the Zimbabwean economy's downturn: the first one was a tendency toward monetary oversupply, which got even worse during 1997, causing an inflation rate of over 30 percent (the Zimbabwean dollar fell from 14 to 25 to the U.S. dollar). Panicked by the consequences, especially vis-à-vis the already cool IMF, the government resorted to massive tax increases, pushing down economic growth for the year to less than 0.5 percent. This resulted in food riots in January 1998, which were brutally repressed by the police.[56] The other problem was the November 1997 announcement by President Mugabe that he would confiscate about fifteen hundred white-owned farms and distribute the land to poor peasants. This was in fact cheap demagoguery because, although the land problem was real enough, previous attempts at "land reform" had only served to confiscate white farms to give them to rich cronies of the Zimbabwe African National Union and the Patriot Front (ZANU/PF), with poor peasants none the better off for it.[57] By June 1998 the farms had not yet been confiscated, but the announcement had been enough to scare off potential investors and to cause tobacco companies (tobacco being one of Zimbabwe's main cash crops) to switch to planting in a variety of other Asian and African countries, leaving a depressed market in Harare. The budget deficit was running at 10 percent of GDP, the currency plunged another 13 percent, and the 300,000-strong Zimbabwe Congress of Trade Union threatened to organize a general strike over new tax increases and what it termed "government parasitism."[58]

Strangely enough, it is that dismal domestic economic situation that goes a long way toward explaining Zimbabwe's intervention in the Congolese crisis. Harare had a large financial stake in the DRC,[59] and though most of it could be classified under the heading of "crony capitalism," President

Mugabe's fuzzy populist vision probably saw it as a fine opportunity for the growth of Zimbabwean business, provided he could keep the South Africans out of the honey pot.[60] As early as July 1997, a few weeks after Kabila's victory, Zimbabwe Defence Industries (ZDI)[61] had landed a small ($500,000) military supply contract. Things developed quickly when Philip Chiyangwa, a well-connected Zimbabwean businessman, arranged a $45 million loan to Kinshasa. It financed vehicle, fuel, and foodstuff imports.[62] From there business grew quickly. By early 1998 ZDI had received orders from the Kinshasa regime totaling about $140 million, and large mining concessions were being negotiated.[63] Because President Mugabe shared Luanda's doubts about South Africa's long-term economic and political aims and because he saw the Congo as Zimbabwe's land of opportunity, this made it imperative for the Kabila regime to survive, debts, commitments, contracts, and all. The presence of South African Secret Service agents in Goma only served to reinforce the doubts about Pretoria's position in the conflict,[64] and the tension with South Africa over the Congo became such that President Mugabe himself felt obliged to deny it publicly.[65]

To carry the day at the SADC Luanda and Harare needed another ally that would look more innocent than they. President Nujoma's Namibia was the ideal patsy. Ever since its breakup with UNITA in 1976, SWAPO had remained in the political shadow of the MPLA.[66] Although Namibia was economically quite prosperous,[67] it was a mere flyspeck on the flank of the South African giant and for that reason kept nudging ever closer to Luanda. UNITA infiltrations in the north even forced the Namibian Defense Force to integrate its operational plans with those of the FAA and to operate as far north as Mavinga, five hundred kilometers into Angola, to protect its border.[68] Thus President Nujoma was in no position to remain aloof from the DRC crisis, and his diplomatic and military support for the Angolan-Zimbabwean intervention was almost automatic.

Between them Mugabe and dos Santos (with Nujoma in tow) rode roughshod over the Pretoria-inspired SADC diplomatic niceties and brought their guns along. South Africa complained, but not to the extent of openly siding with the Rwanda- and Uganda-backed "rebels."[69] Although it was essentially Angola and Zimbabwe who saved Kabila, there were other friendly alignments with their camp that were less remarked upon.

One was with the Sudan. The Congolese involvement of the Sudan was essentially motivated by its confrontation with Uganda.[70] This had led Khartoum to side with the falling Mobutu regime in 1996–1997. But Kabila's victory did not put an end to Sudanese military activity in Congo's Province Orientale. The March 1997 slaughter of WNBLF forces in the Yei ambush had diminished the proxy fighting capacity the Sudanese had been trying to build. But they did not give up and kept resupplying the remnants of both the WNBLF and UNRF II.[71] In addition, they continued to welcome the hard-pressed Rwandese former *Interahamwe* to Juba, and in March 1998 Col. Tharcisse Renzaho, the former prefect of Kigali, and Colonel Ntimi-ragabo, the former Rwandese Garde Présidentielle commander, arrived in Juba from Nairobi to reorganize them.[72] When the war broke out in August they were joined by Idi Amin's son Taban who came to recruit Former Uganda National Army (FUNA) Ugandan West Nilers; both units were later sent to bolster the defense of Kindu in Maniema. When Kindu fell in October a number of Rwandese and Ugandan rebels were captured by RCD-RPA forces; they were often described to the press as "Sudanese" since they had come from Juba.[73]

Then by October the pro-Kinshasa alliance was reinforced by Chadian troops and Libyan aircraft. But the attitudes of the three countries differed in terms of acknowledging their involvement. Khartoum flatly denied any form of military presence, simply invoking "diplomatic and political support" for the Kabila regime.[74] Tripoli simply did not talk to journalists, and Ndjamena declared openly that it had sent an expeditionary force of one thousand men to the DRC "to support the legitimate government."[75]

Kinshasa's foes. The most determined of all these countries was of course Rwanda and, given the security argument later advanced by Kigali to justify its intervention in the Congo,[76] we must pause briefly and try to assess the security situation of Rwanda in early August 1998. As we saw in the preceding chapter, the end of 1997 had been rather bad. There had been regular *Interahamwe*-ALIR attacks since October 1997 and they had increased at the beginning of 1998,[77] a situation that led the RPA to reorganize its forces in the northwest and to put them under the command of Col. Kayumba Nyamwasa, one of the best high-ranking officers in the Rwandese army. Some of the attacks were particularly atrocious, such as the ambush of a taxi minivan at Bulinga (Gitarama Province) on December 17, 1997, in which nineteen travelers were burned alive in their vehicle, and the January 19, 1998, attack on a bus transporting workers from the Bralirwa brewery just outside Gisenyi, in which forty-six people were killed and thirty wounded. To these the RPA responded with a policy of brutal counterinsurgency. Since the *abacengezi* (infiltrators) were trying to recruit the ex-FAR who had been repatriated in November 1996, the army often took to killing them preventively. It also cut down all the banana plantations over a two-hundred-meter swathe on both sides of the road so as to prevent ambushes. This further restricted the peasants' food supplies in an already land-starved agricultural environment where calorie intake in 1998 was 30 percent lower than before the genocide. In spite of the official slogans about "national reconciliation" the Tutsi-Hutu community tensions were worse than ever and the presence of Hutu ministers in the government was a piece of window-dressing that did not convince anybody.[78] The regime did not help when its only answer was to increase the degree of military repression and to concentrate all the power into the hands of General Kagame.[79] The government bought Mil Mi-17 helicopter gunships from Ukraine and hired mercenary pilots, who operated without too much care for the safety of civilian populations. The public execution by firing squad of twenty-two *génocidaires* on April 22, 1998, which might have been understandable four years earlier, worsened the political climate even further.[80] On May 8 the UN Human Rights mission in Rwanda was suspended by New York after a stormy visit by Kofi Annan to Kigali. But strangely enough, what probably contributed to push Kigali beyond the point of no return was the murder of former RPF minister Seth Sendashonga.[81]

Sendashonga and his Forces de Résistance de la Démocratie had been the voice of the moderate opposition to RPF policies. After over a year in the political wilderness they were just beginning to come to the fore as a possibly credible alternative. Sendashonga was a Hutu who was completely acceptable to many Tutsi, especially the "survivors." But he was also a seasoned politician, and the RPF hard core knew that any political combination that would accommodate him and his friends would demand a heavy price and could lead to a fundamental redivision of the power structure. His murder in Nairobi on May 16 cleared the way for extremist policies.

James Kabarebe was in the paradoxical position of heading an army (the FAC), half of which was ready to follow him into a rebellion while the rest wanted him dead. But up to the month of July, when he was eliminated from his position as chief of staff, there had been diverging voices in Kigali about what to do with the growing ALIR threat.[82] Outright invasion of the Kivus looked like a case of military overkill, even if many young ambitious officers in the RPA preferred it for the economic opportunities it could offer them. With Sendashonga dead and Kabarebe kicked out of Kinshasa, the RPA hard-liners had a nice international *casus belli* and a domestically clear field of fire. The invasion-in-the-guise-of-a-rebellion meant carrying out a counterstrike against ALIR and at the same time opening up economic opportunities in the Congo for the young, undereducated, hungry, foreign-born Tutsi who formed the hard core of the RPA officer corps.

Another factor pushing Rwanda into a Congo war was the infighting within the RPF itself. Kagame and several of his close friends were seen, rightly or wrongly, as the center of what the ordinary Rwandese called "the new *akazu*," in parallel with Habyarimana's corrupt kitchen cabinet. The new *akazu* had a majority shareholding in the TriStar Company, which had been awarded all the road contracts financed by UNDP and the European Union and seemed to get its cut of all the foreign aid money. Kayumba Nyamwasa, recently promoted to the rank of brigadier general, and Major Nsesibera, the assistant director of the RPA medical services, were spearheading a (possibly self-interested) anticorruption drive which had taken them close to trying a military coup against the *akazu*.[83] A short and successful war would be a nice way out of that tension and an occasion for all to get their share of the spoils. All the more so because Kigali felt that it had the blessing of the U.S. government, a feeling that had been reinforced by President Clinton's visit in April[84] and by the fact that Kigali's mediation had been solicited by the U.S. State Department in May 1998, when Ethiopia and Eritrea went to war with each other.[85] Thus by August 1998 the Rwandese leadership believed, for a variety of reasons, that it had wide diplomatic leeway, even after Kabarebe's Blitzkrieg attack on the Congolese capital failed. As President Kabila had warned his people, the war was going to be a long one.

The situation was quite different when seen from Kampala. President Museveni's spokeswoman Hope Kivengere immediately denied any Ugandan involvement in the Congo,[86] and when Beni fell to "the rebels" on August 10 Kampala reiterated its denial. This was of course false. The "rebel" occupation of Bunia three days later involved a UPDF contingent.[87] In his careful examination of Kampala's motives for getting involved in the Congo Professor J. F. Clark considers as "the most plausible explanation" the necessity for Museveni to support his Rwandese ally, saying that if the Rwandese regime had fallen this would have damaged Museveni's regional prestige and caused him great difficulties, as large numbers of Tutsi refugees would have poured into Uganda.[88] This seems like a far-fetched explanation because in August 1998 Paul Kagame's regime in Rwanda was in no danger of collapsing at all.[89] Even if the danger had existed there would have been no need to send thousands of troops to take Kinshasa in order to shore up Rwanda's security; a simple broad sweep into the Kivus would have been enough. Professor Clark is right in saying that economic and ideological reasons, even if they were present, were not the main reasons to move into the Congo. The main reason, as in the previous war, was Sudan.

Early in 1997 Museveni had already said, "We have run out of solutions with the Sudan. We are now seeking a solution on the battlefield."[90] Obviously by mid-1998 the solution still had not been found: the UPDF had had to enter Sudan itself on several occasions to strike back at the LRA;[91] the ADF guerrillas who got regular arms air drops from Juba[92] were wreaking havoc in Bundibugyo (there were 50,000 IDPs by late January and 70,000 by July); and when an ADF agent was caught in Mbarara in March and gave the names of his friends, all were Muslims. Amama Mbabazi, security adviser to President Museveni, declared, "Khartoum's plan is to destabilize the region to prepare the ground for the spread of Islamic fundamentalism and Arabism."[93] In addition to the various guerrilla groups (ADF, UNRF II, FUNA, LRA), all supported by Sudan, there were another three thousand hostile troops in Garamba National Park, two hundred kilometers west of Arua, who were also occasionally supplied from Juba.[94] None of these forces had the capacity to overthrow the regime, but together they kept grinding it down and costing it an inordinate amount of money, which Museveni felt was not only spent largely in vain, but tended to create problems with the donors, who reproached him for an oversize military budget. Although fighting Khartoum directly remained an option, the Ugandan government felt that it was better to leave that task to the SPLA[95] and to strike at the wild Congolese northeast, where Sudanese military intelligence operated freely.

The first strategic move of the UPDF as soon as it went seriously over the border was to head for Garamba and clean it up.[96] But does this overriding security concern mean that there was no economic motive in the Ugandan intervention? Hardly. In fact, one strange thing was the fluctuations in Ugandan gold exports around the time of the war.

Uganda Gold Exports (in U.S. $ millions)

1995	1996	1997	1998
23	60	105	19

Source: Economist Intelligence Unit.

One notices a rapid increase in gold exports since the first Congo war and then a sharp drop as Uganda went into the second. Three years later, when the UN commissioned a research panel to investigate the looting of natural resources in the Congo, President Museveni said that the increase in gold exports was due to "liberalization of trade," a not altogether wrong explanation if by this it is understood that wildcat gold-mining products from the Congo were allowed to transit freely though Uganda. The real problem was that from 1995 on, President Museveni started gradually to lose his hold over UPDF finances. In 1991, when the UPDF was 100,000 strong, the cost of keeping these troops was $42 million per year. In 1996, after the demobilization exercise, the cost of only 50,000 troops had climbed to $88 million. Over $400,000 a month was being stolen from the anti-LRA operational budget. In the Congo, where the UPDF had remained on anti-ADF duty with the agreement of Kinshasa, Col. Peter Kerim and his ADC Lt. Col. Napoleon Rutambika were accused of stealing over five million dollars' worth of goods from Congolese traders, and General Kazini admitted that he had only 6,000 men under his command and not 10,000, as shown in his books.[97] When the auditor general James Kahooza produced a report on UPDF finances it read like a catalogue of horrors: a $1.5 million swindle in military equipment customs clearance in Dar-es-Salaam harbor; $1 million vanished from a "special account" opened by Brigadier Kazini; two Mi-24 combat helicopters bought in Belarus for $1.5 million apiece that could never fly; over 30 percent of the T-54 tanks bought in Bulgaria that could not run.[98] In many ways the Congo gold flurries were part and parcel of the same thing. Uganda produced very small quantities of gold at its Kaabong mine in Karamoja,[99] mined by Branch Energy Uganda Ltd.,[100] which denied any responsibility in the massive gold export increases of 1996–1997. It was obvious that since the late 1996 Ugandan involvement in the overthrow of Mobutu, UPDF officers had found ways of quickly enriching themselves in the Congo that were not unique but rather were part of the multifaceted swindle operations the Ugandan army staff had deftly developed. The 1998 drop did not reflect a decrease in illegal gold mining; it simply reflected a rechanneling of product flows through the new possibilities that opened up with the occupation of Kisangani, a city with a strong attraction for seasoned "behind-the-counter" gold and diamond dealers. This, like a similar appetite among their RPA colleagues, explains why a deep thrust into the DRC was preferred to a limited border security operation. It was not an either/or proposition, security or illegal mining. It was a combination of these, wherein the officer corps in both armies hoped to kill two birds with one stone. But there was a major difference between the RPA and the UPDF concerning the attitude toward what could be called "national interest": the Rwandese officers were under a strong obligation to surrender a share of their gains to the Ministry of Defense, which had a special Congo Desk to deal with such matters;[101] not so in Uganda, where the loot remained in the private hands of perhaps up to two hundred well-connected officers, their civilian friends, and their families. As the darling of the IMF, Uganda lived up to its entrepreneurial reputation.

The last of Kinshasa's foes was also the least. Burundi's FAB collaborated with the UPDF and the RPA, but only on a limited scale, both geographically and in terms of numbers. Burundian forces in the Congo were to fluctuate between one thousand and two thousand, and never went very far away from the Uvira-Baraka-Fizi area directly to the west of Lake Tanganyika's northern end. This was the shore facing Burundi and one of the entry points for the FDD guerrillas led by Jean-Bosco Ndayikengurukiye, who had supplanted the tamer CNDD of Léonard Nyangoma in early 1998. Bujumbura's military was not out to overthrow the Kinshasa government, nor was it trying to control gold mines: it was mostly minding its back door. In a paradoxical way, although Burundi never admitted to having troops in the Congo, it was the only one of Kinshasa's foes that could legitimately claim to be there purely for reasons of local security.

Fence-sitters and well-wishers. This was a very large category indeed, regrouping all the governments and ethnic groups whose sympathies or interests linked with one side or the other or, even more incongruously, with *both* sides simultaneously.

The epitome of ambivalence was probably Zambia, where, as we will see, President Chiluba was actively promoting his country's role as a diplomatic go-between while serving at the same time as the main conduit for military supplies going to UNITA.

As for Jonas Savimbi, he had a long-standing relationship with Zambia. Because he had not been particularly welcome there at the time of Kenneth Kaunda in the 1960s (his attacks on the Benguela railway were a security problem for Zambia), he worked with Kaunda's enemy, Simon Kapwepwe. Being in opposition to UNIP, Kapwepwe was bound to be hostile to UNIP's ally, the MPLA. So when Frederick Chiluba swept into power in October 1991 several of his close associates who had won their opponents' spurs with Kapwepwe happened to also be friends of Jonas Savimbi. The situation got so embarrassing after the signing of the Lusaka Peace Protocol in 1994 that Chiluba used the pretext of a failed mini-putsch in October 1997 to sideline some of the most compromised UNITA supporters. But the changes were largely cosmetic because Chiluba needed those men's support. Thus Benjamin Mwila, who had been removed from his position as defense minister, was kept in the cabinet as minister of energy. The minister of commerce and industry, Enoch Kavindele, was removed but kept all his connections within the MMD. Vice President Christian Tembo stayed on. As the war went on things grew dangerously tense between Angola and Zambia, forcing Paris and Washington to use their influence on Luanda to stop the MPLA from attacking Ndola Airport in April 1999.[102] Chiluba kept denying everything and frantically protesting his country's innocence. In a way he was right: it was not the Zambian government helping UNITA, or even the MMD; it was men with private business interests and long-standing friendships. But this in itself spoke eloquently of the state's weakness, when it could not even halt the momentum that could lead to war.[103]

Another uneasily positioned fence-sitter was Tanzania. Dar-es-Salaam had sent six hundred military instructors to train Kabila's fledgling army in May 1997. They were still at the FAC Kamina base when the war broke out and they had to be quickly repatriated.[104] But the presence of the Tanzanian People's Defense Force in Kamina was ambiguous, in that one of their jobs was to train to combat readiness a number of survivors of the Hutu refugee trek across the continent a few months before.[105] In a similar vein, when Seth Sendashonga was seriously thinking of opening up an eastern front against the RPF regime in Rwanda, it was in Tanzania that he found a ready welcome.[106] It was also a well-known fact that the CNDD and later the FDD recruited freely among the huge Burundian refugee population in Kigoma.[107] In spite of all this, Paul Kagame was very careful never to say anything hostile against Tanzania, banking on Mkapa's pusillanimity, Nyerere's desire to achieve peace in Burundi, and the general confusion of the Chama cha Mapinduzi (Party of the Revolution), which made it an unlikely candidate for military adventures. He was eventually proved right, and in spite of many near-misses when Tanzania and Burundi looked like they were going to war with each other, which would have led to an eastward extension of the conflict, things always seemed to mend at the last minute.

A short mention should also be made of Kenya, which remained peripheral to but not uninvolved in the crisis. There were two connections between Nairobi and the exploding Great Lakes crisis: one was the long-standing hostility between Presidents Moi and Museveni;[108] the other was the massive Rwandese *akazu* presence in Nairobi after 1994. Many of the leaders, such as Mrs. Habyarimana herself, her brother Séraphin Rwabukumba, and top Garde Présidentielle officers such as Colonels Nkundiye and Mpiranya, were all in Nairobi, where they bought large houses. They recreated a little *akazu* culture away from home, and for a while their cash bought a lot of influence in Kenyan political circles. This created a climate in which the KANU government was, from the start, hostile to the rebellion. But later, when Rwanda and Uganda fell out after the August 1999 clashes in Kisangani, Nairobi got on much better with Kigali and discreetly squeezed out the old *génocidaire* crowd, whose presence was becoming an embarrassment and whose money and therefore influence had dwindled as time went on. This way Kenya eventually edged a bit closer to true neutrality.

Another quasi-player who never declared its hand until it was unavoidable was Congo-Brazzaville. The Republic of Congo had recently known two periods of armed conflict (in 1993–1994 and again in 1997),[109] which had been characterized by the use of "tribal" militias;[110] a growing fragmentation of the conflict in which southerners of Niari, Lekoumou, and Bouenza first fought among themselves and with central Pool Province dwellers while the northerners from the Sangha and Likouala later took advantage the southerners' divisions to eventually "win" the civil war in October 1997; and a central role for the oil money, which had been used by former president Lissouba till the last moment to keep buying weapons and which the new president Sassou-Nguesso was desperately trying to lay his hands on. Sassou -Nguesso started by trying to persuade Elf into paying $600 million in April 1998, arguing that the company had helped Lissouba fight him.[111] When this failed he scaled down his demands to $180 million, and then finally settled for an increase in government royalties from 17.5 to 32 percent.

In fact, the fighting that had restarted sporadically during April 1998, quickened in August, and finally exploded in December was but a continuation of the two previous bouts of civil war. Same actors, same causes, same methods. There was only one difference: this time the fighting moved away from the capital and focused on the "rebel" areas of the Pool, where the Ninja militiamen of Bernard Kolelas had taken refuge, and in the Niari-Bouenza-Lekoumou (Nibolek) region, where Lissouba's Cocoyes had gone into hiding.[112] But Brazzaville was caught in a web of contradictory loyalties and enmities that made it very difficult this time around to contain the conflict within the borders of the Republic of Congo (or simply to understand what was going on).

- In April 1997 many fleeing Zairian DSP soldiers crossed into the Congo. They later fought for Sassou-Nguesso during the June–October 1997 war.[113] Their presence remained a permanent threat to Kabila.

- There were 11,000 Rwandese Hutu refugees in three UNHCR camps in the Republic of Congo. They had also fought on the side of Sassou's Cobra militia, but when fighting broke out in the DRC the men started leaving the camps and crossing the border to join the FAC and to tangle with Kabarebe's Tutsi.[114]

- Sassou was embroiled in a complicated quarrel with Central African Republic President Ange-Félix Patassé because he had given asylum to a French adviser of former president Kolingba (Patassé's enemy), which had caused Patassé to lend a favorable ear to Lissouba's demands for support. Patassé himself was worried that he could not keep aloof for long from the fighting in the DRC as the war spread northward into the Equateur Province and Congolese rebels were recruiting ethnically friendly tribal fighters in the Central African Republic.

- Sassou, who had received the backing of a four-hundred-strong Chadian expeditionary corps, was forced to mediate between Idriss Deby, president of Chad, and Patassé because Deby was angry at Patassé, a Sara by tribe, alleging his support for Sara rebels in Chad who were endangering oil exploration in the Doba region.

Does the reader at this point want to throw in the towel and give up on the ethnopolitical complexities of the region? I would not blame him, although I can assure him that I am honestly trying to simplify the picture. If we stand back for a moment and try to assess the situation, what do we see?

- *A core conflict* in which the new Rwandese RPF regime was trying, with Ugandan help, to overthrow their rebellious puppet Kabila.

- *A second layer* of powerful players (Angola and Zimbabwe, with Namibia riding shotgun) who could not care less about the Tutsi-Hutu conflict or the Uganda-Sudan confrontation but who, for their own diverse reasons, wanted Kabila to stay in power, albeit as a puppet.

- *A third layer* of actors (Libya, Chad, the Sudan) who felt they had to get involved for reasons that had nothing to do with the Congo itself but had to do largely *with each other* and with their indirect relationship to the core conflict players.

- *A fourth layer* of countries that were peripherally involved because of *geography* and because of *other entanglements* with countries not themselves neutral in the DRC war. This ranged from Burundi, which committed troops to the war (without ever admitting it),[115] to the Central African Republic, which desperately tried to resist being dragged in.[116]

This leaves out one major player, which, although it could not be described as the hidden puppeteer, was nonetheless *the major outside presence* in a conflict it was almost fated to win without ever having to get involved in fighting it. This essential actor was the Republic of South Africa.

South Africa had no direct or indirect security concerns in the Congo; its economic stake there was peripheral to its economic core; it had no political entanglements with anybody involved in the conflict that would have steered it, against its better judgment, in one direction or the other. It never sent troops to any of the areas at war.[117] Its diplomatic role was modest.[118] And its real understanding of the situation remained limited.[119] But South Africa is a very heavy player in a very lightweight environment. Since colonial times South African mining and transport industries have put down very deep roots in the Katanga region of the Congo Free State and later of the Belgian Congo.[120] Apartheid isolationism and Mobutu's economic mismanagement partly (but never completely) prised them apart. By 1997 both had disappeared, and economic logic had reasserted itself. Most of South Africa's actions regarding the Congolese situation were economically motivated.

- Pretoria was engaged in an implicit policy of economic expansion toward the whole of southern, eastern, and central Africa: plans by Trans Africa Railway Corporation to build a rail link to Kenya by way of Morogoro in Tanzania;[121] plans to buy the faltering Uganda Airways and Air Tanzania Corporation as well as shares of Kenya Airways; Eskom attempts at indirectly controlling the sick Congolese electricity parastatal Société Nationale d'Electricité;[122] and everywhere massive exports of South African goods and services. From that point of view Zimbabwe was a rival whose manipulation of the SADC was a constant irritant to Pretoria.

- Gold was at $300 an ounce in 1998, a rather listless price level: prolonged marginalization of the DRC could only be a good thing from South Africa's point of view since Kinshasa was a potential spoiler in the world gold market.

202

- The "rebels" were short of funds and desperate to turn Congolese assets into a rapid cash flow. Their victory was likely to further integrate Katanga's mining economy into the structures of its dominant southern neighbor.

All available indicators pointed to the logic of South African support for the rebels. But up to a point: South Africa's army was not the preferred means of intervention. Pretoria had, and rightly so, much more confidence in its economic clout and in its diplomatic capacity than in its rather inefficient armed forces. South African diplomacy was clumsy and ill-informed, but it had two very powerful trump cards: the guilt accumulated in Western countries by their long toleration of apartheid during the cold war and the eagerness of these same economically developed countries to enter a promising South African market. Both could be mined efficiently to ensure that the not-so-neutral "international community" would never stray too far from whatever positions Pretoria would take.

Fighting down to a stalemate

All the actors in the "Congolese" conflicts met at Victoria Falls in Zimbabwe on September 7, 1998, once the heat of Kabarebe's Blitzkrieg had died down. But the invaders' failure to take the capital had left an indecisive situation in which it was premature to expect any kind of settlement. As we will see, this did not discourage the belligerents from practicing with abandon Mao Zedong's old strategic dictum "Negotiate while you fight." According to this pattern negotiations were usually preceded, accompanied, and followed by the most extraordinary lies and exaggerations. This started right away when FAA Chief-of-Staff João de Matos declared before the Victoria Falls Conference, "Operations have been successfully carried out, the war will end pretty soon."[123] To which Modeste Rutabahirwa, chargé d'affaire at the Rwandese Embassy in Paris, retorted more realistically, "The Congo war is with us and it could last for two, four or even ten years."[124]

The Victoria Falls meeting was in itself a perfect example of deceitful pseudo-diplomacy: General Kagame denied that he had any troops in the DRC, while President Museveni said he had "fifty-one intelligence agents with the rebels and two battalions near our border for self-protection."[125] As for the cease-fire signed on September 7 (there were many more to come), it was broken the next day, when an Angolan Antonov An-12 flying from Kindu bombed Kalemie, killing twenty-five civilians.[126] Everybody went home then, and the war could really start.

Given the discomfiture of the Blitzkrieg force,[127] the next best thing the "rebels" could do was consolidate their control of the east. From their bases in North and South Kivu they could move in two directions: north-north-west to occupy Province Orientale and south-southwest to enter northern Katanga.[128] On the first front the still very thin RCD was to be supported by the UPDF, while the second front was largely an RPA operation, with some UPDF support in terms of artillery and tanks. Isiro was attacked in late August, and Kabila, who did not have the means of defending the northeast, flew to Ndjamena and then on to Tripoli, in defiance of the UN embargo, to request help from his allies. On September 18 the first Libyan planes started to ferry a one-thousand-strong Chadian contingent to the embattled north. But they were flown first to Gbadolite, and rallying the east from there was to prove a slow and difficult business. Kabila had also asked Central African Republic President Patassé and President Sassou Nguesso of the Brazzaville Congo for the Hutu refugees who were living on their territories. The U.S. State Department immediately sent a telegram to its Geneva mission to ask the UNHCR to stop the move at all cost.[129] On September 25 a combined RCD-UPDF-SPLA force occupied Dungu. The Sudanese rebels immediately started looting the town, going as far as dismantling the local power station to take it to Yambio in the Sudan.[130] They also corralled forty-six thousand Sudanese refugees from the local camps and pushed them back into western Equatoria in a rather rough way. From Dungu they moved into the Garamba National Park to scatter the Ugandan guerrillas hiding there and then went on to take Isiro on October 4. The Chadian contingent never made it to the battlefield, but it soon became involved in the fighting anyway because, even if the Chadians did not manage to move eastward, the enemy was now coming westward. Buta, on the edge of Equateur Province, had been taken on the same day as Isiro, and it soon became evident that the force moving into the province had a new component. On November 7 Jean-Pierre Bemba, a son of Mobutu's former crony and president of the Zairian Chamber of Commerce Bemba Saolona, announced the existence of a new rebel movement, the Mouvement de Libération du Congo (MLC). His approach, as he explained to a French journalist, could be characterized as "empirical": "I had identified the possibility of launching an armed movement. So I went looking for serious partners. There were two countries in the region which were interested but I chose to present my dossier to the Ugandans.[131] They liked it and so I went in."[132] When the interviewer asked him whether he had sought the support of rich former Mobutists, he replied with a laugh, "If they want to invest, now is the time. When I get to Kinshasa they'll have to queue up to reach my office."

In fact this was slightly disingenuous. Bemba the younger is a Ngbaka by tribe, that is, a member of the larger Bangala group. As such he could not but be a champion of the north, and if the "rich Mobutists" had not yet flocked to his standard it was only due to diplomatic precautions and also to some doubts about the feasibility of a young Belgian-educated playboy turning overnight into an effective African guerrilla leader.[133] But for the time being he was not doing badly. His Ugandan patrons had flown him into Kisangani on September 29, and from there he had loosely supervised battles fought by the Ugandan army on his behalf since his own movement was still too small to make a serious impact at the military level. The Chadian contingent, which had finally reached the front line, got whipped at Aketi and then at Bondo, losing over 70 men and 120 POWs.[134] A Ugandan helicopter flew Bemba into Aketi as soon as it was taken so that he could show himself and rally potential supporters. He got a rousing welcome and, a few days later, in the company of the Ugandans, his fledgling forces ambushed the Chadians again near Buta, killing 122 and capturing 148.[135]

As Bemba was driving deeper into Equateur the SPLA was finishing its housecleaning in the northeast, bringing ever greater numbers of former Sudanese refugees back into Yambio. The Chadians were frustrated at their poor showing and denied losing more than 250 casualties and over 400 POWs in a few weeks.[136] On November 17 the joint MLC-UPDF forces captured Bumba, 320 kilometers northwest of Kisangani, driving deep into the north. In the next few days the MLC was to recruit over a thousand young boys, all eager to fight for the new Bangala hero.[137] Bemba had earned his spurs, and he flew into Kampala two days later to meet Wamba dia Wamba, Museveni's man at the helm of the RCD. The reason for that meeting was that problems were already beginning to develop inside the rebel camp.

The RCD had never been popular, largely because it was seen as a tool of Rwanda. The preexisting ethnic tensions were brought to a boiling point by the "rebellion," which all the autochthonous tribes perceived as a Rwandese invasion. In late August in Uvira the local populace killed approximately 250 Banyamulenge as the RCD approached the city, and in a reprisal action the RCD massacred over 600 people (Bavira and Bafulero) at Kasika. The RCD found it difficult to recruit local collaborators, and those they could induce to join up were usually disliked by the population. The first RCD governor of South Kivu, Jean-Charles Magabe, was sacked in mid-October and replaced by his more pliable deputy, Benjamin Serukiza. Magabe fled to Brussels, where he passed very severe judgment on the "rebels": "We do not think these people will ever bring any form of democracy to the Congo. I can't see such a minority group fighting for democracy because if there were elections they have almost no chance of getting their people elected.... They just use the word democracy.... I could not support massacres. I could not accept that while pretending to fight for democracy we would install the rule of a tribe or rather of a sub-ethnic group."[138]

There were rumors within the RCD that its president, Ernest Wamba dia Wamba, was not far from sharing such politically incorrect feelings. The fact that Wamba was a Ugandan protégé created tensions between Kampala and Kigali in their management of the war. The creation of the MLC, with obvious Ugandan support, only made matters worse. Jean-Pierre Ondekane, the RCD military leader, tried to keep up the pretence that the MLC was under his command and even claimed the taking of Bumba as his own victory. The Kampala meeting was supposed to bring all the "rebels" and their sponsors together; it resulted in the proclamation of a common RPA-UPDF Military Command in the Congo. This was to remain a purely paper decision, with no effect on the ground.

Meanwhile, Rwandese forces, with some UPDF support, had pushed for a deepening of the southern front. The first step was the taking of Kindu, the capital of Maniema, in mid-October after a no-holds-barred bloody battle[139] in which many of the combatants were non-Congolese. Just as it was mostly Ugandans fighting Chadians in the north, in Kindu many of the five-thousand-strong "Congolese" garrison was made up of Rwandese ex-FAR and *Interahamwe* and Ugandan guerrillas flown in from Juba by the Sudanese army, while the assailants were largely Rwandese and Ugandans. "After the fall of Kindu, roads are now open for the conquest of the entire country," declared RCD Commander Jean-Pierre Ondekane. The "rebel" forces started immediately to push south, potentially a very dangerous move for the Kinshasa regime. Between November 18 and 22 Kabila used his allies' air transport capacity[140] to fly eight thousand ex-FAR and *Interahamwe* to Lodja (418 kilometers west of Kindu) in the hope of stemming the rebel advance, while the Zimbabwean National Army (ZNA) quickly deployed two thousand more troops in Lubao and Kabinda. What they were trying to protect was the obvious next target for the "rebels": Mbuji-Mayi and its diamond mines, the only cash-producing territory the government had left under its control. Kabalo had fallen to the RCD on October 20 and Kongolo had been taken on November 10. From there the Rwando-rebel forces quickly extended their control over northern Katanga, taking Moba, Pepa, Manono, and Kasange. Soon the fighting was down to Pweto on the Zambian border.[141] Further west as well the situation kept deteriorating for the government camp, with Lubao falling on January 27. By March the rebels had pushed to Kabinda, which was under siege.[142] The Rwando-rebel forces pushed desperately because the big diamond prize was nearly theirs. By late March they had gained partial control of Kabinda, where the Zimbabweans were putting up a spirited defense. Fifteen thousand refugees had fled to the Kaputa refugee camp in Zambia, many of them with battle wounds.[143] Since Kabinda was proving such a hard nut to crack, the Rwando-RCD forces tried to go around it, occupying Lusambo on the Sankuru River on June 15 to threaten Mbuji-Mayi from the north. Zimbabwe deployed another three thousand troops in June and Rwanda seven thousand more. Peace talks had started in Zambia, and both sides were hoping for military successes before international pressure proved irresistible. In the north Bemba was doing the same thing: he had captured Gemena on December 30, causing panic in Kinshasa since in his case it was not the diamond mines of Kasai that were at stake, but the capital itself.

In the first days of January 1999 Namibian Boeings and Angolan Tupolev transport planes brought one thousand FAC soldiers to Bangui in the Central African Republic to mount a counteroffensive in Equateur. The Sudanese joined in with daily bombings by Antonov An-12 from Juba. The MLC-UPDF forces could not withstand the pressure and withdrew to Lisala after losing Gemena, Businga, and Libenge. Bemba remarked in disgust, "We are fighting a mixture of Sudanese, Chadians, *Interahamwe* and Central Africans; there are only very few Congolese among the FAC."[144] He conveniently forgot to mention that many of his own men had been recruited in the Central African Republic[145] and that the Ugandan army made up most of his battle corps. In February the "rebels" organized the only combined offensive they were going to be able to manage during the whole conflict. Over sixty thousand men were involved on the "rebel" side if one added up the RCD, the RPA, the MLC, and the UPDF.[146] In the north the targets were Gbadolite, Mbandaka, and down to Kinshasa. In the southeast they were Mbuji-Mayi, Kamina, and Lubumbashi. In case these military plans succeeded only partially, the partition of the country would follow. Bemba went on the offensive and took Ango. The FAC fled across the river into the Central African Republic town of Zemio, where Libyan aircraft came to fly them back to Kinshasa. On their own front the Rwando-RCD forces had widened their control of northern Katanga by taking Kaputo and Kasiki in mid-March, all the while desperately pushing around Kabinda. The ZNA counterattacked too soon and lost over two hundred men at the battle of Eshimba.[147] But the offensive did not have the means to carry on and it progressively lost momentum.

Meanwhile the rivalry between the Rwanda-sponsored RCD and the Uganda-sponsored MLC was growing ever sharper. When Bemba's forces took Kateke and Bondo in mid-April he was careful to point out that "these successes belong to MLC troops, they owe nothing to the RCD."[148] But just like his rivals in Kasai and Katanga he was hoping to achieve decisive victories before the peace talks now under way in Zambia could freeze the military situation. On July 3 he took Gbadolite, Mobutu's former "jungle capital," and then in quick succession kicked out the FAC from Gemena, Bokungu, and Zongo. He now controlled practically the whole of Equateur Province and, contrary to his RCD rivals, without any tension with the civilians. Both he and his movement were popular among the Bangala, who were hoping for a return of the "good old days" of Mobutist northern domination while the relatively disciplined behavior of the Ugandan soldiers also helped when compared to the constant violence of the Rwandese RPA in its own zone of operation. But Bemba could not make it to Kinshasa, at least not with his present strength and not unless the UPDF mounted an all-out offensive to support his move downriver. As for the Rwando-RCD forces, they were similarly stuck in northern Kasai and northern Katanga, where fighting was still violent around Kabinda but where the ZNA blocked all progress toward Mbuji-Mayi. The diamond capital had received large reinforcements of FAC and ZNA and its entire periphery was by now heavily mined. The "rebels" had long hoped that UNITA would cross the border and intervene in the war to break the deadlock. Already in October, at the time of the fighting for Kindu, UNITA forces had started from Tchikapa toward Mbuji-Mayi to coordinate with the Rwando-Ugandan push. But they had to turn back due to Savimbi's needs on other battlefronts. On March 25 Savimbi had met General Kagame, Bizima Karaha, and former Republic of Congo president Pascal Lissouba in Ouagadougou at the invitation of the great west African prestidigitator Blaise Compaore. The hope was to get UNITA to throw its weight into the "Congolese" war as a step to further operations (and victory) in Angola proper. Savimbi thought the plan too complicated and refused to go along with it, in spite of two hours of intense discussions.[149] Without UNITA support (and possibly even with that) the Rwando-Ugandan troops could not swallow the huge chunk of the continent they had bitten. The situation was not that of early 1997, when the AFDL and its continentwide supporters could walk clear across Zaire, practically without opposition. The FAC, weak as they were, were trying their best, contrary to the FAZ two years before. And contrary to the FAZ, they had reasonably strong allies. By mid-April Ondekane could still declare defiantly, "The objective remains the liberation of the whole country and we are pushing on towards Kinshasa," but it sounded increasingly like whistling in the dark. The time had come for "peace talks."

Behind and around the war: domestic politics, diplomacy, and economics

The Congo. Seen from Kinshasa the whole war situation hinged on Laurent-Désiré Kabila, his obsessions, whims, and bizarre cabinet. Kabila's entourage resembled a medieval court in that the paper positions of the cabinet members were only a vague indication of what their actual roles could be and in that the favor of the prince counted for everything. The key man was perhaps Mwenze Kongolo, a thirty-eight-year-old Muluba married to an African American; he was one of the "ANACOZA recruits" of the AFDL days who was also a key member of the president's Baluba inner circle. He had managed to put his trusted man Jean Mbuyu in the important position of Kabila's secretary, which enabled him to oversee everything in the president's office. Another confidant was Didier Kazadi Nyembwe, an eastern Kasai Muluba on his father's side with a Burundian Tutsi mother. Kazadi Nyembwe was a longtime associate of the president and of his son Joseph, whose studies he had supervised in Dar-es-Salaam when the father was away for long periods. His intimate knowledge of the president's affairs put him at the heart of the security system and of his private business deals. In the shadow of his former minder Joseph Kabila acquired steadily growing importance in military affairs after returning from military training in China. When Pierre-Célestin Kifwa, who had been made army chief on July 13, turned out to be completely incompetent, Joseph, who was his deputy, had to replace him impromptu as he floundered helplessly in the midst of Kaberebe's Blitzkrieg.[150] In fact, it was the triumvirate of Mwenze Kongolo, Kazadi Nyembwe, and Joseph Kabila who, together with Didier Mumengi and Yerodia Ndombasi, had held the fort during those decisive days in August when Laurent-Désiré Kabila had safely removed himself to Lubumbashi. Their loyalty was beyond question. Not so with Fernand Tala Ngaï, the finance minister who was sacked in October because he had been too close to the Tutsi component of the AFDL. He was replaced by Mawampaga Mwana Nanga, a Mukongo who had briefly held the position in the early days of the AFDL before his wife was caught trying to smuggle $200,000 out of the country in a shoebox. Pierre-Victor Mpoyo was another Muluba whose long history as an oil middleman doubled as that of an informal representative of Angolan interests.[151]

This "government" was organized like a loose band of freebooters or a hunting pack. Roles could be switched easily,[152] there were no rules or procedures, state business and private business were hopelessly intermingled, and there was a tremendous feeling of precariousness. Failure to win would mean exile or death. The war was run in a most haphazard fashion because there was no army to speak of, and while the FAC were slowly and painfully brought up to standards, the government had to rely on two sources of military support: foreign armies and the Mayi Mayi guerrillas.

Among these foreign troops the most controversial were the Rwandese ex-FAR and *Interahamwe*. Although embarrassing, they had the advantage of being fiercely loyal, both because they hated the new Kigali regime and because they could see no hope in their present situation unless Kabila won. On September 28 Colonels Serubuga, Rwagafilita, and Kibirigi arrived in Kinshasa from their Nairobi exile and met Gen. Augustin Bizimungu, who had just been fighting on the other side of the river for the militia of President Denis Sassou-Nguesso. There they were welcomed by Michael van Krut, the boss of Executive Outcomes in Luanda,[153] who had already seconded about 40 South African and 120 French and Belgian mercenaries to the FAC at the request of the Angolan government.[154] Soon large numbers of Hutu former soldiers flocked to the Congolese capital from Brazzaville, the Central African Republic, Gabon, and as far as Sudan. As the war went on the refugee camps emptied, and within six months "the Rwandese [were] at the forefront of the fighting and there [were] no adult males left in the camps."[155] This was militarily necessary but politically quite damaging for the Kabila regime, which laid itself open to Kigali's propaganda attacks of "preaching genocide."[156]

Another important source of military support for the embattled Kinshasa government was the Mayi Mayi guerrilla forces, which had sprung up spontaneously all over the occupied east. They were reckless, confused, mostly very young, poorly armed and organized, and often so violent that they were feared by the very populations they purported to defend. Almost immediately they became a key element in the eastern theater of operations when they attacked Goma, the RCD "capital," twice during September.[157] The Mayi Mayi were a godsend for Kinshasa for a number of reasons: they fought voluntarily; they gave the regime a certain popular legitimacy to which the president himself, with his Maoist past, was particularly sensitive; they were cheap; and they were a constant thorn in the side of the Rwandese army as it tried to push into Kasai and Katanga. For the Congolese government this largely outweighed the international discredit their real or supposed génocidaire associations brought along.[158] In Kinshasa Faustin Munene, the vice minister of the interior, and General Sikatenda, an old friend and companion of Laurent-Désiré Kabila from his guerrilla days, were in charge of liaising with the Mayi Mayi in the field, but the help they could give them, especially at the beginning of the war, was extremely limited. Nevertheless, supposed "FAC victories" in the east (and even those of the foreign armies fighting alongside them) were often in fact achieved by Mayi Mayi forces.[159]

But the Mayi Mayi phenomenon had tragic consequences for the population in the two Kivus. The Rwandese and their RCD cohorts were widely hated and the Mayi Mayi were the armed expression of that hatred. But because they were militarily weak they could not protect the population from a horribly violent repression. This led to repeated massacres, all of which are not yet fully documented. It started in August with the Kasika massacre (600 killed), followed by the Lemera massacre of December 4 (30 killed), the Ngweshe killings (around 30 killed in early February 1999), the Kamituga slaughter (around 100 victims on March 5), the Burhinyi and Walungu killings of mid-March 1999 (280 killed), 41 villagers burned alive by the RCD in Malemba-Nkuku (Upper Lomani) at around the same time, the big Makobola slaughter of March 15 (814 casualties), the May 1999 "Mayi Mayi surrender massacre" in Kinyogota,[160] and the Uvira slaughter of early August 1999 (119 victims).[161] These outrages are simply the largest and the best known ones, but the whole atmosphere of life in the Kivus became impossible, with a constant stream of murders, carjackings, armed attacks, rapes, theft, arson, highway robberies, and casual looting.[162] Life became so difficult that whole segments of the population took refuge in the forests, where the absence of medical care and the presence of malaria and tropical rains killed many more than did enemy bullets. Agriculture was neglected because women feared being raped when they went to cultivate their fields. Prices rose in the occupied areas as commerce dwindled. The Catholic Church became the last service provider still able to function.[163] This violence in the occupied territories was matched by the casual way the government used the air force (or rather, that of Kabila's allies) to bomb "enemy targets," which were simply civilians living in enemy-occupied areas.

Bombing	Date	Casualties	Nationality of Aircraft
Kalemie	Sept. 8, 1998	25 killed	Angolan
Kalemie	Nov. 25, 1998	20 killed	Zimbabwean 90 wounded
Kisangani	Jan. 12, 1999	40 killed	Sudanese
Goma	May 11, 1999	43 killed	Zimbabwean
Uvira	May 11, 1999	20 killed	Zimbabwean
Uvira	June 3, 1999	3 killed	unknown
Equateur	Aug. 4, 1999	524 killed	Sudanese

Sources: IRIN Bulletins, press agencies, eyewitnesses.

The attack, on August 4, 1999, during which two Antonov An-12 flying from Juba had bombed a series of villages (hitting, among other "targets," a crowded market), was the only one in which soldiers were actually killed (134 MLC and 10 UPDF). But on the ground the FAC did not commit the type of atrocities that were commonly associated with the Rwando-rebel forces simply because they did not have to face a hostile civilian population. There was one exception to that: Equateur Province, where the local people actually supported Bemba and his MLC and where the FAC committed their only known atrocities of the war when they killed about 320 civilians during their short-lived counteroffensive in January.[164]

Political life in such a climate was restricted to a minimum. President Kabila had created the Comités du Pouvoir Populaire on January 21 and he saw this "popular mass organization" as playing the central role of "transmitter belt" between the government and "the masses." On April 20 he convened their first congress, during which he dissolved the AFDL, calling it "a conglomerate of opportunists and adventurers." He railed against the "one hundred parties" of the late Mobutu era, which he said had turned democracy into a joke, and extolled the new organization as "one organization for the people to create their own happiness."[165] A Kinshasa newspaper sadly remarked, "One thought the one-party state had died in 1990 but it is now coming back in another guise."[166] The same blend of aggressive populism and Marxist-Leninist leftovers inspired his diplomacy. He courted Beijing and Pyongyang,[167] letting loose a curiously antiquated rhetoric not particularly calculated to endear him to what he probably saw as "the capitalist

West": "If the American slave traders are planning to occupy the Congo to plunder its wealth as their Rwandan and Ugandan agents are already doing in the occupied territories, the Congolese people will show them ... that they will never passively suffer genocide like the American Indians.... . Imperialist aggression ... is a plot which ultimately aims at reducing all Congolese into slavery. We must unmask the enemy even if he is hiding under a cassock, wearing the mask of a humanitarian organization or that of a diplomat."[168]

His economic policies were perfectly coherent with his general political line. On September 11 he created the Service d'Achat des Substances Minérales Précieuses (SASMIP), which was supposed to centralize all gold and diamond purchasing for the state. The results were eloquent: within one month exports were down by 13 percent. Central Bank Director Jean-Claude Masangu was politely aghast and managed to get the SASMIP disbanded. He also put his foot down on the printing of fresh currency since the Congolese franc had lost 64 percent of its value since August 2 and inflation had risen to 81 percent, though he had previously managed to bring it down to 7.3 percent just before the war.[169] But Kabila was not going to be foiled by his Central Bank director, no matter how clever he was. On January 8 Presidential Decrees 177 and 179 re-created the SASMIP under another name (Bourse Congolaise des Matières Précieuses, or BCMP) and banned dollar trading altogether.[170] De Beers was horrified and tried to talk some sense into the president because it feared that, unless he ordered the treasury to wildly print more currency, Kabila would not be able to mobilize enough Congolese francs every month to finance the fifty million dollars' worth of Congolese diamond exports. Masangu was arrested on January 14 for criticizing the two presidential decrees and for refusing to disburse $17 million (in hard currency) due to Zimbabwe. The Congolese franc immediately fell from 3 to 6.6 to the U.S. dollar on the black market; it eventually had to be devalued by 35.5 percent on April 8, down to $1 = FC 4.5. By then Masangu had been freed from detention to try to save the situation, but the black market rate was up to 8.2. Since the dollar was only at FC 3.6 in the rebel areas, which were in better financial shape due to the free market smuggling of commodities, a juicy traffic was immediately started by the FAC (and even by the allied ZNA and Namibian Defense Force), taking big bundles of Congolese francs over the "front lines" and converting them into dollars at the better rate.[171] When commercialized, the first six months of MIBA diamond production brought only $1.4 million and oil revenue dropped from $36.4 million (1997) to $9.9 million (1998) due to the price distortions.[172] The value of diamond exports fell precipitously as the BCMP was systematically short-circuited and gems were sold on the black market.

Value of Diamond Exports (in U.S. $ millions)

April 1998	December 1998	January 1999	February 1999
50	35	17	16

Source: La Lettre Afrique Energies, 31 March 1999.

Congolese exports were increasingly impounded by court order to cover unpaid import bills: 6,500 cubic meters of precious lumber was seized in Lisbon, 800 tons of cobalt in Johannesburg, 40 tons of cobalt in Antwerp. On April 11 fuel prices were doubled, and the next day Kabila's motorcade was stoned as it rode through Kinshasa. The bodyguards opened fire, killing one bystander and wounding three. The popular singer Papa Wenge composed a new song, "Titanic," and many night clubs picked up the name. The latest dance was called "Firing Position." In spite of the growing threat of AIDS casual love affairs flourished. There was a kind of defiant despair in the air, as if tomorrow would never happen. If people were going to go down, at least they would go down singing.[173]

Angola. The situation had become intractable: it was evident that the MPLA had decided to destroy UNITA as a possible form of alternative power. An emasculated UNITA that would take its (small) share in the looting of the country's wealth would have been acceptable, but one that might demand an equal share or even all was unthinkable. This was in fact a view shared by the international business community, and particularly the Americans. The J. P. Morgan Bank had arranged a $750 million loan backed by oil futures, which implied the continued control of resources by the MPLA,[174] and a major trading company went one step further in July when it arranged a $900 million credit to Luanda against one whole year of oil production. As a qualified observer remarked at the time, "Savimbi has complied with the bulk of the peace protocol six months ago."[175] But it did not matter. On September 4 President dos Santos "suspended the dialogue with UNITA" and sacked UNITA's four ministers and seven vice ministers in the government. Frantically trying to dissociate themselves from Savimbi, whom they felt had a personal fight with the MPLA leadership, several top UNITA commanders "suspended" Savimbi from his position at the head of the movement.[176] Then the charismatic leader Abel Chivukuvuku launched another dis-

214

sident faction that rallied fifty-five UNITA MPs behind it. They had not really understood the nature of the situation, but they soon did, when "somebody" fired several shots at Chivukuvuku's car, missing his wife by inches. The UNITA dissidents never got anywhere. The reality was in the new offshore deep-water oil permits: block 14 to Chevron, block 15 to Exxon, blocks 17 and 32 to Elf, block 19 to Petrofina, and block 20 to Mobil. These brought almost $1.5 billion in advance bonuses, and the MPLA elite had no intention whatsoever of sharing that loot.[177]

At the end of October, on the principle that my enemy's enemy is my friend, Savimbi flew to Kisangani to meet James Kazini and Kayumba Nyamwasa. They discussed the exfiltration of UPDF Brig. Ivan Koreta and his boys, left stranded in the western Congo, and they talked diamonds. Soon Savimbi was to make a big present to the "rebels" by sending them "Papa Felipe," the legendary Belgian diamond dealer Philippe Surowicke, who had long been UNITA's main diamond trader and who used his old Antwerp connections to start trading diamonds in Kisangani in November, drawing on supplies from over two hundred small artisanal mines around the city. But the gift was to prove poisonous because "Papa Felipe" soon came to do business mostly with the Kazini–Salim Saleh group of companies, that is, with the Ugandans, which fed, with dire consequences, into the growing Rwando-Ugandan rivalry in Kisangani.

Meanwhile the war had restarted in earnest on December 4, when the FAA attacked Bailundo. The fighting was extremely hard and no mercy was shown to humanitarians: the UN lost four airplanes shot down between December 11 and January 2; the government and UNITA blamed each other for downing the aircraft. On January 17 Kofi Annan finally admitted, "Peace has collapsed." The MPLA accused Burkina Faso, Togo, Rwanda, Uganda, and Zambia of helping UNITA,[178] which was largely true provided the word "help" is qualified. President Blaise Compaore of Burkina Faso and President Gnassingbé Eyadema of Togo were mostly out to make money and to some extent further their complicated schemes in west Africa. Rwanda and Uganda mostly wanted to get UNITA to support their war in the Congo and in the meantime did not mind serving as a conduit for some of UNITA's diamond exports. As for Zambia, as we already saw, the government was not even involved, but some powerful individuals made money by selling UNITA what it needed. The war flared all over Angola, although the worst-affected provinces were Malange and Huambo. The number of IDPs shot up tragically.

IDP Numbers

January 1998	October 1998	February 1999	March 1999	August 1999
423,000	654,000	881,000	1,200,000	2,000,000

Source: UNHCR.

Fighting was intense, with a massive deployment of tanks and artillery that made the Congolese operations look amateurish by comparison. Large towns such as M'Banza Congo, Maquela do Zombo, and Chinguar would change hands several times in a few months. Paulo Lukamba ("Gato") declared that UNITA would fight until dos Santos agreed to "direct talks,"[179] an offer the MPLA lost no time in turning down, saying instead that it would "wage a final war."[180] The civilian population was caught in the middle in a way that was perfectly summarized by the civil society NGO Angola Forum:

> We [the civil society] are the target of deadly persecution by the regime for having exposed corruption cases in the government… . Senior FAA members have been selling fuel to UNITA… . UNITA is a purely military movement that promotes political instability while President Dos Santos shows a total lack of political solutions on how to shelter the thousands upon thousands of Angolans displaced by the civil war… . To wage [war] more easily the government called for the withdrawal of international community observers but it now wants UN personnel back to take part in humanitarian assistance.[181]

The intensity of the fighting was such and the stakes were so high that the Angolan regime saw any other foreign entanglement as secondary in relationship to the main battlefield. When the survivors of Kabarebe's Blitzkrieg attacked Maquela do Zombo together with UNITA, it prompted an immediate redeployment of FAA forces from the DRC and a counterattack from the Congolese side of the border. Maquela do Zombo was retaken with Zimbabwean help. Luanda's foreign minister, João de Miranda, went to Pretoria in May to try to stop South African support for UNITA. But South African Foreign Minister Alfred Nzo countered by saying that it was all happening outside of his government's control because over one hundred small airfields were used by the smugglers.[182] After the UN Fowler Report came out, saying that UNITA was still getting at least $200 million a year from its diamond smuggling, De Beers suggested a "standardized" Certificate of Origin system, with verification offices in Ouagadougou, Abidjan, Kolwezi, Lubumbashi, Kampala, Ndola, Luanda, and Kiev.[183] That list is as interesting for the diamond smuggling geography it outlines as for the one it hides. Ouagadougou, Abidjan, and Kampala are understandably there.

Ndola recognizes the role of Zambia in the system, and Lubumbashi realistically stands for the Congolese collusion with their allies' enemy. Luanda is even more interesting in that it recognizes that many UNITA diamonds were going through the Angolan capital with the help of corrupt MPLA officials. Kiev is there to annoy De Beers's Russian rivals. But Johannesburg and Antwerp, where De Beers itself operated, are absent. And so is Kigali because in the postgenocide wave of Western contrition it would not be politically correct to suggest that the Tutsi "victims" could also be UNITA diamond smugglers. By then UNITA had turned into everybody's favorite villain: it spoiled the diamond market and could potentially threaten future oil interests by calling into account the huge pre-exploitation bonuses American and French companies had agreed to pay to the MPLA, with no questions asked about how the money was used.[184]

This puts into perspective Angola's interest in the Congolese side of the war: it was both essential—Savimbi should not be allowed to reclaim the rear bases he had there during Mobutu's time—and secondary because the war was not going to be won or lost on the Congolese battlefields. Therefore Luanda was content with letting the Zimbabweans, the FAC, and the Rwandese ex-FAR and *Interahamwe* do all the hard fighting in the Congo while it devoted itself to the purely Angolan military situation. This also explains why Savimbi (who had at the most seventy thousand men under arms) did not agree to send an expeditionary force to the Congo, where his MPLA enemies had kept only a limited contingent of about fifteen hundred men once the threat to Kinshasa receded.

Zimbabwe. The Zimbabwean position was much more simple: it was in the war to protect its past investments in the Kabila regime, to secure new ones, and to block what it saw as a South African–supported attempt at taking over the Congo. This was clearly stated at the highest level, and Minister of Justice Emerson Munangagwa, one of the ZANU-PF heavyweights, had declared, "There is a deliberate effort on our part, as a government, to push Zimbabwean business into the Congo."[185] As later reports were to show, the ZANU-PF government was not too choosy about the nature of that "Zimbabwean business." This had been obvious from the start, when Laurent-Désiré Kabila had signed a rather vague agreement between Gécamines, Ridgepoint Overseas Development Ltd., and the Central Mining Group Corporation on September 29, 1998. The last two companies were in fact branches of Billy Rautenbach's company, Wheels of Africa,[186] which specialized in importing Japanese cars to Zimbabwe, a successful business that was greatly helped by his father's political connections with the ZANU-PF establishment. Mugabe picked Billy as the man best able to make some quick money for the cash-strapped Congolese government, and by late 1998 he was extracting 150 tons of cobalt a month, worth $6 million, from the Likassi slag heaps. On November 6 Kabila, who was delighted with his wonder businessman, made him general manager of the giant Gécamines corporation. But as we saw earlier, the going soon got rough and increasing quantities of cobalt were being seized by foreign creditors of the government in lieu of unpaid bills. The legitimate mining companies were shutting up shop everywhere,[187] and in the following months Rautenbach and his Zimbabwean backers found that the going got much rougher than hitherto.

As for the Zimbabwean army, it was simply the field agent of Zimbabwe's economic interests, something that was painfully clear to the vast majority of that country's people. As time went on, withdrawal from the Congo became one of the strongest demands of the MDC political opposition.

Rwanda and Uganda: a violent friendship. Rwanda's main problem in the early days of the new war were the rebel infiltrations in the northwest of the country. By mid-October there were 478,637 IDPs in the two northern prefectures of Gisenyi and Ruhengeri.[188] By mid-December their numbers had passed the 500,000 mark. But the repression that had started before the war went on unabated and sheer force ended up by prevailing over the guerrillas. After a massacre during which at least 140 civilians were killed on December 19, the insurgency seemed to collapse, and African Rights, an advocacy NGO based in Britain, coyly declared, "The population is no longer prepared to support the insurgents."[189] To better control the situation the Rwandese government moved part of the vast mass of IDPs (they were 508,626 by late March) into the new Imidugudu housing.[190] The donors meekly gave 58 percent of the $37.9 million needed, calling the forced resettlement "an answer to the housing crisis."[191] Rwanda was keenly aware of its dependency on foreign aid and it never lost an opportunity to remind the West of its criminal negligence at the time of the genocide. Thus the war in the Congo was described purely in terms of security concerns. As early as October Rwanda's foreign minister Anastase Gasana had asked the UN "to condemn the genocide of the Tutsi now underway in the DRC."[192] With such "explanations" playing fully on Western guilt it was easy for Kagame to bluntly state, "RPA troops will stay in the Congo as long as Rwanda's national security will be under threat.... . Militarily we have eliminated the insurgency from Rwanda but there is still a threat coming from the DRC.... We shall be in the Congo till a solution is found."[193] As the extreme violence of the Rwandese troops against Congolese civilians became common knowledge, Kigali reacted by trying to blur the issue into a kind of genocidal melting pot, wherein Congolese citizens became assimilated into the *Interahamwe*. Gerald Gahima declared, "We have to protest against the implications that our armed forces have a policy of indiscriminate killings of non-combatants during counter-insurgency operations";[194] he then added in a perfect *non sequitur*, "We ask the international community to take a stand against the spread of the genocide ideology in the Great Lakes region." In reality the former *génocidaires* could never have dreamed up better public relations agents than Kagame's soldiers, as their brutality toward innocent civilians helped to progressively develop an unhealthy retrospective toleration of the genocide among the Congolese population. But the donors remained blind and deaf to the problem, particularly Britain's minister for overseas development Clare Short, who was persuaded of the Rwandese regime's absolute innocence. Since the French were sulking in a corner in the aftermath of their Rwandese debacle, the British, through Short, became Kigali's main advocate in Brussels. It was through her insistence that the European Union finally released in May a $50 million grant it had withheld for the past six months due to criticism of the Rwandese invasion of Congo by other EU members. The accompanying communiqué was sadly amusing, stating, "The amount will be used to support economic reforms."[195] In exchange for their belated kindness the good donors were trying to get some few scraps of niceties for their diplomatic mill. It was at the behest of Susan Rice, U.S. under-secretary of state for African affairs, and Clare Short that Kagame finally admitted—four months after the beginning of the war— that his troops were indeed in the Congo, adding cryptically that there were "good reasons not to acknowledge it before."

Donors also kept harping on the question of "transition." Ever since the collapse of the government of national unity in August 1995 the international community had been hoping for some kind of decently balanced new political dispensation which would be a symbol of national reconciliation. On April 29, 1998, shortly before the war, Kagame had said, "The recent elections could mark the end of the transition period,"[196] and no more was heard on the subject for quite a while. But in June 1999, irritated by constant reminders of the donors, Kigali decided to "extend the transition period," and RPF heavyweight Charles Morigande declared, "Rwanda is a special case and there are challenges to be met." The following month, when the five-year transition period agreed upon in July 1994 came to an end, the Rwandese government simply decided to prolong the transition for another four years. The donors swallowed their objections rather than be reminded for the umpteenth time of their callousness during the genocide.

But the international community was soon to be challenged by another problem. As the war in the DRC broadened and deepened, the invaders increasingly tried to finance their operations directly through the exploitation of Congolese natural resources. This was the period that saw the creation of what would become the notorious "Congo Desk" in the Rwandese Ministry of Defense and in which a Brussels bank created a (modest) "revolving fund" of $10 million financed by "coltan from Butembo, gold from the Sominki mined in Kamituga and Kisangani diamonds."[197] A staggering prize (the more than two hundred artisanal mines around Kisangani had produced $5.3 million between July and October 1997 alone), this particular source of cash was soon to exacerbate the growing difficulties that had begun to develop between the two allies, Rwanda and Uganda.[198]

At this point a word of warning is needed: so much has been made of foreign rivalries over "the looting of Congolese riches" that I must insist on the fact that the growing antagonism between Kigali and Kampala was more than a fight between gangsters sharing the product of a heist. It was both a thuggish fight *and* a political and strategic conflict, and it was the political conflict that came first. Rwanda and Uganda had attacked the Congo together but with different views on almost everything: the relative importance of their own security, the economics of the war, the attitude toward the international community, and, last but not least, what to do in Kinshasa in case of victory. Museveni still retained a basic faith in the tenets of his revolutionary past: the Congolese must be allowed to decide for themselves (with a little help from their friends) and should create an inclusive government of national unity, preferably some sort of "no-party democracy," as practiced in Kampala. For Kagame and the RPF this was pure poppycock; the Congolese were simply to be manipulated into some kind of neocolonial subservience to their natural masters. Of course, these views were never articulated in so many words, but they shone through the actions of the parties. Museveni tried to wheedle and coddle his Congolese; Kagame simply bullied his.

These differences were soon to lead to practical repercussions on the ground. In November 1998 the Ugandans announced the creation of a Joint Military Command (JMC) between them and the Rwandese, an idea that seemed to make sense in purely military terms. The announcement was contradicted five days later by Kigali, which declared that there was no such a thing as a JMC between them and the Ugandans. As early as December 1998 a Ugandan opposition paper echoed stories of limited military clashes between the RPA and the UPDF because of the latter's support for Jean-Pierre Bemba's fledgling MLC.[199] But the divergences were not limited to the MLC/RCD dichotomy; they were also *inside* the RCD. On December 31, as RCD president Wamba dia Wamba was giving his New Year's speech on Radio Goma, the broadcast suddenly went off the air as his rival, Lunda Bululu, cut the power supply. Bululu allegedly did not appreciate the attacks on "former Mobutists who disfigure our movement."[200] In such a climate the first few months of 1999 saw a growing rift between the pro-Kampala and the pro-Kigali wings of the RCD. Wamba had moved his group to Kisangani, while Kigali's friends stayed behind in their original headquarters in Goma. As a result, the two factions became informally known as RCD-K and RCD-G and started to fight a war of propaganda though their respective media, les Coulisses and Radio Goma for RCD-G and Radio Liberté and Kisangani TV for RCD-K. Finally, in early May, Lunda Bululu called an RCD General Assembly in Goma for May 23, but Wamba beat him to the draw by calling another one in Kisangani for May 15. The fight was on.[201]

On May 17 the RCD "dissolved itself" at a meeting hastily convened in Goma and then "recomposed" itself as a "new" organization which comprised only the Kigali faithful (Emile Ilunga, Jean-Pierre Ondekane, Moïse Nyarugabo), that is, fifty-one members of the original 151 in the executive. On May 20 Wamba refused the dissolution and reorganization and was reelected in Kisangani by seventy-five members of the movement's executive. Two days later he organized a demonstration in his own support in Kisangani, but the city's control was split between Rwandese and Ugandan troops, each backing opposite factions of the splintered RCD. There were four people killed and a score wounded and Wamba suspended the RCD-nominated governor. The next day Bizima Karaha and J. P. Ondekane flew into Kisangani, organized an anti-Wamba meeting, and confirmed the governor in his position. Bemba was coolly looking at the situation, declaring, "I am ardently courted by both factions but I am not ready to get married." At this point Wamba declared that he was prepared to meet with Kabila and to organize elections in the territory he controlled. This sent a shock wave into the highly unpopular RCD-G, which organized its own "elections" for governor in Goma on May 24, with RPA units encircling the building where the delegates made their choice, just to be sure the choice was the right one. On May 25 Wamba landed in Goma, protected by five hundred UPDF troops and four tanks. His "negotiation" with RCD-G unsurprisingly yielded no result, and the next day he was escorted out by road to Rutshuru and Kisoro, over to Uganda. With the kind of clumsy frankness that was eventually to cost him dear, President Pasteur Bizimungu declared that Rwanda would continue to fight because "even if the rebellion disintegrated we have our own interests."[202] The war of words was rapidly edging toward a shooting war and the two factions began trading pot shots in Kisangani. On August 2 Rwanda pulled out its usual ideological ultimate weapon, saying that Wamba was recruiting former *Interahamwe* and accusing Uganda of complicity.[203]

Although the crisis was fundamentally politically driven, there was a seedy economic underside to it, and in order to understand that we have to take a look at the exploitation of the local diamond mines since the RCD's occupation of Kisangani.[204]

In August 1998, when the rebels and their foreign friends occupied the city, they immediately closed 150 of its 200 or so diamond export counters. They also found a stash of uncut stones worth $100 million, which they confiscated to finance the war. Prices immediately fell by 30 percent; this was when the Ugandans brought in their famous "Papa Felipe" (Philippe Surowicke) of Angolan repute. He had been unemployed for a while and arrived in Kisangani in December 1998 after much negotiating in Kampala. At the time the surviving counters were paying a 3 percent tax on all diamond transactions to the RCD. "Papa Felipe" offered 10 percent in exchange for a monopoly. But he was working with the Victoria Group of Salim Saleh, Museveni's half-brother, and he dealt exclusively with the pro-Kampala wing of the RCD. In the meantime Kigali had brought in a whole bevy of Lebanese diamond traders who had their own "monopoly." By early 1999 the two sides were staring at each other over the barrels of their Kalashnikovs.

In the meantime Generals Nzimbi and Baramoto, the two Mobutist stalwarts, arrived in Kampala to make contact with Bemba. In January 1999 they all met at the Palm Beach Hotel in Kisangani, where Bemba, flashing his Ugandan support and diamond money, made an overt play for RCD loyalties. This nearly led to an armed clash when the Rwandese tried to arrest the two Zairian generals at the airport. And then on May 10, as the

RCD split was getting under way, the UPDF arrested six Lebanese diamond traders and one Belgian working for the Rwandese under the pretext of unpaid taxes. In a rougher way some of Bemba's men killed two or three "motor bike boys" working for pro-Kigali dealers.[205] This brought the situation to the point of explosion.

So we can see that the final break, which was to end in major combat between the UPDF and the RPA in the streets of Kisangani, was *both* about politics (who will control the RCD) *and* about mineral resources. Actually, the two issues fed into each other at a crucial moment, exactly at the time when the various actors of the war were trying to appease the international community by brokering some kind of a peace agreement.

The Lusaka "peace" charade

What came to be known as the Lusaka Peace Agreement had a long history behind it by the time it was signed on August 31, 1999, and a good part of that long process was marked by the Franco-American differences of views over what was actually going on in the Congo.[206] As early as October 1998 Paris had sent Special Adviser for Africa Michel Dupuch to Kinshasa;[207] Laurent-Désiré Kabila arrived in Paris soon after to take part in the Franco-African Summit, where he was invited as "acting president." On November 27 President Chirac announced a French-brokered ceasefire in the Congo that did not seem to have much support: Thabo Mbeki and Museveni expressed doubts, and two of the main protagonists, Kabila himself and Pasteur Bizimungu, denied that anything had been decided. Kofi Annan and Chirac congratulated each other, and everything went on as before. Officially the Americans shared the politically correct vision, and Kinshasa's U.S. ambassador Bill Swing condemned "the outside intervention of Rwanda and Uganda."[208] What somewhat weakened his declaration was the presence of rebel leader Jean-Pierre Ondekane in Washington at the same time.

In late October U.S. Under-Secretary of State for African Affairs Susan Rice and Special Envoy Howard Wolpe arrived in Luanda to try to mollify President dos Santos. The meeting proved hard for the American envoys as they were kept waiting for two days by the Angolan president, who had just learned of the presence of U.S. mercenaries in South Kivu.[209] Rice, who very likely had been kept in the dark, put on a brave face and stuck to her guns, declaring in Luanda, "The spectre of genocide is once again present in the DRC." She had more trouble three days later, when she met with Kabila in

Kinshasa; he challenged her version of events, saying that what was happening was "not a rebellion but an invasion."[210] Things were easier with Wamba and Bizima Karaha in Kigali the next day, and she took the opportunity to ask them to admit that RPA troops were indeed in the Congo. Caught between the undeclared French bend in Kinshasa's favor and the equally hypocritical favor shown by the United States toward Rwanda and Uganda, the peace process was not getting anywhere, especially as long as the invaders/rebels had a hope of winning militarily.

On November 20 there was an inconclusive "peace meeting" in Botswana, just before the bizarre Paris episode related above. On January 19 Patrick Mazimpaka, a close adviser to Kagame, summarized the process with disenchanted honesty: "The insistence on the signing of an agreement and not on its contents is definitely symptomatic of an impatient world that wants to run away from the problem rather than solve it."[211] He had the hopeless Paris proceedings in mind, but the same could be said of all that was to follow.

On March 23 President Chiluba of Zambia finally got what he had wanted for so long: he was made the official mediator of the peace process. But when a minor breakthrough occurred, it owed nothing to him: on April 17 Kabila signed some kind of a "peace agreement" with Museveni in Sirte, Libya, in the presence of Idriss Deby of Chad and Issayas Afeworki of Eritrea. In fact, the whole thing had been brokered by Colonel Gaddafi, who wanted to disengage himself and his Chadian proxies from what he increasingly saw as an endless and useless conflict. The "agreement" was limited to the northern front (its main purpose was to give the MLC a free hand in the hope that it could march all the way to Kinshasa), and it only served to allow the Chadians a quick and painless withdrawal.[212] Mazimpaka declared on April 25 that Rwanda was not concerned by the Sirte Agreement. Many people expected that the limited peace agreement would extend to the wider conflict, but unfortunately this did not occur; there was no virtuous contagion. There were vague rumors of a possible meeting in Rome, but nothing happened until the Rwandese and Ugandan forces began to run out of steam and feel the pressure of the donors.[213]

Finally, on June 24, "the great meeting" everybody had been waiting for opened in Lusaka, with fifteen countries represented (but not Burundi) and all the "good" fighting movements. There were no representatives of either the loose Mayi Mayi groups (who announced on July 3 that they would not recognize the results of the talks since they were not taking part in them) or, of course, of the "bad" Rwandese and Burundian guerrillas who stank of genocide. It took a couple of weeks to arrive at a draft cease-fire, which was signed on July 11 by all the heads of state present but not by the "rebels," who had fallen out among themselves: both Wamba (RCD-K) and Ilunga (RCD-G) insisted that they were the legitimate representative of the movement and refused to sign if the other did. As for Bemba, he said that the MLC would sign only if the two branches of RCD both signed. RCD-G "expelled" Wamba, accusing him of "high treason," and on July 27 Ilunga walked away from the table because the negotiators had agreed that Wamba could sign. Bemba signed on August 1 but said he would withdraw his signature if the two RCDs did not sign within a week. The two RCDs then agreed to sign, but then did not.

While this confused process was sloshing around it was brutally overshadowed by the military explosion that suddenly threw the "allied" forces of Rwanda and Uganda against each other.[214] For one long week (August 7–16) the RPA and the UPDF battled it out in the streets of Kisangani, using heavy artillery against each other with a complete lack of restraint or care for the Congolese civilian population. Kinshasa accused the two opponents of "a semblance of rivalry . . . aimed at derailing the Lusaka accord."[215] This was false, but the degree of paradoxical confusion that had been reached by then was such that the actors could be forgiven for trying to make sense out of the absurdity. For what was happening in Kisangani was only a portent of things to come: the disintegration of a "rational" war into myriad "privatized," socially and economically motivated subconflicts. But at that stage the international community did not understand the nature of the problem and still believed that it faced a conventional conflict that could be treated by traditional diplomatic methods. So when the various contenders finally agreed to sign on August 31,[216] the document they agreed on was outwardly "normal" but in fact completely unfit for dealing with the reality on the ground.

All along, from the moment the first draft agreement had been put on the table, international diplomats had refused to deal with what could be termed the "reality gap."[217] In spite of the contorted disputes that had nothing to do with the actual contents of the agreement but only came from conflicts of etiquette and legitimacy among the signatories,[218] what was finally signed on August 31 was basically that initial draft document. What did it contain?[219] Basically, an international community wish list: fighting was supposed to stop within twenty-four hours of the signing; then the various armies would form a JMC, which would organize the disarming of the various "negative" militias, such as ALIR and the Burundian CNDD-FDD;[220] forty-five days later all Congolese political forces would open a national dialogue, with the help of a neutral facilitator; then, after four months, all the foreign armies would move out of the Congo and be replaced by a UN force; two months after that, the Kinshasa government and the "rebels" would have integrated their respective armed forces and would sit down to discuss a democratic government of transition.

As a reporter for the *Economist* wrote at the time, "It sounds like a fantasy and it may well turn out to be. Yet underneath the pious hopes lies an element of serious reconsideration. The leaders of the outside countries involved in the war have become increasingly reluctant to go on fighting each other in the jungles of Congo, even though some of them, or their cronies, have done well out of business deals there. They are also under pressure from the western countries that give them aid and can get them assistance from the World Bank or the IMF."[221] This quote perfectly illustrates the contradictions between what could be termed "globalized logic" and the grassroots logic of the contenders. The degree of compliance with the Lusaka wish list—even if after years of delay—was going to be directly proportional to the degree of an actor's implication in the international market diplomacy system. Angola would be the first to quit because of its susceptibility to U.S. pressure. Zimbabwe would follow suit, when its internal situation degenerated so much that it had to concentrate on it to respond to British and Commonwealth pressure. Namibia, as usual, simply followed the Angolans. IMF-sensitive Uganda would tentatively half-withdraw many times before finally quitting in 2003. And Rwanda would improvise ever more complex games because its grassroots interests largely outweighed its international ones. As for the nongovernment actors, ranging from the Congolese NGOs to the Rwandese guerrillas and from the Mayi Mayi to the Burundian fighters, they simply could not rely on a piece of paper nobody was ready to enforce on the ground. The "reality gap" had opened up in the Congo, and it was going to remain open for several years to come.

7

SINKING INTO THE QUAGMIRE
(AUGUST 1999–JANUARY 2001)

"The war is dead, long live the war."[1]

The East: confused rebels in confused fighting. The Lusaka agreements had a temporary restraining effect on the battles taking place on the "real" fronts, such as western Equateur and northern Katanga, where large units using modern equipment were engaged. But in the two Kivus, in Maniema, and in the Province Orientale the confused violence that was typical of the situation in mid-1999 went on unabated. News reports and press dispatches logged an endless litany of skirmishes, massacres, ambushes, and random looting: at Kahungwe, forty kilometers north of Uvira, unidentified "armed men" slaughter thirty civilians on November 2, 1999; on November 22 Mayi Mayi forces attack Butembo airstrip, killing thirty; clashes in Ituri between Hema and Lendu irregulars cause thirty thousand civilians to flee around mid-December; on December 23 *Interahamwe* militiamen coming from the Congo attack the Tamira resettlement village near Gisenyi, inside Rwanda, killing twenty Congolese Tutsi refugees; on December 29 the Congolese ambassador to the UN André Mwamba Kapanga accuses the Rwandese army of having massacred fifteen civilian women in Mwenga District of South Kivu; in January 2000 RCD-K leader Mbusa Nyamwisi starts training his "children's army" at Nyaleke Camp near Beni (median age of the future combatants: thirteen); on January 6, 2000, Lendu militiamen kill 425 Hema civilians at Blukwa village, near Bunia; twelve civilian women accused of supplying Mayi Mayi with food are beheaded by RCD-G rebels in Kasika (South Kivu) on January 28; on February 3 an RCD-RPA offensive retakes Shabunda and its surroundings, which had been in Mayi Mayi and ex-FAR hands for the past month: number of casualties unknown; ex-FAR and FNL guerrillas, who have come into Burundi from the DRC, fight each other north of Bujumbura for two weeks in early February: around three hundred are killed. Early February was also marked by massive IDP displacements in South Kivu, with nearly 150,000 persons on the move.[2] In March the Mayi Mayi forces that had been trained at great cost in Zimbabwe to bolster the FAC fighting capacity in the east went home and started attacking Banyamulenge civilians instead of fighting. Then seven hundred refugees crossed into Burundi. In late March and early April Lemera was taken, lost, retaken, and lost again by Mayi Mayi forces linked with Commander "Willy" Dunia; each change of control of the town was an occasion for a spate of summary executions. On the night of May 14–15 Rwandese and Burundian army units encircled the village of Katogota, where a FAB officer had been murdered the day before, and killed thirty to forty civilians. This list is only very partial and could go on *ad nauseam*, making Lusaka look like a sick joke when seen from an eastern Congo point of view. But the violence that kept unfolding in the area could barely be qualified as "war." It was an unending series of confused clashes in which low military intensity did not mean low casualty figures among civilians. And the political actors often seemed to be in a state of amoral uncertainty about what their military men were doing: when the UN Security Council, spurred on by Ambassador Mawamba Kapanga, challenged RCD-G on the massacre of the fifteen women at Mwenga, Emile Ilunga's cry from the heart would have been funny had it not been horrifying: "But we killed only three women," he said, "and then the other side does it too."[3]

Since its split into pro-Rwandese and pro-Ugandan branches, the RCD was even more organizationally weak than it had been before. Finances were a perennial problem since their Kigali and Kampala sponsors took the first cut, leaving very little for their Congolese agents. The RCD-G resorted to levying taxes on the movement of goods between the area it controlled and that controlled by Wamba in North Kivu, as if the two zones were separate countries. In October furious local traders went on strike and forced the rebels to lift their roadblocks. Then in November 1999, Wamba dia Wamba, ever the absent-minded professor, took up with a certain A. Van Brink of the "First International Bank of Granada." Van Brink, whose real name was Allen Ziegler, was a bankrupt real estate operator from Oregon with a Granadian passport and a genuine international crook on the run from the U.S. Securities and Exchange Commission for a $400,000 swindle. He "secured" a $16 million "loan" for the RCD and promptly used the documents signed by the Congolese as collateral to get more money out of other gullible investors.[4] The RCD never saw a penny of the promised monies.

Wamba had formalized the split by calling his movement RCD-ML (ML standing for Mouvement de Libération), but his control over it was loose and it was riven by suborganizational rivalries. In November 1999 Désiré Lumbu Lumbu, one of the movement's cadres, was arrested in Beni; transferred to Butembo, starved, half-blind from maltreatment, he was finally beaten to death in mid-December by RCD-ML fighters after one month of continual torture. He had been accused of colluding with the Mayi Mayi, but what may have cost him his life were accusations that he was plotting with rivals from RCD-G. Meanwhile in Goma Roger Lumbala, a prominent RCD-G leader, had been arrested for "rebellion," in fact because he was suspected of having transferred his allegiance to RCD-ML. Later freed, he resigned from RCD-G and, after a brief spell with Wamba, created his own "movement" in Bafwasende, the RCD-N (N standing for National).[5] By then the rebels' sponsors were getting nervous at the fissiparousness of their Congolese protégés, and in late December they organized a meeting in Kabale, Uganda, where the MLC, the RCD-G, and the RCD-ML promised to establish a common front. In spite of the promise, this was to remain an elusive goal in the years to come.

Of the three, Wamba's group was the sickest. At Kampala's prompting the RCD-G had created in June 1999 a new "province" called Kibali-Ituri and named a Hema woman, Adèle Lotsove, as its governor. This was an unfortunate choice because since April 1999 the Ituri region of Province Orientale had been in a growing state of upheaval.[6] Wamba soon realized the mistake he had made and replaced Lotsove with a new, ethnically neutral governor, Uring pa Dolo, an Alur.[7] But the UPDF officers, who by then were up to their necks in using the Hema as proxies for their local economic interests,[8] did not approve of Wamba's move. In the short term they could do nothing about it, but they undermined Wamba's position by supporting two of his rivals in the RCD-ML, Jean-Bosco Tibasima Atenyi and Mbusa Nyamwisi. Tibasima was a Hema and Mbusa a Nande from outside the province and both wanted to eliminate Wamba. Soon Tibasima was sending his young men to Uganda to create an independent militia and Mbusa was training his own near Beni.

The interethnic clashes stepped up and Wamba started to lose control of his territory. In November 1999 a UN mission found a "catastrophic humanitarian situation" in Ituri, with an estimated 5,000 to 7,000 deaths due to fighting since April and over 100,000 IDPs.[9] Raphaël Katoto Katebe, a millionaire businessman close to the RCD, declared, "Kabila, Wamba or Ilunga, they have all failed to govern the small areas they control: how do you expect them to rule the whole country?"[10]

By early August 2000 Wamba's men and his rivals' were fighting each other, in the midst of the Hema-Lendu interethnic strife. Ituri waded into a bloodbath. On November 3 Tibasima and Mbusa overthrew Wamba in Bunia, only to be kicked out the next day by UPDF troops. On orders from Museveni himself his proconsul James Kazini had reluctantly sided with the "official" leader of the RCD-ML, but his own officers were wavering because of their business interests. By November 21 there were already forty-one casualties in and around Bunia due to the intra-RCD-ML clashes; the fight eventually spilled into Uganda when the two rival factions tried to take control of the Kasindi border post in December.[11]

While Ituri was sliding into anarchy, the situation was not much better in North and South Kivu. There were around eight different military groups fighting each other in fluctuating patterns of alliance and confrontation: at least three Mayi Mayi groups, only one of whom was—distantly—controlled by Kinshasa; the Rwandese army; the Burundian army; the RCD-G; and the former *Interahamwe* of ALIR. The fighting patterns of the various groups did not always respect what could have been expected, that is, a pro- or anti-rebel dichotomy. Thus the CNDD and ALIR guerrillas, although theoretically allied, at times fought each other; the Mayi Mayi, who were supposed to protect their fellow countrymen from the foreign invading forces, often looted and killed them instead.[12] The RPA, which used the pursuit of the *Interahamwe* militiamen as its rationale for being in the Congo, often protected them instead, as long as it was not targeted by their attacks.

As for the Kinshasa government, it tried to use the mess to weaken the Rwandese and Ugandan forces, without giving too much thought to the sufferings of the local population. Gen. Sylvestre Lwetcha had been named FAC chief of staff in September 1999, immediately following the signing of the Lusaka Agreement. This nomination was greeted with fury by the RCD, which called it "an effort at avoiding his indictment for complicity with the *Interahamwe*."[13] Lwetcha, a Mubembe from South Kivu, was seventy-two years old and his appointment was due to two things: he had been involved with Kabila's anti-Mobutu underground network since 1969 and he had always sided with Kabila in his various quarrels with the guerrillas' old guard.

Kabila knew that he could trust him to try to keep the resurgent Mayi Mayi forces more or less in line with Kinshasa, not an easy job. In spite of his age Lwetcha plunged into it and rallied the east overland from Lubumbashi, partly on foot. Late in the year the RCD-G announced gleefully that he was dead, but he resurfaced in early February 2000 in Kigoma, from where he was transported to Dar-es-Salaam and flown home. He was actually in pretty bad physical shape, but he had managed to coordinate some of the unruly eastern guerrilla forces, and from March 2000 on they started getting better air supplies from the capital.

The situation of the Banyamulenge, still holed up above Uvira on their bastion of the Itombwe plateau, was unusual, to say the least. Used as proxies by the RPF regime since 1996, they had grown progressively disenchanted with their Tutsi cousins from Rwanda. The February 1998 mutiny[14] was the first sign of their growing estrangement from Kigali. Things did not improve as the various rebel factions kept splitting into ever smaller segments, since there were Banyamulenge fighters in all of them and they progressively ended up fighting each other. In late 1999 the Munyamulenge leader Müller Ruhimbika created the Forces Républicaines Fédéralistes to defend Banyamulenge interests without being manipulated by Kigali.[15] This was not an easy task because individual Banyamulenge continued to do things that did not endear them to their autochthon fellow countrymen.[16] But then, how could they trust their neighbors? In mid-July 2000 a gaggle of CNDD Burundian guerrillas operating together with Padiri's Mayi Mayi had climbed up the Itombwe plateau and indiscriminately attacked everybody, killing twenty-two, wounding forty, and burning three hundred houses.[17] Between the Mayi Mayi rock and the hard place of Kigali's RCD "protection," the Banyamulenge felt that they were caught in a double bind. The Forces Républicaines Fédéralistes literature reflects a constant anguish, which did not get much of a sympathetic hearing locally.

Westwards: the river wars. While the eastern witch's cauldron kept simmering, the more organized fronts (the MLC in the northwest and the RCD-G in the center, with their respective Ugandan and Rwandese allies) went into a short recess after Lusaka, just long enough for the actors to test the international diplomatic waters. They soon found them to be conveniently lukewarm, since a combination of Kabila's obduracy and Western toleration for the rebels and their friends made a UN military deployment rather unlikely in the short run. For the rebels the main opportunity was provided by the central front. In fact, given the nature of the terrain and the importance of the waterways as means of communication,[18] both the MLC and the RCD-G were engaged in a river race for the capital, Bemba on the Ubangi and the Rwandese along the Tshuapa. Seen from Kinshasa, the central front seemed to be the major threat, especially as the Rwando-RCD forces had managed to trap over three thousand FAC, Zimbabwean, and Namibian soldiers at Ikela Airport. Mugabe was furious and wanted to relieve his men. So in late November the FAC and Zimbabwean Defense Forces mounted a major offensive from Boende, eventually taking Bokungu after a heavy battle. The fighting then moved upstream toward Ikela, with the government forces managing to approach the town but not to reconquer it, in spite of using combat helicopters and river-borne heavy artillery. They eventually struck a bargain with the Rwandese, who allowed the besieged airport garrison to be airlifted out.

Meanwhile Kinshasa engaged in a series of poorly prepared offensives on the northern front around Imese, Libanda, and Lisala. They lost at least 300 killed and 255 taken as prisoners, which Bemba immediately paraded in front of the foreign press as proof of Kabila's duplicity.[19] Then he went on to build on his first success: within days UPDF reinforcements, American mercenaries, and MLC troops, over three thousand men in all, poured through Libenge and moved on from there to take Dongo. Bemba kept pushing and probing, attacking Likwelo in February. The MLC was recruiting heavily in the Central African Republic, which caused Kinshasa to complain.[20] At a meeting in Victoria Falls on April 21 all the parties to the war very seriously "reaffirmed their commitment to a cease-fire and the withdrawal of all foreign troops from the DRC."[21] Then they went on with the fighting.

The pressure could be felt in the capital. In late April President Kabila began to regain some breathing space when the North Koreans commissioned the new elite 6th Brigade of fifteen thousand men they had just finished training.[22] He immediately set upon preparing a large offensive in Equateur. On the other side Bemba was getting a lot of UNITA artillery that the Angolan movement had evacuated after the fall of Andulo and Bailundo to MPLA troops a few months earlier. Since fighting had broken out again in Kisangani between Rwandese and Ugandan "allies" in May, Kabila felt that the time was now favorable, and a large contingent of troops started sailing upstream. Congolese gunboats seized any river traffic they found, even if the boats carried the Brazzaville or Central African Republic flag, and fuel was soon in short supply in Bangui while river commerce became paralyzed.

Prudently, Central African Republic President Félix-Ange Patassé declared, "Kabila is my brother but Bemba is my son."[23]

To buy time Kabila claimed that he was acting in self-defense in Equateur and that the MLC should withdraw to its July 10, 1999, positions.[24] Then, a week later, his forces went on the offensive, hoping to take Libenge and roll back the MLC, perhaps as far as Gbadolite. Six thousand refugees crossed into the Republic of Congo while the government troops pushed upstream, retaking Dongo and Imese at the end of the month. But the MLC and UPDF forces had deliberately withdrawn to Libenge to prepare a counterattack, and they sprang the trap on August 8: the heavy barges lumbering upriver were attacked with deadly accurate mortar fire while the columns moving along the river bank were ambushed. Over nine hundred troops were killed in one afternoon, including over twenty Zimbabwean "advisers" who were onboard the ships.[25]

Because they had not been consulted about the offensive, Kabila's allies were less than pleased. Angolan army chief João de Matos flew to Kampala with a military delegation, spending three days there in late September,[26] trying to clarify the Ugandan strategy, particularly their degree of collaboration with UNITA. Practically at the same time Jean-Yves Ollivier, the French influence agent, flew Bemba to Paris in his private jet to meet Angolan Foreign Minister João de Miranda, exactly for the same purpose. Bemba tried to lie about his UNITA connection and so failed to convince his Angolan counterpart, who would have preferred him to come clean.[27] On September 25 Kabila rushed to Luanda, begging not to be abandoned. From there he dashed to Harare (September 28), and from Harare to Windhoek (September 29), with the same desperate demand.

Heavy fighting was still in progress on the Ubangi, Kabila's troops were losing, and his allies were getting tired. At the beginning of October the Zimbabweans had to bring back 75 percent of their aviation from the DRC. The deepening economic crisis in Harare restricted spare parts purchases and the Zimbabwean Ministry of Defense did not want to see its planes run the risk of remaining grounded in the Congo.[28] The FAC had finally been beaten at Konongo and had had to withdraw; by then there were 120,000 Congolese refugees across the river in the Republic of Congo. The MLC took Lulonga, sixty kilometers north of Mbandaka, and started to advance on Boende from Basankusu. Beyond Mbandaka, key to the river war, the ultimate target was evidently the capital. But Bemba and his men were to be frustrated of their prize at the last moment due to unexpected military and diplomatic developments.

Rwanda drives south into Katanga. By the spring of 2000 it was evident that Lusaka had become a mantra to be repeated only by despairing UN personnel.[29] After nearly two years of war, the rebels had renewed hopes of winning a military victory,[30] and while Bemba was staking all his cards on taking Mbandaka and sailing on to Kinshasa, Kigali, disappointed by the hard fighting down the Tshuapa, was looking for another possibility. After all, why take power at the center and have to bother with the setting up of another bogus government, which might again decide to turn independent? What mattered more and more as the war went on were the economic interests. And those were in Kasai and Katanga, not in Kinshasa.

In early August Kigali announced that it was ready to unilaterally withdraw two hundred kilometers back from the front lines. With the consummate diplomatic ineptitude typical of the Kabila regime, FAC forces immediately attacked in South Kivu, in alliance with ALIR Rwandese rebels.[31] Most of September was then spent skirmishing around Pepa, and in October Kigali announced it had lost both Pepa and Moba after the FAC landed troops and used gunboats on Lake Tanganyika. Kin Kiey Mulumba declared, sounding pained, "They have attacked us, it's a real war."[32] By November 1 the RCD-G, backed by large RPA regular forces, had retaken Pepa and was pushing south. Zimbabwe, which was getting increasingly distressed at Kabila's clumsiness, declared that it had no intention of taking part in the fighting. Realizing too late the danger of losing Lubumbashi, Kabila rushed reinforcements to northern Katanga. On December 3 the Rwandese forces took Pweto, declaring with indignation, "We had to undertake this operation in response to the general offensive of Mr Kabila and his allies."[33] The fall of Pweto and the collapse of FAC forces on the Katanga front was to have enormous consequences, since it is one of the causes eventually leading to Laurent-Désiré Kabila's assassination. But in the short term thousands of refugees, a mixed crowd of vanquished soldiers and civilians, fled into Zambia. In spite of Harare's denials, there were almost three hundred Zimbabwean troops among the refugees.[34]

On December 14 Kigali said again that it had only been responding to the government's attack and that it "still supported the Lusaka Peace Agreement."[35] Zimbabwe was caught on the hop and had to rush another thousand troops to Katanga or run the risk of seeing Lubumbashi fall. Harare used some of its still flying CASA STOL transport planes to bring the reinforcements practically right up to the front lines, on the shores of Lake Mwelu. The RPA was also bringing supplies and equipment. As Patrick Mazimpaka was to proudly tell me a few weeks later, "There is now nothing standing between us and the taking of Lubumbashi."[36] Emile Ilunga confided to the UN, "[I am] just waiting for the fall of Lubumbashi so that I can become the first RCD Governor of Katanga."[37] Fate—that is, the United States of America—decided otherwise. Clinton was gone, and when Kabila died the international perception of his son started quickly evolving.

Paul Kagame came back from his January 2001 Washington visit knowing that the situation was in complete flux. Some of the old Rwanda supporters in the U.S. administration, such as John Prendergast and Susan Rice, were either marginalized or out. Partial violations of Lusaka had been one thing, but throwing Lusaka entirely out of the window would have been something else, which the new secretary of state, Colin Powell, was not prepared to tolerate. Messages to that effect began to flow to Kigali. The armies froze.

The shaky home fronts

The Congo: an elusive search for national dialogue while the economy collapses.
Today in our country everything is justified in reference to the rebellion. When somebody is arrested it is because of Rwanda, when public money is stolen, it is because of Rwanda. Special advisors who answer to no authority go on missions, terrorize people, arrest civil servants, all because of the rebellion.... But for the last five months politically the rebellion has only existed in virtual form.

This assessment of the Congolese political situation by a Kinshasa magazine[38] was barely exaggerated. Even if it represented an ultimate threat for him, the rebellion was also the perfect excuse for Laurent-Désiré Kabila not to democratize his regime. The veteran opposition politician Joseph Olenghankoy summarized the president's attitude when he declared on foreign radio, "Mr Kabila considers us to be fishes locked up in his aquarium for which he alone can provide the needed oxygen."[39] As if to help him make his point President Kabila cut off *his* oxygen on March 31, when Olenghankoy was arrested as he was trying to organize a national day of protest (the demonstration failed).

The Lusaka Agreement provided for a "national dialogue" on October 15, 1999, forty-five days after the signing. Elements of civil society started to congregate hopefully and organized meetings and conferences, taking the president at his word. But on October 4, as this flurry of activity was about to coalesce into the organization of the first preparatory national conference, the government outlawed it. Seven members of Olenghankoy's FONUS and several journalists were arrested.[40] Kabila wanted "democratization," but on his terms. On February 16 he announced the creation of a Constitutional Assembly—without the rebels, without the political opposition, and outside the Lusaka framework. Consultations on this piece of creative politics started on February 29. But it was a stormy process from the start. The first delegates attending the proposed preparatory assembly declared, "This smacks of Mobutu Sese Seko.... We demand an immediate halt to amateurism and adventurism at the head of the state."[41] Panicked at this crime of *lèse-majesté*, Congolese TV, which was covering the proceedings, went off the air rather than keep broadcasting such subversive talk. The international community complained of this violation of the Lusaka process, which led Foreign Minister Yerodia Ndombasi to brazenly turn the tables, declaring that he rejected Masire's plan for national dialogue,[42] "which violates the Lusaka Agreement."[43]

On July 3, 2000, the National Assembly finally convened. It was made up of 240 members chosen from a list of five thousand candidates drawn up by the government, with Kabila personally adding sixty hand-picked MPs, including his lady friend, Tshala Mwana, and the famous musician Tabu Ley. As could be expected the rebels rejected the proclamation of the National Assembly, which they rightly deemed to be both unrepresentative and in contradiction with the provisions of Lusaka. Popular wits called the new Assembly "the Employment Agency" because most of its members had been unemployed at the time of its creation. But popular voices had more serious things to worry about than the questionable legitimacy of Parliament. The economy was collapsing.

Congolese Economic Production

Commodity	Nov. 1998	Nov. 1999	% change
Copper (tons)	36,086	23,804	-34
Cobalt (tons)	3,688	1,800	-51
Diamonds ('000 carats)	24,463	18,520	-24
Gold (kilos)	135	7	-94
Coffee (tons)	33,716	16,038	-52
Uncut wood (cubic meters)	79,656	27,226	-66
Palm oil (cubic meters)	15,910	5,664	-64

<u>Source</u>: Economist Intelligence Unit, *Congo Country Report 1st Quarter 2000.* The Banque Centrale du Congo (*Condensé d'Informations Statistiques,* February 2000) gives somewhat different figures for some products, but the general trend is the same.

The economic rate of "growth" fell from +0.7 percent in 1998 to –10.3 percent in 1999 and –11.4 percent in 2000. The value of exports, which was still $1.422 billion in 1998, fell to $749 million in 1999 and $685 million in 2000.[44] Inflation rose from 147 percent in 1998 to 333 percent in 1999, pushing the Congolese franc down from 9.5 to 12 to the U.S. dollar on the black market. It was devalued ($1 = FC 9) in January 2000 and again ($1 = FC 23.5) in June, causing the black market rate to jump from FC 30 and then to FC 52. In the rebel areas the Congolese franc was still trading at 12 or 15 to the dollar because of a more limited supply and because dollars were more easily available due to illegal exports. This caused the smuggling of francs from the government to the rebel areas, mostly through Brazzaville. Civil servants were caught with bags full of money as they were about to cross the river; even ministers were involved. The basic problem was the de-dollarization of trade, particularly for diamonds, which had caused massive smuggling of exports and a drying up both of foreign exchange and of tax receipts.[45]

Under such circumstances the government itself had become a kind of sharp operator, ready to make any deal to scrape up a few pennies, often with unforeseen consequences. In July 2000 Kabila arrested two expatriates working for the Bralima brewery under the (true) accusation of currency trafficking. Their foreign employer paid a $500,000 ransom to get them released. But then, to make up for its loss, Bralima started to stockpile its Congolese francs to "cool off" the black market. When franc rates had gone down enough in late September, the brewery suddenly turned all its reserves into dollars, causing the black market rate to jump from less than 70 to over 100 in a few days.[46]

Even when it did not resort to extortion the government just seemed to live on financial improvisation, dealing with ever more questionable partners,[47] such as the Thai businessman Rakesh Saxena, under investigation in Bangkok for an $88 million swindle,[48] and the Israeli Rami Golan, a former diamond "fixer" for Mobutu.[49] Billy Rautenbach, the once crucial *wunderkind* of Zimbabwe and boss of Gécamines, had not lived up to his promises even if his friend and mentor John Arnold Bredenkamp had managed to inject over $50 million into the Kinshasa financial system through his Harare-based Noczim petroleum company.[50] After some stormy exchanges between Rautenbach and Kabila, the young Zimbabwean was fired in March 2000 and replaced by George Forrest, a Katanga-born Belgian who immediately set upon reorganizing Gécamines "in order to restore its international credibility." It was a timely change because by December Rautenbach was embroiled in a series of lawsuits.[51] Always looking for a financial panacea, in July 2000 Kabila signed a monopoly agreement with the Israeli diamond company IDI, a young and untried outfit but one that was promising a minimum floor price for purchases over the next eighteen months.[52]

If the government itself was thus living from hand to mouth, for the ordinary citizens the hand carried less and less to the mouth, particularly in the sprawling capital of six million people.[53] In the midst of agricultural plenty, the war-torn Congo was slowly starving.

Angola: the pressure begins to ease off. After the battle for Maquela do Zombo, in which some forces that had survived the failure of Kabarebe's Blitzkrieg took part alongside UNITA, both Harare and Kinshasa sent troop reinforcements to Uige and Moxico Provinces.[54] Slowly the tide began to turn. In September 1999 the FAA went on a general offensive, using lots of air power. Within three months most of UNITA's conventional military capability had been destroyed and the government occupied the rebellion's "capital" in Jamba (December 1999). FAA forces progressed on all fronts. The last provincial capital in UNITA hands, Cazombo, on the Zambian border, fell to the government in September 2000. By then Angola had few troops remaining in the DRC, even if they still played an essential role in case of need.[55]

Luanda had derived a number of economic advantages from its intervention, such as bringing fuel distribution in the DRC under Sonangol's control via its Cohydro subsidiary, and acquiring a controlling interest in the Congolese Coco offshore wells.[56] But more important than anything else, Luanda acted as the ultimate guarantor of Kinshasa's security. With airborne forces conveniently stationed in Dolisie, Pointe Noire, and Brazzaville since October 1997, the FAA was in a position to militarily stop any foe trying to take the capital. Hence Bemba's (unsuccessful) efforts at convincing Luanda of his innocuousness in relationship to UNITA. Although by late 2000 Angola had become rather disenchanted with Kabila's diplomatic blindness, it had no better choice, for the time being. In October it had reluctantly called a meeting of the Communauté Economique des Etats de l'Afrique Centrale (CEEAC; i.e., the Republic of Congo, Gabon, Equatorial Guinea, and the Central African Republic) in Kinshasa, where it aligned itself with Kabila's demand for a revision of the Lusaka Agreement.[57] The CEEAC was largely a French diplomatic construct, and the move seemed to fit within the usual Franco-U.S. rivalry in west and central Africa. But Luanda's heart was not in it; instead, the government was beginning to explore the possibility of "neutralizing" Kabila. There were enough Luanda men in the regime (Victor Mpoyo, Col. Eddy Kapend, Generals Yav Nawesh and Faustin Munene) to make such an operation possible. By late 2000, with the advantage of a much-diminished UNITA threat, Angola was keeping its options open.

Zimbabwe: trying to make the war pay for itself. Zimbabwe's basic motivations for being in the Congo had not changed: to block the northward creep of South African influence,[58] particularly at the mining level, and to recoup its initial investment in Kabila's rise to power. On September 4, 1998, Kabila and Mugabe had signed a contract providing for the "self-financing" of Zimbabwe's intervention through a 37.5 percent interest in Gécamines; 30 percent of the company's profits were to be earmarked for financing Harare's war effort.[59] But the former giant mining concern was as sick as the rest of the Congolese economy; it had $1 billion in long-term debts and over $50 million in short-term trade liabilities.[60] Harare did not have the money that should have been invested in Gécamines to make it profitable, and Kinshasa's monthly installments soon stopped coming. Moreover, the whole deal rested on Rautenbach's position as head of the company, and his poor management and eventual removal caused the whole deal to fall by the wayside.

Harare then tried several different courses. The Zimbabwean Electricity Supply Authority signed a contact to double its power import from the giant Inga dam at a very low cost. But the power lines had to be built and there was no money to do it. Later, 500,000 hectares of prime farmland in Katanga were given to a large Zimbabwean state farm, which did nothing with the land because it lacked the necessary capital.[61] In late 1999 the so-called Osleg (Operation Sovereign Legitimacy) Company was set up. Kinshasa Minister of Mines Kibassa Maliba immediately gave Osleg the Tshibwa and Senga Senga diamond permits, near Mbuji-Mayi, which had been attributed to MIBA; this caused a furor at De Beers, which, as a minority shareholder in MIBA, considered itself fleeced. Then, using this donation as an asset, Osleg joined with Oryx and Comiex to create the Cosleg Consortium and tried to get it quoted in London to raise more capital for its development. But in June 2000 London's Alternative Investment Market threw out the Cosleg quotation at the behest of the Foreign Office.[62] Cosleg tried to get quoted in Amsterdam and in Dublin but failed in both and in the end achieved almost nothing.[63] Harare's problem was that it had completely failed to realize the degree of decay of the Congolese economy in general and of its mining industry in particular.[64] But by then Zimbabwe, whose own economy was in a tailspin, was getting frantic about making the war pay for its own costs.

Harare admitted to spending $36 million a year in the Congo, but by mid-2000 this fiction was no longer tenable, and even Finance Minister Simba Makoni was forced to admit to having spent at least $200 million during the past two years. The World Bank had already estimated that the real cost was at least $27 million per month and had cut off a much needed $340 million loan to Zimbabwe in retaliation.[65] War costs escalated wildly during 2000, with the purchase of weaponry from China costing $72.3 million, three MiG-23s from Libya for $1.5 million, and spare parts for British-made BAe Hawks fighter bombers costing $5 million to $10 million.[66] By late 2000 the Zimbabwean economy, already reeling from other causes, could no longer sustain the costs of the war in the Congo. A Harare newspaper expressed popular sentiment when it wrote, "The best Christmas present Zimbabweans could get would be the announcement of a troop withdrawal from the DRC."[67]

Rwanda and Uganda: the friendship grows violent. Between August 1999 and April 2000 Rwanda faced a growing internal political crisis which had indirect repercussions on its international political engagement:

- A group of students of the University of Butare fled to Uganda in August after threats of expulsion when they questioned the university's language policy.[68] Although children from the very elite of the RPF, they were brutalized in a way that called into question the internal logic of RPF functioning.[69]

- On August 20 the bishop of Gikongoro, Monsignor Augustin Misago, was charged with complicity in the genocide. The political nature of the trial was obvious from the start.[70] The anti-Catholic mood of the regime was such that the preceding April Jean-Népomucène Nayinzira, leader of the Parti Démocrate Chrétien (which was part of the government "coalition") had changed the "Chrétien" to "Centriste" to keep the PDC acronym on the safe side. After a long drawn-out procedure intended to vilify the Church and although he had been sentenced to death, Misago was finally acquitted on June 15, 2000. Court Public Prosecutor Bernard Kayihura came under threat and promptly fled the country.

- During October 1999 the Transitional National Assembly (TNA), composed entirely of hand-picked MPs, "removed" Anastase Gasana[71] and Minister for Social Affairs Charles Ntakiruntika from their posts. Prime Minister Pierre-Célestin Rwigiema was accused of misappropriation of funds dating back to the period when he had been minister of education in the first postgenocide cabinet. The pressure against him progressively built up to the point where, accused of being an accomplice in the genocide, he resigned in February 2000 and fled the country.[72]

- In early January 2000 Parliament Speaker Joseph Sebarenzi came under fire. Because he was a Tutsi survivor of the genocide he could not be accused of being an accomplice; he was instead denounced for "seeking a cheap popularity."[73] Put into a minority position by the obedient TNA, he resigned and also fled the country. The popular paper *Imboni* printed a special number on the affair which they used to criticize the authoritarianism of the regime.[74]

- On March 5, 2000, RPF cadre Aciel Kabera was shot dead by three military men who were never arrested. Like Sebarenzi he was a Tutsi from Kibuye. With the RPF hard core mostly belonging to the so-called Gahini mafia, regionalist rivalries were beginning to look like the days of Habyarimana's old *akazu*.[75]

- On March 20 President Pasteur Bizimungu went on the air to denounce the role of the TNA in the political crisis; three days later he was forced to resign. His main sin had been to organize a faction within the RPF (together with one of the key Tutsi cadres, Patrick Mazimpaka) and to have tried to influence the composition of the new cabinet that Rwigiema's and Sebarenzi's resignations had made necessary. The *akazu* did not like to share the spoils, and on April 17, dispensing with both the "nonethnic" and the "democratic" fig leaves it had used up to then, the RPF "elected" Kagame as Rwanda's new president.

But by then events in the Congo had forced the internal political crisis to take a back seat to more pregnant developments. Resentment had simmered between Rwanda and Uganda since the Kisangani clashes of August 1999. There were a lot of personal feelings involved, and analyzing them would be an almost Freudian endeavor. The expression most often heard on the Rwandese side was "We cannot accept their 'big brother' attitude," while the Ugandans usually complained of the "ungratefulness" of the Rwandese, "whom we have put where they are." Added to this were the personal rivalries between the top actors. Museveni was bitter and resentful at Kagame's "arrogance,"[76] while his half-brother Salim Saleh was persuaded that at least one of the two murder attempts he had survived during 1999 had been planned in Kigali.[77] As the UN report on the illegal exploitation of wealth in the Congo was soon to make abundantly clear, Salim was up to his neck in Congo looting. And that put him in direct competition with RPA officers, who had sometimes rather abrupt ways of resolving their business quarrels.

241

After the August 1999 fighting "Papa Felipe" had been kicked out of Kisangani by the victorious Rwandese, who replaced him and his apparatus with a Lebanese network headed by a certain Ali Hussein.[78] But the Lebanese network found itself frustrated by the dispersion of the Kisangani-area small diamond mines. In spite of having won the battle for the city, the RPA soon found that its men were unable to access many sites, particularly those north of the Tshopo River and around Banalia, where close to ten thousand creuseurs were at work. This, in addition to Lumbala being in control of the Bafwasende area, made the RPA victory hollow from the mining point of view.[79] The economic resentment deepened the other causes for bitterness, and on the morning of May 5, 2000, the two "allied" armies went at each other's throats in Kisangani.[80] After the first five days of fighting Ugandan proconsul and Salim business associate James Kazini declared, "Rwanda is now an enemy . . . which will be crushed."[81] These martial words contradicted Museveni's; he blamed the whole disaster on "lack of communication."[82] A "demilitarization" of the city was agreed upon, but RCD-G forces refused to move, arguing disingenuously that they feared a Kinshasa airborne attack on the city if they left. In fact, Commander Ondekane feared that the Ugandans would use the nearby MLC forces to occupy Kisangani.[83] "The agreement is null and void if the Goma group does not pull out," fumed a UPDF commander.[84] In any case, the communication must have gone bad again because at 10 a.m. on June 5 the fighting resumed. The battle lasted for a full week and killed about 120 soldiers on both sides, with an estimated 640 Congolese civilian deaths and 1,668 wounded.[85] Later, when General Kagame was asked about the causes of the fighting, he answered with his usual capacity for deflecting embarrassing questions, "The situation in Kisangani is a complex matter which I find hard to explain."[86] In fact, even if the details were indeed complex, the overriding cause was grossly simple: the predators had problems, both internal and with each other, and they were fighting over the carcass of their quarry to settle them.[87]

Before we leave the question of the actors in the conflict I must say a word about the overall human consequences of the war: they were absolutely appalling. In June 2000 the U.S. International Rescue Committee made public the results of a mortality survey carried out in eastern DRC by the competent and dedicated demographer Les Robert. His findings were clear: there were about 1.7 million excess deaths due to the war between August 1998 and April 2000, when he carried out his survey.[88] Only about 12 percent (i.e., around 200,000) were directly attributable to fighting; the vast majority of these deaths resulted from frequent forced population displacements, from the near total collapse of the health system, from the impossibility of carrying out normal agricultural work, from overexposure to the weather and to diseases, and probably from plain despair.

The international dimension: giving aid, monitoring the looting, and waiting for MONUC

During the war international aid went on as usual. The phenomenon was perhaps clearest (and most ambiguous) in the case of the aid for Rwanda. Rwanda had an army of 50,000 to 60,000 men (plus 6,000 gendarmes, or paramilitary police, and 7,000 Local Defense Unit militiamen). Out of this force a minimum of 25,000 to 30,000 were in the Congo.[89] In his careful discussion of the relationship between aid, illegal resource exploitation, and military expenses, Bjorn Willum[90] compares official and unofficial estimates of the Rwandese military budget: for 2001 the IMF accepted the Kigali government's figure of $55.6 million, whereas the International Institute of Strategic Studies estimated the spending reality at $135 million and the International Crisis Group (ICG) at $161.8 million. These two different attitudes toward Kigali's military spending had considerable consequences: by accepting a lower figure the international community could justify its high level of aid in proportion to the budget by arguing that it did not contribute to the war either directly (through misuse of aid) or indirectly (by allowing military spending to be financed extralegally while civilian spending would be taken care of by aid).

Budget Spending Financed through Foreign Aid (in percentages)

	1996	1997	1998	1999
Uganda	36	36	35	39
Rwanda	59	47	44	50

Sources: Uganda: *HIPC Point*, January 2000. Rwanda: *Country Report*, January 2001. Both from IMF.

One of the key questions to be asked was whether the international community was aware of the amount of illegal resource exploitation in the Congo. The first estimates had come in indirectly, through a study commissioned to determine how UNITA could have been suddenly resurrected phoenix-like in late 1998, complete with an expensive new arsenal of heavy military hardware.[91] The report detailed many of UNITA's arms-buying circuits in Eastern Europe, its fuel-purchasing networks in Africa (particularly in the Republic of Congo, Zambia, and Botswana), and, most interestingly, its diamond export networks across the world. It showed that the by then notorious "blood diamonds" from Angola were handled through Burkina Faso, Zambia, South Africa, Zaire (prior to 1997), and Rwanda (since 1998), all channels eventually leading to Antwerp. The Fowler Report noted that "the lax security environment that prevailed in Antwerp seemed to be largely influenced by the often-expressed fear that stricter regulation would simply cause traders to take their business elsewhere" (Section 89). It soon became apparent that this "business realism" excuse extended to many other raw materials and that illegally mined Congolese riches were being bought all over the world by unscrupulous operators. In August 2000 UN Secretary-General Kofi Annan appointed a panel of experts on resource looting in the DRC, led by an Ivorian former minister of justice, Safiatou Ba N'Daw.[92] The panel report was made public in April 2001, finally giving substance to many elements that previously had been known only through rumors.[93] Using this report as well as IMF documents, a final reasonable estimate could be produced.

Estimated Value of Congo-Originating Raw Materials Re-exported by Rwanda and Uganda (in U.S.$ millions)

	Rwanda		Uganda	
	1999	2000	1999	2000
Diamonds				
Official exports	0.4	1.8	1.8	1.3
DRC re-exports	40.0	40.0	36.0	36.0
Re-export net added value	8.0	8.0	7.2	7.2
Gold				
Official exports	0.1	0.1	95.0	89.9
DRC re-exports	29.0	29.0	95.0	89.9
Re-export net added value	5.6	5.4	19.0	18.0
Coltan				
Official exports	24.0	16.6	13.9	—
DRC re-exports	200.0	200.0	13.9	—
Re-export net added value	150.0	150.0	13.2	—
Total value official exports	61.2	68.4	438.8	380.5
Total value DRC re-exports	269.0	269.0	144.9	126.0
Total re-export added value	163.6	163.4	39.4	25.2
As GNP %	8.4	7.1	0.7	0.5
As military spending %	200.0	190.0	34.0	24.0
As public aid %	65.0	110.0	13.0	6.0

Source: S. Marysse and C. André, "Guerre et pillage économique en République Démocratique du Congo," in S. Marysse and F. Reyntjens, eds., L'Afrique des Grands Lacs (2000–2001) (Paris: L'Harmattan, 2001), 326.

These interesting results call for a number of comments:

1. "Re-export added value" means the money actually derived from the re-export of DRC resources once their production and transport costs had been deducted.

2. Diamonds, which are foremost in people's minds when looting is mentioned, in fact constitute a small proportion of the resources illegally exploited. But the fierce competition for their control comes from the fact that, at very high value for a negligible weight, they are easy to steal and transport. There was constant competition between looting for war support and looting for the private enrichment of the officers involved. Generally speaking, RPA officers tended to be more "public-minded" (the feared Congo Desk at the Ministry of Defense was there to remind them of their duty), whereas more loosely controlled UPDF officers tended to look to their personal benefit first.

3. Uganda had a more "transparent" policy (some would say brazen) and declared a lot of its DRC-acquired products to be official exports. The question never asked by the international community was how these had been acquired.

4. Coltan was the product that made the big difference, but its price fluctuated wildly. I would personally tend to minorate the 1999 figures, when prices were hovering around $80/kilo, and increase the 2000 figures when they had risen to $600/kilo. In his estimate Bjorn Willum figures at least a $191 million re-export added value for Rwandese coltan in 2000, which seems high but not unreasonable.

5. The exploitation of Congolese resources was much more essential for Rwanda than for Uganda, both because its military spending in GNP percentage is much higher (4 percent officially, instead of 2.5 percent) and because its export capacity is much lower.

6. The international community had been, to say the least, rather negligent in its evaluation of the situation.

This last point deserves some development because international aid has—rightly—come under heavy criticism both for prolonging the war and for favoring the anti-Kinshasa camp.[94] When the EU commissioner for development Poul Nielsen released €110 million in aid for Rwanda, he declared that the monies would "support government efforts to reduce poverty and consolidate its reform programme both on macro-economic matters and good governance."[95] When the Dutch Ministry of Foreign Affairs decided on added aid to Rwanda in 2000, it justified its decision by "progress made in the area of the economy and good governance."[96] As for the British Department for International Development, it decided to grant £30 million to Rwanda because of "its progress in fiscal, monetary and trade reform."[97] When the World Bank approved a new $75 million loan to Rwanda in February 1999 and questions were asked about whether this might not be used to support the war, Bank economist Chukwuma Obidegwu answered, "The government assured us that it is not interested in continuing the war. Which is satisfactory for us.... . We have no guarantees but we have their word."[98] Should such attitudes be attributed to naïveté or to a political choice? Probably to neither: there was the already mentioned desire of the international institutions to "push money out of the door" (otherwise, why do such institutions exist?) and then the enormous amount of guilt that came from not having done anything about the genocide when it was in the power of the international community to stop it. As a result, even when actors of the Congo looting showed themselves ready to speak, no attention was paid to what they had to say and no further action was undertaken. From that point of view, the testimony of RPA staff officer Deus Kagiraneza to the Belgian Senate Commission of Inquiry on the Great Lakes is an amazing case in point:

In 2000 I was contacted unofficially by a World Bank expert who asked me why was it that there were in Antwerp records of $30m of precious metals imports from Rwanda while there was no trace of that in our national accounting.[99] I told him that I did not know but ... that we had a second set of unregistered books for our national accounting.[100]

This in the year when Poul Nielsen and the Dutch minister for foreign affairs were both finding signs of "good governance" to be rewarded financially. At least in the case of Uganda the donors kept asking for a reduction of the military budget, and $278 million of Heavily Indebted Poor Countries debt relief got delayed because of the war.[101] But in the end, the tolerance was similar.

Lusaka had given the warring parties a precise (perhaps *too* precise) timetable for everything from disarmament to UN deployment. But from the beginning it was obvious that the UN was not going to get much cooperation from the Congolese authorities. Foreign minister Yerodia Ndombasi, not known for his diplomatic niceties, had already declared that he did not see the point of deploying UN personnel "where there are no rebels and no aggressors."[102] In other words, keep your noses out of our business. This attitude, which was quite widespread not only among government members but even among the general population, came from the very ambiguous role played by the UN in the early 1960s, with the accusations of having

connived in Lumumba's murder and of having protected Tshombe's secession.[103] When the first MONUC observers were deployed in November
1999,[104] they were theoretically allowed in Goma, Bukavu, Kisangani, Gbadolite, Lisala, Pepa, Isiro, Kabalo, Bunia, Pweto, Bumba, Kalemie, Moba,
Kongolo, and Kindu. But they were explicitly barred from Mbandaka,
Mbuji-Mayi, Lubumbashi, Kananga, Matadi, and Kamina. This meant that
Kinshasa accepted the MONUC deployment on rebel territory but refused
it on its own, particularly in the places where it had fighting forces or where
it handled military cargo. In fact, MONUC observers (seventy officers to
cover 2.3 million square kilometers) were looked upon by the government
as spies. The noncooperative attitude of the United States did not help. It
was so obvious that U.S. UN Ambassador Richard Holbrooke even tried to
justify it in a contorted way, saying, "We are dragging our feet not because
we are opposed to peacekeeping in the Congo but because we don't want
to write the DPKO [UN Department of Peacekeeping Operations] a blank
cheque, we want to get it right."[105] What "getting it right" meant exactly
was not spelled out. In January 2000 Kofi Annan proposed the deployment of 5,537 UN troops for the MONUC force, a proposal that received
lukewarm U.S. support.[106] Kabila declared that the Lusaka Agreement "was
going to be put into practice within the next two weeks," the first of a long
series of broken promises. In mid-February, as soon as he started working
on his non-Lusaka National Assembly plan, Kabila recanted in practice and
put many complicated conditions in the way of troop deployment. This
sabotage came at the very moment when both the government and the
rebels had finally abandoned all pretence and returned to open warfare. The
UN declared itself "disappointed" by the offensives, which might stop the
deployment. This caused Museveni's diplomatic adviser Amama Mbabazi to
quip, "It should be the opposite; they should deploy and set straight what
they don't like."[107]

In spite of its Chapter Seven mandate, MONUC, which was experiencing serious staffing problems, was not about to deploy in the midst of the
fighting. And by then, on top of Kabila's hostility, the UN had to face
that of the rebels. Emile Ilunga, the RCD-G chief, declared irrationally,
"The Lusaka process has been held to ransom by the international community and Laurent-Désiré Kabila... . There is complicity between Kabila
and the UN... . The cease-fire no longer holds."[108] The reality was simply
that, like Kabila himself, by early 2000 the Rwandese-backed rebels had
renewed hopes of a direct military victory and did not want inquisitive eyes

247

looking on.[109] When Facilitator Masire arrived in the DRC at the end of March, he sat for a week in Kinshasa waiting for flight clearances to various points of the country and finally had to fly home without being able to go anywhere. In early May, as things were still stuck, Holbrooke flew to Kinshasa to plead for MONUC deployment. With the Rwando-Ugandan fratricidal fighting going on in Kisangani, his mission was aborted. The song and dance went on in confused and desultory fashion: Masire met with Wamba, Ilunga, and Bemba, who all assured him of their cooperation and did nothing; MONUC said that the MLC advance southward was a violation of the Lusaka Agreement; Bemba answered that there had been over one hundred violations so far; Kabila refused to meet Masire; Robin Cook appointed Douglas Scrafton as British Great Lakes special representative (he remained underemployed); Museveni declared that unilateral withdrawal of military forces was very dangerous since "it could upset the carefully negotiated sequence of events and lead to the collapse of the cease-fire agreement as a whole,"[110] a somewhat surrealistic statement given the situation; Kabila relented and allowed for MONUC deployment, then, at the last minute, changed his mind and said that UN forces could not be allowed to deploy in government-controlled territory.[111] The RCD-G said it was out of the question that it would evacuate Kisangani. By then Kabila's allies were frantic, especially when their champion "forgot" to show up at the conference that the SADC had organized in Windhoek on August 6 to try to rescue the Lusaka process. Chiluba chased Kabila to Lubumbashi on August 10 and wrangled from him a reluctant consent to attend yet another "summit." Kamel Morjane, the embattled head of MONUC, immediately jumped in and managed to get Kabila to confirm his promise to Chiluba on August 11. He then attended the so-called "last chance summit" in Lusaka on August 14 but left after one day without making any commitment. As the *Economist* wrote, "Congo's ruler is now irritating his allies as well as his opponents,"[112] something which was to have very grave consequences for him. A week later, when he flew to Luanda to ask for more troops for his northern front offensive, he was cold-shouldered and got only a few aircraft.[113] Peeved, he had his minister for human rights, Léonard She Okitundu, announce that Kinshasa had decided to unilaterally suspend the application of the Lusaka Peace Agreement.[114] This time it was too much for dos Santos, who made an angry phone call to Kabila in the middle of the night and told him to stop his obstruction. So Kabila backtracked the next day and declared personally that he was now ready to accept the deployment.[115]

In the midst of this tiring tragicomedy it was sobering that a member of the U.S. mission to the United Nations had the decency to remind whoever cared to listen that "in terms of the number of countries involved this war is probably the greatest threat to peace and security in the world today and, considering the numbers of at-risk civilians, it is one of the greatest humanitarian crises ever."[116]

On August 23, Kabila again unilaterally suspended the application of the Lusaka peace process, a move characterized by Emile Ilunga of the RCD-G as "contradictory and insane."[117] The situation appeared to be so blocked that that perennial diplomatic gadfly Colonel Gaddafi jumped in and organized a meeting in Tripoli calling for the deployment of a "neutral African force" in the Congo that, he said, would have "immediate impact." Enchanted with this new smokescreen, Museveni declared that the African force "should replace all foreign armies," and Rwanda promised "an unconditional and complete withdrawal."[118]

MONUC had been slowly inching upward (although nowhere near its 5,537 personnel deployment target), and it now had 566 people in the DRC. Of these, 117 were local recruits used for administrative and logistic jobs, 205 were expatriate UN civil servants, and only 26 were soldiers. The remaining (218) were "military observers" (i.e., soldiers without weapons) who were stuck in Kinshasa and rarely flew out to the field.[119]

Dos Santos and Chiluba then wearily organized a "last last-chance" meeting in Maputo for November 27. It resulted in catastrophe when Museveni and Kagame stormed out of the conference during the very first session. Kabila had answered their demand for the disarmament of the *Interahamwe* militiamen with the quip that the only two *Interahamwe* in the Congo were Museveni and Kagame themselves.[120] All venues for negotiation seemed definitely blocked. Forty-nine days later the Congolese president was dead.

Mzee's assassination

On Tuesday, January 16, 2001, around noontime, Laurent-Désiré Kabila was sitting in one of the offices of the Presidential Palace in Kinshasa, looking at papers and chatting with Social Affairs Counselor Emile Mota when one of his bodyguards, Rashidi Kasereka, walked up to him as if to whisper something in his ear. Instead, he pulled out an automatic pistol and fired two or three bullets (the various accounts do not agree) at point-blank range into the president. One of the bullets entered the back of the skull and killed him almost immediately. Then things got more uncertain. There was a lot of shooting which seemed to have come from the courtyard, where elements of the president's bodyguard were exchanging fire with a small group of armed men. The murderer ran out of the room. Almost immediately Presidential Aide Col. Eddy Kapend shot a bodyguard whom he later said was Kasereka.[121] After about half an hour of shooting things quieted down at the Palace. The radio then announced that the president had been wounded in an assassination attempt. The same evening, although Kabila had now been dead for several hours, an ambulance took his body to Ndjili Airport and put it aboard a Congolese DC-8 transport, which flew it to Harare, under the pretence of looking for medical help. On Tuesday evening at 6 p.m. Colonel Kapend went on the air, told everybody to stay at home, asked the armed forces to remain calm and disciplined, and announced that all borders were closed. But he did not admit the president's death. At 8 p.m. Interior Minister Gaëtan Kakudji announced a curfew, effective immediately, but still did not acknowledge that the president was dead. That same evening the Belgian Foreign Ministry, which had its own sources of information in Kinshasa, announced that President Kabila had been killed.[122] That message was contradicted the next day by the Congolese ambassador to Zimbabwe Kikaya bin Karubi. Deputy Defense Minister Godefroid Chamulesso, who was visiting Libya, was the first Congolese official to admit that Kabila was dead.[123]

The rebels stressed their support for the Lusaka Agreement,[124] and Zimbabwe pledged continued support for the Congo.[125] Meanwhile, Kabila's staff called the whole diplomatic corps accredited in the capital to the Cité de l'Organisation de l'Unité Africaine, where the diplomats were told solemnly that Joseph Kabila, the president's son, was to be "head of the interim government for the time being."[126]

The official announcement of Laurent-Désiré Kabila's death finally came on Thursday, January 18, at 8 p.m., when Government Spokesman Dominique Sakombi Inongo declared that President Kabila had died from his wounds that same morning at 10 a.m. and announced thirty days of official mourning.[127] The body of the dead president was then flown back from Harare on Sunday, January 21, and a grand national funeral where hundreds of thousands of mourners turned up took place on Tuesday, January 23.

Why all these complications and dissimulations? And why the lie about Kabila's actual hour of death? The reasons are complex and have to do with what lay behind the murder itself.

The best account of the murder, even if incomplete, was published about a month later in the Paris newspaper Le Monde.[128] Although generally well-received, this article was criticized on two levels.[129] First, some people considered that it was too "French-centered," that it "protected" Luanda of any responsibility and that it had been "inspired" by the French Secret Service, both to protect Luanda for oil contract reasons and to try to pin the guilt on Kampala.[130] A second line of criticism was that the story was naïve and that the murder could not have been (as the authors, Smith and Glaser, present it) the act of isolated individuals but that behind this smokescreen lay a vast international conspiracy which was at times attributed to Mobutist circles and Angola[131] and at times to vast, dark, and somewhat imprecise forces of an evil nature.[132] In fact, several of these explanations and criticisms, if taken together and somewhat shifted for better focus, constitute a kaleidoscopic version of the truth. Let us look at some of the elements that went into the killing of Mzee, the man who tricked his puppet masters, surprised his enemies, puzzled the international community,[133] and won the grudging respect of the fellow countrymen he both defended and oppressed.

There are two main strands in the assassination story. The first one could be called the "Kivutian strand" and the other the "Angolan strand." To understand the first one we have to go back, as Smith and Glaser do, to the early days of Kabila's last adventure, during the fall of 1996 in Kivu.[134] Kabila, picked by the trans-African anti-Mobutu crusade leadership, had no military means of his own. From the beginning he knew he would need his own armed group, in the short term to compete with Kisase Ngandu and, perhaps later, to emancipate himself from Rwandese tutelage. He then systematically set about recruiting young local boys to join the newly formed AFDL. To his surprise, they came in droves:[135] massive rural poverty, lack of schooling opportunities, boredom, disgust with Mobutu's decaying rule, all combined to give him in a few months an army of 10,000 to 15,000 *kadogo* ("little ones").[136] They ranged in age from ten to twenty, with a median age of around fifteen. Many were orphans, their parents having died either from diseases[137] or in the Kivu ethnic wars that had been endemic for the past three years.[138] They looked up to the resurrected revolutionary leader as a charismatic father-like figure. It is they who, very early, started to call him *Mzee* ("old man," an expression of quasi-filial respect in Swahili). He, in turn, played with them like an old tomcat with young kittens. They had no social worth; thanks to him they became, first, young adventurers, then apprentice soldiers, and eventually heroes. For *Mzee* they would kill and they would die. He knew it and he used it; then he overused it. The turning point did not come at once; it started with the August 1998 war. There were *kadogo* in the 10th Brigade and there were *kadogo* in the ranks of the FAC units that remained loyal to Kinshasa. Within a month they were fighting each other, an emotionally painful situation that was to last for the next two and a half years; both the *kadogo* who had stayed on the government side and those who had "rebelled" had simply followed their commanding officers. In all these armies of child soldiers, the officers and the boys had developed quasi-familial relationships,[139] and above them stood *Mzee*, father to them all. It was for that reason that the young boys made up his bodyguard, because he trusted them in a way he would not trust the adults: "They can't harm me," he used to say. "They have been with me since the beginning. They are my children."[140]

But slowly things started to go sour. The boys around Mzee could not correspond with their family, if they still had one, because the families were caught on the rebel side and there was no mail or telephones operating between the two camps. Their salaries were very irregularly paid. The FAC medical services treated them like poor relatives, with the limited medical help that was available going to well-connected officers. Those who wanted to go back to school were forbidden to do so. Some who deserted were shot. Then came the arrest and trial of Masasu Nindaga.[141] Masasu had been their man. Slightly older than most of them, without family (his father had deserted the home and left him with an old uncle), a former street boy like many of them, he had managed by sheer force of guts and cunning to become one of the founding members of the AFDL in October 1996.[142] Masasu had been kept in jail until April 2000 and then freed as a lubricant for the secret negotiations then going on with Kigali.[143] But on October 21, 2000, Masasu was rearrested. His crime was going to the Kivus and talking with many people belonging to his old prewar crowd. The conclusions of these conversations were that people hated the Rwandese but that they did not like Kabila very much either. This induced Masasu, who had always been a kind of "Kivu nationalist," to try to strike an independent course and create his own faction within the FAC, based on "his" *kadogo* group, with the ultimate hope of starting a Kivu secessionist movement. This Kabila quickly learned, and he feared that the "third way" guerrilla movement in the east that Masasu had in mind would probably be started with Rwandese help.[144] As the RPA was by then building up its forces for an attack on Pweto, Mzee became sure that this was part of the plot. He ordered Masasu to be transferred to Pweto, probably in the hope of arranging some kind of last-minute bargain with what he saw as a concerted move between Kigali and his prisoner. Whether or not the conspiratorial link existed, Masasu could not deliver the end of a plot he had barely started, and he was shot in Pweto on November 24. All hell then broke loose among the Kivutian *kadogo* in Kinshasa; there were hundreds of arrests, thirty-six were shot, and 250 fled to Brazzaville.[145] RCD-G South Kivu "Governor" Basengezi Katintima was delighted and made sure that everybody in Bukavu heard about the arrests and the executions.[146] Kinshasa clumsily tried to deny the clampdown.[147]

Then came the attack on Pweto which quickly turned into a rout. The *kadogo* had to bear the brunt of the fighting in spite of the fact that they had not been paid or resupplied for months and were almost starving. To make things worse they had received inhumane instructions, ordering them to shoot their wounded comrades "because it would be too expensive to fly them out to Kalemie or to Lubumbashi."[148] When the RPA–RCD-G troops came down on them, they fled across the border into Zambia because they simply did not have the means to fight the enemy's overwhelming force. Most of the boys refused refugee status in Zambia and asked to be repatriated, knowing full well that this meant they would go on fighting. Nevertheless, Kabila publicly disowned them and accused them of cowardice. In the refugee camps in Zambia many died because their wounds went septic and they lacked even basic medical attention. "We have defended a man who has showed little or no interest for our personal lives," one of them declared to an NGO person working among the refugees.[149] As in a nightmare, Mzee, the father figure, had finally turned into an ogre. It was this feeling, coupled with the execution of Masasu and the Kinshasa clampdown on their comrades, that set in motion the desperate and clumsy conspiracy eventually leading to the president's assassination.

But then (and here we have to go beyond Smith and Glaser's account, to which I have substantially adhered so far, even if with some additional details) there was another dimension, "the Angolan connection." It was not a murder plot, properly speaking, but it was a deliberate conspiracy of silence. Luanda was furious at Kabila for squandering the diplomatic opportunities that he could have taken advantage of. The Angolans wanted his regime to survive, but they did not think that his policy of deliberately torpedoing the MONUC deployment, of humiliating Masire, and of mocking the international community was leading him (and them by association) anywhere. They had tried to explain that to him many times, after the Lusaka August 2000 meeting and later, after Maputo I and Maputo II, and each time they had been met with a deaf ear because the former fierce "Afro-Stalinists" who had turned into clever and crooked "petro-diamond capitalists"[150] had no more conceptual common ground with the time capsule–enclosed former companion of Che Guevara. Kabila was locked up in a black-and-white world where the "UN-U.S." represented the epitome of evil. He believed in his own propaganda. His capacity to maneuver did not extend to the succubus in human guise he felt the "international community" to be. He honestly believed that there could be no durable compromise with the imperialist dragon and that only short-term tactical accommodations were possible. These remained pitifully inadequate compared to what his wily Angolan allies would have wished. And as if this was not enough, Kabila then crossed an absolute red line: his constant cash problems caused him to start dealing in diamonds with UNITA. In August 2000 his close aide Commandant Jean-Calvin Kondolo[151] contacted a diamond trader who was a known operator for Savimbi.[152] By October the newsletter *Africa Confidential* could write in the same issue "Recent reports indicate that Savimbi's business allies are again trading diamonds in Kinshasa" and "Several diplomats believe that dropping Kabila might unblock the peace negotiations."[153]

It is at that point that a bizarre event becomes relevant: eleven Lebanese citizens, all related by blood, were killed within days of the president's murder, apparently on orders from Gen. Yav Nawesh and Col. Eddy Kapend. Incredible stories were later invented, saying that Kasereka had carried a list of the eleven names in his pocket because the Lebanese had been the financers or instigators of the assassination.[154] In fact, the Lebanese victims were thought by Luanda to be the diamond-trading link between Kabila and UNITA, and that link had to be brutally cut.[155] Which throws the Nawesh-Kapend radical action into a very peculiar light: both men, and a number of other pro-Angolan officers, were perfectly aware of the fact that the *kadogo* had become desperate and were about to kill their "father." They had warned Luanda, saying at the same time that the plot was so amateurish that any danger of a successful *kadogo* putsch could safely be ruled out.[156] Luanda had apparently told them to keep quiet and to get ready for the transfer of power.[157] On the day before the assassination General Nawesh had ordered the disarmament of a number of units at Camp Tshatshi and Camp Kokolo.[158] These were made up of Balubakat soldiers whom he felt the Angolan camp could not trust if things got rough. And then, during the Wednesday 10 a.m. cabinet meeting, which actually decided what had to be done before the president's death would be announced, Gaëtan Kakudji tried to take over, saying that he was closest to the dead man. It was Eddy

Kapend, firmly seconded by Mwenze Kongolo, who put him back in his place and suggested that Joseph Kabila should exercise interim power. The Angolans had apparently suggested earlier that Victor Mpoyo should take over when the president was killed, but Colonel Kapend had told them that this would be both too obvious and probably impossible, since the Balubakat would not tolerate it.[159] As a Lunda, Kapend was keenly aware of the effect that such a publicly pro-Angola man as Mpoyo (even if he was a Muluba from Kasai) assuming power would have had on the Balubakat. The whole Katangese secession–civil war–deportation issue would have jumped back to the fore at a time when, with the fall of Pweto, Lubumbashi and the whole of Katanga seemed to be within the reach of the Rwandese.[160]

The consensus was that Joseph was the safest bet. He was young, he was inexperienced, he was rumored not to be his father's son, and he had no tribal constituency of his own in the Congo because he had spent practically all of his life abroad. This made him an ideal choice to be used as a front by a pro-Luanda government. So Kakudji was told to sit back and let the young man, who was not even present,[161] assume the appearance of power. The "Nokos" ("uncles," or, more properly, "godfathers") had made their choice, and they felt confident that it would work smoothly. Actually, they, and the rest of the world, were in for a big surprise.

8

NOT WITH A BANG BUT WITH A WHIMPER: THE WAR'S CONFUSED ENDING (JANUARY 2001–DECEMBER 2002)

Li'l Joseph's new political dispensation

"Notwithstanding the formal appointment of Joseph Kabila as interim head of state, a Joint Military Command reportedly retains effective control, with Colonel Eddy Kapend in charge, according to intelligence sources."[1] At first not many observers would have granted much of a political future to the young (twenty-nine years old) taciturn son of the dead president. He was constantly watched by Luanda's men, did not have any real political or tribal constituency of his own, and was closely "protected" by Kapend and his group. In addition, he was caught between the demands of an international community for which his father incarnated everything that was wrong with African politics and those of a close "palace guard" that had decided to carry on with those very policies that had so alienated the dead man from the rest of the world. His chances looked very slim indeed. But the next three months were going to witness an extraordinary political and diplomatic balancing act from which he would emerge as the fragile but triumphant arbiter of the situation.

His first move was to address the Military High Command to pacify them by saying that his intent was to "attain the objective Mzee Laurent-Désiré Kabila had set for them, namely to reconquer all the occupied territories of the country."[2] The next day the word *interim* had disappeared from his title and Mwenze Kongolo said that he would have to be sworn in. But he added, "We all came to the conclusion that this young man was the one we needed to keep things under control for the time being, until we have a President again."[3] The warning was clear, but Li'l Joseph pretended not to hear.[4] Instead he held statesman-like conversations with Presidents dos Santos, Nujoma, and Mugabe, who had come to Kinshasa to attend his father's state funeral.[5] The next day the RCD-G rebels asked Parliament not to recognize him as president.[6] On January 25 he was nevertheless sworn in and immediately met with UN Special Envoy Kamel Morjane, U.S. Ambassador Bill Swing, and EU Special Representative Aldo Ajello. Devoid of any national constituency, he had decided to treat the international community as his power base.

On January 26 he made his first big speech as president. Widely followed on Radio Télévision Nationale Congolaise, it was a careful construction designed to please everybody. For the belligerent Nokos there was a pledge to "demand the immediate withdrawal of the aggressor states" and to "defend the country's unity and territorial integrity." For the human rights advocates there was a "commitment to respect fundamental rights as well as individual and public freedoms." For the international community there was a promise to "examine ways and means to revive the Lusaka Accord" and a pledge to "pursue political openness so that all political actors can exercise their rights." To the business community he promised to "liberalize economic activities, first . . . in the diamond sector and then in the currency exchange sector" and to "propose a new mining code and a new investment code." To Washington he said, "Without beating about the bush, I recognize there has been mutual misunderstanding with the former administration. The DRC intends to normalize bilateral relations with the new administration." He thanked his allies, "particularly Zimbabwe, Angola and Namibia."[7] He declared himself "firmly resolved to improve cooperation with our main partners of the European Union, especially France . . . and Belgium with which we share historical ties." He promised to "collaborate closely with the UN, particularly with the Observers' Mission in the Congo . . . notably with regard to the urgent deployment of its forces on our soil." And he ended with a peroration: "[I salute] the lofty spirit of sacrifice of our brothers and sisters living in the occupied territories... . My military, political and diplomatic efforts will be directed towards your total liberation." Awash with all the right buzzwords, it was an artist's performance,[8] and he lost no time capitalizing on the refreshing effect he produced on his listeners. Two days later he met with South African President Thabo Mbeki. Three days later he held a widely publicized meeting of the Military High Command during which he extracted a personal pledge of loyalty from Colonel Kapend.[9] But unknown to Kapend he had first met secretly with the leaders of the Balubakat community and told them that their help was required as he wanted to arrest all those who had connived in his father's death and could be a threat to his position. He told them they did not have much of a choice; if they abandoned him, the Lunda would sooner or later take over with Angolan help, and it would be the posthumous triumph of Moïse Tshombe, Tshisekedi would make a comeback (which meant the triumph of their hostile Baluba cousins from Kasai) or, worse, there would be chaos and the military victory that the "rebels" and their foreign sponsors had been hoping for all along. None of this was very attractive to the Balubakat and the community pledged its support.

The young, not-quite-yet-president then left the country on the first leg of a whirlwind foreign tour.[10] On January 31 he was in Paris, where he met President Jacques Chirac and his Africa adviser Michel Dupuch. On February 1, together with President Kagame, he attended the Washington Prayer Breakfast organized by President George W. Bush. The same day he met with Secretary of State Colin Powell,[11] and by February 2 he was in New York, where he gave a speech at the United Nations Security Council. In the words of a journalist who attended the event,

When he first appeared, tightly surrounded by his entourage, some people thought he seemed to be a puppet in the hands of his powerful allies. But two and a half hours later, after his speech, UN diplomats were queuing up to shake his hand and congratulate him.... Surprisingly for his age, he had found the right words to put the Security Council members on his side.[12]

Losing no time, he then met with businessmen, earning accolades from the usually no-nonsense Jane Perlez of the *New York Times,* who wrote, "The new young leader has made a case for fresh investment in the Congo."[13] The next day he was in Brussels to meet Prime Minister Guy Verhofsadt, who pledged to support him. He then flew back to Kinshasa's grim world.

There were now 100,000 refugees in the Republic of Congo, fleeing recent fighting between the FAC and the MLC in Equateur; at least four hundred civilians had been killed in Ituri during the past two weeks in clashes around Bunia, and the UPDF had recruited another six hundred Hema child soldiers to be trained in Uganda.[14] Reality was quickly reasserting itself. But the young man knew he had to keep the momentum generated by his trip, if only on the symbolic level. On February 5 all the militants of the peace campaign who had been incarcerated on January 10 as one of his father's last decisions were released, and "P'tit Joseph" declared, "Everything has to be re-started from zero."[15]

Still, the iron hand was very much present inside the velvet glove, and arrests of citizens from the Kivus, both civilians and military, continued unabated.[16] The young president did not want to acknowledge these domestic developments. Instead, he met with Nelson Mandela, who obligingly declared himself "very impressed"[17] with his young host, and then flew to Lusaka to attend the latest summit trying to revive the ailing Agreement. This earned him renewed diplomatically useful kudos, particularly since Kagame, still sulking from his cold-shouldering in Washington, had declined to come. Then, as Joseph flew home, there was another wave of arrests on February 18, unconnected with the Kivus but very much connected with the conspiracy to kill his father: Gen. Yav Nawesh, Colonel Mabila (commander of FAC forces in Mbandaka), the late president's security adviser Nono Lutula, the former ANR director George Leta Mangassa, and three superior officers. The Angolans got nervous and brought eight hundred men from Luanda to reinforce Dolisie in the neighboring Republic of Congo. Six days later the president moved in for the kill and arrested Colonel Kapend himself.

For four days Luanda maintained a stunned silence before it finally acknowledged the situation. When it did, it was to sullenly accept what had happened. The key reason was Angola's nervousness concerning the military situation. Bemba was still extremely reluctant to accept any kind of talks, in spite of Ugandan efforts.[18] This was because UNITA had dispatched six hundred men to Bangui, complete with artillery and transmission equipment, to bolster the MLC forces, which still had Kinshasa in their sights.[19] This made dos Santos quite wary of any major upheaval in the Congo. But just to be on the safe side, Joseph Kabila had closely surrounded himself with a Zimbabwean bodyguard, directly under the orders of the ZDF overall commander in the DRC, Gen. Amos Chingombe.[20] As overthrowing the young upstart president seemed likely to create more problems than it would solve, dos Santos swallowed his pride. After all, he had achieved what he wanted, even if by other channels than those he had planned to use.[21]

Whereas his father had remained a prisoner in a cold war time capsule, Joseph Kabila understood the nature of modern politics: never mind reality, image is all. He gave orders to his personal office to reimburse three million Congolais francs that had been budgeted for a "support march," deriding the proposed "spontaneous demonstration" as "an obsolete practice belonging to the bygone era of the personality cult."[22] In another well-advertised show of public virtue he rebuked veteran Congolese spin doctor Dominique

Sakombi Inongo, who had offered him his usual medicine of heavily personalized publicity spots.

His opponents began to panic and to grasp at straws. Jean-Pierre Bemba huffily declared that Joseph Kabila "is not a president but just the chief of an army which controls only 40% of the Congo." And in an apparent complete non sequitur he "revealed" that the young man was not Laurent-Désiré Kabila's son but that "of the Rwandese Tutsi Kanombe who was killed in Moba."[23] We must stop for a moment to clarify these rumors, which were fed by the complicated and secretive life Laurent-Désiré Kabila had led between his dropping out of the political limelight in the mid-1960s and his political "resurrection" thirty years later. The explanation for the uncertainty of Joseph Kabila's origins can be found in Erik Kennes's splendidly researched biography of the late president.[24] One of L. D. Kabila's companions in the PRP guerrilla group was a certain Adrien Kanambe or Kanambi, a Tutsi from Rutshuru. Kanambe died in June 1985, during the second of the two PRP attacks on Moba, not in combat but apparently shot on Kabila's orders. He had several children, including one, Selemani, who was Joseph's age and his playmate. After Kanambe's execution, the mother of the little Selemani died in a shipwreck on Lake Tanganyika and the boy was raised by another of Kanambe's wives, a Mubembe woman by the name of Vumilia. It is she who later "married" Laurent-Désiré, who then "adopted" the late Kanambe's son. Selemani and Joseph, by then both "Kabila's children," got mixed up in the public imagination.[25] But it is ironic that the previous "democratic questioning" of a succession based on simple biological filiation was now giving way to challenges about that very filiation in order to refute the legitimacy of the power transfer. It showed that even the adversaries of the process had entered its peculiar dynastic logic.[26]

Meanwhile, ignoring such challenges, the young president kept moving ahead with his regime change agenda. On February 22 the free trading of foreign exchange was reauthorized[27] and new, clear regulations were issued concerning the diamond counters, which had to be registered for a reasonable fee ($200,000 per counter per year, plus a $3,000 licensing fee per purchasing agent). They would be charged 1 percent of their export volume to get centralized quality expertise, and they would pay a 4 percent export tax. Minimum yearly turnover was set at $48 million per counter to eliminate the small fry.[28] Implicit in these measures was the termination of dubious contracts such as IDI's.

Elsewhere in the newly opened business world, Cohydro, the national Congolese oil company, signed a $125 million contract with the South African oil company Thebe Petroleum, thereby ending the *de facto* monopoly enjoyed since 1998 by the Angolan state company, Sonangol.[29] This caused some gritting of teeth in Luanda, but by then the Angolans were resigned to the new dispensation being implemented. Since late February the mining investors had smelled money and begun to descend upon Kinshasa. Alfred Sefu, CEO of Gécamines, met with a World Bank mission on March 6 and coolly asked for $150 million.[30] He did not really expect to get it, but what would have been laughable at the time of the late president had suddenly become conceivable. John Bredenkamp was leading the pack of (largely white) Zimbabwean and South African businessmen who now besieged the Kinshasa government offices, causing a Congolese minister to joke, "This is an Afrikaner Renaissance."[31] Brussels decided to second to the Congolese government Alphonse Verplaetse, a former governor of the Belgian Central Bank and a friend of Jean-Claude Masangu, with the mission of reforming the commercial code.[32] On the side, he could also advise his friend on monetary policy, a fact that was going to go a long way in relaxing the attitudes of international financial institutions toward Kinshasa.

To accompany this economic *aggiornamento* Joseph needed hands-on control of the civil service, and this he proceeded to achieve by signing three key decrees on March 12, appointing a whole bevy of "new men." First and most important, Didier Kazadi Nyembwe became the head of Agence Nationale de Renseignements (ANR). To keep four competing secret services under control, a tough and reliable man was needed for the job.[33] At his side was the new security adviser, a very different man, Jean Mbuyu, who had created the Centre for Human Rights in Lubumbashi. As head of his personal staff Joseph appointed Théophile Mbemba Fundu, a Muyeke from eastern Katanga and a long-time Mobutu opponent whom his father had installed as mayor of Kinshasa, a politically dangerous job he had fulfilled honorably. Fundu's righthand man was Evariste Boshab Mbudj, a Mutetela with a doctorate in law from the University of Louvain who had been an academic in France. As a diplomatic adviser the president picked Dieudonné Vangu Mambweni wa Busana, a Mukongo key dignitary of the Kimbanguist Church; he was also a fanatically anti-Tutsi politician who held very extreme opinions. The last two men were described as "Mobutists" because they had served under the Guide. This was quite exaggerated: Vangu was picked mostly for his useful Kimbanguist credentials,[34] because in 1997 he had been an ally of Roberto Garreton in his attempt to inquire into the fate of the "lost" Hutu refugees and, perhaps more slyly, because his presence helped indirectly to exonerate Joseph from his supposed Tutsi ancestry; Mbudj was just a good legal expert. New "president's men" also took over the Press Bureau, the Transport Office, a discreet Financial Bureau, and a roving ambassador's job.

No less important and covered by some of the decrees were the new military nominations. Some were not so new, such as Sylvestre Lwetcha, since September 1999 chief of staff of the FAC. Lwetcha had no education and was quite incapable of really discharging his duties, but he was a former 1960s Simba and later PRP guerrilla; he had done all he could to help the Mayi Mayi in the east and was very popular with the rank and file. It was his new second-in-command, Dieudonné Kayemba, who actually ran the FAC, while veteran Faustin Munene took care of the sensitive position of recruitment and training. Trusted Pierre-Célestin Kifwa became a special adviser on military affairs.

All in all, "P'tit Joseph" had now fairly well secured his immediate administrative surroundings. He could now reach further out, which he did on April 5, when he sacked his whole cabinet. The atmosphere was thick with tension for a week. The Nokos knew what was coming and were belatedly trying to make contact with the Mobutist opposition in Brazzaville. The notorious French mercenary Paul Barril suddenly turned up in Kinshasa, invited by Yerodia Ndombasi. He was immediately arrested and deported.[35] The day the new cabinet was announced (April 14) the army closed the Congo River crossing to Brazzaville as the Nokos half-heartedly thought of trying a coup.[36] But it was too late, they had all been kicked out of the government. Gaëtan Kakudji, Yerodia Ndombasi, Victor Mpoyo, Sakombi Inango, Didier Mumengi, Mawampanga Mwana Nanga—all had disappeared. The only two kept in the new cabinet were Léonard She Okitundu (Foreign Affairs) and Jeannot Mwenze Kongolo (Interior). The rest were either technocrats, like Finance Minister Freddy Matungulu Mbuyambu, a former IMF man, or political activists coming from the civil society, like Labor Minister Marie-Ange Lukiana Mufuankolo. The median age of the ministers was thirty-eight, and the national press dubbed it "a government of strangers."[37] For the new president, this was a perfect cabinet, unencumbered by the weight of the past.

Joseph still largely remained a mystery to his fellow countrymen,[38] but they had begun to get used to him. Foreigners were more responsive, at times too responsive, to a man who seemed to play the political game on their terms, which caused a respected international weekly to ask bluntly, "Is the world soft on Kabila?"[39] The question could reasonably be asked because there were two sides to the man. On the one hand, there was the "modern" politician who, in the course of one month, canceled the IDI monopoly, welcomed back his moderate opponent Arthur Z'Ahidi Ngoma, and charmed $110 million out of the European Union. On the other hand, there was the stealthy Machiavellian who could discreetly arrest over one hundred people, many of them innocent, to terrorize real or alleged "conspirators" linked with his father's murder.[40] The accumulated clichés about his youth, his silences, and his supposed "timidity" did not convince everyone. President Jacques Chirac seemed to have understood him well when he told his ambassador in Kinshasa, "Please stop writing that Joseph Kabila is timid. The fellow is a hundred times better at his job than his father. He knows exactly what he wants and he will go far."[41] But before going further he still had one hurdle to clear: explaining how his father had been killed.

An international commission of inquiry was created on February 9 and reported its conclusions on May 23. The report was a hodgepodge of unproven statements which tried to artificially connect a Kivutian plot, a "Lebanese" plot, and various dark manipulations by security service members, all being coordinated through a Rwando-Ugandan overall conspiracy. The whole thing was so preposterous that even the commission members did not seem too convinced of what they were saying. Rwanda's Foreign Minister André Bumaya simply declared, "Collaboration between Kigali and Kampala would have been in any case impossible given the relations between the two countries which are now very strained."[42] President Museveni wearily denied having anything to do with the whole affair. And Joseph Kabila said nothing. He then let a calculated interval elapse, not too long (he would have been accused of a cover-up) but sufficient to let other events overtake the murder in his fellow countrymen's minds. Then, on March 10, 2002, shortly before the mass trial of 115 "plotters" was to begin, Colonel Kapend's wife and baby were arrested and threatened with dire consequences.[43] Many other innocent family members of the accused were also arrested and detained in rough conditions. The result was that the trial took place in a very quiet atmosphere. When thirty of the accused were condemned to death and another fifty-nine to long prison sentences, there was hardly a ripple, apart from human rights organizations. Kabila's allies did not react, and the whole international community, by then thoroughly smitten with Joseph, declined to comment.

None of the accused was executed, and in well-connected political circles there was the brief rumor of a discreet deal. Then there was silence.[44] The new regime was now firmly installed, and those who had tried to stop it were unlikely to see the light of day for a long time.

Diplomacy slowly deconstructs the continental conflict

The actors start jockeying for position. What was the situation of the continental war in early 2001? First of all, one of weariness. The various actors had entered the conflict out of often unrelated interests, and most of these had started to disassemble. Angola had saved Laurent-Désiré Kabila at the last minute because it feared that the Rwandese adventurers who were trying to overthrow him could at any time broaden their tactical deal with Savimbi into a strategic alliance. In 1998 Savimbi had been a major threat who seemed capable of attacking Luanda. But by 2001 he was a spent force, trying with great difficulty to survive. Zimbabwe had jumped in to protect its investments and to block South Africa's political ascent on the continent. By 2001 it had failed on both counts, and its regime was struggling to survive in the face of mounting opposition, both at home and internationally. Windhoek had joined only because of SADC big boy pressure, and by 2001, faced with the growing indifference of one ally and the exhaustion of the other, it wanted out. As for the "aggressors," they remained involved, but only slightly. Burundi had always been a marginal force, more concerned with securing the Congolese side of its domestic security situation than with a real war of conquest. By 2001 its domestic situation was worse than ever and being in the Congo seemed to be of only marginal interest for improving it. As for Rwanda and Uganda, their mutual bitterness was so intense after the three Kisangani "wars" that it was hard to decide whom they hated most, each other or their supposed common enemy. In addition, President Museveni's grandiose dreams of trans-African statesmanship had come to naught, and he was under continuous donor pressure to reduce his military budget in order to keep Uganda's valuable Heavily Indebted Poor Countries (HIPC) status. Unlike Kagame in Rwanda, he was not under strong demographic or political pressure inside his own country, and the looting of the Congo had been more a factor of personal enrichment for some of the members of his regime than a useful tool of economic imperialism. As a result Kampala's heart was not strongly in the game even if some of the top UPDF officers remained eager to stay for purely financial reasons.[45] This left Rwanda as the only country both able and willing to go on. The reasons were multiple: security, economic benefits, relieving demographic pressure, keeping an oversize army happy,[46] surfing on foreign guilt about the genocide, and following the spirit of the RPF's Spartan political culture, which over the past twenty years had repeatedly considered war to be the solution to all problems. But even if the causes of involvement in the DRC had considerably receded, all the players remained wary of each other and watched their rivals for signs of disengagement before making their own moves.

Kagame was the first to react, declaring that he was ready to evacuate Pweto, "which is beyond our line of deployment but was taken in response to a military offensive launched by Laurent-Désiré Kabila."[47] Three days later he qualified his statement, saying that Rwanda would not leave the DRC until "the full disarmament of the *Interahamwe* militias."[48] Since the Mayi Mayi almost immediately attacked Shabunda he declined to attend the next Lusaka meeting, accusing Kinshasa of being responsible for the offensive. Always the optimist, Department of Peacekeeping Operations boss Jean-Marie Guehenno announced that he saw "a window of opportunity" and that only twenty-five hundred MONUC troops were now needed.[49] RCD-G leader Azarias Ruberwa declared, "War is a form of pressure aimed at forcing the DRC government to negotiate." The Mayi Mayi retorted that they were ready to collaborate in the disarming of the *Interahamwe*, adding, "We want to stress that we are independent from Kinshasa and that no durable solution can be found without us."[50] Joseph Kabila then came back to the controversial question of the Hutu refugee massacres of 1996–1997, declaring to the Belgian journalist Colette Braeckman, "Everything has been done to block the UN inquiry on this.[51] If they want to come back, they will be welcome.... . Can you explain to me how, in the eyes of the international community, the whole of the Congolese people has been turned into *Interahamwe*?"[52] But the diplomatic situation had changed and even the United States was now taking a much stronger line, talking of "firmness towards Kagame," of "grave human rights violations committed by Rwanda and Rwanda-backed troops in the DRC which fall within the mandate of the ICTR."[53] Ugandan Foreign Affairs Minister Eriya Kategaya flew to Kinshasa on April 3 and met with Kabila.[54] Soon after, MONUC started its first serious troop deployment, with Moroccan troops arriving in Kisangani, where they were cheered by the local population after the RCD-G tried to block their arrival.[55] Museveni was by then visibly nervous and making contradictory statements. On April 29 he announced a unilateral UPDF withdrawal, saying at the same time that he was opting out of the Lusaka peace process,[56] and then changing his mind on May 8. Bemba hailed Museveni's decision but added, "I give an ultimatum to Angola, Zimbabwe, Namibia and Rwanda to also pull out or else I withdraw from the Lusaka Peace Process."[57] The French ambassador in New York J. D. Levitte then led a twelve-person UN mission to the DRC, South Africa, Zambia, Tanzania, Rwanda, Angola, Burundi, and Uganda. He declared that thirty-five hundred MONUC troops would be enough to monitor the process[58] and was immediately contradicted by Kabila, who said that this figure was "a joke" and that twenty thousand men were needed.[59] A new meeting was planned in Lusaka for February 2002, where a general troop pullout would be discussed. During his African tour, U.S. Secretary of State Powell declared in Johannesburg, "The U.S. will not support any solution for the Congo crisis which would not respect its territorial integrity."[60]

Meanwhile, the main actors were reorganizing behind the scenes. Since they had to adapt to the new circumstances they were increasingly offering a main "peaceful" front while trying to pursue their various goals through proxy Congolese militias. UPDF Brig. James Kazini had given artillery reinforcements to Bemba to help him fight Mbusa Nyamwisi's RCD-ML, and Kigali had instructed its RCD-G friends to deny UPDF the use of Bangoka Airport in Kisangani for its planned troop withdrawal from the northeast.[61] The Ugandans who left Bafwasende had to do so on foot.[62] The Namibians, who now felt free to go with the flow, started to leave. But the Zimbabweans declared that they would wait for a stronger MONUC deployment before going.[63] As for the RCD-G, it announced that it was "studying" the demilitarization of Kisangani.[64] But by then all the actors had reached the same conclusion: open armed participation in the war was counterproductive, and evacuation was only a question of schedule and modalities. In any case, what would happen later was another matter.

Negotiations, national dialogue, and disarmament in competition. Of these three elements Laurent-Désiré Kabila had hollowed out the first, tried to highjack the second, and stubbornly resisted the third. Now the various actors started to haggle over these three dimensions, each one supposedly a precondition of the others. On August 8 Joseph Kabila signed a decree creating a National Dialogue Preparatory Commission, and a four day predialogue meeting took place in Gaborone on August 20, agreeing that the real thing should begin within six months. Léonard She Okitundu declared, perhaps a bit prematurely, "The war is now over."[65] The UN appointed

Amos Namanga Ngongi, a Cameroonian, to replace Kamel Morjane. Facilitator Masire agreed that the next venue for the talks should be Addis Ababa, where the same delegates who had come to Gaborone would meet again. This caused an immediate uproar from the four hundred or so "political parties" that had been left in limbo since the 1990 Conférence Nationale Souveraine. They were loudly clamoring to have a place in the new political structure they now saw emerging.[66] Zimbabwe then declared that its own troop withdrawal would depend on the outcome of the planned dialogue, and She Okitundu, who had so far insisted on foreign troop departure before the National Dialogue took place, suddenly reversed his stance.[67] UN pressure was by then considerable, and Secretary-General Kofi Annan personally visited the DRC in early September. To impress Rwanda and the RCD-G with the fact that the times had changed, he made a point of going all the way to Kisangani, where he quipped, "A peace process is like a bicycle: once you stop, you fall off."[68] The main sticking point remained the ambitiously named Disarmament, Demobilization, Rehabilitation, Reintegration, and Resettlement (DDRRR) program. To understand the complexity of the process, the fact that there were no homogeneous "negative forces" in the Congo must be kept in mind. Even the limited Burundian rebel presence was divided between the FNL and the CNDD-FDD. As for the Rwandese, they comprised three main groups:

- The old ALIR I in North Kivu: made up of ex-FAR and *Interahamwe*, it was about four thousand strong. In May 2001 they reentered Rwanda in Gisenyi and Ruhengeri. For the first time the *abacengezi* did not get much support from the local population, which was tired of the war. This allowed for quick success for the RPA, which killed over two thousand of them and captured eighteen hundred. After this episode, ALIR I was largely a spent force,[69] even resorting to attacks on Mayi Mayi groups in North Kivu to steal their weapons.

- The new ALIR II operated in South Kivu out of Kinshasa-supported bases in Kasaï and northern Katanga. It had over ten thousand men, and although many of the officers were old *génocidaires* most of the combatants had been recruited after 1997. They were the ones who fought around Pepa, Moba, and Pweto in late 2000.

- The even newer Forces Démocratiques de Libération du Rwanda (FDLR) had about three thousand men, based at Kamina in Katanga. Still untried in combat, they had been trained by the Zimbabweans and were a small, fully equipped conventional army.[70]

The problem was that everybody was playing with loaded dice. Just as the RCD-G was playing Kigali's game, thus Joseph Kabila, discreetly supported by Zimbabwe, dragged his feet in helping MONUC implement DDRRR because many of the "negative forces" targeted by the disarmament exercise were used behind the scenes to "put pressure" on Kigali.[71] The domestic situation was not much more honest, with the ANR constantly harassing and arresting civil society members who thought that the "Republican Pact" signed in Gaborone actually guaranteed them the right of free speech.[72] The Addis Ababa meeting in October, which was supposed to reinvigorate the process, was in fact a nonstarter: the facilitation was confused and short of money, there were only eighty delegates, who kept bickering at each other, and Mwenze Kongolo declared he would not even start without the full quorum of 330 delegates. The talks got bogged down in procedural squabbles and the Kinshasa delegation eventually left abruptly.[73] But not before the increasingly dynamic Pretoria observer team was able to make a convincing offer of reconvening the conference at a later date in South Africa. On December 4 Facilitator Masire announced that a new meeting would soon be held in Sun City, South Africa.

The South African breakthrough. The talks reconvened in Sun City on February 26, 2002. What was going to turn into a big South African diplomatic victory was all the more interesting for coming on the heels of the latest attempt at European conventional diplomacy. Between January 21 and 24, French Foreign Minister Hubert Védrine and his British counterpart, Jack Straw, had traveled to Kinshasa, Kigali, and Kampala in an obsolete display of "great power diplomacy." The common trip was supposed to show to the world that Paris and London had buried their past differences; the problem was that nobody on the ground was very much interested in the white men's hectoring. The two gentlemen told Joseph Kabila that he must carry out DDRRR with his Hutu forces; they told Kagame that he should leave the Congo and Museveni that he should control his army. They were met in all three capitals with barely disguised irritation.[74] It is worth comparing this half-hearted attempt with the uninspired but doggedly persistent South African efforts.[75]

The conference started almost immediately on the wrong foot, with bickering about accreditation which nearly led to an early breakup. Then Kinshasa asked for the expulsion of Ugandan and Rwandese security officers, who were openly consorting with "their" rebel protégés. The RCD-G laughed it off, adding in a rare display of humor that it did not mind the presence of the Angolan and Zimbabwean security men on the other side. Rebels harassed civil society representatives from the occupied areas, accusing them (not without reason) of being pro-Kinshasa. Then there was further wrangling on the accreditation of "journalists," many of whom were fake. The whole thing was markedly chaotic and, in a strange sort of a way, quite cheerful.[76] There was a serious incident when DRC Human Rights Minister Ntumba Luaba declared, "The Congo would explode like Somalia if President Kabila were forced to step down after these talks," and the RCD-G answered that the whole point of the conference was to get him to resign. Kikaya bin Karubi, the press and communication minister, a new regime heavyweight, replied, "The government is prepared to share power but in no way to step down." When talk came around to the possibility of elections, there was a clear lack of interest from all the armed parties (Kinshasa included), while the civil society struggled to make room for that agenda. Veteran 1960s politician Antoine Gizenga said that the survivors of Congo's first Parliament, who were the only ones to have ever been fairly elected, should select the members of the future Assembly. He was politely ignored. In the midst of all this hubbub news suddenly arrived that the RCD-G had stormed the small Lake Tanganyika harbor of Moliro.[77] The Kinshasa delegation withdrew. Then it came back a week later and the RCD-G offered to give Moliro to MONUC if the FAC would evacuate the two outposts of Kayaya and Yayama in northern Katanga. Through all this, the South African mediators never lost hope and kept cajoling their charges, reasoning with them and at times discreetly blackmailing them.

Then suddenly, two days before the talks were going to go into recess, Bemba's representative, Olivier Kamitatu, signed a power-sharing agreement with Kinshasa. This was obviously done in agreement with Kampala, leaving Rwanda out in the cold. The RCD-G was incensed and Azarias Ruberwa declared, "The Congo will not be reunified and there will be no peace."[78] Mwenze Kongolo accused him of "not negotiating freely," that is, of remaining hostage to Kigali's decisions.[79] Kigali desperately tried to put together an anti-Agreement coalition, but, apart from four inconsequential organizations,[80] all it could come up with to join with RCD-G was Tshisekedi's old UDPS. The veteran oppositionist agreed to create the Alliance pour la Sauvegarde du Dialogue Inter-Congolais (ASD) and accused Kabila of "high treason."[81] But the ASD soon discredited itself by its shrill tone and unrealistic proposals.[82]

Meanwhile, the first dividends of the first real diplomatic breakthrough since 1998 started to appear when Equateur began to open up to travel and commerce with the government-held areas. Boat traffic returned to the Congo and Ubangi Rivers, and after a while air travel restarted on the Kinshasa–Lisala–Basankusu–Bumba–Kinshasa route.[83] There was such palpable relief among the civilian population that the RCD-G found it very difficult to enforce its policy on noncooperation, even among its own troops. At 4 a.m. on May 14 part of the Kisangani RCD-G garrison mutinied against their officers and their Rwandese minders.[84] The mutineers' radio call to "throw the Rwandese out of the Congo" was immediately popular, but the uprising was poorly organized;[85] by 8 a.m. loyalists were back in control of the radio and the public buildings and by 4:30 p.m. Antonov An-12 transports arrived from Goma, bringing 216 RPA and RCD-G troop reinforcements. Since the RCD-G unit under Félix Mumbere, who had spearheaded the uprising, was mostly made up of ex-FAZ, all ex-FAZ prisoners were shot, most of them at the bridge over the Tshopo River so that their bodies could be dumped into the water.

Repression went on during the next four days, with particular attention to the Mangobo suburb, where the civilian population had demonstrated in support of the mutiny. The killings were organized by the notorious commander Gabriel Amisi[86] a.k.a. "Tango Four," who was at the time the RCD-G chief of logistics. By May 17 the RCD-G was firmly back in control of the city. But its forces there showed serious signs of weakening as men started to desert at night, stealing canoes and paddling downstream to the now peaceful MLC-held territory. For once MONUC departed from its careful neutrality and published a report squarely placing the blame for the bloodbath on the RCD-G and estimating the number of deaths at 150, later increased to 183.[87] The RCD-G was incensed. It asked for MONUC head Amos Namanga Ngongi's recall and later banned him from traveling to the areas it controlled. The official motive given for this was rather paradoxical, since Adolphe Onusumba accused the UN official of supporting the April 17 Sun City Peace Agreement, something he would be reasonably expected to do. On May 31 the RCD-G expelled from its zone the UN Human Rights director Luc Hattenbruck and two days later added two MONUC functionaries to the expulsion order. This drew condemnation by the UN Security Council on June 5, and Secretary-General Annan appointed two special representatives to disentangle the situation, former Senegalese prime minister Mustafa Niasse and former Eritrean diplomat Haile Menkerios.

These were shrewd appointments: Niasse was a tough and experienced politician and Menkerios had been President Issayas Afeworki's "controller" for the AFDL in 1996–1997 and had an intimate knowledge of the Congolese power structure.

Rwanda's isolation had developed as predicted. Bizima Karaha implicitly acknowledged this on June 7, when he reiterated his demand for Amos Namanga Ngongi's recall but declared at the same time that the RCD-G would "keep collaborating with MONUC." Kigali became frantic and went back to its leitmotiv of terrible *Interahamwe* danger in the Congo, claiming that there were forty thousand *génocidaires* in the DRC. When challenged by MONUC's own figure of around fifteen thousand, Patrick Mazimpaka replied with aplomb, "This concerns only the Kivus and North Katanga. MONUC does not have access to Kinshasa government military camps where these 40,000 are."[88] But on June 27 Belgian Socialist MP Dirk van der Maelen demanded sanctions against all nonsignatory parties to the conflict "to turn the April 17th Agreement from a first step into a comprehensive deal," and the talks restarted in Pretoria on July 18 with Kigali in a difficult position. It was now getting increasingly bad press coverage while "Li'l Joseph" was stealing all the headlines.[89] Rwandese diplomacy then operated a quick about-turn, and on July 30 the RCD-G signed the power-sharing agreement.[90] At first most observers doubted the Agreement's feasibility.

1. With 45 days for the national dialogue, 76 days for disarmament, and 166 for general foreign troop withdrawal, the Agreement seemed to suffer from the same hurried optimism that had defeated Lusaka in 1999.

2. Nobody agreed on "negative forces" strength, estimates varying from a high of 50,000 (Rwanda) to a low of 12,000 (MONUC).

3. The war was no longer two-sided but multisided, and all the nonstate actors (the various Mayi Mayi groups, *Interahamwe*, the Burundian rebels, several ethnic militias such as those of the Ituri and Masunzu's Banyamulenge)[91] were absent from Pretoria.

4. There was no hard figure for RPA deployment in the Congo, estimates varying from 20,000 to 40,000 men.

5. Who would monitor? MONUC had barely 2,500 men on the ground and was not known for its efficiency.

6. Finally, who would pay? The Economic Commission, probably the only serious leftover from the Lusaka process, had earlier computed a need of about $3.5 billion in fresh money for the DRC to restart its economy, with 50 percent coming from the donors and 50 percent from national sources.[92] Neither of the two seemed either willing or able to mobilize the cash.

And yet somehow this behemoth ultimately got the show on the road. Why did Pretoria succeed while Lusaka had failed so abysmally? There are several reasons, none of which is fully convincing but which together add up to a coherent array:

- Everybody was tired, which was not the case in 1999. Hopes for a clear military victory on either side had melted away.

- As mentioned earlier, several of the initial reasons for intervention had either vanished (this was the case for Angola)[93] or failed (this was the case for Zimbabwe and Uganda).

- Unintended domestic consequences of the war had begun to make some of the involved governments suffer (Uganda and especially Zimbabwe).

- The war had degenerated into a confused melee, particularly in the east, where the foreign actors seemed to be losing control over increasingly unmanageable alliance shifts.

- The UN had finally recuperated some marginal efficiency, particularly with the publication of its reports on the looting of national resources.

- The United States had changed its diplomatic stance from partiality toward one camp to neutrality.

- South African diplomacy, for all its shortcomings, was simply more pugnacious and better informed than that of the largely amorphous "international community."

- Last but not least, Laurent-Désiré Kabila was dead and replaced by a man who belonged to the contemporary world.

This, as usual, left Rwanda as the odd man out. The country whose internal crisis had triggered the massive process of what had been for a while a nearly continentwide war remained in a special situation. Traumatized by the genocide, playing on lingering foreign guilt due to the international community's former neglect, under massive internal pressure to reconcile a dictatorial minority government and a "guilty majority" population, steeped

273

in Congolese affairs in a radical way that had no parallel among the other foreign actors, Rwanda remained faced with dangerous and visceral unfinished business.

The bumpy road toward a transitional government. When it became clear that some kind of peace was going to come out of the Pretoria process, all the parties started to scramble in various directions to take care of their special interests, hoping to fit them within the general framework before it was too late. On August 7 the World Bank announced that it would loan $454 million to the DRC through its International Development Association branch, thus starting the process of economic normalization.[94] The same day South Africa decided to commit fifteen hundred men to the peace monitoring. The next day Zimbabwe declared that it would pull out its remaining troops.[95] Museveni announced his umpteenth "complete withdrawal," but for the first time he gave clear details about the forces involved.[96] Then former *génocidaire* Gen. Augustin Bizimungu was suddenly arrested and sent to the ICTR in Rwanda.[97] And on August 16 Museveni signed a complete withdrawal treaty, with no conditions attached. The fact that he chose to do so in Luanda rather than in Kinshasa was a last tribute to the realities of the conflict: that it was a war fought among foreigners on Congolese territory for reasons of their own.

On August 28 Kinshasa's new spokesman Kikaya bin Karubi announced the obvious: that the next step would be to turn the power-sharing agreement into a proper transitional government. Everybody was concerned about how Kigali would react to these developments, and these reactions were confused and ambiguous, as could be expected. Rwanda was constrained by trying to follow two contradictory policies: the first one was to satisfy the international community, without whose financial support it could not keep functioning; the second was to try to preserve its stake in the control of the eastern Congo, which had become a domestic necessity. These two conflicting aims dictated a policy of stealth and proxy operations; DRC Minister-Delegate for Defense Awan Irung soon announced that the RPA had dispatched about a thousand troops to Kasuo, thirty kilometers from Lubero, with the purpose of blocking ex-FAR surrenders.[98] By then the relationship of the Kigali regime with the former *génocidaires* had become increasingly complicated. While in public the RPF government kept selling the position of concern for its security, which had been its official line since the beginning of the conflict in August 1998, on the ground the situation by then encompassed everything from continued fighting to outright cooperation, with all the shades of relations in between (toleration, alliance with some groups to attack others, support for "real" or "false" *génocidaires* used as a pretext for continued occupation, sharing of mineral resources with some ALIR units, and so on). Then there was the new hostility toward Uganda, which often led the RPA to behave as if the main enemy was not Kinshasa anymore but Kampala.[99] A third dimension of Kigali's policies was the forced repatriation to the eastern Congo of Congolese Tutsi who had been refugees in Rwanda, at times since 1994. Of the 31,923 Congolese Tutsi then staying at the Kiziba and Gihemba camps in northern Rwanda, about 9,500 were forcibly bussed to Masisi before protests from UNHCR and local missionaries stopped this dangerous exercise in October.[100]

On September 16 the Americans organized a tripartite meeting between Presidents Bush, Kabila, and Kagame at the UN in New York to reiterate the U.S. resolve to support the peace process. President Kagame then announced a pullout of his forces "within one week."[101] To everyone's surprise, the forces really did pull out, though not within the week but within a month. On October 7, 2002, Kigali announced that it had completed its evacuation, bringing 20,941 men back to Rwanda out of a figure of 23,760 in the Congo. The 2,819 missing were said to be either sick or gone AWOL. Since the total figure had been announced only at the time of the withdrawal, there were immediate doubts about whether the pullout was indeed complete. All the more so because, as soon as the withdrawal had taken place, rumors of foul play began to develop.[102] For example, only 590 Rwandese soldiers had been evacuated from Kindu, though there had been about 2,000 in the garrison there; between October 16 and 20 about 250 RPA troops reentered the Congo near Bukavu and immediately headed for Walungu. In addition, many RPA soldiers were said to have simply changed their uniform and "become RCD-G."[103] In a way this was almost unavoidable since Mayi Mayi forces, which had not been party to the Pretoria Agreement, were now swarming all over the place, trying to take advantage of whatever pullout had actually been carried out by the Rwandese forces or their allies. Kindu fell to them but was later retaken by the RCD-G, which carried out a systematic massacre of the people who had "collaborated" with the Mayi Mayi.[104] Mayi Mayi "General" David Padiri Bulenda took Shabunda on the heels of the retreating RCD-G on October 4 and other commanders occupied Fizi, Baraka, Minembwe, Mwenga, Ubwari, and Walungu. Kabalo and Kindu were still precariously held by the RCD-G, but they were surrounded by Mayi Mayi. Then, on October 13, after two days of intense fighting,

Gen. Lukole Madoa Doa[105] took Uvira and immediately announced his intention of marching on to take Bukavu. The whole of South Kivu looked like it was going to fall into the hands of pro-Kinshasa forces without Kinshasa actually taking part in the fighting. The Rwandese High Command then called an RCD-G general meeting in Kigali to deal with the situation. This seemed like a partial illustration of the remark made slightly earlier by seasoned DRC observer Pierre Bigras on his website: "Everything is now happening as if Uganda, Rwanda and Zimbabwe had agreed not to fight each other directly any more but to exercise control over the different parts of the Congolese territory through the agency of the Congolese parties they are sponsoring."[106]

Why was this situation a "partial" illustration of his remark? Because even if the general drift was correctly analyzed, there was by now a difference in the role distribution: Zimbabwe had completely dropped out of the game, Uganda was limiting its proxy activities to the Ituri region immediately adjacent to its border, and it was Kinshasa that had now burst to the fore, taking a major proxy role in the struggle for the eastern Congo. The only outside actor still fully involved was Rwanda, which could not afford to back off. During the night of October 15–16 seven trucks full of RPA soldiers crossed into South Kivu by way of the Ruzizi 2 border post in Burundi and joined the RCD-G troops on the other side. In Walungu and Kabare supposed *Interahamwe* groups (in fact RPA in civilian clothes who had been left behind) attacked the Mayi Mayi. Both sides were completely disingenuous: Vital Kamerhe, Kinshasa's general commissioner for the Great Lakes, condemned the Rwandese for having left troops behind[107] while at the same time denying any responsibility for the Mayi Mayi attacks. RCD-G authorities denied that the Rwandese army was helping them, but they broke off relations with the government, accusing it of sponsoring the Mayi Mayi offensive. Kigali declared that it was "ex-FAR and *Interahamwe* fighting in Uvira, not Mayi Mayi."[108] On October 19 the RCD-G retook Uvira and said it was now ready to talk again to Kinshasa. Since the beginning of the month 13,000 Congolese and 11,000 Burundian refugees had crossed the border into Tanzania to flee the fighting. Kigali and Kinshasa, the final key actors, had tested each other's resolve; they could now go back to the negotiating table.

On October 25 what was going to be the final session of the Congolese peace talks restarted in Pretoria. Desirous to draw the international community's attention away from its recent Mayi Mayi power play, Kinshasa tried to do a bit of DDRRR by attempting to disarm the FDLR forces in Kamina and send them back to Rwanda. It managed to "treat" 674 of them before the situation exploded.[109] But the dynamics of conflict management (one hesitates to use the word *peace*) had acquired enough momentum so that, to borrow Kofi Annan's expression, there was no more danger of "falling off the bicycle."

On December 17, 2002, an "all-inclusive Peace Agreement" was signed in Pretoria. The war had formally ended, leaving the violence that continued unabated as "residual" and "illegitimate."

What were the provisions of the Agreement? Joseph Kabila would remain as interim president. There would be four vice presidents, one belonging to the government, one to the RCD-G, one to the MLC, and one from the civil society. The government would keep 22 of 120 senators, 94 of 500 MPs, seven ministerial posts out of 36, and 4 vice ministerial positions out of 25. The rest would be apportioned between the RCD-G (22 senators, 94 MPs, 7 ministers, and 4 vice ministers), MLC, and civil society (exactly the same numbers). Some of the lesser forces, such as the RCD-ML and the RCD-N, got smaller portions, and the Mayi-Mayi got 4 senators, 10 MPs, 2 ministers, and 2 vice ministers. The whole exercise, necessary as it was to stop major organized violence, reeked of rewards for crime coupled with pork barrel politics. In the words of the specialized French African affairs newsletter *La Lettre du Continent* (January 1, 2003), "The whole of the Inter-Congolese 'political dialogue' seems to have resulted only in a vast programme of sharing out the jobs." In an equally severe diagnosis, another specialized publication wrote, "The Inter-Congolese Dialogue leaves only minor positions to civil society and the non-armed opposition. This results in offering to the Congolese population in the guise of government a coalition of people who looted their own country, of predatory rebels and of corrupt civil servants."[110] Another comment remarked that the Agreement did not display "the slightest concerns for political legitimacy, ethnic balance or regional equilibrium."[111] All of these were true. But the war had ended. Sort of.

The economy: slowly crawling out of the abyss

Getting the economy back on its legs was the other Herculean task Joseph Kabila had to undertake upon assuming power.[112] The country was in ruins, from every point of view. There were around 2.3 million IDPs scattered to the four corners of the country (with peaks in the eastern provinces) and

326,000 refugees abroad. In addition, due to all the other conflicts surrounding the DRC, it had become home to over 360,000 refugees from seven different countries, with the Angolans representing over half of those.[113] From a level of $630 in 1980, per capita income had fallen so low that it was now hard to measure, various sources giving figures between $78 and $88. This put the DRC squarely at the bottom of the African pile, lower even than Ethiopia; Somalia was perhaps the only country in comparable economic distress.[114] Because of an unrealistic fixed exchange rate that made imports impossible, food imports had diminished by 50 percent in 2000 while domestic food production was dropping at the same time. As a result, in a country where agriculture had never been a problem, 64 percent of the population was now underfed and probably more than 33 percent were malnourished.[115] Up to 3.5 million people had died, perhaps 90 percent of them from these "collateral effects" of the war.[116] GNP had shrunk by 40 percent in the past ten years (it was −11.4 percent during 2000 alone), exports had dropped by 45 percent since 1997, inflation had shot up to 520 percent, and banking was dead, with a 200 percent rate of interest but no cash left to loan out.[117] At the time of Laurent-Désiré Kabila's assassination, the Congolese franc, whose parity was fixed at 50 to the dollar, actually traded at 200, while the external debt had reached astronomical proportions ($13.5 billion, according to Kinshasa; $16 billion, according to the World Bank), completely blocking any hope of repayment or further loans unless a major rescheduling could be arranged.

Faced with this there were two priorities for the government: straighten out the mining industry, which was the only available short- to medium-term source of cash, and try to cut some of the parasitical costs. As early as May 4, 2001, the regime had come out with a new diamond-mining decree embodying a number of commonsense measures: liberalization of licensing, reserved for Congolese only, with a minimum sales figure; no direct exports by unlicensed producers; and compulsory expertise. This was very much needed since smuggling was still widespread. The Antwerp Diamond Office reported that in August 2001 it had received $61 million in contraband stones, as opposed to $24 million in legal ones.[118] The minimum buying rule was hard to enforce, and by early 2002 only three of the licensed counters had achieved their legal monthly minimum of $3.5 million.[119] As a necessary corollary to the mining reforms the Congolese franc was allowed to float, and it immediately shot up to 300 to the dollar.[120] The recovery of official diamond exports was staggering: by late 2002 they had reached

$396 million, a 44 percent increase over the preceding year. Then fuel prices were left free and climbed 400 percent in a week,[121] but transport became available again.

Once the time of the emergency measures was past, the regime issued a full new mining code which embodied 163 new modifications. It was both tight enough to control foreign interests (the state reserved itself a minimum 5 percent participation in any new project, and there would be no more case-by-case contract negotiations with separate companies) and liberal enough to please both the national operators and the IMF (granting mining rights became much more simple, custom tariffs were standardized, a special forex rate was introduced to benefit mining concerns).[122] Almost immediately a medium-size foreign company, Australian Anvil Mining, decided to make the first new outside investment in the DRC since the war began.[123]

In parallel with these developments the government was desperately trying to clean up the administrative environment, where economic operators had to function. On August 7, 2001, Joseph Kabila received a report on the performance of the DRC's fifty-two parastatals, and on August 9 he fired forty-nine of the managers. Two of the organizations that had been vetted positively were not parastatals but rather economic branches of the government: Post and Telecom and the Office of Management of Public Debt. Among the parastatals proper, only MIBA's Jean-Claude Okoto kept his job. It was difficult to find replacements: the newly picked Gécamines CEO, Munga Yumba, was arrested for corruption less than two months later. Some of the parastatals were closed outright. Another report, this time on public service salaries, unearthed new horrors: the state was paying 21,652 "ghost workers" who altogether cost it $619,000 each month. Bad as it was, this was still only a monthly average of $28.59 per worker, ghost or real. Some of the "salaries" at the bottom of the paying scale were discovered to be as low as $2 per month, not much of a material incentive for hard work.[124] In addition, salaries were in arrears by eight to ten months. In rebel areas no salaries had been paid for the past thirty-seven months.[125] Not that the private sector was doing much better: Gécamines, for example, had a $170 million salary backlog for its 24,000 employees.[126] In such circumstances the incentive for civil servants to develop private rackets of their own was considerable. In November 2001 a government report described the conditions of Congo River commerce as "catastrophic." There were no fewer than fourteen different entities "controlling" the river traffic and stealing everything they could. After a police inquiry only four were allowed to remain in place.[127] In a similar vein, fourteen division chiefs of the Finance Ministry were fired in Equateur after a direct check by the minister himself found them guilty of stealing $308,000 worth of civil servants' salaries.[128]

Slowly, the donor community, which had been keeping the Zaire/Congo at arm's length for the past fifteen years, began to stir. The Belgians were the first ones to move, Prime Minister Guy Verhofstadt going to Kinshasa on June 26, 2001, with a €20 million emergency aid package in spite of fairly strong opposition at home.[129] A month later Kinshasa went to the Paris donors' meeting asking for a modest $156 million; it got $240 million. The World Bank and the IMF started discussing between themselves how to arrange for a relay credit of $800 million to pay the DRC arrears, as the only way to clear the old credit logjam that had accumulated. IMF Managing Director Horst Köhler summed up the situation from the donors' point of view when he declared on May 3, 2002, "The DRC has instituted budgetary discipline and tackled exchange rate and price distortions in the economy. The Central Bank has conducted a prudent monetary policy. And there have been important improvements in the judicial and regulatory environment. As a result hyperinflation and the free fall in the value of currency have come to an end." Such good behavior deserved a reward: on June 13 the IMF gave $750 million toward a Poverty Reduction and Growth Facility program. Because at the same time Belgium, South Africa, France, and Sweden had disbursed $522 million to pick up Congo's IMF tab and the World Bank had given $450 million, everything was now ready for including the DRC into an HIPC program.[130] In September the Club of Paris proceeded to reschedule $8.98 billion of the debt,[131] which brought debt service down to $380 million between 2002 and 2005. The Congo could now breathe more freely. The relief was such that even "small" problems, such as a $50 million "hole" in the Central Bank accounts[132] or the February 17, 2003, firing of respected finance minister Freddy Matungulu Mbuyamu, did not cause too much of an uproar.[133]

The Congo was reemerging. Everything seemed to be going in the right direction. Except in the eastern provinces, where, paradoxically, the peace agreement had made things worse.

The eastern sore: the continental conflict shrinks into sub-regional anarchy

In a candid moment, RCD-G leader Azarias Ruberwa had called the eastern Congo "the thermometer of peace."[134] He was right, but he did not see that the approach of peace would be in itself a fever factor, sending everybody scrambling for positions. An important factor in those frenzied movements was the desire to position oneself vis-à-vis the various illegal economic interests that had been developed in the east over the past three years.[135] There was an implicit feeling that, even if "peace" was achieved, it could be years before the eastern Congo would actually fall under Kinshasa's full control. And in the meantime there would be a lot of money to be made for those state or nonstate actors who would know how to position themselves strategically.

On the very day of Laurent-Désiré Kabila's assassination the rebels announced their final "unification" under the Front de Libération du Congo (FLC) label. Wamba, who had never been very enthusiastic about the idea, had criticized it before its proclamation when he had declared to the Ugandan press, "It is easy to talk of unity between us. But what I see is more of us struggling for positions rather than any discussion of issues."[136] In January 2001 he strongly opposed the FLC as being simply a tool of Kampala to control the rebel movement through their man Bemba. Three days after Kabila's murder Ngiti and Lendu warriors attacked Bunia, killing about one hundred Hema. The next day the Hema militia took revenge on Lendu civilians, killing over twenty-five.[137] There was nothing that the FLC could do. Instead it was the FLC that had broken up between MLC and the RCD-ML faction now fully in the hands of Mbusa Nyamwisi. On Museveni's orders Kazini and the UPDF expeditionary corps sided with Bemba and eventually forced him out of Beni.[138] The FLC was in bad shape even before it managed to fully get off the ground. But by then everybody was fighting everybody else: FDD Burundian rebels supported by Zimbabwe attacked RCD-G units reinforced by the Rwandese in South Kivu;[139] Mayi Mayi groups were fighting RPA and RCD-G forces in both Kivus; Mayi Mayi groups were at times fighting each other;[140] and the FAC together with Mayi Mayi forces had attacked RCD-G and RPA units in Pania and Mutembo, north of Mbuji-Mayi.[141] As the prospect of peace negotiations grew closer, the scramble for military positions in the still openly contested east accelerated. And with nine "organized" guerrilla movements plus at least seven or eight Mayi Mayi groups, all of which kept fluctuating to maximize their short-term tactical gains, the situation quickly reached a peak of violence and confusion.

By mid-August 2001 Bemba threw in the towel and agreed to withdraw to Equateur. He and Mbusa agreed that his zone would extend to Bumba in the east, leaving Mbusa's RCD-ML in control of the area from Butembo to Isiro. The in-between zone of Aketi-Buta-Bambesa-Niangara-Dungu remained undefined and was soon to be the scene of fierce fighting between Mbusa's forces and Roger Lumbala's, who had found a job as a proxy for the MLC. The ALIR II–FDD occupation of Fizi and the attack on Kindu (both in October 2001) were part of the jockeying for position before the "serious" peace conversations started.

But it was the northeastern situation that was the worst, because of three factors: (1) the Ugandans desperately wanted to keep a foothold in the area and did not know whom to back in order to achieve this; (2) the Ituri conflict acted as a violence multiplier; and (3) Mbusa Nyamwisi had decided to ally himself with *both* Kampala *and* Kinshasa to push Bemba aside. For this he used the fact that Kazini and Salim Saleh had lost a lot when the FLC was created because, in exchange for his political engagement, Bemba had taken out a large slice of the UPDF officers' benefits. Mbusa Nyamwisi offered more, and he swung them to his side. Then, by mid-October 2001, Mbusa was in Kinshasa, offering his services. He got money to distribute among the various Mayi Mayi groups in North Kivu and Province Orientale. Since Kabila rightly considered Bemba to be the main danger he agreed to follow Mbusa in drifting toward a rapprochement with Uganda.[142] Their common fear of Kigali finally cemented the deal. Fueled by a struggle for gold and diamonds, based on the desire to marginalize Bemba and to isolate Kigali, the war in the northeast could now restart. The U.S. NGO Refugees International was right to call it "a slow-motion holocaust" but wrong to say that it had "no political or strategic rationale." Simply, the nature of the rationale was so cold-bloodedly commercial that few observers dared to believe it. The cynicism of the UPDF and RCD-ML operators was particularly horrible because their strategy, rather noxious in itself, had the added drawback of playing itself out on the background of the Ituri conflict, that is, of a politically septic environment where "outside" elements immediately acquired an enormous "inside" dimension, producing large "unintended" massacres.[143]

Apart from the Ituri there was fighting almost everywhere else in both North and South Kivu, right up to the Pretoria Agreement. In the Itombwe, the Banyamulenge, who were by then desperately trying to distance themselves from their alliance with Rwanda,[144] rose in revolt against the Rwandese army under the leadership of RCD-G deserter Cdr. Patrick Masunzu in February 2002. The RPA turned against them with great violence, deploying Mil Mi-17 combat helicopters.[145] In addition to battling the MLC in the northeast Mbusa's men also fought Mayi Mayi groups, which did not recognize his new alliance with Kinshasa.[146] The situation around Rutshuru and Lubero degenerated into almost complete anarchy, with ALIR I, four Mayi Mayi groups, the RCD-G, and the RCD-ML all fighting each other in total confusion.[147] Worst of all, this horror remained marginal and did not intrude on the main "peace process." When a respected advocacy NGO wrote in a report that "unless a peace process is crafted especially for the Kivus and made central to the government's transition programme and to international efforts, the Pretoria Agreement will fail,"[148] it was—fortunately or unfortunately—not the case. The Kivu slaughterhouse had provided the initial *casus belli* of the war, but once the central actors had decided that the game was no longer worth it, they let it fester without bothering to include that complicated situation in their "peace" calculations. The paradoxes were massive, particularly if one remembers that it was to "save" the Banyamulenge threatened with "genocide" that the Rwandese army had first entered the Congo in 1996. Now that same Rwandese army was attacking the same Banyamulenge with combat helicopters.

The grim truth was voiced by Monsignor Melchisedech Sikulu Paluku, bishop of Butembo, when he said in his Christmas 2001 homily,

In the Congo everybody is now talking about peace. Conferences, dialogues, meetings are happening here and there. But beyond these meetings and dialogues it is clear that it is the very people who pretend to want peace who are fuelling war with all its terrible attending circumstances. And all that in the name of "liberation," "self-defence" or "resistance."

The good prelate was mostly right. But what he perhaps could not comprehend was that the peace the actors had in mind was simply a continuation of the war by other means.

FROM WAR TO PEACE: CONGOLESE TRANSITION AND CONFLICT DECONSTRUCTION (JANUARY 2003–JULY 2007)

The conflict's lingering aftermath (January 2003–December 2004)

The peripheral actors drop off. As we saw in chapter 8, several of the war's protagonists, the peripheral ones, had started to walk away even before the Sun City peace process reached fruition. The term *peripheral* should not be understood here as meaning "unimportant," but rather as "not vitally involved." In many ways, if we examine the bare bones of the conflict, what I called a "continental war" (which it really was, courtesy of its political elites) was fundamentally a war between Rwanda and the Congo. The Tutsi-Hutu conflict in Rwanda had been left unresolved by the genocide, the RPF victory, and the flight of the vanquished into Zaire. The RPF then decided to solve it once and for all and, in a gigantic leap of political faith, tried to vassalize its huge neighbor at the same time. All the rest was anecdotal. This is why the expression "Africa's First World War," used by the Africans themselves, is only partially correct. Yes, Rwanda and the Congo experienced in several ways the anger, the fear, the hatred that were evident in Belgrade, Paris, and Berlin in 1914. But in the case of Angola, Uganda, Zimbabwe, Burundi, and Namibia the pattern of the conflict was much older and prenationalistic: it was more like the Thirty Years' War that had ravaged Europe between 1618 and 1648. For most of the African countries involved, as had been the case for seventeenth-century Sweden, Poland, France, and Lithuania, the war took place purely because of the princes' ambitions, prejudices, and security fears. And the Congo, like Germany in the seventeenth century, was their battlefield. The violence and the meaninglessness were the same. In Burundi and Angola, already ravaged by civil wars of their own, projecting troops into the DRC had just been an extension of internal conflicts, and in Zimbabwe and Uganda, where the Congolese intervention was highly unpopular, it was perceived as an elite strategy that had nothing to do with the ordinary lives of ordinary people. For the really peripheral actors, such as the Sudan, Chad, Libya, and the Central African Republic, the populations were barely aware of their country's involvement in the Congo; if and when they were aware, they saw it as their leaders' political calculations about domestic problems, having almost nothing to do with the Congo itself. None of the nationalistic fervor that was such an essential feature of the First World War was in evidence in any of these countries. This set Rwanda and the Congo, where the mass of the population deeply cared about the war, in a category apart. Logically, the patterns of exit from the war reflected the reasons for getting involved in it.

Angola was probably the one participant in the Congo war that left it completely behind in the quickest and most radical way. This is because it never had a stake in the Congo itself, but only in what the Congo could represent in terms of strategic depth for its own civil war, and also because its enormous mineral wealth enabled it to look to its future without much concern for a secondary war theater that it had been able to finance without any serious economic strain.[1] As soon as Jonas Savimbi was shot dead in February 2002, the war stopped.[2] Around 80,000 rebel soldiers and 300,000 of their relatives came out of the bush and quickly faced a grim situation: half-starving in camps, they did not benefit from the social reinsertion programs that they had been promised.[3] The former UNITA guerrillas turned into a political party, and Isaias Samakuva, long the movement's representative in Paris, became its secretary-general in June 2003. Elections were planned for late 2004 or early 2005, but they did not take place; most recently, they were scheduled for 2007 "at the latest."[4]

During 2002, as the situation got superficially normalized in the Congo, Angola's fears receded and it seemed to lose interest. But although it evacuated the DRC, it kept troops in the Republic of Congo, in Dolisie and Pointe Noire, ready to intervene. And as the pattern of Angolan troop deployment during the October 2006 Congolese election later showed, the loss of interest was more apparent than real, and Luanda's watchful eye remained on Kinshasa.

Zimbabwe was in a very different situation. It had already fallen into a radical phase of internal political decline when it entered the Congo war,[5] and its involvement in the DRC had nothing to do with security and everything to do with money. In a way, the Zimbabwean involvement in the war was, at least partly, a kind of foreign extension of the corruption of its leaders, who hoped to derive real economic benefits from their intervention in the DRC. Unlike in Angola, where the Congo was (correctly) perceived as a secondary theater of operation of the domestic civil war, the Zimbabwean population could not see any arguable reason for being in the DRC and the war was highly unpopular.[6] When the second UN report on the looting of Congo resources was published, the Zimbabwean government declared that it would not think of starting an inquiry about the people whose names were mentioned in the document for the following reason: "We did a good job in the DRC and we will not respond to malicious allegations by the British masquerading as the United Nations."[7] During August 2002 the Zimbabwean government signed no fewer than six different trade agreements with the Congo in a futile attempt at protecting the interests that had been acquired by the Harare "elite network."[8] "We have opened the doors; it is now up to the businessmen and businesswomen of Zimbabwe and DRC to pass through those doors," declared Commander Murerwa during the signing ceremony of one of the agreements.[9] But like most other Mugabe policies this was a complete pipe dream, and many observers realized it: "I think we will see a repeat of what happened in Mozambique," said the political scientist Masipula Sithole. "We did all the donkey work only for South Africa to gain the peace dividends and now Mozambique has overtaken Zimbabwe as South Africa's biggest trading partner."[10] Five years later, not only had Zimbabwe failed to reap any benefit from its Congolese adventure, but it can even be said that this mad foray into a war it did not have to fight became one of the contributing factors to its further collapse.

The smallest of the three government allies was also the one whose involvement in the Congo was the least important. The conflict that Namibia was really involved in was the Angolan civil war, and, at least as much as a desire to remain aligned with its SADC partners, it was the Angolan war that caused Windhoek to get involved in the DRC in the first place. Apart from the need to please Luanda, nobody could see any reason for being in the Congo, and as soon as the Botswana pre-dialogue reunion had taken place, Namibia was the first country to start withdrawing. By September 2001 it had brought back 80 percent of its contingent and announced a complete pullout as soon as possible. By January 2002 there was not a single Namibian Defense Force soldier left in the Congo. When old Sam Nujoma launched his (unconstitutional) drive for a fourth presidential mandate later in the year, the Congo issue had disappeared from the political landscape.

On August 28, 2000, Burundi entered a peace agreement that was supposed to end the civil war existing in the country since the assassination of President Melchior Ndadaye in October 1993, the cause of its involvement in the Congo in the first place.[11] The agreement provided for eighteen months of continued UPRONA government under President Buyoya, followed by another eighteen months under FRODEBU Vice President Domitien Ndayizeye.[12] But because the actual shooting war was fought between the Forces Armées Burundaises (the regular army) and the CNDD-FDD and FNL guerrillas, this "solution" remained an empty paper construct. And because the FAB were in the Congo for purely Burundian reasons, the assassination of Laurent-Désiré Kabila did not mark any sort of turning point.

Things slowly started to change when the actual fighters[13] finally agreed to meet with the government in March 2002. At first the FAB tried to scuttle the peace process by forcing the government to sign a useless draft document with the now dormant Ndayikengurukiye and Mugabarabona[14] factions of CNDD-FDD and FNL. In spite of the peace developments in the Congo, the fighting factions could keep their rear bases in South Kivu because a number of people in the Kinshasa government discreetly kept giving them support.

Then in December 2002 Pierre Nkurunziza finally agreed to sign a ceasefire; a month later, in what was to become its first peacekeeping mission ever, the African Union decided to create the African Mission in Burundi. The turning point was the power transfer between Buyoya and Ndayizeye in May 2003, not because "a Hutu" was now in control of the government (he was not) but because the whole political construct shifted. A political space suddenly opened for CNDD-FDD to challenge FRODEBU as the main representative of the Hutu population. At the same time, a number of war-weary Tutsi (particularly the Muramvya group, which had felt excluded from politics since 1972) saw in the CNDD-FDD a possible alternative to the infernal UPRONA/FRODEBU dichotomy which had polarized and sterilized Burundian politics over the past ten years. In a way it was timidly reminiscent of the early days of independence, when the Tutsi-Hutu question had not yet usurped the center stage of national politics.[15] The October 2003 final peace agreement signed in Pretoria left Agathon Rwasa's group as the only embodiment of the diehard ethnic war position. From then on Burundi's involvement in the Congo decreased proportionately to the success of its own internal peace process. Following the successful elections of August 2005, this left the FNL guerrilla remnants in South Kivu as the last trace of a Burundian presence in the DRC.

This group of actors was quite different from the others, in that its links with the Congolese conflict were always peripheral, whereas their involvement with each other was very strong. In many ways we have here a geopolitical "cluster," which at a certain point got drawn into the Great Lakes–Congolese vortex although it never "belonged" to it.[16]

In this northern cluster Libya was the prime mover. Since 1991 the Lockerbie affair had kept Libyan diplomatic initiatives under a pall. But after years of negotiating, the international sanctions were finally lifted in April 1999. In late 1998 Colonel Gaddafi, who knew he would soon be able to act freely, had restarted the picturesque diplomacy he had been famous for in the 1970s and 1980s. But he had largely changed tack. He publicly declared, "I am tired of my Arabism," and, as a respected weekly wrote, "Qaddafi says farewell Arabia and sets his sights on Africa."[17] The "Guide" was angry at his Arab peers for not giving him support during the period of the sanctions, whereas several African heads of state[18] had visited him to express their solidarity, defy the West, or pick up their checks. Gaddafi's Congolese intervention should be seen in that light, as a lackadaisical "African adventure" rather than a carefully thought-out policy. On the other hand, Khartoum, supported by Gaddafi, wanted to help Kabila for anti-Ugandan reasons[19] but could not do it directly. And Chad's President Idriss Deby was trying to strike an independent course on his oil development program with a pipeline heading west toward Cameroon and not north toward Libya. For Deby, providing the manpower Khartoum wanted and Tripoli was ready to pay for squared the circle, even if the depth of his geopolitical engagement was questionable.

So after the Chadians got drubbed, Gaddafi magnanimously pulled them out of the mess he had put them into. But the complexities and interferences did not stop there. To keep pressure on Chad, even after it withdrew from the Congo, Libya supported President Ange-Félix Patassé of the Central African Republic. Patassé had been "reelected" in December 1998, not only through ballot box stuffing but through a process of "electors without borders," whereby thousands of neighboring foreigners also came to vote: Congolese Ngbaka, Ngbandi, and Yakoma had crossed the border to vote for Patassé's opponent, former president André Kolingba, while thousands of Chadian Sara crossed into the north to vote for Patassé.[20] The result was a fairly unstable regime, and in May 2001 Kolingba, the loser of that bizarre election, tried to overthrow Patassé through a military coup. He failed. But Patassé's savior represented another big problem: it was the Congolese guerrilla leader Jean-Pierre Bemba whose men had crossed the river to thwart the coup.[21] They had fought the insurgents side by side with Libyan troops also protecting Patassé. Thus Tripoli found itself in the strange position of fighting alongside rebels who were trying to overthrow the Kinshasa government Gaddafi supported. This put Patassé in a delicate position. Two years before, already caught between Kinshasa and Bemba's rebels, he had tried to finesse his way out of the situation by saying "Kabila is my brother but Bemba is my son." Now with Kabila Senior dead and Bemba protecting his doorstep, he modified the family relationships: it was Bemba who had become "his brother" and Kabila the Younger was now "his son."[22]

It took a successful coup by Gen. François Bozizé on March 15, 2003, to start clearing the atmosphere. Libyan troops went home, the new regime normalized its relations with Kinshasa within a week, and Bemba's men prudently remained on their side of the river. In an ultimate paradox, six months later the same Jean-Pierre Bemba had become a minister in the new "national unity" government in Kinshasa. As for Khartoum, which had supported Patassé up to the last moment, it superficially reconciled with Bozizé.

Thus by mid-2003, the countries of the northern cluster were completely disengaged from the Congolese conflict, even if their mutual relationships remained fraught with suspicion and shifting attempts at mutual destabilization.

Uganda and Rwanda refuse to give up. During the eighteen months preceding the signing of the final "all-inclusive" peace agreement, the UPDF had progressively withdrawn almost 10,000 of the 13,000 men it had once deployed in the DRC.[23] The idea was that after extensive training, MLC troops would be capable of taking Kinshasa on their own, without embarrassing Kampala. But when that hope eventually faded away and when the question became essentially one of making the most gracious exit possible while safeguarding the greatest possible number of economic interests, the situation became much more complicated, for a number of reasons.

- President Museveni had won a presidential election in circumstances that were not very glorious for his regime. Despite prospects of certain victory, he had harassed his main opponent, Kiiza Besigye, and let his men indulge in limited and unnecessary ballot box stuffing. The result (69 percent of the vote) turned the once "darling of the international community" into just another heavy-handed African politician.[24]

- Practically at the same moment the first UN report on the illegal exploitation of Congolese riches put the Ugandan regime into a very poor light. President Museveni's reaction of pique did not improve his image.[25]

- Then the enmity between Rwanda and Uganda reached such a level that the major military problem for Kampala became, not Kinshasa any more, but Kigali. Once again, as with the Sudan before, the Congo threatened to become a battlefield wherein third-party proxy warfare could develop. Time and time again, London had to intervene to avoid all-out warfare between the two countries.[26]

- The danger of a war with Rwanda and the Congo conflict combined to increase military expenses, creating an added irritant for the donors.[27] To make matters worse, the Lord's Resistance Army (LRA), which had remained relatively quiet for the past two years, suddenly burst forth in renewed violent activity.[28]

- The combination of growing military expenditures and deteriorating relations with the donors caused Kampala to risk losing its extremely lucrative HIPC status, without which the country could not run.[29]

In such a situation the simplest thing to do would have been to cut one's losses and get out of the DRC. But this was not really an open option, for two reasons. First, President Museveni still cherished a certain image of himself as the elder statesman of eastern and central Africa. He had gone to war in the Congo partly because he saw himself as the lawgiver of post–cold war Africa, ready to "open up" the wild and primitive regions to the west of civilized east Africa.[30] Second, in the meantime, UPDF officers had developed their own networks and their own commercial interests. Contrary to what had happened with Rwanda, there was no "Congo Desk" in Kampala. Congo looting was a private sport that hardly benefited the state. But these interests were perfectly ruthless and, among other things, triggered the abominable "ethnic" conflict in the Djugu territory of the Ituri District in Province Orientale. Cleaning that hornets' nest would not be easy.

"Old Africa hands" explained the Ituri bloodshed in ethnic terms, whereas the Congolese themselves saw it as an artificial conflict engineered by "foreign imperialists" in order to exploit Congo's riches.[31] In fact, both explanations were wrong: the conflict resulted from the exploitation by corrupt Ugandan army officers of latent social contradictions (mostly about landholdings) in order to brutally control the local economy. Fostering the conflict helped rough-and-ready short-term economic exploitation, but it also unleashed forces that soon festered beyond the control of the sorcerer's apprentices who had initially put them into motion.[32] Nevertheless, even if the situation was due only to rogue UPDF freebooters masking their greed under the guise of security concerns, Museveni could not dismantle his presence overnight because Rwanda had meanwhile acquired a new ground for anti-Ugandan subversion in the region, just as in Sudan earlier.[33] Hence the strange pattern of Uganda's "disengagement" from Congo's northeast: two steps forward and one step (if not two) back. Although Museveni favored all global solutions to the war (as when he supported, or perhaps even fostered, the April 2002 Sun City "partial agreement" between Kinshasa and the MLC), at the same time he finagled anything having to do with his "immediate neighborhood" in Congo's northeast. And in order to maintain his presence in the northeast he resorted to supporting increasingly violent and increasingly illegitimate tribal militias, who committed atrocities rarely seen before in a war that had been notorious for its cruelty toward civilians.[34]

The September 2002 Luanda Agreement had provided for the quick evacuation of Ugandan troops, but in early 2003 they were still there, and it took a difficult meeting with Joseph Kabila and Angolan Foreign Minister João de Miranda in Tanzania to renew the commitment.[35] Strangely enough, the Ituri Peace Commission, the new neutral body that was supposed to try to get a handle on the situation, was created in faraway Luanda on February 14, perhaps because the Angolans realized that their Congolese protégés were impotent in the northeast and the Ugandans could not be trusted. Museveni had agreed to remove twenty-five hundred men from Bunia, but on March 11 Defense Minister Amama Mbabazi "revealed" the "invasion plans" of the Ituri-based and Kigali-supported People's Redemption Army, saying that this "threat" made a preemptive strike necessary. As a result, the UPDF stayed in the Congo.[36]

The Rwandese threat was initially somewhat controversial,[37] but it became quite concrete after Kigali recruited Thomas Lubanga, warlord chief of the Union des Patriotes Congolais, Uganda's former main proxy in the region. In a last desperate attempt at regaining control of the situation, the UPDF then turned against its erstwhile protégé and on March 6, 2003, took by storm the regional capital of the Ituri, Bunia. A week later the Porter Commission released a report criticizing Museveni's brother Salim Saleh, chief suspect in the looting of northeastern Congo, for "disobeying the President's directive forbidding the Army to trade in the DRC." The reprimand was moderate, but coming from such a tame body, it amounted to an indirect vindication of the UN verdict on the looting of the Congo.[38] From then on the choice was clear: it was either stay in the Congo (with the attendant huge military expenses) and risk losing donor support or else withdraw by any means possible. By then the Ituri catastrophe was complete: the Luanda-born Ituri Peace Commission was powerless to install any form of civilian administration, seven tribal militias were fighting each other in bloody horror and total confusion, and MONUC was impotent to control the situation. In a desultory attempt at maintaining a semblance of local influence the Ugandan army left some of its artillery to its latest and completely unreliable tribal militia proxies[39] when it pulled out in May. The withdrawal was a near rout, and on June 2, 2003, the last elements of UPDF's 53rd Battalion crossed the Semliki River on foot after walking 240 kilometers from Bunia to the border.[40] Meanwhile, the military situation in northern Uganda had escalated to such a point that going back into the DRC was no longer a feasible proposition. In any case the United States, Kampala's main protector, was clear about it. After it had been solicited to help in the anti-LRA fight, the American Embassy in Uganda declared, "A condition attached to disbursing [anti-LRA insurgency] funds is to remain outside the DRC."[41]

As for Rwanda, it remained the odd man out, the last country trying to hang on to its bloody chunk of the Congo. But U.S. support, which had weakened since the beginning of the Bush administration, was waning. Washington was tired of seeing Rwanda exploit its "genocide guilt credit" to justify what appeared more and more like a policy of deliberate deception in the Congo. As U.S. Acting Assistant Secretary of State for African Affairs Charles Snyder put it in his usual blunt language:

We said to Kagame when he was here most recently and we said to Museveni just last week, we need to put things right in the Eastern Congo and that means you need to stay the hell out. Museveni's response was: "I agree" and Kagame's was "I don't think so." . . . So we said privately to him (and we will say publicly if he does anything outrageous) that if MONUC is doing the right thing and demobilizing these ex-*Interahamwe* and if the international community is satisfied, we won't let Rwanda be the odd man out. We will sanction them and we will take them to the UN if it comes to that. But I don't think we'll have to go there, Kagame will let it play out.[42]

In the Congo the Rwandese government was pursuing an ambiguous policy. Just like Uganda, and possibly even more, Rwanda had been fingered by the first report of the UN Panel of Experts on the Illegal Exploitation of Congolese Resources. But the panel made a distinction in the "style" of the exploitation, clearly recognizing that in the case of Uganda the looting was essentially private and due to UPDF rogue elements, whereas in the case of Rwanda it was coordinated by the government and part and parcel of a general policy of financing the war effort. This did not preclude individuals enriching themselves,[43] but it placed their private operations in a secondary role in comparison to the regime-sponsored resource extraction. In that perspective the "military withdrawal" of October 2002 has to be seen as a tactical measure within a global policy and not as a strategic policy reorientation.[44]

At first Kigali simply used its old surrogate, the RCD-G, as a proxy. But after the RCD-G became a "Congolese government" element in December 2002, it was seen by Rwanda as being in an ambiguous position. Where would its future loyalty lie: with Kinshasa or with Kigali? The men of the RCD-G, after all, were Congolese. So by mid-2003 Kigali had developed a new strategy for keeping control of the Kivus, using the Tous Pour le Développement militia of "Governor" Eugène Serufuli in North Kivu[45] and the smaller and less well-organized militia developed in South Kivu by Xavier Chirhibanya.[46]

But the Rwandese regime was quite aware of the progressive change of mood in the international community. And since it depended heavily on international financing for its continued economic survival, it used all the right buzzwords—*reconciliation, democratization,* and *good governance*—while efficiently pursuing its goal of an airtight authoritarian state. Former president Bizimungu, who had been kicked out of the presidency when General Kagame stopped needing a docile Hutu stand-in, had been gradually boxed into an ever tighter corner as he struggled to develop some kind of a democratic civilian opposition. He and his deputy, Charles Ntakirutinka, were at first restricted from leaving Kigali and cut off from outside contact;[47] then they were placed under house arrest in April 2002 and jailed a month later.[48] Finally the former president and his political associates were brought to trial and condemned to long prison sentences in June 2004 for "embezzling state funds and forming a militia that threatened state security."[49]

The press, never very free, was brought under even tighter control. The chief editor of *Umuseso* was arrested in January 2003 simply for printing a cartoon representing the president as King Solomon ready to cut in two a baby labeled "MDR." The cartoon was prescient: a few days later the MDR was actually banned on the ground that it stood for "divisive politics." Amnesty International wrote that "the government was organising a crackdown on the opposition ahead of the planned presidential elections."[50] In late May 93 percent of the voters approved the draft constitution, which would give the president extensive powers during a seven-year renewable mandate.[51] At the beginning of July, in a touching show of unanimity, four political parties joined hands with the ruling RPF to support Paul Kagame's candidacy.[52] With the MDR out of the way, this forced opposition candidate Faustin Twagiramungu to run as an independent. To keep a clear field of fire, a court decided that former president Bizimungu had to stay in jail to answer some more vague charges, which were never officially made. And just in case people had not gotten the message, another court condemned eleven people to death for their participation in the genocide.[53]

The electoral campaign was perfectly organized: Kagame was everywhere, flying all over the country in his presidential helicopter, while Twagiramungu had no airtime, no money, and no posters, and his few supporters were discreetly harassed and accused of inciting ethnic violence. Kagame kept his claws in but never let anybody forget that they were there. His last campaign speech ended on an unforgettable note when he said, "Others are advocating genocide. But you need not be afraid when you elect me on Monday. I will protect you."[54] His audience understood perfectly the meaning of being protected by such a powerful man. In the end, after the security men made sure that everybody voted "well,"[55] Twagiramungu got 3.62 percent of the vote to Kagame's 95 percent.

But the newly elected president still had to deal with his radical wing, and it was at least partly Congo-related. A number of Kagame's top men retained a bellicose nostalgia for the war days. "Commander James" Kabarebe for one did not agree with the 2002 troop withdrawal. This "Congolese" position dovetailed with the ethnic hard-line positions of a group loosely gathered around Kayumba Nyamwasa.[56] The danger for the Congolese peace process then painfully crawling forward was that these Rwandese warmongers had venomous counterparts on the other side of the border.

295

In Kinshasa, a small lobby of "old Kabilists" (Samba Kaputo, Gen. John Numbi, Yerodia Ndombasi) discreetly kept helping the *génocidaire*-linked FDLR guerrillas, in whom they saw a counterweight to Kigali's proxy influence in the Kivus. These were being glared at by a group of former RCD-G officers of Tutsi or Banyamulenge origins who, because the Sun City "all-inclusive" peace agreement was terribly imprecise on army integration, feared being marginalized in the new armed forces due to their background. These antagonisms on the Congolese side of the border, which reflected the extension of the Banyarwanda world into the Kivus, provided the hardliners in Kigali with all the ingredients of an explosion, were they to try to provoke one.

An attempt at violently upsetting the transition. The first intimation of trouble came in February 2004, when Munyamulenge Col. Jules Mutebutsi refused to obey his commanding officer, Gen. Prosper Nabyolwa. The explicit reason for Mutebutsi's defiance was the decision of the Defense Ministry to accept the transfer to Kinshasa of a former RCD-G officer who had been charged in the convoluted Laurent-Désiré Kabila murder trial.[57] Kinshasa backed down and flew the officer back to Bukavu, but the impact of this near mutiny reverberated all over the east, causing everybody to take sides. The Bukavu populace demonstrated (against Mutebutsi), and dissident Ituri warlord Jérôme Kakwaku Bokonde reneged on the armistice he had signed with MONUC two weeks earlier.

Since former U.S. ambassador to Kinshasa William Swing had replaced Amos Namanga Ngongi as head of MONUC in July 2003, the UN mission had taken a higher, more proactive profile. Correctly perceiving it to be the main trouble spot, Swing had just decided to redeploy 80 percent of MONUC's troops in the east, declaring, "The former frontline is now a part of history. We now need to redeploy where our troops are most needed."[58] This gave an added dimension to Mutebutsi's disobedience. It now became a test of wills not only between the remnants of the pro-Kigali factions in the east and the Kinshasa government, but also between those factions and the international community. The transition itself now hung in the balance.

Then, in late April, Kigali security boss Patrick Karegeya denied that Rwanda was massing troops on the border with Burundi,[59] only to declare the next day that there was indeed a heavy troop deployment on the border with Burundi "in anticipation of possible attacks from Hutu rebels."[60] In Bujumbura the FAB chief of staff, Brig. Gen. Germain Niyoyonkana, announced that RPA forces had entered Burundian territory in Cibitoke

Province two days before and were moving in the Kaburantwa Valley. On that same day MONUC reported a positive identification of over one hundred Rwandese troops in South Kivu, near Buganaga.[61] There was panic in Kinshasa, where pro-transition politicians quickly put together some anti-FDLR sweeps to try to remove the pretext of a Rwandese attack. Kinshasa declared that it had killed thirty-nine Rwandese rebels since April 20 in the 8th and 10th Military Regions (i.e., around Rutshuru and Bukavu, respectively), losing three men; fifteen civilians had been killed.[62] Kigali's Special Envoy for the Great Lakes Richard Sezibera gave a long interview to the UN press agency, declaring that the FDLR had recently attacked Rwanda's territory,[63] that the Hutu rebels were afraid of losing their sanctuary after the planned DRC elections, that there was "no doubt" that the present Congolese government was supporting the FDLR, that his government was "not willing to sit back and watch these people come back and complete the genocide," that there were no Rwandese troops at present in the Congo, and that fifteen thousand FDLR guerrillas were amassed in the Kivus and ready to attack Rwanda.[64] The tension grew noticeably, and a week later Jean-Marie Guehenno, the head of the UN Department of Peacekeeping Operations, arrived in Kinshasa to investigate the increasingly explosive situation. Five days after he arrived, the fighting started in Bukavu.

At first it was limited to groups of Banyamulenge soldiers loyal to Colonel Mutebutsi attacking other soldiers loyal to Gen. Mbuza Mabe, 10th Military Region commander of the Forces Armées de la République Démocratique du Congo (FARDC).[65] But four days later over a thousand ex-RCD-G troops arrived in Bukavu from other parts of South Kivu. They claimed to be defending Banyamulenge civilians "who were victims of an attempted genocide." In fact, the rebellion triggered, if not a genocide, at least a wave of cross-ethnic killings: Mutebutsi's soldiers started to kill and rape Babembe and Barega civilians, while civilians of these same ethnic groups and FARDC troops started to kill and rape Banyamulenge and even some Bashi who were supposed to be sympathetic to them.[66] These attacks started an exodus of civilians toward Cyangugu in Rwanda and even more extensively across the Ruzizi plain into Burundi.[67]

On May 31, coming down from North Kivu, Gen. Laurent Nkunda appeared on the scene with around twenty-five hundred troops. Nkunda, a North Kivu Tutsi from Rutshuru, had a long track record as Kigali's man. He had fought as a volunteer with the RPF during the Rwandese civil war and had later become one of the top RCD-G commanders. His soldiers had been deeply implicated in the 2002 massacres in Kisangani, and Nkunda was furious that this was held against him and had prevented him from joining the new FARDC, while some of his former comrades, such as the notorious Gabriel Amisi, a.k.a. "Tango Four,"[68] had received important positions. When Nkunda showed up coming from the north he first occupied the airport, some thirty kilometers outside of town, and then "negotiated" with the Uruguayan MONUC troops who were "defending" Bukavu. To the horror of the civilian population the Uruguayans declined to fight and let Nkunda proceed into town. As soon as he arrived, the violence increased. Refugees were pouring into Burundi.[69] Nkunda was loudly clamoring that he was protecting the Banyamulenge civilians from genocide, omitting to mention the fact that he had started his military move from Goma on May 24, that is, *before* the first killings took place. There were anti-UN riots in Kinshasa, in Kindu, in Kisangani, in Lubumbashi, and even in Goma to protest MONUC's dereliction of duty and indirect role in the violence. Five people were killed and sixty-five wounded.[70] But Nkunda seemed lost about what to do with his "victory," and he eventually pulled out of Bukavu on June 4. His withdrawal meant only that the fighting spread to Walikale, and Kigali closed its border on the night of June 5. Kinshasa decided to deploy twenty thousand troops in the east, and RPF Secretary-General Charles Morigande accused the Congolese government of preparing to invade Rwanda.[71] Kofi Annan warned Uganda, Rwanda, Burundi, and the DRC against going back to war.[72]

The fighting spread quickly as the Tutsi-Banyamulenge insurgents had the support of the Mudundu 40 Mayi Mayi group[73] and of Bashi militia elements. The newly integrated FARDC units were trying to hold their own but not doing very well. MONUC troops seemed demoralized and rudderless. To make things worse the governor of the Burundi province of Cibitoke declared that around a hundred FDLR guerrillas had entered his territory and were heading for Kibira Forest, while at the same time the armistice painstakingly brokered by MONUC on May 14 completely broke down and the militias began to fight each other again in the Ituri.[74] The combat spread to Kalehe, displacing thirty thousand more refugees.[75]

It is in that atmosphere that the Gatumba massacre took place. Gatumba was a refugee camp in northwest Burundi, close to the borders of both Rwanda and the DRC, where about 160 refugees were killed on August 13 "by unknown elements." The FNL Burundian Hutu guerrillas immediately claimed the horror as their work, but it soon transpired that the slaughter had been a joint venture between several fanatically anti-Tutsi groups of Congolese Mayi Mayi, FDLR guerrillas, and indeed the FNL.[76]

The Gatumba massacre finally gave the hard-line Tutsi camp what it considered to be a decisive justification for resuming hostilities. Nkunda said he was going back to war "because of the planned genocide," and FAB Chief of Staff General Niyoyonkana declared, "We have now decisive proof of FNL, Hutu *Interahamwe*, ex-FAR and Congolese Mayi Mayi complicity.... The DRC attacked our country[77] and we will not wait till a second massacre takes place." Burundi (Hutu) President Domitien Ndayizeye tried to calm things down a bit by saying, "It is still early to think of an offensive in the DRC," and Nkunda answered, "Last time I captured Bukavu I withdrew peacefully. But this time once I capture it again I will never withdraw."[78]

Then, on August 23, Azarias Ruberwa, the former RCD-G leader and now national unity vice president of the Kinshasa government, flew to the east and announced that he was suspending his participation in the transition. For one moment it seemed as if the whole process painfully crafted in Sun City had come crashing down. The international community was appalled. Cindy Courville, the U.S. National Security Council person in charge of Africa, flew to Kampala on August 28 to try to whip up an emergency "conference on armed groups." But the main problem was that there were not two institutionally clearly defined camps: the new supposedly "integrated Congolese Army" (FARDC) was divided against itself, with Kinyarwanda speakers poised to fight members of other ethnic groups and to fight among themselves according to the Tutsi-Hutu line of cleavage.[79]

Gen. Mbuza Mabe first retook Minova and later signed what amounted to a nonaggression pact with the 8th Military Region commander Maj. Gen. Obed Rwibasira.[80] By then the Rwandese army had entered the Congo and was fighting FDLR groups around Rutshuru with the help of Nkunda's men. Pro-Rwibasira and pro–Mbuza Mabe groups of FARDC soldiers were fighting each other, and so were "integrated" and "nonintegrated" Mayi Mayi combatants. The international community was falling prey to increased panic; the British government put pressure on MONUC so that it would not mention the presence of the Rwandese troops and their involvement in the fighting in North Kivu.[81]

Meanwhile Kigali had finally brought the crisis to the boiling point. On November 25 a direct phone call to MONUC announced Rwanda's decision to cross the border (it already had, but not officially) and attack the FDLR. On the same day, Aziz Pahad, South Africa's deputy minister of foreign affairs, asked MONUC to attack the FDLR to preempt Kigali's move. What he did not say (did he know it?) was that at the same time South Africa's security chief had gone up to see Kagame and banged his fist on the table.[82] Pretoria was determined to save its Sun City agreement, and for that it was ready to issue threats at the highest level, implying possible war. In Kigali things started to get confused. Kagame wrote to the African Union saying that his troops "would need to stay only two weeks in the Congo" to root out the FDLR, while at the same time his special envoy Richard Sezibera denied that there were any Rwandese troops in the DRC.[83]

The Ugandan-Rwandese tension compounded matters further when Kampala and Kigali began to expel each other's diplomats in what looked like a prelude to a diplomatic relations break while armed clashes took place on their common border.[84] Fighting started in Kanyabayonga, at the limit of the two Kivus, the classical border between the Rwandese area of influence (South) and the Ugandan one (North). In a remarkable display of disingenuousness Richard Sezibera craftily declared, "The current fighting is all intra-Congolese."[85]

But the various actors were slowly beginning to get a handle on the situation. Arguably the key factor was the South African threats, which Kagame took into account—after a decent interval.[86] But in addition, Kinshasa transferred General Rwibasira out of the 8th Military Region while MONUC deployed troops in Kanyabayonga and Lubero, where the recent fighting had uprooted 150,000 people. The fighting receded, then stopped. The very official and diplomatic Comité International d'Accompagnement de la Transition (CIAT)[87] came in a delegation to Goma to talk directly with the actors.[88] On December 26 the European Union, by now persuaded of the need for a stronger, more resolute MONUC, called for its military force to be expanded up to sixteen thousand men. Moreover, it said that it was ready to support the troop increase financially.[89] By Christmas Sezibera could comment off-handedly, "The FDLR no longer constitutes an immediate threat to our government but they are a security problem to people's lives, property *and to our economic growth.*"[90]

Tottering forward in Kinshasa. What was the "transition" that the Rwandese (and in some measure the Ugandans) had tried to upset? It was something that the institutional international community (i.e., the UN, the World Bank, the various chanceries) was "ecstatic about"[91] but that other, more seasoned observers disbelievingly looked upon as some kind of a monster.[92]

300

For a few months after the signing of the Sun City Agreement things had stagnated as the delegates to the Inter-Congolese Dialogue kept debating in Pretoria on how to turn the piece of paper they had signed into some kind of reality. On April 1, 2003, they finally adopted the draft constitution which had been presented to them on March 6, and they agreed on the outline of a transitional government.[93]

On April 7 Joseph Kabila was sworn in as transitional president for a period of two years. Two days later an African summit in Cape Town solemnly warned Rwanda and Uganda against going to war with each other. Everybody knew that if they did, it would be on Congolese territory.[94] Slowly the "peace institutions" moved forward: the vice presidents were chosen[95] and Joseph Kabila abolished the hated Cours d'Ordre Militaire, which had condemned so many people to death in dubious circumstances.[96] On April 28 Azarias Ruberwa arrived in Kinshasa to take up his position, declaring an official end to the war, "which had lasted four years and nine months because the circumstances demanded it."[97] What exactly these circumstances were, apart from the need to propel him into a vice presidential seat, he declined to explain. The swearing in of the transitional government was postponed for several weeks because the various components of the potential cabinet could not agree on the military arrangements. Trust was in limited supply and everybody was looking over their shoulder. There were three types of problems. First, there was the question of sharing positions and of cross-checking the nominations for security. Thus the military commanders were rebels in government areas and government rebels in former rebel territories; they had to be flanked by commanders of the opposite camp to keep tabs on them. Second, there was the problem of some of the commanders picked by the RCD-G who, like Gabriel Amisi, were notorious war criminals. They refused to take up their positions in former government-held areas, saying that "their security was not guaranteed."

MONUC strength was at 8,700 men and a recent UN resolution had decided to increase it to 10,800. Trade slowly restarted on the Congo River, mobile telephones arrived in Kisangani, and dribbles of food aid began (slowly and inadequately, but still to some degree) to answer the IDPs' needs. The first cabinet was finally announced on July 1, and recently named commanders managed to take their positions without fighting. In late November 2003 South African President Thabo Mbeki organized the fourth Kinshasa-Kigali Peace Agreement review meeting in Pretoria. The atmosphere was subdued. Bill Swing was present to promote a revamped

301

version of the Third Party Verification Mechanism, which had evolved from total irrelevancy to mediocre performance, a great leap forward. There was a grudging compliance with its existence and functioning.[98] In Kinshasa the former foes eyed each other warily but without pulling the trigger.

Everything was moving desperately slowly. In January 2004 the CIAT expressed its concern over the delays in the transition schedule, pointing out that none of the five key commissions decided upon in Sun City had yet become operational.[99] Provincial governors were finally appointed in May, re-creating an embryo regional administration,[100] but the whole Rube Goldberg contraption still felt very weak, very provisional. There were periodically mini-coup attempts,[101] betraying the extreme fragility of the security situation. Hence the temptation for Rwanda to see what would happen if the house of cards was given a firm push.

Given the fact that Kigali politics are only slightly more transparent than Pyongyang's, it is difficult to say who and what activated the whole eastern Congo crisis of the second half of 2004. On the Rwandese side there was no doubt an attempt at preempting the Kayumba Nyamwasa–Kabarebe faction from organizing a coup, and later, when the spotlights were off, Kayumba was sent as an ambassador to India and Patrick Karegeya was arrested. But who was responsible for activating the murderous gaggle of genocidal Hutu to hit Gatumba? Hard to say. The relations between the RPF and the former *génocidaires* had become very close by 2004. For example, when FDLR General Rwarakabije was welcomed back into Kigali in November 2003, he had allegedly been dealing in coltan with certain high Rwandese military officials for over a year.[102] These links between the RPF Security and their "enemies" on the other side of the border facilitated a lot of things. But President Kagame's desire to bring down the transition cannot be assumed. He is such an intelligent and wily operator that he might very well have engineered the crisis so that it would fail and discredit the hard-liners' policy. One element that would militate for such a "sideways" strategy is the fact that soon after the destabilization failure of late 2004, Kagame's own personal policies switched radically, from destabilization of the Congo to a developmentalist approach I will try to define further on.

In any case, partly by luck, partly because of resolute international support, and partly through fighting down what seemed to have been a dastardly but poorly organized plot, the transition had survived. Paradoxically, this close call had a cathartic effect on the transition's sluggish process. Suddenly not only the diplomats but the ordinary public and the politicians who were its cynical actors—everybody, in short—started to wonder. The ailing baby had survived a dangerous bout of deadly sickness, so it was stronger than previously believed. Elections stopped being an abstraction and the population as well as the politicians began to factor them into their calculations. Belief was helping to create fact, and the ghost of the transition began to gain substance. The immediate result was to solve (or at least tone down) the problems of the east and to whip up new ones in the newly promoted focus of power: Kinshasa itself.

Slouching toward Bethlehem: the transition slowly turns into reality (January 2005–November 2006)

The pre-electoral struggles. Almost as soon as the elections began to acquire greater credibility, they were called into question. At the beginning of January 2005 Apollinaire Malu Malu, the tough priest who was the head of the Electoral Commission, announced that elections would very likely have to be postponed. In the new pro-election mood this immediately triggered strong reactions, and anti-postponement riots caused four deaths in Kinshasa. Malu Malu said that he was not to blame, that postponement was probable because of the delaying tactics of a number of transition politicians who were benefiting from the present state of affairs and did not want to end it too soon.[103] The UDPS, which had boycotted the transition and was smarting in the wings,[104] was accused of having triggered the riots; it denied this, saying that the riots were the result of popular exasperation with artificial delays in the process. CIAT, which had put up a budget of $280 million for the elections, discreetly concurred.[105] On May 16, in the presence of visiting transition godfather President Thabo Mbeki, Kabila presented the new draft constitution, which was due to be submitted to popular referendum before the end of the year; he used the occasion to confirm the probability of a delay in the electoral calendar. Although he had taken the precaution to add that the process was now irreversible and that elections were indeed going to take place, this triggered new anti-postponement riots, killing two and wounding twelve.[106] Because the population concurred with Malu Malu's argument about the politicians' delaying tactics, rioting spread very quickly, killing over thirty people across the country during the last week of June.[107] The UDPS jumped into the fray and pushed for mass protests everywhere, but its agenda was incoherent since it both denounced the postponement and advocated boycotting the voters' registration process. Vice President Jean-Pierre Bemba did not make things any easier when he announced on his private radio stations that he was "ready to shoot those responsible for electoral sabotage." But Monsignor Monsengwo, the veteran CNS politician, urged people to register without rioting, and the call of the Church slowly calmed things down.

The UDPS continued on its erratic course of criticizing the transition process while advocating boycotting it. But in spite of Tshisekedi's prestige and earlier popularity, his calls fell on increasingly deaf ears, and at the closure of registration on December 10, 24,522,650 men and women had signed up. The old "Lion of Limete" persisted; he advocated boycotting the constitutional referendum, which was held on December 18; in spite of his instructions 62 percent of the electorate voted anyway. The results were interesting, since they anticipated the future electoral map of the coming elections:[108]

- In Kinshasa, the results were 50–50, reflecting the deep distrust of a tired and somewhat disenchanted electorate.

- In the two Kasais, the "yes" vote got 80 percent, but only 20 percent of the registered voters had bothered to vote, showing that Tshisekedi's boycott call still worked in his home territory.

- In Katanga and the east, the war's former theater of operations, the "yes" vote got over 90 percent, as Kabila was seen as the best way to keep Rwanda out.

- In Bas Congo and Bandundu, the "yes" vote got around 70 percent.

- In Equateur only 60 percent voted "yes," showing that in spite of Jean-Pierre Bemba's presence in the cabinet the old "Mobutuland" was not reconciled with the loss of its former symbolically privileged status.

All in all, 84.3 percent of the voters approved the proposed constitution, a resounding triumph for the transition process.

This success had an immediate impact on the now increasingly mercurial Tshisekedi, who changed his mind and announced that he wanted to contest the next elections.[109] But he was in a bad position to run since many of his potential electors had obeyed his recommendation and neglected to register; he then started to agitate—ineffectively—for the voters' rolls to be reopened.[110] His confused strategy unfortunately marginalized the Kasai Baluba from the new political dispensation then taking shape, something that remains one of its weaknesses to this day.[111] But with all its limitations and contradictions, a new shape was emerging on the political scene.

DDRRR, SSR, and assorted security headaches. The main *national* problem of the transition, beyond the vagaries of individual politicians, was—and remains—security. There were of course many other problems: facing the consequences of the dictatorship and the destructions of the war; conjugating national independence with what the Congo specialist Jean-Claude Willame has called, with perhaps a dash of exaggeration, "a state in receivership";[112] the practical problems of organizing elections in a huge half-pacified country with hardly any roads; and the constant problems of poverty's daily grind, of how to think constructively when disease, fear, and hunger remained the daily preoccupation of the vast majority of the people. But all these problems were lived under the shadow of another, bigger problem: how to reintegrate structures of often anomic destruction into new structures of controlled violence. If we recall that the classical definition of the state is an entity having the monopoly of legitimate violence over a certain territory, then, according to that definition, there was no state in the DRC even at the end of the transition. Thus, creating the conditions of national security during that period—a paid, professional, and disciplined army, honest and efficient police forces—was the primary task overshadowing all the others and whose success or failure could make them either productive or irrelevant.

The Sun City Power-Sharing Arrangement had largely been due to a military stalemate rather than to any kind of genuine desire for "peace." The "rebels" were stuck in an endless position war, particularly after the end of the Clinton administration, which had supported, or at least tolerated, the invasion of the Congo between 1996 and 2000. On the other side the government was exhausted and fearful that the Angolan and Zimbabwean support, on which it desperately relied, might wear out over time and lead to the collapse of its own meager, undisciplined, and poorly equipped forces. The "rebels" were first and foremost armed movements without ideology, without any very large civilian constituency,[113] and without any sort of unified cause apart from their hopes of profiting politically and economically from the dissolution of the former Zairian state. So when the new Bush administration cold-shouldered the invaders and when Luanda made it clear to Joseph Kabila that its support was about to end, the belligerents were pushed into peace by force of circumstances rather than by choice. Thus, in the absence of any genuine political consensus, the military arrangements of the Peace Agreement, which were essential for the country's future, were botched and insufficient, and the consequences are still felt to this day.[114] As a result of this oversight[115] the parameters of DDRRR and SSR were (and remain) in a state of almost constant improvisation.[116] What was the situation during the transition, and what is it today (since little has changed in terms of SSR during the past few years)?

The Forces Armées Congolaises were supposed to have 120,000 men at the time of the peace agreement, but a large number of those were "ghost" soldiers who existed on paper only to enable the officers to collect their salaries from the Ministry of Defense. The RCD-G had perhaps 40,000 men, the MLC around 20,000, and the RCD-ML about 8,000. In addition, the eastern militia groups collectively known as Mayi Mayi, who ranged from the Ituri all the way down to northern Katanga, were an unknown quantity which regrouped anywhere between 50,000 and 300,000 combatants, depending on the criteria used to define that word.[117]

The FARDC were set up to fuse the various armed groups into one national army. But the various warlords tended to keep some troops outside FARDC as a kind of military insurance policy, or else to "incorporate" their men in name only, putting them into homogeneous "former rebel" units where the ex-belligerents retained their separate command structures, even within the supposedly "unified" forces. Hence the all-important role of *mixage* and *brassage,* the two steps of the integration of the former troops into supposedly homogeneous units. To this day, *mixage* (when troops of various ethnic origins serve in the same units) and *brassage* (when troops are stationed in parts of the country well away from their ethnic homeland) are still far from completed, in the east particularly, and many units of FARDC are "national" in name only.

The goal was for FARDC to eventually number about 120,000, even though military experts (particularly the South Africans) believed that a tighter, more professional, and better paid force of 60,000 to 70,000 would probably be better adapted to the country's needs. But the main problem remained that of the ghost soldiers. Payments were allocated for 240,000 men, a figure that was obviously cooked.[118] But the foreign military experts had problems deflating these numbers because their Congolese counterparts systematically manipulated the figures, cooked the raw data, and tampered with the computer programs. The government was spending $8 million monthly on soldiers' salaries and at least half of that might have been embezzled. On the official scale junior officers were paid $50 per month and privates $10, a powerful incentive for officers to embezzle and for soldiers to loot. The officer corps was still very confused. At the top levels former FAZ generals who had taken twenty years to reach that rank and had studied in foreign military academies had to cohabit with Mayi Mayi "generals" who were much less educated (if at all) and who had been promoted from bush fighter to brigadier in one year. Various foreign military missions and training teams were trying to put some kind of order and professionalism into all this.[119]

But a measure of the incoherence of the foreign efforts at military restructuring is evident when one considers that the 10,600 MONUC soldiers, who had only limited rules of engagement, cost roughly $1 billion per year, while the 120,000 to 150,000 Congolese soldiers of FARDC had a budget of less than $150 million, even when taking into account all the cheating around ghost soldiers. Army living conditions[120] and salaries were so poor that discipline was and will remain a problem for the foreseeable future.

With about nine thousand men the national police was supposed to be the elite of the police force. In spite of having been trained by the Angolans, the EU, and the French it had remained poorly disciplined and without direction. On November 21, 2006, when a gaggle of fewer than two hundred pro-Bemba demonstrators entered by force the Supreme Court to burn it down,[121] the Police d'Intervention Rapide[122] ran away because some of the demonstrators had guns and were firing in the air. Not only did they abandon their equipment (batons, shields, helmets), they even stripped down to their underwear for fear of being recognized by the population and lynched.[123] As for the 29,000 members of the territorial forces, they were supposed to have been trained by MONUC and by South Africa, but in fact fewer than 5,000 had been. Their salaries were often stolen by their superiors, they are underprofessionalized, and they could not be relied upon to keep law and order. The result was that civil disturbances were usually handled by the FARDC or by special units like the Groupe Spécial de la Sécurité Présidentielle (GSSP), which tended to use disproportionate force and cause massive casualties.

To understand the security problems of the transition, one has to play them on that background. Then they suddenly appear much more understandable and their confused handling much more excusable.

If we forget for a moment the Kigali-induced late 2004 crisis examined earlier, what were the recurrent security problems during the transition period?

- In terms of sheer violence, the Ituri situation. Following the efficient but short-lived French intervention in 2003,[124] MONUC had moved in with about four thousand men and aerial support. It took its Chapter VII seriously and adopted an offensive stance, slowly wearing down the militias. By early 2005 they were sufficiently weakened to allow the arrest of several of the leaders to take place.[125] From then on the situation started to wind down, even if some holdouts remained, such as "Peter Kerim" in the Mahagi area. Over ten thousand militiamen had been disarmed in the Ituri over the past twelve months. But the problem of DDRRR was that the last two "Rs"—reinstallation and reinsertion—were usually missing. At about $50 the demobilization package offered to individual soldiers was insufficient to start any kind of business or even to go back to farming. As a demobilized and not reinserted militiaman told the UN, "It is very difficult for us to survive without the guns. The movement was our income. Now they have to give us jobs."[126] But there were no jobs. So what often happened is that militiamen would get demobilized to get the $50 and a bit of food, and then buy or steal another gun, or dig up one they had buried, and go back to the bush.

- Another area of insecurity was eastern Katanga, where the mystical Mayi Mayi commander known as Gédéon terrorized the Dubie-Kato-Kilwa area.[127] MONUC being overstretched, he was hunted down by one of the first "integrated" FARDC brigades, which behaved with ruthless disdain for human rights and caused almost as much havoc as the man they were supposed to capture.

- A ghost from the past resurfaced in the east: the old Ugandan ADF guerrilla unit. MONUC hunted it down and, in cooperation with FARDC and the UPDF lying in wait on the order side of the border, was able to kill eighty-six ADF combatants in late December 2005.[128]

- A bit in the same way as Rwanda before, but somewhat less dangerously, Uganda tried one last time to sponsor a "rebel" movement in the east. In June 2005, duly steered by operatives of ESO, a number of Congolese guerrilla remnants[129] met at the Crested Crane Hotel in Jinja and given birth to the Mouvement Révolutionnaire Congolais (MRC). In a rare display of boldness, President Museveni declared on March 19, 2006, "If the LRA attacks any part of Uganda we shall follow them into the Congo, with or without approval."[130] On May 25 MONUC, FARDC, RPA, and UPDF officers met in Kinshasa to try to defuse the multiple tensions centered around the LRA presence in Garamba, the ADF skirmishes around the foothills of the Ruwenzori, and the fairly large-scale operations of the Ugandan-sponsored MRC all the way from the Ituri down to the Semliki. The atmosphere was tense, with strong Congolese hostility toward the Ugandans, who were put in the position of having to justify themselves and did not manage to do it very convincingly.[131] A few days later FARDC traded shots with infiltrated Ugandan elements in Garamba;[132] this was the pathetic ending of a miserable attempt, as Bosco Taganda himself soon started to negotiate with the Congolese authorities.

- Last but not least, there was the problem of the FDLR. This last incarnation of the old Rwandese *génocidaire* forces was an altogether different element. The FDLR was a well-organized, nearly conventional army with ranks, paper-work, leaves of absence, and pay for its soldiers.[133] Kigali did not know how to deal with it. The government had failed to uproot it, did not really want to use it as an excuse for offensive operations in the eastern Congo anymore, but could not tolerate it on its borders for fear that one day it might develop into a real threat if something went wrong inside Rwanda itself.[134] So both MONUC and the Congolese regime were asked to deal with it, something they were neither capable of nor really willing to do since it would have meant a large-scale military operation in difficult circumstances and with a doubtful outcome. Non-Banyarwanda FARDC officers had lingering sympathies for a group that had been their ally against Rwanda during the war, and MONUC did not really have the stomach for a large military offensive that seemed a bit much even for their Chapter VII mandate.[135]

So the transition lived on, with its troubled former battlefield areas that it was never able to fully pacify. There were two Congos: the former government territory, which grumbled and complained but lived roughly in peace, and the former war zone, which wondered at times if the war had really ended.

The elections. By early 2006 election fever had started to grip the Congo. The fighting in the east, the security problems, the last-ditch attempts at destabilization were all—rightly—perceived as remnants of the past. But the looming future was both full of hope (perhaps too much; the elections had turned into a Holy Grail) and full of threats. All efforts converged at successfully organizing an enormously difficult exercise. MONUC was both carefully deploying its troops to minimize security risks and preparing to organize a massive logistical operation.[136] In April the European Union con-tributed a $21 million auxiliary military force of two thousand men under a Franco-German coordinated command. Its main point of deployment was Kinshasa itself (MONUC was mostly busy in the east), where the Bemba-Kabila rivalry had created a tense climate. In a much more discreet way, Angola was also preparing for problems at election time, and it had carefully deployed two brigades along its border with the western DRC.[137] Dozens of new "political parties" were springing up (parliamentary elections were due to be held at the same time as the presidential); these were parties in name only since they were mostly tribal or regional gatherings around the name of one or two well-known local politicians. The president had his own party, of course, the Parti Pour la Reconstruction et le Développement (PPRD); but it was not built on the model of "presidential parties" elsewhere in Africa. It was a fairly modest thing, and its secretary-general, Vital Kamerhe, was only one of the president's men.[138] There were thirty-three presidential candidates, seven of them considered to be "serious": Joseph Kabila, Jean-Pierre Bemba, Oscar Kashala, Pierre Pay Pay, Antoine Gizenga, Azarias Ruberwa, and Diomi Ndongala.[139] But everybody knew that, barring a last-minute surprise, the basic contest was between Kabila and Bemba. So both of them tried to gather momentum and attend to the small but vital elements that would make a decisive difference. This in itself was a momentous shift in the political landscape; albeit in a crude way, the politics of democratic seduction had entered the picture. There was still gunplay in the east, there were all kinds of rumors of plots and destabilization, and the former actors of the war all kept fingering their weapons. But Africa's core quasi-continental "country" had entered a new world, that of rough but democratic politics.

This was immediately evident in the choice of the candidates' public relations maneuvers. On June 17 transitional president Joseph Kabila married his long-time girlfriend, Marie-Olive Lembe da Sita. This was a masterful tactical move since Kabila's support came from the east, and the west resented a man seen as representing "the ignorant Swahilophones."[140] "Madame Olive," as she quickly became known, was a Mukongo. She was also good-looking, politically savvy, and a good public speaker who quickly became a tremendous asset for her husband during the campaign and helped him minimize his losses in the western DRC. Socially, though Kabila was not even a Roman Catholic and though he and Lembe da Sita had been "living in sin" for the past six years (they had a five-year-old son), he nevertheless got married in a lavish Roman Catholic ceremony blessed by Kinshasa's Cardinal Frédéric Etsou, a key Catholic power broker. To make it more ecumenical, President Kabila, a free-thinker but nominal Anglican, had his marriage blessed by a Protestant bishop as well.

Both candidates pulled out all the stops; every argument, including unfair ones, was used. Bemba's slogan was "Vote Mwana Mboka," meaning "Vote for a native son," this to play on the rumors of Kabila's supposedly "foreign" (i.e., Rwandese) ancestry. The cannibalism practiced by Bemba's troops in Ituri during the war resurfaced as an electoral issue. Each candidate flexed his muscles, just this side of organized violence. Kabila let the men around him (not himself, he never did it himself) discreetly "remind" the electorate that the Maison Militaire Présidentielle (Presidential Military Establishment), not in theory but in practice, gave orders to all the civilian and military secret services and to the fifteen-thousand-strong GSSP, the only semi-serious military outfit in the country. As for Bemba, he used his popularity in the capital to the hilt and even a bit further. On July 27, three days before the polls, he organized a huge meeting of 100,000 supporters at the Tata Rafael Stadium in Kinshasa. The crowds were ecstatic and they trashed the Haute Autorité des Médias building to punish the commission for what they considered the media's unfair coverage of their candidate's campaign. When the police tried to interfere, Bemba's guards opened fire, killing six. Demonstrators burned down a bar, raped a journalist, and ransacked a church.[141]

On July 30 eighteen million voters (out of the twenty-five million registered) went to the polls. Then the suspense started; in that huge country, it would take weeks to know the results. Meanwhile, the pressure mounted, so when the results were finally known on August 20, things came to a head. First the PPRD stalwarts, frustrated at the fact that their candidate had not won an absolute majority in the first round (Kabila had 44.81 percent of the vote to Bemba's 20.03 percent), tried to push the Electoral Commission to "rectify" the results so that the president would be immediately declared a winner.[142] They also sent the GSSP to try to prevent Malu Malu from announcing the results. Soon armed clashes broke out in front of Bemba's CCTV station, causing six fatalities; the next day, August 21, tanks were out in the streets, with the PPRD diehards hoping to provoke a level of violence sufficient to justify a cancellation of the election in order to proclaim Kabila the winner. The CIAT ambassadors rushed to Bemba's residence to try to get him to publicly accept the score and quiet things down, but as they were inside the house, GSSP forces arrived on the scene and opened fire. The whole thing nearly ended up in a diplomats' holocaust as the house was riddled with bullets and Bemba's helicopter set on fire.[143] Kabila managed to rein in his overzealous followers and save the diplomats. There was still some light fighting on the 22nd, but Bemba and Kabila met on the 23rd and the tension was defused. All in all, twenty-three people had been killed and forty-three wounded.

The main surprise in the election results was how well veteran Lumumbist politician Antoine Gizenga had done. With 13 percent of the vote he came third behind Kabila and Bemba and thus assumed a kingmaker position. His bastion was Bandundu, where he got more votes than all the other candidates put together, and both frontrunners' camps courted him. Nzanga Mobutu, one of the late dictator's sons, had managed to get 5 percent of the vote by coming in second in Equateur behind Bemba. Another result of note (which was not a real surprise) was the collapse of the RCD-G and its candidate, Azarias Ruberwa. The man who was identified with the hated Rwandese invaders got barely 2 percent of the vote. But the really worrying thing was the deep division in the country: a Swahili-speaking east and south solidly behind Kabila and a Lingala-speaking west and north (almost) solidly behind Bemba. If one calculated only demographics, Kabila's victory was unavoidable, as "his" regions simply had more people than Bemba's. But the problem came from Bemba's popularity in the capital and the neighboring areas, which gave him a massive nuisance capacity.

As for the legislative elections, the five-hundred-member Parliament inaugurated on September 22, 2006, had two positive characteristics: it was reasonably representative of the state of public opinion in the Congo and it was freely elected. It also has two negative characteristics: it did not have a UDPS representation and it was incredibly fragmented.

First there were two (relatively) big chunks of MPs directly linked to the two presidential candidates: the PPRD had won 111 seats (about 21 percent) and Jean-Pierre Bemba's MLC had obtained 64 seats (around 13 percent). But it was significant that the two main presidential contenders had, between them, managed to attract only 34 percent of the electorate, while a majority of the MPs either belonged to small or even tiny parties or to no party at all.[144]

Then there were eleven medium to small parties who had MPs. By order of diminishing importance, there was the Parti d'Action Lumumbiste Unifié (PALU), Gizenga's party, which had 34 seats (7 percent), mostly won in Bandundu, where PALU got 80 percent of the vote. PALU was part of the new Alliance pour la Majorité Présidentielle (AMP) coalition, Kabila's new anti-Bemba loose coalition. The Mouvement Social pour le Renouveau, led by Pierre Lumbi, who was not a presidential candidate, had 27 seats and represented about 5 percent of Parliament. It was also a member of Kabila's AMP. The Forces du Renouveau, Mbusa Nyamwisi's party, had 26 seats, and the Rassemblement Congolais pour la Démocratie (RCD), led by former vice president and rebel leader Azarias Ruberwa, had gained only 15 seats (3 percent). The various Christian Democratic parties together got 37 seats, but being divided among four different organizations they failed to exercise the influence they could have had if united. The Union des Démocrates Mobutistes (UDEMO), led by Nzanga Mobutu, won 9 seats in Equateur Province, where it represented a minority vote among the Bangala, competing with J. P. Bemba's MLC for the same tribal vote. The last of the "real" parties, the Union Nationale des Fédéralistes du Congo (UNAFEC), led by rabble-rousing Katangese politician Kyungu wa Kumwanza, was the direct heir to the old Mobutu-era UNAFER anti-Balubakat party. It won only 7 seats but nevertheless represented a real danger in Katangese politics because of the demagogic and violent populist tactics of its leader. UNAFEC was a member of the presidential AMP, but a fairly unpredictable one.

Then came the first layer of the swamp: a gaggle of forty-three "political parties" that each had only one or two MPs. Together this confused mass represented 55 seats. Most of these "parties" were in fact simple vehicles for well-known individuals who needed a party label for their respectability: Joseph Olenghankoy (FONUS), Boboliko Lokonga (Parti Démocrate Social Chrétien), Diomi Ndongala (Démocratie Chrétienne), Roger Lumbala (RCDN), Augustin Kisombe (MDD), and Olivier Kamitatu (ARC). Kamitatu, a former member of Bemba's MLC, was the only one who stood to emerge from the mass because his party was already busy recruiting independents to broaden its influence.

The fourth and last layer of MPs was that of the independents. Together they occupied 63 seats, and if the elections had not been held according to a bizarre electoral system designed to favor small parties to the detriment both of the large ones and of the independents,[145] these independents might have seated over 100. They were tribal chiefs, well-known figures, successful businessmen, or even former warlords, big men of the provinces, a floating and unruly mass, fairly well-grounded in their local realities but often devoid of any larger view, potentially prey to strong emotions, winking at the big guys, often waiting to be bought if the price was right.

After the August clashes the situation remained tense between the Bemba and Kabila camps. There was a lot a haggling in the aisles and, predictably, "Li'l Joseph" and his allies were better at it than Bemba.[146] The key electoral alliance they managed to win for the second round was to get the support of Gizenga and his PALU. This was a masterful stroke because, even if Gizenga could not bring 100 percent of his vote to Kabila, he could reasonably be expected to get between 60 and 70 percent. This provided Kabila with a modicum of western support which he sorely lacked and deprived Bemba of the possibility of creating a homogeneous western bloc. Then, less important but also useful, the AMP got the support of Nzanga Mobutu and his UDEMO. This did not make much of a difference, since everybody knew Bemba would get the vast majority of the Equateur vote, but it opened a little split in the Bangala vote and prevented it from producing a solidly hostile mass in the north. The final stroke was to get Kyungu wa Kumwanza and his UNAFEC to support the AMP. Katanga was going to give a majority vote to Kabila anyway, but the young president's support would essentially be among the Balubakat, and UNAFEC could add a strong Lunda-Tshokwe "southern Katanga" component to what was a basically "northern Katanga" plus Lubumbashi power base.

The second round of voting took place on October 29 and the results were known two weeks later: Kabila had won with 58 percent of the vote to Bemba's 42 percent; turnout had been 65.4 percent of the registered voters.[147] The next day Bemba rejected the results of the polls and started court proceedings to challenge them.[148]

What can be made of these claims of rigging? First, if the election was not always fair, it was free. Of course, in the Congo's immense space and confusion a few ballot boxes here and there got stuffed or "lost." But these minor mishaps did not significantly alter the validity of the results. There was no systematic rigging, as had been known to occur in other African countries. Why? The answer is not clear, but it was probably a mixture of causes: first, the AMP was bound to win without rigging; second, the elections were fairly well monitored; third, there was a diffuse feeling on everybody's part that heavy rigging would be counterproductive since the population, exasperated by years of suffering and political violence, *wanted* a clean election; and last but definitely not least, large-scale rigging would have been extremely difficult to organize given the country's size and circumstances.

When the Supreme Court rejected Bemba's claims of rigging, his militiamen, who had strong popular support in Kinshasa, invaded and burned down the Supreme Court building after the police had run away.[149] There was a tense standoff for a few days while everybody waited to see if Bemba would comply with a presidential ultimatum to remove his men to Camp Maluko, outside the capital. He finally agreed but finagled the numbers and eventually did not fully comply.[150]

But the elections were now over, with a minimum of disruption. The east-west split was wide and visible, but it had not materialized violently. The international community's partiality in favor of Joseph remained embarrassingly obvious. Jean-Pierre Bemba was a very poor candidate for leading a constructive opposition, and the AMP was indulging in a "winner-take-all" attitude not very conducive to good governance. But all in all, given the Congo's past history and its spectrum of possibilities, it was a rather normal situation. Expecting more would have been unrealistic. The friends of the Congo were cautiously optimistic, and Bill Swing breathed a sigh of relief.

The morning after syndrome (November 2006–July 2007)

The risk of internal political paralysis. In a report issued in June 2007, the advocacy NGO International Crisis Group wrote, "More than six months after the Kabila inauguration, challenges are piling up with no long-range strategy for addressing them in sight."[151] The assessment is both true and perhaps a bit too severe. But there are some very weak points in the new regime which perhaps still considers its very existence with a certain degree of disbelief.

First, the AMP is an incoherent gaggle. It is not a "government" in the proper sense of the word, but rather a coagulation of groups operating out of completely mercenary interests (several of the smaller parties) or outdated and almost mystical ideological strands (PALU). Antoine Gizenga, who was made prime minister both to reward his support and because his puritanical integrity could be used as a bulwark against corruption, is not a real government leader. His authority over his unruly ministerial stable is weak and his impotence serves the palace clique that surrounds the president. In theory, the presidential cabinet, which was reorganized on March 17, 2007, could run the government from behind the scenes. But its boss, the technocrat Raymond Tshibanda, is too timid and not well-connected enough to exert a real counterweighing influence. As a result, the old palace guard (Augustin Katumba Mwanke, the man for financial and mining deals; Samba Kaputo, the security adviser; Denis Kalume and Brig. John Numbi for internal affairs; Marcellin Cishambo for unofficial diplomacy) are the ones actually running things. Because their interest is of course not to reform or change or streamline government operations, they have a vested interest in "personally fruitful" stagnation.

Then there is a disturbing tendency to "solve" problems through the use of often disproportionate force administered in confused and unprofessional ways. This first became evident in the way the rebellious members of the Bundu dia Kongo (BDK) politicoreligious sect were dealt with in January 2007. The situation came about when the AMP slate for the Bas Congo governorship "won" by 15 votes to the 14 given to the MLC slate.[152] The head of the BDK political sect, Ne Muanda Nsemi, was a candidate for the vice governorship and he was irked at being "beaten" by AMP candidate Deogratias Nkusu Nkuuzi because Nkuuzi and his boss, Mbatshi Batshia, had paid more and gotten the MLC MPs (who are a majority in the Regional Assembly) to vote for the AMP slate. This resulted in riots that left 138 people dead. The reason for the exaggerated violence was the intervention of the Angolans.[153]

What happened when Jean-Pierre Bemba refused to disband or remove his militia is another case in point. On November 13, 2006, President Kabila had issued a decree requiring the vice president's personal guards to be included in the army. Yerodia Ndombasi and Arthur Z'ahidi Ngoma complied, Ruberwa negotiated a good deal for the reintegration of his boys, and Bemba kept silent and did nothing. The MLC leader has a difficult personality, and his mixture of adventurism and genuine fears requires kid glove handling. Instead, on March 6, 2007, General Kisempya, the FARDC chief of staff, gave him nine days to get his men out of Kinshasa. The deadline passed without any action being taken and Bemba felt he had again gotten away with it. Then, on Thursday, March 22, around noon, troops of the GSSP attacked elements of Bemba's bodyguard in the downtown Kinshasa area of La Gombe. They were quickly repulsed, and Bemba's men started to fan out from their positions. They went down to the Nguila Beach and to Ndolo Airport, from where they could call in reinforcements from former FAZ in Brazzaville. Government forces had melted away, and it took a strong intervention by the Angolan-trained commandos to bring things back under control. But they did it their way, using light artillery, heavy machine guns, mortars, and RPG-7 anti-tank rocket launchers, with no special care toward the civilians; 348 people were killed and several hundred wounded.[154] Bemba had abandoned his men and taken refuge in the South African Embassy as soon as the fighting started, finally leaving the country on April 11 to go to Faro in Portugal, where he owns a villa. Thus a mixture of political incoherence, military incompetence, and gross brutality resulted in both a massacre and a politico-diplomatic deadlock.[155]

The economy: donors, debts, and the Great Mining Robbery. We saw in the previous chapter that by late 2002 the previously disastrous state of the economy had started to improve. The foreign donors were an essential part of that process; the first serious global effort by multilateral financial institutions had begun in September 2001, when debt rescheduling lowered the (multilateral) debt service to about $160 million a year.[156] A year later the Club of Paris debt was restructured. Out of $10.3 billion, $4.6 billion was canceled[157] and $4.3 billion was rescheduled, leaving another $55 million still owed yearly to service the commercial debt. Thus by the beginning of 2007, the DRC could live with a debt service of about $215 million to $220 million a year. But there was still a lot of resentment against the international community at having to pay even this amount since it corresponded mostly (about 90 percent) to debts accumulated by the Mobutu regime, which were directly attributable both to the West's toleration of his corruption and to the political support the dictator had been able to muster. Thus the fundamentally orthodox monetary option chosen by Budget Minister Adolphe Muzito in 2007 came under heavy fire for pandering to "foreign interests," even though Muzito himself was a member of the radical PALU.[158] The quarrel is both understandable (paying for Mobutu's debts rankles the public) and unrealistic: without satisfying these unpleasant technical requirements it would not have been possible to bring in the fresh money that has been coming since 2002, when $1.7 billion of cofinancing was arranged through the World Bank. Every year since then there has been a sustained effort, culminating in 2005, when the Bank approved eighty-six different loans addressing the needs of fourteen different economic sectors and totaling $3.62 billion.

And dealing with the Congolese authorities has not always been easy for the international community. Due to pork barrel politics in an election year, the 2006 budget was overspent by 141 percent, and this led to the suspension of relations with the World Bank and the IMF. The international financial institutions had desperately tried to save the Congo from itself by offering a Programme Relai de Consolidation, whose period of application was supposed to be from April to December 2006, but it has not been adhered to. A rather desperate "Plan for Corrective Measures" implemented in October of that same year did not work either, which resulted in the complete suspension of the DRC from collaboration with the international financial institutions. In Kinshasa in February 2007 Paul Wolfowitz, chairman of the World Bank, promised a new facility of $1.4 billion for 2008, after a new structural plan would be devised in collaboration with the new Ministry of Finance and the Congolese Central Bank, whose governor, Jean-Claude Masangu, personally retained the trust of the IMF and the World Bank. But the whole thing got embroiled in Wolfowitz's personal problems at the World Bank, and an exceptional facility of $180 million had to be disbursed in March to plug the gap. These rigorous monetary and budget policies are beginning to bear fruit: inflation has sharply receded to probably around 10 percent, and for the first time since the end of the war, the Congolese franc has strengthened appreciably against the U.S. dollar.

Congolese Franc Exchange Rate against the U.S. Dollar

Nov. 1997	Jan. 2000	Dec. 2003	July 2005	Feb. 2007	May 2007
5	200	375	470	570	500

The rate of exchange is essential because of the massive dollarization of the economy. The U.S. currency circulates everywhere, and DRC monetary policy is thus indirectly in a symbiotic relationship with U.S. financial policies. The tax base has shrunk to less than 4 percent of GDP, and a major problem is now looming on the horizon with the planned administrative reforms of the provinces and with decentralization.[159] If the whole set of measures goes through as planned, the central government will be starved of tax money. And if it does not, this might cause violent reactions in some of the more politically unstable provinces. The fine line between these two extremes will be a difficult one to toe.

With an insufficient tax base and a negative balance of trade, public finances still rely heavily (over 40 percent) on aid. Whatever is not in the peasant self-produced and nearly nonmonetary sector of the economy is under direct foreign perfusion. The only services available to the people are foreign-created, foreign-run, and foreign-financed. The UN and NGOs together spend $3 billion a year running hospitals, providing transport, paying the army, and supporting the school system. The only media organ with a national reach, Radio Okapi, is a UN-NGOs joint venture.

But one of the main problems of this aid, a problem typical of many postconflict situations but particularly preoccupying here, is the very poor coordination between projects and implementing agencies. Duplication, confusion, and waste are rife. This lack of coordination is particularly damaging because of the endless levels of corruption typical of the DRC. This is probably where the consequences of the thirty-two years of Mobutist dictatorship have had the worst impact. Mobutism as a system implied and presupposed corruption, even elevating corruption to the level of an institution.[160] This created a political and administrative culture wherein the stealing of government funds was seen as normal, even praiseworthy; civil servants would boast to each other of their achievements in theft. This culture has survived Mobutu and is still causing havoc in the economy today. The problem is not only a moral one, it is a financial and economic one: the extent of corruption is such that the government is largely economically dysfunctional. The coexistence of middle-ranking civil servants paid $50/month working in parastatal companies under bosses who are often paid up to $15,000/month (and who steal quite a bit beyond these opulent salaries) has a demoralizing effect on the workforce.

But the mining situation overshadows everything else in the economy, and the way it is handled will be a make-or-break test for the new regime. The mining industry is in a state of flux and confusion, hovering between rich memories (the colonial days and the Mobutu regime before 1985–1988), a descent into hell (the late Mobutu period), and a state of piratical endeavors during the war and immediately after. By 1997 the Zairian mining industry was in such a state of disarray that junior companies were in a position to raid it with the hope of parlaying their freebooters' expeditions either into cash (reselling their permits) or into joint ventures with major companies.[161] From that point of view the 2003 mining code is an ambiguous document, as it was prepared by President Kabila's advisers to bring along to Sun City to seduce the mining interests (and the South African government) into helping Kinshasa. It largely worked, but the price has been an almost supine deference to predatory mining interests and a slanted tax system whereby some of the richest mining assets in the world contribute at present a meager $40 million a year to the national treasury.[162] Thus the thirty-two joint ventures that Gécamines has entered into with foreign "partners" often amount to asset-stripping and unequal "leonine" contracts, which have come under fire since the end of the transition. Other, formerly prosperous parastatals (OKIMO, MIBA, SOMINKI) are now nearly bankrupt after signing partnership agreements amounting to a form of legal swindle.[163] In April 2007 Mining Minister Martin Kabwelulu launched a commission charged with reviewing the most suspect of the contracts.[164] A partial list includes the various activities of such groups as Australian Anvil and the Belgian-Congolese George Forrest Group, the shocking contract concluded for the Tenke Fungurume Mining site with the U.S. giant Phelps Dodge[165] just before the elections, the KOV contract and all the activities of the Dan Gertler/Barry Steinmetz association, the MotoGold contract with OKIMO, and the Kamoto tailings contract. Forestry contracts, although carrying less of a taxable potential, are also an important economic resource that has been abused by unscrupulous operators since the war.[166] Together with the security situation, the future of the mining industry will probably be the other key factor in the ultimate success—or ultimate failure—of the electorally approved transition process.

The east refuses to heal. The whole debt, aid, financial management, and contractual analysis business was addressed by different segments (World

Bank, IMF, BAD) of the international community than the political problems, which remained the preserve of the UN and of what would have once been called "the Great Powers" assembled within CIAT. Contrary to the "financiers," who tended to be very technical, those other segments of the international community considered the elections to be the be-all and end-all element that was going to put an end to the regional wars and restabilize the Congo. But even if the elections were critically important, this was an oversimplified view of the situation.[167] Apart from the economy, security remained essential—and "security" was another name for the eastern problem. Bad as the Kinshasa clashes and the Bas Congo BDK massacre had been, they did not have the capacity to durably and fundamentally damage the country. The recurring and apparently intractable character of the eastern violence was considerably more problematic *because it preexisted the war,*[168] *had been made worse by the war, and would not stop even if the war stopped.* This meant at least two things. First, military problems were perhaps more fundamental than electoral problems. This was put bluntly by South African observers: "The possible consequences of inaction and of not supporting a new national Army are much more dangerous than any delays in the electoral process. The incomplete process of demobilization and disarmament and of the creation of the new national Army could contribute significantly to a return of major hostilities."[169] Although the possibility of renewed major hostilities seems low (the foreign factor has slowly been deconstructed), the danger of continued anomic violence remains high, with all its disastrous corollaries in terms of national self-image, diplomatic weakness, and damage to foreign investment possibilities. Second, the military problems could not be dealt with in exclusively military terms. FARDC power had to be there as a deterrent and an ultimate recourse, but the real solutions in the east were historical, ethnic, geographical, economic, political, and cultural, in that order. Such a deconstruction of complicated and toxic patterns dating back to colonial days could not be achieved easily, were not really within the competence of the UN, and would take much more time than it took to organize an election.

Meanwhile, regardless of the successful completion of the elections, the east did not heal. Military violence in the east has often been treated as a kind of whole, although it is in fact a series of different problems coming from groups whose impact is global but whose origins, structures, and motivations are quite separate.

The less dangerous (although not the least violent) are probably the various Mayi Mayi groups (Willy Dunia in Fizi, Capt. Bendera Kilelwa on the Ubwari peninsula, several groups loosely linked to Padiri Kanero in North Kivu, Gédéon's former fighters in northern Katanga) who refuse to recognize anybody's authority and keep a system of shifting alliances.[170] In many ways they are "social bandits" whose problem is chiefly economic. As a local UN worker in charge of DDRRR said, "There has been a lot of talk about disarming and reintegrating Mayi Mayi fighters back into society but so far no one is really doing anything."[171] This is a problem that should not be addressed at the level of the leaders only, but also—even more—at the level of the rank and file, which is socially desperate and keeps shifting between groups in order to eat.

The various warlords (Cobra Matata, Peter Kerim) who have survived amid the debris of that civil-war-within-the-civil-war in the Ituri are not very different from the Mayi Mayi, but they are more regionally and tribally grounded. They also have for a long time had the support of Uganda, which kept clumsily trying to fish in increasingly bloody waters. They are now being "integrated" into FARDC at fairly high levels.[172] But as the recent International Crisis Group report remarked, "They [the warlords] have refused to leave Ituri and prevented most of their troops from going to designated assembly areas since they fear arrest and want to keep a reserve force in case the deals do not work out."[173] Here too dealing with the leaders has been an inefficient shortcut since the men who really matter are the disenfranchised and criminalized ordinary fighters.[174]

The third group of uncontrolled armed men in the east, the "foreigners," is more serious because of its real or imagined potential for regional destabilization. It comprises various foreign guerrilla groups, such as the Ugandan LRA and ADF, the Burundian FNL, and the biggest, best organized, and potentially most dangerous, the Rwandese FDLR. The LRA and ADF are vastly overrated. The LRA is a "cultural" guerrilla force, the product of Acholi alienation from the mainstream of Ugandan social evolution since 1986. Poisonous as its military behavior can be, it has no capacity for spreading beyond its initial social group; particularly in the DRC, it is a kind of rootless "Thugs without Borders" outfit, moving aimlessly between the province of western Equatoria in Sudan, the southeast of the Central African Republic, and the Garamba National Park in the Congo. Even though it will die kicking, its days are numbered. The ADF, which still survives in the foothills of the Ruwenzori, has evolved from a guerrilla group into a rogue mining company. The recent fighting on the Ugandan border[175] was almost purely motivated by an attempt at controlling the border trade.[176] As for the FNL, its last few fighters survive on the Burundian border, largely by fishing in the lake. President Museveni periodically threatens to cross the border and hit the LRA inside the Congo. This is most likely motivated by his irritation at still having to deal with an armed opposition that has been around for twenty-one years and one that Museveni's rational nature completely fails to understand. These angry presidential outbursts are more a sign of frustration than a political response to a real threat. The ADF and the FNL are—rightly—perceived in Kampala and Bujumbura as carryovers from the past rather than dangers for the future. This nevertheless leaves the Congo forced to deal with what are actually, for all practical purposes, bandits.

The FDLR, which still has a fighting strength of perhaps six thousand men, is in another category if only because, through its genocide image, it still retains the capacity to trigger strong reactions in Kigali.[177] But the FDLR problem, contrary to what it was in the past, is neither an invasion threat for Rwanda (in the present) nor a pretext for Kigali's armed actions in the DRC. As Richard Sezibera said very clearly in December 2004, at the end of the last "Rwandese" crisis in the east, the problem with the FDLR lies in its capacity to hinder Rwanda's economic effort. The FDLR is perceived by the Kigali regime as a weight rather than a danger, but the RPF leaders, who came to power through a somewhat similar phenomenon (they were the armed remnants of an earlier crisis in Rwanda, in the 1960s), cannot completely discard the idea that one day, after some unforeseeable events, they might have to face a revamped and aggressive FDLR which could be an instrument of Hutu revenge. In the meantime, given the large Kinyarwanda population in the eastern Congo, which has its own Congolese and even "Kivutian" problems, the FDLR presence acts as a kind of permanent irritant in the relations between (a) the Tutsi and Hutu on the Congolese side, (b) the Banyamulenge community and the other Kinyarwanda speakers, (c) all of the above and the so-called *originaires* (native) tribes.

Which brings us to the last and perhaps most dangerous segment of the armed groups in the East, that of Gen. Laurent Nkunda. After 1998 he became one of the main officers of the RCD-G; his troops played a key role in the Kisangani massacre of 2002.[178] He was later indicted with crimes against humanity by the International Criminal Court, accusations he rejects, which caused him not to come to Kinshasa when he was appointed in the new army because he feared a trap.[179] He lay low after the May–June 2004 attempt to capture Bukavu, but then in November 2006 he rebelled again and attacked Goma, probably intending to hold it as a bargaining chip in any future negotiations. After losing about three hundred of his fighters to the firepower of MONUC's Pakistani battalion, he went to the negotiating table and agreed to see his men enter mixage.[180] He then used his *unités mixées* to carry out a thorough cleaning-up of the "Petit Nord" region, that is, the Walikale-Rutshuru area, where his soldiers went on the offensive against the FDLR, causing large civilian loss of life and displacements. These "victories" gave Nkunda the idea of widening his "crusade" beyond the local level, and on December 30, 2006, he created the Congrès National pour la Défense du Peuple (CNDP), which was in fact a political armed militia but which he tried to present as a political tool to "clean up Congolese politics." His discourse kept oscillating between minimalist demands (jobs) and flights of demagogic rhetoric in which he demanded the resignation of the government and his own assumption of power in Kinshasa. In the meantime he complained about his various pet hates: the shabby way he had been treated by FARDC; his innocence in the Kisangani massacres; the betrayal of his erstwhile friend and political boss, former RCD-G president Azarias Ruberwa, who became vice president in Kinshasa during the 2002–2006 transition but nevertheless had done nothing for him;[181] and the tragic fate of his Banyamulenge friends at the end of the war. But what soon made him more dangerous was that, under the fold of his demagogic populist CNDP banner, he started to recruit all sorts of malcontents, mostly Tutsi of course, but also Hutu Banyarwanda from Masisi and even flotsam and jetsam from various tribes who began to drift toward him as the pressure from MONUC and its demobilization programs from other regions liberated a lot of former fighters into military unemployment. He went further and started actively using allied Mayi Mayi groups such as Mundundu 40 to network and recruit for him. He even went across the borders and started to recruit young unemployed Tutsi men in both Rwanda and Burundi, offering them spurious hopes of nonexistent civilian jobs. Some of them deserted and surrendered to MONUC when they found out about the scam after crossing the border into the Congo, but some, who had nothing much to go back to, stayed and joined his "army."

By his own account Nkunda now has around twelve thousand men.[182] But the worst aspect of his maneuvering is that he has kick-started the FDLR back into life and reopened all the sores of the east; his repeated attacks in the Walikale-Rutshuru area were the cause of brutal *génocidaire* retaliation when they massacred a whole village in cold blood at Kanyola in South Kivu on May 29, 2007. In his own "Petit Nord" area the various former anti–RCD-G tribes, such as the Banande, the Bahunde, and the Banyanga, started to mobilize their young men to fight him. As a result the whole region, from the southern Ituri down to the edge of northern Katanga, experienced a sudden return to a state of tension previously forgotten.

Does all this mean that we are back in July 1998 and about to see the Congo explode into another civil war?[183] Most likely not. Why? Because there are several fundamental differences:

- Rwanda, even if it is involved, is involved only at a marginal level. In 1998 it had mobilized its whole army for an invasion.

- In 1998 pro-Kigali elements such as Jean-Pierre Ondekane controlled large segments of the FAC, which was then the Congolese national army. The initial onslaught was carried out through an internal rebellion of the armed forces. Not so today. Nkunda controls an army only of unofficial militiamen.

- In 1998 the regime of Laurent-Désiré Kabila was very weak, hardly legitimate, and did not have any serious international support. Today his son is strongly supported by the international community after achieving a clearly democratic election.

- In 1998 the Congolese economy was in complete disarray; today it is slowly picking up.

- Before 1998 Kagame could count on almost unlimited sympathy from the international community, which felt guilty for its neglect during the genocide. Today his moral credit has been seriously damaged by the horrors committed in the Congo during 1998–2003.

The danger comes from the belligerence of some former members of Laurent-Désiré Kabila's entourage in Kinshasa, combined with the timidity of the international community and Nkunda's own near desperate gambit. The recent FARDC reshuffle in the region is good,[184] but the transfer by Kinshasa of large amounts of heavy weapons to the east around mid-May is worrying. Interior Minister Denis Kalume and Minister of Defense Chikez Diemu both favor a military offensive to crush Nkunda once and for all.

Will the east finally heal? That remains an open question at the time of this writing.[185] But the Goma Roundtable Conference of January 2008 has significantly brought things forward. For once, a UN initiative was taken seriously by the local participants. President Kabila picked Father Apollinaire Malu Malu as chairman, a controversial but good choice. Malu Malu was the chairman of the Electoral Commission for the Congolese national elections of 2006 and did a commendable job in difficult circumstances. But more than that, he is himself an easterner and a very special one. He is a Nande from Butembo and as such the "prince" of the "Autonomous Republic of Butembo."[186] This gives him considerable clout in regional affairs because the Kinshasa minister of foreign affairs, Mbusa Nyamwisi, is a Nande as well and largely dependent on the good father for his local political support. And Mbusa is not in fact the real foreign minister (this job goes directly to the president himself); he is truly and really *the minister of the Great Lakes.* When he was a rebel during the war he dealt constantly with Kagame and Museveni, and he knows them through and through. His job in the cabinet is to deal with them and with the broader eastern situation. Father Malu Malu's appointment did not please Nkunda too much because the good father knows the eastern situation like the back of his hand, is a tough customer, is a devoted Kinshasa supporter even if not a "centralist," and belongs to a tribe that the Kivu Tutsi cannot accuse of genocide (the Nande were on their side during the civil war) but whom they fear for their numbers, organization, and economic clout.

At the same time, this appointment was a guarantee that the conference was not going to be another session of empty babbling. The Goma conference was top news in the Kinshasa press because everybody realized that this was a very important step in the final postwar normalization. To drum up support all ministers in Kinshasa were asked to contribute 10 percent of their salaries for the financing of the conference; Prime Minister Antoine Gizenga voluntarily gave up 50 percent of his.[187] Nkunda was under a lot of pressure from the region (both nationally and internationally) to shape up and work toward a solution. His bogus screams of "Genocide! Genocide!" simply were not enough any more to replace a political program. On the other side, Father Malu Malu is one of the few people who might be able to talk some sense into the autochthonous tribes and tell them that Rwanda or no Rwanda, they cannot take out their anger and frustration on the Congolese rwandophone populations and that they have to accept some kind of a deal on a new citizenship law.[188]

The problems of the east are (in this order) demographic, agrarian, ethnic, and economic. The first problem is a given which cannot change in the short to medium term; the second is the heart of the matter. But agrarian problems touch the heart of the people's livelihood, so they are directly tied to the ethnic problem because land belongs to tribes and most of the struggles have been to displace or kill the other tribe in order to get their land. This whole demographic-agrarian-ethnic nexus is exactly what was at the root of the war back in the 1990s.[189] Which is where the fourth problem kicks in: the only way not to have agrarian reform work as a zero-sum game is to inject money into a static rural economy through the cash nexus, which in the Kivus means transport and mining. And transport and mining mean *security,* which in turn presupposes some kind of a working settlement between Nkunda's Tutsi, the various Mayi Mayi bands still plundering the area, the Banyamulenge, the autochthon tribes, and, yes, the FDLR *génocidaires,* who, although "foreign," are part and parcel of the problem and therefore need to be included in any kind of solution.[190]

Therefore, a way out of what I have called elsewhere "the recurring Great Lakes crisis"[191] lies in brokering a temporary security deal that can bring enough security to restart the mining operations and get the economy moving out of its present doldrums, in which a gun is a more useful tool to earn a living than either a hoe or a shovel. The conference in Goma is tackling the essential questions, whose answers have been postponed for years.[192] This is understood in Kinshasa, where the press wrote, "Finally we are now dealing with the basics." Mere window dressing simply won't do. We are dealing here with a problem as basic as that of the enclosure system in seventeenth-century England.

Whether the sense of urgency will be enough for the actors to rise to the occasion (and that includes the international community) remains to be seen. Meanwhile, the question of the relationship between Rwanda and the Congo has stood very much at the forefront of the conference.[193] Today President Kagame does not try to control "the Congo" anymore but simply to control enough *mining interests* in the Congo to help finance his great dreams of turning Rwanda into the Singapore of Africa. The money comes from a variety of nonferrous metals (niobium, cassiterite, not much coltan these days since the Australians got back into the market) extracted from mines controlled by local Congolese militias[194] who export their product to Rwanda in light planes. President Kagame has to deal with a resolute opposition *within* his militarized party that still regrets the good old days of Congo plundering. These people, like his chief of staff, James Kabarebe, are the ones who underhandedly helped Nkunda in December 2007 and who were less than enthusiastic about the Goma conference.[195]

Goma might not be the final and complete attainment of peace, but it is a positive step along that road.

10

GROPING FOR MEANING: THE "CONGOLESE" CONFLICT AND THE CRISIS OF CONTEMPORARY AFRICA

After most of the sound and fury of war had died down (leaving large pockets of territory where it still reverberated) outside observers were left with an impression of both inevitability and painful absurdity. Thirty-two years of Mobutism could not but have ended in catastrophe. But then what? Were the nearly four million victims of the war a typically Congolese problem? Or were they the result of a more general crisis of the African continent after half a century of decolonization? Were foreigners well-meaning Samaritans eager to help? Or evil manipulators of the crisis? Were they baffled bystanders in spite of all their control rhetoric? Or were they simply indifferent, as the limited reporting of these monstrous events might tend to suggest? What were the deep underlying causes of such a large-scale conflict: the anarchic violence of unstable states? an African version of old-style territorial imperialism? a confused grabbing of natural resources by predatory self-appointed elites? Was "conflict" a pertinent category, and was "conflict resolution" a realistic goal or just snake oil sold by smooth operators? Did our familiar tools of diplomacy, media exposure, and humanitarian action actually function as advertised, or did they get waylaid into perverse unintended consequences? We will not of course succeed in answering all these questions since doing so would entail a capacity to solve most of the core problems both of Africa studies and even, to some extent, of the social sciences. But in this last chapter I will try to look *analytically* at those years of turmoil, at their historical structure, at their relation to the rest of the world, and at their pertinence to the general paradigm of an "African crisis."

The war as an African phenomenon

The purely East African origins of the conflagration. Global as they later appeared, the workings of the Congolese continental crisis must be seen as the last link in a chain of events that were triggered by a very precise and localized upheaval back in 1959. For it is in that year that the *muyaga*[1] brutally splintered Rwandese society, causing several years of civil disturbances that sent a sizable number of Tutsi into exile. These Tutsi went into exile in various African, and non-African, countries but kept in touch with each other as an organized diaspora. Their efforts at a homecoming and/or regaining power proved fruitless, and they stopped trying after 1963. But this left unfinished business with a potential for future problems which was not perceived at the time.[2] In 1981 civil war broke out in Uganda after the rigging of an election that had been designed to give the country a proper democratic government after the fall of Gen. Idi Amin's dictatorship. Because President Milton Obote, the spurious "victor" of these rigged elections, manipulated ethnic contradictions in western Uganda to undercut the guerrilla movement fighting his regime, the Rwandese refugees living there found themselves involuntarily caught in the repression and joined the guerrillas in self-defense. By January 1986 they found themselves sharing a certain amount of power in Kampala, but not automatically welcomed by native Ugandans, who resented their often overbearing presence in the new Museveni regime. Disenchanted with the results of their victory, they gradually started to question their "Ugandan" identity[3] and to look at the country of their parents as a promised land. They reorganized in exile and invaded Rwanda in October 1990.[4] The war lasted nearly four years and ended up precipitating the genocide of the "interior" Tutsi (April to June 1994), who were seen by the Hutu extremist elements of the Kigali regime as a fifth column ready to side with the invaders.

Up to then these conflicts had remained penned up in one little corner of the Great Lakes area of eastern Africa. Their causes and lineaments were known only to specialized academics, a handful of diplomats, and a few spies who had not made it to front-line cold war assignments. The genocide brutally changed all that, first by causing worldwide emotional shock and then by involving an uncomprehending international community in an obscure local problem that had suddenly exploded into universal relevance. France was the first external power involved in Rwanda, without understanding the true nature of its involvement. It acted there in the same way as it had in other parts of French-speaking Africa since the 1960 decolonization, propping up an authoritarian regime it believed was sympathetic to Paris. But because the place had been a Belgian rather than a French colony, the actors of that policy in Paris were largely ignorant of the history and the problems of the region. They thought they were dealing with a little war they could fight not too expansively in terms of either money or diplomatic exposure.[5] And then they suddenly found themselves sitting on top of a heap of 800,000 corpses they had not seen coming. They were horrified and tried to deny any responsibility. But meanwhile the United Nations, that supposed repository of the world's conscience, had joined them in opprobrium by frantically doing nothing and avoiding any responsibility in the third and last genocide of the twentieth century, although they had a military force deployed in the country at the time. By then millions of politically embarrassing Rwandese refugees had crossed the border into Zaire, and it was obvious that the situation could no longer remain a parochial east African affair.

Antigenocide, the myth of the "new leaders," and the spread of democracy in Africa: the world projects its own rationale on the situation. When a number of African countries, spearheaded by Rwanda, invaded Zaire two years later in September 1996, two different sets of variables found themselves in competition to try to make sense of the now growing storm. First there was the explanation that regional Africa specialists derived from a historical appreciation of the facts. For reasons of cold war expediency the West had tolerated, even supported, a monstrously inefficient and predatory regime in the Congo/Zaire. The result was a catastrophe waiting to happen, an enormously mismanaged blob of a country, in the very heart of the African continent but without shape or capacity to handle itself. In a dangerous paradox, this sick monster was potentially one of the richest countries in the world, the repository of immense mineral wealth which could not be rationally exploited because the polity "owning" it was by then incapable not only of doing the job for itself but even of ensuring the necessary conditions for somebody else to do it. With the end of the cold war this monstrous system suddenly appeared for what it was: an anachronism waiting for some kind of a (probably brutal) overhaul. Facing this dying monster was a bevy of energetic regimes led by mostly former communist sympathizers who secretly rejoiced at the idea of taking revenge on their old cold war foe; were groping for some kind of a new, continentwide, post–cold war dispensation; and carried the smelly luggage of all kinds of former unresolved conflicts which they hoped to solve all at once in one decisive action.

331

On the other side of the paradigmatic divide were the foreigners looking at this suddenly convulsing Africa. The foreign vision of the continent was dominated by two broad ideas: economic retardation and the existence of a dangerous breeding ground for communist subversion. In the euphoria following the end of the cold war, which Western egocentrism was mistaking for the End of History,[6] the second view suddenly appeared obsolete. The West, buoyed by its own generosity at supporting the end of apartheid in South Africa, felt that it had to cheer the continent along as it finally joined the rest of the world in a kind of reconciled modernist, capitalist, human-rightist democratic utopia.[7] The link between these grandiose views and the somewhat grimmer African realities was the very group of "New Leaders" and their associates[8] who were then attacking Zaire. Thus in the Western world and in the diplomatic view, the war against Mobutu appeared as a kind of holy crusade of the new against the old, of virtue against vice, an epic of reformed communists who had seen the light of capitalism and were going to bring free trade and the computer revolution to Africa. Ugly Mobutu and his bloody *génocidaire* cohorts provided the perfect Darth Vaders to these lightly cavalcading Luke Skywalkers. The show was on.

The real actors of that fantasmatic soap opera immediately realized the advantages that could accrue to them from playing along with this exciting new scenario. And they understood that the link between the old and the new had to be that existential continental divide: the Rwandese genocide. The words *genocide* and *genocide prevention* became a mantra through which the West would atone for all its Africa-related sins, past and present, and by means of which Africa would tragically access modernity, in the same way the West had done in 1945 after purging the Nazi evil.[9] The New Leaders were to be Moses ushering Africa into that Brave New World, and antigenocide was to be their miraculous rod.[10]

Paul Kagame was probably in the best position as the main communicator from the African side. As the leader of the exemplary victims, his intelligence, his ruthless determination, his capacity to fine-tune white guilt as a conductor directs an orchestra put him miles ahead of his lesser associates. He presented the West with a very convincing storyboard: prevent a supposed genocide of the Banyamulenge[11] and remove the border threat created by armed elements of the former *génocidaire* Rwandese government. Both suggestions fit well with the Western view of the situation and had a reasonable relationship to the reality on the ground. The first target, which was the most ambiguous, was quickly achieved; the second one was successfully completed by December 1996. But then the attackers, emboldened by their success, did not stop; they moved on to another and larger agenda: the removal of the Mobutu regime itself. This, although a bit more daring, could be seen as an extension of the virtuous cleaning of the African Augean stables that had just been launched. But how truly reformist was that second stage of the New Leaders' enterprise? Could not another, perhaps "imperialistic" element be detected in their endeavor? By early 1997 a certain uneasiness was beginning to develop around the perception and explanation of what was happening.

The "New Congo": between African renaissance and African imperialism. For people who had known the situation for a long time, the "new" dispensation was simply the (astonishing) triumph of certain components of the regional problem. Just as Museveni's assumption to power had been less of the "new dispensation" that he pretended it to be,[12] Kagame's victory in Rwanda was the return under a new guise of something that had been known before. But the extension of these two phenomena, in partnership with a number of others, eventually led to something truly new, although it was far from the ideological dreams of the West: the first known instance of postcolonial imperial conquest in Africa by an African country.

There had of course been many cross-border conflicts in Africa since the end of colonization, but straight open warfare had been rare,[13] and most of the other cases were cross-border *subversions* rather than *invasions,* and the support of the subverting states was routinely denied even if everybody knew it to be true.[14]

The Rwanda-Congo conundrum that was producing the first case of clear-cut African imperialism was quite different. It was neither subversion nor straight foreign invasion; it was Trojan-horsing. Although cross-border tribal interlocking is an extremely common situation all over the continent, the case of the Congolese Kinyarwanda speakers was special in that *they were not a tribe shared between two countries*[15] but *a national group from a nation-state extending into the territory of a neighboring multiethnic state.* Thus the Congolese Banyarwanda of what was known as "uncertain nationality" were in a particularly controversial situation because they had *both* strong state and nonstate loyalties and because one of their segments had just been massacred by the other, turning support for the non-génocidaire group into a matter of politically correct transborder commitment. In such a context, the new regime in Kigali could claim to be the *guarantor* of its non-Rwandese (but Banyarwanda) brothers' safety. This was an infrequent configuration worldwide and without any parallel in Africa.[16]

But the Banyarwanda whom Kigali claimed to defend were impacted in what was probably the weakest state in a continent of weak states, even though this weakest of weak states was buoyed by an extremely strong feeling of nationalism.[17] Given the pride of the Zairian Congolese, the sorry economic state of the country drove this nationalism to higher and more abstract levels, akin to those of a religion.[18] In the difficult Zairian economic environment of the late Mobutu years, the "hated foreigner" was the uninvited guest at the native's poorly served table. As a result, political representation for the Kivus at the Conférence Nationale Souveraine in 1990 was highly contentious.[19] The Rwandese civil war had only made matters worse, since the Habyarimana regime on one side and the RPF on the other had both tried to use the Hutu and Tutsi segments of the Congolese Banyarwanda communities.[20] Thus the genocide argument used by Kigali in relation to the Kivus was a powder keg, since its consequences could potentially irradiate the whole of the Great Lakes area, down into Burundi and up to Uganda's Bufumbira region. As for the "dangerous refugee" argument, which drew on a completely different body of justification, that is, the rational-legal one used by the international community, it provided the necessary international camouflage for the operation. It meant that even if it began to have second thoughts, the embarrassed international community was hard put to challenge something it had so enthusiastically supported shortly before.

In many ways Africa was—and remains—the bad conscience of the world, particularly of the former colonialist powers of the Western world. They entertain a nagging suspicion, played upon by the Africans themselves, that perhaps the continent wouldn't be in such a mess if it hadn't been colonized.[21] So in the ten years that followed jettisoning the heavy African baggage of apartheid, the international community was only too happy to support the so-called African Renaissance, the New Partnership for Africa's Development, the New Millennium Goals, and the Peer Review Mechanism of the newly revamped African Union. Within this new paradigm the continental war began as a seemingly bright illustration of the new trend, but then began to evoke an embarrassing reincarnation of some very old ghosts. Caught in the web of its own tangled guilt—that of having long supported the gross Mobutu regime, combined with the more recent sin of *not* having helped the Tutsi in their hour of need—the international community tried

to hang on to the image of the new Tutsi colonizers of the Congo as basically decent men devoted to making Africa safe for democracy. Of course,
there was a bit of a problem factoring in the personality of the leader they
had put in power as their Congolese surrogate. It was difficult to smoothly
include Laurent-Désiré Kabila in the New Leader movement because the
others were *reformed* communists whereas he was an *unreformed* one and his
democratic credentials were hard to find. So, in a way, when the break occurred in 1998 and the Rip Van Winkle of Red African politics sided with
the surviving *génocidaires*, it was almost a relief: the good Tutsi could go on
incarnating Africa's decent future while the fat Commie could symbolize its
refusal to change.[22] The massacre of a number of Tutsi in Kinshasa and the
obliging incendiary remarks of Yerodia Ndombasi helped the international
community integrate the new war into its pro-democracy and antigenocide
ideology. But there were lots of contradictions, and it was going to be a
harder and harder conjuring trick to pull off as time went on.

From crusading to looting: the "new leaders" age quickly. August 1998 in Africa resembled in some ways August 1914 in Europe: the same mindless
automatism in acting militarily on previous diplomatic engagements, the
same bad faith, and the same brandishing of supposed moral wrongs as
thin covers for grossly material interests. The only thing that was lacking
was the nationalistic fervor that inebriated the European crowds on the eve
of the First World War. Except for two countries: Rwanda and the Congo.
For these core actors of the conflict it was a fight to the death. As I noted at
the beginning of the previous chapter, the other countries involved in the
war were there because of elite choices that had no real grounding in the
population. Thus the best image one can give of what happened is that of
a geographical hollow, the Congo Basin, entirely surrounded by a chain of
otherwise unconnected storm clouds which were all drawn toward the low-
pressure zone that had suddenly developed. Was this a product of typical
characteristics of the controversial "African state"? Yes and no. The traits
usually attributed to African states—their authoritarianism, their lack of
democratic control, the monopolization of power by a small and corrupt
elite, their patrimonial structures—all played key roles in involving Angola,
Namibia, Zimbabwe, Uganda, and even little Burundi into the global confrontation. And the same goes for the peripheral actors who either did not
fight directly or fought only for a brief duration. But the core conflict was of
a different nature and was absolutely specific to its geographical and cultural
theater. Which is also why it is the core that is proving so intractable and

why the eastern Congo is still, if not in a state of open warfare, at least in a situation of very high insecurity six years after the conflict officially ended. This is also one reason why a correct diagnosis was so difficult: the problem was (and remains) rooted in history, an element that the West looks upon as irrelevant and tries to evacuate through the abstract bureaucratic language of "peace and security," while the local actors manipulate it with furious alacrity. The gap between the two approaches has been enormous.[23]

In a situation wherein the new war was a decision by elites fought by poor countries but in which the core actors were at the same time fighting about essential gut feelings that made the conflict intractable,[24] looting and ultraviolence became the normal tools of the conflict. The notion that wars can be regulated by certain moral principles began in Europe in the thirteenth century, when the Church tried its hand at the first forms of violence control, even if they remained an ideal that was not much adhered to. The creation of the Red Cross after the horrors of the Crimean War and the later signing of the Geneva Convention were further steps in the same direction. But World War II, with the Nazi death camps and the indiscriminate bombing of civilians by both sides, was a major setback. Contrary to popular perception, most African wars, both precolonial and postcolonial, were not worse from the humanitarian point of view than wars in other parts of the world. At first this was the case with the new conflict. But things soon degenerated, largely because this was a real war and not a military walkover, like the 1996–1997 conflict that had toppled Mobutu. African wars can be carried out only part time. The "total war" concept invented by Germany during World War I and since then seen to apply to many conflicts worldwide[25] cannot apply in Africa because the means are simply not available. Military action is largely disconnected from the rest of socioeconomic life and cannot be sustained relentlessly. Thus, if war can be carried out only part time because of financial constraints, the combatants sooner or later tend to privatize their action. And if looting can at times be supervised by the state, as in the case of Rwanda, it is a "natural" tendency for all the combatants to practice it on a large scale, particularly for those belonging to nonstate militias, who are usually left without pay for long periods of time.

In this respect, as in several others, the Great Lakes or "Congolese" conflict resembles the European Thirty Years' War (1618–1648), in which looting was one of the fundamental activities of the contending armies. Even when they are relatively efficiently used by the state, the combatants devise strategies of economic relevance that turn "war" into something Western observers cannot recognize as the kind of "real military conflict" we have been used to identify due to its extensive use in the past three hundred years. Here economic predation, trafficking of all kinds, and looting both at the individual and at the collective level become essential features of the conflict because they are essential means of financing it.[26] This has massive consequences on the way the war is fought. Because civilians are the ones from whom the military can take its means of survival, armed violence is more often directed at civilians (including, at times, those of one's own camp) than at the enemy army. Direct armed confrontation is often avoided, and straightforward military victory is only one of the various options in the field. It is actually this nonstate, decentralized form of violence that makes the conflicts so murderous and so hard to stop. Looting and its attendant calamities (arson, rape, torture) become routine operations for the "combatants," who are soon more akin to vampires than to soldiers. Even the regular armies—and here the parallel with the Thirty Years' War is inescapable—all use militias to supplement or reinforce their own capacity. After a while there is a kind of "blending" between the so-called regular forces (who in Africa are usually poorly paid and poorly disciplined) and the militias they have recruited as auxiliaries. This blending leads more to the de-professionalization of the regular forces than to the professionalization of the militias. This was a key factor in the grotesque fighting between the Rwandese and Ugandan armies in Kisangani, where the invaders seemed to have lost even the most elementary vision of what they were doing in the Congo and turned to fighting each other like dogs over leftover bones.

These problems move straight to the fore when the war ends. In an environment in which economic alternatives are extremely limited or even nonexistent, the well-meaning DDRRR plans of the foreigners are often almost completely impracticable, since war has become a way of life for those involved in it. In the Congo this is the main difference between the intractable east and the rest of the country: in the east (and from that point of view the east includes northern Katanga) civilian militias have taken war to the village level, whereas in other areas of the country it was the various armies (Congolese, Rwandese, Angolan, Zimbabwean) who fought semi-professionally and therefore could be physically stopped and evacuated elsewhere. But in the eastern war zone, because there had never been a unified command capable of carrying out a coherent centralized strategy, bringing under control the myriad feuding units was akin to trying to harness a bunch of wild horses to a cart.

This is what explains the tragic casualty structure of the war,[27] in which, although there were no massive weapons resources (aviation, heavy artillery), the deaths were largely civilian. Civilians died partly because the soldiers killed them but, more often, because their living conditions (absence of health care, impossibility of steady cultivation, impossibility of trade, lack of shelter during the rainy season, constant displacement) caused their death. War is never very much fun. But the Congolese continental conflict was particularly horrible, not only because it caused the deaths of nearly four million human beings but because of the massive suffering it visited on the surviving civilian populations.

The war as seen by the outside world

What did all the diplomatic agitation actually achieve? Much has been written on the supposedly important U.S. involvement in the Great Lakes conflict, an involvement that has often been described as driven by allegedly large U.S. strategic and economic ambitions in the Congo basin. I hope that this post-Leninist bogey was somewhat laid to rest in the last pages of chapter 3.[28] The veteran American Africanist William Zartman was much more realistic when writing in 2000, "The U.S. is engaged in the Congo willy-nilly . . . and since we are held accountable anyhow, it might as well be on the basis of a coherent policy."[29] Apparently this policy never materialized because a year later the same author declared, "The hallmark of the Clinton administration policy towards Africa has been one of overwhelming rhetoric with no follow-through."[30] Nevertheless, as we saw earlier, the first period of the conflict was a moment of definite U.S. engagement in support first of the AFDL and later of the anti-Kabila forces. Why so? This support seems to have been rooted in cultural traits that, though "imperialistic," had little to do with conventional "imperialism." Since the collapse of the "Evil Empire," the United States, which already considered itself "God's country," blossomed into an overweening sanctimoniousness that attributed its victory in the cold war to an innate cultural superiority. Since September 11, 2001, this has morphed into complex feelings of persecution, election, and revenge akin to those of the Hebrews.[31] But since God's people are by definition good, the United States was deeply embarrassed at having passively connived in a genocide and tried to make up for that by turning the RPF into a black Israel. In addition, Zaire remained an embarrassing albatross in U.S. cold war memories. President George Bush Sr. was still declaring as late as 1989, "Zaire is among America's oldest friends and President Mobutu one of our most valued friends on the whole continent of Africa."[32]

In practice U.S. involvement in Mobutu's regime had gone through three phases: active support and promotion in the wake of the first Congo civil war of 1960–1965, disinterest for the next ten years, and then sudden reengagement after 1975, when Angola jumped to the forefront of Washington's cold war worries and Henry Kissinger decided Mobutu was the man to help the United States confront that threat. But the cold war had ended and democracy blossomed everywhere, which turned Mobutism into a skeleton in the American cupboard. Then, completely unexpectedly, the Rwandese "problem from hell"[33] exploded, and with his customary repulsive aplomb Mobutu embraced the surviving demons. The groan of disgusted embarrassment from Bill Clinton was almost audible as the former U.S.-supported dictator welcomed the *génocidaires* the White House had so carelessly failed to curb. For a great power sure of its greatness and its goodness, the whole spectacle was unsavory. In typical Clintonian fashion, the president's reaction was emotional and personalized[34] but only superficially worked out in practical terms. During the summer of 1995, as tension was growing between Kigali and Kinshasa, Joseph Nye and Vincent Kern, the Department of Defense numbers two and three, went to Rwanda. Ambassador Rawson told them the State Department had just sent a cable saying it wanted Kagame warned not to cross the border in reprisal attacks. But the pragmatic State Department approach was behind the times. The Department of Defense was taking over the U.S. Great Lakes policy and would not let it go for the next few years; Kern told the ambassador not to deliver the message because it did not agree with the Department's policy.[35] This muscular moralism resulted in incredibly simplified versions of reality being bandied about. When Assistant Secretary of State for African Affairs Susan Rice came back from her first trip to the Great Lakes region, a member of her staff said, "Museveni and Kagame agree that the basic problem in the Great Lakes is the danger of a resurgence of genocide and they know how to deal with that. The only thing we have to do is look the other way."[36]

American support for Rwanda, Uganda, and the "rebels" they backed did not come from a Machiavellian plan to dismember the Congo and take over its mineral riches. It came simply from a deep sense of unease on the part of President Clinton, mirroring that of a large segment of U.S. public opinion, which could not conceive of an America that wasn't on the side of the "good guys." As Africa ranked very low on the scale of Pentagon security concerns,[37] the White House did not feel constrained by official obligations and could afford a very subjective level of engagement. Thus trusted aides like Susan Rice, John Prendergast, and Ambassador Richard Bogossian, who shared the president's regrets and his somewhat simplified view of the resulting situation, would be allowed to act on their personal feelings and deeply influence policies.

During 1997–1998 this trend briefly tied in with the short-lived craze over the alleged phenomenon of the "New African Leaders."[38] There was a naïve gushing enthusiasm in the media ("Museveni sounds like Ronald Reagan. He's bought the whole gospel"),[39] and doubters were seen as party-poopers.[40] The former Marxist born-again market economy Democrats were seen as leading Africa forward, and Mobutu's fall embodied the (brief) triumph of young virtue over stale habit. Even when the "friends" jumped at each other's throats[41] there remained a lingering sympathy for the dead concept, and in the Congo the simplified idea of "struggling against the *génocidaires*" became embedded as an article of faith in U.S. policy.

Its limited means and simplified ideas did not prevent Washington from having a strong influence on the situation, simply through its sheer symbolic weight. Thus John Prendergast could write without exaggeration, "The leverage of the United States cannot be judged solely on the amount of aid it provides. There is a cachet U.S. involvement brings to any initiative which should not be minimized."[42] Physical intervention could be dispensed with since virtual political blessings sufficed at this highest stage of altruistic imperialism. This was particularly visible in February 2001, when Paul Kagame and Joseph Kabila came to Washington at the same time, leading to a change in the U.S. relationship with Rwanda "from a warm embrace to a cordial handshake."[43] For Kigali this was a fifteen-second catastrophe and a fundamental turning point in the war. This new type of American influence could be effective only when the blessing or cold-shouldering was "for real," meaning that it had a strong U.S. domestic grounding, for U.S. diplomacy is secondary to domestic concerns, and Africans know this very well. Thus Richard Holbrooke's December 1999 "Congo crisis tour" had little impact because elections were due eleven months later and it was so obvious that Holbrook was campaigning for his own hoped-for position as President Gore's future secretary of state[44] that all actors preferred to camp on standby.

During the presidential campaign Republican candidate George W. Bush candidly declared, "Africa is not part of U.S. strategic interests."[45] And in American eyes September 11 was to deal the final blow to the continent. As

Assistant Secretary of State for African Affairs Charles Snyder told me short-ly after the events, "Before that Africa did not figure very high on our list of priorities. Now with this thing it's completely gone off our radar screens."[46] But by then South Africa had picked up the diplomatic ball in the Congo and was running almost alone. The African vision of U.S. diplomacy sank back to the simplicities of the Africa Growth and Opportunity Act[47] and the "war on terrorism."[48]

France's intervention in the Great Lakes crisis stands in almost complete contrast to that of the United States. This is not because of their alleged (and greatly exaggerated) rivalry but because of the radical heterogeneity of their cultural views of the continent. Louis de Guiringaud, once a foreign minister under President Giscard d'Estaing, said back in the 1970s, "Africa is the only continent which is a possible field of action for France, the only one where, with 500 soldiers, she can still change the course of history."[49] The immediate question from the puzzled non-French reader is why would she want to? Which takes us back to the differences with U.S. policy. U.S. policy toward Africa has been one of benign neglect interspaced with limit-ed periods of sharp activism targeting one particular problem: Soviet threats, real or perceived (the Congo 1960–1965, Angola 1975–1988, Ethiopia 1985–1991), humanitarian public relations (Somalia 1992–1993, Darfur since 2004), and guilt politics (the Great Lakes 1996–2001). Since Septem-ber 2001 two new items have crept onto the agenda: secure west African oil supplies and fight Islamic terrorism.[50] France has never known these spurts of enthusiasm followed by long periods of disinterest because the basic drive behind French foreign policy is ontological: a systematic geopo-litical perspective and a desperate quest for vanished grandeur, resulting in a diplomatic version of *Remembrance of Things Past.*[51] Because that concern is constant and because, as Guiringaud noted, Africa is one of the few areas where this obsession has some chance of playing itself out, Africa has re-mained at the forefront of French diplomatic concerns since the ambiguous "independence" of its colonies in 1960. In the French view of international relations, a diabolical conspiracy by the "hyperpower" (read: United States) is permanently unfolding with the help of its British sidekick, with the aim of "lowering" France and humiliating its qualitatively superior culture.[52] In this view, the courageous Gallic Don Quixote fights the "Anglo-Saxon" conspiracy with the help of his little African Sancho Panzas. Of late, the size of the windmills has become quite awesome.

341

This led to a reiteration *ad nauseam* that the whole of the Great Lakes crisis could be explained by the rivalry of Paris with Washington and London. Many journalists bought this interpretation because it was so pat, so convenient, and seemed to give such a welcome gleam of sophisticated veneer to what many readers would otherwise have perceived as just another obscure scuffle between savages in the heart of the Dark Continent. France did have a *pré carré* (reserved area) in Africa. Its unstated but evident purpose was to prop up France's world rank and shine in the international arena.[53] Taking advantage of this motive, a whole bevy of rather unsavory characters squatted the concept to further often dubious business interests.[54] But this was limited to its former French-speaking colonies. The "tragedy" of Rwanda[55] was that, because of a misconceived linguistic pride, François Mitterrand felt obliged to defend the integrity of something that had never been within the confines of that nostalgic preserve. The French governmental Commission of Inquiry on Rwanda, whose report came out in December 1998, was a curious mixture of guilty admissions, convoluted denials, and poker-faced sophistry. It was more eloquent in its avoidance of embarrassing subjects than in its reticent admissions. More than anything else it was an exercise in futility: its chairman, Paul Quils, and all its members belonged to the Socialist Party and could not dissociate themselves from the policies of Mitterrand.[56] Most French politicians of a certain generation, regardless of their political side, saw Africa as a necessary prop of French grandeur. "Mistakes" had been made, but not to the point of crime. Which, from their point of view, was true: France had for forty years tolerated recurrent violence on the part of its protégés. Killings (preferably in limited numbers) were regrettable but necessary tools in the exercise of power in Africa. Concerning Rwanda, nobody at the Elysée Palace had ever dreamt that little murders between friends would escalate to such an apocalyptic level.

Then the 1996–1997 "Mobutu war" came at the tail end of the Rwandese horror and Paris gamely persisted in its mistakes till the predictable bitter end. The whole *pas de deux* of the multinational force was an exercise in almost unbelievable bad faith, on both sides. The French pretended to want to save the Rwandese refugees when they actually wanted to save Mobutu, and the Americans pretended that all the refugees had gone home because they wanted their recently anointed New Leaders to rid them of the old cold war Frankenstein still hunched over the banquet table.

The New Leaders did kill the old monster, even if this was not the end of the story but the beginning of a new one. And in that new episode, the

French were clueless. They had lost their familiar bearings in the scuffle, and besides, at home a certain amount of weariness was beginning to develop around African issues. For a new generation of politicians the continent was increasingly seen as a faraway, exotic, and dangerous place, largely irrelevant to the modern world except as a recipient of charity. Without realizing it, civil society critics of French corruption in Africa had the unintended effect of turning disgusted public opinion from further involvement. The whole Foccart–de Gaulle generation was now either dead or in retirement, and their epigones were tiring of what increasingly looked like a rearguard action. During 1998, as the Great Lakes crisis grew into a continental war, Paris closed down its Ministry of Co-operation and integrated it into the Ministry of Foreign Affairs. For a non-Frenchman this might seem like a small matter, but in terms of Franco-African relations it was an earthquake: the Ministry of Co-operation had been a latter-day Ministry of (Neo)Colonies, where French-sponsored regimes got preferential treatment.[57] With the blending of the two ministries there was a feeling that Africa was "abandoned" and left to the European bureaucrats in Brussels:

It is now in Brussels that African delegations have to face cold-blooded European examiners to answer interrogations about human rights, good governance and democratic agendas... . Today there is nothing left of what De Gaulle had wanted and which Foccart tried to preserve... . [Without Africa] France will soon sink to the level of Spain and Italy, second-rate powers.[58]

An era was indeed coming to a close. Rwanda and the fall of Mobutu was the watershed that marked the end of a certain conception of France's action in Africa, even if many other forces were at work to bring it to an end. But it was psychologically easier to blame "Anglo-Saxon plots" for this demise of grandeur than to have to admit that the world had changed and that the Gaullist dream of a Françafrique was dead.[59]

Did the international community actually act? Well, yes and no. It all depends how one defines acting. In the new, politically correct age ushered in by the demise of the "Evil Empire," actual action is not as important as its representation. What matters is image perception. Therefore the international community tried to offer the picture of (virtuous) action, in the same way that the United States wanted to be seen as recuperating a clean soul and France as shoring up its tottering grandeur. It is my contention that none of the state actors actually cared about what was *really* happening.[60] This does not apply of course to civil society actors and NGOs. But the various states making up the amorphous body of the "international community" were happy to go through the motions of aggrieved concern, without any of the urgency that was so obvious during the cold war period, when actual physical involvement, financial and military, was essential.[61] Actually, a large part of the misreading of the situation by the Congolese themselves was due to their mechanical projection of obsolete cold war patterns onto the new dispensation of the 1990s. "Classical" imperialism was dead, replaced by media diplomacy. The reasons were simple: there were no more "real" (i.e., strategic or economic) stakes, and in the wake of the Rwandese horror, image juggling was the paramount preoccupation. There was of course a vague concern about "destabilization," but, as September 11 was soon to show, this was an "Islamic" problem, never taken very seriously as far as Africa was concerned.

A special passing mention has to be made of "African diplomacy," as this was the period of a growing fashion for "African solutions to African problems," actually an elegant way of passing the devalued buck of African geopolitics from those who could to those who could not.[62] The Great Lakes crisis exploded just as this new "policy" started to develop. Washington had dreamed up its African Crisis Response Initiative just as the French paralleled their military disengagement from the continent[63] with their RECAMP program. Neither of the two initiatives ever worked, and the sick baby was left in the hands of the African actors themselves, particularly the regional organizations. If we forget about the (O)AU, whose absolute impotence had by then become legendary, this meant the Southern African Development Community in the case of the Congo. But the SADC was a house divided against itself, with Zimbabwe and Angola siding with Kinshasa while South Africa could not be expected to cooperate with its geopolitical rivals.[64] The result was endless meetings about "peace" that did not change anything in the way the conflict was unfolding. In the meantime the United Nations was left in its usual thankless position of having to manage what member states did not want to touch directly. The UN was sliding into complete insolvency as its Department of Peacekeeping Operations had over thirty-eight thousand troops deployed worldwide by 2000 (with many in Africa) at a cost of $2.2 billion per year, while at the same time the United States owed it $1.69 billion and other member states $1.21 billion.[65] Starting with the December 11, 1998, Security Council statement on *The Situation in the DRC*, UN pronouncements on the conflict were the ultimate experience in toothlessness. After failing so miserably to stop the genocide in Rwanda and to solve the resulting refugee crisis, the UN did not feel it could condemn outright the invaders of the Congo who had looked as if they were righting the UN wrongs in 1996–1997 and who still surfed on their anti-Mobutu credentials. Kofi Annan kept asking for "thousands of troops,"[66] knowing very well that the member states had neither the will to intervene nor the courage to say so. Resolution 1291 of February 24, 2000, authorized the deployment of 5,537 men for MONUC, which would not actually be deployed for over two years, and Resolution 1304 of June 16, 2000, asked foreign troops to leave the Congo, but without specifying a deadline.[67]

For the actors of the war, in line with the image diplomacy of postmodern times, the stakes in dealing with the international community were essentially media-oriented. This should be understood restrictively. Contrary to some past African horrors (the Biafran war, apartheid, the Ethiopian famine of 1984–1985, and finally Somalia in 1992), the Congolese continental conflict was never a "hot topic" for the media. Thus media positioning by its actors did not angle for the massive international aid which was unlikely to ever materialize, particularly in military terms. Rather, the parties to the war aimed more modestly at a "good image" among a select circle of specialists in order to receive "development" international aid, which would then enable them to channel their own resources into fighting the war while the foreign Good Samaritans would foot the domestic bills. As we saw earlier, Uganda and Rwanda were way ahead in that game, whereas Laurent-Désiré Kabila's Congo never understood how to play it and even thought they could do without it. It is largely the economic results of this image gap that enabled the two rather poor countries of the east to keep chewing away at their giant neighbor for four years. With a dash of exaggeration one could say that the game was over the moment the old Marxist the international community loved to hate got killed and was replaced by a young, lean, smooth operator who understood the rules of postmodern diplomacy. Since the end of the cold war reality has become a poor second to image. But fighting a war still means mobilizing resources, and image manipulation has turned into the new way for the poor to mobilize the resources they do not have.[68]

Regardless of the various capacities at image formation, international mobilization in the widespread African conflict always remained far below what was devoted to other, more important parts of the world. If we take, for example, 1999, the core year of the African conflict as well as the year of the Kosovo crisis, the following summary is quite eloquent.

	Great Lakes Region	Kosovo
Population (millions)	86	3

UN Consolidated Appeal ($m)	314	471
Foreign troop deployment	0	30,000

A discreet unspoken racism could always be rephrased as "a question of strategic priorities."

It is interesting to see that MONUC, which, under Bill Swing's leadership, eventually became a serious factor in the postwar transition period, had to wait until South African diplomacy had leveled the ground before it could take off. International involvement was still too timid to be pioneering.

Moral indignation in lieu of political resolve. The media treatment of the Rwandese genocide was largely dealt with in moral terms. Involving as it did a complex mixture of anthropology, history, geography, African politics, and colonial guilt, the political analysis of what happened was abandoned to "specialists." The still largely unexplained tragedy was soon left behind, officially attributed to the evils of human nature and, perhaps more subjectively, to the "darkness" Europeans tend to perceive in Africa. Meanwhile the serious business of dealing with the consequences was contracted out to "realistic" professionals.[69] But because these practitioners were left to face a gaping intellectual and political black hole, "moral" formulas were called on to explain away the gap. This is why the next three subsections of this chapter are in fact arbitrary and can be seen as three different aspects of a constant interplay between morality, efficiency, and understanding, with "moralism" too often used as an excuse for a lack of hard analysis and a weak political resolve.

In a book written when only the first part of the Great Lakes tragedy had unfolded,[70] the professional and practitioner John Prendergast could call his first chapter "The Seven Deadly Sins" and the second one "Good Intentions on the Road to Hell." After being overglorified in the 1970s and 1980s, humanitarian organizations were criticized in the 1990s as naïvely romantic at best and self-serving business concerns at worst.[71] Criticism has tended to concentrate on three areas, and all three came to the fore during the Congo war:

- Humanitarian organizations are not what they are touted to be, and too much of their budget goes into administration, publicity, and fund raising.[72]

- They are either blind or complicit when their resources are hijacked by the fighting parties in a conflict.[73]

346

- They are naïve and don't even understand what is going on under their noses.[74]

Paradoxically the demand for their services had grown exponentially at the same time as criticism piled up. The reason was simple. As the cold war waned so did strategic interest in what used to be called "the Third World." But local conflicts did not recede; far from it. As a result humanitarians had to fill in for delinquent politicians. Even diplomacy tended to turn away from being an extension of politics to internationally furthering charitable concerns.[75] This mushrooming moral treatment of politics tended to obscure issues rather than clarify them.

In central Africa it had started even before the genocide crisis was completely over. The two main *political* problems—how to stop the genocide and how to deal with its perpetrators—were both left hanging. While completely unwilling to intervene militarily the international community kept asking for a cease-fire, without realizing that this amounted to an incitement to finish the genocide. And it did nothing about the retreating *génocidaires* because as hundreds of thousands of Hutu refugees were fleeing into Zaire and a cholera epidemic had broken out, the instinctive international response was charitable.[76] This set the stage for the next catastrophe: the direct confrontation between triumphant military adventurers and unrepentant *génocidaires*. There was a sharing of tasks. The pure humanitarian component of the international community fed indiscriminately the refugees and their evil minders in Goma, while the diplomats brought their moral embarrassment with them to Kigali. This added to two parallel mistakes: on the one hand, neglecting the degree of control the former regime still had over the refugees and the degree of militarization of the camps, and on the other hand, not analyzing the nature of the new Rwandese government and promoting General Kagame as a kind of Rwandese Konrad Adenauer bent on peace, reconciliation, and extirpating the evils of ethnicism. Both camps, for different reasons, were deemed worthy of "humanitarian" help, and both were prepared to use it for their political and military ends. But rushing into humanitarian action had four advantages for the international community: (1) it allowed it to do what it knew best; (2) it was the cheapest alternative to any form of durable military commitment; (3) it was the most consensual course of action, apparently value-free—Who could be against feeding starving children?—thus avoiding unpleasant arguments about the political responsibilities of some major UN members before and during the genocide; and (4) it was highly visible for the media and could provide world public opinion with a low-cost alternative to real political action. This is of course not to say that humanitarian action was not *needed*. The situation both in Rwanda and in the camps was atrocious and deserved to be dealt with. But what was not acceptable was the role of political substitute that humanitarianism was asked to play. To their honor some (not all) of the humanitarian NGOs present in the camps understood this and withdrew from a crooked game. Those working in Rwanda never looked twice, the horror of the genocide acting as a kind of magic screen, hiding any further reality. As for the UN agencies that did not have a choice, their situation got progressively worse as time went on. Sadako Ogata's struggle with New York to obtain some kind of political commitment became tragic. The anti-Mobutu war of 1996–1997 pushed humanitarian schizophrenia to new heights when the partial return of the Hutu refugees to Rwanda became enough to exonerate the international community from any further concern about their fate.

Compared to that first period, humanitarian action was much more muted during the second conflict of 1998–2001, precisely at a time when it was needed more than ever because "civilian losses and the destruction of infrastructures [had] become military objectives as such and [were] not any more simply collateral damages of the war."[77] Part of the problem was that as the humanitarian situation got progressively worse,[78] the Congolese reaction to it grew more defensive, not to say paranoid. The January 2, 1999, decree on the state of siege severely curtailed humanitarian activities in the noncombat zones, while the fighting put at least one-third of the county practically off-limits to humanitarian organizations. Apart from the ICRC, humanitarian agencies found their work severely hampered in the areas where they were most needed. This demonstrated the tragic limitations of the humanitarian approach to what were coyly termed "complex emergencies." The same absence of political will that had replaced politics by humanitarianism *after* the worst of the crisis in 1994 was powerless to support humanitarian work *at the height* of another crisis, which was largely the product of the nontreatment of the previous one. Faced with this the international community could only utter truisms, such as the central message of the Brahimi Report: "The key conditions for the success of future complex operations are political support, rapid deployment with a robust force posture and a sound peace-building strategy."[79] Who could quarrel with that? But equally truly, who was ready to do it?

Set up by a UN resolution dated November 8, 1994, the ICTR has been plagued by monumental problems from day one. To be fair, how could it be otherwise for an international court manned by people of eighty-seven nationalities whose mandate was to investigate in agreement with modern legal standards a massive genocide organized largely by word of mouth?[80] But even if we accept the technical premises, there were numerous difficulties in both conception and functioning. First of all, the tribunal's mandate was limited to acts committed between January 1 and December 31, 1994. At the time of its creation that period seemed reasonable. But nobody foresaw that December 31, 1994, would be far from the end of the story and that hundreds of thousands more were still to die in events related to the genocide.

The ICTR was conceived of as a neat tool that would bring a messy and ambiguous situation to a tidy conclusion by 2008 at the latest. But reality refused to let itself be penned up in that convenient enclosure. To make matters worse, the court soon combined three different evils: it was an embodiment of the worst aspects of UN bureaucratic inefficiency; a muted, closed arena for jousting over all the unacknowledged political contradictions of the genocide; and a swamp of nepotistic and corrupt practices. The first aspect is perhaps the most visible because it reduced the pace of the trials to a crawl. Every single type of bureaucratic malpractice that can be imagined has been present at the court: lengthy procedures lasting at times nearly two years, endless indictments,[81] the hiring of suspected *génocidaires* as investigators for the tribunal, the hiring of staff who did not know French when 80 percent of the documents made available to the court were in that language, no simultaneous translation in the chambers until 2001 although the majority of the witnesses spoke nothing but Kinyarwanda, a thoroughly insufficient and largely incompetent translation service, files getting lost, experts and witnesses being discouraged from working with the court because of its sheer confusion and incompetence,[82] and completely erratic behavior at the highest levels.[83] The result was that, whereas it had taken the Nuremberg Tribunal one year (from November 1945 to November 1946) to judge twenty-four Nazis and hang ten, the ICTR had managed to carry out only twenty procedures in ten years at a cost of around $700 million.

The second failing of the ICTR, its role in confusing politicomoral issues even further, is perhaps graver. From the beginning Kigali said that it wanted quick and expeditious justice. The sincerity of this claim can be questioned, and I will do so further on. But at least the public intention was there and, in the aftermath of the genocide, it was difficult to dispute it. But the display of public confusion and bickering at the ICTR was such that the first two prosecutors (Judge Richard Goldstone of South Africa and Judge Louise Arbour of Canada) did not fulfill their mandate. For Kigali this was a godsend. In 1996, at the time of the attack on Zaire, and then later at a variety of junctures (the 1997 northern infiltration-cum-repression, the Garreton inquiry into the fate of the disappeared Hutu refugees, the 1998 invasion of the Congo), it was most useful diplomatically for General Kagame to be able to keep playing on the guilt feelings of the Western countries, and particularly of the United States. The ICTR mess gave him a clear line of fire: you (meaning the international community) cannot give us justice; therefore we have to take justice into our own hands. The fine line between self-administered justice and violent military action thus became conveniently blurred. This put the Rwandese government indirectly in control of the ICTR: because 80 percent of the casework for the accusations rested on the use of witnesses, Kigali would fine-tune the release or blocking of testimonies according to what it needed from the tribunal. This was, diplomatically speaking, a magnificent piece of work, with the Rwandese literally running circles around a clumsy and incompetent ICTR that, being largely ignorant of the long and complicated history of the region,[84] most of the time did not even understand that it was being manipulated. The main fear of the Kigali regime was that it itself would be accused of the massacres it had committed after the genocide. Because the ICTR was not supposed to look at facts posterior to December 31, 1994, the bulk of those massacres would not fall under its mandate anyway. But this posed the question of reopening the Gersony Report file, something the UN was most unwilling to do, given the fact that it had suppressed the facts unearthed by Robert Gersony in September–October 1994, that is, well within the court's mandate. This would have put into question the moral and political stance of both Secretary-General Boutros Boutros Ghali and then Secretary-General Kofi Annan. Thus the UN found itself in a *de facto* alliance with Kigali in not looking any further into RPF crimes against humanity, even if only a very small portion of those would fall under the ICTR mandate.[85] In late 2003 this was to be at the heart of the controversy about renewing Carla del Ponte's mandate.[86] The relationship between Kigali and the ICTR was best described by the Human Rights Watch researcher Lars Waldorf: "Rwanda has the Tribunal over a barrel. They can hold it hostage because they know that it needs witnesses to come and testify in important cases in the genocide."[87] And talking publicly about certain things could be a very risky business: "Each time I say something a member of my family is either killed or put in jail," declared former defense minister James Gasana, who is living in exile in Switzerland, "and my case is only one among many."[88]

Last but not least were the massive corruption problems at the tribunal. Even if we overlook the freewheeling ways in which some of the ICTR staff treated their professional expense accounts, there were even more damaging practices, such as fee splitting, by which lawyers kicked back from $2,500 to $5,000 a month to their clients to be allowed to work for them.[89] This did not make for a speedy treatment of the files. "Go slow" was the prevailing attitude; those ICTR investigators who worked too fast were accused by their colleagues and superiors of spoiling the game.[90]

The case seems to be clear: if we add up all these dysfunctionalities the net result is that the ICTR is a nonperforming asset.[91] But was it ever an asset at all? This is far from certain. After long experience of working with the tribunal, the court expert André Guichaoua wrote, "Having in a way managed to unite all Rwandese sensibilities against itself the ICTR has finally lost even the support of the democratic elements in Rwanda which were attached to its existence, thus freeing the way for the extremists."[92] Western concepts of justice can be extremely foreign to an African culture, especially one that has just been so thoroughly traumatized by such a violent event as the genocide. Unintended paradoxes abound: for example, the survivors' associations complained that women infected by HIV during the rape sessions of the genocide had not received any form of medical help, while the accused in Arusha had benefited from full medical care. In many ways Arusha is seen as providing creature comforts for criminals by people who live on less than $1 a day, and very few of them *really care* about that *Muzungu* justice. For the RPF regime this is not a bad deal: fast, expeditious justice would have weakened its capacity not only to play on the guilt feelings of the foreigners but to keep the Damocles' sword of collective guilt hanging over the heads of the Hutu.

In the conclusion of my book on the genocide I wrote:

The immensity of the crime cannot be dealt with through moderate versions of European criminal law made for radically different cases.... Only the death of the real perpetrators will have sufficient symbolic weight to counterbalance the legacy of suffering and hatred *which will lead to further killings if the abscess is not lanced* [emphasis in the original].... This is the only ritual through which the killers can be cleansed of their guilt and the survivors brought back to the community of the living.... If justice does not come, then death will return—and will duly be covered by an eager media for the benefit of a conventionally horrified public opinion which will finance another round of humanitarian aid.[3]

I am not trying to give myself the benefit of prescience, but after all, this is pretty much the way things have gone.

International media coverage of the conflict years in central Africa varied enormously. It was intense in the wake of the genocide, as there was questioning about what had just happened. It receded considerably during 1995 (the only stories were about the refugee camps, a rather dull topic for non-specialists), only to flare up wildly during the 1996–1997 "Mobutu war," which was rightly seen as the ultimate consequence of the cold war in Africa.[94] The secrecy, the deception, the cleverness of RPF media manipulation,[95] the fact that for the first time the combatants were clearly media-conscious, the lingering effects of the genocide—all these factors helped make the conflict a major "media event."[96] Interest dropped as soon as the new government was installed in Kinshasa and tended to limit itself to specialized publications on Africa. There was a brief flare-up in August 1998, when the rebels attempted to take the capital by storm and failed, and then the media coverage sank to fourth-page status for the next three years, with brief surges of interest at the time of the Lusaka conference in 1999 and later of the Sun City Power-Sharing Agreement, although its protracted character did much to dilute media interest. The net result was that the most murderous conflict since World War II remained seen (if at all) through the prism of the Rwandese genocide.

This variable treatment of the events is more a reflection of the priorities and interests of world opinion than of the importance of the events themselves. The 800,000 victims of the Rwandese genocide were news because they threw the developed world back to the memories of some of the ugliest pages of its own recent past. The nearly four million victims of the "Congolese" conflict were not really news because they belonged (together with Angola, Uganda, Ethiopia, Somalia, the Sudan, Burundi, Liberia, and Sierra Leone) to the abominable and hardly comprehensible world of African civil wars.[97] That particular war was simply a bit bigger than the others, but it did not mean anything more. Apart from linking it to the Rwandese genocide, the only twist that would catch readers' attention was the dark and sinister allusions to Congo's mineral wealth, which were often used as a kind of catch-all explanatory device.

This poverty of media coverage throws us back on a major fact: everything that happened in central Africa had to be measured by its relationship to the genocide phenomenon because this was the way the outside world could understand it. It was also definitely the way the Rwandese government wanted it to be seen for maximum media effect. The Congolese, who of course saw it differently, had to fight a permanent uphill battle to remind the media that it was not *they* who had killed 800,000 Tutsi in 1994, and that they had to pay the price for that abomination was fundamentally unfair.[98] Any discussion of Rwandese violence in the Congo was immediately countered by reminders of the horrors of the genocide (and of the fact that the West had done nothing about it) in order to block any objective examination of the situation. But by late 2000 the Rwandese claim to be in the Congo *purely* to fight the evil *Interahamwe* had begun to wear thin. The end of the Clinton administration, whose guilt largely allowed the success of RPF media tactics, also put an end to that simplified view of the war. Later, as the war receded into confused postconflict civil violence, coverage practically disappeared. From that point of view Darfur, which is a perfect example of the fact that nothing seems to have been learned, had a disastrous media effect on coverage of the Congo. While specialized NGOs such as the International Rescue Committee still noted that in late 2005 (i.e., one year before the Congolese elections) over thirty thousand people died every month of war-related causes, media coverage of the Congo practically *disappeared*. During 2005 1,600 articles were published on the Darfur crisis; only 300 were published on the DRC.[99] Which means that media coverage of the Darfur crisis was over five times that of the Congo, though the Congo situation killed over three times as many people as Darfur. Some corpses are more media-sexy than others, not in the absolute but within a certain time frame. After thirty-seven years of studying Africa, I remember the sexy emergencies: Ethiopia in 1985–1986, which was the mother of all emergencies[100] and set the ground rules for all those that followed; Somalia in 1992; Rwanda in 1994; Zaire in 1994–1995; and Darfur since 2004. And then the unsexy ones: the Ugandan civil war (1981–1986), southern Sudan from day one in 1983 to the present, the whole 1998–2003 "Congolese" continental war, and Somalia after 1995.

Intellectually the hegemonic position of the Rwandese genocide as a global frame of explanation was all the more tragic because it was almost impossible to achieve a reasonable modicum of objectivity on the topic. I have often asked myself why it was that there could be so many white Hutu and white Tutsi, so eager to prove the virtue of their adopted camp and the evil of the opposite one. The reasons are quite complex and mostly anterior to the genocide, although the genocide was to bring them to a boiling frenzy.

Prior to 1990, practically all those interested in the Great Lakes[101] were pro-Hutu, with the lone exception of Jean-Pierre Chrétien. There were several reasons for this:

- The Hutu were perceived as the "little guys," victims of the aristocratic Tutsi oppression for centuries. They had courageously freed themselves through the 1959 "revolution," whose ambiguities were usually glossed over.

- For the Western camp in the cold war, the Hutu were the allies who had fought against the Tutsi "Red aristocrats" linked with Beijing.[102]

- After the 1960s the Tutsi also turned to a pro-West diplomatic stance, thereby losing any previous claim to the sympathy of the "socialist" camp.

- Hutu-led Rwanda was virtuous (the 1959–1963 massacres were glossed over), whereas Tutsi-led Burundi was evil (the 1972 "selective genocide" was remembered by some, and the corruption and authoritarianism known by many).

- The Catholic Church, which likes to always be right ("infallibility" dies hard), tried to have public opinion forget its half-century of pro-Tutsi prejudice in line with the colonial oppression to regain an ideological virginity by supporting the allegedly "anticolonial" Hutu movement.

With Jean-Pierre Chrétien holding out as the lone expression of sympathy for the Tutsi, the lines of ideological battle were sharply drawn.[103] The polemics would have remained buried within the pages of scientific publications if the genocide in Rwanda had not suddenly propelled its actors (all of them remarkably competent academics, even if at times savagely opposed to each other) to the forefront of the world's media. Apart from one or two cases, Rwanda and Burundi had largely remained a French-speaking academic preserve.[104] But as soon as the area of "expertise" widened the new "experts"[105] joined with gusto the ethnic battle lines. Given the horror of the genocide, almost all of the newcomers were pro-Tutsi.[106] The pro-Hutu "old guard" either remained limited to the Christian Democratic circles close to the Catholic Church[107] or else recruited new marginal adepts with exotic ideological axes to grind.[108] Later, the old pro-Hutu academics mellowed out into much more balanced positions. Given what I mentioned earlier about the importance of image building for diplomacy, these Western ideological quarrels were of the utmost importance for the contenders in the war. Foreign academics, journalists, and NGOs were either "friends" or "enemies." They themselves clung desperately to the idea of their own "objectivity" in order to better support what they saw as the "right" position.[109] But finding the "right" and "objective" position was not always so easy. Rather than point at the partisanship of some of my colleagues (a process that would make my future social life rather unpleasant), I will use my own case as an example of the difficulty of attaining objectivity and academic detachment. And of the consequences of failing to do so.

Take two precise points: in my book *The Rwanda Crisis: History of a Genocide* I offered certain interpretations of the story of Fred Rwigyema's death and the problem of the so-called Gersony Report.[110] Fred Rwigyema, the first commander of the RPF, was killed on the second day of the attack on Rwanda. In my previous work I mentioned the fact that a French diplomat in Kampala had told me the story of his being murdered by Peter Banyingana, only to immediately discount this fact as unlikely. Nevertheless I established later from incontrovertible evidence (including an interview with an eyewitness to the killing) that this story was true. Why did I discount it at first? For two reasons: my sympathy for the RPF at the time and the fact that the person telling me the story was a French official whom I suspected of feeding me a slanted line. Pretty much the same goes for the Gersony Report story: although I met people who told me about its contents I decided that "it did not exist."[111] There again, the reason for "selecting facts" was my sympathy for the RPF and my refusal at the time to believe that it could be cold-bloodedly killing people. This of course gained me the status of "friend of the RPF," something of a mixed blessing in academic and political terms.[112] When I came to realize that the RPF was not the White Knight I had expected it to be and when I talked about its violations of human rights, there were no reactions, and Kigali concentrated instead on the evil intent of the journalist Stephen Smith.[113] Reactions started to come when I published a second edition of *The Rwanda Crisis* with an additional chapter called "Living in a Broken World," which attempted to describe life in postgenocide Rwanda and which contained a critical assessment of the first two years of the RPF government.[114] But the reactions were muted and there seemed still to be a hope that I would come back to a "better position."[115] That position slipped further away in 1997, after a confidential report written for UNHCR[116] was put by mistake on that organization's website. The blast came from the boss of the Rwandan Office of Information, Maj. Wilson Rutayisire.[117] It would be tedious to review here the various points used in this clumsy character assassination, but suffice it to say that to call this text "a eulogy for genocide" requires a rather creative stretch of the imagination. The final break came in 2000, after I had collaborated with the African Union in the publication of its report on the Rwandese genocide.[118] A communiqué from Kigali accused me of "having revised [my] book and [my] points of view on the genocide . .

. to reinforce [my] newly acquired revisionist ideology and [my] position of solidarity with the authors of the genocide." This is typical of the relentless Manichaean tone surrounding the Rwandese genocide and, by extension, the Congo war. In such a context any examination of the RPF's human rights violations is described as "revisionist ideology" and seen as support for the genocide.[119] This line of argumentation was used liberally, not only against me, but against anybody who constituted a target for the RPF at any given moment. The advocacy NGO International Crisis Group was thus denounced publicly[120] and some of its employees accused of being secret agents of the French government. This relentless pressure was clumsily mirrored by the (much less efficient) work of the pro-Hutu negationists trying to deny that the genocide had ever occurred.[121] Swamped by this frantic struggle for the moral high ground,[122] outsiders were seized by a kind of moral vertigo, which led to the growth of the "double genocide" theory. Some tenants of the "double genocide" theory were perfectly aware of what they were doing: "There has been in Rwanda a double genocide: the one against the Tutsi committed after 6 April 1994, which has caused 500,000 victims, and the one against the Hutu since October 1990 . . . whose victims amount to around one million."[123] This emanated from the Vatican's highest authorities,[124] trying to show that there were twice as many Hutu killed as there were Tutsi. In addition it gave October 1990 (i.e., the beginning of the Rwandese civil war) as the starting point of an alleged genocide against the Hutu, none of which was a historically tenable position. But the mention in the same article of the arrest of Monsignor Misago, saying that "this is part of a strategy by the Rwandese government to deny the pacifying role the Church has had in Rwandese history, both in the past and today," shows what lay behind this distortion of history: the recurrent defense of the Church as an institution. For many other weary bystanders, the "double genocide" theory (which I find absolutely unacceptable for reasons ranging from historical evidence to intellectual coherence) was just a convenient shelter in a situation of moral overkill.

Interestingly, while the passion slowly died out in the rest of the world, it remained quite intense in France, where the charges proffered by Judge Bruguière against President Kagame, whom he accused of having shot down Habyarimana's aircraft, have kept the wounds (relatively) open.[125] Since the end of the war no fewer than fourteen "political" books on the Rwandese genocide have been published in France, ranging from anguished soul searching[126] to ideologically motivated distortions-cum–personal attacks.[127]

The tone is polemical, violent, and *ad hominem*, very different from the efforts at ideological evaluation produced in the English-speaking world.[128]

Why so much misguided passion? And especially by academics who could have been expected to be more objective on such a foreign topic? I am tentatively tempted to identify three different lines of causality. The first one is touched upon in a book on the Kennedy years reviewed by Gary Wills, who stresses what he calls "abusive simplification":[129] "[Hersh] does not see how specific incidents fit into larger patterns or respond to competing pressures. He personalizes situations as if each actor he studies has complete control of the situation he is in. Whole structures disappear while his villains act in a vacuum." There is a tendency of the human mind to strive for coherence. Many writers routinely warn about "complexity" and "contradictions" and then immediately proceed to re-create a coherence that contradicts the wise warnings they have just uttered. And the situation in the Great Lakes is so horribly complex, so contradictory that one does not have to be American to fall victim to the syndrome of desperately wanting to find "good guys" and "bad guys" who could restore meaning and clarity to such moral gloom.

A second line of thought has to do with why people choose a particular side rather than another. Timothy Garton Ash gives us a useful tip on how to find the logic of what Jean-Paul Sartre used to call *engagement:*

Political perception, like treason, is a matter of date. If you want to judge anything written by a foreigner about a country, you need to know when the writer first went there. Was it in the bad old days? Or perhaps for him they were the good old days? Was it before the revolution, war, coup, occupation, liberation or whatever the local caesura is? Of course the writer's own previous background and current politics are important too. But so often the first encounter is formative. Emotionally and implicitly, if not intellectually and explicitly, it remains the standard by which all subsequent developments are judged.[130]

This does apply to me. Getting to know the Tutsi exiles in Uganda during 1986–1989 was my "formative experience," later reinforced by visiting the RPF front in Byumba in June 1992. My friend Lieve Joris, a person of impeccable honesty, admitted that at first she did not like the Tutsi "because I first came to the Kivus in 1998." Later, when she was writing *L'heure des rebelles,*[131] which can loosely be described as the biography of a Muyamulenge RCD commander, a new empathy emerged. I could easily extend that chronological explanation to several of my colleagues.

Finally comes the genocide phenomenon itself. Citizens of postmodern times cannot accept the radical heterogeneity of their world. Phenomena have to fit within the parameters of a "filtered" experience, preferably Western. The result is a constant comparison with Germany and the genocide of the Jews, which is why what happened in the Congo is often literally "not seen" because it does not fit such a format. The view of many observers (and this includes seasoned diplomats, politicians, and NGO activists) is limited as to whether or not an element of the situation can be linked to pro- or antigenocide formations, even fantasized ones, meaning "Nazi" or "anti-Nazi." Since the word *Nazi* has acquired in modern times the moral equivalence of the Devil in medieval parlance, it acts as a kind of intellectual anaesthesia in any attempt at analyzing the specifically complex present rather than reaching for a parallel with a more familiar past.

To conclude this last part, and perhaps to sum up the chapter thus far, I would like to comment briefly on what could be called the "feel-good factor." It is a factor common to diplomacy, to humanitarianism, to the need to impose a legal order upon chaos, and to what I called "the struggle for the moral high ground." It is the need to make the world pleasant, or at least understandable. We wish for things that are good to hear. We wish to restore our surroundings to some kind of predictability. We wish to believe that we are good upright human beings, doing the right thing and (hopefully) better than the brutes out there doing those other things. Most of the social, political, judicial, intellectual, and humanitarian devices used in dealing with the "Congolese" conflict from the outside have tended toward that smoothing out of the world. The whole thing was too awful; better to not really get into it.

I do not mean that we did not care about the populations involved. But I contend that the factor that was predominant in the way we dealt with them was our own peace of mind. Thus the most vicious ad hominem attacks on colleagues, researchers, and assorted writers are perhaps motivated less by a desire to crush the adversary than by a preoccupation with keeping or regaining our own internal balance. The violence of what has happened in eastern and central Africa has left few of those who looked at it from up close completely intact.

An attempt at a philosophical conclusion

Having reached this point, what can I say about the consequences of the central African situation as the clouds of war have largely melted away but left looming masses of further uncertainties behind them?

The "Congolese" conflict has, in many ways, been the last gasp of the dying order of the cold war. Communism was no longer part of the cognitive map, and democracy, up to then an empty word on the continent, had begun a life of its own since the fall of the Berlin Wall. Along with the removal of the apartheid regime in South Africa, it had created a new readiness to challenge the injustices of the past, real or imagined, but along fault lines the international white establishment was unfamiliar with, especially because democracy in Africa meant taking everything back to the drawing board: regimes, tribes, nations, borders, economic networks, the states themselves. The 1993 failure at establishing a democratic regime after free and fair elections in Burundi was a warning shot. Without communism and away from colonialism, African problems would now have to be taken seriously, for themselves and in themselves. And African problems were enormous.

This is why later efforts at "bringing things back to normal" cannot be taken seriously. Things were not normal in the first place. By 1996 the Zairian core of the continent had become a hologram flickering on the brink of its own extinction. The United States was fed up with its old accomplice of so many years and dreamed of nothing better than to see him go and be replaced by—who knows, a "democracy" perhaps. But how? Did anybody in Washington really *see* the reality of Zaire in 1996, apart from a few old Africa hands who were often dismissed as doomsayers? As for Rwanda, Burundi, and the two Kivus, the ghosts of genocide, past or future, real or fantasized, were all conveniently attributed to an evil and conveniently overthrown regime. "Democracy" would take root there too. How? The answer remained fuzzy, and asking the question too forcefully brought about suspicions of sympathies for the *génocidaire* regime. General Kagame was an African Adenauer who would commit the tropical Nazis to oblivion. Uganda, which had barely recovered from its own civil wars, was seen as the new bulwark of a specifically African form of quasi-democratic government; its connection with Rwanda was perceived as benevolent and its own internal contradictions were attributed to negligible holdovers from an obscure "tribal" past. Sudan's civil war was systematically blamed on the new radical Muslim regime that had taken power in 1989, conveniently forgetting that Sadiq al-Mahdi's "democracy" had fueled it and that it had been started in the early 1980s by the destructive policies of that great friend of the West, President Jaafar al-Nimeiry. Further south, Angola had been involved in a titanic struggle between good and evil. But since the collapse of the Soviet Union, the good ones had become evil and vice versa. After the cold war logic did not apply any more; a new oil-based economic logic now came into play. But the real sociological and cultural nature of the two well-funded entities that wanted ultimate triumph even at the cost of their nation's survival was never seriously looked into.

But once we have surrounded Zaire with such a ring of pain and uncertainty, does it all add up to some coherent whole, to some kind of a geopolitical interlocking of conflicts? Not really. Many Africans have called the conflict that was about to begin over the Congo Basin "our first World War." It is not an altogether false comparison because of the automatic state loyalties linking regimes. But this multiple interlocking nature hides a basic difference: the treaty-bound rivalries of competing European imperialisms around the Balkans before 1914 were different because popular loyalties, everywhere, went centrally to the states. Not so here. Contrary to Europe in 1914, loyalties did not go to the states as such but were divided among myriad cellular identities, among which citizenship in the formal sense was only one.

Nevertheless some lines are now beginning to take shape. First of all, if we start with preconflict situations, one thing is certain: the African states that became involved were not nations. All were at varying degrees of integration, from fairly homogenized (Zambia) to split in two (the Sudan, Angola) by way of low-intensity rivalries (Central African Republic) capable of suddenly bursting into flames if properly fanned for external reasons (Congo-Brazzaville). But no state was *internally* safe. Any form of outside subversion could always find internal helpers for several different and cumulative reasons:

1. Boundaries were arbitrary and tribal identities crossed them. Though not overly preoccupying in some cases (the border between the Central African Republic and Congo-Brazzaville, for example), it could be a major cause of conflict, such as when considering "persons of uncertain identity" in eastern Zaire. Everybody politely acknowledged the 1963 OAU Charter principle on the intangibility of borders inherited from colonization. But now that communism was dead and the Western enforcers were not really willing to stand for African abstractions anymore, everybody violated it in practice.

2. These states were universally weak because they lacked both legitimacy and money. Legitimacy was the biggest problem because even those states that did or could have money, such as the mining states, were also weak. Loyalty to the state is not an internalized feeling in today's Africa. Which does not mean that nationalism is unknown, but that nationalism is essentially reactive. In a difficult economic environment the "hated foreigner" is simply the uninvited guest at somebody's poorly served table. Internally states are seen as cows to be

milked. But because there is little milk and the cow can go dry at any time, it would perhaps be better to say that the state is a cow to be *bled* quickly before it slips into somebody else's hands. The state is an asset for the group in power, but that asset is fragile, there are no commonly accepted rules for future devolution of power, and things have to be grabbed while they last. The notion of a common good to which everybody contributes and which deserves respect for that reason is very dim. The state is always *somebody's* state, never *the State* in the legal abstract form beloved of Western constitutional law. It is the Museveni dictatorship for the Acholi, the Arab state for the southern Sudanese, the *mestiço* state for UNITA, or the Tutsi state for the Hutu. When tribes are not the main problem, pseudo-tribes or other groupings will do. So much for tribalism as a "resurgence of the past"; it is in fact more of a raw material for the transformations of the present.

3. The reason the political struggles were not primarily state struggles (although the states did play enormous roles in them) is due to the combination of point 1 and point 2. The state is weak, whereas identities are strong but multiple and overlapping. And behind all these we increasingly find *individuals*. Individualism has grown exponentially in postcolonial Africa, and individuals did play a tremendous role in the conflicts. But not independently. Individuals belong to a state. They also belong to tribes, religious groups, regions, age groups, economic networks, without any monocausality. So powerful individuals will try to use the state for the group's benefit (and also for their own personal benefit), and groups perceived rightly or wrongly as powerful will try to instrumentalize one another and together will try to instrumentalize the state. The notion of an "objective" state above the melee is a touching Western ideological construct. Hence the later difficulties of diplomats, who, by definition, are used to dealing with relatively autonomous states and not with weak but voracious multifaceted entities.

4. Why do we have such a process? Because of economics. The poverty is so massive, so grinding, that anybody with a minimum of perception can be relied upon to activate his or her identity segments into some kind of a militant pseudo-globality if it brings economic rewards. This is why it is always easier to recruit militias in towns and in cities than in the countryside: city people *know* they are poor because they have the means (radios, TVs, cinemas, newspapers) and the references (rich people, foreigners) that tell them about their poverty. Deep in the bush poverty can still be experienced as "traditionalism," at least for some of the people and for some of the time, for lack of a vantage point. The international community is often in the position of the well-meaning charitable passerby offering a sandwich or a few coins to aggressive slum dwellers violently demanding an end to their misery. To its horror the charitable international community will discover that this can very well mean killing most of the people they see as responsible for their own dire situation. The

international community usually does not know how to react to such crude prejudices and tries to keep the situation in a polite limbo, where the myth of a possible future consensus can be entertained. The economic distress and instinctive exclusion of the competitors are often the unspoken background of the outwardly polite "peace negotiations." This is often explained off the record as "ethnic hatred," as if ethnicity were a structurally given fact, like a geological structure, and not the product of dynamic historical interaction.

5. Finally, the very substance of the new African international politics that unfolded with the war freely remained radically different from politics in the West, even if the same "democratic" vocabulary has now been widely put in use. Power is both more tangible and more magical than what Western countries expect it to be. Here too their own past could be a guide. But their own past has been forgotten in two steps, the first one in 1945, the second one in 1989. OECD countries often seem to act *as if they had always lived under a legal-bureaucratic system*, a rather amnesic attitude if one still remembers the first half of the twentieth century. In Africa charismatic leadership is the rule, not the exception. The magic component of that charisma is never far from the surface. And the routinization of charisma is difficult due to a lack of both funds and internalized shared values. As for the legal-bureaucratic governments that rich donor countries talk about, it is a possible future ideal, but in the present it is largely an abstraction. Nevertheless, actions will often be undertaken "as if" it were a reality.

This leaves us with an essential question: Could it all happen again? One of the unintended consequences of the war has been the mushroom-like proliferation of a conflict-oriented cottage industry. Hundreds of NGOs, think tanks, and "conflict resolution centers" have sprung up all over, both in Africa and in the developed world. Staffed by hordes of eager young graduates under the guidance of seasoned para-academic entrepreneurs, they churn out enormous amounts of rather colorless and uncontroversial material which seems mostly designed to ensure future funding from that revered target audience of the business, the "donors."[132] The business is doing fairly well, but because the number of conflicts in Africa over the past ten years has steadily decreased, the sector's activity is now increasingly geared toward more abstract categories, such as "good governance," "security reform," "conflict prevention" (rather than just plain old "resolution"), or even, more ambitiously, "genocide prevention." HIV, gender-based politics, and child soldiers are frequently mined sidelines. What is the impact of that industry on the reality of African conflicts? Not huge, it seems. At the level of actual existing conflicts it is largely an ammunition provider. The conflict actors bombard each other with reports, variably described as "authoritative," "controversial," or (more rarely, since the war of words is muted) "questionable." The UN and various governments have entered this paper game, but their documents are only marginally more influential than those of the NGOs. As for conflict prevention, this seems a little bit like planning for the prophylaxis of a disease you do not know how to cure.

But once this paper fog is seen for what it is, as more of an ideological smokescreen than a real determining factor, there are a number of *real* parameters that have changed if we compare today's situation with that of fifteen years ago:

- First of all, there are some stirrings of economic development in Africa. These should not be exaggerated, since the six "economic dynamos" of the continent (i.e., those with 5 percent or more of yearly economic growth) are *all* mining economies, with the exception of Mozambique.[133] And then the rate of growth has of course to be seen as calculated in relation to an often incredibly low baseline. But this is a small change, and hopefully the beginning of a bigger one.[134]

- The end of the cold war has deprived dictatorships of the excuse of being allies of the "Free World" in order to secure their regimes against the danger of democratization. There are now worrying signs that the "war on terror" so beloved of Washington's strategists is beginning to play the same role.[135]

- The general political *Zeitgeist* has changed to a point where naked violence in the exercise of power *à la* Idi Amin is not permissible today. It has to be somewhat hidden from view, and even "protected" regimes like Equatorial Guinea or Chad have to help their protectors through concerted efforts at believable hypocrisy. But even if we agree with Oscar Wilde that hypocrisy is the homage rendered by vice to virtue, it remains better than the naked displays of violence that were tolerated in the 1970s and 1980s. Hypocrisy puts its purveyor in the ambiguous position of having to permanently justify himself, which is better than being able to shamelessly flaunt his violence.

- African economies are getting more internationalized and therefore more conscious of their overseas link.[136] This is of course counterbalanced by the growth of a Chinese influence which is not particularly interested in human rights and which can be used as a shield against the West.[137]

Are these finally relatively small changes sufficient to prevent a recurrence of the monstrous conflict that tore up one-third of the continent between 1996 and nearly now? The answer is probably not. Does it mean that such a violent conflict could happen again? Here again, the answer is probably not. The death (and rebirth) of Zaire is a unique case. No other country in Africa today, probably not even Nigeria or South Africa,[138] has the potential of creating such a continentwide upheaval. Existing conflicts, such as in the Sudan, Chad, and Somalia, are structurally circumscribed. This does not make them less tragic, but their potential for contamination is much more limited.

It is in this way that "Africa's First World War" will probably remain a unique phenomenon, but one that was, here again like the Thirty Years' War in Europe, a *transforming moment* in the history of the continent. Albeit in ways that are quite far from the international community-approved ways, Africa has now entered the modern age. Following its own rocky road.

APPENDIX I

SETH SENDASHONGA'S MURDER

The first attempt on Seth Sendashonga's life (1951–1998) took place in February 1996, in Nairobi, where he had been living in political exile after being fired from his position as Minister of the Interior in the National Unity Cabinet of Rwanda on 29 August 1995 (see Chapter 1). Seth was called at home by a fellow Rwandese exile who offered to give him documents proving that there had been an attempted mutiny within the RPA. He went to the appointment only to fall in an ambush where two men repeatedly shot at him with pistols. Two bullets, which did not endanger his life, hit him but his young nephew who had gone with him was seriously wounded. Before falling unconscious he had recognized one of his would-be killers as one of his former bodyguards when he had been a minister. The other gunman was Francis Mugabo, a staff member of the Rwandese Embassy in Kenya who was caught with the proverbial smoking gun in the toilet of a service station where he was trying to dispose of the pistol used in the attack. The Kenya government asked Rwanda to lift Mr. Mugabo's diplomatic immunity, which Kigali refused. This led to a major row between the two countries, resulting in the closure of the Rwandese Embassy in Nairobi and a break in diplomatic relations. When the attempt on Seth's life had been carried out he was just about to fly to Brussels to launch his new opposition movement, the Forces de Résistance pour la Démocratie (FRD) with his old friend and colleague, former Prime Minister Faustin Twagiramungu. He carried out his plans after recovering from his wounds and FRD was officially launched in April 1997. A sizable portion of the party's political platform was given to a detailed and unsparing analysis of the Rwandese genocide. "You cannot imagine the difficulty I had to convince my friends to include that analysis in the document," he later told me when I visited him in Nairobi. When I remarked that this part of his party's platform was

365

on the contrary a very valuable contribution because it was an honest and realistic assessment of the genocide from a mostly Hutu political group he answered me with a sigh:

I know; and this is why I wanted it to be included. But many people told me "This is just a way of giving aid and comfort to the enemy." Gérard, I am afraid we still have a long way to go before they understand that the enemy are not the Tutsi but the RPF or rather what Kagame has turned it into.

Seth went on with his political activity for another year and the regular FRD communiqués were among the most informative elements to document the increasingly violent drift of Rwandese politics. Seth had called for help for the Rwandese refugees in Zaire in 1996, warning against any gross amalgam along the then often fashionable line of *refugees = génocidaires*. And like everybody else he had watched helplessly as the refugees were butchered or starved and walked to death through the jungle. By late 1997, as the situation was decomposing further in the "new" Congo, he was again a frustrated witness as the former génocidaire leadership managed to coerce or seduce disenfranchised young Hutu peasants into the growing ranks of ALIR. He knew all of them, the Nkundiye, the Mpiranya, the Kibiligi, the Rwabukwisi, and, as he said: "They are just old vampires trying to get new blood. Their only political program is to kill Tutsi." He was also aware of Kagame's remark about the Hutus at the end of January 1998: "We don't have to kill them all. It is enough to beat them hard enough so that they don't bite, so that all the dogs remain sitting." It had been reported to him by some of his former RPF Tutsi associates who wanted to keep him informed. They felt that he would be needed at some point, when the violent solutions would have finally failed. This is what made Seth a dangerous man because he embodied a recourse, an alternative to the twin parallel logics of madness that were developing and feeding each other in Rwanda. But Seth was fed up with always playing the good guy and of always finishing last.

"I have got to make my move," he told me in early 1998 during one of our meetings in Nairobi. "Everybody uses a gun as a way of sitting at the negotiation table one day. If I always refuse to use guns, I'll be marginalized when the time comes. But then should I do it? There has been so much blood spilt and so few results to show for it. Should I take the responsibility to add to that?"

About six hundred men and around forty officers of the ex-FAR had gathered around him. They were ready to follow him into battle because they could bear neither the RPF regime in Kigali nor its ALIR challengers, both representing in their eyes opposite but symmetrical forms of violent racism. Tanzania had agreed to host his training camps but he wanted support from what he felt to be the only decisive and progressive force in the region, that is, the Museveni regime in Uganda. He asked for my help in talking to Kampala and I arranged the necessary contacts. On Sunday, 3 May 1998, he met in Nairobi with Salim Saleh, President Museveni's brother. Things were far from rosy between Kampala and Kigali, and Salim was quite open to the idea of helping a new moderate force enter the game. A few days later Seth met Eva Rodgers from the U.S. State Department and briefed her on his intentions. The reply was noncommittal but not hostile. It is probably then that some people in Kigali decided that he had crossed the danger line.

On Saturday 16 May at 5:00 p.m., as he was being driven home along Nairobi's Forest Road in his wife's UN car, Seth was shot, together with his driver Jean-Bosco Nkurubukeye, by two unknown assailants firing AK-47s. Both victims were dead within minutes. The subsequent Kenyan police inquiry was a sad joke. Three men were arrested: David Kiwanuka, Charles Muhaji, and Christopher Lubanga. The first was supposed to be a Rwandese, in spite of his typically Ugandan/Muganda name while the two others were indeed Ugandans. All three had been arrested after being denounced to the police by a Kenyan cab driver called Ali Abdul Nasser who said they had contacted him to hire him as a paid killer because Sendashonga had stolen $54m from Kiwanuka's father. The theft story, obviously fed by rather untalented Kigali security operatives, gained a bit of flesh in the next few days when the Nairobi police organized a ridiculous press conference (22 May 1998) during which Kiwanuka said that Seth, then Interior Minister of the Rwandese government, had stolen the money in cahoots with his father who had been at the time Kigali's Director of Immigration Services and that he had later killed him to defraud him of his share of the loot. The problem was that the man in question, called Charles Butera, surfaced a few days later to say that not only was he quite alive but that he had no son called Kiwanuka, that he had only known Sendashonga superficially and that nobody, either him or the late minister, had ever stolen $54m, an absurdly high amount in 1994 Rwanda.[1] Everybody in Nairobi knew that Seth was basically surviving on his wife's UN salary. The theft-cum-murder story died down but the three accused remained in jail. The case dragged on and on. In December 2000 during a hearing Seth's widow, Cyriaque Nikuze, declared to the court that the Kigali government was guilty of her late husband's murder and she added two supplementary motives for his killing: he was due shortly to testify before both the International Criminal Tribunal for Rwanda and the French Parliamentarian Commission of Inquiry. In both cases, she said, the Rwandese government feared what he could reveal. She named a Rwandese Embassy official called Alphonse Mbayire as the organizer of the assassination. Mbayire, a high-ranking Secret Service operator who often used the aliases "Alphonse Mbabane" and "Ernest Neretse," was Rwanda's acting ambassador at the time of the assassination. Prosecution witness John Kathae, a police officer with the Kenyan Criminal Investigation Department (CID), testified under cross-questioning that he had not found the accused's story credible and that he felt that the murder had political motivations. He added that the pistol proffered in court was not the murder weapon. He also revealed that a Rwandese Embassy diplomat, Alphonse Mbayire had had frequent contacts in the past with the accused Kiwanuka, but that when he had wanted to question Mbayire for the inquiry, he had been forbidden to do so.[2] Alphonse Mbayire was recalled by his government in January 2001, shortly before the Sendashonga murder case was supposed to come up again for a new hearing.[3] He returned to Rwanda only to be shot dead by two unidentified gunmen in a Kigali bar on 7 February 2001. The trial re-started in Nairobi five days later and the defence lawyers argued that the real killers were not in court. On 31 May 2001, more than three years after the murder, the three accused men were finally released after the court had decided that "the State has failed to prove beyond reasonable doubt that the accused had committed the offence." Justice Msagha Mbogoli added that in the court's opinion the murder was political and that it was linked with the deceased "having fallen out with the government of Rwanda."[4]

NOTES

Introduction

1.   Robert Klitgaard, *Tropical Gangsters: One Man's Experience with Development and Decadence in Deepest Africa* (London: Basic Books, 1990).The book is centered on Equatorial Guinea, perhaps the worst-case African scenario, and the tone is harsh. But the contents are painfully familiar for people intimately plunged into the real Africa.
2.   The father of slave emancipation during the 1848 revolution, he is buried in the Pantheon in Paris.
3.   P. Chabal and J.P. Daloz, *Africa Works: Disorder as Political Instrument* (Oxford: James Currey, 1999).
4.   This is the title of a key World Bank document published in 2000.

Chapter 1

1.   Since I started writing this book in 1998, a huge body of work on postgenocide Rwanda has been published. For a good overview, see Phil Clark and Zachary Kaufman, eds., *After Genocide: Transitional Justice, Post-Conflict Reconstruction and Reconciliation in Rwanda and Beyond* (London: Hurst, 2008).
2.   For this episode of the conflict, see Gérard Prunier, *The Rwanda Crisis (1959–1994): History of a Genocide* (London: Hurst, 1995), chapter 8; Olivier Lanotte, "L'Opération Turquoise au Rwanda," Ph.D. diss., Catholic University of Louvain, 1996.
3.   Mahmood Mamdani, "Rwanda in a Dilemma," *New Vision,* September 6, 1995.
4.   Foreign terms can be found in the glossary.
5.   *Lettre du CLADHO,* no. 4 (August–September 1995).
6.   Private communication from a relative, Brussels, November 1999.
7.   *Rwanda Rushya,* no. 62 (August 1995).
8.   Private communication, Nairobi, January 1995. Being a member of the single-party MRND was almost a requirement for any businessman in prewar Rwanda, whether he was Tutsi or Hutu.
9.   Private communication, Kigali, February 1995.
10.   Human Rights Watch Africa, *Rwanda: A New Catastrophe?* New York, December 1994.
11.   Private communication, Kigali, February 1995.
12.   For a very honest picture of these tragic complexities by an eyewitness, see

Charles Karemano, *Au-delà des barrières: Dans les méandres du drame rwandais* (Paris: L'Harmattan, 2003).

13. See African Rights, *Rwanda, Killing the Evidence: Murder, Attacks, Arrests and Intimidation of Survivors and Witnesses,* London, 1996.

14. Joseph Matata, "Au Rwanda, des syndicats de délateurs," *Dialogue,* no. 186 (October–November 1995).

15. See Anne Moutot, "Au Rwanda, la diaspora tutsie contre les rescapés," *Libération,* November 28, 1995; Vincent Hugeux, "Les démons du Rwanda," *L'Express,* December 7, 1995.

16. This in no way changes the fact that the vast majority of the victims were Tutsi. But the marginalization of the Hutu victims changed the meaning of the phenomenon.

17. The following section on immediately postgenocide Rwanda is based on my visit to the country in January 1995, my first after the genocide.

18. For a strong indictment of the Catholic Church's behavior during the genocide, see Groupe Golias, *Rwanda: L'honneur perdu de l'Eglise* (Villeurbanne, France: Editions Golias, 1999). For more dispassionate but still damning research, see the work of Timothy Longman, notably "Church Politics and the Genocide in Rwanda," *Journal of Religion in Africa* 31, no. 2 (2001): 163–186.

19. *Lettre d'un groupe d'Abbés à Sa Sainteté le Pape,* Goma, August 2, 1994.

20. See Rev. Roger Bowen [CMS], "Rwanda: Missionary Reflections on a Catastrophe. J. C. Jones Lecture 1995," *Anvil* 13, no. 1 (1996). See also C. Rittner, J. K. Roth, and W. Whitworth, eds., *Genocide in Rwanda: The Complicity of the Churches* (New York: Paragon House, 2004), which constitutes an effort at objectively assessing the role of all the Christian churches in the genocide.

21. See Patrick de Saint-Exupéry, "Loin de Biarritz, le Rwanda," *Le Figaro,* November 8, 1994; author's interviews with several cabinet members, Kigali, January 1995.

22. *Africa Analysis,* September 30, 1994; "Abandoned Rwanda," *Economist,* November 26, 1994.

23. "L'Union Européenne débloque une aide de 440m de francs," *Le Monde,* November 27–28, 1994.

24. Mouvement Démocratique Républicain, *Position du parti MDR sur les grands problèmes actuels du Rwanda,* Kigali, November 6, 1994.

25. See, for example, the criticism of democracy by Privat Rutazibwa, one of the regime's leading ideologues, in *La crise des Grands Lacs et la question tutsi* (Kigali: Editions du CRID, 1999).

26. See "The Black Hole of Rwanda," *Economist,* March 25, 1995; Human Rights Watch Africa, *Rwanda: The Crisis Continues,* New York, April 1995.

27. Afsané Bassir Pour, "Rwanda: Le gouvernement ne souhaite plus la création d'un tribunal international," *Le Monde,* November 1, 1994.

28. Colette Braeckman, "Rwanda: Le temps du révisionnisme," *Esprit,* December 1994.

29. Radio Rwanda as reported by the *BBC Summary of World Broadcasts* (henceforth *BBC/SWB*), December 8, 1994.

30. See "Le débat public entre le Premier Ministre et le Vice Président sur le problème de la sécurité," *Umukororombya,* no. 3 (January 9, 1995).

31. Paul Kagame with Colette Braeckman, "A propos de la sécurité et de la réconciliation au Rwanda," *Le Soir,* April 7, 1995.

32. For an early overview of the tribunal and its problems, see J. F. Dupaquier,

ed., *La Justice internationale face au drame rwandais* (Paris: Karthala, 1996). D. Patry, *Rwanda: Face à face avec un génocide* (Paris: Flammarion, 2006) gives the point of view of a defense lawyer at Arusha, while T. Cruvelier, *Le tribunal des vaincus* (Paris: Calmann-Lévy, 2006) analyzes the later developments of the tribunal's functioning.

33. For an overview of the justice situation, see "La justice rwandaise au banc des accusés," a special issue of *Dialogue,* no. 186 (October/November 1995).

34. "Le Premier Ministre rwandais veut faire juger au moins 30.000 personnes," *Le Monde,* August 4, 1994.

35. *Abakada* is the Kinyarwanda transformation of the French word *cadre.* These were young men recruited by the RPF to be its eyes and ears in the rural areas. Their power was largely unchecked.

36. Radio Rwanda in *BBC/SWB,* March 9, 1995.

37. Personal communication, Paris, May 1995.

38. Radio France Internationale in *BBC/SWB,* July 5, 1995.

39. For a description of the conditions of detention, see Fédération Internationale des Droits de l'Homme, *Conditions mortelles de détention à la prison de Gitarama,* July 6, 1995; "The Black Hole of Rwanda," *Economist,* March 25, 1995.

40. The International Committee of the Red Cross (ICRC) spent $53 million in Rwanda during 1994–1995, that is, 20 percent of its budget for the whole of Africa.

41. To understand the state of underprofessionalization of the Rwandese justice system even before the genocide, one must read F. X. Nsanzuwera, *La magistrature rwandaise dans l'étau du pouvoir exécutif* (Kigali: CLADHO, 1993).

42. Human Rights Watch Africa, *Rwanda: The Crisis Continues.*

43. François Misser, "Searching for the Killers," *New African,* April 1995.

44. "Kenya, base arrière des Hutus rwandais," *La Lettre de l'Océan Indien,* April 1, 1995; "Kenya Harbours Rwanda Killers," *New African,* September 1995.

45. Human Rights Watch Africa, *Rwanda: The Crisis Continues;* Amnesty International, *Concerns and Recommendations for Fair Trials in Rwanda,* London, March 1996.

46. F. X. Nsanzuwera, "Pour l'indépendance de la magistrature rwandaise," *Dialogue,* no. 186 (November 1995). Nsanzuwera, a magistrate well known for his personal integrity under the former regime, had been made procuror general of Kigali by the new government. Faced with the impossibility of discharging his duties and fearing for his security, he chose to go into exile in May 1995.

47. For example, former minister Casimir Bizimungu, himself one of the leading *génocidaires,* said that more Hutu were killed by the Tutsi during the genocide than vice versa and that he was ready to stand in court to testify to this. Radio France Internationale in *BBC/SWB,* January 27, 1995. Some "academics" (Helmut Britzke, Christian Davenport) later tried to give some respectability to this criminal fallacy.

48. For a broader debate on the issue of moral responsibility and contradictory forms of propaganda concerning the genocide and the forms of violence that followed it, see the section in chapter 10 titled "Struggling for the Moral High Ground."

49. There is an abundant literature of varying interest on the political convulsions of Uganda between 1979 and the mid-1990s. Among the most interesting works, one could mention C. P. Dodge and M. Raundalen, eds., *War, Violence and Children in Uganda* (Oslo: Norwegian University Press, 1987); A. B. K. Ka-

sozi, *The Social Origins of Violence in Uganda (1964-1985)* (Montreal: McGill University Press, 1994); R. Gersony, *The Anguish of Northern Uganda* (Kampala: USAID, 1997); Ondoga ori Amaza, *Museveni's Long March* (Kampala: Fountain Publishers, 1998); Sverker Finnström, *Living with Bad Surroundings: War and Existential Uncertainty in Acholiland, Northern Uganda* (Uppsala, Sweden: Uppsala University Press, 2003); Pecos Kutesa's lively *Uganda's Revolution (1979–1986): How I Saw It* (Kampala: Fountain Publishers, 2006). These should be contrasted with the ideologically sanitized version of the same events given by General Kagame in his book of interviews with François Misser, *Vers un nouveau Rwanda? Entretiens avec Paul Kagame* (Brussels: Luc Pire, 1995), chapters 3–5.

50.   During the Ugandan civil war, since Museveni was a Munyankole Muhima, Obote's thugs of the Uganda Peoples Congress (UPC) Youth Wing attacked and killed Rwandese Tutsi refugees in Ankole whom they assimilated to their Bahima cousins.

51.   Here I must offer my apologies to the readers of *The Rwanda Crisis,* where on pp. 94–96 I give a totally false account of Rwigyema's death. My only excuse is that, in a book written in the immediate aftermath of the genocide, I still wanted to believe in the relative innocence of the RPF and therefore accepted the cooked version of the facts it provided me with, in spite of several warnings that I was wrong. For the problem of author's subjectivity in the social sciences, see "Struggling for the Moral High Ground" in chapter 10.

52.   The following account is the result of several interviews in Kampala, Paris, Kigali, and Bujumbura conducted between 1992 and 2000 with former RPF members or members of the RPF support network.

53.   See G. Prunier, *The Rwanda Crisis,* 23–24, for a quick summary. For specialists a much more detailed version can be found in Jan Vansina, *Le Rwanda ancien: Le Royaume Nyiginya* (Paris: Karthala, 2001), chapter 7.

54.   For those familiar with Great Lakes contemporary history, the parallel with Prince Rwagasore in Burundi is very strong.

55.   See the open letter to the Rwandese government written by former RPF member Jean-Pierre Mugabe on http://www.strategicstudies.org (July 1999). Mugabe denounces by name Brig. Gen. Kayumba Nyamwasa, Lt. Col. Jacson Rwahama, and Maj. Steven Balinda for ordering these killings. He accuses them all of belonging to the so-called Gahini mafia, a small group of "Ugandan" refugees bent upon totally controlling the RPF structure. These very serious accusations were repeated to me in a variety of interviews with former RPF supporters, including relatives of the dead boys, during 1996–2000.

56.   UNHCR Situation Report no. 12 for the Kagera region by Mark Prutsalis of Refugees International, May 20, 1994.

57.   Human Rights Watch Africa, *Leave None to Tell the Story,* New York, 1999, particularly 705–712.

58.   See in particular the letter by Eric Gillet quoted in Human Rights Watch Africa, *Leave None to Tell the Story,* 700 note 28. Alan Kuperman, "Provoking Genocide: A Revised History of the Rwanda Patriotic Front," *Journal of Genocide Research* 6, no. 1 (2004): 61–84, goes further when he writes, "The Tutsi rebels expected their challenge to provoke genocidal retaliation but viewed this as an acceptable cost of achieving their goal of attaining power in Rwanda" (79). Whether or not the RPF actually expected a genocide to take place is impossible to know. But its indifference to the fate of the Tutsi civilians once it did

happen is not in doubt. See Romeo Dallaire, *Shake Hands with the Devil* (New York: Carroll & Graf, 2004), especially 358 and 410–411. See also General Dallaires's testimony to the Arusha tribunal, Fondation Hirondelle, Arusha, June 8, 2004.

59. For the story of the Gersony Report as seen from the UNHCR perspective, see Sadako Ogata's memoirs *The Turbulent Decade* (New York: Norton, 2005), 190–194.

60. This treatment of the Gersony Report is based on direct discussions with Robert Gersony himself, whom I met in New York in 1998. Having been personally hoodwinked into disbelieving the very existence of his report (see Prunier, *The Rwanda Crisis,* 323–324), I was particularly interested in discussing the circumstances of his fieldwork.

61. At one point in Butare prefecture Gersony and his team stumbled by mistake upon a detail of pink-uniformed prisoners burying freshly killed bodies. Since the genocide had ended two months before they began to ask questions. The armed escort arrived running and told them to move off. They were told that these were genocide victims. Interview with Robert Gersony, New York, 1998.

62. One close participant-observer of this period later offered an interesting hypothesis for why the RPF killed Tutsi and Hutu indiscriminately in its area of control. According to this theory the rebel movement was not sure of acquiring power and, in case of failure, wanted to partition Rwanda and create a "Tutsi homeland" in the North (Byumba prefecture and Mutara); it conceived of such a zone as a "refugee area" to be populated purely by "old caseload refugees" over which it had complete political control, contrary to the Tutsi of the interior. See James Gasana, *Rwanda: Du Parti-Etat à l'Etat-Garnison* (Paris: L'Harmattan, 2002), 263–264.

63. Interview with Seth Sendashonga, Nairobi, April 1998.

64. Thus Sixbert Musamgamfura, head of the Prime Minister's Security Unit, tried to tell me that things were "basically all right in spite of some problems," although he was better placed than anybody to know that this was not the case. After he had to run away in 1995, he changed his stance and denounced the massacres he had tried to deny. Both Seth Sendashonga and Prime Minister Twagiramungu also lied to me at the time, only to apologize later and explain that they had done so in the hope of helping national unity.

65. Interview with Dr. Théogène Semanyenzi, Nairobi, February 1, 1995. Dr. Semanyenzi and his Tutsi wife themselves narrowly escaped death at the hands of the *Interahamwe* near Cyangugu before being evacuated by French soldiers in August 1994.

66. See Monique Mujawamaliya, *Rapport d'une visite effectuée au Rwanda du 1er au 22 septembre 1994,* mimeo, Montréal, October 1994.

67. Human Rights Watch Africa, *Leave None to Tell the Story,* 713, 714, 719.

68. Interview with Marianne Baziruwiha, Washington, DC, October 1997.

69. A typical feature of the period, experienced by all foreigners who were in Rwanda in 1994–1995, was the travel restrictions enforced by the RPF under a variety of dubious pretexts. When a UN helicopter landed unexpectedly in Gabiro camp and hundreds of civilians rushed to try to talk to the UN personnel, the crowd was beaten back and prevented from making contact. This developed into a major diplomatic incident between the UN and the government. Human Rights Watch Africa, *Leave None to Tell the Story,* 722.

70. Human Rights Watch Africa, *Leave None to Tell the Story,* 721–722; Stephen

Smith, "Enquête sur la terreur Tutsie," *Libération,* February 27, 1996; Nick Gordon, "Return to Hell," *Sunday Express,* April 21, 1996.

71. Seth Sendashonga, Nairobi, May 1997.

72. See chapter 2.

73. See African Rights, *A Waste of Hope: The United Human Rights Field Operation in Rwanda,* London, March 1995.

74. This gentleman was W. R. Urasa, the same person who had answered the UN special rapporteur on Rwanda that the Gersony report "did not exist" when he had had a summary in his hands. See Human Rights Watch Africa, *Leave None to Tell the Story,* 727–731.

75. That is, Tutsi coming back from exile. They were unlikely to denounce RPF killings.

76. UNHCR Archival Fund 19 Sub-Fund 7, Records of the Regional Bureaux/ Great Lakes (henceforth referred to as UNHCR 19/7), *Report of a Mission to Rwanda (23 October to 22 December 1995).*

77. Interview with a former RPF member, Paris, October 1999.

78. Gen. Guy Tousignant, the new UNAMIR commander, had spoken quite sharply to the government after the Gersony report episode.

79. This is what Sendashonga called "le syndrome de la funeste conférence" (the fateful conference syndrome). He had desperately wanted economic aid, only to discover that in the absence of any human rights conditionality the $598 million pledged in Geneva in January 1995 had a perverse effect. The RPF knew that the international community was aware of the killings since the Gersony Report and it took the money as a tacit nod of approval. Seth Sendashonga, Nairobi, May 1997.

80. Parti pour l'Emancipation des Bahutu, the first anticolonial nationalist political party in Rwanda, created just before independence in 1958.

81. General Rusatira alludes here to the fact that many of the former FAR officers and men who joined the RPA were later killed.

82. Quoted in *Le Monde,* January 5, 1996, emphasis mine.

83. For example, in spite of being present in Rwanda at the time I do not know to this day whether the Busanze camp incident of January 7, 1995, in which eleven IDPs were killed by RPA soldiers was an accident or a deliberate killing.

84. Killed by his own bodyguards on March 4, 1995.

85. Kidnapped by "men in uniforms" on May 12, 1995; found dead nine days later.

86. Arrested in April 1995 he "suddenly" died in jail on July 1, 1995, without apparent causes.

87. Which makes his progressive transformation into a "business developmentalist" during 2004–2007 all the more fascinating (see chapter 9).

88. Quoted in Nick Gowing, "Dispatches from Disaster Zones: The Reporting of Humanitarian Emergencies," paper presented at ECHO Conference, London, May 27–28, 1998.

89. The most notorious case was that of President Pasteur Bizimungu, who was removed from power, then arrested and finally condemned to fifteen years in jail on trumped up charges of "forming a militia group which threatened state security." Integrated Regional Information Network (IRIN) Press dispatch, Kigali, June 8, 2004.

90. I have been challenged on this problem of obedience to authority, particularly

in relationship to obeying orders to commit genocide. See Barrie Collins, *Obedience in Rwanda: A Critical Question* (Sheffield, UK: Hallam University, 1998); C. Vidal, "Questions sur le rôle des paysans durant le genocide des Rwandais tutsi," *Cahiers d'Etudes Africaines* 38, nos. 2–4 (1998): 331–346. Collins tends to attribute the genocide to a breakdown of the central authority, a theory that seems definitively disproved by the authoritative account of the genocide written by Alison DesForges in Human Rights Watch Africa, *Leave None to Tell the Story*. Vidal puts forth two rather disconnected arguments: Rwandese children are brought up sweetly, and my position is "essentialist," that is, attributing obedience as a sui generis quality to Rwandese culture. Both points seem irrelevant. First, cultures socialize their young ones into broad patterns; behavior does not constitute a sui generis expression of preexisting essence. Second, Rwandese respect for (legitimate) authority does not stem from any inborn quality but from education. Whether or not this authority is evil is another point, quite distinct from the "sweetness" of childhood manners. I still stand by what I wrote in *The Rwanda Crisis*: that respect for authority is a fundamental trait of Rwandese culture, instilled in children from a very young age and periodically reinforced during maturity by a complex social code. On this, see the remarkable work of the Belgian anthropologist Danielle de Lame, *A Hill among a Thousand: Transformations and Ruptures in Rural Rwanda* (Madison: University of Wisconsin Press, 2005). See also the recent work by Scott Straus, particularly *Intimate Enemy: Images and Voices of the Rwandan Genocide* (New York: Zone Books, 2006).

91. In April 1995, six thousand dead bodies were dug up and reburied in large ceremonies designed to commemorate the anniversary of the genocide.

92. For an overview of this flight, see Prunier, *The Rwanda Crisis,* chapter 8; Kazadi Bob Kabamba, "Une deuxième génération de réfugiés: La fuite des populations Hutu après le génocide d'avril–mai 1994," in A. Guichaoua, ed., *Les crises politiques au Rwanda et au Burundi (1993–1994)* (Villeneuve d'Ascq, France: Université des Sciences, 1995), 349–357. The refugee problem became almost immediately a politically sensitive subject, giving birth to ideologically conflicting reports. The most balanced general assessment can be found in Joël Boutroue, *Missed Opportunities: The Role of the International Community in the Return of the Rwandan Refugees from Eastern Zaire* (Boston: MIT Press, UN-HCR, 1998).

93. UNHCR figures.

94. Florence Aubenas, "La longue marche vers Kigali," *Libération,* August 2, 1994.

95. For a good analysis of the leadership and sociology of the camps, see Johan Pottier, "Relief and Repatriation: Views by Rwandan Refugees and Lessons for Humanitarian Aid Workers," *African Affairs,* no. 95 (1996): 403–429.

96. Jean-Pierre Godding quoted in Dirk De Schrijver, "Les réfugiés rwandais dans la région des Grands Lacs," in S. Marysse and F. Reyntjens, eds., *L'Afrique des Grands Lacs: Annuaire 1996–1997* (Paris: L'Harmattan, 1997), 221–246.

97. For example, in Kibumba camp, it was found that 40 percent of the refugees received less than 2,000 kcals/person, while 13 percent received over 10,000 kcals/person. Joint Evaluation of Emergency Assistance to Rwanda, John Borton et al., *Humanitarian Aid and Effects,* vol. 3 of *International Response to Conflict and Genocide: Lessons from the Rwanda Experience* (Copenhagen, 1996), 96.

98. Raymond Bonner, "Aid Is Taken Hostage in Rwanda Camps," *International*

Herald Tribune, November 1, 1994; Laurent Bijard, "Les tueurs Hutus se portent bien," *Le Nouvel Observateur,* November 3–9, 1994.

99. "Armored vehicles" in French. This was the ironic term used by the refugees to talk about their round, smooth, and windowless plastic shelters.

100. UNHCR field notes, October 1995.

101. See interview of UN Special Representative Shaharyar Khan, Radio France Internationale, in *BBC/SWB,* September 8, 1994.

102. See Chris MacGreal, "Hutu Exiles Are in Training," *Guardian,* December 19, 1994; "Crime and Nourishment," *Economist,* April 1, 1995. In this latter article there is a picture of fully armed ex-FAR soldiers in a camp, with the caption "These are refugees."

103. Not only did they sell part of the stolen international food aid and tax "their" population, but they even made money through various kinds of local commercial activities, including trade and transport, using the vehicles taken with them at gunpoint during their retreat.

104. In January 1995 I met in Bukavu a former army officer working for UNHCR who had seen South African–manufactured 155mm artillery pieces in a refugee camp. These weapons and others were transported by road from South Africa to Zambia, taken apart at Mpulungu harbor, and then shipped by lake freight to Kalemie or Uvira. Zairian custom officers were bought on a routine basis.

105. Interview with an operative from a European secret service, Geneva, October 1994. The occasion is reported in a slightly different form in Human Rights Watch, *Rwanda/Zaire: Rearming with Impunity. International Support for the Perpetrators of the Rwandan Genocide,* Washington, DC, May 1995, 16.

106. Mark Hubbard, "UN Alert Urged as Arms Pour into New Rwanda War," *Observer,* March 26, 1995.

107. An Israeli company was mentioned, and when the RPA smashed the camps in November 1996 it found invoices from an Isle of Man–registered and British-based military supplies company run by two Kenyan Asians. Deliveries seem to have totaled around $6 million.

108. See Amnesty International, *Rwanda: Arming the Perpetrators of the Genocide,* London, June 1995.

109. See Prunier, *The Rwanda Crisis,* 278. Previous support had been extended by every and all possible means, the French going as far as bringing in weapons and ammunition in the planes used for the humanitarian Operation Amaryllis on April 8, 1994. See testimony by Belgian colonel Luc Marchal, an eyewitness to the events, in *Le Monde,* August 23, 1995; I was later able to confirm the story from Rwandese sources.

110. From that point of view, the "facts" concerning France in Human Rights Watch Africa, *Rwanda/Zaire: Rearming with Impunity,* do not really stand up to serious examination. See Stephen Smith, "Livraisons d'armes au Rwanda: Retour sur un rapport contestable," *Libération,* July 31, 1995.

111. See chapter 2.

112. François Misser and Alan Rake, "Mobutu Exploits the Rwanda Crisis," *The New African,* November 1994. Mobutu knew that the French were behind him in his effort at an international comeback. For firsthand testimony to this, see Prunier, *The Rwanda Crisis,* 279 note 139.

113. Haut Conseil de la République/Parlement Transitoire (HCR/PT), the transitional Zairian national assembly, demanded immediate refugee repatriation in April 1995 because it feared vote rigging.

376

114. When Robin Cook, British shadow minister for foreign affairs, accused Zaire of complicity in rearming the ex-FAR after a visit to Goma, Mobutu created a Commission of Inquiry, which promptly denied everything (April 1995).

115. For perhaps too sympathetic a view of that predicament, see J. P. Godding, *Réfugies rwandais au Zaire* (Paris: L'Harmattan, 1997).

116. For a good study of the RDR, see Tom Ndahiro, "Genocide Laundering: Historical Revisionism, Genocide Denial and the Role of the RDR," in Phil Clark and Zachary Kaufman, eds., *After Genocide: Transitional Justice, Post-Conflict Reconstruction and Reconciliation in Rwanda and Beyond* (London: Hurst, 2008).

117. *The East African,* May 15–21, 1995.

118. Radio Rwanda in *BBC/SWB,* May 15, 1995.

119. The failure of the international intervention in Somalia has spawned a massive literature of criticism and self-examination, at times short on analysis. J. G. Sommer, *Hope Restored? Humanitarian Aid to Somalia (1990–1994)* (Washington, DC: Refugee Policy Group, 1994) gives an honest global presentation; W. Clarke and J. Herbst, eds., *Learning from Somalia: The Lessons of Armed Humanitarian Intervention* (Boulder, CO: Westview Press, 1997) has clarity of analysis; and M. Marren, *The Road to Hell: The Ravaging Effects of Foreign Aid and International Charity* (New York: Free Press, 1997) is to be commended for its politically incorrect frankness.

120. The case about the tragic lack of proper grasp of the political situation was repeatedly made by the best evaluation studies on the genocide, such as Human Rights Watch Africa, *Leave None to Tell the Story,* 141–179, 595–634; Joint Evaluation of Emergency Assistance to Rwanda, *International Response to Conflict and Genocide,* 1: 46.

121. Pottier, "Relief and Repatriation," 423.

122. From that point of view the massive UN official document on Rwanda, *The United Nations and Rwanda 1993–1996* Books Series vol. 10 (New York: UN Department of Public Information, 1996), makes for fascinating reading. Everything is there: all the proper procedures, all the careful wording. And everything repeatedly fails.

123. The following account is directly based on Robert Gersony's experience.

124. The information given was confusing enough so that the journalists either did not believe the story (Michel Bührer, "Rwanda: Massacres, rumeurs et vérité," *Le Journal de Genève,* October 8–9, 1994) or when they did, they saw it as a tale of revenge ("Revenge," *Economist,* October 8, 1994).

125. UN Commission of Expert Report, October 3, 1994.

126. From Mrs. Sadako Ogata, UNHCR high commissioner.

127. Boutroue, *Missed Opportunities,* 45.

128. Radio France Internationale in *BBC/SWB,* December 6, 1994.

129. The camps were permanently teeming with rumors that kept interfering with the humanitarians' work. See Amnesty International, *Rwanda and Burundi: The Return Home: Rumours and Realities,* London, January 1996.

130. *Economist,* March 23, 1996.

131. For different reasons, there were no problems with either Tanzania or Burundi.

132. Boutroue, *Missed Opportunities,* 28.

133. Following limited humanitarian involvement after the genocide, the U.S. Army had started a training program for the RPA and several U.S. officers were quite impressed by the professionalism of their counterparts. Maj. (later Lt. Col.)

Rick Orth, the U.S. military attaché in Kigali, played a key role in that warming relationship between RPA and the U.S. Department of Defense.

134. Radio Tanzania in *BBC/SWB,* April 4, 1996.
135. Prunier, *The Rwanda Crisis,* 355.

Chapter 2

1. *Kinyamateka,* no. 1425 (July 1995).
2. *Economist,* June 17, 1995.
3. Marie-Laure Colson, "Rwanda: Des veuves laissées pour compte," *Libération,* May 6, 1996.
4. Randolph Kent, "The Integrated Operations Centre in Rwanda: Coping with Complexity," in J. Witman and D. Pecock, eds., *After Rwanda: The Coordination of United Nations Humanitarian Assistance* (London: Macmillan, 1996), 66.
5. Ibid., 73.
6. Ibid., 64.
7. Manuel Da Silva, *Personal UNREO End of Mission Report,* New York, January 1996. Christine Omutonyi, the RPF stalwart who ran the NGO circus from the government side, was quite good at keeping a tight rein on what she saw either as worthless youngsters or, in the case of the more seasoned humanitarians of Médecins Sans Frontières and Oxfam, as dangerously nosy quasi-spies.
8. Ibid.
9. Ibid. All this would come in very handy later to give detailed reports of the massacre.
10. Anonymous IOC memo, April 12, 1995.
11. Kent, "The Integrated Operations Centre in Rwanda," 78.
12. IOC Situation Report, April 5, 1995. In another report dated April 10, UNREO was writing that "the population of Kibeho, Ndago and Kamana camps has grown substantially of late…. The population of Kamana camp has grown by over 4,500 people in the week since 5 April."
13. Col. P. G. Warfe [Australian Army], "Address on the Kibeho Massacre," Australian Red Cross Conference on Humanitarian Law, Hobart, Australia, July 22–23, 1999.
14. Interview with Seth Sendashonga, Nairobi, April 1997.
15. The figure was widely disputed, with estimates ranging from 50,000 to 150,000. This is due to the fact that numbers had to be subtracted for people running away to Zaire or Burundi in anticipation of the catastrophe, and added to for refugees coming from Burundi fleeing the violence there, for more IDPs either returning from repatriation or making a dash for the camp after a massacre in the hills, and so on. The best estimate from an IOC staffer who followed the situation day by day is between 80,000 and 100,000 (interview in Paris, June 1999).
16. There were about eighty Zambian soldiers from UNAMIR at Kibeho.
17. Linda Polman, "The Problem Outside," *Granta,* no. 67 (September 1999).
18. Interview with former UNREO member, Washington, DC, October 1996.
19. Ministère de la Réhabilitation et de l'Intégration Sociale, Kigali, *Closure of Displaced People's Camps in Gikongoro,* April 25, 1995.
20. IOC Situation Report, April 23, 1995, 2330 hrs.
21. Jean-Philippe Ceppi, "60.000 déplacés disparus au Rwanda," *Libération,* June

23, 1995. Sixty thousand might be a high figure, but it is likely that between 20,000 and 30,000 IDPs were killed *after* they left Kibeho.

22. This was totally false. When the so-called hard core (i.e., 311 men, 581 women, and 954 children) were finally evacuated from Kibeho on May 8, what was found behind were two assault rifles (one AK-47, one G-3), two half-empty boxes of ammunition, five machetes, and one grenade. Radio Rwanda quoted in *BBC Summary of World Broadcasts* (henceforth *BBC/SWB*), May 9, 1995.

23. T. E. S. Kleine-Ahlbrandt, *The Protection Gap in the International Protection of Internally Displaced Persons: The Case of Rwanda* (Geneva: Institut Universitaire des Hautes Etudes Internationales, 1996).

24. Kigali Public Prosecutor François-Xavier Nsanzuwera, who had already been frustrated at the way justice was handled, quietly left the country on April 26, finally pushed over the brink by the Kibeho horror.

25. Interview with Seth Sendashonga, Nairobi, April 1997.

26. Jean-Pierre Mugabe, *Le Tribun du Peuple,* no. 48 (April 1995). Although an RPF veteran, Mugabe was an "interior" Tutsi and a francophone. As such he quickly became aware of the monopoly of power exercised within the RPF by the small group of anglophone Tutsi nicknamed "the Gahini mafia," from their common place of origin in Kibungo prefecture. See chapter 1, note 53.

27. Radio France Internationale, in *BBC/SWB,* April 28, 1995.

28. The prison population, which stood at 9,000 in February 1995, had jumped to 44,000 by June.

29. Radio Rwanda, in *BBC/SWB*, May 26, 1995.

30. Radio Rwanda, in *BBC/SWB,* May 15, 1995

31. Radio Rwanda, in *BBC/SWB,* June 8, 1995.

32. Major Kabuye was quite close to Kagame. During the war she had been the one taking care of all his domestic needs, and later she tried to run Kigali as a prim governess, closing down the discos that did not respect her restrictive hours of business, running the prostitutes out of town, and so on. Kagame liked this virtuous approach.

33. *Le Monde,* June 15, 1995.

34. Stephen Smith, "Le Rwanda passé au crible du renseignement militaire," *Libération,* July 18, 1995. It was Seth Sendashonga himself who had leaked the memo to Stephen Smith.

35. Radio Rwanda, in *BBC/SWB,* August 12, 1995.

36. Sendashonga's brother Abel Furera had been bourgmestre of Rwamatamu commune in Kibuye prefecture at the time of the genocide and was accused of having some responsibility for the slaughter. In fact he had been in Kigali when the massacres started and he had returned to Rwamatamu on April 17, only to be an impotent witness to the liquidation of three thousand Tutsi by the gendarmerie. When the calumny campaign started he had asked his brother to get him out of the country. Sendashonga refused and Furera was arrested in December 1994, after a perfunctory two-hour inquiry. The story was dug up in the summer of 1995 and Sendashonga was accused of having tried to illegally protect his brother. See "Les frères [*sic*] du ministre Sendashonga sont coupables," *Imboni,* no. 13 (July 1995).

37. Interview with Seth Sendashonga, Nairobi, April 1997.

38. Radio Rwanda, in *BBC/SWB*, August 28, 1995.

39. Radio Rwanda, in *BBC/SWB*, August 29, 1995

40. I consider the presence of the Rwandese refugees in Burundi (270,000 in late

1994) in the next section.

41. Since the failure of the Conference Nationale Souveraine (CNS) at the national level and since the end of the cold war, Mobutu's standing with his former supporters abroad (Belgium, the United States, France to a degree) had deteriorated considerably (see chapter 3).

42. Something that nobody had forgotten locally and everybody seemed to have forgotten internationally (see chapter 3).

43. The Rwenzururu movement in Uganda started as an anticolonial rebellion which extended all the way into the 1990s and contributed to the anti-Museveni Allied Democratic Forces (ADF) guerrillas. For its origins and up to the birth of the ADF, see A. Syahuku-Muhindo, "The Rwenzururu Movement and the Democratic Struggle," in M. Mamdani and J. Oloka-Onyango, eds., *Uganda: Studies in Living Conditions, Popular Movements and Constitutionalism* (Vienna: JEP Books, 1994), 273–317.

44. The three crucial steps of that process of neglect are perfectly documented in the excellent study on the genocide by Human Rights Watch Africa, *Leave None to Tell the Story,* 1999.

45. This is a colonial term meaning "local tribes." Still commonly used today, it has acquired deeply racist undertones.

46. Roland Pourtier, "La guerre au Kivu: Un conflit multidimensionel," *Afrique Contemporaine,* 4th quarter (1996): 20.

47. The Banande, the largest autochthon tribe, held its ground better and felt less threatened, and as a result was initially less hostile toward the Kinyarwanda speakers.

48. Johan Pottier and James Fairhead, "Post-Famine Recovery in Highland Bwisha, Zaire," *Africa* 61, no. 4 (1991): 444. See also James Fairhead, "Fields of Struggle: Towards a Social History of Farming Knowledge and Practice in a Bwisha Community, Kivu, Zaire," PhD diss., School of Oriental and African Studies, London, 1990.

49. This was the so-called Kanyarwanda (Sons of Rwanda) rebellion of 1965, mostly a fight between the Banyarwanda and the majority Banande autochthon tribe.

50. Down from 2.16 hectares (5.4 acres) in 1958. J. C. Willame, *Banyarwanda et Banyamulenge* (Brussels: CEDAF, 1997), 44.

51. This decree was appended to the MPR statutes and voted on with them, later to be turned into Law 72-002.

52. For a good discussion of the new law, see Oswald Ndeshyo-Rurihose, *La nationalité de la population zaïroise d'expression kinyarwanda au regard de la loi du 29 juin 1981* (Kinshasa: CERIA, 1992). The author, a former dean of Kinshasa University Law Faculty, remarked, "Since Zaire has nine borders with other countries and that many tribes are divided by these borders, this law puts the country in a dangerous situation for future security." These were prophetic words indeed.

53. The Banyarwanda were running very profitable smuggling operations with Rwanda. Up to 1990 there was no Tutsi-Hutu split in those operations, many Zairian smuggling bosses being Tutsi and most of their over-the-border counterparts being Hutu.

54. Médecins Sans Frontières, "Des conflits fonciers aux luttes inter-ethniques dans la zone de santé de Masisi," Goma, April 1993.

55. See Aloys Tegera, "Les réconciliations communautaires: Le cas des massacres au Nord Kivu," in *Les crises politiques au Burundi et au Rwanda* (Villeneuve d'Ascq,

France: Université des Sciences et Technologies de Lille, 1995), 395–402; Faustin Ngabu, "Massacres de 1993 dans les zones de Walikale et de Masisi," *Dialogue,* no. 192 (August–September 1996): 37–46.

56.   Willame, *Banyarwanda et Banyamulenge,* 76.

57.   For an introductory view of this much talked-about group, see G. Weis, *Le pays d'Uvira* (Brussels: ASRC, 1959); J. Hiernaux, "Note sur les Tutsi de l'Itombwe," *Bulletin et Mémoires de la société d'anthropologie de Paris* 7, series 11 (1965).

58.   Alexis Kagame, *Abrégé de l'ethno-histoire du Rwanda,* vol. 1 (Butare: Editions Universitaires du Rwanda, 1972). Kagame mentions the fact that some troops of Mwami (king) Kigeli II Nyamuheshera had settled across the Ruzizi. But Kagame has a tendency to exaggerate the power of the old Rwanda kingdom.

59.   Catherine Newbury, *The Cohesion of Oppression* (New York: Columbia University Press, 1988), 48–49. Mwami Kigeri "Rwabugiri" was a great conqueror who unified Rwanda by force and brought many noble lineages into submission to the new centralized royal power. He died in 1895.

60.   Simba (lions) was the name the pro-Lumumba anti-Western Congolese rebels gave themselves in the 1960s.

61.   A few younsters had joined the rebels on a personal basis. This limited participation does not prevent *munyamulenge* author Joseph Mutambo from writing, "The Banyamulenge, like the Bafulero and the Babembe, massively joined the rebellion." *Les Banyamulenge* (Kinshasa: Imprimerie Saint Paul, 1997), 83. It is false, but it shows the Banyamulenge as good anti-Mobutu "patriots," like their neighbors, a useful stance at the time the book was written, and even more later.

62.   For a scholarly assessment of these events, see Muzuri Gasinzira, "Evolution des conflits ethniques dans l'Itombwe des origines à 1982," BA thesis, University of Lubumbashi, History Department, 1983. For a more militant one by an actor in the 1990s conflicts, see Müller Ruhimbika, *Les Banyamulenge du Congo-Zaïre entre deux guerres* (Paris: L'Harmattan, 2001).

63.   Between 1970 and 1984 the population of Uvira grew from 14,000 to 138,000.

64.   See the interview with the Belgian geographer Georges Weis: "Ils sont devenus les Banyamulenge en 1973," *La Libre Belgique,* October 30, 1996.

65.   Quoted in Willame, *Banyarwanda et Banyamulenge,* 87.

66.   See Baraza la Kivu, *Open Letter to Mr Kumar Rupeshinge, Secretary General of International Alert,* Montreal, October 25, 1996.

67.   This is the figure given by Mutambo, *Les Banyamulenge,* 23–26.

68.   These and other similar points of ideology will be discussed in more detail in chapter 10.

69.   After the war this was to be the ideological underpinning of the 2006 rebellion by Gen. Laurent Nkunda.

70.   During the Clinton administration, when the U.S. government was keen to have people forget its disgraceful role in the Rwandese genocide. Without the same burden of guilt, the Bush administration was later to prove much more even-handed.

71.   Rather than "pro-anything," since its supporters are a mixed bag, from devious revisionist ideologues to honest Zairian civil society backers.

72.   For this episode, see Gérard Prunier: *The Rwanda Crisis (1959–1994): History of a Genocide* (London: Hurst, 1995), 299–305.

73.   Joël Boutroue to Kamel Morjane, November 21, 1994, UNHCR Archive 19/7.

The archive also contains copies of the memos exchanged during the following days.

74.   By this the authors of the memo meant the local Zairian Hutu.

75.   Letter from Mrs. Sadako Ogata, UNHCR high commissioner, to UN Secretary-General Boutros Boutros Ghali, August 30, 1994, in the high commissioner's private archive.

76.   See chapter 1.

77.   UNHCR Goma Situation Report no. 22, April 20, 1995, UNHCR archive 19/7, Geneva.

78.   The old grand master of France's African policies under Gen. de Gaulle had returned to the position of political adviser to Jacques Chirac, first behind the scenes in 1993 and then officially when Chirac was elected to the presidency in 1995.

79.   Interview with a high-ranking French civil servant, Paris, March 1998.

80.   A. Glaser and S. Smith, "Le retour en grâce négocié de Mobutu," *Libération,* September 2–3, 1995; "Expulsions Part of Mobutu's Master Plan," *Africa Analysis,* September 8, 1995; "Zaire: En direct de l'Elysée," *La Lettre du Continent,* September 21, 1995.

81.   W. R. Urasa to A. Liria-Franch, December 13, 1995, UNHCR archive 19/7, Geneva.

82.   Colonel Bizimungu was then moving freely around Zaire and was a frequent guest at Mobutu's palace in Gbadolite. Interview with a Belgian former close confidante of President Mobutu, Brussels, October 1999. Nevertheless Mobutu promised Jimmy Carter everything he wanted when they met at Faro, Portugal, in September 1995.

83.   Mrs. Sadako Ogata to UN Secretary-General Boutros Boutros Ghali, May 9, 1995, UNHCR archive 19/7, Geneva.

84.   From a confidential UN memo excerpted in *La Lettre du Continent,* June 22, 1995.

85.   *Sunday Times* (London), November 10, 1996.

86.   *Washington Post,* November 10, 1996. The camps received eight thousand to nine thousand tons of food per month, plus a lot of medicines, which meant good contracts for the suppliers.

87.   Radio France Internationale, in *BBC/SWB,* May 9, 1996.

88.   On October 22, 1995, he met President Museveni at the UN in New York and agreed both on Carter's continuing mediation and on elections for May 1997.

89.   In early April an Air Zaire Boeing 737 was forced to land in Cyangugu by bad weather while on a Bukavu–Goma flight. It was found to be carrying weapons. Radio France Internationale, in *BBC/SWB,* April 9, 1996.

90.   Victor Bourdeau, "Mokoto en exil," *Dialogue,* no. 192 (August–September 1996): 95–102.

91.   A. Akodjenou to K. Morjane, notes on a meeting with Gen. Elukia Monga Aundu, May 29, 1996, UNHCR archive 19/7, Geneva.

92.   Human Rights Watch Africa, *Forced to Flee: Violence against the Tutsi in Zaire,* Washington, DC, July 1996.

93.   U.S. Committe for Refugees, *Masisi down the Road from Goma: Ethnic Cleansing and Displacement in Eastern Zaire,* Washington, DC, June 1996; Human Rights Watch Africa, *Forced to Flee.*

94.   For a good overview of the events of October 1993 and their immediate consequences, see Human Rights Watch Africa, *Commission internationale d'enquête*

sur les violations des droits de l'homme au Burundi depuis le 21 octobre 1993, Brussels, July 1994, 14–53.

95. FDD-CNDD received strong support from some top Zairian officers. Generals Baramoto and Eluki Mpondo Aundu sold them, through the agency of the notorious Mrs. Goolam Ali, a large quantity of the weapons the ex-FAR had brought into Zaire when they fled Rwanda. See Kisukula Abeli Meitho, *La désintégration de l'armée congolaise de Mobutu à Kabila* (Paris: L'Harmattan, 2001), 65–69. This was an added irritant in the relationship between Kinshasa and the new regime in Kigali.

96. Vice President Christian Sendegeya was a Tutsi opponent of the so-called Bururi mafia. Since independence all the presidents of Burundi and many of their close associates had come from the same area around Bururi. This caused hostility among the erstwhile high lineages of northern Muramvya province, who considered the Bururi people uncouth. The result was a steady tradition of northern Tutsi opposition that could even in some cases go as far as allying itself with the Hutu.

97. Jean-Philippe Ceppi, "Dans un maquis Hutu du Burundi," *Libération,* January 19, 1995; François Misser, "Terreur à Bujumbura," *La Cité,* February 9, 1995.

98. On June 12, 1995, Tutsi Sans Echec militiamen killed thirty Hutu students in one night in their dormitories. FDD retaliated on July 21 by infiltrating a commando which managed to kill eight Tutsi students before being flushed out of the university by the army on the next day.

99. He was traveling in President Habyarimana's plane and was killed with him. He was replaced by Sylvestre Ntibantunganya.

100. This was the title of an article on Burundi by John Edlin and Colin Legum in *The New African,* February 1994.

101. "Tutsis and Hutus: More Blood to Come," *Economist,* July 22, 1995.

102. Radio France Internationale, in *BBC/SWB,* July 30, 1994.

103. Filip Reyntjens, *Burundi, Breaking the Cycle of Violence,* London, Minority Rights Group, March 1995.

104. Radio Burundi, in *BBC/SWB,* February 18, 1995.

105. For the continuing Tutsi-UPRONA dominance of the civil service, justice, and diplomacy, see FRODEBU, *Un Apartheid qui ne dit pas son nom,* Bujumbura, August 1997.

106. Barnabé Ndarishikanye, "Quand deux clientélismes s'affrontent," *Komera,* no. 3 (March–April 1994).

107. Ibid.

108. See Jacqueline Papet, "La presse au Burundi," *Dialogue,* no. 180 (January–February 1995): 75–77; Reporters Sans Frontières, *Burundi: le venin de la haine,* Paris, June 1995.

109. In its issue no. 32 (May 27, 1994).

110. In its issue no. 47 (October 28, 1994).

111. The Catholic paper *Ndongozi,* the independent *La Semaine,* and the government papers *Le Renouveau* and *Ubumwe* tried to save journalistic honor in Burundi in those years.

112. "Burundi: Bubbling Over," *Economist,* January 6, 1996.

113. Colette Braeckman, "Hantise du génocide au Burundi," *Le Monde Diplomatique,* March 1996; Cyrus Vance and David Hamburg, "A Move to Stop Burundi's Spiral," *International Herald Tribune,* March 11, 1996.

114. Africa no. 1 (Libreville), in *BBC/SWB,* March 16, 1996.

115. "Des Hutus contre une intervention étrangère au Burundi," *Le Monde,* July 3, 1996.
116. See "UN Ponders Burundi Force," UPI dispatch, New York, July 24, 1996.
117. Private communication, Washington, DC, October 1996.
118. USIA dispatch, Washington, DC, 9 August 1996.
119. Bagaza played a key role in the last stages of Museveni's war in 1985, when he allowed Libyan weapons to be flown to Bujumbura and then transported by truck through Zaire to NRA-occupied western Uganda. Author's field notes, Kampala, February 1986.
120. Interview with FDD cadre, Bukavu, February 1995.
121. Whether he later changed his views is unclear. His reluctant adoption of multiparty elections in 2005 felt more like a grumpy bending to donor pressure than a genuine conversion to open democracy.
122. In an internal PARENA memo dated July 8, 1995 (in the author's possession), former president Bagaza wrote, "If we lose the war we will not be able to carry out guerrilla warfare inside Burundi because the Hutu are everywhere and you cannot fight a guerrilla if you cannot melt in the population… . We will have to evacuate all the women and the children to Rwanda, the only country with which we have a common border and which is not hostile to us."
123. In June 1995, thirty thousand desperate refugees tried to flee the camps toward Tanzania to escape these attacks. Radio Burundi declared, "The cause of departure of those refugees is not known." In *BBC/SWB,* June 17, 1995.
124. See eyewitness accounts in Archidiocèse de Bukavu, Bureau diocésain de Développement, *Enquête auprès des réfugiés burundais au Zaïre,* Bukavu, August 1996.
125. Fifteen thousand were expelled in July. The UNHCR could only accompany the move, which, compared to the fate of IDPs inside Rwanda itself, was not too rough.
126. Radio France Internationale, in *BBC/SWB,* August 31, 1996.
127. The Gendarmes Katangais were there, but Laurent-Désiré Kabila had not been invited. James Kazini was in charge of the military follow-up. Ugandan political source, Kampala, March 1998.
128. And that included dealing with Zanzibar's maverick island government.
129. This was so at the time, of course. Since then they went back to it, and the situation is still not resolved at the time of this writing (end of 2007).
130. Jean-Marie Mutandikwa, "Le Burundi, le Rwanda et le Zaïre au seuil de la guerre?" *Rwanda Libération,* no 17 (July 31, 1996).
131. Interview with a high-level Ugandan politician, Kampala, March 1998.
132. Interview with M. Mamdani in *Weekly Mail and Guardian* (South Africa), August 8, 1997.
133. He later became minister of the interior when Gérard Kamanda wa Kamanda was given the foreign affairs portfolio.
134. Interviews with Congolese civil society members, including eyewitnesses, Paris and Brussels, September and October 1999. Some of these weapons were destined for the Hutu militias in North Kivu, who took a very dim view of the fact that these were sold to "the enemy." On November 11, 1995, they tried to blow up Gen. Eluki Monga Aundu's plane in Goma. Crazy as this behavior may seem, it was not new in Zaire, and the FAZ had indeed sold their equipment to the enemy in 1977, during the invasion of Shaba Province by the Gendarmes Katangais.

135. Interview with Banyamulenge RPA veterans, Kampala, January 2000.
136. HCR-ZRE-UVI memo 0372, UNHCR Archive 19/7, Geneva.
137. F. Swai to W. R. Urasa, Cyangugu, September 16, 1996, UNHCR Archive 19/7, Geneva. This was of course playing into the hands of General Kagame, who later admitted with a smile to Colette Braeckman, "In a way we were lucky. They even gave us a pretext for this war." *L'enjeu congolais* (Paris: Fayard, 1999), 27.
138. A. Mahiga to L. Franco, September 19, 1996, UNHCR Archive 19/7, Geneva.
139. Aliou Diallo, UNHCR representative in Kinshasa, to Boutros Boutros Ghali, September 14, 1996, UNHCR Archive 19/7, Geneva.
140. Confidential note by W. R. Urasa, ref. RWA/MSC/HCR/1561 of September 17, 1996, UNHCR Archive 19/7, Geneva.
141. The arms embargo on Rwanda was lifted by the UN on August 17, 1995, and Kagame went down to South Africa three weeks later with a $100 million letter of credit countersigned by the Ugandan government to purchase weapons. Confidential information from the arms trading milieu, Geneva, September 1995. After denying the contracts, South African Minister of Defense Joë Modise finally admitted to them publicly (Agence France Presse dispatch, Pretoria, October 30, 1996) before officially "suspending" them on November 6, 1996.
142. Radio France Internationale, in *BBC/SWB*, September 23, 1996.
143. Casimir Kayumba, "Le Zaire en voie de désintégration: Quel est le rôle du Rwanda?" *Ukuri*, no. 11 (September 1996). This was only the latest in a long series of similar warning signs. See Filip Reytjens, "La rébellion au Congo-Zaïre: Une affaire de voisins," *Hérodote*, no. 86/87, 4th trimester (1997): 69.
144. This map was initially drawn from indications from Abbé Alexis Kagame for his *Abrégé de l'ethno-histoire du Rwanda* (Butare: Editions Universitaires du Rwanda, 1972). The eminent historian was also a fierce nationalist who always tended to exaggerate the outreach of the old kingdom. See D. Newbury, "Irredentist Rwanda: Ethnic and Territorial Frontiers in Central Africa," *Africa Today* 44, no. 2 (1997): 211–222. Later the same map was reproduced unquestioningly in *Atlas du Rwanda*, published in Paris in 1981 by Editions du CNRS. It is this particular reprint that President Bizimungu brandished on October 3, 1996.
145. Khassim Diagne to Liria-Franch, October 4, 1996, UNHCR Archive 19/7, Geneva; Radio Rwanda, in *BBC/SWB*, October 3, 1996; interviews with eyewitnesses.
146. *La Voix du Zaire* (Bukavu), in *BBC/SWB*, October 6, 1996.
147. UN Integrated Regional Information Network, bulletin, October 14, 1996.

Chapter 3

1. The first Angolan political movement supported by Zaire was the FNLA. But the FNLA could hardly be characterized as an "interloper" since it was born and bred on Zairian territory.
2. In 1977 the communist regime in Angola used the surviving combatants of the Katangese independence movement of the 1960s to invade Zaire and try to overthrow the pro-U.S. Mobutu regime. They were defeated with the military assistance of France, Belgium, and Morocco.
3. This statement has to be qualified: there was a whole spectrum of beliefs in the West about the necessity of Mobutu's survival, running from the French at 100

percent to the United States at 10 percent. Ultimately, just as his career had been made by foreigners, his downfall was to come from the withdrawal of their support.

4.   The best overall presentation of this horror remains Adam Hochschild, *King Leopold's Ghosts* (New York: Houghton Mifflin, 1998).

5.   Michel Merlier, *Le Congo, de la colonisation belge à l'indépendance* (Paris: Maspéro, 1962), 166. Michel Merlier was the pseudonym of the left-wing and anticolonialist Belgian colonial civil servant André Maurel. His book was later (1992) reissued by the Paris publisher L'Harmattan under his real name.

6.   African dissent had traditionally been dealt with by massive shooting. When the Belgian reformist Van Bilsen wrote his *Thirty Years Plan for the Emancipation of Belgian Africa* in 1956 he was greeted with derision and called a communist. Less than five years later the Belgians abandoned the Congo, with hardly any planning about what to do.

7.   There is a very rich literature on the man and his regime. Among the best overall scholarly treatments are Thomas Callaghy, *The State Society Struggle: Zaire in Comparative Perspective* (New York: Columbia University Press, 1984); C. Young and T. Turner, *The Rise and Decline of the Zairian State* (Madison: University of Wisconsin Press, 1985); Jean-Claude Willame, *L'automne d'un despotisme* (Paris: Karthala, 1992). Michela Wrong, *In the Footsteps of Mr Kurtz: Living on the Brink of Disaster in the Congo* (London: Fourth Estate, 2000) is a most perceptive literary essay on a phenomenon that transcends normal scholarship. The documentaries of Belgian film director Thierry Michel (see bibliography) are remarkable works.

8.   See next section.

9.   The construction of his "Versailles-in-the-jungle" palace at his native town of Gbadolite had only increased that tendency.

10. They had been banned during the Zairianization program of 1973.

11. See P. Digekisa, *Le massacre de Lubumbashi* (Paris: L'Harmattan, 1993). The students had roughed up a number of secret service informers the day before and beaten up or raped the daughter of General Baramoto, a Mobutu crony, who had been a student there.

12. The nickname was bestowed by Colette Braeckman in her book *Le dinosaure* (Paris: Fayard, 1992).

13. For a detailed description of the period, see G. de Villers, *Zaïre: La transition manquée (1990–1997)* (Brussels: CEDAF, 1997).

14. Ironically the worst-behaved unit was perhaps the 31st Paratroops Brigade which the French colonel Matthiote had reformed and retrained after its poor showing during the second Gendarmes Katangais invasion.

15. Although close cousins who share the same language, the Luba from Kasai (their original home) are perceived by the Luba from Katanga as unwanted interlopers. But they were the key actors in many businesses.

16. Kasaï revolted when Prime Minister Birindwa had tried to impose the new devalued currency on the province, which continued using older notes to keep inflation at bay, and violence broke out in Kivu between autochthons and Banyarwanda.

17. For this section, see G. Prunier, "Rebel Movements and Proxy Warfare: Uganda, Sudan and the Congo (1986–1999)," *African Affairs* 103, no. 412 (2004): 359–383. For a good assessment of the Sudanese nationalist movement and the early days of independence, see Muddathir Abd-er-Rahim, *Imperialism and Na-*

tionalism in the Sudan (Oxford: Clarendon Press, 1969); Mohamed Omar Beshir, *Revolution and Nationalism in the Sudan* (London: Rex Collings, 1974).

18.   For Sudanese political life of the 1960s and 1970s, see Peter Bechtold, *Politics in the Sudan* (New York: Praeger, 1976). For Uganda during its years of strife, the best book is A. B. K. Kasozi, *The Social Origins of Violence in Uganda (1964–1985)* (Montreal: McGill University Press, 1994). For the first Sudanese civil war (1955–1972), see Dunstan Wai, ed., *The Southern Sudan: the Problem of National Integration* (London: Frank Cass, 1973); Dunstan Wai, *The African-Arab Conflict in the Sudan* (New York. Africana Publishing, 1981).

19.   The best introduction to the complex political problems that resulted in the civil war and in Museveni's victory can be found in T. V. Sathyamurthy's *The Political Development of Uganda (1900–1986)* (London: Gower, 1986), a near encyclopaedic compendium (781 pages) of Uganda's politics since colonization. Though suffering the handicap of being a president's memoir, Yoweri Museveni's *Sowing the Mustard Seed* (London: Macmillan, 1997) is refreshingly candid about the civil war.

20.   The SPLA did not need Uganda because at the time it could rely on solid support from communist Ethiopia.

21.   This did not prevent the theory's being revived in 1996, this time by Western journalists who were trying to explain the logic behind the sudden appearance of an anti-Mobutu alliance. To make things intellectually more tidy, Laurent-Désiré Kabila, who was almost old enough to be Museveni's or Garang's father, was also said to have been a student at DSM University in the 1960s.

22.   Author's field notes, Kampala, October 1990.

23.   This should have (but has not) buried the often-heard bizarre notion that Museveni was put in power by the United States to stop Muslim fundamentalism in Central Africa, a triple error because (a) in 1986 the Reagan administration looked upon Museveni's left-wing record with extreme distaste; (b) in 1986 the NIF was not in power in Khartoum; and (c) in 1986, within the framework of their collaboration with CIA activities in Afghanistan, the United States was on excellent terms with Hassan al-Turabi and the NIF.

24.   The clearest English-language overall assessment of the NIF regime's rise to power can be found in Abdel Salam Sidahmed, *Politics and Islam in Contemporary Sudan* (London: Curzon, 1997).

25.   And at the time, in the somewhat exaggerated words of a covert operation specialist, "Uganda was America's African beachhead." Wayne Madsen, *Genocide and Covert Operations in Africa (1993–1999)* (Lewiston, ME: Edwin Mellen Press, 1999), 37. The U.S. turnaround toward Museveni had occurred gradually after Uganda's 1987 monetary reform and embrace of free-trade economics.

26.   There was even the hope of a worldwide Islamic revolution that would extend to the West; see Hassan al-Tourabi, *Islam, avenir du monde: Entretiens avec Alain Chevalérias* (Paris: J. C. Lattès, 1997).

27.   The Acholi and Langi Nilotic tribes of northern Uganda were the ethnic base of the Obote II regime.

28.   See Gérard Prunier, "Alice Lakwena: Un prophétisme politique en Ouganda," in J. P. Chrétien, ed., *L'invention religieuse en Afrique* (Paris: Karthala, 1993), 409–419. For a more anthropological approach to the Alice phenomenon, see Heike Behrend, *Alice Lakwena and the Holy Spirits* (Oxford: James Currey, 1999)

29.   In 1992 the LSA changed its name to the Lord's Resistance Army (LRA). For this

period, see Behrend, *Alice Lakwena,* chapter 10; Robert Gersony, *The Anguish of Northern Uganda* (Kampala: USAID, 1997), 20–35; Sverker Finnström, *Living with Bad Surroundings: War and Existential Uncertainty in Acholiland, Northern Uganda* (Uppsala, Sweden: Uppsala University Press, 2003).

30. The Kakwa sit astride the triple border between Uganda, Zaire, and the Sudan. They are equally at home throughout the region, regardless of formal citizenship.

31. See Kirsten Alnaes, "Songs of the Rwenzururu Rebellion," in P. H. Gulliver, ed., *Tradition and Transition in East Africa* (London: Routledge and Kegan Paul, 1969), 243–272. For a detailed history of the movement up to 1986, see Arthur Syahuku-Muhindo, "The Rwenzururu Movement and the Democratic Struggle," in M. Mamdani and J. Oloka-Onyango, eds., *Uganda: Studies in Living Conditions, Popular Movements and Constitutionalism* (Vienna: JEP Books, 1994), 273–317.

32. Jean-Claude Willame, *Banyarwanda et Banyamulenge* (Brussels: CEDAF, 1997), 71. Marandura had been one of the 1964–1965 Simba leaders in South Kivu.

33. See chapter 2, p. 67.

34. *New Vision,* June 18, 1994. This was a local effect of the general decomposition of the FAZ rather than a planned operation.

35. Radio Uganda, in *BBC Summary of World Broadcasts* (henceforth *BBC/SWB*), September 2, 1994.

36. Agence France Presse dispatch, Kampala, August 30, 1994. There were still seventeen thousand Ugandans in northeastern Zaire who had fled there at the fall of Idi Amin in 1979.

37. On August 25 a grenade was tossed into the White Rhino Hotel in Arua, killing one and wounding four; on August 30 a pickup truck got blown up by a mine near Gulu, killing eight and wounding ten. Accusations kept flying back and forth between Kampala and Khartoum.

38. The personal accusation is probably false but relies on real facts: in 1979, as Amin's troops were retreating, a number of Muslims were killed in the Mbarara area as revenge for Muslim domination during the dictatorship.

39. This relates to an obscure episode of the 1981–1986 civil war. It seems more likely that the Nyamitaga massacre was committed by Obote troops fighting the UFM, a guerrilla group that was a rival of the NRA and operated in the Mpigi area.

40. The Uganda Muslim community was in a state of permanent upheaval due to factional infighting; see G. W. Kanyeihamba, *Reflections on the Muslim Leadership Question in Uganda* (Kampala: Fountain Press, 1998). By 1994 there were at least four main factions vying for the potentially lucrative Arab-funded leadership of the Muslim community.

41. Prince Badru Kakungulu was then the uncontested leader of the Uganda Muslim communities, Baganda or not. Interviews with Princess Elizabeth Bagaya, Kampala, November 1997, and with Professor Abdu Kasozi, Kampala, March 1998.

42. See Gérard Prunier, "The Uganda Monarchic Restorations," in Gérard Prunier, ed., *Uganda Monarchies in Transition* (unpublished ms).

43. See, for example, the *Memorandum of Detailed Grievances against the National Resistance Government,* December 30, 1996. Museveni is accused of having deprived Ugandans of democracy, of being Rwandese, of having murdered Burundi president Melchior Ndadaye, and of having killed three hundred thou-

sand innocent civilians during the bush war of 1981–1986.

44. Interview with ADM members, London, April 1999 Kabaka Yekka was the ultramonarchist party of the 1960s that precipitated the confrontation with Obote without having the means to win it. For a short and lucid analysis of this period, see I. K. K. Lukwago, *The Politics of National Integration in Uganda* (Nairobi: Coign Publishers, 1982).

45. For an overview of twentieth-century Islam in Uganda, see A. B. K. Kasozi, *The Spread of Islam in Uganda* (Khartoum: Oxford University Press, 1986); *The Life of Prince Badru Kakungulu Wasajja (1907–1991)* (Kampala: Progressive Publishing House, [1997]).

46. Author's field notes, Uganda, 1996–1998.

47. For a broad (but quite pro-NRM) view of Ugandan society since 1986, see the four volumes edited by Holger Bernt Hansen and Michael Twaddle, *Uganda Now* (1988), *Changing Uganda* (1991), *From Chaos to Order* (1994), and *Developing Uganda* (1998). All are published by James Currey Publishers in Oxford.

48. Interviews with ADM-ADF cadres, London, April 1999.

49. The majority of the fighters came from eastern Uganda and were recruited among the Basoga, Bakedi, and Bagisu tribes. But there were also Banyoro and Baganda. The northerners were very few since northern enemies of Museveni would tend to join either the WNBLF or the LRA.

50. For its origins and development, see Muhammad Khalid Masud, ed., *Travellers in Faith: Studies of the Tablighi Jama'at as a Transnational Islamic Movement for Faith Renewal* (Leiden: Brill, 2000).

51. See S. Simba-Kayunga, "Islamic Fundamentalism in Uganda: The Tabligh Youth Movement," in Mamdani and Oloka-Onyango, *Uganda*, 319–363.

52. Given the interstate tension between Sudan and Uganda, Sudanese help for the Muslim radicals tended to be channeled through Pakistani or Bangladeshi intermediaries. Thus in November 1997 Mohamed Izz-ed-Din, a Bangladeshi national who was director of the Uganda branch of the Islamic African Relief Agency, was deported after being accused of using his NGO as a cover for recruiting ex-FAR soldiers into the ADF.

53. Although much diminished, the ADF still exists at the time of this writing (December 2007).

54. Interestingly enough, although several analysts questioned my etiology of the ADF movement, it has been confirmed by a series of later military captures in which some of the prisoners were Tabliq Muslims (including strangely enough, women) and others hailed from the former NALU. See *New Vision*, May 1, 2001, and May 5, 2001. All had been recruited in 1996.

55. Radio Uganda, in *BBC/SWB*, January 8, 1996.

56. Radio Uganda, in *BBC/SWB*, April 22, 1996.

57. *Indian Ocean Newsletter*, July 6, 1996.

58. This from a high point of 120,000 men in 1992.

59. By September 1996 the Sudanese had achieved the necessary military synergy to bring together UMLA, ADM, Tabliq, NALU remnants, and Rwandese *Interahamwe* to form the Allied Democratic Forces (ADF), which started operating from the Zairian side of the Ruwenzori into Bundibugyo and all the way to Kasese.

60. The best work to follow this belated process is René Pélissier, *Les guerres grises: Résistances et révoltes en Angola (1845–1941)* (Orgeval, France: Self-published, 1977).

61. Gervase Clarence-Smith, "Capital Accumulation and Class Formation in Angola," in David Birmingham and Phyllis Martin, eds., *History of Central Africa* (London: Longman, 1983), 2: 163–199.

62. They were estimated to be twenty-six thousand in 1950, quite likely an underestimation.

63. Among the best introductions to the Portuguese colonial system are Gerald Bender, *Angola under the Portuguese* (Trenton, NJ: Africa World Press, 2004) and Christine Messiant, *L'Angola colonial: Histoire et société* (Basel: P Schlettwein Publishing, 2006).

64. Clarence-Smith, "Capital Accumulation," 192.

65. J Marcum, *The Angolan Revolution*, vol. 1: *The Anatomy of an Explosion (1950– 1962)* (Cambridge,MA: MIT Press, 1969).

66. The only African ethnic group that adhered to the MPLA in large numbers was the Mbundu, probably because of the long-standing commercial and social links derived from their geographical proximity to Luanda .

67. Holden Roberto had even married a sister of Joseph-Désiré Mobutu.

68. It is ironic to think that Savimbi's initial plan was to join the MPLA. But he was blocked, both by Neto's insistence on Soviet-style "democratic centralism" and by the cold-shouldering of the mestiços. On Savimbi and UNITA, see Fred Bridgland, *Jonas Savimbi: A Key to Africa* (London: Hodder and Stoughton, 1988); Jonas Savimbi: *Combats pour l'Afrique et la Démocratie* (Paris: Favre, 1997).

69. For proofs of Savimbi's collaboration with the Portuguese, see W. Minter, *Operation Timber: Pages from the Savimbi Dossier* (Trenton, NJ: Africa World Press, 1988).

70. This was the famous Operation Carlotta in which Fidel Castro brought ten thousand soldiers over from Cuba, with strong Soviet logistical support. See P. Gleijes, *Conflicting Missions: Havana, Washington and Africa (1959–1976)* (Chapel Hill: University of North Carolina Press, 2002).

71. Savimbi did not hesitate to accept CIA and South African support and, with absolute pragmatism, immediately forgot his earlier Chinese connections. What he retained from the "Chinese phase" of his experience was the militarized, centralized, and almost sect-like forms of organization along which he ran UNITA.

72. See Ronald Dreyer, *Namibia and Southern Africa: Regional Dynamics of Decolonization (1945–1990)* (London: Kegan Paul International, 1994), 44–50. The reason for the link with Savimbi was that UNITA had good bases in southern and eastern Angola, close to Ovamboland, where the passage of SWAPO fighters could be facilitated either in and out of Zambia or for hit-and-run raids into South West Africa. An added reason was that the Angolan Ovambo were usually UNITA members.

73. J. Marcum, *The Angolan Revolution*, vol. 2: *Exile Politics and Guerrilla Warfare (1962–1976)* (Cambridge, MA: MIT Press, 1978), 271.

74. United Nations Resolution no. 435, September 29, 1978.

75. Dreyer, *Namibia and Southern Africa,* 158.

76. Reproduced in *Survival* 23, no. 6 (December 1981). The speech was delivered on August 29, 1981.

77. The 27th Congress of the Communist Party of the Soviet Union (February 1986) defined a new foreign policy in direct contradiction with the support for Third World "wars of national liberation" decided ten years before by Leonid

Brejnev at the 25th Congress, then basking in the euphoria of the Soviet victory in Vietnam.

78. J. Marcum, "A Continent Adrift," *Foreign Affairs* 68, no. 1 (1989): 173.

79. Mike Hough, director of South Africa's Institute of Strategic Studies, quoted in Dreyer, *Namibia and Southern Africa,* 176.

80. It was the beginning of the end for the apartheid regime. Three months after the New York Agreement on Namibia Pieter Botha had to make way for Frederik De Klerk and a policy of progressive political opening.

81. See Global Witness, *A Crude Awakening,* London, 2000.

82. See Global Witness, *A Rough Trade,* London, 1999.

83. Empresa Nacional de Diamantes de Angola (Endiama) has a monopoly issuing licenses for diamond mining and is supposed to collect a 2.5 percent tax on all legal diamonds. Working around it is a national sport for the nomenklatura, up to and including the families of the highest members of the government.

84. Everyday life in Angola provides plenty of evidence of that attitude: in Luanda an African name is often a passport to petty humiliations and social slights, and when Savimbi came to the capital in 1992 the fact that he dared give his public speeches in Ovimbundu and not in Portuguese was denounced as "primitive" and "racist." Skin color is less important than cultural markers: a totally black assimilado who speaks only Portuguese will look down on the equally black but Kikongo- or Ovimbundu-speaking matumbo.

85. After some fighting inside Namibia in early 1989 the SADF left the country in November and fairly democratic elections were held in November, giving a 57.3 percent majority to SWAPO. Sam Nujoma was elected president in February 1990 and Namibia became independent on March 21, 1990.

86. Agostinho Neto died in Moscow in September 1979, and Eduardo dos Santos, a typical assimilado MPLA apparatchik born in Sao Tome and married to a Russian wife, succeeded him.

87. FAPLA was then over 100,000 strong and FALA had at least 50,000 or 60,000 men. The problems of demobilization were not seriously considered.

88. In 1990 oil exports brought $2.748 billion and diamonds $214 million, while debt service stood at $1.011 billion.

89. Actually the massive arms purchases that had progressively switched from the Eastern Bloc to Western suppliers were not purely motivated by military concerns. They were also an opportunity for large kickbacks to the members of the nomenklatura who were allowed to negotiate the deals.

90. The best account of this period for the international point of view can be found in Margaret Anstee, *Orphan of the Cold War: The Inside Story of the Collapse of the Angolan Peace Process (1992–1993)* (London: Macmillan, 1996).

91. With about 3 percent of the vote the FNLA had signed its own death certificate. It had not even been able to mobilize the Bakongo ethnic vote, and even less to attract another electorate.

92. Savimbi, *Combat,* 137.

93. Symptomatically UNITA's few mestiço (Honoria Van Dunem) or white (De Castro, Fatima Roque) cadres were spared, while their black comrades were shot. M. A. Africano, *L'UNITA et la deuxième guerre civile angolaise* (Paris: L'Harmattan, 1995), 160–161.

94. One of the worst ones (two hundred killed) was committed in the southern city of Lubango, where the FAPLA shot up and invaded the UNAVEM compound. Anstee called it "a government riposte to curb the spread of UNITA's tentacles

across the country" (*Orphan of the Cold War*, 357).

95. J. M. Makebo Tali, "La chasse aux 'Zaïrois' à Luanda," *Politique Africaine,* no. 57 (March 1995): 71–84.

96. This is what he eventually did on May 19, 1993.

97. Former interior minister Charles Pasqua flew to Luanda in February 1997 in the company of Bernard Guillet and Daniel Leandri, two of his close aides, whose names were later to come up during the notorious "Angolagate" scandal of 2001. Unbeknown to French public opinion, two French arms merchants had already started delivery on the enormous $633 million weapons contract I discuss below.

98. AFP dispatch, July 22, 1997, quoted in A. Rozès, "Un pays en déshérence et au bord de la guerre totale: L'Angola 1994–1998," in *L'Afrique Politique 1998* (Paris: Karthala, 1999), 193.

99. United Nations, *Report of the Panel of Experts on Violations of Security Council Sanctions against UNITA,* March 2000, 14. In February 2001 Romania was added to the list of probable UNITA suppliers.

100. Although both men were French citizens they also held citizenship in a variety of countries: Venezuela for Falcone, who was also a U.S. resident; Israel and Canada for Gaydamak, who was a naturalized Russian with excellent former KGB connections dating back to the days he worked at the Soviet Embassy in Paris.

101. The supplier was a Czech-registered company that purchased the arms in the former USSR. But Falcone then went through his French-registered company, Brenco, apparently because one condition the Angolans had put in the contract was the supply of high-tech French-manufactured electronic listening devices the Russians could not provide. Although this component of the contract was worth only about $30 million, it was a key part and required authorizations from highly placed sources in Paris. The case was later prosecuted in France. See "Falcone et Cie, armes en tous genres," *Libération,* December 13, 2000; "Charles Pasqua et ses réseaux sous surveillance," *Libération,* January 11, 2001; "Les hommes de l'Angolagate," *Le Monde,* January 13, 2001; "Gaydamak parle," *Libération,* March 6, 2001. Things dragged on and have not yet been settled judicially at the time of writing. See "L'enigmatique monsieur Gaydamak," *Le Nouvel Observateur,* September 28–October 4, 2006.

102. SOFREMI is the public company used by Paris to market French military hardware. The "discovery" of the SOFREMI-Brenco scandal by mainstream French media in late 2000 is amusing since the specialized *Lettre du Continent* had documented it as early as mid-1996.

103. United Nations, Department of Humanitarian Affairs. *Revised Consolidated Appeal for Angola (February–December 1994),*mimeograph, September 1994.

104. The white population culminated at 72,000 in 1958, compared to the black African population of 2.3 million.

105. The South African Anglo-American mining giant dominated. The other companies were British and paid their taxes directly in London.

106. For a clear history of the federation, see Patrick Keatley, *The Politics of Partnership: The Federation of Rhodesia and Nyasaland* (Harmondsworth, UK: Penguin Books, 1963).

107. B. Turok, *Zambia: Mixed Economy in Focus* (London: Institute for African Alternatives, 1989), 113.

108. For this compensatory aspect of Zambia's diplomacy, see Daniel Bourmaud,

"La Zambie dans les relations internationales: La quête désespérée de la puissance," in J. P. Daloz and J. D. Chileshe, eds., *La Zambie Contemporaine* (Paris:
Karthala, 1996), 69–87. It is interesting to note that this trait later survived
the UNIP regime, with Chiluba's pro-U.S. free enterprise rhetoric replacing
Kaunda's exhausted "socialist humanism" but with the same frantic quest for
outside approbation to help shore up a crumbling internal situation.

109. "Basic decency" should be taken here to describe a certain overall quality of life
and social relationships. As we will see, the government seemed to do its best to
belie that tradition as time went on.

110. A favorite trick was to use tourist facilities such as the Mluwe airstrip in Lu-
angwa National Park or Zambezi Lodge, near the Cazombo Angolan border
salient.

111. For the chapter subheading here, I borrow this formula from Pierre Kalck's
remarkable *Histoire Centrafricaine des origines à 1966* (Paris: L'Harmattan,
1992).

112. The definitive work on this subject is Catherine Coquery-Vidrovitch, "Le Congo français au temps des grandes compagnies concessionnaires (1898–1930),"
PhD diss., Sorbonne, 1970.

113. Often they were Belgians who were sacked from the Congo administration for
excessive violence or theft.

114. Kalck, *Histoire Centrafricaine,* 183.

115. André Gide, *Voyage au Congo* (Paris: Gallimard, 1927). Some of the cases he
documented included torture and the burning alive of women and children.

116. Albert Londres, *Terre d'ébène: La traite des noirs* (Paris: Albin Michel, 1927).

117. In the French "assimilationist" system, contrary to the British colonies, which
were supposed to develop various degrees of self-rule *in their territories,* political development was conceived of as an increased participation of the colonies
in the metropolitan political life. Thus many among francophone Africa's first
generation of politicians were at one time or another MPs in Paris during the
1940s and 1950s, and some, such as Houphouet-Boigny, even became cabinet
ministers.

118. The whites who worked for what was left of the Grandes Compagnies Concessionnaires hated Boganda, who had been instrumental in finally getting compulsory labor outlawed in 1946. They also hated his intelligence, which was
unsettling to their view of black inferiority.

119. With full French support, since Goumba was supposed to be left-leaning. See
Kalck, *Histoire Centrafricaine,* 302–312.

120. Max Weber, *Economy and Society* (Berkeley: University of California Press,
1968), 241–242.

121. The French ambassador was able to persuade him at the last moment that it was
a bit too gross.

122. Bokassa's personality fostered a whole sensationalistic literature in France. For a
more thoughtful view of the violence without the prurient interest, refer to E.
Germain, *La Centrafrique et Bokassa (1965–1979): Force et déclin d'un pouvoir
personnel* (Paris: L'Harmattan, 2000). For a more theoretical approach (with
which I am not really in agreement but which has the merit of objectivity), see
Didier Bigo, *Pouvoir et obéissance en Centrafrique* (Paris: Karthala, 1988).

123. Germain, *La Centrafrique et Bokassa,* 190–191. There are good reasons to suspect that it was actually the French Secret Service trying to poison him.

124. Since Bokassa never tried to hide any of his killings (on the contrary), it is

possible to evaluate their numbers. Germain (*La Centrafrique et Bokassa,* 123) arrives at about 400, a very small amount if compared to Idi Amin's 200,000 or Macias Nguema's 300,000.

125.   De Gaulle found it particularly irritating and once told him in public, "I am not your father." But given the way Bokassa's real father had been murdered by agents of French power, the insistence amounted to a Freudian transfer.

126.   They were valued at around $100 million at the time he was deposed, a large figure for the Central African Republic but a very modest one if compared to Mobutu's standards.

127.   There were numerous accusations of cannibalism, and when he was overthrown two human bodies were found in the palace's cold room among the carcasses of sheep and oxen.

128.   "As a British soldier Amin had internalised the most nationalistic British values. But these were peripheral, not central. When they were combined with the interiorisation of new nationalistic values it produced a state of *aggressive anglophilia, very different from Anglophobia.*" Ali Mazrui, "Racial Self-reliance and Cultural Dependency: Nyerere and Amin in Comparative Perspective," *Journal of International Affairs* 27, no. 1 (1973): 105–121. Replacing Mazrui's terms with "*aggressive Francophilia, different from Francophobia*" would depict perfectly Bokassa's attitude toward his former colonizers, the killers of his father and his army superiors.

129.   Or so they thought. But Bokassa was still a French citizen and he eventually took refuge in France itself, where his embarrassing behavior eventually caused considerable difficulties and played a key role in President Giscard d'Estaing's electoral defeat in April 1981.

130.   He flew back to the Central African Republic in one of the French army transport planes.

131.   See Bigo, *Pouvoir et obéissance,* 262–263. Kolingba was no simple French stooge. He managed to turn around his secret service minder, Col. J. C. Mantion, and get him to defy his Paris superiors for the sake of an independent "power behind the throne" role in Central Africa. The Kolingba years could equally well be termed the Mantion years.

132.   Kolingba was a Yakoma, one of the biggest "river tribes."

133.   J. P. Ngoupande, *Chronique de la crise centrafricaine (1996–1997)* (Paris: L'Harmattan, 1997), 108.

134.   He was hoping to get Gaddafi's support to overthrow Dacko, then just brought back to power by the French.

135.   See a scathing exposé in the French magazine *Lui,* September 1996.

136.   Ngoupande, *Chronique,* 24–30.

137.   Bangui is ethnically mixed but with a Gbaya-Banda-Mandja majority.

138.   Highway robbers, often coming from Chad and the Sudan. The government had lost control over at least 30 percent of the territory, particularly along the northern and eastern borders.

139.   With almost half the Congo's population the capital has such a powerful effect on the rest of the country that it has been described as "a suburb of Brazzaville." See the special issue of *Politique Africaine,* no. 31 (October 1988) entitled "Le Congo, banlieue de Brazzaville."

140.   Just as Ubangi-Chari was the ugly duckling of the AEF family, the Congo was its child prodigy. In a rather interesting development this has led practically all the contemporary politicians (Marien Ngouabi, Denis Sassou-Nguesso, Pas-

cal Lissouba, Bernard Kolelas, and others) to write books about their views of politics. This is a very French tradition; de Gaulle of course, but even Giscard d'Estaing, François Mitterrand, Nicolas Sarkozy, and a whole bevy of lesser political figures have all written books, a necessary element for "serious" political recognition in France.

141. De Gaulle's chief Africa adviser, Jacques Foccart, regretted not intervening when he saw Youlou replaced by the left-leaning Massamba-Debat. So when President Léon Mba was overthrown by a popular movement in Gabon in February 1964, Foccart convinced de Gaulle to send his army to put him back in power in what was the first of Paris's many military interventions in sub-Saharan Africa.

142. Massamba-Deba was a Mukongo, but not a Lari like Youlou. Lissouba came from the small Nzabi tribe, whose majority lives across the border in Gabon.

143. Aloïse Moudileno-Massengo, *La République Populaire du Congo, une escroquerie idéologique* (Paris: Maisonneuve et Larose, 1975).

144. The PCT was a full-fledged communist party, with references to Marx and Lenin. The republic was "popular" and its flag was red with a yellow star, a hammer, and a hoe instead of a sickle.

145. For a good political history of the Brazzaville-Congo up to the PCT downfall in 1991, see Rémy Bazenguissa-Ganga, *Les voies du politique au Congo: Essai de sociologie historique* (Paris: Karthala, 1997).

146. Brazzavillian life is vividly portrayed in E. Dorier-Apprill et al., *Vivre à Brazzaville: Modernité et crise au quotidien* (Paris: Karthala, 1998).

147. Gen. Denis Sassou-Nguesso played a key role in the events surrounding the death of Ngouabi.

148. It was the sixth constitution the Congo had known since independence. Although all had regularly been violated, the intellectually inclined Congolese retained a particular fondness for fundamental texts.

149. André Bassinet, "Congo: À qui profite la rente pétrolière?" *Imprecor*, no. 173 (May 14, 1984): 30–34, quoted in R. Bazenguissa-Ganga, *Les voies du politique au Congo*, 274.

150. For the effects of this speech on Rwanda, see G. Prunier, *The Rwanda Crisis: History of a Genocide* (London: Hurst, 1995), 88–89.

151. This is where the various strands of the Congo's social contradictions came together: overurbanization, youth unemployment, a very lively antiestablishment youth subculture (the *sapeurs* or "smart dressers" and the music and bar groups). The presidential militia had no recruitment problem, quite the contrary. Other politicians soon followed suit.

152. See Global Witness, *A Rough Trade*, particularly 13–14 and notes 46–52.

153. And the old commitments as well: by May 1993 salaries in the bloated civil service were already seven months in arrears.

154. Elf produced 75 percent of Congo's oil and commercialized 90 percent of it. Since 1979 oil revenues represented between 50 and 80 percent of the government's fiscal base. Yitzhak Koula, *La démocratie congolaise brûlée au pétrole* (Paris: L'Harmattan, 1999), 173–174.

155. Mouvement Congolais pour le Développement et la Démocratie Intégrale, the political party created by Bernard Kolelas.

156. They were never computed, but the estimates vary from 2,000 to 5,000.

157. For a description of the phenomenon, see R. Bazenguissa-Ganga, "Milices politiques et bandes armées à Brazzaville, enquête sur la violence politique et sociale

des jeunes déclassés," *Les Etudes du CERI,* no. 13 (April 1996).

158.   Sassou-Nguesso had wisely removed himself to his village in the north and let Kolelas and Lissouba slug it out, giving only some calculated support to the MCDDI leader. He considered Lissouba the stronger of the two since he had parts of the state apparatus at his disposal. The Lissouba militia was called the Zulu, while the Kolelas militia went by the name Ninja. There were other, smaller militias, such as the Requins (Sharks) and Faucons (Falcons), with different ethnic or pseudo-ethnic identities.

159.   This was particularly clear for the many "ethnic half-castes." See Dorier-Apprill et al., *Vivre à Brazzaville,* 314–315: the story of the half-Lari Zulu militia boy who "hated Lari" when he fought their Ninja militia and then forgot his hatred after the war was over. The militias hardened ethnic identities or even replaced them altogether since they could integrate people who did not have the "right" ethnic identity.

160.   If the "Niboleks" joined the Zulu it was the same thing on the other side, where various Teke and Lari groups who joined the Ninja were also far from acting out clearly identified ethnic identities.

161.   U.S. Vice President Al Gore's visit to Brazzaville in December 1995 was frowned upon in Paris.

162.   A false assumption: by 1996 the various "foreign" oil companies (the U.S. Oxy, Chevron, and Exxon; the South African Engen; the Anglo-Dutch Shell; the Kuwaiti Kufpec; and the Italian Agip) had received together less than 45 percent of the exploration permits, and most of those had gone to Agip, with very few to the U.S. companies.

Chapter 4

1.   It had in fact been signed in a Kigali hotel; the Lemera location was announced only to make it sound more "authentically Congolese." This small piece of deception was typical of the larger artificiality of the whole process.

2.   His nom de guerre was "Douglas," which was later mistakenly said to be his first name.

3.   This Conseil National de Résistance pour la Démocratie was the new denomination of the old Parti de la Libération Congolais.

4.   His mother was a Tutsi refugee from Rwanda in 1959. This and the fact that he had fought in the RPF during the Rwandese war of 1990–1994 made him Kagame's favorite among the AFDL leaders. Interview with his uncle, Aristide Chahihabwa Bambaga, Kampala, January 2000.

5.   For general views of the first Congolese civil war, see Benoit Verhaegen, *Rébellions au Congo,* 2 vols. (Brussels: CRISP, 1966–1969); C. Coquery-Vidrovitch et al., eds, *Rébellions-Révolution au Zaïre (1963–1965),* 2 vols. (Paris: L'Harmattan, 1987); Madeleine Kalb, *The Congo Cables* (New York: Macmillan, 1982). On the war in Katanga, see Kabuya Lumuna Sando, *Nord-Katanga (1960–1964): De la secession à la guerre civile* (Paris: L'Harmattan, 1992); Christophe Goosens, "Political Instability in Congo-Zaire: Ethno-Regionalism in Katanga," in R. Doom and J. Gorus, eds., *Politics of Identity and Economics of Conflict in the Great Lakes Region* (Brussels: VUB Press, 2000), 243–262. On Kabila himself we now have an excellent biography by Erik Kennes: *Essai biographique sur Laurent-Désiré Kabila* (Tervuren, Belgium: CEDAF, 2003). The following information on Kabila is mostly drawn form Kennes's work.

6. Although his mother was Lunda. But the Baluba are strongly patrilineal.

7. CONAKAT, led by Moïse Tshombe, eventually led the secession of Katanga.

8. Kabila was largely self-educated, never having finished secondary school. But during his travels in Eastern Europe in 1964 and later during several trips to China in the late 1960s he progressively became reasonably familiar with Marxism.

9. It is then that he fell out with Sendwe, who had veered toward opportunist politics and who was murdered by the "Mulelists" in June 1964, when they took Albertville (Kalemie). That murder would later remain an unresolved problem between Kabila and the mainstream Balubakat.

10. The whole episode is chronicled in William Galvez, *Che in Africa* (Melbourne: Ocean Press, 1999). Guevara hoped that the Congo could become a *foco de guerrilla* for the whole continent, a mistake he was to repeat two years later in his assessment of the situation in Bolivia.

11. Tshombe had by then graduated from heading the Katanga secession to being prime minister in Leopoldville.

12. They were mostly based in Cairo.

13. "The only man who has the genuine qualities of a mass leader is in my view Kabila. But to carry a revolution forward it is essential to have revolutionary seriousness, an ideology that can guide action, a spirit of sacrifice that accompanies one's actions. Up to now Kabila has not shown that he possesses any of these qualities. He is young and he can change … but I have grave doubts about his ability to overcome his defects in the environment in which he operates." Ernesto "Che" Guevara, *The African Dream: Diaries of the Revolutionary War in the Congo* (London: Harvill Press, 2000), 244.

14. Laurent-Désiré Kabila and a few friends (Ildephonse Masengo, Jeanson Umba, Gabriel Yumbu) remained in the Fizi-Baraka area and created the Parti de la Révolution Populaire (PRP) in December 1967 to continue the struggle against the Leopoldville authorities.

15. "Pure air" in Swahili; this was the name given by the PRP combatants to their "liberated zone."

16. For details of the *hewa bora* days, see W. B. Cosma, *Fizi 1967–1986: Le maquis Kabila* (Brussels: CEDAF, 1997).

17. E. Kennes, "L. D. Kabila: A Biographical Essay," in D. Goyvaerts, ed., *Conflict and Ethnicity in Central Africa* (Tokyo: Institute for the Study of Languages and Cultures of Asia and Africa, 2000), 146. This is an earlier version of the text later developed in book form.

18. Interview with Didi Mwati, Paris, November 1999.

19. He did a bit of everything: dealing in smuggled gems and gold, ivory, insurance brokerage, commercial fishing, and fraudulent sale of stolen Gécamines cobalt. In 1989 he even met Mobutu to facilitate a deal between the Zairian president and Sudanese rebel leader John Garang to sell some tropical lumber from Equatoria through Zaire. The SPLA had no French speakers on staff, and Kabila was "supplied" to Garang as an interpreter courtesy of the old communist networks working with Ethiopian president Menguistu Haile Mariam. Interview with an eyewitness to the meeting, Paris, March 1997. See also *Libération*, January 7, 1997.

20. Interview with Adonya Ayebare, Washington, DC, October 1999.

21. Interview with a Tanzanian security officer, Arusha, August 1999.

22. Monsignor Munzihirwa, bishop of Bukavu, *Open Letter to the International*

Community, October 11, 1996.

23. *Refugee International Bulletin*, October 11, 1996.
24. *Le Monde*, October 20–21, 1996.
25. USIA communiqué, October 25, 1996.
26. They were in fact Bahunde and Banyanga Mayi Mayi combatants who had decided to ally themselves with the Rwandese, believing that the encroaching ex-FAR and *Interahamwe* were the main enemy for the time being.
27. *IRIN Bulletin*, October 26, 1996.
28. Radio Rwanda, in *BBC Summary of World Broadcasts* (henceforth *BBC/SWB*), October 28, 1996.
29. Radio France Internationale, in *BBC/SWB*, October 29, 1996.
30. Interviews with eyewitnesses, Paris, October and November 1999. The man who shot Munzihirwa was known only by his nickname, "Sankara." In a situation typical of the paradoxes of this fratricidal conflict Munzihirwa had just come down from the Alfajiri College, where he had hidden some Tutsi nuns whom he feared might be killed in the violent anti-Banyamulenge and anti-Tutsi climate, when he was stopped at a roadblock by Banyamulenge militiamen and shot by "Sankara."
31. Reuters dispatch, Paris, October 30, 1996. President Bongo and Biya had flown to Paris the day before and consulted with Chirac. Elysée Secretary-General Dominique de Villepin and Secret Service Adviser Fernand Wibaux told them that Mobutu had asked Paris to help him recruit mercenaries. *Africa Confidential* 37, no. 23 (November 15, 1996).
32. Agence France Presse dispatch, New York, October 31, 1996.
33. The lake attack had an interesting dimension: the rubber dinghies used by the Rwandese army belonged to the American NGO International Rescue Committee and were apparently loaned and not commandeered. Interviews with eyewitnesses, Paris, March 1997, and Kampala, December 2000. This was the first visible sign of any U.S. involvement in the Rwandese invasion plan.
34. Radio Rwanda, in BBC/SWB, November 3, 1996.
35. *IRIN Bulletin*, November 5, 1996.
36. It was usually possible to know who had done the killing because the FAZ seemed mostly to kill with bayonets, machetes, or clubs, whereas the attackers shot their victims. The difference was due to the greater availability of ammunition on the assailants' side. Interview with an eyewitness, Paris, December 1996.
37. Both headlines appeared side by side in the November 6, 1996, issue. Mobutu had undergone surgery for prostate cancer in Switzerland in August, leaving the Kinshasa political elite to its own devices and petty conspiracies throughout the whole crisis.
38. Some of the South Kivu refugees arrived after walking up the western shore of the lake.
39. Nicholas Burns, U.S. State Department spokesman, Reuters dispatch, Washington, DC, November 6, 1996.
40. In early November 1996 I received a telephone call from the U.S. State Department asking "Who is this Kabila anyway?" I suggested that since there were strong probabilities that the ongoing invasion had received a fair amount of U.S. blessing I was sure that the State Department had full access to Kabila's CIA file, where his kidnapping of three U.S. citizens in 1975 must have been duly recorded at the time. There was a gasp of horror, followed by a pained si-

lence, and then a request to please elaborate since "the Agency is not always very generous with its documentation." Similarly, Ambassador Simpson in Kinshasa kept bombarding the State Department with telegrams about a "Rwandese invasion," which Ambassador Gribben in Kigali flatly denied had ever happened.

41. John Pomfret, "Rwandans Led Revolt in Congo," *Washington Post,* July 9, 1997.

42. There were men of Kisase Ngandu's and of Masasu Nindaga's groups. Kisase's fighters were multiethnic; Masasu's were mostly Banyamulenge with some Bashi.

43. It is extremely likely that they had been recruited through what a former U.S. intelligence officer called "the second-echelon little black book," managed by a Los Angeles–based mercenary company run by retired U.S. top brass who have kept good Pentagon contacts. Interview, Washington, DC, October 1999. On government-sanctioned operations such as the Croatian offensive in the Krajina, they use what is known as "first-echelon" people (i.e., former U.S. army personnel with honorable discharges). For the "black operations" (i.e., covert operations about which Congress is kept in the dark) they use second-echelon men who are also former GIs but with shady records of drug offenses, theft, or sexual offenses. These men are contacted indirectly, through "friendly" private companies, and can include foreigners. Colette Braeckman, in *L'enjeu congolais* (Paris: Fayard, 1999), 43, mentions that this company recruited a number of Liberian Krahns for the Congo mission. As late as October 2007 U.S. government officials were still trying to convince me that the whole operation had never existed.

44. Their last operation during the Kivu campaign was the taking of Kamituga on December 16. There was no fighting, since the FDD, which had taken four Belgian SOMINKI employees as hostages, withdrew after a gentleman flew in from Brussels and paid them a $20,000 ransom. The American mercenaries, who were under the orders of a Ugandan officer, withdrew on the 18th and were taken back to Goma. They later moved west and fought at Kindu and Shabunda. Interview with one of their former Congolese guides, Paris, November 1999.

45. *Time,* November 8, 1996.

46. For a detailed treatment of the vagaries of the international community over the MNF question, see P. Dupont, "La communauté internationale face à l'intervention humanitaire lors de la rébellion (octobre–novembre 1996)," in S. Marysse and F. Reyntjens, eds., *L'Afrique des Grands Lacs: Annuaire 1996–1997* (Paris: L'Harmattan, 1997), 205–220.

47. See "Struggling for the Moral High Ground" in chapter 10.

48. His worry was that the humanitarians had been forced to leave Goma on November 2 and that the camp supply system had seized up. But his remark was also politically motivated; the UN secretary-general knew that he could not count on American support for his reelection and he was therefore putting his hopes on a voting bloc made up of France, the African Francophone countries, and the Arab states.

49. Tony Barber, "The West Delays Sending Peace Force to Zaire," *Independent,* November 8, 1996.

50. Afsane Bassir Pour, "Washington freine toujours l'envoi d'une force multinationale au Zaïre," *Le Monde,* November 10–11, 1996.

51. *Le Monde,* November 13, 1996.

52. Colette Braeckman, "Le Kivu s'interroge sur ses nouveaux maîtres," *Le Soir,* November 6, 1996.

53. *International Herald Tribune,* November 14, 1996. Clinton mentioned one thousand men.

54. *Le Monde,* November 15, 1996.

55. They were stopped by the Ugandan army under Cdr. Peter Kerim at the Karambi trading center, forty kilometers west of Kasese. See *New Vision,* daily from November 14 to 20, 1996; G. Prunier, "Rebel Movements and Proxy Warfare: Uganda, Sudan and the Congo (1986–1999)," *African Affairs* 103, no. 412 (2004): 359–383.

56. Interview with a high-ranking Uganda government member, Kampala, November 1997.

57. *Crusader,* November 21, 1996.

58. *New Vision,* November 22, 1996. For an analysis of the complexities of ADF, see Prunier, "Rebel Movements and Proxy Warfare."

59. These figures have been suspected of being too high. But according to an internal memo of the Special Rwanda-Burundi Unit in Geneva dated February 14, 1996, the overcounting due to the refugees trying to get more supplies by overestimating their numbers (and to the NGOs doing the same) could not possibly be put at more than 10 percent and was probably less. This estimate is corroborated by two experienced Médecins Sans Frontières doctors who were on the spot, J. H. Bradol and A. Guibert, "Le temps des assassins et l'espace humanitaire: Rwanda/Kivu 1994–1997," *Hérodote,* no. 86/87, 4th trimester (1997): 137. So we could rely on a bracket of 990,000 to 1,100,000 for the Rwandese and of 135,000 to 150,000 for the Burundians, for a grand total of 1,125,000 to 1,250,000 people.

60. UNHCR, *The State of the World's Refugees* (Oxford: Oxford University Press, 1997), 23.

61. *IRIN Bulletin,* no. 106 (February 21, 1997). For a skeptical evaluation of the "self-repatriation" concept, see Johan Pottier, "The 'Self' in Self-Repatriation: Closing Down Mugunga Camp, Eastern Zaire," in R. Black and K. Khoser, eds., *The End of the Refugee Cycle? Refugee Repatriation and Reconstruction* (Oxford: Berghahn, 1999): 142–170.

62. UNHCR, *The State of the World's Refugees,* 23.

63. *IRIN Bulletin,* no. 25 (November 15, 1996).

64. *Libération,* November 16–17, 1996.

65. Reuters dispatch, Kinshasa, November 18, 1996.

66. For the figures between Wednesday, November 20, and Sunday, November 24, I have systematically taken the high estimate to make things clearer because during these days the flow fluctuated between 2,000 and 5,000 daily. *IRIN Bulletin,* no. 29 (November 18, 1996, for figures up to that date, then eyewitness reports after the 18th.

67. Nevertheless by November 20 UNHCR Rwanda already had 575,813 registered returnees in the country. What happened was that many people inside Rwanda managed to get on the list, which was useful both for them because of the proffered aid and for the government because it did not want large numbers of refugees left in Zaire to be used as a pretext for MNF creation. As UN Rwanda ambassador Gidéon Kayinamura asked innocently, "Now that the refugees are flowing by the thousands into Rwanda, would a multinational force still

be necessary?" A few days later the Rwandese government was asking for $739 million in emergency aid for the returnees. Reuters dispatch, Kigali, November 23, 1996.

68.   On November 21, the day Mazimpaka made his statement, UNHCR counted 241 returnees, most of them Rwandese Tutsi, and 1,959 refugees from South Kivu with their families, Interview with UNHCR officer, Geneva, March 2000. The final Cyangugu returnee count at the end of November stood at 5,229.

69.   *Financial Times,* November 16–17, 1996.

70.   *Le Monde,* November 19, 1996.

71.   Charles Correy, USIA dispatch, New York, November 22, 1996.

72.   FRD communiqué 22/96, November 20, 1996. The FRD (Forces de Résistance Démocratiques) was the moderate Rwandese opposition group created in exile by former interior minister Seth Sendashonga. It was based in Nairobi.

73.   *IRIN Bulletin,* no. 33 (November 20, 1996).

74.   On November 13 the U.S. Air Force brought two Lockeed P-3C Orion patrol planes to Entebbe with a C-141 transport for the logistics. But they were doing their job only too well; after a week in operation the P-3C flights were suspended "due to a possible shooting from the ground." Reuters dispatch, Washington, DC, November 20, 1996. For a detailed discussion of the media-humanitarian battle around the photographic operations, refer to Nick Gowing, *Dispatches from Disaster Zones,* ECHO paper, May 1998.

75.   Interview with Kisase Ngandu's former army cameraman, Kampala, January 2000.

76.   Reuters dispatch, Goma, November 17, 1996.

77.   *IRIN Bulletin,* no. 26 (November 26, 1996).

78.   See "Massacres au Zaïre: Le témoignage qui réveille les Occidentaux," *Libération,* March 10, 1997.

79.   The Church later transferred him to another parish in Mali.

80.   Letter from Father Balas to the author, dated October 28, 1998.

81.   Lynne Duke, "Africans Use Training in Unexpected Ways," *Washington Post,* July 14, 1998. The author added, "Rwanda…is not the prototypical weak client state seeking military help from a powerful patron. Its relationship with Washington is built on a complex mix of history, personal relationships, shared geopolitical objectives and, not least some would say, guilt." At the top of the "personal relationship" column figured Ambassador Gribben himself. A former Peace Corps volunteer in Kenya (1968–1970), he had been Rwanda desk officer at the State Department (1977–1979), U.S. Embassy number 2 in Kigali (1979–1981), and then number 2 at the Kampala Embassy (1989–1991) in the early days of the RPF attack. His second in command, Peter Whaley, evidently admired the RPF, as did his military attaché, Lt. Col. Richard Orth. Together they worked toward implementing strategic goals that seem to have emanated perhaps more clearly from the Defense Intelligence Agency (DIA) of the Pentagon than from the State Department.

82.   There was also a specific army dimension to it, based on admiration and almost envy. Still shaken by their Vietnam defeat and their poor showing in Somalia, U.S. army officers loved Kagame and the RPA who, as one American colonel told me, "really knew how to kick ass." In the frustrated macho environment of the 1990s U.S. army this was an important factor in bending the rules to help the RPA.

83.   All these facilities were closed after Kabila's victory. In March 1997 when *New*

Vision's chief editor William Pike tried to publish a story about the Fort Portal facility, the U.S. Embassy intervened with Museveni to stop him, something the Ugandan president almost never did, as Pike had always been left quite free to operate. Personal communication.

84.   Author's direct personal observations and several interviews with journalists, both foreign and local, Kigali and Kampala, 1995 and 1996.

85.   Interviews with Directorate-General for External Security officers, Paris, May 1997, and with UPDF officers, Kampala, November 1997.

86.   Peter Whaley was the real field operator of the U.S.-AFDL cooperation, to the point that foreign Kigali residents at the time nicknamed the conflict "Whaley's war." He had thirty to forty meetings with Kabila between November 1996 and April 1997. When he was awarded the State Department's Outstanding Reporter of the Year Medal in September 1997, an official from the British Foreign and Commonwealth Office wryly remarked to me off the record, "I know diplomats are supposed to lie, but it is usually for the benefit of their country, not of the country they have been posted to."

87.   *RTBF*, in BBC/SWB, November 27, 1996.

88.   Reuters dispatch, Kampala, December 4, 1996.

89.   Crawford Young and Thomas Turner, *The Rise and Decline of the Zairian State* (Madison: University of Wisconsin Press, 1985), 266.

90.   In fact it had only 6,000 men, out of which a mere 3,000 were operational. Erik Kennes, "La guerre au Congo," in F. Reyntjens and S. Marysse, eds., *L'Afrique des Grands Lacs: Annuaire 1997–1998* (Paris: L'Harmattan, 1998), 247.

91.   All the more so since the previous two chiefs of staff, Generals Eluki Monga Aundu and Marc Mahele Lieko Bokungu, were cousins belonging to the Budja tribe. Although also from Equateur they were rivals of the Ngbandi.

92.   It was the heir of the old FAS and FIS, the "special units" under the command of Mobutu's security adviser Honoré N'Gbanda Nzambo Ko Atumba, whose sweet disposition had earned him the nickname "Terminator." FIS was responsible for the Lubumbashi campus massacre in 1990, and they both were disbanded in 1991 at the express request of the CNS. Mobutu immediately recreated them as SNIP.

93.   They were shamelessly budgeted by their superiors as 140,000 men. Kennes, 247.

94.   International Institute for Strategic Studies, *The Military Balance 1996/1997* (London: IISS, 1996), 268.

95.   Honoré N'Gbanda Nzambo Ko Atumba, *Ainsi sonne le glas: Les derniers jours du maréchal Mobutu* (Paris: Editions Gideppe, 1998), 49.

96.   See Kisukula Abeli Meitho, *La désintégration de l'armée congolaise de Mobutu à Kabila* (Paris: L'Harmattan, 2001), chapter 2.

97.   Honoré N'Gbanda Nzambo Ko Atumba, *Ainsi sonne le glas,* 54.

98.   The result was constant harassment of Tutsi or Tutsi-looking people in the large cities. Dozens had been killed since the beginning of the war. Those who lived in Kinshasa had taken refuge across the river in Brazzaville, and those of Lubumbashi had fled to Zambia.

99.   Paradoxically, not for his corruption or ineptitude but because he complained of not receiving enough help to "fight off the invaders."

100.   This polemical concept was developed during the 1990s by the French NGO Survie through the work of its director, François-Xavier Verschave, who wrote a book under that title (Paris: Stock, 1998). It refers to the incestuous political,

military, and economic confusion of interests between Paris and its various clients states in sub-Saharan Africa (see chapter 10).

101. See chapter 4, note 31.

102. It did business selling satellite telephones to the FAZ through a Mobutu crony. It also sold Thomson radar equipment to Serbia. Connecting its two fields of operation, it offered Wibaux "one hundred Serb commandos who will invade Kigali in support of the FAZ and ex-FAR." *La Lettre du Continent,* May 8, 1997. The Serbs were, in the words of an experienced French mercenary, "not fighters, just killers of little old grandmothers." Wibaux, who was in his seventies, acted as a proxy for Jacques Foccart, then in his eighties and ailing. They bought that ridiculous scheme and put Colonel Tavernier, a mercenary veteran of the 1960s Congo civil war, in command of the whole show.

103. Agir Ici-Survie, *France Zaïre Congo (1960–1997): Échec aux mercenaires* (Paris: L'Harmattan, 1997), 124–145.

104. In March 1997 an MB-326 pilot in a show-off display of aerobatics even managed to crash directly onto a Mi-24 Serb pilot who was on the ground having a beer. Both men were killed. *Le Monde,* May 10, 1997.

105. In Kisangani they tortured to death a number of people, including two Protestant clerics they falsely accused of being AFDL agents. Interview with Alphonse Maindo, Paris, April 2000.

106. Interview with a Belgian former resident of Kisangani, Brussels, February 1999.

107. *La Lettre du Continent,* January 23, 1997.

108. Almost two thousand UNITA fighters were lost that way during November 1996. *La Lettre du Continent,* March 20, 1997.

109. Kennes, "La guerre au Congo," 240.

110. This is what Mobutu himself seems to have thought. In early 1997 the director of a large mining and mercenaries company offered Mobutu an army to fight the AFDL, with some gold mining concessions in payment. Mobutu refused, saying, "The head of this Kabila is not even worth one gold mine. He is perfectly harmless." The story is told by eyewitness Pierre Janssen (Mobutu's Belgian son-in-law) in his book *A la cour de Mobutu* (Paris: Michel Lafont, 1997), 227–229.

111. They were called *kadogo* ("the little ones" in Swahili) because they were usually between eight and fifteen years old. They were volunteers, and they came from all the Kivu ethnic groups, with a slight majority of Bukavu area tribes (Bashi, Babembe, Barega, Bafulero). Since the feud had been passed on to the younger generation there was quite a bit of tension between them and their old 1965 enemies, the Banyamulenge. This tension was to be at the heart of all the further problems in the eastern Congo (see chapters 6 and 7).

112. This account of Kisase's death is based on two separate interviews, one with a Mukongo CRND member who deserted from AFDL after Kisasu's murder (Kampala, April 1997), the other with Kisase's former cameraman, a Mushi from Bukavu (Kampala, January 2000).

113. Kabila was also glad to see Kisase get shot because he had begun to resent his popularity. As for the Rwandese, they wanted him, their obedient *ndiyo bwana,* in charge of the now unified AFDL without having to deal with the dangerous nationalistic competition Kisase Ngandu represented.

114. *Le Monde,* January 4, 1997.

115. Braeckman, *L'enjeu congolais,* 265.

116. These dated back to early 1993, when Savimbi gave $1 million to the RPF. For him it was a small amount, but for the then impoverished Tutsi guerrilla force it was a small fortune. The gift was typical of Savimbi's strategy of buying himself potentially important friends all over the continent. The January 1993 RPF offensive had attracted his attention and he was willing to bet some money on the newcomers. Interview, Kigali, April 1997.

117. Kennes, "La guerre au Congo," 262. The Tigres, or Tropas de Infanteria e Guerrilla Revoluçionaria, were the descendants of the famous Gendarmes Katangais who had fought for Tshombe before seeking asylum in Angola, where they fought for the Portuguese against Holden Roberto's FNLA. After 1976 they switched allegiance and served the MPLA against UNITA. They invaded Shaba in 1977 and 1978 on Luanda's orders. Although by now Portuguese speakers, they still considered themselves at least partly Congolese and in any case fully Katangese.

118. Radio Kampala, in BBC/SWB, January 31, 1997.

119. It was the first operation in which the new Angolan-Katangese Tigers took part.

120. Two American mercenaries fighting for the Alliance were killed on the Osso River in late January. The French army, which had a secret Commandement des Opérations Spéciales commando unit on the other shore of the river for observation purposes, discreetly returned the bodies of their dead "enemies" to the United States. Interview with ESO officer, Kampala, November 1997. The Economist, February 8, 1997, wrote in an article entitled "Fashoda Revisited," "By African proxy France and the U.S. are at war."

121. Agence France Presse dispatch, Kampala, January 31, 1997.

122. New Vision, January 2, 1997.

123. New Vision, January 22, 1997.

124. Uganda National Rescue Front II (UNRF II, since the original UNRF had fought against Obote in the 1980s) was a small West Nile Muslim guerrilla group drawn from the Aringa tribe.

125. Two months later 746 of them were tried in a mass trial and released after a symbolical condemnation. New Vision, April 23, 1997. Most of them eventually joined the Ugandan army.

126. Le Monde, February 19, 1997.

127. One of the POWs was Capt. Jean-Marie Magabo, of the former Rwandese FAR. He said that about five hundred ex-FAR entered Sudan in late December 1996 and were now incorporated in the Sudanese forces fighting the SPLA. New Vision, May 7, 1997.

128. New Vision, March 17, 1997.

129. Libération, March 14, 1997.

130. IRIN Bulletin, no. 130 (March 18, 1997).

131. At his funeral on March 24, in the presence of Cooperation Minister Jacques Godfrain and all the Françafrique barons, all those present had the feeling they were witnessing the passing of an era.

132. Everybody followed suit, and by late April there were 2,500 Belgian, British, U.S., and French troops in Brazzaville, all ready to evacuate a smaller number of civilians from Kinshasa.

133. He went to France again, on January 9, for cancer treatment.

134. Kakudji was Kabila's cousin who had spent the past twenty-five years in Brussels doing menial labor; Bizima Karaha, a South Africa–trained medical doctor, in-

troduced himself as a Munyamulenge but was in fact the son of 1959 Rwandese Tutsi refugees who had fled to South Kivu.

135. President Chirac had one weakness: he always found it difficult to arbitrate between collaborators who were fighting each other. Dupuch had tried many times to get rid of Wibaux, who was an old Foccart associate, but without success. Chirac had kept both: Dupuch at the official desk at 2 rue de l'Elysée, his rival a hundred yards away as "special adviser" at 14 rue de l'Elysée. The arrangement was a source of consternation in RPR circles and of amusement for the Socialists.

136. *Libération,* March 27, 1997.

137. *Le Monde,* March 29, 1997. Mukamba was nevertheless arrested and sent to Goma. Jean-Pierre Moritz, the MIBA general administrator, paid $3.5 million in ransom into the Brussels account of an old PRP front company Kabila was still using. *La Lettre Afrique Energie,* July 16, 1997.

138. The problem came from his Tutsi ancestry; he was accused by street demonstrators of having "sold the country to the foreigners."

139. Interview with Aubert Mukendi, Paris, June 2000.

140. By now there were almost four thousand "Tigers" operating in Zaire. They were mostly the children of the Gendarmes Katangais operating together with some Angolan Lunda in the 36th FAA regiment. They were serving under the orders of Rwandese officers, with whom they often had a difficult relationship. Interview with Adonya Ayebare, Washington, DC, October 1999.

141. For a picturesque description of Lubumbashi's last days under Mobutist rule, see Crispin Bakatuseka, *La libération de Lubumbashi* (Paris: L'Harmattan, 1999).

142. In a paradoxical development typical of the general confusion, Brig. Delphin Muland, the Tigers' commander-in-chief, found himself faced with thousands of Hutu refugees streaming down toward the Angolan border as he and his troops were coming up by way of Luachimo. The refugees were being chased by RPA elements, and because they were obviously harmless civilians Muland fired on the RPA to let the refugees flee. This caused him to be imprisoned for six months in Kinshasa after the war was over on orders from the RPA officers, who were furious at having lost their quarry. Interview with Deogratias Symba, Washington, DC, March 2000.

143. *La Lettre du Continent,* April 17, 1997. This could be seen as an interesting case of the sorcerer's apprentice premonition since that fear only anticipated what was going to happen a little more than fifteen months later.

144. Quoted in *Le Canard Enchaîné,* May 21, 1997.

145. Jonas Savimbi, interview in *Politique Internationale,* no. 85 (Autumn 1999): 365–366.

146. Wayne Madsen, *Genocide and Covert Operations in Africa (1993–1999)* (Lewiston, ME: Edwin Mellen Press, 2000), 94. Well documented and fully paranoid, this book is an entertaining example of conspiratorial history in which the U.S. government roughly plays the role of the devil.

147. Although, given the simultaneous French fascination for anything American, it might be more fitting to adapt here again the concept forged by Ali Mazrui to describe Gen. Idi Amin's feelings toward the British and to talk in this case about "aggressive americanophilia." See chapter 3, note 128.

148. In the late 1980s, before statistics became very unreliable, the valuof private foreign investment in Zaire was estimated at $800 million for the Belgians, $200

million for the Americans, $60 million for the British, and only $10 million for the French. Economist Intelligence Unit, *Zaire Country Report,* 1994.

149. Cluff Mining was an Anglo–South African company 65 percent owned by South African mining giant AAC (Anglo-American Corporation); Banro was Canadian.

150. Although Zaire was considered Francophone, its economic orientation had traditionally been toward Belgium, not France. This made it a very different case from that of the West African former French colonies.

151. Reading S. E. Katzenellenbogen, *Railway and the Copper Mines of Katanga* (Oxford: Clarendon, 1973) is an absolute must for anybody who wants to understand the complex alliances and rivalries of the Belgian and South African mining interests in the Congo since the late nineteenth century. Their structures and effects remain astonishingly relevant for our times.

152. This is the 1995 figure from the French Ministry of Industry (oil excluded). This corresponds to value actually produced and sold, not to the unexploited Congolese reserves, which are enormous. But putting them into production presupposed a minimum of political stability, a working legal structure, and a minimum of $10 billion to $15 billion in investments over the next ten years. As a point of comparison, in 1995 the biggest mineral seller (excluding oil) worldwide was Australia, with 13.2 percent of the market, followed by South Africa with 8 percent. In 1988 Zaire's share of the world market was still nearly 7 percent.

153. This rough overview is the product of discussions with Zaire expert Willet Weeks and diamond expert François Misser and of perusing a variety of printed sources, *all* invariably described by specialists as unreliable.

154. There was one in 1995, a bizarre scheme concocted by Prime Minister Kengo to put the whole Zairian mining industry into the hands of the Swiss-based company SWIPCO. It was vetoed by the World Bank and by the HCR/PT because there was no public tendering and the whole thing seemed unfeasible. See J. C. Willame, *L'odyssée Kabila* (Paris: Karthala, 1999), 79.

155. *Africa Analysis,* November 15, 1996.

156. This brief portrait of Jean-Raymond Boulle is based on Marc Roche, "Le triomphe de Jean-Raymond Boulle, l'homme d'affaire financier des rebelles," *Le Monde,* May 18–19, 1997, on conversations with African mining expert Antoine Glaser in Paris, and with Congolese mining expert friends in Lubumbashi.

157. Much was made of the fact that former president Bush and former Canadian prime minister Brian Mulroney were members of Barrick Gold's board of directors. But Barrick acquired Kilomoto perfectly legally from the Mobutu government and did not need to start a war to steal its own property. And not only did it not try to have any dealings with Kabila (apart from giving him $7 million, according to *La Lettre du Continent,* May 8, 1997), it even had to close up its mining operation later due to war damages and generalized theft.

158. It is interesting to note that earlier (December 26, 1996) Kabila had issued an "ultimatum," ordering the mining companies back to work in AFDL-controlled areas and threatening them with cancellation of contracts if they did not show up. At the time nobody moved or even answered him.

159. Tenke Mining was the first company to actually come up with cash, giving $50 million to Kabila in March 1997.

160. Mawampanga, who had done a PhD in economics at Penn State University, was

one of the so-called ANACOZA recruits into AFDL. The All North American Conference on Zaire (ANACOZA) was created in April 1996 on the basis of the Internet site Zaire List, which had existed since August 1994. Kabila was so short of trained personnel that he began to scan the ANACOZA Internet site to pick up interesting prospects for his staff.

161. *International Herald Tribune,* May 10–11, 1997.

162. *New Vision,* April 18, 1997.

163. *Africa Confidential* 38, no. 9 (April 25, 1997).

164. *La Lettre de la CADE,* no. 19 (April 1998).

165. For a clear map of the refugee movements, see Sadako Ogata, *The Turbulent Decade* (New York: Norton, 2005), 205.

166. Remark made to the author, Paris, November 1996.

167. See chapter 2.

168. At the time the Mayi Mayi still considered the Hutu to be the main enemy. The next day they killed many more refugees in Nyakatariba. Both villages were in the Masisi area. AZADHO (Association Zairoise des Droits de l'Homme), *Nord Kivu: Existence de charniers et de fosses communes,* March 1, 1997.

169. Human Rights Watch Africa/Fédération Internationale des Ligues des Droits de l'Homme, *Attacked by All Sides: Civilians and the War in Eastern Zaire,* March 1997, 10. This poses an important moral and historical question: Were the refugees fleeing willingly or unwillingly? The question is obscured by the partisan choices of pro-Tutsi (they were compelled to flee by the *Interahamwe* and ex-FAR) and pro-Hutu (they were fleeing because they feared returning to Rwanda) authors. The reality is mixed; I discuss it in the section titled "Struggling for the Moral High Ground" in chapter 10. My impression is that in November 1996 most refugees did not want to go back to Rwanda; this is also the feeling one gets from the only developed account of the refugees' flight: Béatrice Umutesi, *Fuir ou mourir au Zaïre: Le vécu d'une réfugiée rwandaise* (Paris: L'Harmattan, 2000). It is true that the *Interahamwe* tried to dissuade, often by force, those who wanted to return. But in the massive confusion, forcing the flight of over half a million people west would have been beyond the capacity of the representatives of the former regime if the refugee population had been really desirous to go back.

170. A U.S. military mission came back to Kigali after spending one week in Kivu, declaring that there were "175,000 refugees left in Eastern Zaire while 600,000 had returned." Radio Rwanda, in BBC/SWB, November 23, 1996. The fact that this left a gap of over 300,000 people unaccounted for did not seem to worry anybody.

171. French Foreign Affairs Minister Hervé De Charrette, *The Times* (London), November 26, 1996.

172. *Le Soir,* November 25, 1996.

173. James MacKinley, "How the Refugee Crisis Wound Down," *International Herald Tribune,* November 28, 1996.

174. *The Guardian* (Dar-es-Salaam), November 26, 1996.

175. Fund 19, Records of Regional Bureaux, Sub-fund 7, Dar-es-Salaam Office, November 27, 1996, UNHCR Archives, Geneva.

176. Although the Tanzanian camps were not as politicized as those in Zaire refugees did not want to go back: there were only 6,427 voluntary returns in 1995 and 3,445 in 1996 out of a total of 472,811 refugees. UNHCR Statistics.

177. Report by W. R. Urasa, UNHCR representative in Kigali, Fund 19, Sub-Fund

7, Kigali Office, December 30, 1996, UNHCR Archives, Geneva.

178. *IRIN Bulletin,* no. 95 (February 6, 1997); *Le Monde,* February 7, 1997.

179. *IRIN Bulletin,* no. 98 (February 11, 1997). The *Guardian* (London) remarked in an article (February 13, 1997), "The goal of the Rwandese government is to exterminate the Hutu fighters for fear that one day they would come back for revenge." For an eyewitness account of the massacres, see Anonymous: "Massacre des réfugiés Hutu à Shabunda," *Dialogue,* no. 221 (March–April 2001): 75–82.

180. They were the ones the Angolan Tigers were to come across in April, still being chased by the RPA.

181. *IRIN Bulletin,* no. 89 (January 29, 1997).

182. He was soon going to be in Brazzaville, where the deteriorating political situation would provide him with another window of opportunity.

183. It is this group that was soon going to bolster the insurgency in northwestern Rwanda (see chapter 5).

184. This and many following details are taken from the excellent Médecins Sans Frontières USA report *Forced Flight: A Brutal Strategy of Elimination in Eastern Zaire,* May 1997.

185. The fate of that group of refugees who eventually stumbled all the way to Mbandaka, 2,000 kilometers on foot across Zaire, losing thousands of dead in their wake, is the one described in Umutesi, *Fuir ou mourir au Zaïre.* Ogata, the UNHCR high commissioner, assessed the situation by simply saying, "What was unfolding in the field was really a story of terror and killing." *The Turbulent Decade,* 242.

186. Pro-Tutsi groups treated the situation as if all the refugees were *génocidaires,* while pro-Hutu circles were, on the contrary, trying to talk about the refugees as if the ex-FAR and *Interahamwe* had never existed.

187. USIA dispatch, Geneva, April 1, 1997; *Le Monde,* April 3, 1997.

188. *IRIN Bulletin,* no. 140 (April 1, 1997).

189. *Libération,* April 20–21, 1997.

190. Which was false: the 2,000 to 3,000 ex-FAR left behind after the main body of the former army had gone on toward Mbandaka moved to Opala, 140 kilometers to the west of Ubundu, in late February. Médecins Sans Frontières USA, *Forced Flight,* 3.

191. Interview with an Ubundu camp survivor, Nairobi, March 1998. This is a man whom I had known previously in Rwanda, who was a PSD member and who had barely survived the genocide. For a similar testimony, see Véronique Parqué and Filip Reytjens, "Crimes contre l'humanité dans l'ex-Zaïre: Une réalité?" in Reyntjens and Marysse, *L'Afrique des Grands Lacs 1997–1998,* 285–286. Karenzi Karake, later Congolese army chief of staff and RPA second in command, was said to have been in command of the hit team.

192. Not everybody was dead because some of the refugees had managed to hide in the jungle, coming back later when UNHCR and NGO workers were allowed to return. But since only about 40,000 refugees made it to Mbandaka, a minimum of 40,000 to 45,000 must have been slaughtered in Kasese and Biaro. As for the Mbandaka survivors, at least 340 (*IRIN Bulletin,* no. 181 [May 26, 1997]) and possibly up to 2,000 (Robert Block, "Congo Villagers Describe Horrific Killings of Refugees," *Wall Street Journal,* June 6, 1997) were killed on May 13 by the RPA, at the very end of their run. Mbandaka residents remember to this day the scenes of carnage in the streets of their town.

193. Ogata was the first official voice to point out what was going on when she declared to the UN Security Council on September 9 that she had to suspend operations in Zaire as "the most basic conditions for protecting Rwandan refugees in the Democratic Republic of the Congo have ceased to exist." *The Turbulent Decade,* 247. But she stopped sort of explaining what was forcing her to desist.

194. *Het Laatse Nieuws,* February 22–23, 1997. Moreels had reportedly seen U.S. satellite pictures of the massacres but had not been allowed to keep them and make them public.

195. Except for France. But because France had such a political responsibility in making the genocide possible, its "humanitarian" complaints during the slaughter of the refugees sounded partisan.

196. Thus UNHCR Field Coordinator Filippo Grandi declared in Goma, "There is nothing to prove the existence of organised massacres . . . .The international community should not play around with words as serious as *genocide.*" *IRIN Bulletin,* no. 111 (February 28, 1997). The next day UNHCR Spokeswoman Pamela O'Toole said, "We receive every day more and more shocking reports of *massacres,*" USIA dispatch, Geneva, April 29, 1997. *Massacres* and *genocide* are the key words. We will return to this question of an emotionally and politically loaded vocabulary in chapter 10.

197. Nations Unies, Commission des Droits de l'Homme, *Rapport sur la situation des droits de l'homme au Zaïre présenté par Mr Roberto Garreton, Rapporteur Spécial,* January 1997.

198. UN General Assembly, *Allegations of Massacres and Other Human Rights Violations Occurring in Eastern Zaire (now Democratic Republic of the Congo) since September 1996,* July 1997.

199. *The State of the World's Refugees 1997–1998.*

200. Interview with Sakado Ogata, Geneva, March 2000. Her words were: "My personal conclusion is that there have very likely been more than 300,000 dead." Slightly mitigating this figure was the fact that around 40,000 refugees came back from the Congo to Rwanda during 1999–2000. UNHCR figure; AFP dispatch, Goma, February 13, 2001. So, for want of a clearer figure, we can conclude on a minimum of 213,000 dead and a maximum of 260,000 to 280,000. In a well-researched article Emizet Kisangani arrives by other methods at a figure of 233,000: "The Massacre of Refugees in the Congo: A Case of UN Peacekeeping Failure and International Law," *Journal of Modern African Studies* 38, no. 2 (2000): 163–202.

Chapter 5

1. For a remarkable description of daily life in the Congo during this whole period, see Lieve Joris, *La danse du léopard* (Arles: Actes Sud, 2002);

2. *Africa Confidential* 38, no. 14 (June 4, 1997).

3. He had been an assessor in a Philadelphia court for several years.

4. In fact, he had been Lacan's driver and had married the famous psychoanalyst's secretary. *Libération,* April 13, 2001.

5. Interview in *Le Soir,* October 31 –November 2, 1997.

6. This is the expression used by Justine M'Poyo Kasa Vubu in the book she wrote about her experience as civil service minister and later ambassador to Belgium for Kabila's government: *Douze mois chez Kabila (1997–1998)* (Brussels: Le

Cri, 1998).

7. Dr Fabrice Michalon from MDM who had been arrested for "spying" on May 4, 1998, only to be released without explanation or excuses on July 11.

8. Dr. Michalon's interview in *Le Figaro*, July 23, 1998.

9. The only cabinet member from Equateur was Paul Bandoma (Ngbaka), the minister of agriculture. But he was there more as a UDPS member than as an Equatorian.

10. For some examples, see B. C. Wilungula, *Fizi 1967–1986: Le maquis Kabila* (Brussels: CEDAF, 1997).

11. It does not mean that there would have been no ethnic rivalries within the regime if it had not been for the president's manipulations. But he not only made things worse, he also soon lost control over them because of their independent dynamics and his own lack of experience in Zairian ethnopolitics over the past ten to fifteen years.

12. Minister of Finance Mawampanga had been accused of currency trafficking in July, briefly detained, then freed and reinstated at his post after a humiliating ritual of public accusation.

13. Gaëtan Kakudji, a cousin of Kabila who had become one of his most trusted advisers, was made governor of Katanga and had then arrogated to himself the right to oversee Gécamines.

14. There was significant fighting throughout September when the Rwandese had tried to resettle a number of Tutsi driven away from Masisi in 1993 back to their land. They met stiff opposition from local Mayi Mayi militias. *IRIN Bulletin*, nos. 242 and 243 of September 5 and 9, 1997.

15. Marie-France Cros, "Les Tigres Katangais menacent l'AFDL," *La Libre Belgique*, September 27, 1997.

16. Which did not prevent both Emile Ilunga and Deogratias Symba from later joining the anti-Kabila rebellion of August 1998, their dislike of the Rwandese notwithstanding.

17. Radio Télévision Nationale Congolaise, in *BBC Summary of World Broadcasts* (henceforth *BBC/SWB*), February 16, 1998.

18. "The old one," a respectful way of greeting a person in Swahili. Kabila was beginning to encourage this way of being addressed by his close associates.

19. Kakudji, acting as his master's voice, declared, "The Alliance is the only Movement and the opposition parties should join it." *Le Monde*, July 6–7, 1997.

20. A Lunda former truck driver of vaguely Lumumbist persuasion, he later became minister of youth and sport.

21. Author's interview with Eriya Kategaya, Ugandan minister of foreign affairs, Kampala, March 1998.

22. Interview in *Le Soir*, September 23, 1997.

23. *IRIN Bulletin*, no. 195 (June 17, 1997).

24. Interview in *Libération*, August 6, 1997.

25. *IRIN Bulletin*, no. 219 (July 29, 1997); *Le Monde*, July 27–28, 1997.

26. See G. de Villers and J. C. Willame, eds., *Congo: Chronique politique d'une entre-deux-guerres (octobre 1996–juillet 1998)* (Brussels: CEDAF, 1998), 95.

27. He had tried to organize his own celebration of that anniversary. Kabila clearly intended to claim a monopoly on Lumumba's image for himself and did not appreciate any trespassing on "his" political territory, including from Lumumba's own family.

28. Amnesty International, *DRC: Civil Liberties Denied*, February 1998.

29. About sixteen delinquents shot publicly in Lubumbashi, see, for example, "21 Criminals Shot at Camp Tshatshi," *IRIN Bulletin*, no. 342 (January 28, 1998); "Ex-Zaïre: Éxécution collective," *Libération*, March 4, 1998.. Although brutal, this violent repression was relatively popular among the ordinary population, who hoped that it would bring down the common crime rate. It did not.

30. De Villers and Willame, *Congo*, 208–209. Gizenga and Parti Lumumbiste d'Action Unifié ran a distant third with 8 percent of the vote at the presidential level and only 4 percent at the legislative level.

31. *IRIN Bulletin*, no. 450 (July 2, 1998).

32. This "realistic" position was true of Western governments, not of the NGOs. For a clear indictment of the new regime's record during the "transition," see Human Rights Watch, *Uncertain Course: Transition and Human Rights Violations in the Congo*, December 1997.

33. Author's interview with Aubert Mukendi, Paris, June 2000.

34. It was George Nzongola-Ntalaja who first drew my attention to these points, in Stockholm, May 1998.

35. Expression used in a public lecture by Professor Elikia M'Bokolo, Le Mans, May 1998.

36. *Monitor,* April 6, 1997.

37. *New Vision,* May 7, 1997.

38. J. C. Willame, "La victoire de seigneurs de la guerre," *La Revue Nouvelle*, nos. 7–8 (July–August 1997): 19. Papain is a complex enzyme obtained from the unripe fruit or the latex of the paw paw tree (*carica papaya*), which is used by the food industry.

39. *Le Potentiel*, September 17, 1997, quoted in Wamu Oyatambwe, *De Mobutu à Kabila* (Paris: L'Harmattan, 1999), 95. The amount mentioned was $19.7 million, which could only be a fraction of what the AFDL actually owed to its allies.

40. Philip Gourevitch, "Continental Shift: A Letter from the Congo," *New Yorker*, August 4, 1997.

41. This point will be discussed again in the section "Struggling for the Moral High Ground" in chapter 10. But even if one finds it hard to agree with the Rwandese general, there is a sneaking suspicion that, for the French at least and for their friends in Africa, the refugee massacres were a godsend that allowed them to disentangle themselves from the accusations of complicity in the genocide. And for the others, finding fault with the victims provided a form of moral excuse by mixing their own past guilt with somebody else's more recent one.

42. Since Nyerere's death his place has been taken by Nelson Mandela. But to understand the moral and political weight Nyerere had in Africa one can refer to C. Legum and G. Mmari, *Mwalimu: The Influence of Nyerere* (London: James Currey, 1995).

43. *IRIN Bulletin*, no. 177 (May 20, 1997).

44. C. Braeckman, *L'enjeu congolais* (Paris: Fayard, 1999), 134.

45. In an interview with John Pomfret, "Rwandans Led Revolt in Congo," *Washington Post*, July 9, 1997.

46. *Le Monde*, July 17, 1997. Then, in a BBC interview (July 16), Kagame adviser Claude Dusaidi innocently said that Pomfret had "misunderstood" his boss, who had simply "trained" the AFDL, not led it.

47. *IRIN Bulletin*, no. 208 (July 9, 1997).

48. USIA dispatch, Geneva, May 12, 1997.

49.   Interview with eyewitness Aristide Chahahibwa Bambaga, Kampala, January 2000. Chahahibwa Bambaga was an uncle of Masasu Nindaga and was then a refugee in Uganda. He went missing in May 2001.

50.   I will come back to this point in the section dealing with the east and the army situation.

51.   For a summary, see V. Parqué and F. Reyntjens, "Crimes contre l'humanité dans l'ex-Zaïre: Une réalité?" in F. Reytjens and F. Marysse, eds., *L'Afrique des Grands Lacs (1997–1998)* (Paris: L'Harmattan, 1998), 295–302.

52.   Guy Mérineau, "Scènes de massacres dans l'ex-Zaïre," *Le Monde,* July 13–14, 1997.

53.   *Le Monde,* July 15–16, 1997.

54.   This was the title used in the communiqué, a first and last effort at reviving the vocabulary of a bygone era in what was presented as a "new revolution."

55.   For a conventionally conspiratorial view, see W. Madsen, *Genocide and Covert Operations in Africa (1993–1999)* (Lewiston, ME: Ewin Mellen Press, 1999), chapters 1 and 7. For an educated debunking, see M. Ottaway, *Africa's New Leaders: Democracy or State Reconstruction?* (Washington, DC: Carnegie Endowment for International Peace, 1999).

56.   *IRIN Bulletin,* no. 227 (August 12, 1997).

57.   *IRIN Bulletin,* no. 238 (August 29, 1997). On August 30 five thousand people demonstrated "spontaneously" against him in the streets of Kinshasa.

58.   *IRIN Bulletin,* no. 244 (September 9, 1997).

59.   *IRIN Bulletin,* no. 246 (September 11, 1997).

60.   *IRIN Bulletin,* no. 247 (September 12, 1997).

61.   The commission was submitted to "spontaneous" demonstrations which were orchestrated by Masasu Nindaga. As we will see he later fell out with Kabila, and during his trial he explained that the president had given him $15,000 per group that he could bring to demonstrate. Joris, *La danse du léopard,* 334.

62.   *Washington Post,* September 22, 1997.

63.   *Economist,* September 27, 1997.

64.   *Washington Post,* October 5, 1997.

65.   *La Lettre du Continent,* October 16, 1997. This was picked up by U.S. Ambassador to the UN Bill Richardson, who declared at a hearing of the House of Representatives Foreign Affairs Committee, "Kabila is eager to re-start the inquiry…. There have been many abuses by all sides." USIA dispatch, Washington, DC, November 6, 1997.

66.   *Le Soir,* November 4, 1997.

67.   *IRIN Bulletin,* no. 307 (December 5, 1997).

68.   *IRIN Bulletin,* no. 314 (December 16, 1997).

69.   Radio France Internationale, in BBC/SWB, March 6, 1998.

70.   The publication of the Human Rights Watch report *What Kabila Is Hiding* in October 1997 decisively undermined the argument of those who still insisted that Kabila's good faith had been abused.

71.   *IRIN Bulletin,* no. 383 (March 26, 1998).

72.   Author's interview with John Prendergast, special adviser, U.S. State Department, Washington, DC, October 1998.

73.   *Le Monde,* April 12–13, 1998.

74.   *IRIN Bulletin,* no. 449 (July 1, 1998).

75.   This brief description of the Zairian economic downfall is based on World Bank statistics, on the quick overview given in the article "Business at War," *Africa*

Confidential 38, no. 9 (April 25, 1997), and on the paper "Reconstruction and Foreign Aid" prepared for the UN Congo Expert Group Meeting of May 1–3, 1998, by Dr. M'Baya Kankwenda.

76. A bill is deemed "dead" when its real purchasing power falls below U.S. $0.02.

77. There were theoretically 580,000 civil servants even if in fact many existed only so that ministry accountants could draw their "ghost" pay. But even those who did actually exist seldom did any work because although many were still willing to work, they had no means at their disposal to do so. Monthly salaries for civil servants ranged (in 1992) from $91 for a ministry permanent secretary, down to $59 for the head of a service and $9 for an unskilled clerk. Civil service average pay was $14/month, but this remained theoretical as salaries were often delayed for months on end.

78. This was already an unrealistic estimate because there was no way tax collection could be improved in just a year to enable the new Congo to contribute its share of over one billion dollars.

79. There was a lot of resentment against the Rwandese military presence, even though people admitted that their efficiency had reduced criminality. But they had arrogant manners, and the Congolese population particularly resented their extensive use of the whip in public and their unpleasant habit of spitting into people's mouths in order to humiliate them. Interviews with many different Congolese from the Kivus, from Kisangani, and from Kinshasa, New York, Paris, Kampala, Bunia, October 1997 to November 2000.

80. As usual with Kabila, the issue was mostly psychopolitics. Ms M'Poyo Kasa Vubu remembers how, when she broached with the president the subject of Claes, whose detention was also ruining relations with Belgium, he shouted at her, "We will not be dictated by these people." Kasa Vubu, *Douze mois chez Kabila,* 133. When she asked him what the charges against Claes were, he could not remember.

81. Faced with bankruptcy, the Intercontinental preferred to close down for a while.

82. Interview with Aubert Mukendi, Paris, December 2000.

83. The feeling was also that widespread poverty combined with the absence of even the most modest beginnings of outside economic aid contributed to killing any idealism the AFDL could have brought along; see J. C. Willame's section on "La gestion de l'Etat: Défaite de la corruption?" in *L'odyssée Kabila* (Paris: Karthala, 1999), 119–124.

84. *Africa Confidential* 38, no. 16 (August 1, 1997). This was of course partly due to completely stopping the printing of new money. But this improvement in the rate of exchange was also due to the fact that there were fewer and fewer manufactured products to be bought on the market and that the demand for dollars was declining rather than that the intrinsic value of the NZ was improving.

85. *Le Monde,* December 4, 1997.

86. Kasa Vubu, *Douze mois chez Kabila,* 66.

87. This included $36 million from Gécamines, $12 million from MIBA, and $9.9 million in oil revenue, leaving almost nothing from nonmineral exports.

88. Mining Minister Kibassa Maliba and Finance Minister Tala Ngai had introduced a new licensing system for the diamond purchasing counters where taxes had to be paid in advance. *La Lettre Afrique Energies,* February 11, 1998.

89. For an overview of the interrelationship between diplomacy and aid, see C. Collins, "Congo-ex-Zaire: Through the Looking Glass," *Review of African Political Economy,* April 1998, 114–123.

90. *IRIN Bulletin,* no. 328 (January 8, 1998).

91. *La Lettre Afrique Energies,* January 14, 1998.

92. *La Lettre Afrique Energies,* May 13, 1998.

93. J. Maton and A. Van Bauwell, "L'économie congolaise 1997–2000: Le désenchantement et les échecs possibles," in F. Reyntjens and S. Marysse, eds., *L'Afrique des Grands Lacs: Annuaire 1997–1998* (Paris: L'Harmattan, 1998), 204. By early 1999 the tax proportion of GNP had risen to 11 percent.

94. The "automatic alliance system" was already at work: Sassou Nguesso having had close relations with Mobutu was seen as pro-Habyarimana, which brought the Tutsi RPF close to Lissouba.

95. The pro-Lissouba militias (Zulu, Cocoye, Aubevillois) had theoretically been included in the regular army, but in reality they had kept separate financial and command structures. Interview with Rémy Bazenguissa-Ganga, Paris, January 1998.

96. "Congo Brazzaville: A Dictator Returns," *Africa Confidential* 38, no. 21 (October 24, 1997).

97. The best objective analysis on that war can be found in the special issue of *Afrique Contemporaine,* no. 186 (April–June 1998) edited by Roland Pourtier on the Brazzaville Congo (articles by R. Pourtier, P. Yengo, R. Bazenguissa-Ganga, E. Dorrier-Apprill, and A. Kouvouma). The best book on these events is Y. Koula, *La démocratie congolaise brûlée au pétrole* (Paris: L'Harmattan, 1999), which is anti-Sassou without being pro-Lissouba. N. Dabira, *Brazzaville à feu et à sang* (Paris: l'Harmattan, 1998) is a colorful document by a Soviet-trained officer who became one of Sassou's main militia commanders.

98. Césaire to the French Ministry of Foreign Affairs, May 10, 1995, quoted in *La Lettre du Continent,* May 18, 1995.

99. FIBA was Elf's private bank, used for its dubious deals with foreign heads of state and oil ministers. It was later closed down when Elf was bought by TOTAL.

100. "Congo/Angola: La paix pétrolière," *La Lettre du Continent,* October 30, 1997. August 31 was the expiration date for Lissouba's presidential mandate. Sassou's irritation was partly due to the fact that when he won the war he found documents in the presidential palace proving that the oil fees had been directly transferred to pay for Lissouba's weapons: see Dominique Gallois, "Le jeu ambigu d'Elf au Congo," *Le Monde,* October 30, 1997.

101. Lissouba had subcontracted a lot of his security to UNITA and FLEC-Renovado, which were taking care of the Pointe Noire Airport while Lissouba's militias were battling it out with Sassou's Zulus in the capital.

102. This rivalry between Kabila's two main backers over Congo Republic policies went largely unnoticed at the time. But it was a forerunner of the radical split that was to occur a year later, showing the largely illusory nature of the whole "new African leaders" theory.

103. *IRIN Bulletin,* no. 268, October 13, 1997. For a discussion of the political context of the interventions, see Y. Koula, *La démocratie congolaise,* 104–109.

104. R. Bazenguissa-Ganga, "Les milices politiques dans les affrontements," *Afrique Contemporaine,* no. 186 (April–June 1998): 55.

105. Quoted in ibid., 52.

106. For details of that return to war, see Human Rights Watch, *Angola Unravels: The Rise and Fall of the Lusaka Peace Process,* New York, 1999.

107. For the immediate consequences, see ICRC communiqué, Geneva, June 18, 1997, and WFP communiqués of October 1, 1977 (Kinshasa) and November 17, 1997 (Nairobi).

108. An overview of how the Kivu problems led to the war can be found in G. Prunier, "The Catholic Church and the Kivu Conflict," *Journal of Religion in Africa* 31, no. 2 (2001): 139–162.

109. For a good description of how the democratic opening worked in antidemocratic ways for the east, see K. Vlassenroot, "The Promise of Ethnic Conflict: Militarisation and Enclave Formation in South Kivu," in D. Goyvaerts, ed., *Conflict and Ethnicity in Central Africa* (Tokyo: Institute for the Study of Languages and Cultures of Asia and Africa, 2000), especially 72–74. Generally speaking, Vlassenroot offers the best short analysis of the relationship between land, ethnicity, politics, and violence in the Kivus since independence.

110. The perfect example was the way the Bashi got split into pro- and antigovernment groups when Faustin Birindwa, a Mushi, was made prime minister by Mobutu.

111. The same could be said later of the Lusaka Agreement of July 1999. Even though it was roughly implemented at the *international* level, it did not solve the *domestic problem* of the Kivus, as became abundantly clear during 2002–2003 when the national situation improved while that of the east worsened. Even now, in the aftermath of the 2006 elections, implementing the final 2002 peace settlement remains a daunting task in the east.

112. *IRIN Bulletin*, no. 201 (June 26, 1997).

113. *IRIN Bulletin*, no. 240 (September 3, 1997).

114. *IRIN Bulletin*, no. 243 (September 8, 1997).

115. *IRIN Bulletin*, no. 245 (September 10, 1997).

116. For a detailed description, see African Rights, *Rwanda: The Insurgency in the Northwest,* London, September 1998, 94–98. What the Rwandese government called *abacengezi* ("infiltrators") the local population often called *abacunguzi* ("liberators"). They were mostly ex-army regulars who had turned back during the Zaire campaign and had been reorganized as the Armée de Libération du Rwanda (ALIR) under the command of former FAR officers (Major Rwabukwisi, Colonel Mpiranya, General Kabirigi). They received support from some of the civilian returnees who had "voluntarily" crossed the border in mid-November 1996.

117. Amnesty International, *Rwanda: Ending the Silence,* London, September 1997, 36.

118. Author's interviews with UNHRFOR employees, Kigali and Butare, April 1997.

119. On the events of this period, see G. Prunier, "Rwanda: The Social, Political and Economic Situation in June 1997," *Writenet Analysis Network,* July 1997.

120. See Human Rights Watch, *Uprooting the Rural Poor in Rwanda,* New York, May 2001. The Rwandese government was incensed at the publication of this report, which damaged the virtuous image it depended on for continued foreign financial support. Interestingly, my somewhat sketchy field notes dating back to April 1997 fully corroborate the more detailed Human Rights Watch document.

121. See *IRIN Bulletin*, no. 259 (September 30, 1997) for the North Kivu Provin-

cial Security Commission denial. The facts were confirmed to me by a former AFDL eyewitness. Interview, Kampala, January 2000. The dead were said to number 500. The real figure could have been around 200 to 300.

122. *IRIN Bulletin*, no. 293 (November 17, 1997).

123. For a description of how the new government's policies made a bad situation worse, see J. C Willame, "Les relations du régime Kabila avec le Kivu," in G. de Villers and J. C. Willame, eds., *Congo*, especially 240–255.

124. *IRIN Bulletin*, no. 300 (November 26, 1997).

125. Interview with his uncle Aristide Chahihabwa Bambaga, Kampala, January 2000.

126. *IRIN Bulletin*, no. 303 (November 29, 1997). An unconfirmed report published in the *New York Times* said there were eighteen casualties in the shootings. Two days later Kabila created his new secret service, the Direction Militaire des Activités Anti-Patrie (DEMIAP), which was given the job of carrying out internal political repression.

127. *IRIN Bulletin*, no. 304 (December 2, 1997).

128. *IRIN Bulletin*, no. 305 (December 3, 1997). Masasu's subsequent stormy trial in Lubumbashi is vividly described in Joris, *La danse du léopard*, chapter 10. The Masasu Nindaga episode was the distant beginning of the chain of events that eventually led to Kabila's assassination in January 2001.

129. See Willame, "Les relations," 247–252.

130. Kabila had many relatives of Masasu arrested, both in Kinshasa and in South Kivu. Upon arrest they were told that their crime was "to have consorted with the USA and France," a perfect display of how the president's mind was stuck in the 1960s groove, when all the "imperialists" had worked in alliance. Interview with Aristide Chahihabwa Bambaga, Kampala, January 2000.

131. Quoted in Willame, "Les relations," 261–262.

132. For a description of the rough treatment meted out to the former FAZ, see Kisukula Abeli Meitho, *La désintégration de l'armée congolaise de Mobutu à Kabila* (Paris: L'Harmattan, 2001), chapter 6.

133. On the causes of the mutiny, see *Memorandum de la Communauté Banyamulenge à Son Excellence le Président de la République Démocratique du Congo, eut égard à la situation sécuritaire qui prévaut au Sud Kivu*, Bukavu, February 24, 1998.

134. This was a logical development given the fact that many Banyamulenge families had relatives in Burundi and that several more had taken refuge there to escape from FDD attacks. The FAB had had troops in South Kivu since October 1996 to counter FDD infiltrations.

135. See *IRIN Bulletin*, no. 366 (March 3, 1998). Commenting on the Ugandan involvement following in the steps of the Burundese intervention in South Kivu, the *Deutsche Tageszeitung* was the first paper to speculate on the possibility of "a future regional war of invasion" (February 27, 1998).

136. Interestingly enough, the third large group of dissenters (i.e., the Baluba from Kasaï) remained on the sidelines, biding their time, hoping for a Tschisekedi breakthrough at some point.

137. Up to the time when their shabby treatment in his hands led them to revolt (see chapter 6).

138. The attempts at recruiting former Mayi Mayi logically proved disappointing. Their differences with Kabila had to do with the Rwandese; once they sensed an imminent fallout between the two, they were bound to side with the president,

even if they had few illusions about him.

139. Charles Petrie, *Report to the UN Office for the Co-ordination of Humanitarian Affairs*, Goma, June 16, 1998.

140. The Congolese journalist Bapuwa Mawamba had recently written, "One is almost surprised that war has not yet broken out in Kivu. All the ingredients are there for a conflagration which could set fire to the whole region." *Jeune Afrique Economie*, June 1–14, 1998.

141. See Gérard Prunier, "Convoitises multiples sur le Kivu: Une poudrière au cœur du Congo Kinshasa," *Le Monde Diplomatique*, July 1998. It is difficult to resist the temptation of quoting what I was writing a month before the war started: "Kivu is on the verge of blowing up and nobody is trying to find the scissors to cut the fuse. There will be time later to write long reports about international financing, 'lessons learned' and other adequate recommendations for the next crisis."

142. It is interesting to note that even at that late stage the Mayi Mayi were still considered by Kinshasa to be the major danger.

143. République Démocratique du Congo, Présidence de la République, Communiqué de Démenti, June 8, 1998 (extract of an interview with Didier Mumengi, minister of information, on June 5, 1998).

144. Chamuleso was the leader of the dwindling band of real or supposed survivors of Che Guevara's adventure in South Kivu. After having spent years living in Cuba he came back to the Congo in 1997 and was instrumental in promoting a modicum of help for Kabila from the Castro regime.

145. *IRIN Bulletin*, no. 468 (July 28, 1998).

146. *IRIN Bulletin*, no. 469 (July 29, 1998).

147. Kabarebe had been replaced a few weeks before by Pierre-Célestin Kifwa, Kabila's brother-in-law.

148. Interview with a relative of one of Kabila's bodyguards who witnessed the scene, Kampala, January 2000. This gung-ho mad dog attitude is rather typical of a certain category of RPA "Ugandan" officer and was later to prove an important factor in the conduct of the war.

Chapter 6

1. For the situation on the eve of the war as seen from North Kivu, see International Crisis Group, *North Kivu, into the quagmire?* Brussels, August 1998. For the general situation in the Kivus, see Bapuwa Mawanda's article in *Jeune Afrique Economie* and mine in *Le Monde Diplomatique:* "Convoitises multiples sur le Kivu: Une poudrière au cœur du Congo Kinshasa," July 1998.

2. The first official pronouncement of a rebellion came on August 2 at 4:00 p.m. from Cdr. Sylvain Mbuki, commanding officer of the FAC 10th Battalion in Goma, who declared, "We, the Army of the DRC, have taken the decision to remove President Laurent-Désiré Kabila from power." SWB/Radio Rwanda, August 2, 1998.

3. "This is an affair that concerns only Congolese soldiers, the Rwandese Army is not involved in the movement," declared Cdr. Ilunga Kabambi, the FAC deputy commander for Kivu. SWB/AFP, August 3, 1998. Anastase Gasana, Kigali's minister for foreign affairs, insisted that the "crisis now arising in Kinshasa and the eastern part of the DRC is purely an internal matter and the government of Rwanda is not involved in it in any way." SWB/Radio Rwanda, August 3, 1998.

4.   *IRIN Bulletin*, no. 473 (August 4, 1998). RPA commandoes highjacked a number of commercial and cargo planes of various nationalities from the airport in Goma and used them to ferry troops clear across the Congo to Kitona during the next few days. With guns put to their heads, the pilots had no choice. See, in *Libération*, August 22–23, 1998, the story of the Nigerian pilot Raymond Niang, who managed to get away and fly his Boeing 707 to Lagos. Most of the money for the operation was quickly raised from the old Mobutists Nzimbi, Baramoto, and their friends, who rushed to Kigali. Interview with a former RPA officer, Washington, DC, October 1999.

5.   REC report 8 (August 31, 1998). Most of the forty-eight officers shot (and the majority of their bodyguards) were former Katangese Tigers, and the massacre immediately drove a wedge between the mostly eastern rebels and their Balunda comrades-in-arms. Many of those later deserted the rebellion and went back either to Katanga or to Angola, where they fought against UNITA.

6.   In addition, several hundred young Banyamulenge recruits who were being trained at Kasindi were massacred by the government forces on the assumption that they would join the rebellion.

7.   The same goes for the political local cover of the makeshift rebellion: AFDL Health Minister Jean-Baptiste Sondji declared on TV a few days later that he had been contacted on August 2 at 1 p.m. by a defecting member of his staff who wanted him to come over to Goma and join the leadership of the rebellion. SWB/Radio Television Nationale Congolaise (RTNC), August 5, 1998.

8.   Interview with a former RPF cadre, Brussels, February 1999.

9.   Telephone interview with the freelance journalist (later Human Rights Watch employee) Corinne Dufka, Freetown, April 1999.

10.   Some of the officers were bought outright with quite large amounts of cash (up to $150,000 in some cases; see the September 1999 testimony of one of the FAC officers kindly communicated by Mauro de Lorenzo). Jealousies and rivalries developed around who got how much, but the rumors of loose cash led to quite a few cases of loyalty switching. See G. de Villers, J. Omasombo, and E. Kennes, *Guerre et politique: Les trente derniers mois de L. D. Kabila (août 1998– janvier 2001)* (Tervuren, Belgium: CEDAF, 2001), 18.

11.   The rebels eventually occupied Kisangani on August 23, but their hold on the city remained precarious. The population rose against them three days later in a bloody counteruprising in which twenty-eight people were killed and dozens wounded. Interview with Alphonse Maindo, Paris, December 1999.

12.   Kabarebe himself had put them there when he was FAC chief of staff and he was partly responsible for their poor treatment. The majority were ex-FAZ but there were also Angolan UNITA elements and former Lissouba militiamen from Brazzaville.

13.   He eventually came to have about eight thousand men under his command. But their military fitness varied enormously depending on whether they came from Goma or Kitona. Many of the ex-FAZ were of no use.

14.   *IRIN Bulletin*, no. 475 (August 6, 1998). The very fact that he felt obliged to say that spoke volumes about the perceived reality of the situation.

15.   *IRIN Bulletin*, no. 476 (August 7, 1998). The defense minister's declaration was somewhat disingenuous: if it was true that the FAB had not crossed the border it was because they had been in the DRC all along. Bujumbura had stationed about two thousand troops on the Congo side of Lake Tanganyika to try to prevent FDD guerrilla incursions into Burundi.

16.   *IRIN Bulletin*, no. 478 (August 11, 1998).

17.   Hundreds more crossed the river and took refuge in Brazzaville. Popular anger against the Tutsi was such that quite a few Tutsi-looking people (mostly Somali traders) were lynched by angry mobs. For a description of the situation in Kinshasa at that time, see Lieve Joris, *La danse du léopard* (Arles: Actes Sud, 2002), chapter 12; J. B. Gervais, *Kabila, chronique d'une debâcle annoncée* (Villeurbanne, France: Editions Golias, 1999). Gervais, himself a Tutsi half-caste, gives an honest description of the reasons Banyamulenge were disliked in the capital (68–70) and of the resulting violence against them, in which he himself was caught (128–152).

18.   Thus the Bunia radio issuing calls to kill "those tall and slim ones with the long noses who want to dominate us" (SWB/RTNC, August 8, 1998) just a few days before the town fell to rebel forces. There were similar anti-Tutsi pogroms in Lubumbashi, driving hundreds of Banyaviura refugees into Zambia. Although this was a godsend for Kigali's propaganda mill (on August 11 Cdr. Sylvain Mbuki aired the first rebel accusation about Kinshasa, making use of *Interahamwe* militiamen), the largely spontaneous Congolese lynch mobs were quite differently motivated than the Rwandese *génocidaires* of 1994.

19.   *IRIN Bulletin*, no. 477 (August 8–10, 1998).

20.   This was actually a dangerous strategy because he would have been fully dependent on South African electrical supply to Katanga, as the Inga line would have been cut off. See *La Lettre Afrique Energies,* August 26, 1998. And, as we will see, South Africa's attitude toward Kinshasa was by then extremely ambiguous.

21.   His tenure as Mobutu's prime minister in the early 1990s had been so bad that his nickname among Kinshasa's populace was Ndunda Bololo, "bitter vegetable."

22.   J. C. Willame, *Congo: Nouvelle crise dans les Grands Lacs,* Geneva, Writenet Report, August 1998.

23.   *IRIN Bulletin*, no. 482 (August 18, 1998). Tschisekedi was biding his time, both because he did not like Kabila and because Z'Ahidi Ngoma had mentioned in public that the "UDPS should be part of the future government."

24.   His father had just made him acting army chief of staff.

25.   *IRIN Bulletin*, no. 484 (August 20, 1998).

26.   The reason for his hesitation was that he had among his forces large numbers of ex-FAZ who were broadly sympathetic to the anti-Kabila movement. But once the MPLA swung its weight against it he had to follow, because since UNITA and FLEC still backed what was left of Lissouba's forces he could not afford to do without Luanda's full support. As for Museveni, his threat was largely rhetorical since he did not have the means to intervene that far from his border.

27.   An average of three planes a day landed at Kitona from Goma between August 5 and 21. But the Rwandese army could not match the equipment and firepower of the FAA, who killed over seven hundred of their enemies in three days of fighting. Telephone interview with eyewitness Corinne Dufka, March 1999.

28.   I later heard in Washington a persistent (but uncorroborated) rumor according to which they had been hired courtesy of the U.S. Defense Intelligence Agency. In any case the whole operation was monitored by two U.S. navy surveillance warships anchored just outside the harbor of Banana. *Le Soir,* September 19, 1998; interviews with DIA personnel, Washington, DC, October 1999. As for the FAA, they waited and let the Rwandese expeditionary force reembark, prob-

ably to avoid antagonizing Washington by crushing them.

29.   This poses the still unanswered question of whether the logistics of the evacuation were improvised or had been discussed beforehand between UNITA and the Rwandese. Other defeated rebel or RPA troops also transited through Brazzaville, where both Sassou-Nguesso and his Angolan protectors looked the other way as they were passing through.

30.   See de Villers, Omasombo, and Kennes, *Guerre et politique,* 26–31. This desperate attempt at taking Ndjili Airport even as the main force was being evacuated had to do with two things: first, the bedraggled bands that entered Kinshasa on the 26th were mainly not Rwandese but rather ex-FAZ from Kitona who were fleeing forward more than they were attacking; second, it seemed that Kabarebe had gotten rid of them by promising to pick them up by plane if they could take Ndjili. The promised planes never materialized and Kabarebe's main force left western Congo by the morning of August 29.

31.   For garish descriptions of the street massacres, see "Kinshasa Mobs Torch Retreating Rebels," *Times* (London), August 28, 1998; "Comment Kabila s'est fait chasseur de Tutsi," *Libération,* August 28, 1998; "Les rebelles congolais sont pourchassés dans les rues de Kinshasa," *Le Monde,* August 29, 1998. For a more complex analysis of the mobs' motivations, see Adrien de Mun, "Les Kinois ont participé à la chasse aux rebelles," *La Croix,* September 5, 1998.

32.   SWB/RTBF, August 27, 1998.

33.   Both sides had been lobbing accusations of genocide and/or ethnic cleansing at each other on an almost routine basis since the first days of the war, whether it was Wamba dia Wamba accusing Kabila of "intended genocide" (SWB/RFI, August 13, 1998) or the same Yerodia Ndombasi saying that the rebels "want to exterminate the Bantu authochtones" (SWB/RTNC, August 27, 1998). Tutsi living in Belgium later sued Yerodia Ndombasi for these utterances.

34.   About two thousand invading troops remained trapped in the western Congo, half of them Rwandese and half belonging to the 23rd and 31st UPDF battalions under Brig. Ivan Koreta. These were elite troops of the Ugandan army who had been trained by U.S. instructors as part of the African Crisis Response Initiative (ACRI). The Americans repatriated the UPDF force discreetly in September but later barred Uganda from further participation in ACRI.

35.   *IRIN Bulletin,* no. 492 (September 1, 1998).

36.   Leaving behind a total body count of 7,731 victims. REC report, October 30, 1998.

37.   This was partly due to an unfortunate off-the-cuff remark from Cooperation Minister Charles Josselin, who had said in early August, "Kabila is perhaps not fit to be the president of a continent-sized country." François Soudan, "RD Congo: Les dessous de la guerre," *Jeune Afrique,* September 1, 1998. Arthur Z'Ahidi Ngoma later praised France's "understanding" of the situation. *Le Figaro,* August 18, 1998. When two French diplomats were expelled from Kinshasa, Prime Minister Lionel Jospin was spurred to state the obvious by denying any support for the rebels. SWB/RFI, August 19, 1998.

38.   "Angola's Endless Wars," *Economist,* September 25, 1999.

39.   Washington, Moscow, and Lisbon.

40.   *Lettres d'Angola,* no. 16 (April 1998). The incident was hurriedly ascribed to a "mechanical failure" and the promised Commission of Inquiry never reported its conclusions.

41.   *Nord-Sud Export,* November 6, 1998. "Ben Ben" was the brother of Elias Salu-

peto Pena, who had been murdered by the MPLA in Luanda in 1992. His death was ascribed to "acute malaria."

42. For further details of the MPLA's extermination of UNITA cadres from May 1997 onwards, see Francois Misser's article in *New African*, "Stumbling towards Peace," May 1998.

43. For example, Savimbi's status was supposed to allow him to travel and speak freely, but the UN sanctions prohibited him from doing so.

44. Since mid-1996 half a dozen mining companies (the Australian Ashton, the Brazilian Oudebrechts, the South African De Beers, the Russian Alrosa, the Canadian Diamond Works) had invested over $400 million in the Angolan diamond industry. *Africa Analysis,* January 23, 1998. They immediately expanded their operations to the Kwango Valley as it came under MPLA control.

45. *Libération,* June 18, 1998.

46. USIA transcript of Susan Rice's speech in Luanda on October 29, 1998.

47. Interview with Radio France Internationale on August 30, 1998.

48. SWB/Radio Nacional de Angola, July 20, 22, and 25, 1998; *Le Monde,* September 2, 1998.

49. Interview with a U.S. State Department specialist, Washington, DC, October 1999.

50. Interview with EU Special Envoy Aldo Ajello, Brussels, February 1999. To try to sway dos Santos much was made in Kigali and Kampala of alleged diamond dealings on UNITA's behalf by Kabila's entourage.

51. *La Lettre du Continent,* August 27, 1998. The late Michel Pacary was well known for his role in the illegal financing of the Gaullist political party RPR, which eventually brought him to face the courts. He was also a lobbyist for FLEC and a personal friend of Z'Ahidi Ngoma, whom he had known when he worked at UNESCO in Paris.

52. Interview with a CIA operative, Washington, DC, October 1999.

53. The joke notwithstanding, this rough attitude might have played a part in the later sidelining of De Matos by the president.

54. Particularly since they enjoyed Washington's support.

55. After several sour exchanges and reciprocal visits the Angolan government ended up asking for international sanctions against South Africa for failing to stop arm flows to UNITA. IRIN, September 15, 1998.

56. Six people were killed, scores wounded, and eight hundred arrested. SAPA News Agency, Johannesburg, January 22, 1998.

57. After the war of independence in 1980 Mugabe promised to resettle 162,000 families in five years. Fifteen years later only 70,000 families had benefited from the program, but the 270 biggest farms had gone to the ruling elite. "Buying the Farm," *Africa Confidential* 38, no. 24 (December 15, 1998); various interviews with Zimbabwe specialist Daniel Compagnon, Paris, 2000.

58. "Zimbabwe: Poorer and Angrier," *Economist,* August 15, 1998.

59. Jakkie Potgieter from the Pretoria-based Institute for Security Studies estimated that Zimbabwe had a $200 million stake in Kabila's regime, mostly due to war loans in 1996–1997 and later to emergency financial support for the faltering regime. *Business Day* (South Africa), August 21, 1998.

60. Zimbabwe was still smarting from the situation at the end of the war in Mozambique, where Harare did all the hard military work in support of FRELIMO only to see South African companies get all the lucrative reconstruction contracts after the conflict was over.

61.   ZDI is a government-owned military products company which was created with British and South African help during the period of Ian Smith's minority regime (1965–1979), when Rhodesia had to fight the nationalist guerrillas with its own means. It was later developed with French and Chinese help by the ZANU regime after 1980.

62.   "Zimbabwe: Cap sur l'ex-Zaïre," *La Lettre de l'Océan Indien,* October 11, 1997.

63.   The Kapushi zinc mines that were being discussed had been promised to Anglo-American. This riled both the South African giant and some of its mining allies. See Donald McNeil Jr., "Congo Exiles Group Seeks Kabila's Ouster," *New York Times,* September 2, 1998; "Zimbabwe/Congo: Les mines au coeur de l'alliance," *La Lettre de l'Océan Indien,* September 5, 1998.

64.   SWB/SAPA News Agency, August 20, 1998. There were only three South African security operatives in Goma, but they had come there as part of Foreign Affairs Minister Alfred Nzo's and Defense Minister Joe Modise's visiting delegation to Rwanda and Uganda.

65.   SWB/Radio Harare, August 20, 1998.

66.   See chapter 3.

67.   Its per capita income of $1,890 put it among the middle-income economies.

68.   Defense spending had reached $90 million in 1998, that is, over 10 percent of the total budget. *Nord Sud Export,* January 26, 2001.

69.   Former South African Ambassador to the DRC (1999–2006) Sisa Ngombane later told me, "This was the wisest decision we ever took." Interview in Pretoria, November 2007.

70.   See G. Prunier, "Rebel Movements and Proxy Warfare: Uganda, Sudan and the Congo (1986–1999)," *African Affairs* 103, no. 412 (2004): 359–383.

71.   For these developments, see chapter 3.

72.   Interview with Seth Sendashonga, Nairobi, April 1998.

73.   See Peter Strandberg, "With the Rebels in the Congo," *New African,* February 1999.

74.   See *IRIN Bulletin,* no. 501 (September 12–14, 1998). Khartoum countered Ugandan accusations of military intervention on the Kindu front by saying that UPDF troops were fighting alongside SPLA forces in El Jebeleyn and Torit. While it was true that Kampala was providing logistical support to the Sudanese rebels, Ugandan troops were not involved directly on the battlefield. But just in case, both countries denied everything.

75.   I will discuss more fully Tripoli and Ndjamena's reasons for coming into the war in the next section. For the moment let me just say that Libya's involvement was largely motivated by Colonel Gaddaffi's larger-than-life diplomatic delusions, while Chad was in the game only because Sudan needed a proxy and President Idris Deby could not refuse anything to the men in Khartoum who had put him in power, with French help, in 1990.

76.   As early as late August Kagame was declaring to the French journalist François Soudan (*Jeune Afrique,* September 1, 1998), "*Interahamwe* militiamen are trained by Kabila and are receiving a military formation in Kamina and in the Garamba National Park." Later, Kagame's first admission that RPA troops were indeed fighting in the Congo (November 6, 1998) was accompanied by a statement saying that they were there "specifically to ensure our national security." *Libération,* November 7–8, 1998.

77.   ALIR was the new name under which the ex-FAR and former *Interahamwe*

reorganized in the Congo. See Rémy Ourdan, "Les combats s'intensifient dans la région des Grands Lacs," *Le Monde,* January 4–5, 1998; Laurent Bijard, "Les Hutus ressortent les machettes," *Le Nouvel Observateur,* January 22–28, 1998; Vincent Hugueux, "Rwanda: La guerre sans fin," *L'Express,* February 5, 1998.

78. "Any trust that had been built between Tutsi and Hutu is waning. You can see it at receptions, they avoid eye contact, even among ministers." Alan Thompson, "The Killing Continues," *New African,* May 1998.

79. The RPF Congress held in Kigali on February 14–16, 1998, had made him president of the Party in addition to his positions as vice president and minister of defense.

80. What made the execution even worse than its timing was the fact that at least one of the victims (Silas Munyagishali) and possibly two others (Déogratias Bizimana and Egide Gatanazi) were known to be innocent and to have been lumped together with the guilty parties for reasons of political vengeance. Interviews with Rwandese political refugees, Nairobi, May 1998.

81. For a short assessment of Sendashonga's position at the time and of his murder, see the appendix.

82. For an evaluation of the situation in mid-1998, see "Rwanda: North West Nightmare, *Africa Confidential* 39, no. 15 (July 24, 1998).

83. Author's interview with a high-ranking member of a European Secret Service (not France's!) who carried out a mission of evaluation in Rwanda for his government in mid-1998.

84. Clinton's apology for his neglect during the genocide was only proper. But it was coming too late and at the wrong time. It was perceived by the RPF *akazu* as a tool with which to manipulate U.S. support.

85. The Ethio-Eritrean war and Kigali's failure at mediation seriously damaged the U.S. discourse on the "new African leaders." The later Rwanda-Uganda military confrontation in Kisangani in 1999 finally put paid to that rhetoric.

86. *IRIN Bulletin,* no. 475 (August 6, 1998).

87. It was at the same time that hijacked aircraft flew Brig. Ivan Koreta and his men to Kitona.

88. John F. Clark, "Explaining Ugandan Intervention in Congo: Evidence and Interpretations," *Journal of Modern African Studies* 39, no. 2 (2000): 261–287.

89. This is, for example, a fundamentally different situation from that of Burundi in 1996, whose fragility indeed precipitated Kagame's decision to move into Zaire.

90. Agence France Presse, Kampala, January 31, 1997.

91. See, for example, the description of the joint UPDF-SPLA operation carried out inside southern Sudan in early April 1997, killing 153 and taking 210 prisoners, followed a few days later by another battle wherein sixty Sudanese soldiers and sixty-eight LRA fighters were killed. *New Vision,* April 12 and 18, 1997. By mid-1998 there were over 170,000 IDPs in northern Uganda.

92. See *New Vision,* November 14, 1997; interviews with UPDF officers in Bundibungyo, March 1998.

93. In a conversation with visiting Dutch Deputy Prime Minister Hans van Mierle on January 17, 1998.

94. These were a gaggle of WBNLF, SPLA deserters, ex-FAZ, and Sudanese soldiers cut off by the March 1997 joint UPDF-SPLA operation on Yei. But contrary to what Kagame claimed at the time, there were no *Interahamwe*; even if there had been, it would have been quite beyond the power of Laurent-Désiré Kabila

to "train" them in that isolated wilderness.

95. In terms of political philosophy Museveni was in favor of rebels fighting their own battles rather than foreign armies taking on the brunt of their struggle. This difference of philosophy was later to resurface devastatingly in the Congo, where Kigali simply wanted to kick Kabila out and put a puppet government in Kinshasa while Museveni was hoping to foster a friendly but home-grown Congolese movement.

96. *La Lettre de l'Océan Indien,* August 29, 1998.

97. Crespo Sebunya, "Uganda: Trouble in the Army," *New African,* October 1997.

98. *La Lettre de l'Océan Indien,* June 13, 1998. None of these cases led to prosecution.

99. Even that did cause trouble since it increased the clashes between the Upe section of the Karimojong tribe (to which government Security Adviser David Pulkol belonged) and the hostile Pian clan, which did not get any benefit from the gold mining. Author's field notes, Karamoja, November 1997.

100. Branch Energy Uganda Ltd. was a subsidiary of Heritage Oil and Gas run by former SAS officer Tony Buckingham, a close associate of Executive Outcome's Eben Barlow. In December 1996 Branch Energy received a 4,800-square kilomter oil research permit on the shores of Lake Albert, where TOTAL, Petrofina, and UGWEC had previously made rather desultory attempts at oil exploration.

101. This probably had to do with the postgenocide survival syndrome, whereby most Tutsi of military age felt that they had to stick together, no matter what. There was no such feeling among Ugandans. Similarly, the Rwandese Congo Desk made sure that a thick slice of the pie would go to Defense. Again there was nothing comparable in Kampala.

102. Institute for Security Studies expert Jackkie Potgieter, quoted in *Afrique Express,* April 29, 1999. Ndola was used as a transshipment point for UNITA fuel coming from abroad into Zambia.

103. It also led the Congolese government to express strong reservations about Chiluba's neutrality in acting as a peacemaker. These reservations were most likely groundless: the Zambian regime wanted *both* to make money with UNITA and to ingratiate itself with the donors by brokering a peace deal in the DRC, never acknowledging the contradiction between the two.

104. South African aircraft carried out the evacuation after a personal conversation between President Mkapa and not-yet-president Thabo Mbeki. Author's interview with a French diplomat, Paris, January 2000.

105. Colette Braeckman, "Les opposants rwandais ne manquent pas d'armes," *Le Soir,* October 8, 1998.

106. Personal interview with Seth Sendashonga, Nairobi, April 1998. (See Annex One.)

107. UNHCR registered 350,000 Burundian refugees in Tanzania, but the total population was huge, possibly up to 800,000, and many had been settled there for over twenty years, slowly retreating into their own world. On this, see Lisa Malkki's wonderful book *Purity and Exile: Violence, Memory and National Cosmology among Hutu Refugees in Tanzania* (Chicago: University of Chicago Press, 1995).

108. It went back to August 1985, when Moi tried to act as a peacemaker between the Ugandan Military Council of Basilio Okello and Museveni's guerrillas after the overthrow of Obote. Museveni played along with Moi, used him, ridi-

culed him, and then went back to war, eventually upsetting the Kenyan peace arrangements. Moi never forgave him and tensions eventually led to border clashes in 1987, followed by grudging but never honestly felt reconciliation. Author's personal reminiscences from 1985 to 2000 in Nairobi and Kampala.

109.   See chapter 3. To understand the political evolution that brought about the Brazzaville-Congo creeping violence, see Rémy Bazenguissa-Ganga, *Les voies du politique au Congo: Essai de sociologie historique* (Paris: Karthala, 1997).

110.   For the very complex meaning of the word *tribal* used in relationship to Brazzaville tribal militias, see Elizabeth Dorier-Apprill, "Guerre des milices et fragmentation urbaine à Brazzaville," *Hérodote,* no. 86/87, 4th quarter (1997): 182–221; Rémy Bazenguissa-Ganga, "Milices politiques et bandes armées à Brazzaville: Enquête sur la violence politique des jeunes déclassés," *Etudes du CERI,* no. 13 (April 1996).

111.   *Nord Sud Export,* May 29, 1998. Lissouba had declared somewhat undiplomatically on French TV M6, "Elf has helped me in the war effort because I asked them." But the tactic was hardly convincing because Lissouba had earlier tried to sue Elf for supporting Sassou Nguesso against him. See Stephen Smith, "La plainte de Lissouba contre Elf irrecevable," *Libération,* January 15, 1998.

112.   Fédération Internationale des Ligues des Droits de l'Homme, *Congo Brazzaville: L'arbitraire de l'Etat, la terreur des milices,* June 1999, 7.

113.   *IRIN Bulletin,* no. 204 (July 2, 1997).

114.   Agence France Presse dispatch, Brazzaville, November 10, 1998.

115.   Because it feared the Congo-based FDD rebels and tried to court Rwanda's favor against them.

116.   In spite of its problems with Chad, with the Republic of Congo, and with Congo itself once the war got to the Central African Republic border.

117.   Until extremely late in the game (July 2003), when it sent a peacekeeping force to Kindu, to help the Mission des Nations Unies au Congo (MONUC). The peacekeeping force sent to Burundi in 2001 does not count since it always remained strictly limited to that country, where it did not achieve much anyway.

118.   This was to change later in the war.

119.   The best (or worst) anecdote at this level was told to me by Ugandan Foreign Minister Eriya Kategaya, who had once been asked by South African Foreign Minister Alfred Nzo, "I can't remember: the country where the Tutsi have always been in power: is it Rwanda or Burundi?"

120.   S. E. Katzenellenbogen, *Railways and the Copper Mines of Katanga* (Oxford: Clarendon Press, 1973) is the best introduction to the interlocking complexities of the South African, Rhodesian, and Katangese economies.

121.   "Kenya Wary of SA Link in Africa Rail," *East African,* October 26, 1998.

122.   *Afrique Energies,* November 18, 1998.

123.   *IRIN Bulletin,* no. 494 (September 3, 1998).

124.   Quoted in *La Croix,* September 18, 1998.

125.   Stephen Smith, "La partition de l'ex-Zaïre semble inévitable," *Libération,* September 9, 1998.

126.   *IRIN Bulletin,* no. 497 (September 8, 1998).

127.   The few Rwandese remnants in the West crossed over into Angola and joined UNITA forces, which unsuccessfully attacked Maquela do Zombo in early September.

128.   The central basin, with its thick forest cover, absence of roads, and limited population was not a preferred axis. In early 1999 RPA-RCD forces eventually

made their way to Ikela, where they clashed inconclusively with the Zimbabwe-ans for months, leaving the central front something of a backwater.

129. "Records of the Regional Bureaus (Great Lakes)," Fund 19, Sub-fund 7, UN-HCR Archives, Geneva. The refugees joined the war anyway.

130. *REC Bulletin,* no. 10/98 (October 30, 1998).

131. The other country was very likely Rwanda.

132. Jean-Philippe Rémy, "Rébellion-business au Congo," *Libération,* August 13, 1999.

133. Jean-Pierre Bemba had been sent to Belgium by his father at a very young age and had spent more time in Europe than in Africa. He was more at ease speaking French than Lingala.

134. *New Vision,* November 4, 1998.

135. Agence France Presse dispatch, Kisangani, November 13, 1998.

136. *IRIN Bulletin,* no. 541 (November 9, 1998). To explain these large losses one should keep in mind that the Chadians were fighting in a very unfamiliar environment and for a cause they did not even understand.

137. This is part of the ambiguity of the boy-soldiers phenomenon. Unnatural as it may seem to a Western mind, we should remember that most child-soldiers are volunteers. A taste for adventure and an almost total lack of opportunities, especially at the educational level, explain the phenomenon. To condemn it without working for serious alternatives is merely moralistic, not practical. It would also be honest to remember the revolutionary and Napoleonic wars, in which children of fifteen and sixteen commonly fought, partly because they were press-ganged and partly because of the excitement of the times.

138. Interview in *L'Autre Afrique,* October 28, 1998.

139. On October 10 the RCD shot down a Congo Airlines Boeing 737 with forty passengers on board. *IRIN Bulletin,* no. 521 (October 12, 1998).

140. Both Angolan and Zimbabwean planes were involved.

141. *IRIN Bulletin,* no. 566 (December 12–14). It was the ZNA that bore the brunt of the fighting, and it got severely mauled in Pweto, losing several tanks, one Alouette helicopter, one jet fighter bomber, and over a hundred men.

142. *IRIN Bulletin,* no. 634 (March 22, 1999). The ZNA got hit again, with one "Mig" shot down and many soldiers killed. Communiqués routinely described the Zimbabwean Air Force fighter bombers as "Migs," while the force had none on strength. In fact they were probably old Hawker Hunters or possibly more modern Bae Hawks.

143. *IRIN Bulletin,* no. 637 (March 25, 1999).

144. Interview with Agence France Presse, Lisala, January 14, 1999.

145. Bemba had more success in recruiting in the Central African Republic than Kinshasa did because many of the riverine tribes, such as the Sango, Yakoma, and Buraka, were close relatives of the Congolese Equateur tribes. Bemba's own Ngbaka actually lived on both sides of the Ubangui.

146. Xinhua Press Agency dispatch, Harare, February 16, 1999.

147. In fact about 130 of them were Rwandese ex-FAR integrated into the ZNA. Interview with a former FAC officer, Paris, February 2000.

148. Agence France Presse dispatch, April 20, 1999.

149. Interview with an American intelligence operator, Washington, DC, September 1999.

150. Joseph Kabila was to remain only briefly as army head. He was replaced on October 20 by Col. Eddy Kapend, a Lunda officer linked to Angolan politics

through his Katangese "Tiger" connections.

151. Working for the French oil company Elf in Angola had made him a rich man and left him with a wide-ranging network of connections.

152. When the cabinet was reshuffled in March 1999, this amounted largely to a game of musical chairs.

153. Interview with a former AFDL member, Paris, March 1999.

154. *Mail and Guardian,* August 27, 1998.

155. IRIN/UNHCR Report, February 12, 1999.

156. These were the words used by Rwanda's foreign minister Anastase Gasana, who added, "The DRC is a den of armed groups who are bent upon destabilising the region." *IRIN Bulletin,* no. 540 (November 6, 1998). Given the position of the Clinton administration at the time, this was a pretty effective line of talk.

157. See *IRIN Bulletin,* no. 502 (September 15, 1998) and no. 508 (September 23, 1998). In those early days of the war the Mayi Mayi exclusively fought against the Rwandese forces and left the Ugandans alone. This was an important sign both of the differential perceptions of the two invading armies and of the eastern ethnic imbroglio in which the Banyarwanda were caught, whereas the Ugandans did not have any significant split ethnic groups on the border, the Alur factor in Province Orientale being negligible.

158. Rwandese propaganda systematically tried to equate the Mayi Mayi with the *Interahamwe* both because of the opprobrium the word carried with it and because recognizing the Mayi Mayi as nationalist guerrillas would have seriously undermined the "rebel" claims of the Rwanda-supported RCD. As for the reality of the claim it was quite variable. In some areas the Mayi Mayi would ally themselves with ex-FAR and *Interahamwe* (and even more frequently with Burundian FDD in South Kivu); in others they would go their separate ways; and in some instances, particularly in Masisi, Walikale, and Butembo, they even fought each other. Interviews with Mayi Mayi supporters, Paris and Brussels, 1999 and 2000.

159. Such as when the Zimbabweans said they had taken Fizi in December. In fact Fizi and Baraka were briefly occupied in late December and early January by a gaggle of Mayi Mayi and FDD guerrillas under the command of ex-FAZ colonel Njabiola. *IRIN Bulletin,* no. 581 (January 6, 1999). The same group later unsuccessfully attacked Bukavu, which was defended by the RPA.

160. This one was particular in that it was not a mass killing of civilians but the machine-gunning to death of over one hundred Mayi Mayi fighters who were trying to surrender. Interview with an RCD deserter eyewitness, Kampala, January 2000.

161. Many of these horrors are chronicled in the Human Rights Watch Report *DRC: Casualties of War: Civilians, Rules of Law, Democratic Freedoms* published in New York in February 1999.

162. Part of it could be attributed to the Mayi Mayi or to the *Interahamwe.* But in spite of Kigali's claim to "keep order" in the Kivus, all the large-scale massacres and many of the "ordinary" crimes could be attributed to the RPA forces and their RCD allies.

163. For glimpses of these grisly circumstances, see some of the reports produced by local NGOs in South Kivu: *Chronique d'une guerre injustifiée* (anonymous), Bukavu, November 1998; SOS Droits de l'Homme, *Rapport sur la situation des droits de l'hommes dans les zones d'Uvira et de Fizi,* Uvira, July 1999. For the role of the Catholic Church, see Gérard Prunier, "The Catholic Church and the

Kivu Conflict," *Journal of Religion in Africa* 31, no. 2 (2001): 139–162.

164. Marie-Laure Colson, "Dans l'ex-Zaïre la stratégie de la terreur gagne du terrain," *Libération,* January 15, 1999.

165. Agence France Presse dispatch, Kinshasa, April 20, 1999.

166. *La Référence Plus,* April 24, 1999.

167. From which he got a limited amount of military aid in exchange for exploration rights for uranium.

168. SWB/Radio Télévision Nationale Congolaise, April 2, 1999.

169. *IRIN Bulletin,* no. 528 (October 21, 1998).

170. Given the rapidly eroding value of the Congolese franc, about 80 percent of all gold and diamond deals were done in U.S. dollars. *L'Observateur* (Kinshasa), March 31, 1999.

171. This was particularly easy in Equateur, where the MLC had soon infiltrated its agents into Mbandaka, where they were in contact with the government side. This was much less common in Katanga and Kasaï, where the fighting was more serious.

172. *IRIN Bulletin,* no. 593 (January 22, 1999).

173. This atmosphere of tragic fun, of desperate enjoyment, is vividly illustrated in the remarkable collection of popular paintings gathered in B. Jewsiewicki and B. Planksteiner, eds., *An/Sichten: Malerei aus dem Kongo (1990–2000)* (Vienna: Museum für Völkerkunde, Springer Verlag, 2001).

174. See "Angola: Les banquiers contre l'UNITA," *Nord-Sud Export,* June 26, 1998.

175. *Africa Confidential* 39, no. 16 (August 7, 1998).

176. They included the former secretary-general Eugenio Manukavola and the former minister of tourism Jorge Valentim.

177. For a good assessment of Angola's oil-driven predatory economy, see Tony Hodges, *Angola from Afro-Stalinism to Petro-Diamond Capitalism* (Oxford: James Currey, 2001), particularly chapter 6, "Oil and the Bermuda Triangle."

178. IRIN, January 25, 1999.

179. IRIN, May 12, 1999. What he actually meant was that UNITA wanted a revision of the 1994 Agreement, with supplementary security guarantees.

180. SWB/Radio Lisbon, May 26, 1999.

181. SWB/Lusa Website, May 25, 1999. The remarks about "international observers" had to do with the fact that in January dos Santos had asked the UN not to renew MONUA's mandate when it expired on February 26. But MONUA had a $1.5 billion budget, which was sorely needed to face the massive IDP problem. Dos Santos wanted the money, but not the prying eyes.

182. SWB/SAPA News Agency, May 18, 1999. This was partly disingenuous because, although the smuggling to UNITA was indeed private and decentralized, the smugglers had enough government contacts to make sure that they would not be bothered by the police. It was often the same people, using the same airstrips, who supplied weapons to Rwanda. Diamonds were smuggled out of Angola by the same circuit.

183. IRIN, June 8, 1999.

184. UNITA was aware of the problem, and as its forces were nearing Soyo, the oil industry supply base on the coast, its secretary-general Paulo Lukamba ("Gato") declared, "Foreign oil interests will not be harmed." *La Lettre Afrique Energies,* May 19, 1999. But it was too late because the oil industry remembered the taking of Soyo in January 1993 and Savimbi's threats to "renegotiate" the oil

contracts.

185.   *Economist,* October 24, 1998.
186.   *La Lettre Afrique Energies,* October 7, 1998.
187.   Banro had closed down in the east and Tenke Mining declared force majeure for its Fungurume operation in Katanga in February 1999. *IRIN Bulletin,* no. 620 (March 2, 1999).
188.   *IRIN Bulletin,* no. 524 (October 16, 1998).
189.   *IRIN Bulletin,* no. 598 (January 29, 1999). The insurgents were as brutal as the government. They periodically slaughtered not only their Tutsi enemies (as when they killed fifty-three people at the Nyarutovu camp for Congo refugees on April 10, 1998) but even their Hutu supporters when they proved reluctant. On the very day of the Nyarutovu massacre they decapitated twenty-four villagers (including children) in Musambira. Government forces had no more humanity, but they had much better firepower and organization.
190.   Imidugudu was the name given to the new housing program supposedly designed to make up for the genocide's destructions. It was in fact closer to the Ethiopian villagization program of the 1980s, caused by the same security obsession and equally indifferent to the people's welfare. For an overall view, see Human Rights Watch, *Uprooting the Rural Poor in Rwanda,* New York, 2001.
191.   *IRIN Bulletin,* no. 635 (March 23, 1999).
192.   *IRIN Bulletin,* no. 517 (October 6, 1998).
193.   *IRIN Bulletin,* no. 643 (April 6, 1999). To give his words a heavier propaganda impact, Kagame gave that speech during the ceremonies of the genocide's fifth anniversary, complete with the spectacular reburial of thousands of corpses.
194.   *IRIN Bulletin,* no. 645 (April 8, 1999). Gahima was responding to a critical memo addressed by Michel Moussali of UNHCR to the UN Human Rights Commission.
195.   *IRIN Bulletin,* no. 674 (May 19, 1999). With Paris taking a back seat in matters Rwandese, criticism of the RPF regime was left to Belgium and Germany. But such criticism always remained muted and could not stand up to Clare Short's moral bulldozing.
196.   He was alluding to the internal RPF "elections" which had brought him to the direction of the front in February 1998.
197.   Colette Braeckman, *Le Soir,* February 5, 1999.
198.   For a good study on the Kisangani diamonds, which were to become the main apple of discord between Rwanda and Uganda, see Jean Omasombo Tshonda, "Les diamants de Kisangani," in L. Monnier, B. Jewsiewicki, and G. de Villers, eds., *Chasse au diamant au Congo/Zaïre* (Paris: L'Harmattan, 2001), 77–126.
199.   *Monitor,* December 24, 1998. In Kisangani Ugandan staff officers Chefe Ali and Peter Kerim organized the training of about fifteen hundred young Congolese to strengthen the MLC. Other batches were being trained in Beni, Bunia, Isiro, and Bafwasende.
200.   Author's interview with Wamba dia Wamba, Kampala, September 2000.
201.   The following account is drawn from a variety of interviews with RCD cadres, various Ugandan actors, and UN and NGO personnel in Kampala, Nairobi, Paris, and Brussels between June 1998 and early 2000. Unfortunately, there is very little input from the Rwandese side, as the author's relationship with Kigali had by that time degenerated into name-calling and threats of physical violence.

202. Reuters dispatch, Nairobi, May 25, 1999.

203. *New Times* (Kigali), August 2, 1999.

204. I am much indebted for treatment of this section to my friend Peter Tygesen, who gave me the benefit of his extensive knowledge of the Kisangani diamond situation (Kampala, March 1998, and Paris, October 2000).

205. Since the diamond mines were small and spread over a vast territory, uncut gems were brought back to the Kisangani counters by boys riding trail bikes through the bush. These couriers were highly vulnerable.

206. For a detailed analysis of the agreement itself, see International Crisis Group, *The Agreement on a Ceasefire in the DRC*, August 20, 1999. For a global overview of the peace process, both before and after Lusaka, see J. C. Willame, *L'accord de Lusaka: Chronique d'une négociation internationale* (Tervuren, Belgium: CEDAF, 2002).

207. *Le Monde*, October 8, 1998. For the Elysée, Laurent-Désiré Kabila had become again an acceptable partner now that the hated "Anglo-Saxons" had dropped him and appeared to support the invasion. But this vision was not shared by the Socialist prime minister Lionel Jospin (the Socialists had won the legislative elections in May 1997 and France was again going through a period of split executive known as "cohabitation"), who was not very keen on inviting the Congolese president to the forthcoming Franco-African summit in Paris. President Chirac overrode his objection.

208. *Le Monde*, October 17, 1998.

209. Interview with U.S. State Department personnel, Washington, DC, October 1999. The U.S. mercenaries seem to have been recruited on the same basis as those used earlier, during the first Zairian war (see chapter 4, notes 43 and 44). There were about 150 of them based on the small Lake Kivu island of Wahu just east of Idjwi, in Rwandese territorial waters, where they occupied a former Peace Corps rest camp. Later they rented several floors of the Hotel Umumbano in Bukavu for fifty of their number, who rotated with the reserves on Wahu Island. They fought regularly side by side with the RPA in South Kivu and suffered some losses, including two prisoners whose hands were cut off by a Mayi Mayi chief (September 1998) as a warning to others. Various interviews with Bukavu residents, March 1999.

210. *IRIN Bulletin*, no. 538 (November 4, 1998).

211. *IRIN Bulletin*, no. 591 (January 20, 1999). Unfortunately that quote could be applicable to a lot of other internationally sponsored "peace agreements" in Africa, notably in the Sudan.

212. A part of the Chadian expeditionary force was redeployed in Bangui to ensure the security of President Patasse, something Gaddafi definitely cared more about than the Congo.

213. Given his greater transparency (and lack of marketable genocide resources) Museveni was under the greater pressure. In May the IMF had refused to disburse a previously agreed upon $18 million loan because of the skyrocketing Defense budget, which had gone up 130 percent between 1997 and 1998. *IRIN Bulletin*, no. 665 (May 6, 1999).

214. This new fighting was in addition to the intense combats pitting the Rwandese against the Zimbabweans around Mbuji-Mayi, which never stopped during the negotiations.

215. Reuters dispatch, Kinshasa, August 8, 1999.

216. Following massive pressure from the international community, particularly

from the U.S. delegation.

217.   The denial persisted for years. In late 2001 I was still arguing with Howard Wolpe, one of the U.S. godfathers of the Agreement, trying unsuccessfully to convince him that Lusaka had been dead from the start.

218.   Which, interestingly, goes a long way toward showing the flimsiness of their claim to represent all or part of the mythical "Congolese people" they kept grandly invoking.

219.   For a complete text, see Willame, *L'accord de Lusaka,* 35–37.

220.   In spite of the fact that Burundi was not a signatory.

221.   "The war is dead. Long live the war," *Economist,* July 17, 1999.

Chapter 7

1.   Title of an article in the *Economist,* July 17, 1999.

2.   The United Nations estimated that there were about 826,000 IDPs in the Congo in November 1999. By early February 2000 the numbers had risen to 1,120,000. *IRIN Bulletin,* no. 863 (February 17, 2000).

3.   *IRIN Bulletin,* no. 924 (May 16, 2000).

4.   See *La Lettre de l'Océan Indien,* September 4, 1999; *Africa Intelligence,* September 7, 2000. "Van Brink" was finally deported from Uganda to the United States in May 2004 to face the charges against at him.

5.   In January 2000 he was sent by Wamba to regain control of Bafwasende, where the RCD-ML thought it had a force of one thousand men. Upon arrival he found about seventy sick and hungry fighters who had not been paid for months. Using his outside connections in Kampala he proceeded to put into exploitation the local small diamond mines, buying the stones from the creuseurs at a fair price and paying his soldiers. Soon he had forty-five hundred men flocking to his standard and could have had more had he been able to buy more guns. In spite of being a Luba from Kasaï, he had no problem commanding local loyalty. "I was a good warlord," he told me. "I paid my men. Too many people want the boys to fight for them for free." Interview with Roger Lumbala, Paris, March 2001.

6.   The Ituri District of Province Orientale is a multiethnic area (thirteen tribes are present) where tensions had long existed between the Hema and the Lendu, neither of which are autochthons (the Lendu originally came from southern Sudan and the Hema are close cousins of Uganda's Banyoro). In April 1999 the Ugandan army entered the fray in support of a Hema landlord who had confiscated Lendu coffee farms, triggering a succession of massacres and countermassacres that were to last for the next four years with varying degrees of intensity. See ASADHO, *Rapport sur le conflit inter-ethnique Hema-Lendu en territoire de Djugu,* Bunia, December 1999; G. Prunier, "The 'Ethnic' Conflict in Ituri District," in J. P. Chrétien and R. Banegas, eds., *The Recurring Great Lakes Crisis* (London: Hurst, 2008), 180–204.

7.   Lotsove immediately switched to the MLC and agitated for Bemba's occupation of the Ituri.

8.   Apart from the coffee, they exploited illegally the Kilo Moto gold mines around Mongbwalu.

9.   IRIN DRC chronology, February 28, 2000.

10.   *New Vision,* April 17, 2000.

11.   *New Vision,* December 6, 2000.

12.   In November 1999 the Batembo tribal chiefs gave Mayi Mayi leader Padiri
       Kanero thirty days to stop his aggressions against civilians, saying that he and
       his *Interahamwe* Rwandese allies had caused over two thousand deaths in the
       community during the past year. Because he was a Mutembo, Chief Katola
       Ndalemwa threatened to have him "outlawed." *IRIN Bulletin*, no. 1,062 (No-
       vember 29, 1999).

13.   Trying to equate Mayi Mayi, whether or not supported by Kinshasa, with
       the "negative forces" defined in the terms of the Lusaka Agreement was a con-
       stant theme of rebel propaganda.

14.   See chapter 5.

15.   For his assessment of the Banyamulenge predicament, see his book: *Les Banya-
       mulenge du Congo-Zaïre entre deux guerres* (Paris: L'Harmattan, 2001). By then
       he was living in exile in Germany after unknown parties had tried to murder
       him in Bujumbura.

16.   In early July 2000 Banyamulenge militiamen killed eight Babembe boys "sus-
       pected" of having Mayi Mayi contacts; a few days later several boys joined yet
       another "false *Interahamwe* attack" on Kabare village, outside Bukavu. Inter-
       view with Congolese NGO workers, Bukavu, November 2000.

17.   *IRIN Bulletin*, no. 975 (July 26, 2000).

18.   While most of the roads were extremely poor and next to impassable, the huge
       network of navigable rivers flowing into the Congo constituted a major trans-
       port facility of key military importance.

19.   Reuters dispatch, Lisala, January 18, 2000. By then the international com-
       munity was beginning to realize that the Lusaka process was in poor health.
       Bernard Miyet, the UN Department of Peacekeeping Operations under-sec-
       retary, admitted, "There has been a serious deterioration during the last three
       months."

20.   *IRIN Bulletin*, no. 836 (January 11, 2000). Former Central African Republic
       president André Kolingba was helping in the recruitment, making it doubly
       embarrassing for Patasse.

21.   Associated Press dispatch, Kigali, April 22, 2000.

22.   Agence France Presse, Kinshasa, April 27, 2000.

23.   *IRIN Bulletin*, no. 915 (May 3, 2000).

24.   *IRIN Bulletin*, no. 972 (July 21, 2000).

25.   *IRIN Bulletin*, no. 987 (August 11, 2000). For spectacular pictures of the river
       battle, see the military buff magazine *Raids*, no. 171 (August 2000).

26.   *New Vision*, September 26, 2000.

27.   *La Lettre de l'Océan Indien*, September 30, 2000. The part about De Miranda's
       reaction comes from an interview with a French Foreign Affairs civil servant
       who was present at the meeting (Paris, October 2000).

28.   *IRIN Bulletin*, no. 1,024 (October 3, 2000).

29.   "We are fighting every day; there is no ceasefire," declared Kin Kiey Mulumba,
       the RCD-G spokesman, on April 2.

30.   Some of them were more lucid. Alexis Thambwe, who had just resigned from
       the RCD-G, declared to Agence France Press in Paris on April 13, "Both the
       rebels and Kabila believe in a military victory. But a military victory cannot be
       expected. So we are getting mired in a status quo which is slowly leading to the
       partition of the Congo."

31.   International Crisis Group, *Scramble for the Congo: Anatomy of an Ugly War*,
       Brussels, December 2000.

32.   *IRIN Bulletin*, no. 1,041 (October 27, 2000).

33.   *IRIN Bulletin*, no. 1,065 (December 4, 2000).

34.   On December 11 the pro-government *Herald* wrote that the Zimbabwean troops "had not run away but had complied with the recent decision of the Harare conference on security to effectuate a 15 km pull-back."

35.   *IRIN Bulletin*, no. 1,075 (December 14, 2000). There were also over two thousand ALIR Rwandese rebels.

36.   Meeting with the author, New York City, January 2001. This meeting took place at the end of the first week of January, that is, while Laurent-Désiré Kabila was still alive.

37.   Interview with a MONUC employee, Paris, May 2001.

38.   *Les Coulisses,* no. 77 (January 15–February 15, 2000).

39.   SWB/RFI, 17 January 2000.

40.   Amnesty International communiqué, October 5, 2000.

41.   *IRIN Bulletin*, no. 877 (March 8, 2000).

42.   Sir Ketumile Masire, former head of state of Botswana, had been chosen by the United Nations as mediator in charge of helping to carry out the Lusaka provisions. Gentle and urbane, he was somewhat ineffective, first, because he spoke only English and, second, because he was too much of a gentleman to deal realistically with the likes of Kabila, Bemba, and Ilunga.

43.   SWB/RFI, April 24, 2000.

44.   F. Kabuya Kalala and Tschiunza Mbiye, "L'économie congolaise en 2000–2001: Contraction, fractionnement et enlisement," in S. Marysse and F. Reyntjens, eds., *L'annuaire des Grands Lacs (2000–2001)* (Paris: L'Harmattan, 2001), 175–194. World Bank figures for exports are slightly different ($1.214 million for 1998, $974 million for 1999, $892 million for 2000), but they reflect the same pattern.

45.   The average value of the exported carat had fallen from $14.68 in 1998 to $7.49 in 1999 due to the fact that all good jewelry quality stones were by then smuggled out, leaving only the inferior quality industrial gems on the official market. *La Lettre Afrique Energies,* November 24, 1999.

46.   Interview with an expatriate eyewitness, Kampala, November 2000.

47.   *La Lettre Afrique Energies,* September 29, 1999.

48.   *Nord-Sud Export,* September 24, 1999.

49.   *La Lettre Afrique Energies,* November 10, 1999.

50.   The financial support to Kinshasa was largely interested since Bredenkamp was, by his own admission, Congo's main private supplier of weapons.

51.   See Chris MacGreal, "The Napoleon of Africa and the Motiveless Murder," *Guardian* (London), December 16, 1999.

52.   IDI was created in 1996 by a fairly inexperienced young man, Dan Gertler, who was soon to prove insolvent in the purchases over which he had acquired a monopoly. See *Jeune Afrique,* August 15–28, 2000; *Africa Mining Intelligence,* November 1, 2000. His role in the sale of the 267.82 carats "wonder diamond" sold by FECODI president Alphonse Ngoy Kasanji for $17.9 million in October 2000 was questionable.

53.   For the plight of the ordinary people in the government-controlled areas, see Th. Trefon, "Population et pauvreté à Kinshasa," *Afrique Contemporaine,* no. 194 (June 2000): 82–89; Colette Braeckman's article in *Le Soir,* December 21, 2000; monthly reports on food security from the Food and Agriculture Organization of the United Nations; the zonal reports from the United Nations

Office for the Coordination of Humanitarian Affairs, *Humanitarian Impact of the Socio-Economic Environment*, Kinshasa, April 2000. On a regular basis the monthly reports of the Brussels-based Réseau Européen Congo are an invaluable source.

54. Luanda being short of manpower, some former *Interahamwe* militiamen and even CNDD Burundians went along.

55. Thus in December 2000, Kinshasa's allies had to plug up the Pweto gap opened by the Rwandese Zimbabwe did not have the long-range planes to bring its troops to Lubumbashi, and so the job was carried out by large Angolan Ilyushin Il-76s. The Zimbabweans then took care of the last leg of the trip with their smaller CASA planes.

56. *Energy Compass*, March 12, 1999, quoted in ICG, *Scramble for the Congo: Anatomy of a Dirty War*, Brussels, December 2000.

57. Reuters dispatch, Kinshasa, October 28, 2000.

58. In early 2000, after President Thabo Mbeki had hosted Etienne Tshisekedi during his visit to Pretoria, Kabila launched searing attacks on South Africa, accusing it of selling weapons to Kigali and Kampala. *New Vision*, January 20, 2000.

59. *Africa Confidential* 40, no. 21 (November 5, 1999).

60. *African Business*, September 1999.

61. Reuters dispatch, Harare, September 29, 1999.

62. Osleg, which was financed by Zimbabwe Defense Industries, had 40 percent of Cosleg. Oryx, which held 40 percent, was headed by the son of a former oil minister from Oman with business interests in Zimbabwe. Comiex, which had 20 percent of Cosleg, was a Congolese company linked directly with the Kabila family. *Africa Confidential* 41, no. 12 (June 9, 2000).

63. Apart from the British hostility to Mugabe, which had caused the London stoppage, other stock exchanges were wary of Cosleg for two reasons: the "blood diamonds" campaign then under way and also, in a more mundane fashion, the fear that the "one billion dollars" concessions in Mbuji-Mayi were both overvalued and resting on dubious legal grounds.

64. On this last point, see Erik Kennes, "Le secteur minier au Congo: Déconnexion et descente aux enfers," in F. Reyntjens and S. Marysse, eds., *L'Afrique des Grands Lacs (1999–2000)* (Paris: L'Harmattan, 2000), 299–342.

65. *Financial Times*, October 8, 1999.

66. Mungbalemwe Koyame and John F. Clark, "The Economic Impact of the Congo War," in John F. Clark, ed., *The African Stakes of the Congo War* (New York: Palgrave/Macmillan, 2002), 216.

67. *Daily News*, November 10, 2000.

68. All Tutsi from "Ugandan" families, they had grown up speaking English and could not take their exams in French, as the university required them to. Although willing to learn French they had never been given the means to do so. They were nevertheless faced with dismissal after "failing" their exams in a language they did not know. Interviews with students, Kampala, January 2001.

69. During a secret meeting about the crisis RPF Secretary-General (and former Butare University vice chancellor) Charles Morigande called them "well-fed brats" and suggested they should be arrested to make an example. Security men attending the meeting suggested killing one or two to deter any further demonstrations. This scared the parents (some of whom were present at the debate), who helped their children run away "back home," that is, to Kampala. "If we,

their children, could be treated so roughly, it made me wonder about the fate of the Hutu," a young Tutsi student confided to me.

70. See "Rwanda Bishop's Trial Puts Church on the Dock," *New Vision,* August 29, 1999; "State v. Church," *Economist,* September 18, 1999.

71. The long-serving former foreign affairs minister had previously been demoted to minister without portfolio in the President's Office. But he was still trying to reorganize the MDR to change it from its forced rubber-stamp role back into the real political party it had once been. This was not deemed acceptable by RPF stalwarts.

72. If the first accusation may have been right, the second was politically motivated. There again the "kinglet of the Hutu," as Rwigiema was desultorily called in RPF extremist circles, was mainly "guilty" of having acquired an independent political base.

73. *Daily Nation* (Nairobi), January 8, 2000. Sebarenzi was indeed popular, both among Tutsi survivors and moderate Hutu. This was the cause of his downfall.

74. *Imboni,* February 2000. One of the articles joked, "By now some people are so scared of the DMI (Directorate of Military Intelligence) that they are afraid to dream." As if to prove that point, three *Imboni* journalists were later arrested for putting together "a politically obscene publication."

75. The "Gahini mafia" were Protestant Tutsi from the eastern part of the country (Kibungo, Mutara, and Byumba) who were entrusted with 80 percent of the top political and administrative jobs. As for the old expression *akazu,* it was by then again in common popular use, among both Tutsi and Hutu.

76. Interview with one of President Museveni's top advisers, Kampala, September 2000.

77. *La Lettre de l'Océan Indien,* July 24, 1999; interviews in Kampala, September 2000. The first attempt took place at Salim's Kampala home and the second at Minakuru (Gulu district). In the highly personalized East African context, such events, far from being anecdotal, acquire considerable political significance.

78. Ali Hussein was the brother of an associate of Naim Khanafer, the former "king of diamond smuggling" in late Mobutu Zaire. Prime Minister Kengo had tried to expel him from Kinshasa in 1995, but he failed because Khanafer enjoyed Baramoto's and Nzimbi's protection. Later his network was subdivided into two branches, that of Ali Hussein, who worked with the Rwandese, and that of "Khalil," Mohamed Hassan, and "Talal," who worked for Salim Saleh's Victoria Enterprises Group. See the report by Pierre Lumbi's Observatoire Gouvern-ance-Transparence, *Guerre en RDC: Ses enjeux économiques, intérêts et acteurs,* Kinshasa, April 18, 2000. Both branches of the Khanafer network collaborated in Antwerp through common subsidiaries.

79. Here again I am deeply indebted to my friend Peter Tygesen and his precious knowledge of the Kisangani mining scene. Interview, Paris, October 2000.

80. The UPDF had built up its forces during the past few days in anticipation of a showdown. But the Rwandese were quicker and, as in 1999, fought better. In-terviews with UPDF officers who took part in the battle, Kampala, September 2000.

81. *IRIN Bulletin,* no. 920 (May 10, 2000).

82. *IRIN Bulletin,* no. 923. (May 15, 2000).

83. That fear was aggravated by the fact that Bemba had recruited a battalion of Banyamulenge hostile to Kigali and the RCD-G, with whom they had previ-ously served. Interview with a pro-FRF Munyamulenge former fighter, Kam-

pala, September 2000.

84.   Colonel Semakula, talking to Africa 1, in BBC/SWB, May 19, 2000. This was the beginning of a long series of so-called evacuations, wherein the RPA used the RCD-G as an "independent" proxy.

85.   ICRC and UN estimates a week after the fighting was over. Neither the RPA nor the UPDF ever precisely acknowledged their military losses. There was one Rwandese political victim, Maj. Wilson Rutaysire, the former head of the Rwandan Office of Information, who was shot by his friends because he opposed the war with Uganda.

86.   Interview in *New African,* July/August 2000.

87.   The Rwandese victory was again hollow from the mining point of view because the small mines of the Kisangani basin were scattered over a vast area and remained out of their reach. In November 2000 Kigali sent the RCD-G north in an attempt at reaching the Banalia zone and occupying the mines, but their men were stopped by a combined RCD-N–MLC force at Kondolole and beaten back to Kisangani. Interview with Roger Lumbala, Paris, March 2001.

88.   International Rescue Committee, *Mortality Survey in Eastern DRC,* Bukavu, June 2000. Roberts's findings have been criticized on the basis of having too small a sample (1,011 households with 7,339 people). But his methodology is serious, and, even if his results are to be considered as an order of magnitude rather than a precise figure, the overall result is the same.

89.   International Institute for Strategic Studies, *The Military Balance 1999/2000,* 2000.

90.   Bjorn Willum, "Foreign Aid to Rwanda: Purely Beneficial or Contributing to War?" PhD diss., University of Copenhagen, 2001.

91.   *Letter dated 28 February 2000 from the Chairman of the Panel of Experts established by the Security Council pursuant to Resolution 1237 (1999) addressed to the Chairman of the Security Council Committee established pursuant to Resolution 864 (1993) concerning the situation in Angola* (henceforth referred to by the name of its panel chairman, Robert Fowler, as the Fowler Report).

92.   *IRIN Bulletin,* no. 990 (August 16, 2000).

93.   United Nations, *Report of the Panel of Experts on the Illegal Exploitation of Natural Resources and Other Forms of Wealth of the Democratic Republic of the Congo,* New York, April 2001. The report was dismissed by Kigali and Kampala as "French-inspired" because of the nationality of the panel's chairperson. This accusation is not serious since there were people of several nationalities on the panel, including a U.S. citizen. A later updated report produced under the chairmanship of the Egyptian Mahmood Kassem, though it tended to delve more deeply into the looting carried out by the Zimbabweans, did not invalidate the first set of conclusions concerning Rwanda and Uganda.

94.   See, for example, C. André and L. Lozolele, *The European Union's Aid Policy towards Countries Involved in the Congo War: Lever for Peace or Incitement to War?* Brussels, Réseau Européen Congo, May 2001.

95.   *IRIN Bulletin,* no. 879 (March 10, 2000).

96.   Quoted in Willum, "Foreign Aid to Rwanda," 105.

97.   United Kingdom, Department for International Development, *Rwanda: A Country Strategy Paper,* September 1999, 3.

98.   Reuters dispatch, Kigali, February 8, 1999.

99.   In fact, the exact amounts were $35.5 million (1997) and $29.8 million (1998). The two amounts were in complete contradiction, both with total Rwandese

exports to Belgium ($4 million/year) and with total registered Rwandese gold exports ($9.8 million). See UK Economist Intelligence Unit, *Rwanda Country Profile,* 2001, 27.

100. Sénat de Belgique, Commission d'Enquête Parlementaire, "Grands Lacs," Compte-rendu de l'audition du 1er mars 2002. The point about the separate bookkeeping was confirmed by the next report of the UN panel on illegal exploitation of Congolese resources (October 2002).

101. Reuters dispatch, Kampala, May 12, 2000. The Heavily Indebted Poor Countries program had enabled Kampala to reduce its debt service from 27 percent of its budget in 1997–1998 to 11 percent in 2000–2001. In comparison, Defense stood at 30 percent. *La Lettre de l'Océan Indien,* April 1, 2000.

102. *IRIN Bulletin,* no. 786 (October 25, 1999).

103. For the facts, see Madeleine Kalb, *The Congo Cables* (New York: Macmillan, 1985). For the (well-articulated) myth, see Katete Orwa, *The Congo Betrayal: The UN-US and Lumumba* (Nairobi: Kenya Literature Bureau, 1985).

104. MONUC stands for Mission des Nations Unies au Congo. Congolese popular wits soon turned it into "Monique," because "like a beautiful woman it does nothing and costs a lot of money."

105. *IRIN Bulletin,* no. 828 (December 22, 1999).

106. The deployment was authorized on February 24 by Resolution 1,291 with a tentative budget of $200 million for the first six months.

107. IRIN interview, Kampala, March 22, 2000.

108. *New Vision,* March 24, 2000.

109. It was exactly the same for the Ugandan-backed MLC, but they were clever enough not to say it out loud.

110. *IRIN Bulletin,* no. 933 (May 29, 2000).

111. *IRIN Bulletin,* no. 974 (July 25, 2000).

112. "Congo: A Snub from Kabila," *Economist,* August 19, 2000.

113. *La Lettre du Continent,* August 24, 2000.

114. *Le Monde,* August 25, 2000.

115. *Le Monde,* August 26, 2000. The story of the midnight telephone call from dos Santos was told to me by a French businessman who had unrestricted access to the Futungo Palace (Paris, November 2000).

116. *IRIN Bulletin,* no. 983 (August 7, 2000).

117. *IRIN Bulletin,* no. 998 (August 28, 2000).

118. *IRIN Bulletin,* no. 1,049 (November 9, 2000). This Gaddafi initiative was linked to his plan for replacing the OAU with a new organization (today's African Union), over which he hoped to have ultimate control due to his financial clout.

119. *IRIN Bulletin,* no. 1,050 (November 10, 2000). During October, twenty-one of the thirty-two flights for which MONUC had asked for clearance were canceled by the government.

120. Radio Television Nationale Congolaise, in *BBC Summary of World Broadcasts* (henceforth *BBC/SWB*), November 28, 2000. The RTNC reported only the storming out of Kagame and Museveni, not the reason for their sudden departure, which I learned during an interview in Kampala with a member of the Ugandan delegation (January 2001).

121. It most likely was not, and Laurent-Désiré Kabila's assassin probably managed to flee to Brazzaville, where his trail went cold. Private information from a businessman based in the Republic of Congo.

122. La Chaine Info (Paris), in BBC/SWB, January 16, 2001.
123. ZBC Radio (Harare) and Libyan TV (Tripoli), in BBC/SWB, January 17, 2001. Chamulesso later recanted, pretending that he had made a mistake and that Kabila was only wounded.
124. IRIN Press dispatch, Nairobi, January 17, 2001.
125. ZBC Radio, in BBC/SWB, January 18, 2001.
126. RTNC/Kinshasa, in BBC/SWB, January 17, 2001.
127. RTNC/Kinshasa, in BBC/SWB, January 18, 2001.
128. Stephen Smith and Antoine Glaser, "Ces enfants-soldats qui ont tué Kabila," *Le Monde,* February 10, 2001.
129. For a good discussion of the account itself and of the criticisms it drew, see G. de Villers, Jean Omasombo, and Erik Kennes, *Guerre et politique: Les trente derniers mois de L. D. Kabila (août 1998–janvier 2001)* (Tervuren, Belgium: CEDAF, 2001), 320–323.
130. This is the position adopted by Pierre Bigras at his website, www.obsac.com (February 5–11, 2001).
131. This is hinted at in F. Ryckmans, "Joseph Kabila, un mois après," *Politique,* no. 20 (March–April 2001): 50–53.
132. This is the position of C. Braeckman, *Les nouveaux prédateurs: Politique des puissances en Afrique Centrale* (Paris: Fayard, 2003), 113–124. But since that author's general thesis is that Central Africa is the locus of the vast geopolitical designs of foreign powers, it is logical that she would see the president's murder as fitting within that pattern.
133. Upon Kabila's death French Foreign Minister Hubert Védrine commented, "He was quite unbelievable, he looked like a character out of *Star Wars.*"
134. See chapter 4.
135. Interview with several former AFDL officers, Kampala, January 2001, and Nairobi, October 2001.
136. For a general treatment of the child soldiers phenomenon in Central Africa, see Hervé Cheuzeville, *Kadogo: Enfants des guerres d'Afrique Centrale* (Paris: L'Harmattan, 2003), particularly 173–296, which deal with the DRC. See also Amnesty International, *DRC: Children at War,* London, September 2003.
137. AIDS started as a regional pandemic during the late 1970s, spreading at first when the Tanzanian army advancing into Uganda to overthrow Idi Amin went through Karagwe and Rakaï, which were perhaps the two "original" AIDS regions.
138. See chapter 2.
139. I am indebted for that insight to Lieve Joris, who first mentioned it to me in early 1999 in Paris while talking about the death of a *kadogo* who served under the Munyamulenge officer who later became the hero of her "real-life novel" *L'heure des rebelles* (Arles: Actes Sud, 2007). She knew the man to be a ruthless fighter. But when he came home splattered with the blood of his thirteen-year-old aide who had been shot next to him in an ambush, he was crying.
140. Smith and Glaser, "Ces enfants-soldats qui ont tué Kabila."
141. See chapter 5.
142. His social climbing was achieved through the South Kivu NGO network during the 1990s, and he had always kept a very sharp ear for Kivutian popular moods. Interview with his uncle Aristide Bambaga Chahihabwa, Kampala, January 2001.
143. The Rwandese president placed very high hopes on Masasu because he had a

438

Tutsi mother and had worked for the RPF during the anti-Habyarimana war. During his face-to-face meeting with Kabila in Eldoret on June 2, Kagame asked the Congolese president, who had recently freed Masasu, to give him back an important position in the FAC. Interview with a Ugandan ESO agent, Kampala, November 2000.

144. It is at this point that some observers see possible Rwandese input in the murder plot because certain politicians, such as Patient Mwendanga, who were later to play secessionist politics in South Kivu with Kigali's support, were part of Masasu Nindaga's network. Interview with Kivutian exiles, Washington, DC, October 2003.

145. See CODHO, *Rapport succinct sur la persécutions dont sont victimes les ressortissants des provinces du Nord Kivu, Sud Kivu et Maniema à Kinshasa,* Kinshasa, December 30, 2000, quoted in de Villers et al., *Guerre et politique,* 325, and Amnesty International communiqué, January 9, 2001.

146. After Laurent-Désiré Kabila's assassination RCD-G tried to cash in on Masasu's personal aura by digging up his body and organizing a solemn reburial in Bukavu. The local population was not impressed and stoned the funeral convoy. Misna website, April 17, 2001.

147. Radio Television Nationale Congolaise/Kinshasa, in BBC/SWB, December 16, 2000.

148. *IRIN Bulletin,* no. 1,076 (December 19, 2000). The story of these inhuman orders was gathered by humanitarian workers taking care of the boys after they fled to Zambia.

149. Ibid.

150. I am referring here to Tony Hodges's brilliant characterization of the Angolan regime's evolution used in the title of his book *Angola: From Afro-Stalinism to Petro-Diamond Capitalism* (Oxford: James Currey, 2001).

151. In August 2001 he was charged with conspiring to overthrow President Joseph Kabila.

152. *La lettre du Continent,* August 24, 2000. The fact that the president kept diamonds in his office was well known; after he was shot one of his assistants, Annie Kalumbo, quickly sneaked into his office and stole a bag containing several thousand dollars worth of gems. See www.obsac.com, October 14–20, 2002. She was later caught and tried.

153. *Africa Confidential* 41, no. 20 (October 13, 2000).

154. In another apocryphal story the Lebanese and Kabila had all been killed because of a gangland-like settling of accounts between diamond traffickers. As for Colette Braeckman (*Les Nouveaux prédateurs,* 112), she mistakes the whole murdered Khanafer family, children included, for "a commando" supposedly in charge of killing L. D. Kabila.

155. The suspicion could have been true since four of the murder victims (Mohamed Khanafer and his three sons) were close blood relatives of Naïm Khanafer, the old Zaire "diamond king." But six of the victims were younger than eighteen, including three young children. AFP dispatch from Aynatta in Lebanon, March 9, 2001. Mwenze Kongolo said they had been shot by soldiers who thought them responsible for the president's assassination and called the massacre "an unfortunate incident." Associated Press dispatch, Kinshasa, March 7, 2001.

156. A postassassination communiqué by the CNRD claiming that it had been behind the president's killing was simply an effort to revive a dead movement and to claim posthumous vengeance for Kisase Ngandu. This is the only point

439

where Smith and Glaser got it wrong: the group of kadogo who organized Kabila's murder had nothing to do with either Uganda or the ghost of the CNRD.

157. Confidential information given by two independent sources, one Angolan and one French, Paris, February and March 2001.

158. This was noted in the International Crisis Group report *From Kabila to Kabila: Prospects for Peace in the Congo,* Nairobi/Brussels, March 2001, note 47. It was confirmed to me by the above-mentioned Angolan source and by a high-ranking member of Mzee's entourage (who later managed to fit nicely in Joseph Kabila's circle of close advisers).

159. Interview with Antoine Rozès, Paris, February 6, 2001. Kapend added that the Zimbabweans would not like it either.

160. Kapend also had a politically loaded past: he had been in charge of Governor Kyungu wa Kumwanza's security during the expulsion of the Kasaïan Baluba from Shaba (Katanga) in 1992–1994.

161. He was still in Lubumbashi, where he had retreated after taking part in the defeat at Pweto.

Chapter 8

1. IRIN Press dispatch, January 18, 2001.

2. RTNC/Kinshasa, in *BBC Summary of World Broadcasts* (henceforth *BBC/SWB*), January 19, 2001.

3. RFI, in *BBC/SWB,* January 21, 2001.

4. Popular talk in Kinshasa had dubbed the interim president "P'tit Joseph" (Li'l Joseph).

5. Agence France Presse dispatch, Paris, January 23, 2001.

6. They were not alone in questioning his right to office. Kinshasa opponent Joseph Olenghankoy declared in an interview, "On what grounds was he 'appointed' to handle the transition? That boy has no training, he knows nothing of life and he does not even speak French." *Le Soir,* January 19, 2001.

7. Even the ranking order of gratitude was precisely calculated.

8. This is what Colette Braeckman called, deprecatingly, "giving up on all that his father has refused." *Les nouveaux prédateurs* (Paris: Fayard, 2003), 136. The speech was immediately criticized by the old Maoist militant Ludo Mertens, who had been an enthusiastic supporter of his father.

9. RTNC/Kinshasa, in *BBC/SWB,* January 31, 2001.

10. Interview with a Mulubakat leader, Paris, July 2001. This particular gentleman supported P'tit Joseph's takeover but thought that it gave the Balubakat a special political edge. He later ended up in jail.

11. Powell had seen Kagame the day before and had told him bluntly, "This is the end of the free ride." Interview with a member of the U.S. State Department, Washington, DC, February 2001. In the State Department, more diplomatic official words describing the relationship with Rwanda, so close under Clinton, had changed "from an embrace to a handshake." *New York Times,* February 1, 2001.

12. Agence France Presse dispatch, New York, February 3, 2001.

13. *New York Times,* February 2, 2001.

14. *IRIN Bulletin,* no. 1,107 (February 6, 2001).

15. African Press Agency dispatch, Kinshasa, February 5, 2001.

16. See the ASADHO open letter to the president, February 14, 2001.

17. RTNC Kinshasa, in *BBC/SWB,* February 13, 2001.

18. Author's meeting with Ugandan Foreign Minister Eriya Kategaya, Paris, February 21, 2001.

19. Author's meeting with UNITA leader Isaac Samakuva, Paris, February 28, 2001.

20. Angolan Foreign Affairs Minister Joao Bernardo Miranda later felt obliged to deny that there was any tension between Zimbabwean and Angolan forces in the DRC. *IRIN Bulletin,* no. 1,203 (June 19, 2001).

21. Joseph waited until April 24 to go to Luanda, when he was sure that everything was safe. By then he had solidified his relationship with the international community, taken control of his secret services, replaced his cabinet, put the Nokos back in their place, and consolidated his internal support. Dos Santos, always the pragmatist, knew a winner when he saw one, and Kapend was abandoned to his fate.

22. African Press Agency dispatch, March 19, 2001.

23. *New Vision,* February 25, 2001.

24. Erik Kennes, *Essai biographique sur Laurent-Désiré Kabila* (Tervuren, Belgium: CEDAF, 2003). The relevant pages to clarify Joseph's filiation are 39, 291, and 300–302.

25. Since the late Kabila had had at least a dozen "wives" and over twenty children, getting confused about the family was understandable.

26. The last episode in the filiation saga occurred on April 15, 2002, when L. D. Kabila's eldest son, Etienne Taratibu, suddenly surfaced in Sun City during the peace negotiations and denounced Joseph's "illegitimate" origins. *La Libre Belgique,* April 17, 2002. It is more than likely that he was put up to it by some of the parties then negotiating, who seemed to hope that his supposed "Rwandese" ancestry would translate into political weakening. Even if that had been proven, it is not certain that it would have had the expected effect. During the data collection for the BERCI opinion poll "Les cent jours de Joseph Kabila" (April 27–29, 2001) many young respondents volunteered their opinion that "Joseph Kabila is one of us. For the first time we have a young person as President. Who cares if he is a Rwandese Tutsi! At least that means he won't have tribal preferences!" If one keeps in mind that the under-twenty-five group represents nearly 70 percent of Congo's population, this point of view is of some relevance.

27. PANA dispatch, Kinshasa, February 28, 2001.

28. *Africa Mining Intelligence,* April 25, 2001.

29. *La Lettre du Continent,* April 26, 2001.

30. *Africa Mining Intelligence,* March 14, 2001.

31. *Africa Confidential* 42, no. 6 (March 23, 2001).

32. *Le Soir,* March 17, 2001.

33. The four services were DEMIAP, PIR, PNC/SS, and ANR. Kazadi Nyembwe, born in Burundi and later adopted by a Mulubakat trader who had remarried his divorced Tutsi mother, is a former bank robber and escaped convict with a colorful past. His close relationship with Laurent-Désiré Kabila dated from 1979 and was based on shared business interests. Kennes, *Eassai biographique,* 266–268. His closeness to Joseph came from the fact that during his rather solitary youth, as L. D. Kabila traveled all over, "Didi" Nyembwe used to take care of him in Dar-es-Salaam, almost as a substitute father.

34. The Kimbanguist Church was the largest of the many messianic movements that had developed in the Lower Congo during colonial times. On this topic, see Martial Sinda, *Le messianisme congolais et ses incidences politiques* (Paris: Payot, 1972); Susan Asch, *L'Eglise du Prophète Kimbangu, de ses origines à son rôle actuel au Zaïre* (Paris: Karthala, 1983).

35. *Le Soir,* April 21, 2001.

36. *IRIN Bulletin,* no. 1,157 (April 16, 2001) and 1,161 (April 20, 2001).

37. *Le Potentiel,* April 17, 2001. An element of peevishness could be detected because the usual Kinshasa political rumor mill had been taken aback and was feeling bypassed. The same phenomenon was to be repeated in February 2007, when a new cabinet of largely unknown persons was proclaimed after the elections.

38. *Le Monde* correspondent Stephen Smith called him "a levitating extra-terrestrial."

39. *Economist,* July 28, 2001.

40. *IRIN Bulletin,* no. 1,185 (May 24, 2001).

41. *Le Monde,* April 29–30, 2001.

42. Agence France Presse dispatch, Kinshasa, May 24, 2001.

43. La Voix des Sans-Voix, *La famille du Colonel Eddy Kapend martyrisée par le Parquet,* Kinshasa, March 12, 2002.

44. The silence thickened further on October 5, 2004, when State Prosecutor Col. Charles Alamba was condemned to death for a murder alledgedly committed in September 2003. He was not executed, but no more was heard from him.

45. Conversations with UPDF middle-ranking officers showed that quite a few would have preferred a war with Rwanda rather than the continuation of the war in the DRC, which mostly benefited their superiors (Kampala, November 2000).

46. The HIV-positive status of a lot of the officers made it imperative for them to secure the necessary money for treatment, which their normal army salaries could not buy. Given the essentially military nature of the RPF power structure, their feelings could hardly be neglected.

47. Agence France Presse dispatch, New York, February 7, 2001.

48. PANA dispatch, February 10, 2001.

49. *IRIN Bulletin,* no. 1,113 (February 13, 2001). A year before the UN Security Council had authorized 5,537 men for MONUC.

50. *IRIN Bulletin,* no. 1,114 (February 14, 2001).

51. He was conveniently "forgetting" his own role at the time.

52. *Le Soir,* March 7, 2001.

53. Confidential U.S. State Department memo dated March 20, 2001, transmitted to the author.

54. Museveni was worried both by increased tension with Rwanda and by the discussions then going on in New York about the data gathered by the first UN report on the illegal exploitation of Congolese resources (see next section, on the economic situation).

55. *IRIN Bulletin,* no. 1,160 (April 20, 2001).

56. *New Vision,* May 1, 2001.

57. *New Vision,* May 2, 2001. The inclusion of Rwanda in the list was symptomatic of the tensions between Rwanda and Uganda.

58. See *IRIN Bulletin,* no. 1,179 (May 16, 2001), 1,183 (May 22, 2001), 1,187 (May 28, 2001), and 1,189 (May 30, 2001).

59. Associated Press dispatch, Kinshasa, May 21, 2001.

60. African Press Agency dispatch, Kinshasa, May 27, 2001.

61. Uganda had already withdrawn 6,000 troops during late 2000. It was now in the process of taking out another 4,000 from various locations in Equateur, leaving about 3,000 in Buta, Bunia, and the Ruwenzori slopes. *La Lettre de l'Océan Indien,* May 26, 2001.

62. Some of them walked for two months, accompanied by mechanical equipment that constantly broke down.

63. *IRIN Bulletin,* no. 1,207 (June 25, 2001).

64. *IRIN Bulletin,* no. 1,227 (July 19, 2001). The UN did not manage to speak with one voice on Kisangani since Jean-Marie Guehenno accepted the RCD-G "temporary stay" and J. D. Levitte asked for a speedy application of UN resolutions 1304 and 1355.

65. IRIN dispatch, August 27, 2001.

66. The scramble was all the fiercer because nobody knew the rules of the game anymore. The fifteen political parties present in Gaborone had unilaterally decided to multiply their representation by four for the Addis-Ababa meeting and had then started to sell their delegates' seats to excluded parties. The MLC, on the contrary, which had only a skeleton leadership, co-opted three ex-RCDs (Alexis Thambwe, Jose Endundo, and Lunda Bululu) as members, while announcing its intention to become a political party. *La Libre Belgique,* September 4, 2001.

67. IRIN dispatch, August 29, 2001.

68. Agence France Presse dispatch, Kisangani, September 3, 2001.

69. IRIN dispatch, June 19, 2001.

70. Interview with European Union Great Lakes Political Officer Christian Manahl, Nairobi, September 2001.

71. For a good analysis of this double game, see International Crisis Group, *Disarmament in the Congo: Jump-starting DDRRR to Prevent Further War,* Brussels, December 2001.

72. See *IRIN Bulletin,* no. 1,279 (October 3, 2001), chronicling the harassment of Voix des Sans Voix human rights NGO members.

73. Author's own observations at the conference, Addis-Ababa, October 2001.

74. Museveni even denied his obvious troop redeployment in the Ituri.

75. The following account of the conference is drawn from interviews with both Congolese participants and foreign observers in a series of meetings in Nairobi, Addis-Ababa, Paris, and Washington between February and October 2002.

76. See the article by Jonathan Katzenellenbogen, "Sun City: Colourful Delegates Eclipse the Holiday Crowd," *Business Day* (Johannesburg), March 6, 2002.

77. The main reason was that Moliro was used by Kinshasa to run guns by boat to the various "negative forces" (the FDD in Kigoma, ALIR II and Willy Dunia's Mayi Mayi in the Fizi-Baraka area). Kigali wanted to show to the participants that force remained an ultimate option which circumscribed their discussions.

78. Agence France Presse dispatch, Sun City, April 17, 2002.

79. This was confirmed in a confidential EU report dated April 21, 2002 obtained by the author, which stated, "RCD-G margin for manoeuvre has been severely constrained by constant Rwandese interference... . By refusing to give RCD-G reasonable freedom for negotiating . . . Rwanda has manoeuvred itself into dangerous isolation. The perspective is now of Uganda becoming an ally of the new transitional government, leaving Rwanda and RCD-G isolated."

80. One of them (COCEAN) was a tiny Congolese student group in the United States.

81. IRIN dispatch, April 26, 2002.

82. On May 7 ASD declared that the Bemba-Kabila accord was "the consecration of trickery, intending to make the National Dialogue fail.... This satanic agreement is a coup against Lusaka.... The signatories were corrupted by giving them each $1,000." Tshisekedi then toyed briefly with the idea of starting his own armed movement or of setting up a separate government in Kisangani. Outside Kasaï these confused moves lost him a lot of credibility.

83. African Press Agency dispatch, May 7, 2002.

84. Misna website, May 14, 2002. The mutiny took place a day after the failure of separate government talks with RCD-G organized by the South Africans in Capetown.

85. This brief description of the uprising and its consequences is based on a meeting with a survivor of the mutiny in Brussels in May 2002 and on several off-the-record interviews with MONUC personnel in Nairobi in February 2003.

86. His role in slaughtering over two hundred people in four days was denounced by Human Rights Watch Africa on August 20, which caused a problem when the transition government later came into being and the perpetrator of this atrocity was picked by RCD-G to head a military district for the unified army. Another perpetrator was the commander of the 7th Brigade, Col. Laurent Nkunda, later to become one of the main security problems of the late transition period (see next chapter).

87. The figure was underestimated but reasonable. Reuters dispatch, Geneva, June 27, 2002. RCD-G admitted only thirty-nine fatalities.

88. Radio France Internationale, in *BBC/SWB,* June 9, 2002. The 40,000 figure was of course grossly inflated, but the 15,000 MONUC figure was probably underestimated. The real total was likely between 20,000 and 25,000.

89. See, for example, the Associated Press piece "Congo's Kabila Tries to End War," July 27, 2002, wherein "human interest" tidbits slanted the interview to make the young president appear a sympathetic figure.

90. This did not influence in the least Kigali's policy on the ground, where it went ahead with its control plans. On June 24, for example, the RCD-G imposed the monetary circulation of the Rwandese franc in all territories under its control (see its internal memo 075/2PFBP/RCD/2002).

91. For these last two elements, see the section on the continued conflict in the east.

92. IRIN dispatch, March 27, 2002.

93. Even more so since Jonas Savimbi had been killed in an ambush on February 22, 2002.

94. For details on the economic situation, see next section.

95. *Business Day* (Johannesburg), August 8, 2002. On August 24 Zimbabwe signed a whole bevy of trade agreements with Kinshasa, desperately trying to preserve some of the fragile economic advantages it had acquired during the war.

96. *New Vision,* August 12, 2002. The Ugandan president said he would take out the 19th and 53rd Battalions and later the two elements of the 35th Battalion still guarding Gbadolite Airport and garrisoning Buta.

97. He was said to have been "discovered" in a UNITA demobilizing camp. This was most likely a face-saving device provided by the Angolans to help Joseph Kabila, since the notorious general had been on Congolese territory all along.

See Agence France Presse dispatch, Kigali, August 13, 2002: "Le Général Bizimungu arrêté en RDC, pas en Angola."

98.   IRIN dispatch, August 28, 2002.

99.   In late August Kinshasa attracted the attention of the international community because the RPA was infiltrating North Kivu and Ituri on the heels of the retreating UPDF.

100. The repatriation was presented by Kigali as voluntary. See Agence France Presse dispatch, Kigali, September 3, 2002; IRIN dispatch, September 5, 2002; Jesuit Refugee Service communiqué, September 17, 2002.

101. *East African,* September 16, 2002; IRIN dispatch, September 16, 2002.

102. The best overall view of the confused situation at the time of the Rwandese "evacuation" is to be found in the Réseau Européen Congo reports of October 2 and 16, 2002.

103. This was all the harder to detect because a large proportion of the RPA troops in the Congo were by then Hutu. They were a mixture of civilian prisoners from Rwanda formerly accused of genocide and freed on condition of joining the army, rallied *génocidaires* POWs, and Congolese Hutu locally recruited in North Kivu.

104. The RCD-G commander responsible for the repression cynically boasted on the movement's radio about having escaped punishment for his behavior in Kisangani the preceding May.

105. The veteran Yermos Lukole Madoa Doa was a former companion of Laurent-Désiré Kabila from the days of the 1960s Hewa Bora guerrillas. He had been commissioned as a brigadier in the FAC.

106. Obsac website, September 15, 2002.

107. *Le Potentiel,* October 15, 2002.

108. *East African,* October 21, 2002.

109. In fact, the whole operation was supervised by the South African Secret Service operative Billy Masethla and a small team of his men working with Congolese Security. On October 31, after they had forcibly repatriated to Kigali some of the FDLR leadership who had initially been promised political asylum in Brazzaville, there was a revolt during which seven FAC soldiers and an FDLR colonel were killed. Over fifteen hundred FDLR troops managed to run away from the camp and headed for South Kivu. IRIN dispatch, November 4, 2002.

110. *Nord-Sud Export,* November 8, 2002.

111. Obsac website, December 17, 2002.

112. The best overview of the situation can be found in the March 22, 2002, *Nord-Sud Export* special report on the state of the DRC economy.

113. Office of Foreign Disasters Assistance, *Annual Report,* Washington, DC, May 22, 2002.

114. World Bank, *African Economic Indicators,* Washington, DC, 2003, 33.

115. FAO report, quoted in IRIN dispatch, October 25, 2001.

116. International Rescue Committee, *Mortality in the DRC,* Washington, DC, [third report], April 2003.

117. World Bank communiqué, Paris, July 3, 2001.

118. *CID Bulletin,* October 15–25, 2001.

119. The three (IDI, Primogen, and Tofen) were all Israeli. IDI had fallen back in the common lot and was not operating as a monopoly any more. The first counter to be fined for nonperformance was Top International, which had to pay $796,952 in April 2002. *Africa Mining Intelligence,* April 17, 2002.

120. But by July it had climbed back down to 210, reflecting a growing confidence in the economic stabilization.

121. *IRIN Bulletin,* no. 1,191 (June 1, 2001).

122. *Africa Mining Intelligence,* July 3, 2002.

123. *Africa Mining Intelligence,* July 17, 2002. This was the Dikulushi copper mining project, which implied about $20 million in new investment.

124. *IRIN Bulletin,* no. 1,268 (September 18, 2001).

125. This later developed into a major political row, since, to boost its position at the negotiating table, Kinshasa decided to start paying civil servants' salaries in rebel areas. The MLC promptly confiscated the first instalment and the RCD-G refused the money. The public relations benefit for Kinshasa was considerable.

126. *Africa Mining Intelligence,* February 6, 2002. In July 2002 Gécamines started negotiating with the unions to lay off 10,000 of its now largely redundant 24,000 workforce. *Africa Mining Intelligence,* July 17, 2002.

127. ONATRA, the police, OFIDA (customs), and DGM (migrations). African Press Agency dispatch, November 15, 2001. Some of those asked to leave had to be threatened with physical force to make them go.

128. Réseau Européen Congo Report, January 21, 2002.

129. By late 2001 the situation had improved sufficiently for a whole group of Fédération des Entreprises de Belgique companies to attend the Kikwit meeting at which their work in rebel-held areas was discussed. Joseph Kabila magnanimously declared, "The last three years, we should forget them." *Africa Mining Intelligence,* September 26, 2001.

130. *Nord-Sud Export,* June 21, 2002. By then money was coming in in reasonable quantities: the Ninth European Union FED program had earmarked €120 million for the Congo and discussions were under way to untangle the DRC mess at the BAD, whose Congolese debts arrears of $813 milion represented 60 percent of the Bank's liabilities and therefore had to be dealt with to avoid its possible collapse into insolvency.

131. The Club of Paris held between $9 billion and $10.2 billion of the total Congolese debt, depending on whether a global figure of $12.47 billion or $14.3 billion was adopted (the difference came from the calculation of the arrears). See Prosper Mamimami Kabare, *Dette extérieure de la RDC: Encours, gestion et perspectives d'annulation,* Kinshasa, FODEX, September 2002.

132. *Nord-Sud Export,* December 20, 2002.

133. Matungulu was sacrificed to appease the old Kabilist hard core, which accused him of having refused money to Zimbabwe (Harare had taken to claiming $1.8 billion from Kinshasa since the beginning of 2003), of not disbursing funds for extrabudgetary military expenses, and of not using recently acquired monies to reimburse the internal debt. This last accusation was silly because Matungulu was contractually obliged to use these funds for ADB and World Bank reimbursements. But Yerodia Ndombasi and the Comités du Pouvoir Populaire (CPP) kept attacking "international capitalism," for which the finance minister seemed to be the local symbol. They also agitated against the Pretoria Agreement, which they called "a sellout." This led President Kabila to eventually disband the CPP on March 8, 2003.

134. *IRIN Bulletin,* no. 1,148 (April 3, 2001).

135. From that point of view the first *Report of the UN Panel of Experts on the Illegal Exploitation of National Resources in the DRC* (April 2001) was a major political breakthrough. The history of the struggle to prevent or modify its publication,

due not to the African names named but rather to those of their European and American business partners, would in itself deserve an article.

136. *New Vision,* August 18, 2000. This sadly realistic observation could have later been used as a commentary on the results of the Pretoria peace process.

137. For an overview of the Ituri up to late 2003, see G. Prunier, "The 'Ethnic' Conflict in the Ituri District," in J. P. Chrétien and R. Banegas, eds., *The Recurring Great Lakes Crisis* (London: Hurst, 2007), 180–204.

138. Radio France Internationale, in *BBC/SWB,* June 11, 2001.

139. Net Press dispatch, Bujumbura, March 31, 2001. Mugabe's idea was to deflect the war from the Congo and take it to Rwanda and Burundi. It was the same policy that led to the ALIR I attack on northern Rwanda in May–June 2001.

140. The Rwandese DMI had done a fairly good job of turning around several Mayi Mayi groups. Some, like the Mudundu 40 movement, had become regular allies of Kigali.

141. RTNC-Goma, in *BBC/SWB,* April 4, 2001.

142. *La Libre Belgique,* January 9, 2002.

143. For an evaluation of this contagion phenomenon, see Human Rights Watch Africa, *Ituri: Covered in Blood,* Washington, DC, July 2003; Prunier, "The 'Ethnic' Conflict in the Ituri District."

144. The question of their citizenship, which had been one of the key pretexts of the war, was bound to resurface in any kind of in-depth inter-Congolese dialogue.

145. IRIN dispatch, April 2, 2002.

146. Mbusa's main lieutenant, Sylvain Mbuki, was killed along with eleven of his men in Mbigi, between Butembo and Kanyabayonga. *New Vision,* December 11, 2001.

147. Réseau Européen Congo report, November 29, 2001.

148. International Crisis Group, *The Kivus: Forgotten Crucible of the Congo Conflict,* Brussels, January 2003.

Chapter 9

1. Angola was aiming for a daily oil production of one million barrels in 2003 and has over $15 billion of assessed diamond reserves. *Nord-Sud Export,* September 20, 2002.

2. By February 2002 UNITA was already in desperate straits. Even if the story according to which Savimbi was located by U.S. GPS tracking of his satellite telephone is true (there are strong doubts because during the guerrilla leader's last few days his phone battery was dead), this was only a marginal factor: Savimbi was defeated and on the run, desperately trying to take refuge in Zambia. Confidential interview, Addis-Ababa, November 2002.

3. International Crisis Group, *Dealing with Savimbi's Ghost: The Security and Humanitarian Challenges in Angola,* Brussels, February 2003, 5. Most of the war's vanquished are still languishing to this day.

4. President dos Santos quoted in Economic Intelligence Unit, *Angola Country Profile,* 2006, 6.

5. The German advocacy NGO Stiftung Wissenschaft und Politik could already call its December 1998 study of Zimbabwe *A Conflict Study of a Country without Direction.*

6. In December 2000, three hundred Zimbabwean soldiers had been court-martialled for refusing to serve in the Congo. *Financial Gazette* (Harare), January

11, 2001. The popular singer and former freedom fighter Thomas Mapfumo, who was sharply critical of the war on his 1999 album *Chamurorwa,* was eventually forced to leave the country.

7.   *Financial Gazette* (Harare), February 13, 2003. This later remained the official position of the Zimbabwean authorities. In December 2003, during a conference on the Great Lakes conflict held in Dar-es-Salaam, I was still taken to task by representatives of the Harare government for having suggested that the Zimbabwean intervention in the Congo had had economic motives. They offered instead a purely legalistic explanation linked with the respect of SADC rules on aggrieved national sovereignty.

8.   This is the expression used in a UN report (October 2002) which was published soon after.

9.   *Herald* (Harare), August 24, 2002.

10.   *Zimbabwe Independent,* August 9, 2002. Between 1982 and 1992 Zimbabwe sent fifteen thousand soldiers to Mozambique to help the government fight the RENAMO insurgency.

11.   Both CNDD-FDD and FNL guerrillas still have important rear bases in the DRC.

12.   For a clear analysis of the Agreement and its consequences, see International Crisis Group, *Burundi: Ni guerre, ni paix,* Brussels, December 2000.

13.   Jean-Bosco Ndayikengurukiye and Pierre Nkurunziza for the CNDD-FDD, Agathon Rwasa and Cossan Kabura for the FNL. Both organizations were split between "moderate" and "radical" wings, the difference being largely due to the degree of proximity to the fighters on the ground. The leaders who had been abroad for too long, like Ndayikengurukiye, who was Kabila's man in Lubumbashi, tended to be rejected by the more aggressive rank and file.

14.   Alain Mugabarabona replaced Cossan Kabura as the head of FNL. But he failed to displace Agathon Rwasa, who retreated, especially after he was wounded by his rivals in May 2002, into an increasingly convoluted mystical world wherein the Hutu symbolically took the place of the Babylon-suffering Jews in the Old Testament. Many radical Hutu followed Rwasa and his righthand man, Pasteur Habimana, into their flight from reality. Conversations with René Lemarchand, Dar-es-Salaam, December 2003.

15.   For an interesting retrospective view of this period, see Augustin Nsanze, *Le Burundi contemporain: L'Etat-Nation en question (1956–2002)* (Paris: L'Harmattan, 2003), 61–149, as well as the works by M. Manirakiza Nsanze refers to.

16.   For a reflection on this geopolitical interface between central-Sahelian Africa and the Great Lakes, see Gérard Prunier, "Les Grands Lacs ont-ils coulé jusqu'en Afrique Centrale?" *Enjeux* (Yaoundé), no. 17 (October–December 2003).

17.   *Economist,* April 24, 1999.

18.   Including Nelson Mandela.

19.   On the Sudan-Uganda conflict in the Congo, see Gérard Prunier, "Rebel Movements and Proxy Warfare: Uganda, Sudan and the Congo (1986–1999)," *African Affairs* 103, no. 412 (2004): 359–383.

20.   Patasse is a Central African Republic Sara while Kolingba is a Central African Republic Yakoma. In both cases transborder electoral support came from fellow tribesmen of a different nationality.

21.   The motivation was tactical: Bemba needed Bangui's support to fly in supplies and to truck in fuel. It was also political: a number of rival Mobutists, including Jean Séti Yale and General Baramoto, were trying to turn Patasse against him to

replace him at the head of the Equateur-based guerrilla group.

22.   IRIN dispatch, Nairobi, June 19, 2001.

23.   *La lettre de l'Océan Indien,* May 26, 2001.

24.   See "Tarnished Victory," *Economist,* March 17, 2001; "Ungracious Winner," *Africa Confidential* 42, no. 7 (April 6, 2001).

25.   *La lettre de l'Océan Indien,* April 21, 2001.

26.   "Sommet rwando-ougandais à Londres pour éviter la guerre," *Le Monde,* November 6, 2001; "Kagame, Museveni in Peace Meeting," IRIN dispatch, Nairobi, November 6, 2001.

27.   The Congo conflict was estimated to cost $60 million/year. Institute of Strategic Studies, *The Military Balance 2001–2002,* London, 2002.

28.   *New Vision,* February 25, 2002. This renewed northern threat was soon to develop into the major security nightmare of the Ugandan regime.

29.   Fifty-six percent of Uganda's recurrent expenditure budget and 100 percent of its development budget were financed by foreign aid. At the beginning of 2002 Denmark slashed $3.2 million from its aid package as a warning, specifically linking this reduction with Kampala's military expenditure and the Congo war. *New Vision,* February 6, 2002.

30.   Museveni's attitude often strangely echoed the White Man's Burden outlook of yesteryear. When the first UN *Report on the Illegal Exploitation of Congolese Resources* put Uganda on the spot, his instinctive reaction was to pour scorn on the Congo: "They say we are there to get gold and diamonds. But for me, each time I have been there, I have only seen people eating monkeys and caterpillars."

31.   For a lucid debunking of that typically Congolese myth, see René Lefort, "Les ennemis rapprochés du Congo," *Libération,* August 1, 2003.

32.   For a historical and political treatment of the Ituri horror, see Gérard Prunier, "The 'Ethnic' Conflict in Ituri District," in J. P. Chrétien and R. Banegas, eds., *The Recurring Great Lakes Crisis* (London: Hurst, 2008), 180–204.

33.   Actually, in several cases Kigali tried to "recycle" exactly the same guerrilla groups (ADF remnants, the FUNA of Taban Amin, bits and pieces of UNRF II) that Khartoum had used in the past. Rwanda's problem was that these organizations, never very strong in the first place, had by then largely degenerated into banditry.

34.   By 2003 there were 50,000 deaths and 500,000 IDPs and cannibalism was a common practice. The best description of this human rights catastrophe can be found in Human Rights Watch Africa, *Ituri: Covered in Blood: Ethnically Targeted Violence in North-Eastern Congo,* New York, July 2003.

35.   AP dispatch, Dar-es-Salaam, February 10, 2003.

36.   *New Vision,* March 12, 2003.

37.   The People's Redemption Army was a very shadowy outfit; in its only verified fight against it, the Ugandan army said it had killed three and captured twenty-two. *New Vision,* March 19, 2003. But Kigali protested that they were "people who have been paid money to pretend they are rebels with the aim of tarnishing our government." *New Times* (Kigali), March 24–26, 2003.

38.   The Porter Commission was set up as a counterweight to the UN panel on the illegal exploitation of Congolese resources. Its conclusions were only a partial exoneration of Ugandan government activity in the Congo. *New Vision,* May 15, 2003.

39.   By then the Lendu FNI and "Commander" Jerome Kakwavu Bokonde's multi-

ethnic FAPC in Mahagi. When Amnesty International Secretary-General Irene Khan denounced this criminal association during a trip to East Africa, she was rebuked indignantly by the Ugandan authorities. IRIN dispatch, Kampala, October 22, 2003.

40.   *New Vision,* June 4, 2003.
41.   IRIN dipatch, Kampala, October 28, 2003.
42.   Press conference, Washington, DC, November 14, 2003.
43.   In a particularly rough display of gallows humor, many of the big new houses built in Kigali during the past four or five years were nicknamed "vive le génocide" (long live the genocide) since all the owners were Tutsi.
44.   While it was extremely difficult to verify the number of RPA troops left behind after October 2002, it does not seem to have been very large (probably around four thousand) because Kigali's strategy was increasingly to train local militias rather than to fight directly. The exceptions had to do with technical personnel. Interview with diplomatic sources, Dar-es-Salaam, December 2003.
45.   Tous Pour le Développement was entirely made up of local Hutu, many of them former members of MAGRIVI, the pro-Kigali network during the 1990–1994 war. Thus the old "Hutu Power" supporters remained at the service of the Rwandese regime, even if it was now Tutsi-led.
46.   For detailed (even if partisan) information on these new networks of Rwandese influence in the Congo, see ASADHO, *Rapport sur les manoeuvres en cours dans l'Est et le Nord-Est de la RDC,* Kinshasa, August 2003; Observatoire Gouvernance Transparence, *Le Rwanda plante le décor d'une nouvelle guerre d'agression à l'Est de la RDC,* Kinshasa, September 2003.
47.   The means employed could be a bit rough. One of Bizimungu's assistants, Gratien Munyarubuga, was shot dead by "persons unknown" after visiting the former president at home. See Human Rights Watch Africa report, New York, January 13, 2002.
48.   IRIN dispatch, Nairobi, April 25, 2002; *Le Monde,* May 21, 2002.
49.   IRIN Press dispatch, Kigali, June 8, 2004.
50.   Amnesty International communiqué, April 24, 2003.
51.   *Economist,* May 31, 2003.
52.   PSD, Parti Libéral, the Islamic Party, and the tiny Parti Syndical Rwandais. *East African,* July 7, 2003.
53.   IRIN dispatch, Nairobi, August 8, 2003.
54.   "President Uses Memory of Genocide to Win Votes," *Guardian,* August 25, 2003.
55.   Voting was done by putting one's fingerprint opposite the name of the candidate of one's choice. When "wrong" votes were inadvertently forgotten they could always be canceled by the simple process of putting a second fingerprint in front of another box, thereby nullifying the ballot. Interview with the journalist Jean-Philippe Rémy, an eyewitness, on August 31, 2003. The international observers were not fooled, but they gave a passing verdict anyway. See "Kagame Won, a Little Too Well," *Economist,* August 30, 2003.
56.   Which included the powerful intelligence operative Patrick Karegeya.
57.   See chapter 8.
58.   IRIN dispatch, Kinshasa, February 18, 2004.
59.   IRIN dispatch, Kigali, April 22, 2004.
60.   IRIN dispatch, Kigali, April 23, 2004.
61.   IRIN dispatch, Kinshasa, April 24, 2004.

62. IRIN dispatches, Kinshasa, April 27 and 30, 2004. FDLR prisoners declared that their officers were trying to prevent them from going back to Rwanda, even shooting those who tried.

63. There were no media reports of these attacks.

64. IRIN dispatch, Kigali, May 12, 2004.

65. Mbuza Mabe, a tough career general with a good track record, had replaced Nabyolwa as head of the 10th Region. He was particularly disliked by the Banyamulenge troops because, as a Mobutu general, he had been one of the few FAZ officers to fight them successfully (in March 1997 in Mbandaka).

66. Interviews in Bukavu, November 2006.

67. The reason for preferring to flee into Burundi came from a political calculation: the Banyamulenge civilians, who hoped to come back to the Congo after a while, did not want to be accused of being "Rwandese" and of having run to "their country." Burundi was seen as much less ideologically connoted.

68. See chapter 8.

69. There were 22,000 by mid-June and 34,000 by the end of the month.

70. AP and AFP dispatches, Kinshasa, June 2, 2004.

71. *New Vision,* June 21, 2004; IRIN dispatch, June 22, 2004.

72. *New Vision,* June 24, 2004.

73. Multiethnic but with a lot of Congolese Hutu among its fighters.

74. Several of them (FNI, FRPI, FAPC) were in fact directly or indirectly controlled by Rwanda and/or Uganda, and the resumption of hostilities in the north was most likely linked with the South Kivu events.

75. AFP dispatch, Bukavu, July 31, 2004.

76. The Tutsi and their Banyamulenge cousins were systematically targeted by the killers, who would inquire about ethnic identities and spare the Bashi refugees. Telephone interviews with NGO workers in Bujumbura, August 2004.

77. Note the amalgam of all "Hutu forces" into one murderous gaggle and the assimilation of "the DRC" to these same "negative forces."

78. IRIN dispatches, Bukavu and Bujumbura, August 18, 2004.

79. There was one small element of hope in that fanatical mess: the fact that Muyamulenge commander Patrick Masunzu, who had lost any illusions about the RPF a long time before, allied himself with Mbuza Mabe and pushed fellow Muyamulenge officer Jules Mutebutsi down to Fizi, later forcing him to take refuge in Rwanda.

80. It might seem strange to see two commanding officers of the same army agreeing not to fight each other. But Rwibasira was Mutebutsi's brother-in-law, and his attitude during the crisis was ambiguous (he closed the Goma Airport, blocking Ruberwa on the ground at a time when restricting the vice president's movements could have proved disastrous).

81. Confidential interview with MONUC officers, Kinshasa, October and November 2006.

82. Ibid.

83. *New Vision,* December 3, 2004.

84. *East African,* December 5, 2004; IRIN dispatch, Kampala, December 8, 2004.

85. IRIN dispatch, Kigali, December 15, 2004.

86. Confidential interview with a person close to the Rwandese president, Nairobi, April 2005.

87. CIAT was the body set up by the international community to support the transition process (see next subsection).

88.   Reuters dispatch, Goma, December 22, 2004.
89.   *East African,* December 26, 2004.
90.   Author's emphasis. Interview with ICG in Kigali, late December 2004; ICG, *Congo: Solving the FDLR Problem Once and For All,* Brussels, May 2005.
91.   The expression was used by the *Economist* in an article aptly called "Good News from the Congo," August 9, 2003.
92.   The French Africanist journalist Christopher Ayad called it "une usine à gaz," a slang expression that roughly translates in American English as "a Rube Gold-berg contraption." *Libération,* July 24, 2003.
93.   Agence France Presse dispatch, Sun City, April 1, 2003.
94.   Reuters dispatch, Capetown, April 9, 2003.
95.   Yerodia Ndombasi for the former government, Jean-Pierre Bemba for the MLC, Azarias Ruberwa for the RCD-G, and Arthur Z'Ahidi Ngoma for the unarmed opposition.
96.   *La Libre Belgique,* April 29, 2003. The president used the occasion to pardon about seven hundred political detainees. But none of the accused in the murder trial of his father were included in the pardon.
97.   IRIN dispatch, Kinshasa, April 28, 2003.
98.   Still, it did not work in the case of a very serious crisis, as it became painfully clear during the Bukavu fighting of 2004.
99.   They were the Truth and Reconciliation Commission, the Ethics and Anti-Corruption Commission, the media watchdog Haute Autorité des Médias, the National Human Rights Observatory, and the National Electoral Commis-sion.
100.   IRIN dispatch, Kinshasa, May 18, 2004.
101.   On March 28, 2004, some former DSP soldiers coming from Brazzaville, and then on June 10 an attempt by disgruntled Balubakat, who felt that Joseph was not enough on their side.
102.   Interview with Adonya Ayebare, Dar-es-Salaam, December 2003.
       This is one reason Rwarakabije did not manage to bring back many of his men into Rwanda with him: his rallying the government was seen by them as the continuation of a strategy of personal enrichment.
103.   Senators and members of Parliament were earning $2,000 a month and each vice president had a total budget (salary plus expenses) of $5.5 million a year in a country where the average salary, for the man lucky enough to be employed, averaged $6 a month. *Le Potentiel,* September 18, 2003.
104.   Veteran UDPS chief Etienne Tschisekedi seemed irresolute and contradictory in his strategy. He had refused to participate in the Electoral Commission and was calling for a boycott of the whole process, while at the same time criticizing its imperfect implementation.
105.   IRIN dispatch, Kinshasa, January 11, 2005.
106.   IRIN dispatch, Mbuji-Mayi, May 17, 2005.
107.   See Reuters dispatch, June 28, 2005; IRIN dispatch, June 30, 2005; AFP dis-patch, July 2, 2005. Voter registration, a tremendously difficult exercise in a country of 2,345,000 square kilometers with poor communications, started on June 20 and people wanted to feel they were not making the huge effort to register in vain.
108.   The text of the constitution, too complicated and technical to elicit gut reac-tions, was almost irrelevant. Voters voted "yes" or "no" as a show of support or rejection for the transition politicians, particularly President Joseph Kabila.

109. Reuters dispatch, Kinshasa, January 4, 2006. The old fighter seemed oddly unresponsive to the new political environment, and the often-heard remark about him was that "he was frozen in 1992," the year of his greatest glory, when he had become prime minister of the Conférence Nationale Souveraine during Mobutu's aborted "democratic transition."

110. IRIN dispatch, Kinshasa, February 22, 2006.

111. Given the importance of the tribe and especially its high profile in the public administration, durably alienating it is a dangerous development.

112. J. C. Willame, *Les faiseurs de paix au Congo: Gestion d'une crise internationale dans un état sous tutelle* (Brussels: GRIP/Editions Complexe, 2007).

113. Even adding the civilian northern supporters of the MLC and the Banyarwanda supporters of the RCD, one does not reach a critical mass of the population representing a civil war constituency on the model of the Sudan or even of Biafra.

114. For a good overview of the postconflict security problems, see the ICG report *Security Sector Reform in the Congo,* Brussels, February 2006.

115. Which might have been intentional since *precise* security arrangements might have been impossible to negotiate at the time without dragging an already overlong process into further delays.

116. In international newspeak, "DDRRR" means Disarmament, Demobilization, Repatriation, Reinstallation, and Reinsertion; "SSR" means Security Sector Reform. They logically should follow each other, but they often overlap.

117. Even in the world of the notoriously ill-disciplined Congolese soldiery, Mayi Mayi fighters were the worst. Initially formed by volunteers who wanted to protect the civilians from foreign invading armies and their proxies, they ended up preying on the population they were supposed to protect and proved at times as bad a scourge as the invaders. They tend to be heavily segmented according to their tribal recruitment.

118. After Sun City the belligerents even tried to pretend that their combined forces numbered 340,000.

119. The biggest component is Belgian, with a strong participation from France, Angola, and South Africa. An EU mission (EUSEC) acts as a kind of supervisory body. In addition to its peacekeeping role MONUC has tried to have a hand in FARDC integration, but its quick officer turnover has considerably limited its effectiveness.

120. Soldiers often live in substandard housing and diseases are rife among the troops due to a very poor medical system.

121. See next section on the elections.

122. In a play on the phonetics of the French acronym, PIR, the always cheeky Kinshasa public calls it "Pire que tout" (Worse than all).

123. I was an eyewitness to the debacle. But the "Angolan" units, often made up of Portuguese-speaking former Zairian refugees in Angola, are definitely of a tougher (perhaps too tough) material.

124. For a quick overview, see G. Prunier, "The 'Ethnic' Conflict in the Ituri," 199–202.

125. Floribert Njabu and two of his aides were arrested in early March and Thomas Lubanga two weeks later. IRIN dispatch, March 22, 2005. The arrest of the long-feared UPC warlord acted as a positive psychological shock in the Ituri. Chief Kahwa Pandro Manga was then arrested in April for trying to stop disarmament. IRIN dispatch, April 12, 2005.

126.   IRIN dispatch, Bunia. April 8, 2005.

127.   See ICG, *Katanga: The Congo's Forgotten Crisis,* Brussels, January 2006.

128.   *New Vision,* December 29–30, 2005.

129.   There were representatives from UPC, FNI, FRPI, and FAPC. The key player was Bosco Taganda, a North Kivu Tutsi friend of General Nkunda who had also sent members of his Mouvement de Libération de l'Est du Congo, even if those usually tended to be closer to Rwanda. Interview with Jason Stearns, Nairobi, November 2006.

130.   *New Vision,* March 24, 2006. The LRA maintained a shadowy presence in the Garamba National Park in the extreme north of the DRC. Its capacity to attack Uganda in any serious way from there was almost nil and it mostly preyed on the few local inhabitants. But at the same time Mouvement Révolutionnaire Congolais guerrillas were wreaking havoc from the Ituri down to Rutshuru in North Kivu.

131.   By then the Rwandese had withdrawn into a much more neutral stance and they directed a lot of their complaints at the Kampala representatives, voicing considerable doubts about the Peoples Redemption Army they were accused of sponsoring against Uganda and whose existence was strongly in doubt.

132.   *New Vision,* May 30, 2006.

133.   For an excellent study of the FDLR, see Multi Country Demobilization and Recovery Program, *Opportunities and Constraints for the Disarmament and Repatriation of Foreign Armed Groups in the DRC (FDLR, FNL and ADF/NALU),* written by Hans Romkema, De Vennhoop, April 2007.

134.   RPF officers only had to consult their own memories to remember how an organized military force outside of Rwanda could use favorable circumstances to attack and overthrow an embattled regime in Kigali.

135.   In addition, MONUC troops were a mixed bag, with very different combat capabilities. For their at times lackluster military performance, see the hard piece published in the *Telegraph* (London), May 1, 2005.

136.   There were 50,045 polling stations spread over the huge national territory, and with its sixty helicopters, 104 aircraft, and thousands of vehicles MONUC was a key element in helping out. As Bill Swing liked to boast, MONUC was by then the second largest airline in Africa after South African Airways.

137.   The FAA troops were in Soyo facing Muanda, in Ango Ango facing Matadi, and in the Cabinda Enclave facing Tshela. Security reports also detected the presence of Angolan Secret Service men in plainclothes gathering information. JMAC, *Report on Bas Congo,* October 2006.

138.   But he ran a very tight campaign and was to emerge reinforced and strengthened from the elections.

139.   Mbusa Nyamwisi, who had initially been a "serious" candidate, desisted shortly before the last lap of the campaign and chose to back Joseph Kabila. This was an important switch since Mbusa Nyamwisi could bring him the support of the so-called independent republic of Butembo, that is, of the well-organized Nande networks.

140.   These were the words used by Roman Catholic priests in Bas Congo who had been preaching in church against voting for the president.

141.   *Africa Confidential* 47, no. 16 (August 4, 2006).

142.   Confidential interview with a MONUC officer, Kinshasa, November 2006. Such a move would have been a disaster since this was exactly what Bemba was hoping for to have a legitimate recourse to extralegal means.

143.   These disgraceful events seem to have been typical of the degree of confusion and low professionalism of the "security" forces. Contrary to what was later asserted, if the presidential camp had wanted to kill Bemba, there would have been better and more discreet ways of doing it than shooting up his house when it was full of foreign diplomats.

144.   Both leading candidates had in fact a somewhat larger reach through the coalitions they had created. But these coalitions, particularly Bemba's, were fragile, making the creation of a working parliamentary majority (or of a coherent opposition) a real headache.

145.   This complicated system, called *proportionnelle au plus fort reste* (proportional vote, with the seat going to the candidate with the highest rest), had been designed by a Lebanese UN voting expert. Because of both his personal cultural inclination and UN pressures (originating in the United States) hoping to favor the Kinyarwanda RCD electorate, this system had contributed to fragmentation without independent representation and to the multiplication of bogus "small parties."

146.   Jean-Pierre Bemba has a rough and at times violent personality. His overbearing manner tended to alienate potential allies, and many of this top men (Jose Endundo, Olivier Kamitatu, Alexis Thambwe) were driven away from the MLC by their leader's authoritarian streak.

147.   IRIN dispatch, Kinshasa, November 16, 2006.

148.   IRIN dispatch, Kinshasa, November 17, 2006.

149.   IRIN dispatch, Kinshasa, November 21, 2006.

150.   He pretended having only 800 men when he probably had around 1,200; he then promised to evacuate 600 and in the end moved only about 100. Interview with Bill Swing, Kinshasa, April 2007,

151.   ICG, *Congo: Consolidating the Peace,* Brussels, July 2007, 7.

152.   Governors and vice governors, like the senators, were elected indirectly by the regional assemblies. They *all* bought their "victories" (even those who could have won without corruption), because the regional MPs told them that even if they were popular, this was not a reason to avoid paying.

153.   Luanda did not want the BDK anywhere near power in Bas Congo because the sect stands for a restoration of the old Kongo kingdom, an event that, if it came near realization, would trigger secessionist movements in both the Brazzaville-Congo and Angola itself, where Bakongo tribesmen live in large numbers. The areas that would be affected are regions of considerable oil production.

154.   Figure obtained by the author in April 2007 from three Kinshasa NGOs after visiting the city morgues. The government never released any official figure.

155.   The former CIAT (it no longer existed officially but still functioned informally) later kept insisting on Bemba's return as a sign of democratic normalization. That would have been symbolically true, even though in reality it would probably prove more of a headache than anything else, given the man's vision of his role as opposition leader.

156.   The rescheduling did not apply to the whole debt but only to the approximately $9 billion owed to the multilateral institutions.

157.   This corresponded to the amount of the arrears accumulated since Zaire was suspended from the IMF in 1992 for nonpayment.

158.   See, for example, the article by J. P. Mbelu, "Les options fondamentales du budget: Une menace pour le Congo," *Le Potentiel,* June 26, 2007. In fact Muzito, Finance Minister Athanase Matenda Kyelu, and Central Bank Governor

Jean-Claude Masangu were engaged in a desperate struggle to get for Congo the still elusive Heavily Indebted Poor Countries status it has been running after since 2002.

159.   According to the new constitution voted in December 2005, the number of provinces has to be brought from eleven to twenty-six and their budgets will be financed directly by the taxes they raise, which, instead of being centralized in Kinshasa, should see 40 percent of their amount kept directly at the source. The problem is, of course, 40 percent of what? Some provinces will be very poor, and some taxes, particularly those paid to the Direction des Grandes Entreprises, will be excluded from the locally retained 40 percent.

160.   Mobutu deeply distrusted honest civil servants (there still were some) because he suspected them of using their honesty to further oppositionist political agendas. He did not *tolerate* corruption, he actively *encouraged* it.

161.   See chapter 4.

162.   Interview with the mining lawyer Marcel Yabili, Lubumbashi, April 2007.

163.   There is a large and growing literature on the subject. See Global Witness, *Rush and Ruin: The Devastating Mineral Trade in Southern Katanga, DRC,* London, September 2004; Global Witness, *Reforming the DRC Diamond Sector,* London, June 2006; Global Witness, *Digging in Corruption,* London, July 2006; Human Rights Watch, *The Curse of Gold,* New York, 2005; Government of the Democratic Republic of the Congo, *Rapport de la commission spéciale chargée d'examiner la validité des conventions à caractère économique et financier conclus pendant les guerres de 1996–1997 et de 1998,* Kinshasa, June 2005. Known as the Luntundula Report, this report is available on the Web but has never been officially published.

164.   The Kabwelulu Commission's findings were made public in March 2008, after five months of behind-the-scenes bargaining with the companies had ended in deadlock. The result is probably going to be a series of protracted court cases between the Congolese state and the big mining groups.

165.   Later bought by the even bigger Freeport MacMoran for $26.6 billion.

166.   See Global Witness, *Same Old Story: A Background Study on Natural Resources in the DRC,* London, June 2004.

167.   This is a recurrent shortcoming in the approach of the international community when it deals with Africa. Elections and "peace agreements" are too often taken as an end in themselves, without factoring in the context within which they start and later develop. The 1993 Burundi elections were one of the factors leading to the civil war; the Sudanese so-called Comprehensive Peace Agreement (January 2005) is unraveling as I write; and the Darfur Peace Agreement (May 2006) did not for one moment stop the violence in that part of the Sudan. Legal constructs are too often mistaken for realities. Although the DRC elections were quite real, they were not sufficient to directly address the whole of Congolese reality.

168.   See chapter 2, "The Refugees and the Kivu Cockpit."

169.   S. Wolters and H. Boshoff, *Situation Report,* ISS (Pretoria), July 2006.

170.   For example, the Mundundu 40 group in North Kivu, which, although it has many Hutu fighters, has made an informal but efficient alliance with Laurent Nkunda's Tutsi forces.

171.   IRIN dispatch, Bunia, January 3, 2006.

172.   Thus the thuggish "Cobra Matata" (a nom de guerre) who became a FARDC colonel in November 2006, barely more than two months after attacking the

FARDC at Cingo, sixty kilometers to the south of Bunia. See *Le Potentiel,* October 5, 2006, for the attack; IRIN dispatch, Kinshasa, November 30, 2006, for the promotion.

173. ICG, *Congo: Consolidating the Peace,* 14.

174. DRC human rights organizations protested against the appointment as FARDC colonels of two notorious war criminals. IRIN dispatch, Kinshasa, October 11, 2006.

175. On March 26, 2007, the ADF crossed into Uganda and attacked Bundibungyo, losing thirty-four of its men. This was the third clash of this kind in a week. *New Vision,* March 27, 2007.

176. Interview with Bill Swing, Kinshasa, April 2007.

177. As already mentioned (note 134), the best study on all these "foreign" armed groups is the Multi Country Demobilization and Recovery Program's *Opportunities and Constraints for the Disarmament and Repatriation of Foreign Armed Groups in the DRC (FDLR, FNL and ADF/NALU).*

178. Se chapter 8, "The South African Breakthrough."

179. Nkunda is very resentful about his treatment because several of his accomplices in the 2002 Kisangani massacres (Gabriel Amisi, Sylvain Mbuki, Obed Rwibasira) not only were not charged but received high positions in the FARDC.

180. But not *brassage.* In *mixage* the former rebels are put together with other types of troops but their units are not dissolved, they are juxtaposed. In *brassage* they would have been melted down and even geographically reshuffled.

181. He reportedly said in October 2006 at the time of the elections, "Ruberwa f****d me over." Interview in Bukavu, November 2006.

182. About 1,500 in the "Grand Nord," his main battle corps of 8,000 in the "Petit Nord," and another 3,000 in South Kivu.

183. On June 12 UN Human Rights Chief Louise Arbour solemnly warned that "Central Africa was on the brink of yet another major conflict."

184. Mostly the firing of the 8th Military Region, Gen. Louis Ngizo, who was replaced on May 15 by Gen. Vainqueur Mayala, the man who had managed to slowly squeeze FNI into resilience in the Ituri.

185. March 2008.

186. For the past eight years, the Butembo area and the surrounding countryside has, for all practical purposes, been an independent political and economic unit. Although there has never been talk of secession, the "Republic" has its own tax system, produces its own electricity, maintains its own roads, and pays its own militia. The "government" is run jointly by the Catholic and Protestant bishops, with representatives of civil society. But it takes part in the national political life and has elected members at the Parliament in Kinshasa.

187. All participants are supposed to get a $135/day per diem, which adds up to quite a bit since a lot of the international financing for the conference fell through at the last minute. The per diems were essential because for once there is genuine participation of the civil society, which means ordinary people who are usually flat broke.

188. Citizenship laws in the Congo have been a headache since independence and have been changed several times. Each time, the change, although theoretically "national" and "objective," was in fact completely political and driven by the need to deal with the Rwandophone population of the east.

189. See chapter 2, "The Refugees and the Kivu Cockpit."

190. In addition, the Rwandese Hutu have largely "gone native": they marry local

women, live in local villages, raise their children locally, and till the local fields. The problem is that they are also the friendly neighborhood local killers and rapists.

191. This is the title of a book edited by Richard Banegas and J. P. Chrétien, published by Hurst in 2008.
192. Conference subcommittees were still at work in March 2008.
193. Kigali has not sent a full official team to Goma, but only observers.
194. And by the FDLR.
195. Kabarebe and the internal opposition are the worse for Kagame. But on top of that he has to contend with his diaspora enemies (J. P. Mugabe, the king, Sebarenzi), with marginalized RPF (Kayumba Nyamwasa, who is ambassador to India; Karenzi Karake, who has been sent to Darfur), and with rogue elements of his security apparatus (cf. the December 2007 "legal limbo jailbreak" of Security Chief Patrick Karegeya, who had been detained without trial for the past two years). Compared to these Tutsi threats, his Hutu FDLR enemies in the Congo are negligible.

Chapter 10

1. This Kinyarwanda word means a strong but variable wind with unpredictable consequences. It is by that name that the Rwandese refer to the violent events that marked the end of Belgian rule.
2. There is a distinct parallel with the case of the Palestinian refugees after 1948 or later with that of the Pashtun Afghan refugees in Pakistan. Their "problem" refused to go away.
3. For many this was not an obvious move. The men who later were to run Rwanda, including President Kagame himself, had never even seen "their" country till they were in their thirties.
4. For the connection between the Rwandese refugee situation and the Ugandan political world, see G. Prunier, *The Rwanda Crisis: History of a Genocide* (London: Hurst, 1995).
5. They had done so before, in Cameroon in the early 1960s and in Chad in the 1970s and 1980s, without suffering any adverse consequences.
6. This poses the problem of Francis Fukuyama's famous book *The End of History and the Last Man* (New York: Free Press, 1992). Fukuyama's mistake was not so much to have announced the "end of history," a point that could be defended, but to have surmised that since the developed world had come to this fateful moment, the rest of the planet, which functioned along radically different lines, would simply follow suit. In other words, he overestimated the depth of the cultural reach of globalization. What happened on September 11, 2001, was probably the strongest way that point could be made. In a less momentous way, Africa's continental war fits within the same cognitive dissonance: unassimilated historical elements that have survived the homogenization of economic globalization suddenly challenge the dominant worldview.
7. There is an interesting comparison to be made with the combination of Western hubris and ignorance of local circumstances that led President George W. Bush and his administration to invade Iraq in 2003 in the hope of provoking a kind of democratic shock therapy for the whole Middle East.
8. The core group of the New Leaders was made up of Meles Zenawi, Issayas Afeworqi, Yoweri Museveni, and Paul Kagame. Their positively viewed associates

were Eduardo dos Santos, Thabo Mbeki, and even for a while Laurent-Désiré Kabila, all of them supposedly "reformed communist" sinners. They were first promoted by Dan Connell and Frank Smyth in "Africa's New Bloc," *Foreign Affairs*, March–April 1998, and later taken down a peg or two by Marina Ottaway in "Africa's New Leaders: African Solution or African Problem?" *Current History*, May 1998.

9. The Rwandese *génocidaires* were ceaselessly described as "tropical Nazis" and their evil was assigned the same founding role in the supposed new African episteme as the German Nazis had for the Western world. Just as post-Nazi Europe had been the victorious battlefield of democracy, post-Rwanda genocide (and postapartheid Africa) was going to usher in a new era for the continent.

10. It is amusing that the most enthusiastic supporters of the New Leaders paradigm were both former Leftists like Claire Short, with a soft spot for what they saw as a modern reincarnation of their old beliefs, and those most aggressive promoters of the new triumphant globalized capitalist orthodoxy, the IMF and the Word Bank.

11. For an introduction to their nature and their problems, see Mauro DeLorenzo, "Notes for a Historical Ethnography of the Banyamulenge," paper presented at the Conference on Grassroots Perspectives on the DRC Conflict, University of Ghent, Belgium, May 26–28, 2004.

12. Upon assuming power in January 1986 President Museveni said, "This is not a simple changing of the guard, this is a new dispensation." But twelve years later the fact that 56 percent of Uganda's budget was financed by aid, that it remained plagued by a host of minor insurgencies, and that its "no-party democracy" system was more of an enlightened despotism than a real democracy was systematically shoved aside by an international community that desperately wanted at least one African success story. This deliberate blindness was probably not so much willed for the sake of Africa itself as an attempt to show that the new quasi-magic economic recipes that triumphant free-market economists thought they had discovered were absolutely right and universally applicable.

13. The Somali invasion of the Ethiopian Ogaden in 1977 and the Tanzanian occupation of Uganda in 1979 were the only cases. But both were short, sharp, and motivated by clearly limited war aims.

14. Sudanese support for the Eritrean guerrilla movements, Ethiopian support for southern Sudanese rebels, Somali support for southern Ethiopian insurgents, Zairian support for the anticommunist Angolan guerrillas, Libyan support for warring Chadian factions, and Liberian insurgents, to name but a few.

15. As the Bakongo can be between Angola and the Congo or the Sara between Chad and the Central African Republic. These cases are different in that the *divided tribe* has no central connection with a *single ethnic state* next door.

16. The same phenomenon was used in other parts of the world by ideologically very diverse states such as post–World War I Greece (when it attacked Turkey to defend the Greek Aegean diaspora), Hitler's Germany (with its aggressive defense of the Volckdeutsch in central Europe), and Turkey (when it invaded Cyprus in 1974, claiming to protect the Turkish minority after the failed attempt at an Athens-sponsored *Enosis*). Serb military action in Bosnia in the 1990s was based on a similar rationale.

17. The large literature on Mobutu's Zaire tends to focus mostly on political abuse and economic predation. But Mobutu's only achievement, the creation of a strong feeling of nationalism, perhaps compensatory for the feeling of domes-

459

tic frustration, has received less attention; for this point, see G. de Villers, *De Mobutu à Mobutu: Trente ans de relations Belgique-Zaïre* (Brussels: DeBoeck, 1995); Michela Wrong, *In the Footsteps of Mr Kurtz: Living on the Brink of Disaster in the Congo* (London: Fourth Estate, 2000).

18.   See Isidore Ndaywel è Nziem, *La société zaïroise dans le miroir de son discours religieux* (Brussels: CEDAF, 1993).

19.   For a detailed description of this period, see G. de Villers, *Zaïre: La transition manqué (1990–1997)* (Brussels: CEDAF, 1997).

20.   The Banyamulenge, having long ago "Tutsified" themselves, were automatically seen as an RPF fifth column.

21.   This was made explicit by British Prime Minister Tony Blair in 2006 when he said that Africa's situation was "a blemish on the conscience of the world."

22.   This was of course a godsend for the RPF regime. So when the Rwandese were finally forced to evacuate the Congo and were pushed back to their overcrowded microstate, they tried to parlay this one asset into an attempt at turning Rwanda into some kind of Singapore. They managed to enlist foreign acolytes into that project, at times reaching amusing levels of sycophancy; see, for example, Colin Waugh, *Paul Kagame and Rwanda* (Jefferson, NC: MacFarland Publishing, 2004); Stephen Kinzer, "Big Gamble in Rwanda," *New York Review of Books,* March 29, 2007.

23.   In a seminal paper on war and peace in Africa Ken Menkhaus remarked, "One of the recurring problems hampering external interventions in Africa has been misdiagnoses of the crises." "A Sudden Outbreak of Tranquillity: Assessing the New Peace in Africa," *Fletcher Forum on World Affairs* 28, no. 2 (May 2004). The Western refusal to take African history seriously usually goes hand in hand with the "ancient ethnic hatreds" approach: in spite of today's politically correct discourse, Africa is still often unconsciously seen by foreigners as "prehistorical." President Sarkozy's surrealistic speech in Dakar shortly after his election is another proof of this almost unconscious mental attitude.

24.   Recognition of the essential emotional elements overdetermining the Rwanda-Congo historical situation implies in no way adhering to its prejudices on the part of the author.

25.   On the African continent the Angolan civil war and the Eritrean war of independence were the only conflicts to which the "total war" concept was applied.

26.   For studies of such conflicts, see F. Jean and J. C. Rufin, eds., *Economie des guerres civiles* (Paris: Hachette, 1996) (not available in English, but there is a German version published by Hamburger Verlag in 1999). The only (partial) exception to this privatization was the case of the Angolan army because Angola was the only country involved in the war that had enough money to pay its own way.

27.   For this, refer to B. Coghlan et al., "Mortality in the Democratic Republic of the Congo: A Nationwide Survey," *Lancet,* no. 367 (2006): 44–51

28.   See the subsection on the mining interests.

29.   William Zartman, "To Restore the Congo," unpublished paper, Washington, DC, February 2000.

30.   William Zartman, interview with IRIN press agency, Washington, DC, February 2001.

31.   This is one of the reasons why U.S. foreign policy has more than ever before taken Israel under its wing, as from one God-chosen people to another. It is for

the same reason that the French who feel that "quality of life" is their exclusive preserve cannot stand what they perceive as American arrogance, so similar to theirs in its manifestations, so different in its causes.

32.   Official speech by President Bush Sr. at a White House reception in honor of President Mobutu on June 29, 1989, quoted in Peter J. Schraeder, *United States Foreign Policy towards Africa* (New York: Cambridge University Press, 1994).

33.   Samantha Power, *A Problem from Hell: America in the Age of Genocide* (New York: Basic Books, 2002). A good part of the American unease toward the Rwandese genocide is the sneaking suspicion that such horrible phenomena might not be safely sealed away in the distant past (i.e., the first half of the twentieth century) but could linger on, throwing into doubt the naïve optimism born out of the Post-Reagan Era of Triumph.

34.   This was in direct continuation of his aberrant reaction to the genocide, when, according to Power, the president's only concern seems to have been with the physical safety of Rwandese human rights activist Monique Mujawamaliya, whom he had met personally. When he learned that she was all right, he lost interest, "as if she had been the only Rwandese in danger."

35.   Confidential interview, Washington, DC, October 1997.

36.   Conversation with Peter Rosenblum, Washington, DC, March 2000.

37.   When I asked about U.S. Department of Defense official policy toward Africa, the answer was that it ranked seventh in the list of its concerns in the world. Interview with Department of Defense official, Washington, DC, October 2000.

38.   See Connell and Smyth, "Africa's New Bloc."

39.   James Walsh, "Shaking up Africa," *Time,* April 14, 1997.

40.   Ottaway, "Africa's New Leaders."

41.   Ethiopia and Eritrea in May 1998, Rwanda and Uganda against Kabila in August 1998, and then against each other in May 1999. I remember the dismay of John Prendergast in 1998 as he was trying to use Kagame to reconcile Issayas Afeworqi and Meles Zenawi: "They are completely obstinate, they don't want to understand any form of reason" was his comment. The impression he gave was that he perceived the Ethiopian and Eritrean governments as nasty obstinate children who could not see the light of good logical American theories.

42.   John Prendergast, "Building Peace in the Horn of Africa: Diplomacy and Beyond," USIP, Washington, DC, June 1999. The Oxford Dictionary of the English Language defines *cachet* as "a characteristic feature conferring prestige, distinction or high status."

43.   See chapter 8, note 11.

44.   Just as the young Alex Laskaris, who was accompanying him on the tour, was mooted to be the next under-secretary for African affairs.

45.   On February 16, 2000, in a speech wherein he approved Clinton's lack of response to the Rwandese genocide, although he judged it "something which we would not have liked to see on our TV screens." The comment was typical. Blood off-screen hardly exists at all.

46.   Interview at the U.S. State Department, Washington, DC, late September 2001. At the time Snyder was simply an aide to Assistant Secretary Walter Kansteiner.

47.   The Africa Growth and Opportunity Act of 1996 was supposed to save Africa economically by relying on "trade, not aid."

48.   Although there remained some lingering traces of the pro-Kigali attitude for a

461

long time, such as when National Security Council member Cindy Courville remarked in February 2005, "I would understand it if Rwanda felt compelled to reoccupy the Congo again." Interview with MONUC personnel, Kinshasa, November 2006.

49.   Quoted by Eric Fottorino in *Le Monde*, July 25, 1997.

50.   The first item is a perfectly sensible geopolitical goal, whereas the second, spreading a thin cordon of U.S. troops, supplies, and instructors from Mauritania to Djibouti in a latter-day echo of Truman's containment policy, is a largely fantastical one. Both will be briefly discussed further on.

51.   For a discussion of this syndrome, I refer the reader to my *Rwanda Crisis*, 100–106.

52.   For a witty and not unsympathetic assessment of this worldview, see the review by Tony Judt of Hubert Védrine's *Les cartes de la France à l'heure de la mondialisation* (Paris: Fayard, 2000) in the *New York Review of Books*, April 12, 2001. Védrine loves to refer to the United States as "the hyper power."

53.   Hence the French obsession with a still hoped-for "Great Lakes Conference." Nobody seemed to know very well what purpose it would serve beyond an aggrandizement of French diplomacy, but its mere mention around the Quai d'Orsay was enough to make French eyes gleam.

54.   There have been ample writings on the subject, which François-Xavier Verschave and the advocacy NGO Survie have turned into their stock in trade. The notorious trial of a number of former Elf-Aquitaine top executives in 2002–2003 showed that government-sponsored corruption interlinking arms, politics, and oil in Africa had consistently operated at the highest levels of the state during the past forty years.

55.   The tragedy was quite real on the ground. But what was felt in Paris was not the reality of the gushing blood, it was another symbolic reality of political, cultural, and diplomatic decadence.

56.   A few months before the report came out, Foreign Minister Hubert Védrine wrote in *Le Débat*, no. 95 (May–August 1997), "Abominations have been written about François Mitterrand and Rwanda…. If one could make a criticism it would be of not having been conservative enough, of having ignited the La Baule fire near the Rwandese powder keg." Since the La Baule speech in 1990 was made by Mitterrand in support of democratization in Africa, what Védrine reproaches the late president for is an excess of democratic feeling.

57.   The African Unit at the Elysée was another locus of incestuous relations. When I worked there (as a volunteer activist of the Socialist Party) in the 1980s I saw staff having to deal with such matters as the shopping needs of an African president's wife, the police arrest of another president's kleptomaniac daughter, and the slow dying from AIDS of a third president's son.

58.   "Pourquoi la France lâche l'Afrique?" (Why is France abandoning Africa?), *Jeune Afrique*, April 2, 2000. It is symptomatic that *Jeune Afrique*, a typical product of the 1960s Gaullist "respectful anticolonialism," considered questions about human rights and democracy to be "cold-blooded" intrusions into the supposed privacies of African regimes. *Jeune Afrique*'s founder-director Beshir Ben Yamed had long had a soft spot for African and Arab dictatorships, particularly "progressive" (and generous) ones.

59.   The expression was invented by Ivory Coast President Houphouët-Boigny in the 1960s. In his mind this was a highly positive slogan, implying fruitful cooperation. But in recent years the word has acquired a distinctly sinister con-

notation in French political parlance.

60.   The morally repulsive neglect of the Darfur crisis since 2004 is a further case in point. See Gérard Prunier, *Darfur: The Ambiguous Genocide* (London: Hurst, 2005).

61.   For particularly telling examples of the international concerns of that time, see Madeleine Kalb, *The Congo Cables* (New York: Macmillan, 1982); Piero Gleijeses, *Conflicting Missions: Havana, Washington and Africa (1959–1976)* (Chapel Hill: University of North Carolina Press, 2002).

62.   James Wolfenson's interview with IRIN in Dar-es-Salaam, July 18, 2002.

63.   French troop strength in Africa had gone down from 8,000 to 5,000 in 1996–1997. See Ph. Vasset, "The Myth of Military Aid: The Case of French Military Co-Operation in Africa," *SAIS Review* 7, no. 2 (Summer 1997).

64.   See "Tangled Web of Alliances Makes the SADC a Poor Regional Peacekeeper," www.stratfor.com, posted August 2000. This is one of the few commentaries bold enough to mention the politically incorrect South African support for UNITA that the African National Congress had inherited from the apartheid regime.

65.   *Economist*, September 18, 1999.

66.   AFP dispatch, New York, June 16, 1999.

67.   It was the British and the Americans who opposed the very notion of a deadline that the secretary-general had requested. This constant unacknowledged support for Rwanda and Uganda was rooted in the guilt feelings I outlined earlier (Great Britain had been one of the most vocal advocates of UN nonintervention during the genocide) and in a lingering hope that Museveni and Kagame, the "modern leaders," would somehow "set things right" by eliminating Kinshasa's embarrassing human anachronism.

68.   The present Sudan crisis (2007) is an interesting case in point. Khartoum having mobilized *real* resources through its Chinese alliance can dispense with having a good image.

69.   "Professionals" and "specialists" are two different things. "Specialists" are esoteric folklorists with a recognized competence in certain exotic areas. They are "consulted" by the international community for purposes of intellectual legitimization, but their advice is hardly ever followed. "Professionals," on the other hand, have a competence in a certain field deemed to be universally applicable to any part of the world; they need not know the country it is applied to. Some rise to the level of actually influencing policies. I am a "specialist," not a "professional."

70.   John Prendergast, *Frontline Diplomacy: Humanitarian Aid and Conflict in Africa* (Boulder, CO: Lynne Rienner, 1996).

71.   For a sample of the first type of criticism, see P. Dauvin and J. Siméant, *Le travail humanitaire: Les acteurs des ONG, du siège au terrain* (Paris: Presse des Sciences Politiques, 2001). For an example of the second, see D. Sogge, ed., *Compassion and Calculation: The Business of Private Foreign Aid* (London: Pluto Press, 1996).

72.   See, for example, Michael Maren, "A Different Kind of Child Abuse," *Penthouse*, December 1995, remarking that the Save the Children Fund spent only $35.29 out of every $240 pledged for child support on actually supporting the child itself, the rest going to administration, general expenses, and fund raising.

73.   A typical media treatment is the long article by John Pomfret, "Aid Dilemma:

Keeping It from the Oppressors," *Washington Post,* September 23, 1997, describing how Mobutu's army used UN planes to fly weapons to retreating *génocidaires* in March 1997 while Kabila's men appropriated UN fuel to ferry supplies to the Lubumbashi front.

74. See the UN Report by Charles Petrie, Goma, June 16, 1998, describing how, for New Year's Eve 1995, a large international NGO organized a party attended by many expatriate workers at which a famous Hutu singer close to the *Interahamwe* performed and sang songs composed during and in support of the genocide without anybody in the audience realizing what was going on.

75. Old-style left-wingers found it hard to adapt and kept looking for "imperialist" remnants in the oddest places. See, for example, some of the polemics in the European press in late 1992 trying to explain U.S. intervention in Somalia by claiming supposed oil interests there.

76. See my *Rwanda Crisis,* 299–304.

77. United Nations/OCHA, *Impératifs Humanitaires en RDC,* Kinshasa, March 2000. This short document is one of the best summaries of the problems and contradictions of humanitarian action during the second phase of the conflict.

78. The number of affected persons (i.e., IDPs and refugees) in the Congo went from one million in 1998 to three million at the beginning of 2003, with over two million more war-related cases in the neighboring countries (Uganda, Rwanda, Burundi, Tanzania).

79. United Nations, *Report of the Panel on United Nations Peace Operations,* New York, August 2000, 1.

80. Stealth and lying are always at the core of the genocidal phenomenon, as if the perpetrators knew deep down that their acts were evil and had to be hidden from view. One should keep in mind that no clear, firm order for the genocide of the Jews has ever been found (the closest thing to it being the minutes of the Wansee Conference), in spite of the meticulously organized nature of the German bureaucracy.

81. The accused Laurent Semanza, arrested in March 1996, was not indicted until October 1997. In the case of the Coalition for the Defence of the Republic ideologue Jean-Bosco Barayagwiza, this allowed the accused to get the Appeals Chamber of the tribunal to throw his case out of court in November 1999 because "the accused's rights to a speedy trial have been violated." Barayagwiza was ordered to be set free, thereby precipitating a major crisis between the Rwandese government and Prosecutor Carla del Ponte. Barayagwiza was later rearrested under a confused pretext, and at the time of this writing (December 2007) remains detained in a kind of judicial limbo.

82. I have had long conversations on that point with my friend and colleague, the Great Lakes historian Jean-Pierre Chrétien, who, in spite of his willingness to help the court, finally got completely discouraged by its confusion, contradictions, and absolute lack of professionalism.

83. Judges would leave abruptly for personal reasons, leaving a position vacant for months afterward. At least one refused either to attend the proceedings *or* to resign, and personal quarrels blocking the work were constant.

84. To realize how far the ICTR was from understanding (or even being willing to understand) the history and politics of the region which gave the inescapable counterpoint to the trials, refer to Alison DesForges's testimony in the notorious "Media Trial" (www.diplomatiejudiciaire.com, June 2002) in which the witness, one of the very best specialists of recent regional history, was bullied,

suspected, and almost accused by the defense, without any reaction from the court.

85. When I contacted the ICTR through an intermediary in March 2000 to ask whether they would be interested in discussing the topic, even off the record, I got the answer that this was not desirable.

86. Other arguments were used (i.e., the difficulty of running two tribunals—for the former Yugoslavia and for Rwanda—at once, or Del Ponte's frequent stays in The Hague). But these were pretexts; it was well-known that what led UN Secretary-General Kofi Annan not to renew her contract was his reluctance at supporting her announced desire to prosecute RPF crimes.

87. IRIN Press Agency, "Focus on the UN Tribunal," Dar-es-Salaam, February 3, 2004.

88. *Le Monde,* June 8, 2001. Gasana had lost his mother, one sister, and one brother. He could hardly be accused of being a génocidaire since he had left Rwanda almost a year before the slaughter and, during his time as a minister, had steadily tried to fight the growing influence of his permanent secretary Col. Théoneste Bagosora.

89. Hirondelle Press Service dispatch, Arusha, March 13, 2002. Lawyers were paid by the ICTR to the tune of $80 to $110 per hour and they were allowed to charge up to $175 per hour per month.

90. Interview with former ICTR investigator Ibrahima Dia, Paris, March 2001. Since many of the staff exploiting the situation for their benefit happened to be West Africans, Prosecutor Louise Arbour was accused of "racism" when she refused to renew their contracts. See Hirondelle Press dispatch, Arusha, May 21, 2001.

91. The best book on the tribunal is probably Thierry Cruvelier, *Le tribunal des vaincus: Un Nuremberg pour le Rwanda* (Paris: Calmann-Lévy, 2006).

92. *Le Monde,* September 4, 2002.

93. Prunier, *The Rwanda Crisis,* 354–355.

94. Hence the taste of the media for playing up the Franco-American rivalry, which could be mooted as a kind of poor man's substitute for the old scary attention-catcher.

95. "We used communication and information warfare better than anyone. We have found a new way of doing things." General Kagame in an April 8, 1998, interview with Nick Gowing.

96. This is well reflected in the captivating study by Nick Gowing, *Dispatches from the Disaster Zones,* OCHA, London: May 1998.

97. The African Catastrophe Book has become a kind of minor literary genre of its own. For some of the most recent additions, see (in English) R. Kapuscinski, *The Shadow of the Sun* (New York: Knopf, 2001); (in French) S. Smith, *Négrologie* (Paris: Calmann-Lévy, 2003).

98. The parallel with the Jewish Holocaust, the state of Israel, and the price the Palestinians have had to pay for a crime they did not commit is hard to escape. Kigali immediately understood the media advantage it could bring and did all it could to develop good relations with Israel. This led the U.S. Jewish community, particularly Jewish academics, to show a systematic partiality toward the RPF regime.

99. See Nexis, *Index of Major World Publications,* 2006.

100. Before that there were simply plain wars and massacres. The Idi Amin regime in Uganda and the Red Terror in Ethiopia (I lived through both) were *not* "emer-

gencies."

101.   There were few. The Great Lakes were looked upon as a kind of intellectual backwater up to the 1990s, compared with "hot" parts of the continent such as South Africa, Angola, or Zaire.

102.   There was no mention of Che Guevara because his Congolese adventures remained a secret until the 1990s.

103.   See the various polemics between Jean-Pierre Chrétien, Filip Reyntjens, and René Lemarchand around the concept of "the Franco-Burundian historical school" in 1988–1990.

104.   The exceptions were Mr. and Mrs. Newbury, who proved largely reluctant to enter the media circus, and Alison DesForges, who, before shooting to the forefront of the mediatized experts as a member of Human Rights Watch, had also had a discreet career. But in the immediate aftermath of the genocide French-speaking academics enjoyed a quasi-monopoly over the discourse on Rwanda and the Great Lakes.

105.   Often with fresh and dubious claims to "expertise," especially in the case of the journalists.

106.   With the lone exception of the German academic Helmut Strizek.

107.   For a good assessment of the phenomenon, see Léon Saur, *Influences parallèles: L'Internationale Démocrate-Chrétienne au Rwanda* (Brussels: Luc Pire, 1998).

108.   The generally "pro-American" pro-RPF consensus drew some lunatic fringe left-wingers to the pro-Hutu side (see Deirdre Griswold, "Rwanda: The Class Character of the Crisis," on the Workers World Service, www.nyxfer.blythe.org; the literature of the Lyndon LaRouche group), which paradoxically put them in the same camp as the very conservative Christian Democrats.

109.   For a telling illustration of the problems of "objectivity," see the polemics between the "pro-Kigali" NGO African Rights (*Rwanda: The Insurgency in the Northwest,* September 1998) and the "anti-Kigali" NGO Amnesty International (*Rwanda: A Public Statement in Response to Criticisms of Amnesty International by African Rights,* March 1999).

110.   See Prunier, *The Rwanda Crisis,* 91–96, 323–324, as well as this book, chapter 1.

111.   This was technically true because there were only field notes. Robert Gersony later told me that knowing full well that it would never be published, he had never done the work of writing out a fully developed version, keeping it only in synthetic documentary form.

112.   Given the intellectual climate of the immediate postgenocide period, it is interesting that, with one or two rare exceptions, reviews of my book did not fault it for its general pro-RPF slant.

113.   This interview was with the French newspaper *Libération,* where Stephen Smith worked.

114.   Prunier, *The Rwanda Crisis* (2nd ed., 1997), 358–372.

115.   Many Tutsi and Hutu seem to *expect* partisanship on the part of their European friends. In 1993, when the freelance journalist Catherine Watson, long known as a supporter of the then struggling RPF, expressed her disgust at seeing them toast the murder of Burundi Hutu President Ndadaye, their bewildered answer was "But we thought you were our friend." Interview with Catherine Watson, Kampala, March 1994.

116.   "Rwanda: The Social, Political and Economic Situation in June 1997," Writenet, October 17, 1997.

466

117. Rwandan Office of Information, "Gerald [*sic*] Prunier: A Eulogy for Genocide," Kigali, October 23, 1997.

118. African Union, *Rwanda: The Preventable Genocide,* Addis-Ababa, July 2000.

119. Symmetrically many in the pro-Hutu camp seem to think that if only they can prove that General Kagame ordered the shooting down of President Habyarimana's aircraft, this will exonerate them from the guilt of the genocide.

120. The Rwandese government went as far as buying full-page ads in some newspapers to denounce the organization's "naked propaganda" in favor of Kinshasa. See *East African,* November 25, 2002, 34.

121. See, for example, the bizarre document by a certain Neil Tickner ("Rwandan Genocide 10th Anniversary: Correcting the Record") posted at www.genodynamics.com on March 30, 2004, or the strange "research work" of Christian Davenport.

122. When the Paris publisher L'Harmattan published the memoirs of a Hutu survivor of the massacres in Zaire (Béatrice Umutesi, *Fuir ou mourir au Zaire,* 2000) it was immediately deluged by e-mails denouncing this "revisionist propaganda." Most of the e-mails seemed to originate from people who had not read the book.

123. *Osservatore Romano,* May 19, 1999.

124. The article is unsigned but marked *** which is usually used for a piece authorized by the Curia.

125. See "Rwanda: Les oeillères du juge Bruguière," *Le Nouvel Observateur,* February 1–7, 2007.

126. Patrick de Saint-Exupéry, *L'inavouable: La France au Rwanda* (Paris: Les Arênes, 2004).

127. Pierre Péan, *Noires fureurs, Blancs menteurs: Rwanda 1990–1994* (Paris: Mille et Une Nuits, 2005).

128. See, for example, Nigel Eltringham, *Accounting for Horror: Post-Genocide Debates in Rwanda* (London: Pluto Press, 2004).

129. Gary Wills, "A Second Assassination," a review of Seymour Hersh, *The Dark Side of Camelot* (New York: Little, Brown, 1997) *New York Review of Books,* December 18, 1997.

130. Timothy Garton Ash, "The Curse and Blessing of South Africa," *New York Review of Books,* August 14, 1997.

131. Lieve Joris, *L'heure des rebelles* (Arles: Actes Sud, 2006).

132. There are of course perfectly bona fide NGOs and think tanks that produce excellent material on African conflicts. The distinction between pap and real food is usually the degree of knowledge of the terrain and of the ground analysis provided. For an exercised eye, the difference between formulaic and real analysis in a report can usually be made in less than three minutes.

133. The example of Equatorial Guinea (+21.3 percent of "economic" growth in 2006) is the epitome of the danger of relying blindly on unrelativized economic indicators.

134. World Bank, *Africa Development Indicators,* Washington, DC, 2007. The rate of continentwide per capita income change has been –0.9 percent during the 1980s, –0.3 percent during the 1990s, and +1.9 percent since 2000. An improvement, but hardly of the Asian type.

135. The most obvious perverse effect of the "war on terror" has been the sanctuarization of the Sudanese regime, which is simultaneously denounced as violating all sorts of human rights and then protected because it contributes to President

George W. Bush's crusade.

136.   Given President Kagame's entrepreneurial ambitions, this factor has been a powerfully restraining influence on Rwandese politics vis-à-vis the Congo.

137.   Here again, the case of the Sudanese regime is particularly exemplary.

138.   I am not saying that either country is on the point of exploding. I am simply trying, for the sake of the argument, to envision what kind of impact a prolonged violent conflict in these countries would have for the continent.

Appendix I

1.   I have in my possession a letter from Seth addressed to me from Nairobi on 4 May 1998, where he was writing: "With very limited means we carry on our fight … . I hope that you keep up with your search for funds and that you can get us some small support. I beg you not to neglect any effort because we are so hard up. It has reached such a point that we have barely enough money to send our mail." Hardly the words of a man who has managed to salt away $54m!

2.   In 1999 the Rwandese government had again refused to waive the diplomatic immunity of their employee when the Kenyan CID wanted to question him about the murder. But in the meantime the relations between Rwanda and Kenya had taken a great turn for the better and diplomatic relations interrupted in 1996 after the first attempt on Seth's life had been resumed. Nairobi simply accepted Kigali's refusal of the diplomatic immunity waiver and no more was heard of it.

3.   He was by then in hot waters with his superiors not only because of what he knew about the Sendashonga assassination but also because his RPF brother-in-law Jean-Baptiste Cyusa had quarrelled with the Minister of Education Colonel Karemera, a RPF heavyweight. Mbayire had tried to protect his brother-in-law and had failed. Cyusa was briefly jailed but he managed to get out through personal contacts. He then fled to the United States where the RPF leadership feared that he would join the growing Tutsi opposition.

4.   Fondation Hirondelle Press Release on the Court's Decision. Arusha, 31 May 2001.

BIBLIOGRAPHY

This is not meant to be an exhaustive bibliography on the general crisis of the African continent, or even on Rwanda and the former Zaire. This is a bibliography on Rwanda after the genocide, on the ensuing Zaire/Congo crisis, and on the impact of these events on the rest of Africa since 1994. Items concerning countries other than Rwanda or the Democratic Republic of the Congo have been chosen for their pertinence to the conflict rather than for their relevance to other countries' internal situations. For fuller references on Rwanda and the genocide, see the bibliography in my *Rwanda Crisis (1959–1994): History of a Genocide* (London: Hurst, 1995), which contains items published before May 1995. For authors (incuding myself) with extensive publications on the region, the only items included here are those not already mentioned in the previous bibliography. In addition, items on Rwanda relevant to the period prior to that date but published later have been included here.

Global and Periodical Documentation

A number of sources are of global and sustained interest for information on the Great Lakes crisis and its wider reaches. The daily bulletins of the UN-sponsored Integrated Regional Information Network (IRIN) issued from Nairobi are a key source for ongoing developments; they are supplemented on an ad hoc basis by assorted documents of interest. These can be accessed at www.irinnews.org. Filip Reyntjens and Stefaan Marysse, both from the University of Antwerp, have published every year since 1997 a useful compendium of topical articles on the region under the title *L'Afrique des Grands Lacs* at L'Harmattan publishing house in Paris. Details of the most interesting articles appear in the Books and Articles section of this bibliography. During the war the Scandinavian Nordiska Afrikainstitutet in Uppsala published under the editorship of Lennart Wohlgemuth periodical collections of bibliographical data and special papers on the crisis, and the

Réseau Européen Congo in Brussels published under the direction of Jules Devos detailed monthly reports of the situation in the Democratic Republic of Congo that can be accessed at www.perso.wanadoo.fr/dan.cdm/dem/rec-doc.htm. The International Documentation Network on the Great African Lakes Region based in Geneva has been issuing at regular intervals since 1996 compact discs containing thousands of relevant documents of all origins. Their website is www.grandslacs.net. Economic documentation is best obtained from the Economist Intelligence Unit in London, which, concerning the countries involved in the wider Congolese conflict, issues quarterly reports as well as a yearly report on Rwanda and Burundi, the Democratic Republic of the Congo, the Brazzaville-Congo, Sudan, Libya, South Africa, Zimbabwe, and Uganda. These can be found at www.economist.com/countries and www.economist.com/search. The Rwanda News Agency issues dispatches reflecting the Rwandese government's position. Its website is www.ari-rna.com. There is a website on Namibia at www.Namibian.com.na and one on Sudan at www.sudan.net. The UNHCR website, www.reliefweb.int, is a source of information on refugees. In addition, there are several discussion sites on the region, such as www.altern.org/rwandanet, http://groups.yahoo.com/groups/rwanda-1, and www.altern.org/zairenet, but these are only moderately useful. *Grands Lacs Confidentiel* is a stridently militant anti-Kigali information bulletin irregularly posted through e-mail at glac@travel-net.com. The website of the Ugandan ADF guerrillas is www.adm-uganda-adf.com/. The quarterly *Dialogue* published in Brussels gives the Catholic White Fathers' viewpoint. *Traits d'Union Rwanda* is a bulletin of information published by a group of Belgian NGOs. The website www.StrategicStudies.org irregularly posted documents produced by the dissident RPF member Jean-Pierre Mugabe. A variety of documents on Zaire/Congo is also available at www.marekinc.com; www.congo.co.za is a Kinshasa government site. The former Maoist and political activist Ludo Mertens created the www.ptb.be/congo website, with a strongly anti-imperialist tone. A very informative site on Congo and central Africa is www.obsac.com, which gave good coverage of the conflict and later of the transition, with a pro-Kigali slant. The website of the Banyamulenge community is http://mulenge.blogspot.com. The U.S. government's human rights reports for the relevant countries are at www.state.gov/www/global/human_rights. Information on illegal resource extraction in the Democratic Republic of Congo can be found (inter alia) at www.pole-institute.org/ or at www.broederlijkdelen.be/publicaties/coltan14–1.doc. Good general political analysis sites such as www.statfor.com, www.southscan.net, and www.oxan.com have had periodical briefs on the region, and the Stanford University site www.-sul. stanford.edu/depts/ssrg/africa/guide.html has many useful links on Congo and the Great Lakes. The MONUC website is www.monuc.org. A discussion forum in English on the Democratic Republic of Congo is available at www.congokin.com. The Bakongo community website is www.ne-kongo. net. A number of Congolese newspapers have websites; see, for example, www.lesoftonline.net, www.groupelavenir.net, www.lepotentiel.com, and www.eveil.info. An online news site on politics, the economy, and social affairs in the Congo is at http://perso.club-internet.fr/tumba/lettre-ouverte. html. The website of the UDPS is www.udps.org; www.congorcd.org is the website of the RCD political party. A (somewhat unreliable) website for some of the Mayi Mayi groups is www.congo-mai-mai.net. Both www. nkolo-mboka.com and www.robertyanda.populus.ch offer political documents and analyses on the Congo. The website of the International Rescue Committee, with figures on the human losses of the war, is www.theirc.org. In addition, many of the NGO reports listed in the relevant section of this bibliography can be found on their websites, which are indicated after the first mention of their name. London-based *Africa Confidential* and Paris-based Indigo Group Publications (*La lettre de l'Ocean Indien, La Lettre du Continent, Africa Mining Intelligence, La Lettre Afrique Energies*) offer weekly or bimonthly coverage of the political and business situation. They have paying commercial websites.

Films and Albums of Photographs

Valentina's Story. London, BBC TV, 1997. 30 minutes.

Zaïre: le fleuve de sang. Paris, 1997. 120 minutes.

La tragédie des Grands Lacs. Paris, Capa/Arte TV, 2001. 140 minutes.

Aghion, A., dir. *Au Rwanda, on dit ...* Paris, Arte TV, 2006. 52 minutes.

Bellefroid, B., dir. *Rwanda, les collines parlent.* Paris. 52 minutes.

Burdot, E., and E. Van Hove, dirs. *L'incontournable Mr Forrest.* Paris, Thema TV. 30 minutes.

Caton-Jones, M., dir. *Shooting Dogs.* London, 2006. 114 minutes (fiction).

Chappell, P., and G. Lanning, dirs. *The Bank, the President and the Pearl.* London, BBC-TV, 1998. 90 minutes (on Uganda and the World Bank).

Cowan, P. M., dir. *Le prix de la paix.* Paris, Arte TV. 90 minutes (on the UN operations in Ituri).

Fleury, J. P., dir. *Rwanda, génocide, justice?* Paris, Médecins du Monde Video, 1995. 16 minutes.

Freedman, P., dir. *Rwanda: Do Scars Ever Fade?* 2004. 70 minutes.

Genoud, R., dir. *La France au Rwanda, une neutralité coupable* Paris. 52 minutes.

George, T., dir. *Hotel Rwanda.* Hollywood, United Artists, 2004. 122 minutes (fictionalized account).

Glucksman, R., D. Hazan, P. and Mezerette, dirs. *Tuez les tous: Histoire d'un "genocide sans importance."* Paris, France 3 TV, 2004.

Heinz, W., dir. *Chaos au pays du coltan.* Paris, Thema TV. 52 minutes.

Jewsiewicki, B., and B. Plaksteiner, eds. *An/Sichten: Malerei aus dem Kongo (1990–2000).* Vienna: Springer Verlag, 2001. (Based on the February–July 2001 exhibition in Vienna's Museum für Völkerkunde, this is a collection of two hundred remarkable popular Congolese paintings, highly relevant to life in the DRC during its last tormented years.)

Jihan el-Tahri and P. Chappell, dirs. *L'Afrique en morceaux.* Paris, Capa Productions, 2000. 100 minutes.

Kiley, S., dir. *Congo's Killing Fields.* London, Channel 4 TV, 2003. 90 minutes.

Klotz, J. C., dir. *Kigali, des images contre un massacre.* Paris, ADR/Capa/Arte. 94 minutes.

Laffont, F., dir. *Rwanda: Maudits soient les yeux fermés.* Paris, Arte TV, 1995. 80 minutes.

Lainé, A., dir. *Rwanda, un cri d'un silence inouï.* Paris, France 5 TV, 2006. 55 minutes.

Meurice, J. M., dir. *Elf, une Afrique sous influence.* Paris, Arte TV, 2000. 100 minutes.

Michel, T., dir. *Zaire, le cycle du serpent.* Brussels, 1996. 80 minutes.

———. *Mobutu, roi du Zaire.* Brussels, 1999. 125 minutes. (An interesting review of this film is by Victoria Brittain, "King Congo," *The Guardian,* June 11, 1999.)

———. *Congo River, au-delà des ténèbres.* 2006. 116 minutes.

———. *Congo River, au-delà des ténèbres.* Brussels: La Renaissance du Livre, 2006 (an album of photographs accompanying the film, with text by Lye Mudaba Yoka and Isidore Ndaywel è Nziem).

Nachtwey, J. "The Hidden Toll of the World's Deadliest War." *Time,* June 5, 2006 (photographs with accompanying text by S. Robinson and V. Walt).

Peress, G. *Le silence.* Zürich: Scalo Verlag, 1995 (a collection of powerful black-and-white pictures on the Rwandese genocide).

Puech, R., and Ch. Bernard, dirs. *Guerre et paix selon l'ONU.* Paris, Capa, 2006. 60 minutes (on UN operations in Ituri).

Smith, S. *Le fleuve Congo.* Paris: Actes Sud, 2003 (photographs by P. Robert).

Tasma, A., dir. *Opération Turquoise*. Paris, 2007. 52 minutes.

Van der Wee, A., dir. *Rwanda: The Dead Are Alive*. Toronto: Wild Heart Productions, 1998.

Literary Works Based on the Rwandese Genocide and the Congo Wars

Abdourahman Waberi. *Moissons de crânes: Textes pour le Rwanda*. Paris: Le Serpent à Plumes, 2000.

Courtemanche, G. *A Sunday at the Pool in Kigali*. Edinburgh: Canongate Books, 2003.

Hatzfeld, J. *La stratégie des antilopes*. Paris: Le Seuil, 2007.

Joris, L. *La danse du léopard*. Arles: Actes Sud, 2002.

————. *L'heure des rebelles*. Arles: Actes Sud, 2007.

Le Carré, J. *The Mission Song*. New York: Little, Brown, 2006.

Leonard, E. *Pagan Babies*. New York: HarperCollins, 2002.

Rusesabagina, P. *An Ordinary Man*. London: Penguin, 2007.

Sehene, B. *Le feu sous la soutane: Un prêtre au cœur du génocide rwandais*. Paris: L'Esprit Frappeur, 2005.

Tadjo, V. *L'ombre d'Imana: Voyage jusqu'au bout du Rwanda*. Arles: Actes Sud, 2000.

Documents Produced by Governments and International, Nongovernmental, Religious, and Political Organizations

African Centre for Peace and Democracy (ACPD). *Bi-yearly Reports on Human Rights Violations in Eastern DRC*. Bukavu, DRC. January 2001–.

African Rights. www.users.globalnet.co.uk/~afrights. *Rwanda: A Waste of Hope: The United Nations Human Rights Field Operation*. March 1995.

————. *Rwanda: Not So Innocent. When Women Become Killers*. August 1995.

————. *Rwanda, Killing the Evidence: Murders, Attacks, Arrests and Intimidation of Survivors and Witnesses*. April 1996.

————. *Lettre ouverte à Sa Sainteté le Pape Jean-Paul II*. May 13, 1998.

————. *Rwanda: The Insurgency in the Northwest*. September 1998.

————. *Zimbabwe: In the Party's Interests?* June 1999.

————. *The Cycle of Conflict: Which Way Out in the Kivus?* December 2000.

————. *Left to Die: The Stories of Rwandese Cvivilians Abandoned by UN Troops on 11th April 1994*. April 2001.

————. *Colonel Tharcisse Renzaho: A Soldier in the DRC?* October 2001.

African Union. *Rwanda, the Preventable Genocide*. Written by the Eminent Personalities Panel led by Q. K. J. Masire. Addis Ababa. IPEP/OAU. July 2000.

Agir Ici/Survie. *France-Zaïre-Congo 1960–1997: Échec aux mercenaires.* Paris: L'Harmattan, 1997.

Allied Democratic Movement. *Manifesto.* London. January 1995.

Amnesty International. www.amnesty.org. *Reports of Killings and Abductions by the Rwandese Patriotic Army (April–August 1994).* October 1994.

———. *Cases for Appeals.* November 1994.

———. *Arming the Perpetrators of the Genocide.* June 1995.

———. *Burundi: Targeting Students, Teachers and Clerics in the Fight for Supremacy.* September 1995.

———. *Rwanda and Burundi: The Return Home: Rumours and Realities.* February 1996.

———. *Memorandum to the Rwandese Government: Concerns and Recommendations for Fair Trials in Rwanda.* March 1996.

———. *Burundi: Armed Groups Kill without Mercy.* June 1996.

———. *Zaire: Violent Persecution by State and Armed Groups.* November 1996.

———. *Rwanda: Alarming Resurgence of Killings.* August 1996.

———. *Burundi: Leaders Are Changing but Human Rights Abuses Continue Unabated.* August 1996.

———. *Human Rights Overlooked in Mass Repatriation.* January 1997.

———. *Les réfugiés en Afrique droits de l'homme bafoués, réfugiés et personnes déplacées en danger.* March 1997.

———. *Unfair Trials: Justice Denied.* April 1997.

———. *Burundi: Forced Relocations: New Patterns of Human Rights Abuses.* July 1997.

———. *Rwanda: Ending the Silence.* September 1997.

———. *No One Is Talking about It Any More: Appeal Cases.* October 1997.

———. *Open Letter to Governments Hosting Refugees from Burundi, Rwanda and the Democratic Republic of Congo: A Call for the Safety and Dignity of Refugees.* October 1997.

———. *Rwanda: Civilians Trapped in Armed Conflict.* December 1997.

———. *Deadly Alliances in Congolese Forests.* December 1997.

———. *Mémorandum au gouvernment burundais sur le projet de loi relatif au génocide et aux crimes contre l'humanité.* March 1998.

———. *Rwanda: The Hidden Violence: Disappearances and Killings Continue.* June 1998.

———. *Burundi: Justice on Trial.* August 1998.

———. *DRC: A Long-Standing Crisis Spinning out of Control.* September 1998.

———. *Response to Criticisms of Amnesty International in the African Rights Report: "Rwanda: Insurgency in the Northwest."* March 1999.

――――. *Republic of Congo: An Old Generation of Leaders in New Carnage.* March 1999.

――――. *Burundi: No Respite without Justice.* August 1999.

――――. *Rwanda: The Troubled Course of Justice.* April 2000.

――――. *DRC: Killing Human Decency.* May 2000.

――――. *Burundi: Between Hope and Fear.* March 2001.

――――. *DRC: Deadly Conspiracies?* March 2001.

――――. *DRC: Rwandese-Controlled East: A Devastating Human Toll.* June 2001.

――――. *Burundi: Preparing for Peace.* August 2001.

――――. *DRC: Torture: A Weapon of War against Unarmed Civilians.* June 2001.

――――. *DRC: Memorandum to the Inter-Congolese Dialogue.* November 2001.

――――. *Burundi: Confronting Torture and Impunity.* December 2001.

――――. *République Centrafricaine: Réfugiés en fuite, discrimination ethnique et coupables impunis.* June 2002.

――――. *Punishing the Population: Reprisal Killings Escalate in Burundi.* July 2002.

――――. *Rwanda: Gacaca: Une question de justice.* November 2002.

――――. *DRC: Children at War.* September 2003.

――――. *DRC: Arming the East.* July 2005.

Article XIX, International Centre against Censorship. *Broadcasting Genocide: Censorship, Propaganda and State-Sponsored Violence in Rwanda, 1990–1994.* London. October 1996.

ASADHO. *L'Ouganda sacrifie la population civile congolaise.* Kinshasa, DRC. February 2001.

――――. *Rapport sur les manœuvres en cours dans l'Est et le Nord-Est de la RDC.* ASADHO/DEJA/Justice Plus. Kinshasa, DRC. August 2003.

Baraza la Kivu. *Open Letter to Kumar Rupeshinge, Director of International Alert.* Written by Kasangati K. W. Kinyalolo. Montreal. October 1996.

Caritas Italiana. *Goma, citta dei rifugiati.* Parma. Edizioni AlfaZeta. 1996.

Centre for International Policy Studies. *Burundi Reports.* Written by Jan van Eck. University of Pretoria. 1998.

――――. *Burundi Reports.* Written by Jan van Eck. University of Pretoria. 1999.

――――. *Burundi Reports.* Written by Jan van Eck. University of Pretoria. 2000.

――――. *Burundi Reports.* Written by Jan van Eck. University of Pretoria. 2001.

Collectif d'Action pour le Développement des Droits de l'Homme (CAD-DHOM). *Yearly Reports.* 1999–.

Collectif des ONG rwandaises au Zaire. *Analyse de la situation socio-politique au Rwanda.* Bukavu, DRC. July 1994.

Comité d'Action pour le Développement des Droits de l'Homme. *Territoires occupés: La loi de la barbarie et de la mafia.* Paris. March 2001.

Concertation Chrétienne pour l'Afrique Centrale. *L'Afrique Centrale intéresse-t-elle encore la France et ses partenaires européens?* Brussels. December 2000.

Conference for Legal Education and Development in Africa. "Rwanda: Le tribunal pénal international et le droit à la justice." Paper presented to the 14th Congress of the International Association of Democratic Lawyers. Capetown. March 1996.

Eglises Protestantes de Suisse. *Désarmer les cœurs: Démarche rwandaise pour une réconciliation.* Written by Laurien Ntezimana and Modeste Mungwarareba. Lausanne. March 1997.

Environmental Defense (with the Bank Information Centre). *Report of a Trip to the Democratic Republic of Congo.* N.p. June 2006.

Fédération Internationale des Ligues des Droits de l'Homme (FIDH). *Vies brisées: Les violences sexuelles lors du génocide rwandais et leurs conséquences.* Paris. January 1997.

———. *Congo-Brazzaville: L'arbitraire de l'état, la terreur des milices.* Paris. June 1999.

Forces de Résistance pour la Démocratie. *Plateforme politique.* Brussels. March 1996.

———. *Lettre Ouverte à Mr Michel Rocard.* Nairobi. December 8, 1997.

Forum on Early Warning and Early Response. *Early Warning and Humanitarian Intervention in Zaire (March to December 1996).* Written by Howard Adelman. London. March 1999.

Front Patriotique Rwandais Inkotanyi. *Programme Politique.* [Bujumbura, Burundi. 1992].

Front pour la Démocratie au Burundi. *Le chemin de la démocratie au Burundi.* Bujumbura, Burundi. September 1991.

———. *Un apartheid qui ne dit pas son nom.* Bujumbura, Burundi. August 1997.

Global Witness. *A Rough Trade: The Role of Companies and Governments in the Angolan Conflict.* London. [1999].

———. *A Crude Awakening: The Role of the Oil and Banking Industries in Angola's Civil War and the Plunder of State Assets.* London. [2000].

———. *Branching Out: Zimbabwe's Resource Colonialism in the Democratic Republic of the Congo.* London. February 2002.

———. *All the President's Men: The Devastating Story of Oil and Banking in Angola's Privatised War.* London. 2003.

————. *Same Old Story: A Background Study on Natural Resources in the DRC.* London. June 2004.

————. *Rush and Ruin: The Devastating Mineral Trade in Southern Katanga, DRC.* London. September 2004.

————. *Reforming the DRC Diamond Sector.* London. June 2006.

————. *Digging in Corruption.* London. July 2006.

Government of Belgium. *Rapport de la Commission d'Enquête Parlementaire concernant les évènements du Rwanda.* Sous la direction de MM. Mahoux et Verhofstadt. Brussels. December 1997.

Government of the Democratic Republic of the Congo. *Rapport de la commission spéciale chargée d'examiner la validité des conventions à caractère économique et financier conclues pendant les guerres de 1996–1997 et de 1998.* [Known as the Luntundula Report, this report is available on the Web but has never been offcially published.] Kinshasa, DRC. June 2005.

————. *Constitution de la République Démocratique du Congo.* Kinshasa, DRC. February 2006.

————. *Programme du gouvernement (2007–2011).* Kinshasa, DRC. February 2007.

Government of France. *La tragédie du Rwanda.* By M. Gaud. Paris. Service de la Documentation Française. Dossiers Politiques et Sociaux 752. July 1995.

————. *Enquête sur la tragédie rwandaise (1990–1994).* Paris. French National Assembly Report 1271, coordinated by P. Quilès, P. Brana, and B. Cazeneuve. 4 vols. December 1999.

Government of Rwanda. *Programme de réconciliation nationale, de réhabilitation et de relance économique.* Geneva. January 1995.

————. *Closure of Displaced People's Camps in Gikongoro.* Ministère de la Réhabilitation et de l'Intégration Sociale. April 1995.

————. *Memorandum on the Economic and Financial Policies of the Government of Rwanda.* Kigali. March 1997.

————. *Post Conflict Rehabilitation: A Framework of Economic Policies, 1997–1998.* Kigali. April 1997.

————. *Women Parliamentarians and Peace-Building in the Great Lakes Region. The Role of Parliamentarians in Conflict Prevention and Resolution.* Kigali. February 1998.

Groupe d'Action et de Réflexion pour la Démocratie au Congo-Zaïre. *Aux sources du "complot rwandais" contre le Congo.* Brussels. September 1998.

Groupe d'Action pour le Développement de la Promotion Sociale. *Rapport annuel sur la situation des droits de l'homme dans la Province du Kasai Occidental* Kananga, DRC. March 2000–.

Groupe de Recherche et d'Information sur la Paix et la Sécurité (GRIP). www. grip.org. *La guerre du Congo-Kinshasa: Analyse d'un conflit et des transferts d'armes vers l'Afrique Centrale.* Written by G. Berghezan and F. Nkundabagenzi. Brussels. 1999.

———. *Qui arme les Maï-Maï?* Written by Charles Nasibu Bilali. Brussels. 2004.

———. *RDC: Ressources naturelles et transferts d'armes.* Written by Anne Renauld. Brussels. 2005.

Groupe Golias. *Rwanda: L'honneur perdu de l'Eglise.* Written by Christian Terras. Villeurbanne, France: Editions Golias, 1999.

Groupe Jérémie. *La question dite des Banyamulenge.* Bukavu, DRC. March 2002.

Groupe Lotus. *Le calvaire des populations rurales: Rapport sur la situation sécuritaire des droits humains à l'intérieur de la Province Orientale.* Kisangani, DRC. October 2001.

———. *Les foyers d'insécurité et de violations des droits de l'homme à Kisangani.* Kisangani, DRC. December 2001.

Human Rights Watch. www.hrw.org. *Angola: Civilians Devastated by a 15 Years War.* New York. February 1991.

———. *Zaire: Inciting Hatred: Violence against Kasaiens in Shaba.* New York. Human Rights Watch Africa. June 1993.

———. *Angola: Arms Trade and Violations of the Laws of War Since the 1992 Election.* New York. Human Rights Watch Africa. 1994.

———. *Rwanda: A New Catastrophe? Increased International Efforts to Punish Genocide and Prevent Further Bloodshed.* New York. Human Rights Watch Africa. December 1994.

———. *Rwanda/Zaire: Rearming with Impunity; International Support for the Perpetrators of the Rwandan Genocide.* Washington, DC. Human Rights Watch Arms Project. May 1995.

———. *Angola between War and Peace: Arms Trade and Human Rights Abuses Since the Lusaka Protocol.* Washington, DC. Human Rights Watch Arms Project. February 1996.

———. *Forced to Flee: Violence against the Tutsi in Zaire.* New York. Human Rights Watch Africa. July 1996.

———. *Zaire: Transition, War and Human Rights.* New York. Human Rights Watch Africa. April 1997.

———. *Uncertain Course: Transition and Human Rights Violations in the Congo.* New York. Human Rights Watch Africa. December 1997.

———. *Stoking the Fires: Military Assistance and Arms Trafficking in Burundi.* Washington, DC. Human Rights Watch Arms Division. December 1997.

————. *Les civils pris pour cibles: Une guerre civile par personnes interposées au Burundi.* Brussels. March 1998.

————. *DRC: Casualties of War: Civilians, Rule of Law and Democratic Freedoms.* New York. February 1999.

————. *In the Name of Security: Forced Round-Ups of Refugees in Tanzania.* New York. Human Rights Watch Africa. July 1999.

————. *Angola Unravels: The Rise and Fall of the Lusaka Peace Process.* New York. Human Rights Watch Africa. September 1999.

————. *Burundi: Neglecting Justice in Making Peace.* New York. March 2000.

————. *Rwanda: The Search for Security and Human Rights Abuses.* New York. April 2000.

————. *L'Est du Congo dévasté: Civils assassinés et opposants réduits au silence.* New York. May 2000.

————. *Uganda in Eastern DRC: Fuelling Political and Ethnic Strife.* New York. March 2001.

————. *Uprooting the Rural Poor in Rwanda.* New York. May 2001.

————. *"To Protect the People": The Government-Sponsored "Self-Defence" Program in Burundi.* New York. December 2001.

————. *Rwanda: Observing the Rules of War?* New York. December 2001.

————. *RDC: La guerre dans la guerre: Violence sexuelle contre les femmes et les filles dans l'Est du Congo.* New York. June 2002.

————. *DRC: War Crimes in Kisangani.* New York. August 2002.

————. *Ituri Covered in Blood: Ethnically Targeted Violence in Northeastern DRC.* New York. July 2003.

————. *Seeking Justice: The Prosecution of Sexual Violence in the Congo War.* New York. March 2005.

————. *DRC: The Curse of Gold.* New York. April 2005.

————. *RDC: Attaque contre les civils au Nord Kivu.* New York. July 2005.

————. Angola Chapters of Human Rights Watch. *World Reports.* New York. 1998.

————. Angola Chapters of Human Rights Watch. *World Reports.* New York. 1999.

————. Angola Chapters of Human Rights Watch. *World Reports.* New York. 2000.

Human Rights Watch, in collaboration with FIDH. *Commission internationale d'enquête sur les violations des droits de l'homme au Burundi depuis le 21 octobre 1993.* Washington, DC/Paris. July 1994.

Human Rights Watch, in collaboration with FIDH. *What Kabila Is Hiding: Civilian Killings and Impunity in Congo.* New York. October 1997.

Human Rights Watch, in collaboration with FIDH. *Leave None to Tell the Story: Genocide in Rwanda.* New York. March 1999.

Humanitarian Law Consultancy. *Burundi's Regroupment Policy: A Pilot Study on Its Legality.* The Hague. July 1997.

Humanitarianism and War Project. *Report on the Impact of Sanctions on Burundi.* Brown University. March 1997.

Independent Commission of Inquiry into the Actions of the United Nations During the 1994 Genocide in Rwanda. *Report.* [Also known as the Carlsson Report from the name of the Commission's chairman.] New York. December 1999.

Independent International Commission of Inquiry on the Events at Kibeho, April 1995. *Report.* Kigali. May 1995.

International Alert. www.international-alert.org. *Tour Report of Kivu (Zaire).* Written by Karen Twining. October 1996.

———. *L'égalité d'accès à l'éducation, un impératif pour la paix au Burundi.* Written by Tony Jackson. June 2000.

International Center for Transitional Justice. *Les premiers pas: La longue route vers une paix juste en République Démocratique du Congo.* Written by Federico Borello. New York. October 2004.

International Crisis Group. www.crisisweb.org. *Burundi: Lever les sanctions, relancer la transition.* Brussels. April 1998.

———. *Burundi: Négociations à Arusha: Quelles chances pour la paix?* Brussels. July 1998.

———. *North Kivu, into the Quagmire?* Brussels. August 1998.

———. *La rébellion au Congo: Acteurs internes et externes à la crise.* Brussels. October 1998.

———. *Africa Seven Nations War.* Brussels. May 1999.

———. *Burundi: Internal and Regional Implications of the Suspension of Sanctions.* Brussels. May 1999.

———. *Burundi: Proposals for the Resumption of Bilateral and Multilateral Cooperation.* Brussels. May 1999.

———. *How Kabila Lost His Way.* Brussels. May 1999.

———. *The Agreement on a Ceasefire in the Democratic Republic of Congo.* Brussels. August 1999.

———. *L'effet Mandela: Evaluation et perspectives du processus de paix burundais.* Brussels. April 2000.

———. *Uganda and Rwanda: Friends or Enemies?* Nairobi. May 2000.

———. *Burundi: Les enjeux du débat: Partis politiques, liberté de la presse et prisonniers politiques.* Brussels. July 2000.

———. *Burundi, ni guerre ni paix.* Brussels. December 2000.

———. *Scramble for the Congo: Anatomy of an Ugly War.* Brussels. December 2000.

————. *From Kabila to Kabila: Prospects for Peace in the Congo.* Nairobi. March 2001.

————. *Burundi: Sortir de l'impasse. L'urgence d'un nouveau cadre négociations.* Brussels. May 2001.

————. *Tribunal pénal international pour le Rwanda: L'urgence de juger.* Nairobi/Arusha, Tanzania/Brussels. June 2001.

————. *Disarmament in the Congo: Investing in Conflict Prevention.* Nairobi/Washington, DC/Brussels. June 2001.

————. *Zimbabwe in Crisis: Finding a Way Forward.* Brussels. July 2001.

————. *Burundi: Cent jours pour retrouver le chemin de la paix.* Brussels. August 2001.

————. *"Consensual Democracy" in Post-Genocide Rwanda: Evaluating the March 2001 District Elections.* Brussels. October 2001.

————. *Zimbabwe: Time for International Action.* Brussels. October 2001.

————. *The Intercongolese Dialogue: Political Negotiations or Game Bluff?* Brussels. November 2001.

————. *Disarmament in the Congo: Jump-starting DDRRR to Prevent Further War.* Brussels. December 2001.

————. *Rwanda/Uganda: A Dangerous War of Nerves.* Brussels. December 2001.

————. *Zimbabwe's Elections: The Stakes for Southern Africa.* Brussels. January 2002.

————. *All Bark and No Bite? The International Response to Zimbabwe's Crisis.* Brussels. January 2002.

————. *Zimbabawe at the Crossroads: Transition or Conflict?* Brussels. March 2002.

————. *Après six mois de transition au Burundi: Poursuivre la guerre ou gagner la paix?* Brussels. May 2002.

————. *Storm Clouds over Sun City.* Brussels. May 2002.

————. *Zimbabwe: What Next?* Brussels. June 2002.

————. *Tribunal Pénal International pour le Rwanda: Le compte à rebours.* Brussels. August 2002.

————. *The Burundi Rebellion and the Ceasefire Negotiations.* Brussels. August 2002.

————. *Fin de transition au Rwanda: Une libéralisation politique nécéssaire.* Brussels. November 2002.

————. *Dealing with Savimbi's Ghost: The Security and Humanitarian Challenges in Angola.* Brussels. February 2003.

————. *Angola's Choice: Reform or Regress.* Brussels. April 2003.

————. *Les rebelles Hutu rwandais au Congo: Pour une nouvelle approche du désarmement et de la réintégration.* Brussels. May 2003.

———. *Congo Crisis: Military Intervention in Ituri.* Brussels. June 2003.

———. *Tribunal Pénal International pour le Rwanda: Pragmatisme de Rigueur.* Brussels. September 2003.

———. *Réfugiés et déplacés au Burundi: Désamorcer la bombe foncière.* Brussels. October 2003.

———. *Pulling Back from the Brink in the Congo.* Brussels. July 2004.

———. *Maintaining Momentum in the Congo: The Ituri Problem.* Brussels. August 2004.

———. *Back to the Brink in the Congo.* Brussels. December 2004.

———. *The Congo's Transition Is Failing: Crisis in the Kivus.* Brussels. March 2005.

———. *The Congo: Solving the FDLR Problem Once and For All.* Brussels. May 2005.

———. *Katanga: The Congo's Forgotten Crisis.* Brussels. January 2006.

———. *Security Sector Reform in the Congo.* Brussels. February 2006.

———. *Congo's Elecctions: Making or Breaking the Peace.* Brussels. April 2006.

———. *Escaping the Conflict Trap: Promoting Good Governance in the Congo.* Brussels. July 2006.

———. *Securing Congo's Elections: Lessons from the Kinshasa Showdown.* Brussels. October 2006.

———. *Burundi: Democracy and Peace at Risk.* Brussels. November 2006.

———. *Congo: Staying Engaged after the Elections.* Brussels. January 2007.

———. *Congo: Consolidating the Peace.* Brussels. July 2007.

International Peace Information Service (IPIS). *Network War: An Introduction to Congo's Privatised Conflict.* Written by Tim Raeymaekers. Antwerp. April 2002.

International Rescue Committee (IRC). www.theirc.org. *Mortality in Eastern DRC: Results from Five Mortality Surveys.* Written by Les Robert. Bukavu, DRC. June 2000. Updated March 2001, April 2003.

———. *Congo: Nearly Four Million Dead in Six Year Conflict.* New York. December 2004.

———. "Mortality in the Democratic Republic of the Congo: A Nationwide Survey." Written by B. Coghlan et al. *The Lancet,* 367 (2006): 44–51.

Joint Evaluation of Emergency Assistance to Rwanda. *The International Response to Conflict and Genocide: Lessons from the Rwanda Experience.* 5 vols. Copenhagen/Odense. March 1996.

———. *A Review of Follow-Up and Impact Fifteen Months after Publication.* Copenhagen. June 1997.

Lawyers Committee for Human Rights. *Zaire: Repression as Policy.* New York. August 1990.

Médecins Sans Frontières [France]. *Des conflits fonciers aux luttes inter-ethniques dans la zone de santé de Masisi.* Goma, DRC. April 1993.

―――. *Breaking the Cycle.* Goma, DRC. November 1994.

―――. *La population civile, cible systématique du conflit burundais.* Paris. November 1995.

―――. *Deadlock in the Rwandan Refugee Crisis.* Paris. July 1995.

―――. *Epidemiological Survey of Rwandan Refugees in Ndjoundou Camp, Congo, July 1997.* Paris. October 1997.

―――. *Violence and Access to Health in the DRC.* Paris. December 2001.

―――. *Silence, on meurt.* Paris: L'Harmattan, 2002.

―――. *Ituri: Unkept Promises? A Pretense of Protection and Inadequate Assistance.* Paris. July 2003.

Médecins Sans Frontières [USA]. *Ethnic War in Eastern Zaire: Masisi, 1994–1996.* New York. November 1996.

―――. *Forced Flight: A Brutal Strategy of Elimination in Eastern Zaire.* New York. May 1997.

Minority Rights Group. *Selective Genocide in Burundi.* Written by René Lemarchand. MRG Report 20. London. July 1974.

―――. *Burundi Since the Genocide.* Written by Reginald Kay. MRG Report 20 (updated). London. 1984.

―――. *Burundi: Breaking the Cycle of Violence.* Written by Filip Reyntjens. London. 1995.

―――. *Burundi: Prospects for Peace.* Written by Filip Reyntjens. London. November 2000.

Mouvement de Libération du Congo. *Les structures du M.L.C.* Gbadolite, DRC. September 1999.

Multi Country Demobilization and Recovery Program. *Opportunities and Constraints for the Disarmament and Repatriation of Foreign Armed Groups in the DRC (FDLR, FNL and ADF/NALU).* Written by Hans Romkema. De Vennhoop. April 2007.

Netherlands Institute for Southern Africa. *The State versus the People: Governance, Mining and the Transitional Regime in the DRC.* Amsterdam. 2006.

Observatoire Gouvernance et Paix (OGP). *Congo, poches trouées: Flux et fuites des recettes douanières au Sud Kivu.* Coordinated by Eric Kajemba. Bukavu, DRC: Smart, 2006.

Observatoire Gouvernement Transparence (OGT). *Guerre en RDC: Ses enjeux économiques, ses intérêts, ses acteurs.* Written by Pierre Lumbi. Kinshasa, DRC. April 2000.

―――. *Le Rwanda plante le décor d'une nouvelle guerre d'agression à l'Est de la RDC.* Kinshasa, DRC. Septembre 2003.

Organization for Peace, Justice and Development in Rwanda. *Memorandum on the 1994 Assassination of Juvenal Habyarimana, President of the Republic of Rwanda.* Written by Félicien Kanyamibwa. N.p. December 1999.

Oxfam. *Poverty in the Midst of Wealth.* London. January 2002.

Paix pour le Congo. *La guerre en République Démocratique du Congo et les aides financières de l'Union Européenne aux pays impliqués dans le conflit.* Parma. October 2000.

Parti Armé Pour la Libération du Rwanda. *Lettre ouverte à la communauté internationale and other documents.* Gisenyi, Rwanda. January 26, 1998.

Pole Institute. *Le coltan et les populations du Nord Kivu.* Goma, DRC. 2001.

———. *Shifting Sands: Oil Exploration in the Rift Valley and the Congo Conflict.* Written by Dominic Johnson. Goma, DRC. March 2003.

Reporters Sans Frontières. *Médias de la haine ou presse démocratique.* Paris. November 1994.

———. *Burundi, le venin de la haine: Étude sur les médias extrémistes.* Paris. June 1995.

———. *Rwanda: L'impasse? La liberté de la presse après le génocide.* Paris. October 1995.

———. *La désinformation au Rwanda: Enquête sur le cas Sibomana.* Paris. December 1995.

———. *Burundi, la presse en otage.* Paris. February 1996.

———. *Enquête sur la mort d'André Sibomana.* Written by Hervé Deguine. Paris. October 1998.

Réseau Européen Congo. www.perso.wanadoo.fr/dan.cdm/dem/recdoc.htm. *Eléments indicatifs de la coopération entre l'Union Européenne et les pays ACP impliqués dans la guerre en République Démocratique du Congo (RDC).* Written by Catherine André and Laurent Luzolele Lola. Brussels. June 2000. Reprinted in S. Marysse and F. Reyntjens, eds., *Annuaire des Grands Lacs (2000–2001).* Tervuren, Belgium: CEDAF, 2001.

———. *Congo: Fini Lusaka? Vive Lusaka!* Brussels. December 2000.

———. *The European Union's Aid Policy towards Countries Involved in the Congo War: Lever for Peace or Incitement to War?* Written by Catherine André and Laurent Luzolele Lola. Brussels. May 2001.

———. *RD Congo: État des lieux de la "transition."* Brussels. March 2003.

———. *MONUC in the DRC: Strengthen Its Mandate, Denounce the Warmongers.* Brussels. June 2003.

Save the Children (UK). *Background Notes on the Current Emergency in the Northwest of Rwanda.* London. February 1999.

———. *No End in Sight: The Human Tragedy of the Conflict in the Democratic Republic of the Congo.* London. August 2001.

Stiftung für Wissenschaft und Politik. *Zimbabwe: A Conflict Study of a Country without Direction.* Ebenhausen. December 1998.

———. *The Internal and Regional Dynamics of the Congo Crisis in 1999.* Brussels. February 5–6, 1999.

Table de Concertation sur les Droits Humains au Zaïre. *Zaïre 1992–1996: Chronique d'une transition inachevée.* 2 vols. Paris: L'Harmattan, 1996.

Un Groupe de Prêtres de Kigali. *Des prêtres rwandais s'interrogent.* Bujumbura, Burundi: Presses Lavigerie, 1995.

Union Démocratique pour le Progrès Social (UDPS). *Le dialogue intercongolais doit absolument se tenir et il doit absolument réussir.* Brussels. October 2001.

United Nations. *Rapport sur la situation des droits de l'homme au Rwanda soumis par Mr René Degni-Ségui.* New York. Commission des Droits de l'Homme. November 1994.

———. *Collected Documents on the Rwanda Roundtable Conference.* Geneva. January 1995.

———. *Reports and Documents on the Kibeho Crisis.* Kigali. Integrated Operations Centre. April 1995.

———. *Situation Report on Masisi, North Kivu, Zaire.* Nairobi. Department of Humanitarian Affairs. February 26, 1996.

———. *The United Nations and Rwanda, 1993–1996.* Introduction by Boutros Boutros Ghali. New York. UN Blue Books Series, vol. 10. May 1996.

———. *Final Report of the United Nations International Commission of Inquiry for Burundi.* New York. July 1996.

———. *Report of the Secretary General on the Situation in Burundi.* New York. August 1996.

———. *Third Report of the International Commission of Enquiry on Rwanda.* New York. October 1996.

———. *The Conflict in South Kivu (Zaire) and Its Regional Implications.* Nairobi. Department of Humanitarian Affairs. October 1996.

———. *Rapport sur la situation des droits de l'homme au Zaïre présenté par Mr Roberto Garreton, Rapporteur Spécial, conformément à la résolution 1996/77.* January 1997.

———. *Les antécédents politiques de la crise rwandaise de 1994.* Written by André Guichaoua. Arusha, Tanzania. International Criminal Tribunal for Rwanda. April 1997.

———. *Tanzania Refugee Situation Report.* Nairobi. Department of Humanitarian Affairs. April 1997.

———. *Report of the Joint Mission Charged with Investigating Allegations of Massacres and Other Human Rights Violations Occurring in Eastern Za-*

ire (Now Democratic Republic of the Congo) Since September 1996. New York. July 1997.

———. *Report of the Secretary General on the Situation in Burundi.* New York. July 1997.

———. "Population Displacements in the Great Lakes Region of Africa." in UNHCR: *The State of the World's Refugees.* 20–23. Oxford: Oxford University Press, 1997.

———. *Population Movements in the Great Lakes Region.* Nairobi. Department of Humanitarian Affairs. December 1997.

———. *Missed Opportunities: The Role of the International Community in the Return of the Rwandan Refugees from Eastern Zaire (July 1994–December 1996).* Written by Joël Boutroue. Cambridge, MA. UNHCR/MIT Center for International Studies. February 1998.

———. *Report of the Panel of Experts on Violations of Security Council Sanctions against UNITA.* [Also known as the Fowler Report after the name of the panel's president.] New York. March 2000.

———. *Report of the Panel on UN Peace Operations.* Under the direction of Lakhdar Brahimi. New York. August 2000.

———. *The Situation of Human Rights in the Democratic Republic of Congo.* Written by Roberto Garreton. New York. UN General Assembly. September 2000.

———. *Rapport sur la situation des droits de l'homme en République Démocratique du Congo.* Written by Roberto Garreton. New York. Conseil Economique et Social. February 2001.

———. *Report of the Panel on the Illegal Exploitation of Natural Resources and Other Forms of Wealth of the Democratic Republic of the Congo.* Edited by Mrs. Safiatou Ba N'Daw. New York. April 2001. *Addendum.* Edited by Mahmood Kassem. November 2001.

———. *First Assessment of the Armed Groups Operating in the Democratic Republic of the Congo.* Kinshasa, DRC. Mission de l'Organisation des Nations Unies au Congo (MONUC). April 2002.

———. *Report of the Panel on the Illegal Exploitation of Natural Resources and Other Forms of Wealth of the Democratic Republic of the Congo.* Edited by Mahmood Kassem. New York. October 2002.

———. *Report of the Panel on the Illegal Exploitation of Natural Resources and Other Forms of Wealth of the Democratic Republic of the Congo.* Edited by Mahmood Kassem. New York. October 2003.

United States Agency for International Development. *The Anguish of Northern Uganda.* Written by Robert Gersony. Kampala. August 1997.

———. *A Primer on the Historical Context of the Humanitarian Relief Effort in the DRC.* Prepared by Herbert Weiss. Washington, DC. September 2004.

United States Committee for Refugees. *Transition in Burundi: The Context for a Homecoming*. Washington, DC. September 1993.

―――. *Inducing the Deluge: Zaire's Internally Displaced People*. Written by Renée G. Roberts. Washington, DC. October 1993.

―――. *Masisi down the Road from Goma: Ethnic Cleansing and Displacement in Eastern Zaire*. Washington, DC. June 1996.

―――. *Site Visit to Eastern Congo/Zaire: Analysis of Humanitarian and Political Issues*. Written by Eleanor Bedford. Washington, DC. June 1997.

―――. *Life after Death: Suspicion and Reintegration in Post-Genocide Rwanda*. Washington, DC. February 1998.

United States Institute of Peace. www.usip.org. *Refugees and Rebels: The Former Government of Rwanda and the ADFL Movement in Eastern Zaire*. Written by William Cyrus-Reed. Washington, DC. 1997.

―――. *Angola's Last Best Chance for Peace: An Insider's Account of the Peace Process*. Written by Paul Hare. Washington, DC. 1998.

―――. *Reconstructing Peace in the Congo*. Written by John Prendergast and David Smock. Washington, DC. August 1999.

―――. *Post-Genocidal Reconstruction: Building Peace in Rwanda and Burundi*. Written by John Prendergast and David Smock. Washington, DC. September 1999.

―――. *Dealing with Savimbi's Hell on Earth*. Written by John Prendergast. Washington, DC. October 1999.

United States Government. Committee on International Relations, House of Representatives. 104th Congress, 2nd Session. *Refugees in Eastern Zaire and Rwanda*. Hearing before the Subcommittee on Africa. December 4, 1996.

―――. Committee on International Relations. House of Representatives. 105th Congress, 1st Session. *Zaire: Collapse of an African Giant?* Hearing before the Subcommittee on Africa. April 8, 1997.

―――. Bureau of Democracy, Human Rights and Labor. U.S. Department of State. *Report on Human Rights Practices in the Democratic Republic of the Congo*. February 1998.

―――. Bureau of Democracy, Human Rights and Labor. U.S. Department of State. *Report on Human Rights Practices in the Democratic Republic of the Congo*. February 1999.

―――. Bureau of Democracy, Human Rights and Labor. U.S. Department of State. *Report on Human Rights Practices in the Democratic Republic of the Congo*. February 2000.

―――. Bureau of Democracy, Human Rights and Labor. U.S. Department of State. *Report on Human Rights Practices in the Democratic Republic of the Congo*. February 2001.

————. Bureau of Democracy, Human Rights and Labor. U.S. Department of State. *Report on Human Rights Practices in Rwanda*. February 1998.

————. Bureau of Democracy, Human Rights and Labor. U.S. Department of State. *Report on Human Rights Practices in Rwanda*. February 1999.

————. Bureau of Democracy, Human Rights and Labor. U.S. Department of State. *Report on Human Rights Practices in Rwanda*. February 2000.

————. Bureau of Democracy, Human Rights and Labor. U.S. Department of State. *Report on Human Rights Practices in Rwanda*. February 2001.

————. Bureau of Democracy, Human Rights and Labor. U.S. Department of State. *Report on Human Rights Practices in Angola*. February 1998.

————. Bureau of Democracy, Human Rights and Labor. U.S. Department of State. *Report on Human Rights Practices in Angola*. February 1999.

————. Bureau of Democracy, Human Rights and Labor. U.S. Department of State. *Report on Human Rights Practices in Angola*. February 2000.

————. Bureau of Democracy, Human Rights and Labor. U.S. Department of State. *Report on Human Rights Practices in Angola*. February 2001.

————. *Diamonds and Conflic: Policy Proposals and Background*. Written by Nicolas Cook. Washington, DC. Congressional Research Service. February 2001.

————. *Global Humanitarian Emergencies: Trends and Projections, 2001–2002*. Written by David Gordon. Washington, DC. National Intelligence Council. September 2001.

World Bank. *Adjustment in Africa: Reforms, Results and the Road Ahead*. Washington, DC.

————. *Can Africa Claim the 21st Century?* Washington, DC. 2000.

————. *Conflict Diamonds*. Written by Louis Goreux. Washington, DC. February 2001.

————. *Greater Great Lakes Regional Strategy for Demobilization and Reintegration*. Washington, DC. March 2002.

————. *Post-Conflict Recovery in Africa: An Agenda for the Region*. Written by S. Michailof, M. Kostner, and X. Devictor. Washington, DC. May 2002.

World Council of Churches. *The Angels Have Left Us: The Rwanda Tragedy and the Churches*. Written by H. McCullum. Geneva. 1997.

Zimbabwe Human Rights NGO Forum. *The Unleashing of Violence: A Report on Political Violence in Zimbabwe*. Harare. May 2000.

Unpublished Theses

Fairhead, J. "Fields of Struggle: Towards a Social History of Farming Knowledge and Practice in a Bwisha Community, Kivu, Zaire." PhD diss., School of Oriental and African Studies, London, 1990.

Lanotte, O. "L'Opération Turquoise au Rwanda." MA thesis. Université Catholique de Louvain, Department of Political Science, 1996.

Mouzer, F. "Diaspora et pouvoir dans le Rwanda post-génocide." MA thesis. Paris Sorbonne, Department of African Studies, 2002.

Rozès, A. "Angola: Guerre civile et interventions extérieures (1975–1988)." PhD thesis. University of Nantes, Department of Political Science, 1996.

Torrenté, N. de. "Post–Conflict Reconstruction and the International Community in Uganda (1986–2000)." PhD thesis. London School of Economics, 2001.

Willum, B. "Foreign Aid to Rwanda: Purely Beneficial or Contributing to War?" Dissertation for the Candidate Degree in Political Science, University of Copenhagen, October 2001.

Books and Articles

Adelman, H., and Rao, G. C., eds. *War and Peace in Zaire/Congo: Analyzing and Evaluating Intervention (1996–1997)*. Trenton, NJ: Africa World Press, 2004.

Adelman, H., and Suhrke, A., eds. *The Path of Genocide: The Rwanda Crisis from Uganda to Zaire*. Uppsala, Sweden: Nordiska Afrikainstitutet, 1999.

Africano, M. A. *L'UNITA et la deuxième guerre civile angolaise*. Paris: L'Harmattan, 1995.

Aguilar, M. I. *The Rwanda Genocide and the Call to Deepen Christianity in Africa*. Eldoret, Kenya: Gaba Publications, 1998.

Ali, A. A. G., and P. Collier, eds. Special Issue on Aid of the *Journal of African Economies* 8, no. 4 (December 1999).

Ambrossetti, D. *La France au Rwanda: Un discours de légitimation morale*. Paris: Karthala, 2000.

André, C., and L. Luzolele. "Politique de l'Union Européenne et effets pervers pour le conflit des Grands Lacs." In S. Marysse and F. Reyntjens, eds., *L'Afrique des Grands Lacs (2000–2001)*, 365–396. Paris: L'Harmattan, 2001.

André, C., and J. Ph. Platteau. "Land Relations under Unbearable Stress: Rwanda Caught in the Malthusian Trap." *Journal of Economic Behaviour and Organization* 34, no. 1 (February 1998): 1–47.

Anonymous. "Memorandum du Département des Affaires Etrangères du Zaïre." *Politique Africaine*, no. 41 (March 1991): 102–110.

———. *RPF Riding Herd*. Report written by a middle-ranking U.S. civil servant. Posted on the Internet, dated January 26, 1999.

———. "Africa's Great Black Hope: A Survey of South Africa." Supplement to *The Economist*, February 24, 2001.

Ansoms, A. "Résurrection après la guerre civile et le genocide: Croissance économique, pauvreté et inégalité dans le Rwanda post-conflit." In F. Reyntjens and S. Marysse, eds., *L'Afrique des Grands Lacs: Annuaire 2005–2006. Dix ans de transitions conflicturelles*, 373–387. Paris: L'Harmattan, 2006.

Anstee, M. *Orphan of the Cold War: The Inside Story of the Collapse of the Angolan Peace Process (1992–1993)*. London: Macmillan, 1996.

Ayittey, G. *Africa in Chaos*. New York: Saint Martin's Press, 1998.

Bakajika-Banjikila, Th. *Epuration ethnique en Afrique: Les Kasaïens (Katanga 1961–Shaba 1992)*. Paris: L'Harmattan, 1997.

Bakatuseka, C. *La "libération" de Lubumbashi (1997)*. Paris: L'Harmattan, 1999.

Banegas, R., and B. Jewsiewicki, eds. "RDC, la guerre vue d'en bas." Special Issue of *Politique Africaine*, no. 84 (December 2001). [With texts by G. de Villers and J. Omasombo, A. Maindo, L. N'Sanda Buleli, J. Kabulo, F. van Acker and K. Vlassenroot, S. Jackson, and J. F. Ploquin.]

Barnett, M. "The Politics of Indifference at the United Nations." *Cultural Anthropology*, November 1997.

———. *Eyewitness to a Genocide: The United Nations and Rwanda*. Ithaca, NY: Cornell University Press, 2002.

Bassinet, A. "Congo: À qui profite la rente pétrolière?" *Imprecor*, no. 173 (May 14, 1984): 30–34.

Bayart, J. F. *The State in Africa: The Politics of the Belly*. London: Longman, 1993.

———. "La guerre en Afrique: Dépérissement ou formation de l'état? *Esprit*, no. 247 (1998): 55–73.

———. "L'Afrique dans le monde: Une histoire d'extraversion." *Critique Internationale*, no. 5 (Autumn 1999): 97–120.

Bayart, J. F., S. Ellis, and B. Hibou. *The Criminalisation of the State in Africa*. Oxford: James Currey, 1999.

Bazenguissa-Ganga, R. "Milices politiques et bandes armées à Brazzaville, enquête sur la violence politique et sociale des jeunes déclassés." *Les Etudes du CERI*, no. 13 (April 1996).

———. *Les voies du politique au Congo: Essai de sociologie historique*. Paris: Karthala, 1997.

———. "Les milices politiques dans les affrontements." *Afrique Contemporaine*, no. 186. (April–June 1998): 46–57.

Ben Hammouda, H. *Burundi: Histoire économique et politique d'un conflit*. Paris: L'Harmattan, 1995.

Berghezan, G. *Trafics d'armes vers l'Afrique: Pleins feux sur les réseaux français et le "savoir-faire" belge*. Brussels: Editions Complexe, 2002.

Berghezan, G., and F. Nkundabagenzi. *La guerre du Congo-Kinshasa.* Brussels: GRIP, 1999.

Berman, E., and K. Sams. *Peacekeeping in Africa: Capabilities and Culpabilities.* Geneva: United Nations Institute for Disarmament Research, 2000.

Bernault, F. "La communauté africaniste française au crible de la crise rwandaise." *Africa Today* 45, no. 1 (1998): 45–58.

Bertrand, J. *Rwanda: Le piège de l'histoire. L'opposition démocratique avant le génocide (1990–1994).* Paris: Karthala, 2000.

Bizimana, J. D. *L'Eglise et le genocide au Rwanda.* Paris: L'Harmattan, 2000.

Blanc, Th. "Diamonds Are Forever: Le Zimbabwe, les diamants et la guerre en République Démocratique du Congo." *Afrique Contemporaine,* no. 197 (January–March 2001): 34–46.

Boissonnade, E. *Le mal zaïrois.* Paris: Hermé, 1990.

———. *Kabila, clone de Mobutu?* Paris: Moreux, 1998.

Booh Booh, J. R. *Le patron de Dallaire parle: Révélations sur les dérives d'un général de l'ONU au Rwanda.* Paris: Editions Duboiris, 2005.

Bradol, J. H., and A. Guibert. "Le temps des assassins et l'espace humanitaire: Rwanda-Kivu 1994–1997." *Hérodote,* no. 86/87 (1997): 116–149.

Braeckman, C. *Le dinosaure.* Paris: Fayard, 1992.

———. *Terreur Africaine: Burundi, Rwanda, Zaïre. Les racines de la violence.* Paris: Fayard, 1996.

———. *L'enjeu congolais.* Paris: Fayard, 1999.

———. *Les nouveaux prédateurs: Politique des puissances en Afrique Centrale* Paris: Fayard, 2003.

Braeckman, C., et al. *Kabila prend le pouvoir.* Brussels: GRIP/Editions Complexe, 1998.

Brauman, R., S. Smith, C. and Vidal. "Politique de terreur et privilège d'impunité au Rwanda." *Esprit,* nos. 266–267 (August–September 2000): 147–161.

Bridgland, F. *Jonas Savimbi, a Key to Africa.* Johannesburg: Macmillan, 1986.

———. "Savimbi et l'exercice du pouvoir: Un témoignage." *Politique Africaine,* no. 57 (March 1995): 94–102.

Brittain, V. *Death of Dignity: Angola's Civil War.* London: Pluto Press, 1998.

Brunschwig, H. *Le partage de l'Afrique Noire.* Paris: Flammarion, 1971.

Bowen, R. "Rwanda: Missionary Reflections on a Catastrophe. J. C. Jones Lecture 1995." *Anvil* 13, no. 1 (1996).

Buchet, J. L., and A. De Silva, eds. "Un an après, le Congo de Kabila." Special Issue of *Jeune Afrique,* no. 1948 (May 12–18, 1998).

Bucyalimwe Mararo, S. "La société civile du Kivu: Une dynamique en panne?" In S. Marysse and F. Reyntjens, eds., *L'Afrique des Grands Lacs 1998– 1999,* 237–271. Paris: L'Harmattan, 1999.

Bulambo Katambu, A. *Mourir au Kivu.* Paris: L'Harmattan, 2001.

Cain, K., H. Postlewait, and A. Thomson. *Emergency Sex (and Other Desperate Measures): True Stories from a War Zone.* New York: Random House, 2004.

Calderisi, R. *The Trouble with Africa: Why Foreign Aid Isn't Working.* New Haven, CT: Yale University Press, 2006.

Callaghy, T. M. *The State Society Struggle: Zaire in Comparative Perspective.* New York: Columbia University Press, 1984.

———. "Africa and the World Political Economy: More Caught between a Rock and a Hard Place." In J. W. Harbeson and D. Rothchild, eds., *Africa in World Politics: The African State System in Flux,* 42–82. Boulder, CO: Westview Press, 2000.

Cassimon D., and S. Marysse. "L'évolution socio-économique au Rwanda et au Burundi (2000–2001) et la politique financière internationale." In S. Marysse and F. Reyntjens, eds., *L'Afrique des Grands Lacs (2000–2001),* 1–20. Paris: L'Harmattan, 2001.

Cavalieri, R., et al. *Burundi: Democrazia in calvario.* Parma: Alfa Zeta Editore, 1994.

———. *Bujumbura, citta dell' odio.* Parma: Alfa Zeta Editore, 1995.

———. *Balcani d'Africa: Burundi, Rwanda, Zaire: oltre la guerra etnica.* Torino: Edizioni Gruppo Abele, 1997.

Chabal, P., and J. P. Daloz. *Africa Works: Disorder as a Political Instrument.* London: James Currey, 1999.

Cheuzeville, H. *Kadogo, enfants des guerres d'Afrique Centrale.* Paris: L'Harmattan, 2003.

Chrétien, J. P. *Burundi, l'histoire retrouvée.* Paris: Karthala, 1993.

———. "Burundi: The Obsession with Genocide." *Current History,* May 1996, 206–210.

———. *Le défi de l'ethnisme: Rwanda et Burundi 1990–1996.* Paris: Karthala, 1997.

———. "Le Rwanda piégé par son histoire." *Esprit,* nos. 266–267 (August–September 2000): 170–189.

———. *The Great Lakes of Africa: Two Thousand Years of History.* New York: Zone Books, 2003.

———, ed. *Rwanda: Les médias du génocide.* Paris: Karthala, 1995.

Chrétien, J. P., and J. F. Dupaquier. *Burundi 1972: Au bord des génocides.* Paris: Karthala, 2007.

Chrétien, J. P., and G. Prunier, eds. *Les ethnies ont une histoire.* Paris: Karthala, 1989.

Chrétien, J. P., et al., eds. *Rwanda, un génocide du XXème siècle.* Paris: L'Harmattan, 1995.

492

Cilliers, J., and P. Mason, eds. *Peace, Profit or Plunder: The Privatisation of Security in War-Torn African Societies.* Pretoria: Institute for Security Studies, 1999.

Clark, J. F. "Democracy Dismantled in the Congo Republic." *Current History,* May 1998, 234–237.

———. "Explaining Ugandan Intervention in Congo." *Journal of Modern African Studies* 39, no. 2 (2000): 261–287.

———, ed. *The African Stakes of the Congo War.* New York: Palgrave Press, 2002.

Clark, P. "When the Killers Go Home: Local Justice in Rwanda." *Dissent,* July 2005.

Collins, B. *Obedience in Rwanda: A Critical Question.* Sheffield, UK: Hallam University Press, 1998.

Compagnon, D. "Terrorisme électoral au Zimbabwe." *Politique Africaine,* no. 78 (June 2000): 180–190.

———. "Zimbabawe: L'alternance ou le chaos." *Politique Africaine,* no. 81 (March 2001): 7–25.

———. "Mugabe and Partners (Pvt) Ltd ou l'investissement politique du champ économique." *Politique Africaine,* no. 81 (March 2001): 101–120.

Coret, L., and F. X. Verschave, eds. *L'horreur qui nous prend au visage: L'état français et le génocide au Rwanda.* Paris: Karthala, 2005.

Corten, A. "Le discours de la réconciliation et les nouvelles églises au Rwanda." *Afrique Contemporaine,* no. 200 (October 2001): 65–81.

Cosma, W. B. *Le maquis Kabila: Fizi 1967–1986.* Brussels: CEDAF, 1997.

Crépeau, P. *Rwanda, le kidnapping médiatique.* Hull, Quebec: Vents d'Ouest, 1995.

Cros, M. F., and F. Misser. *Géopolitique du Congo (RDC).* Brussels: Ed. Complexe, 2006.

Cruvelier, T. *Le tribunal des vaincus.* Paris: Calmann-Lévy, 2006.

Dabira, N. *Brazzaville à feu et à sang (5 juin–15 octobre 1997).* Paris: L'Harmattan, 1998.

Dallaire, R. *Shake Hands with the Devil: The Failure of Humanity in Rwanda.* New York: Carroll and Graff, 2004.

Debré, B. *Le retour du Mwami: La vraie histoire du génocide rwandais.* Paris: Ramsay, 1998.

———. *La veritable histoire des génocides rwandais.* Paris: Jean-Claude Gawsewitch, 2006.

De Herdt, T. "Nourrir Kinshasa en période de guerre." In S. Marysse and F. Reyntjens, eds., *L'Afrique des Grands Lacs (2000–2001),* 195–218. Paris: L'Harmattan, 2001.

de la Pradelle, Géraud. *Imprescriptible: L'implication française dans le génocide tutsi portée devant les tribunaux.* Paris: Les Arènes, 2005.

DeLorenzo, M. "Notes for a Historical Ethnography of the Banyamulenge." Paper presented at the Conference on Grassroots Perspectives on the DRC Conflict. Univesity of Ghent. May 26–28, 2004.

DesForges, A. "Burundi: Failed Coup or Creeping Coup?" *Current History,* May 1994, 203–207.

———. "Land in Rwanda: Winnowing Out the Chaff." In F. Reyntjens and S. Marysse, eds., *L'Afrique des Grands Lacs: Annuaire 2005–2006. Dix ans de transitions conflicturelles,* 353–371. Paris: L'Harmattan, 2006.

DeSoto, H. *The Mystery of Capital: Why Capitalism Triumphs in the West and Fails Everywhere Else.* London: Basic Books, 2000.

De Temmerman, E. "The ADF Rebellion: From Guerilla to Urban Terrorism." *New Vision,* May 21, 2007.

Devisch, R. "Frenzy, Violence and Ethical Renewal in Kinshasa." *Public Culture* 7, no. 3 (Spring 1995): 593–629.

———. "La violence à Kinshasa ou l'institution en négatif." *Cahiers d'Etudes Africaines* 38, nos. 2–4 (1998): 441–469.

De Waal, A. *Famine Crimes: Politics and the Disaster Relief Industry in Africa.* Oxford: James Currey, 1997.

———, ed. *Who Fights? Who Cares?* Trenton, NJ: Africa World Press, 2001.

Diangitukwa, F. *Qui gouverne le Zaïre?* Paris: L'Harmattan, 1997.

———. *Le règne du mensonge politique en RD Congo: Qui a tué Kabila?* Paris: L'Harmattan, 2006.

Dietrich, C. "Commercialisme militaire sans éthique et sans frontières." In S. Marysse and F. Reyntjens, eds., *L'Afrique des Grands Lacs (2000–2001),* 333–364. Paris: L'Harmattan, 2001.

Digekisa, P. *Le massacre de Lubumbashi.* Paris: L'Harmattan, 1993.

Doom, R., and J. Gorus, eds. *Politics of Identity and Economics of Conflict in the Great Lakes Region.* Brussels: VUB University Press, 2000.

Dorier-Apprill, E. "Guerre des milices et fragmentation urbaine à Brazzaville." *Hérodote,* 4th quarter, no. 86/87 (1997): 182–221.

Dorier-Apprill, E., et al. *Vivre à Brazzaville: Modernité et crise au quotidien.* Paris: Karthala, 1998.

Dorlodot, Ph. de. *Marche d'espoir: Kinshasa, 16 février 1992.* Paris: L'Harmattan, 1994

———. *Les réfugiés rwandais à Bukavu au Zaïre: De nouveaux Palestiniens?* Paris: L'Harmattan, 1996.

Douglas, M. *Purity and Danger.* London: Routledge and Kegan Paul, 1967.

Dumont, R. *False Start in Africa.* London: Deutsch, 1966.

Dumoulin, A. *La France militaire et l'Afrique.* Brussels: GRIP/Editions Complexe, 1997.

Dungia, E. *Mobutu et l'argent du Zaïre.* Paris: L'Harmattan, 1993.

Dupont, P. "La communauté internationale face à l'intervention humanitaire lors de la rébellion (octobre–novembre 1996)." In S. Marysse and F. Reyntjens, eds., *L'Afrique des Grands Lacs: Annuaire 1996–1997,* 205–220. Paris: L'Harmattan, 1997.

Easterly, W. *The White Man's Burden: Why the West's Efforts to Aid the Rest of the World Have Done So Much Ill and So Little Good.* Oxford: Oxford University Press, 2006.

Eltringham, N. "The Institutional Aspect of the Rwandan Church." In D. Goyvaerts, ed., *Conflict and Ethnicity in Central Africa,* 225–250. Tokyo: Institute for the Study of Languages and Cultures of Asia and Africa, 2000.

———. *Accounting for Horror: Post-Genocide Debates in Rwanda.* London: Pluto Press, 2004.

Failly, D. de. "Coltan: Pour comprendre." In S. Marysse and F. Reyntjens, eds., *L'Afrique des Grands Lacs (2000–2001),* 279–306. Paris: L'Harmattan, 2001.

Fairhead, J. "Paths of Authority: Roads, the State and the Market in Eastern Zaire." *European Journal of Development Research* 4, no. 2 (December 1992): 17–35.

Ferrari, A., and L. Scalettari. *Storie de ordinario genocidio: La guerra del Kivu.* Bologna: Editrice Missionaria Italiana, 1997.

Ferreira, M. E. "La reconversion économique de la *Nomenklatura* pétrolière en Angola." *Politique Africaine,* no. 57 (March 1995): 11–26.

Franche, D. "Généalogie du génocide rwandais. Hutu et Tutsi: Gaulois et Francs?" *Les Temps Modernes,* June 1995, 1–58.

———. *Rwanda, généalogie d'un génocide.* Paris: Mille et Une Nuits, 1997.

French, H. W. *A Continent for the Taking: The Tragedy and Hope of Africa.* New York: Vintage Books, 2005.

Fusaschi, M. *Hutu-Tutsi, alle radici del genocidio rwandese.* Torino: Bollati-Boringhieri, 2000.

Galvez, W. *Che in Africa: Guevara's Congo Diary.* Melbourne: Ocean Press, 1999.

Gasana, J. K. *Rwanda: Du parti-état à l'état garnison.* Paris: L'Harmattan, 2002.

Gaud, M. "Rwanda: Le génocide de 1994." *Afrique Contemporaine,* no. 174 (April–June 1995).

Gaud, M., ed. *Du Zaïre au Congo.* Special Issue of *Afrique Contemporaine,* no. 183 (July–September 1997) [with articles by Roland Pourtier, Robert Giraudon, Marc Le Pape, Michel Gaud, and Laurence Porgès.]

Gervais, J. B. *Kabila, chronique d'une débâcle annoncée.* Villeurbanne, France: Golias, 1999.

Gibbs, D. N. *The Political Economy of Third-World Intervention: Mines, Money and U.S. Policy in the Congo Crisis.* Chicago: University of Chicago Press, 1991.

Godding, J. P.*Réfugiés rwandais au Zaire.* Paris: L'Harmattan, 1997.

Goossens, Ch. "Political Instability in Congo-Zaire: Ethno-Regionalism in Katanga." In R. Doom and J. Gorus, eds., *Politics of Identity and Economics of Conflict in the Great Lakes Region,* 243–262. Brussels: VUB Press, 2000.

Gorus, J. "Ethnic Violence in Katanga." In D. Goyvaerts, ed., *Conflict and Ethnicity in Central Africa,* 105–126. Tokyo: Institute for the Study of Languages and Cultures of Asia and Africa, 2000.

Gourevitch, Ph. "The Poisoned Country." *New York Review of Books,* June 6, 1996.

———. "Neighborhood Bully: How Genocide Revived President Mobutu." *New Yorker,* September 9, 1996.

———. *We Wish to Inform You That Tomorrow We Will Be Killed with Our Families.* New York: Farrar, Straus and Giroux, 1998.

Gouteux, J. P. *Un génocide secret d'état: La France et le Rwanda 1990–1997.* Paris: Editions Sociales, 1998.

———. *Le Monde, un contre-pouvoir? Désinformation et manipulation sur le génocide rwandais.* Paris: L'Esprit Frappeur, 1999.

———. *La nuit rwandaise: L'implication française dans le dernier génocide du siècle.* Paris: L'Esprit Frappeur, 2002.

Gowing, N. "Dispatches from Disaster Zones: The Reporting of Humanitarian Emergencies." Paper presented at ECHO Conference, London. May 27–28, 1998.

Gribbin, R. E. *In the Aftermath of Genocide: The U.S. Role in Rwanda.* Universe Com. Inc., 2005.

Guevara, E. *The African Dream: The Diaries of the Revolutionnary War in the Congo.* London: Harvill Press, 2000.

Guichaoua, A., ed. *Exilés, réfugiés et déplacés en Afrique Centrale et Orientale.* Paris: Karthala, 2004.

Hakizimana, D. *Burundi: Le non-dit.* Vernier, Switzerland: Editions Remesha, 1991.

Hall, R. *My Life with Tiny: A Biography of Tiny Rowlands.* London: Faber and Faber, 1987.

Harbeson, J. W. "Externally Assisted Democratization: Theoretical Issues and African Realities." In J. W. Harbeson and D. Rothchild, eds., *Africa in World Politics: The African State System in Flux,* 235–262. Boulder, CO: Westview Press, 2000.

Harding, J. *Small Wars, Small Mercies.* London: Penguin, 1994.

Hatungimana et al. *L'arméee burundaise et les institutions démocratiques.* Brussels: Privately printed, 1994.

Hatzfeld, J. *In the Quick of Life.* London: Serpent's Tail, 2005.

———. *A Time for Machetes.* London: Serpent's Tail, 2005.

Hawkins, T. "Le déclin économique du Zimbabwe: À qui la faute?" *Afrique Contemporaine,* no. 197 (January–March 2001): 47–63.

Herbst, J. "Western and African Peacekeepers: Motives and Opportunities." In J. W. Harbeson and D. Rothchild, eds., *Africa in World Politics: The African State System in Flux,* 308–323. Boulder, CO: Westview Press, 2000.

———. *States and Power in Africa: Comparative Lessons in Authority and Control.* Princeton, NJ: Princeton University Press, 2000.

Hiernaux, J. "Note sur les Tutsi de l'Itombwe." *Bulletin et Mémoires de la Société d'Anthropologie de Paris,* series 19, no. 7 (1965): 361–379.

Hodges, A. *Angola, from Afro-Stalinism to Petro-Diamond Capitalism.* Oxford: James Currey, 2001.

Hoyveghen, S. van. "The Disintegration of the Catholic Church in Rwanda: A Study of the Fragmentation of Political and Religious Authority." *African Affairs,* no. 95 (1996): 379–401.

———. *From Humanitarian Disaster to Development Success? The Case of Rwanda.* Centre for Development Studies Working Paper, University of Leeds. March 2000.

Ingelaere, B. "Changing Lenses and Contextualizing the Rwandan Post-Genocide." In F. Reyntjens and S. Maryssè, eds., *L'Afrique des Grands Lacs: Annuaire 2005–2006. Dix ans de transitions conflicturelles,* 389–414. Paris: L'Harmattan, 2006.

Jackson, S. "Nos richesses sont pillées: Economies de guerre et rumeurs de crime au Kivu." *Politique Africaine,* no. 84 (December 2001): 136–146.

Jean, F., and J. C. Rufin, eds. *Economie des guerres civiles.* Paris: Hachette, 1996.

Jefremovas, V. *Brickyards to Graveyards: From Production to Genocide in Rwanda.* Albany: State University of New York Press, 2002.

Jewsiewicki, B., ed. *Zaïre.* Special issue of *Canadian Journal of African Studies* 18, no. 1 (1984) [with articles by Catharine Newbury, Benoit Verhaegen, George Nzongola-Ntalaja, Jean-Claude Willame, Bogumil Jewsiewicki, Wamba Dia Wamba, René Lemarchand].

————. "The Formation of the Political Culture of Ethnicity in the Belgian Congo." In L. Vail, ed., *The Creation of Tribalism in Southern Africa,* 324–349. Berkeley: University of California Press, 1989.

————. *Naitre et mourir au Zaïre.* Paris: Karthala, 1993.

Kabagema, E. *Carnage d'une nation: Génocide et massacres au Rwanda (1994).* Paris: L'Harmattan, 2001.

Kabamba Nkamany, V. *Pouvoirs et idéologies tribales au Zaïre.* Paris: L'Harmattan, 1997.

Kabulo, J. "Fuir la guerre au Kivu." *Politique Africaine,* no. 84 (December 2001): 86–102.

Kabuya Kalala, F., and Tshiunza Mbiye. "L'économie congolaise en 2000–2001: Contraction, fractionnement et enlisement." In S. Marysse and F. Reyntjens, eds., *L'Afrique des Grands Lacs (2000–2001),* 175–194. Paris: L'Harmattan, 2001.

————. "La politique économique revisitée en RDC: Pesanteurs d'hier et perspectives." In F. Reyntjens and S. Marysse, eds., *L'Afrique des Grands Lacs: Annuaire 2005–2006. Dix ans de transitions conflicturelles,* 307–326. Paris: L'Harmattan, 2006.

Kajiga, G. "Cette immigration séculaire des ruandais au Congo." *Bulletin Trimestriel du Centre d'Etudes des Problèmes Sociaux Indigènes,* no. 32 (1956): 5–64.

Karemano, C. *Au-delà des barrières: Dans les méandres du drame rwandais.* Paris: L'Harmattan, 2003.

Katzenellenbogen, S. E. *Railways and the Copper Mines of Katanga.* Oxford: Clarendon Press, 1973.

Kayimahe, V. *France-Rwanda, les coulisses du génocide: Témoignage d'un rescapé.* Paris: Dagorno, 2002.

Keen, D. *The Economic Functions of Violence in Civil Wars.* Adelphi Paper 320. London, 1998.

Kennes, E. "La guerre au Congo." In F. Reyntjens and S. Marysse, eds., *L'Afrique des Grands Lacs: Annuaire 1997–1998,* 231–272. Paris: L'Harmattan, 1998.

————. "L. D. Kabila: A Biographical Essay." In D. Goyvaerts, ed., *Conflict and Ethnicity in Central Africa,* 127–153. Tokyo: Institute for the Study of Languages and Cultures of Asia and Africa, 2000.

————. "Laurent-Désiré Kabila (1939–2001): Un espoir déçu?" *Afrique Contemporaine,* no. 197 (January–March 2001): 31–33.

————. "Le secteur minier au Congo: 'Déconnexion' et descente aux enfers." In F. Reyntjens and S. Marysse, eds., *L'Afrique des Grands Lacs: Annuaire 1999–2000,* 299–342. Paris: L'Harmattan, 2000.

———. *Eassai biographique sur Laurent-Désiré Kabila.* Tervuren, Belgium: CEDAF, 2003.

Kent, R. "The Integrated Operations Centre in Rwanda: Coping with Complexity." In J. Witman and D. Pecock, eds., *After Rwanda: The Coordination of United Nations Humanitarian Assistance,* 63–85. London: Macmillan, 1996.

Khadiagala, G. M. *Security Dynamics in Africa's Great Lakes Region.* Boulder, CO: Lynne Rienner, 2006.

Kisangani, E. F. "Confronting Leaders at the Apex of the State: The Growth of the Unofficial Economy in the Congo." *African Studies Review* 41, no. 1 (April 1998): 99–137.

———. "The Massacre of Refugees in the Congo: A Case of UN Peacekeeping Failure and International Law." *Journal of Modern African Studies* 38, no. 2 163–202.

Kisukula Abeli Meitho. *La désintégration de l'armée congolaise de Mobutu à Kabila.* Paris: L'Harmattan, 2001.

Kleine-Ahlbrandt, S. T. E. *The Protection Gap. The Protection of Internally Displaced Persons: The Case of Rwanda.* Geneva: Institut Universitaire des Hautes Etudes Internationales, 1996.

Koula, Y. *La démocratie congolaise brûlée au pétrole.* Paris: L'Harmattan, 1999.

———. *Pétrole et violences au Congo Brazzaville.* Paris: L'Harmattan, 2006.

Kuperman, A. J. "Rwanda in Retrospect." *Foreign Affairs,* January–February 2000, 94–118.

———. *Genocide in Rwanda: The Limits of Humanitarian Intervention.* Washington, DC: Brookings Institution, 2001.

———. "Provoking Genocide: A Revised History of the Rwandan Patriotic Front." *Journal of Genocide Research* 6, no. 1 (March 2004): 61–84.

Lame, D. de. *A Hill among a Thousand: Transformations and Ruptures in Rural Rwanda.* Madison: University of Wisconsin Press, 2005.

Lancaster, C. "Africa in World Affairs." In J. W. Harbeson and D. Rothchild, eds., *Africa in World Politics: The African State System in Flux,* 208–234. Boulder, CO: Westview Press, 2000.

Lanning, G. *Africa Undermined: Mining Companies and the Underdevelopment of Africa.* London: Penguin Books, 1979.

Lanotte, O. *Congo: Guerres sans frontières.* Brussels: GRIP, 2003.

———. *La France au Rwanda (1990–1994).* Pieterlen, Switzerland: Peter Lang Verlag, 2007.

Lanotte, O., C. Roosens, and C. Clement, eds. *La Belgique et l'Afrique Centrale de 1960 à nos jours.* Brussels: GRIP, 2000.

LeBor, A. *Complicity with Evil: The United Nations in the Age of Modern Genocide.* New Haven, CT: Yale University Press, 2008.

Lecompte, D. "Une ville africaine dans la tourmente: La guerre à Bujumbura." *Afrique Contemporaine,* 4th trimester (1996): 160–172.

———. "Burundi: Conséquences géo-économiques des guerres civiles." In *L'Afrique Politique 1997,* 55–84. Paris: Karthala, 1997.

Leloup, B. "Le Rwanda dans la géopolitique régionale." In S. Marysse and F. Reyntjens, eds., *L'Afrique des Grands Lacs (2000–2001),* 75–94. Paris: L'Harmattan, 2001.

Lemarchand, R. *Rwanda and Burundi.* London: Pall Mall Press, 1970.

———. *Burundi: Ethnocide as Discourse and Practice.* Cambridge, UK: Cambridge University Press, 1994.

———. "Patterns of State Collapse and Reconstruction in Central Africa." *Afrika Spectrum,* no. 32 (1997): 173–193.

———. "Genocide in the Great Lakes: Which Genocide? Whose Genocide?" *African Studies Review* 41, no. 1 (April 1998): 3–16.

———. "The Fire in the Great Lakes." *Current History* 98, no. 628 (May 1999): 195–201.

———. "La politique des Etats-Unis dans l'Afrique des Grands Lacs." In S.Marysse and F. Reyntjens, eds., *L'Afrique des Grands Lacs (1998–1999),* 355–369. Paris: L'Harmattan, 1999.

———. "Aux sources de la crise des Grands Lacs.» *Dialogue,* no. 218 (September–October 2000).

———. "Pour dissiper les malentendus sur le génocide.» *Dialogue,* no. 227 (March–April 2002).

———. "The Crisis in the Great Lakes." In J. W. Harbeson and D. Rothchild, eds., *Africa in World Politics: The African State System in Flux,* 324–352. Boulder, CO: Westview Press, 2000.

———. "Hate Crimes." *Transition,* no. 81/82 (2000): 114–132.

———. "The Democratic Republic of the Congo: From Failure to Potential Reconstruction." In Robert I. Rotberg, ed., *State Failure and State Weakness in a Time of Terror,* 29–69. Washington, DC: Brookings Institution Press, 2003.

———. "The Geopolitics of the Great Lakes Crisis." In F. Reyntjens and S. Marysse, eds., *L'Afrique des Grands Lacs: Annuaire 2005–2006. Dix ans de transitions conflicturelles,* 25–54. Paris: L'Harmattan, 2006.

Le Pape, M. "L'exportation des massacres du Rwanda au Congo-Zaïre." *Esprit,* nos. 266–267 (August–September 2000): 162–169.

Leslie, W. J. *Zaire: Continuity and Change in an Oppressive State.* Boulder, CO: Westview Press, 1993.

Leys, C. *The Rise and Fall of Development Theory.* Oxford: James Currey, 1996.

Loanda, G. de. "La longue marche de l'UNITA jusqu'à Luanda." *Politique Africaine,* no. 57 (March 1995): 63–70.

Longman, T. P. "Christianity and Democratisation in Rwanda: Assessing Church Response to Political Crisis in the 1990s." In Paul Gifford, ed., *The Christian Churches and the Democratisation of Africa*, 188–204. Leiden: E. J. Brill, 1995.

———. "Empowering the Weak and Protecting the Powerful: The Contradictory Nature of Churches in Central Africa." *African Studies Review* 41, no. 1 (April 1998): 49–72.

———. "Church Politics and the Genocide in Rwanda." *Journal of Religion in Africa* 31, no. 2 (2001): 163–186.

Lubala Mugisho, E. "Interventions militaires au Kivu: Prevention de genocide ou voie de puissance?" In S. Marysse and F. Reyntjens, eds., *L'Afrique des Grands Lacs (1998–1999)*, 284–308. Paris: L'Harmattan, 1999.

———. "La contre-résistance dans la zone d'occupation rwandaise au Kivu (1996–2001)." In S. Marysse and F. Reyntjens, eds., *L'Afrique des Grands Lacs (2000–2001)*, 251–278. Paris: L'Harmattan, 2001.

Lugan, B. *François Mitterrand, l'armée française et le Rwanda.* Paris: Editions du Rocher, 2005.

———. *Rwanda: Contre-enquête sur le génocide.* Paris: Editions Privat, 2006.

MacGaffey, J. *The Real Economy of Zaire.* London: James Currey, 1991.

Maier, K. *Angola: Promises and Lies.* London: Serif, 1996.

Maindo Mnga Ngonga, A. "Survivre à la guerre des autres: Un défi populaire en RDC." *Politique Africaine,* no. 84 (December 2001): 33–58.

Malan, M., and J. Gomes Porto, eds. *Challenges of Peace Implementation: The UN Mission in the Democratic Republic of the Congo.* Pretoria: Institute for Security Studies, 2004.

Malkki, L. H. *Purity and Exile: Violence Memory and National Cosmology among Hutu Refugees in Tanzania.* Chicago: University of Chicago Press, 1995.

Mamdani, M. *When Victims Become Killers: Colonialism, Nativism and the Genocide in Rwanda.* Princeton, NJ: Princeton University Press, 2001.

Manning, C. "The Collapse of Peace in Angola." *Current History* 98, no. 628 (May 1999): 208–212.

Maquet, J. J. "Les pasteurs de l'Itombwe." *Science et Nature,* no. 8 (March–April 1955): 3–12.

Marysse, S. "Balbutiements de la 'Renaissance Africaine' ou somalisation?" In S. Marysse and F. Reyntjens, eds., *L'Afrique des Grands Lacs (1998–1999)*, 309–335. Paris: L'Harmattan, 1999.

Marysse, S., and C. André. "Guerre et pillage en République Démocratique du Congo." In S. Marysse and F. Reyntjens, eds., *L'Afrique des Grands Lacs (2000–2001)*, 307–332. Paris: L'Harmattan, 2001.

Mathieu, P., and A. Mafikiri Tsongo. "Guerres paysannes au Nord Kivu (1937–1994)." *Cahiers d'Etudes Africaines* 38, nos. 2–4 (1998): 385–416.

Mathieu, P., A. Mafikiri Tsongo, and J. C. Willame, eds. *Conflits et guerres au Kivu et dans la région des Grands Lacs.* Brussels: CEDAF, 1999.

Maton, J. "Congo 1997–1998: Évolution de la situation macro-économique et perspectives." In S. Marysse and F. Reyntjens, eds., *L'Afrique des Grands Lacs (1998–1999)*, 180–200. Paris: L'Harmattan, 1999.

May, J. F. "Policies on Population, Land Use and Environment in Rwanda." *Population and Environment* 16, no. 4 (March 1995): 321–334.

———. "Pression démographique et politiques de population au Rwanda (1962–1994)." *Population et Sociétés*, no. 319 (December 1996).

Mbavu Muhindo, V. *Le Congo-Zaïre d'une guerre à l'autre, de libération en occupation (1996–1999).* Paris: L'Harmattan, 2003.

———. *La RD Congo piégée: De Lusaka à l'AGI (1999–2005).* Paris: L'Harmattan, 2005.

Médard, J. F. "The Underdeveloped State in Tropical Africa: Political Clientelism or Neo-Patrimonialism?" In C. Clapham, ed., *Private Patronage and Public Power: Political Clientelism in the Modern State*, 162–192. London: Frances Pinter, 1982.

———. "L'état néo-patrimonial en Afrique Noire." In *Etats d'Afrique Noire*, 323–353. Paris: Karthala, 1991.

Mehdi Ba. *Rwanda 1994, un génocide français.* Paris: L'Esprit Frappeur, 1997.

Melvern, L. R. *A People Betrayed: The Role of the West in Rwanda's Genocide.* London: Zed Books, 2000.

———. *Conspiracy to Murder: The Rwandan Genocide.* New York: Verso, 2004.

Meredith, M. *Our Votes, Our Guns: Robert Mugabe and the Tragedy of Zimbabwe.* Washington, DC: Perseus Books, 2002.

———. *The State of Africa: A History of Fifty Years of Independence.* London: Free Press, 2005.

Messiant, C. "Angola: Les voies de l'ethnisation et de la décomposition (1975–1991)." Part 1, *Lusotopie.* no. 1/2 (1994): 155–210.

———. "Angola: Les voies de l'ethnisation et de la décomposition (1975–1991)." Part 2, *Lusotopie*, no. 3 (1995): 181–212.

———. "Angola entre guerre et paix." In R. Marchal and C. Messiant, eds., *Les chemins de la guerre et de la paix*, 156–208. Paris: Karthala, 1997.

———. "Angola: Une 'victoire' sans fin?" *Politique Africaine*, no. 81 (March 2001): 143–162.

Miles, W. F. S. "Post-Genocide Survivorship in Rwanda." *Bridges.* Fall–Winter, 2002.

Misser, F. *Vers un nouveau Rwanda: Entretiens avec Paul Kagame.* Brussels: Luc Pire, 1995.

Moghalu, K. *Rwanda's Genocide: The Politics of Gobal Justice.* New York. Palgrave, 2005.

Monnier, L., B. Jewsiewicki, and G. De Villers, eds. *Chasse au diamant au Congo/Zaire.* Tervuren, Belgium: CEDAF, 2001.

M'Poyo Kasa-Vubu, J. *Douze mois chez Kabila.* Brussels: Le Cri, 1999.

Mujawamariya, M. "Rapport d'une visite effectuée au Rwanda." September 1994.

Mukagasana, Y. *La mort ne veut pas de moi.* Paris: Documents Fixot, 1997.

———. *N'aie pas peur de savoir.* Paris: Robert Laffont, 1999.

———. *Les blessures du silence.* Arles: Actes Sud, 2001.

Mukendi, G., and B. Kasonga. *Kabila, le retour du Congo.* Ottignies, Belgium: Quorum, 1997.

Mukeshimana Ngulinzira, F. *Boniface Ngulinzira, un autre Rwanda possible.* Paris: L'Harmattan, 2001.

Mungbalemwe Koyame, with John F. Clark. "The Economic Impact of the Congo War." In John F. Clark, ed., *The African Stakes of the Congo War,* 101–223. New York: Palgrave/Macmillan, 2002.

Musabyimana, G. *La vraie nature du FPR/APR d'Ouganda en Rwanda.* Paris: L'Harmattan, 2003.

Mushikiwabo, L., with J. Kramer. *Rwanda Means the Universe: A Native Memoir of Blood and Bloodlines.* New York: St. Martin's Press, 2006.

Mutamba Lukusa, G. *Congo/Zaire: La faillite d'un pays. Déséquilibre macro-économique et ajustement (1988–1999).* Brussels: CEDAF, 1999.

Mutambo, J. *Les Banyamulenge.* Kinshasa, DRC: Imprimerie Saint Paul, 1997.

Muyambo Kyassa, J. C. *La réalité Katangaise.* Johannesburg: Bureau Ed., [2006].

Mwamba Tshibangu. *Joseph Kabila: La vérité étouffée.* Paris: L'Harmattan, 2005.

Naipaul, V. S. "A New King for the Congo: Mobutu and the Nihilism of Africa." *New York Review of Books,* June 26, 1975.

Ndahayo, E. *Rwanda: Le dessous des cartes.* Paris: L'Harmattan, 2001.

Ndarishikanye, B. "Les rapports état-paysannerie au centre du conflit ethnique au Burundi." *Cahiers d'Etudes Africaines* 38, nos. 2–4 (1998): 347–384.

Ndaywel è Nziem, I. "La société zaïroise dans le miroir de son discours religieux." *Cahiers du CEDAF,* no. 6 (1993).

———. *Histoire générale du Congo.* Brussels: Duculot, 1998.

———. "Du Congo des rébellions au Zaïre des pillages." *Cahiers d'Etudes Africaines* 38, nos. 2–4 (1998): 417–440.

Ndeshyo-Rurihose, O. *La nationalité de la population zaïroise d'origine kinyar-wanda au regard de la loi du 29 juin 1981.* Kinshasa, DRC: CERIA, 1992. Reprinted in *Dialogue,* no. 192 (August–September 1996): 3–32.

Ndikumana, L. "Institutional Failure and Ethnic Conflict in Burundi." *African Studies Review* 41, no. 1 (April 1998): 29–47.

Nduwayo, L. *Giti et le genocide rwandais.* Paris: L'Harmattan, 2002.

Nest, M. "Ambitions, Profits and Loss: Zimbabwean Economic Involvement in the Democratic Republic of the Congo." *African Affairs* 100, no. 400 (July 2001): 469–490.

Nest, M., F. Grignon, and E. F. Kisangani. *The Democratic Republic of the Congo: Economic Dimensions of War and Peace.* Boulder, CO: Lynne Riener, 2006.

Newbury, C. "Ethnicity and the Politics of History in Rwanda." *Africa Today* 45, no. 1 (1998): 7–24.

Newbury, D. "Understanding Genocide." *African Studies Review* 41, no. 1 (April 1998): 73–97.

Ngabu, F. "Les massacres de 1993 dans les zones de Walikale et de Masisi." *Dialogue,* no. 192 (August–September 1996): 37–46.

Ngaruko, F., and J. D. Nkurunziza. "An Economic Interpretation of the Conflict in Burundi." *Journal of African Economics* 9, no. 3 (2000).

N'Gbanda Nzambo Ko Atumba, H. *Les derniers jours du Maréchal Mobutu.* Paris: Editions Gideppe, 1998.

———. *Crimes organisés en Afrique Centrale: Révélations sur les réseaux rwandais et occidentaux.* Paris: Editions Duboiris, 2004.

Nguya-Ndila Malengana, C. *Nationalité et citoyenneté au Congo: Kinshasa.* Paris: L'Harmattan, 2001.

Niwese, M. *Le peuple rwandais, un pied dans la tombe.* Paris: L'Harmattan, 2001.

N'Sanda Buleli, L. "Le Maniema, de la guerre de l'AFDL à la guerre du RCD." *Politique Africaine,* no. 84 (December 2001): 59–74.

Nsanze, A. *Le Burundi contemporain: L'état-nation en question (1956–2002).* Paris: L'Harmattan, 2003.

Nzongola-Ntalaja, G. "Les classes sociales et la révolution anti-coloniale au Congo: Le rôle de la bourgeoisie." *Cahiers Economiques et Sociaux* 8 (1970): 371–388.

———, ed. *The Crisis in Zaire: Myths and Realities.* Trenton, NJ: Africa World Press, 1986.

———. *From Zaire to the Democratic Republic of the Congo.* Uppsala, Sweden: Nordiska Afrikainstitutet, 1998.

———. *The Congo, from Leopold to Kabila: A People's History.* London: Zed Books, 2001.

Odom, Th. *Journey into Darness: Genocide in Rwanda.* Austin: University of Texas Press, 2005.

Off, C. *The Lion, the Fox and the Eagle.* Toronto: Random House, 2000.

Ogata, S. *The Turbulent Decade: Confronting the Refugee Crises of the 1990s.* New York: Norton, 2005.

Okoko-Esseau, A. "The Christian Churches and Democratisation in Congo." In Paul Gifford, ed., *The Christian Churches and the Democratisation of Africa,* 148–167. Leiden: E. J. Brill, 1995.

Omasombo, J., and E. Kennes. *Biographies des acteurs de la transition (juin 2003–juin 2006).* Kinshasa, DRC: CEP, 2006.

Onana, C. *Les secrets de la justice internationale: Enquêtes truquées sur le génocide rwandais.* Paris: Editions Duboiris, 2005.

Ottaway, M. "Post-Imperial Africa at War." *Current History* 98, no. 628 (May 1999): 202–207.

Ould Abdallah, A. *La diplomatie pyromane.* Paris: Calmann-Lévy, 1996.

———. *Burundi on the Brink (1993–1995): A UN Special Envoy Reflects on Preventive Diplomacy.* Washington, DC: United States Institute for Peace, 2000.

Pabanel, J. P. "La question de la nationalité au Kivu." *Politique Africaine,* no. 41 (March 1991): 32–40.

Parqué V., and F. Reyntjens. "Crimes contre l'humanité dans l'ex-Zaïre: Une réalité?" In F. Reyntjens and S. Marysse, eds., *L'Afrique des Grands Lacs: Annuaire 1997–1998,* 273–306. Paris: L'Harmattan, 1998.

Patry, D. *Face-à-face avec un génocide.* Paris: Flammarion, 2006.

Péan; P. *Noires fureurs, Blancs menteurs: Rwanda 1990–1994.* Paris: Mille et une Nuits, 2005.

Périès, G., and D. Servenay. *Une guerre noire: Enquête sur les origines du génocide rwandais.* Paris: La Découverte, 2006.

Ploquin, J. F. "Dialogue intercongolais: La société civile au pied du mur." *Politique Africaine,* no. 84 (December 2001): 136–146.

Ploquin, J. F., and P. Rosenblum, eds. *Zaïre 1992–1996: Chronique d'une transition inachevée.* 2 vols. Paris: L'Harmattan, 1996.

Poincaré, N. *Gabriel Maindron, un prêtre dans la tragédie.* Paris: Les Editions Ouvrières, 1995.

Polman, L. "The Problem Outside." *Granta,* no. 67 (September 1999): 219–240.

Pottier, J. "Relief and Repatriation: Views by Rwandan Refugees and Lessons for Humanitarian Aid Workers." *African Affairs,* no. 95 (1996): 403–429.

———. "The 'Self' in Self-Repatriation: Closing Down Mugunga Camp, Eastern Zaire." In Richard Black and Khalid Khoser, eds., *The End of the*

Refugee Cycle? Refugee Repatriation and Reconstruction, 142–170. Oxford: Berghahn, 1999.

———. *Re-imagining Rwanda: Conflict, Survival and Disinformation in the Late Twentieth Century.* Cambridge, UK: Cambridge University Press, 2002.

Pottier, J., and J. Fairhead. "Post-Famine Recovery in Highland Bwisha, Zaire." *Africa* 61, no. 4 (1991).

Pouligny, B. *Peace Operations Seen from Below: UN Missions and Local People.* London: Hurst, 2006.

Pourtier, R. "La guerre au Kivu: Un conflit multidimensionnel." *Afrique Contemporaine,* 4th quarter (1996): 15–38.

———. "Congo-Zaïre-Congo: Un itinéraire géopolitique au cœur de l'Afrique." *Hérodote,* 4th quarter, no. 86/87 (1997): 6–41.

———. "Brazzaville 1997: Les raisons d'une guerre incivile." *Afrique Contemporaine,* no. 186 (April–June 1998): 7–32.

———, ed. "Afrique Centrale." Special Issue of *Afrique Contemporaine,* no. 215 (2005) [with texts by R. Pourtier, J. Damon, G. de Villers, B. Leloup, T. Vircoulon, and M. A. Lagrange].

Power, S. "Bystanders to the Genocide." *Atlantic Monthly,* September 2001.

———. *A Problem from Hell: America and the Age of Genocide.* New York: Basic Books, 2002.

Prunier, G. *Burundi: Descent into Chaos or Manageable Crisis?* Writenet UK, March 1995. [Other reports on Burundi were written in August 1995, February 1996, and June 1996.]

———. "Conflict in the Great Lakes and the International Community." Paper presented at the IPPR Conference on European Union Policy towards Potential Regions of Migration, London. January 19–20, 1996.

———. "The Great Lakes Crisis." *Current History* 96, no. 610 (May 1997): 193–199.

———. "Rwanda, the Social, Political and Economic Situation in June 1997." Geneva. Writenet. July 1997. [Other reports on Rwanda were written in April, August, October, and December 1995, March 1996, and February 1998.]

———. "La crise du Kivu et ses conséquences dans la région des Grands Lacs." *Hérodote,* 4th quarter, no. 86/87 (1997): 42–56.

———. "Rwanda: La mort d'un juste." *Libération,* June 16, 1998.

———. "Une poudrière au cœur du Congo-Kinshasa." *Le Monde Diplomatique,* July 1998.

———. "The Rwandan Patriotic Front." In Christopher Clapham, ed., *African Guerrillas,* 119–133. Oxford: James Currey, 1998.

————. "Grands Lacs: Les clés d'une guerre sans fin." *Politique Internationale,* no. 82 (January 1999): 364–376.

————. "Ein Krieg von kontinentalem Ausmass." *Der Überblick* 35, no. 2 (June 1999): 31–36.

————. *Les conversations de paix sur le Burundi à Arusha.* Report to the French Ministry of Foreign Affairs, July 1999.

————. "L'Ouganda et les guerres congolaises." *Politique Africaine,* no. 75 (October 1999): 43–59.

————. "Congo-Kinshasa: La première guerre inter-africaine." *Géopolitique Africaine,* no. 1 (Winter 2000–2001): 127–149.

————. "The Catholic Church and the Kivu Conflict." *Journal of Religion in Africa* 31, no. 2 (2001): 139–162.

————. "Africa, el continente perdido." *Letras Libres* [Mexico], 4, no. 43 (July 2002): 42–46.

————. "The Tall and the Short: How Colonial Rule Brought Death to the Lakeside." Review essay on Jean-Pierre Chrétien's *Great Lakes of Africa. Times Litterary Supplement,* August 8, 2003.

————. "Les Grands Lacs ont-ils coulé jusqu'en Afrique Centrale?" *Enjeux,* no. 17 (October–December 2003): 11–14.

————. "Rebel Movements and Proxy Warfare: Uganda, Sudan and the Congo (1986–1999)." *African Affairs* 103, no. 412 (2004): 359–383.

————. "The Economic Dimensions of Conflict in the Region." In Gilbert M. Khadiagala, ed., *Security Dynamics in Africa's Great Lakes Region,* 103–120. Boulder, CO: Lynne Rienner, 2006.

————. "The 'Ethnic' Conflict in Ituri District." In J. P. Chrétien and R. Banegas, eds., *The Recurring Great Lakes Crisis,* 180–204. London: Hurst, 2007

Rafti, M. "Rwandan Hutu Rebels in Congo/Zaire: An Extra-territorial War in a Weak State?" In F. Reyntjens and S. Marysse, eds., *L'Afrique des Grands Lacs: Annuaire 2005–2006. Dix ans de transitions conflicturelles,* 55–83. Paris: L'Harmattan, 2006.

Reno, W. "Africa's Weak States, Non-State Actors and the Privatization of Interstate Relations." In J. W. Harbeson and D. Rothchild, eds., *Africa in World Politics: The African State System in Flux,* 286–307. Boulder, CO: Westview Press, 2000.

Reyntjens, F. *Rwanda: Trois jours qui ont fait basculer l'histoire.* Paris: L'Harmattan, 1995.

————. "La rébellion du Congo-Zaïre: Une affaire de voisins." *Hérodote,* 4th quarter, no. 86/87 (1997): 57–77.

————. *Talking or Fighting: Political Evolution in Rwanda and Burundi 1998–1999.* Uppsala, Sweden: Nordiska Afrikainstitutet, 1999.

————. *La guerre des Grands Lacs.* Paris: L'Harmattan, 1999.

————. "Evolution politique au Rwanda et au Burundi." In S. Marysse and F. Reyntjens, eds., *L'Afrique des Grands Lacs 1998–1999,* 124–158. Paris: L'Harmattan, 1999.

————. "Chronique politique au Rwanda et au Burundi 2000–2001." In S. Marysse and F. Reyntjens, eds., *L'Afrique des Grands Lacs (2000–2001),* 21–52. Paris: L'Harmattan, 2001.

————. "Les transitions politiques au Rwanda et au Burundi." In F. Reyntjens and S. Marysse, eds., *L'Afrique des Grands Lacs: Annuaire 2005–2006. Dix ans de transitions conflicturelles,* 3–23. Paris: L'Harmattan, 2006.

Rist, G., ed. *Les mots du pouvoir: Sens et non-sens de la rhétorique internationale.* Geneva: Cahiers de l'IUED, 2002.

Rittner, C., J. Roth, and W. Whitworth, eds. *Genocide in Rwanda: The Complicity of the Churches.* New York: Paragon House, 2004.

Rombouts, H. "Organisation des victimes au Rwanda: le cas d'Ibuka." In S. Marysse and F. Reyntjens, eds., *L'Afrique des Grands Lacs (2000–2001),* 123–142. Paris: L'Harmattan, 2001.

Rosenblum, P. "Endgame in Zaire." *Current History* 96, no. 610 (May 1997): 200–205.

Rothchild, D. "The Impact of U.S. Disengagement on African Intrastate Conflict Resolution." In J. W. Harbeson and D. Rothchild, eds., *Africa in World Politics: The African State System in Flux,* 160–187. Boulder, CO: Westview Press, 2000.

Rozes, P. "Un pays en deshérence et au bord de la guerre totale: L'Angola (1994–1998)." In *L'Afrique Politique 1999,* 179–199. Paris: Karthala, 1999.

————. "L'Angola d'une impasse à l'autre: Chronique d'une guerre sans issue (1998–2001)." *Afrique Contemporaine,* no. 197 (January–March 2001): 76–96.

Ruhimbika, M. *Les Banyamulenge (Congo-Zaïre) entre deux guerres.* Paris: L'Harmattan, 2001.

Rusatira, L. *Lettre ouverte au Dr Charles Murigande, Secrétaire-Général du FPR.* Brussels, June 7, 1999.

Rusesabagina, P. *An Ordinary Man: An Autobiography.* London: Penguin Books, 2005.

Rutazibwa, P. *Espérance pour mon peuple et pour le monde.* Kigali: Editions Centrales, 1995.

————. *Les crises dans la région des Grands Lacs et la question Tutsi.* Kigali: Editions du CRID, 1999.

Ruzibiza, A. J. *Rwanda: L'histoire secrète.* Paris: Editions du Panama, 2005.

Saint-Exupéry, P. de. *L'inavouable: La France au Rwanda.* Paris: Les Arènes, 2004.

Saint-Moulin, L. de. *Atlas de l'organisation administrative de la République Démocratique du Congo.* Kinshasa, DRC: CEPAS, 2005.

Salopek, P. "Torrents of Civil War Pound Ravaged Congo." *Chicago Tribune,* December 10, 2000.

———. "River of Blood Flows in War-Torn Congo." *Chicago Tribune,* December 11, 2000.

———. "City of Five Million Reduced to Mere Survival." *Chicago Tribune,* December 12, 2000.

Saquet, J. J. *De l'UMHK à la Gécamines.* Paris: L'Harmattan, 2000.

Sathyamurthy, T. V. *The Political Development of Uganda (1900–1986).* London: Gower, 1986.

Saur, L. *Influences parallèles: L'Internationale Démocrate-Chrétienne au Rwanda.* Brussels: Editions Luc Pire, 1998.

Savimbi, J. "L'an prochain à Luanda?" Interview with Stephen Smith. *Politique Internationale,* no. 85 (Autumn 1999): 359–72.

Schatzberg, M. *Politics and Class in Zaire.* London: Africana Publishing Company, 1980.

———. *The Dialectics of Oppression in Zaire.* Bloomington: Indiana University Press, 1988.

Schraeder, P. *United States Foreign Policy towards Africa.* Cambridge, UK: Cambridge University Press, 1994.

———. "France and the Great Game in Africa." *Current History* 96, no. 610 (May 1997): 206–211.

———, ed. "The Clinton Administration and Africa (1993–1999)." Special Issue of *Issue* 36, no. 2 (1998) [with articles by J. F. Clark, D. P. Volman, S. Leanne, W. Reno, P. Schraeder and B. Endless, J. W. Harbeson, and D. Rothchild].

Sebasoni, P. *Les origines du Rwanda.* Paris: L'Harmattan, 2000.

Sebudandi, G., and P. O. Richard. *Le drame burundais.* Paris: Karthala, 1996.

Sehene, B. *Le piège ethnique.* Paris: Dagorno, 1999.

Shaharyar, M. Khan. *The Shallow Graves of Rwanda.* London: I. B. Tauris, 2001.

Sibomana, A. *Gardons espoir pour sauver le Rwanda.* Paris: Desclée de Brouwer, 1997.

Simba Kayunga, S. "Islamic Fundamentalism in Uganda: The Tabligh Youth Movement." In M. Mamdani and J. Oloka-Onyango, eds., *Uganda: Studies in Living Conditions, Popular Movements and Constitutionalism,* 319–363. Vienna: JEP Books, 1994.

Sindayigaya, J. M. *Sortir de la violence au Burundi*. Bujumbura, Burundi: Presses Lavigerie, 1991.

Sitbon, M. *Un génocide sur la conscience*. Paris: L'Esprit Frappeur, 1998.

Smith, S. *Négrologie*. Paris: Calmann-Lévy, 2003.

Sogge, D., ed. *Compassion and Calculation: The Business of Private Foreign Aid*. London: Pluto Press, 1996.

Stengers, J. "A propos de l'Acte de Berlin ou comment nait une légende." *Zaïre*. October 1953, 839–844.

———. *Congo, mythes et réalités: Cent ans d'histoire*. Louvain-la-Neuve, Belgium: Duculot, 1989.

Storey, A. "The World Bank's Discursive Construction of Rwanda: Poverty, Inequality and the Role of the State." Unpublished paper. Queen's University, Belfast. School of Sociology and Social Policy. October 2001.

Straus, S. *Intimate Enemy: Images and Voices of the Rwanda Genocide*. New York: Zone Books, 2006.

———. *The Order of Genocide: Race, Power and War in Rwanda*. Ithaca, NY: Cornell University Press, 2006.

Syahuku Muhindo, A. "The Rwenzururu Movement and the Democratic Struggle." In M. Mamdani and J. Oloka-Onyango, eds., *Uganda: Studies in Living Conditions, Popular Movements and Constitutionalism*, 273–317. Vienna: JEP Books, 1994.

Tayler, J. *Facing the Congo: A Modern-Day Journey into the Heart of Darkness*. New York: Three Rivers Press, 2000.

Taylor, Ch. *Terreur et sacrifice: Une approche anthropologique du génocide rwandais*. Toulouse: Octarès, 2000.

Tegera, A. "Le réconciliation communautaire: Le cas des massacres du Nord-Kivu." In A. Guichaoua, ed., *Les crises politiques au Burundi et au Rwanda (1993–1994)*, 395–402. Villeneuve d'Ascq, France: Université des Sciences et Technologies de Lille, Faculté des Sciences Économiques et Sociales, 1995.

Terry, F. *Condemned to Repeat? The Paradox of Humanitarian Action*. Ithaca, NY: Cornell University Press, 2002.

Thibon, Ch. "L'expansion du peuplement dans la région des Grands Lacs au XIXème siècle." *Canadian Journal of African Studies* 23, no. 1 (1989): 54–72.

———. "*Amagume*, l'impasse burundaise." In *L'Afrique Politique*. Paris: CEAN/CREPAO, Pédone éditeur, 1995.

Torrenté, N. de. "L'Ouganda et les bailleurs de fonds: L'ambiguïté d'une lune de miel." *Politique Africaine*, no. 75 (October 1999): 72–90.

———. "Ouganda: Les limites d'un cas d'école." *Vivant Univers*, no. 456 (November–December 2001): 18–23.

Trefon, Th. "Population et pauvreté à Kinshasa." *Afrique Contemporaine,* 2nd quarter, no. 194 (2000): 82–89.

———. *Reinventing Order in the Congo: How People Respond to State Failure in Kinshasa.* Kampala: Fountain Publishers, 2004.

Tull, D. *The Reconfiguration of Political Order in Africa: A Case Study of North Kivu.* Hamburg: Institut für Afrika Kunde, 2005.

Turner, Th. "Angola's Role in the Congo War." In John F. Clark, ed., *The African Stakes of the Congo War,* 75–92. New York: Palgrave/Macmillan, 2002.

Turner, Th., and C. Young. *The Rise and Decline of the Zairian State.* Madison: University of Wisconsin Press, 1985.

Umurerwa, M. A. *Comme la langue entre les dents.* Paris: L'Harmattan, 2000.

Umutesi, M. B. *Fuir ou mourir au Zaïre: Le vécu d'une réfugiée rwandaise.* Paris: L'Harmattan, 2000.

Umwantisi [pseudonym of an Italian diplomat]. *La guerra civile in Rwanda.* Milano: Franco Angeli, 1997.

Uvin, P. *Aiding Violence: The Development Enterprise in Rwanda.* West Hartford, CT: Kumarian Press, 1998.

———. "Difficult Choices in the New Post-Conflict Agenda: The International Community in Rwanda after the Genocide." *Third World Quarterly* 22, no. 2 (2001): 177–189.

Vallée, O. *Pouvoirs et politiques en Afrique.* Paris: Desclée de Brouwer, 1999.

Van Acker, F. "La 'pembenisation' du Haut Kivu: Opportunisme et droits fonciers revisités." In S. Marysse and F. Reyntjens, eds., *L'Afrique des Grands Lacs (1998–1999),* 201–236. Paris: L'Harmattan, 1999.

Van Acker, F., and K. Vlassenroot. "Les Maï-Maï et les fonctions de la violence milicienne dans l'Est du Congo." *Politique Africaine,* no. 84 (December 2001): 103–116.

Vandeginste, S. "Justice for Rwanda and International Cooperation." Paper of the Centre d'Etudes de la Région des Grands Lacs, University of Antwerp. September 1997.

Van Hoyweghen, S. *From Humanitarian Disaster to Development Success: The Case of Rwanda.* Working Paper, University of Leeds, Centre for Development Studies. March 2000.

———. "The Rwandan Villagisation Programme: Resettlement for Reconstruction?" In D. Goyvaerts, ed., *Conflict and Ethnicity in Central Africa,* 177–208. Tokyo: Institute for the Study of Languages and Cultures of Asia and Africa, 2000.

Van Hoyweghen, S., T. Trefon, and S. Smis, eds., *State Failure in the Congo: Perceptions and Realities.* Special Issue of *Review of African Political Economy* 29, no. 93/94 (September–December 2002).

Vansina, J. "The Politics of History and the Crisis in the Great Lakes." *Africa Today* 45, no. 1 (1998): 37–44.

———. *Le Rwanda ancien: Le royaume Nyiginya*. Paris: Karthala, 2001.

Verhaegen, B. *Rébellions au Congo*. Vol. 1. Brussels: CRISP, 1966.

———. *Rébellions au Congo*. Vol. 2. Brussels: CRISP, 1969.

———. *Femmes zaïroises de Kisangani: Le combat pour la survie*. Paris: L'Harmattan, 1992.

Verschave, F. X. *La Françafrique, le plus long scandale de la République*. Paris: Stock, 1998.

———. *Noir silence*. Paris: Les Arènes, 2000.

———. *L'envers de la dette: Criminalité politique et économique au Congo-Brazza et en Angola*. Marseille: Agone, 2001.

Verschave, F. X., B. B. Diop, and O. Tobner. *Negrophobie*. Paris: Les Arènes, 2005.

Vidal, C. "Questions sur le rôle des paysans durant le génocide des Rwandais tutsi." *Cahiers d'Etudes Africaines* 38, nos. 2–4 (1998): 331–346.

———. "La politique de la France au Rwanda de 1990 à 1994: Les nouveaux publicistes de l'histoire conspirationniste." *Les Temps Modernes,* no. 642 (January–February 2007).

Villers, G. de. *De Mobutu à Mobutu: Trente ans de relations Belgique-Zaire*. Brussels: De Boeck, 1995.

———. *Zaïre, la transition manquée (1990–1997)*. Tervuren, Belgium: CEDAF, 1997.

Villers, G. de, with Laurent Monnier and Bogumil Jewsiewicki. *Chasse au diamant au Congo/Zaïre*. Tervuren, Belgium: CEDAF, 2001.

Villers, G. de, with Laurent Monnier and Bogumil Jewsiewicki. *Manières de vivre: Economies de la "débrouille" dans les villes du Congo-Zaïre*. Tervuren, Belgium: CEDAF, 2002.

Villers, G. de, with J. Omasombo and E. Kennes. *République Démocratique du Congo: Guerre et Politique. Les trente derniers mois de L.D. Kabila (août 1998–janvier 2001)*. Tervuren, Belgium: CEDAF, 2001.

Villers, G. de, and J. Omasombo Tshonda. "La bataille de Kinshasa." *Politique Africaine,* no. 84 (December 2001): 17–32.

Villers, G. de, and Willame, J. C. *République Démocratique du Congo: Chronique politique d'un entre-deux guerre (Octobre 1996–Juillet 1998)*. Tervuren, Belgium: CEDAF, 1998.

Vines, A. "La troisième guerre angolaise." *Politique Africaine,* no. 57 (March 1995): 27–39.

Vlassenroot, K. "The Promise of Ethnic Conflict: Militarisation and Enclave Formation in South Kivu." In D. Goyvaerts, ed., *Conflict and Ethnicity in Central Africa,* 59–104. Tokyo: Institute for the Study of Languages and Cultures of Asia and Africa, 2000.

Wagner, M. D. "All the *Bourgmestre's* Men: Making Sense of the Genocide in Rwanda." *Africa Today* 45, no. 1 (1998): 25–36.

Walle, N. van de. "Africa and the World Economy: Continued Marginalisation or Re-Engagement?" In J. W. Harbeson and D. Rothchild, eds., *Africa in World Politics: The African State System in Flux,* 263–285. Boulder, CO: Westview Press, 2000.

Wallis, A. *Silent Accomplice: The Untold Story of France's Role in the Rwandan Genocide.* London: I. B. Tauris, 2006.

Wamba Dia Wamba, E. *A New Congo for a New Millenium.* Lawrenceville: Red Sea Press, 1999.

Wamu Oyatambwe. *Eglise catholique et pouvoir politique au Congo-Zaïre.* Paris: L'Harmattan, 1997.

―――. *De Mobutu à Kabila, avatars d'une passation inopinée.* Paris: L'Harmattan, 1999.

Warfe, P. G. *Address on the Kibeho Massacre to the Australian Red Cross Conference on International Humanitarian Law.* Hobart, Australia. 22–23 July 1999.

Waugh, C. M. *Paul Kagame and Rwanda: Power, Genocide and the Rwandan Patriotic Front.* Jefferson, NC: MacFarland, 2004.

Weiss, H. *War and Peace in the Democratic Republic of the Congo.* Uppsala, Sweden: Nordiska Afrikainstitutet, 2000.

Weissman, S. *A Culture of Deference: Congress's Failure of Leadership in Foreign Policy.* New York: HarperCollins, 1995.

Wild, E. "Is It Witchcraft? Is It Satan? Is It a Miracle? Mai Mai Soldiers and Christian Concepts of Evil in North-East Congo." *Journal of Religion in Africa* 38, no. 4. (1998): 450–467.

Willame, J. C. *L'automne d'un despotisme.* Paris: Karthala, 1992.

―――. *L'ONU au Rwanda (1993–1995).* Brussels: Labor, 1996.

―――. *Les Belges au Rwanda: Le parcours de la honte.* Brussels: GRIP/Editions Complexe, 1997.

―――. "Gestion verticale et horizontale des crises identitaires: Le cas du Kivu montagneux." *Hérodote,* 4th quarter, no. 86/87 (1997): 78–115.

―――. *Banyarwanda et Banyamulenge: Violences ethniques et gestion de l'identitaire au Kivu.* Brussels: CEDAF, 1997.

―――. *Congo: Nouvelle crise dans les Grands Lacs.* Writenet Report, Geneva. August 1998.

―――. *L'odyssée Kabila.* Paris: Karthala, 1999.

―――. *L'accord de Lusaka: Chronique d'une négociation internationale.* Tervuren, Belgium: CEDAF, 2002.

————. *Les faiseurs de paix au Congo.* Brussels: GRIP/Editions Complexe, 2007.

Wrong, M. "The Emperor Mobutu." *Transition,* no. 81/82 (2000): 92–112.

————. *In the Footsteps of Mr Kurtz: Living on the Brink of Disaster in the Congo.* London: Fourth Estate, 2000.

Yanacopoulos, H., and J. Hanlon, eds. *Civil War, Civil Peace.* Oxford: James Currey, 2006.

Yengo, P. "Chacun aura sa part: Les fondements historiques de la reproduction de la guerre à Brazzaville." *Cahiers d'Etudes Africaines* 38, nos. 2–4 (1998): 471–504.

Young, C. *Politics in the Congo: Decolonization and Independence.* Princeton, NJ: Princeton University Press, 1965.

————. "The Heritage of Colonialism." In J. W. Harbeson and D. Rothchild, eds., *Africa in World Politics: The African State System in Flux,* 23–42. Boulder, CO: Westview Press, 2000.

Young, C., and T. Turner. *The Rise and Decline of the Zairian State.* Madison: University of Wisconsin Press, 1985.

Zarembo, A. "Judgement Day." *Harper's Magazine,* April 1997.

Zartman, W. "Inter-African Negotiations and State Renewal." In J. W. Harbeson and D. Rothchild, eds., *Africa in World Politics: The African State System in Flux,* 139–159. Boulder, CO: Westview Press, 2000.

Zeebroek, X. *Les humanitaires en guerre: Sécurité des travailleurs humanitaires en mission en RDC et au Burundi.* Brussels: Editions Complexe, 2004.

INDEX